The New Chronology of the Bronze Age Settlement of Tepe Hissar, Iran

University Museum Monographs 142

The New Chronology of the Bronze Age Settlement of Tepe Hissar, Iran

Ayşe Gürsan-Salzmann

UNIVERSITY OF PENNSYLVANIA MUSEUM OF ARCHAEOLOGY AND ANTHROPOLOGY

PHILADELPHIA

LIBRARY OF CONGRESS CATALOGING-IN-PUBLICATION DATA

Names: Gürsan-Salzmann, Ayşe, author.
Title: The new chronology of the Bronze Age settlement of Tepe Hissar, Iran / Ayşe Gürsan-Salzmann.
Description: Philadelphia : University of Pennsylvania Museum of Archaeology and Anthropology, 2016. | Series: University Museum monographs ; 142 | Includes bibliographical references and index.
Identifiers: LCCN 2015050324| ISBN 9781934536834 (hardcover : alk. paper) | ISBN 1934536830 (hardcover : alk. paper) | ISBN 9781934536841 (eISBN)
Subjects: LCSH: Hissar Tepe (Iran) | Bronze age--Iran--Hissar Tepe. | Iran--Antiquities.
Classification: LCC DS262.H57 G87 2016 | DDC 935/.7--dc23
LC record available at http://lccn.loc.gov/2015050324

© 2016 by the University of Pennsylvania Museum of Archaeology and Anthropology
Philadelphia, PA
All rights reserved. Published 2016

Published for the University of Pennsylvania Museum of Archaeology and Anthropology by the University of Pennsylvania Press.

Printed in the United States of America on acid-free paper.

About the cover art: One of the five modeled mouflon heads from Tepe Hissar, made of gold foil and decorated with repoussé technique. Dated to ca. 1900 BC from hoard 1 at Treasure Hill. Drawing by Han A. Salzmann.

Table of Contents

LIST OF FIGURES		vii
LIST OF TABLES		xiii
LIST OF SECTIONS		xv
LIST OF MAPS		xvii
ACKNOWLEDGMENTS		xix
	Tepe Hissar, an Introduction	1
1	Erich F. Schmidt Excavations (1931–32)	13
2	Stratigraphy and Architecture	41
3	Analysis of Ceramic Complexes of the Main Mound and the North Flat	71
4	Burial Stratigraphy: The Main Mound and the North Flat, 1931–32 and 1976	167
5	Death and Burial Culture of Tepe Hissar	217
6	Concluding Remarks	267
APPENDICES		299
1	Pottery Charts	299
2	Low and High Outlier Burial Tables	319
3	Maps	350
4	Radiocarbon Dates from the 1976 Restudy Project	371
BIBLIOGRAPHY		375
INDEX		383

Figures

0.1	Topographic map of Iran and sites mentioned in the text	2
0.2	Damghan Plain, ringed by snow-capped Elburz Mountains	3
0.3	Aerial view of Tepe Hissar	3
0.4	The Tehran-Meshed Railroad cuts through the site	4
0.5	Modern eroded landscape of Tepe Hissar	4
0.6	First day of excavations on the Main Mound	5
0.7	Late Islamic town citadel at Damghan	5
0.8	Eric Schmidt's registry for Tepe Hissar excavations	8
0.9	Database created from Schmidt's field register	8
0.10	Salzmann database for 1931–32 small finds	9
0.11	Salzmann database for 1931–32 small finds	10
0.12	Salzmann database for 1931–32 burial assemblages	11
1.1	Schmidt's excavation staff (1931–32)	13
1.2	Main Mound burial: DF18 x13	14
1.3	Superimposed construction phases on the Main Mound	16
1.4	Schmidt's plots of burials from the Main Mound	17
1.5	Schmidt's excavated areas by period	19
1.6	Excavations in square DF09	20
1.7	Schmidt's chronological scheme, with transitional periods	27
1.8	Plan of Main Mound with burials	29
1.9	Schmidt's revised archival plan of Main Mound Buildings	30
1.10	Double row of "crescent shaped niches" found in square DF09, Building 1	31
1.11	Plan and photos of Burned Building, Period IIIB	33
2.1	Map of Tepe Hissar, 1976 Project, superimposed on 1931–32 map	43
2.2	Main Mound 1976: DF09 baulk 12, and south face of Pinnacle	44
2.3	Deep test and block and baulk 12	45
2.4	Main Mound 1976: DF09 baulk 13	45
2.5	Vincent Pigott and Susan Howard cleaning baulks DF09–CG90	46
2.6	Correlation of levels, periods, and radiocarbon dates for Tepe Hissar sequence	47
2.7	DF09–CG90 sections on Main Mound	49
2.8	DF09 looking northwest, baulk 12 (center), CG90P (right)	50

2.9	Site photograph showing architectural features in Main Mound squares DG00 and CG90	51
2.10	Site photograph of the remains of Building 2 on the Main Mound	52
2.11	Plan of Main Mound areas investigated, showing Buildings 1, 2, and 3	53
2.12	Two site photographs of a cleaned Building 2 on the Main Mound	54
2.13	Upper rebuilding stage of Building 2, DG00–10	55
2.14	Tepe Hissar 1976: Building 3	55
2.15	Main Mound: Looking southeast, overall view from CG90 through DG00 to DG01	56
2.16	Main Mound: DG00, Building 3, trench through room 12	57
2.17	Main Mound: DG00 Area 11 sketch; photo looking northwest from DG01 to DG00	58
2.18	Grey burnished vessel h76-70	59
2.19	Main Mound: Plan and photographs of DG00	61
2.20	Main Mound: Site photographs of CG90 showing kitchen	61
2.21	Key plan of architectural remains on the North Flat	62
2.22	North Flat: looking southwest over Burned Building and above it (building level 1)	63
2.23	North Flat: CF37 Burned Building; W. Remsen documenting north stairs with hearth	63
2.24	North Flat: CF48–27 Burned Building; looking northwest; buttresses	64
2.25	North Flat: CF27 BB; Remsen taking measurements of north stairs with hearth; looking west-southwest	64
2.26	North Flat: CF37–27; looking northeast; Burned Building north stairs with hearth; Photo Remsen taking measurements; hearth reconstruction	65
2.27	North Flat: CF37 Burned Building Room 1, north stairs with hearth	65
2.28	North Flat: CF37–47; Burned Building looking north; cleaning [8] Schmidt's base of the "tower"; [3] entryway to Burned Building	66
2.29	North Flat: CF37–47 Burned Building storeroom 2, filled with pithoi	66
2.30	North Flat: CF58 exterior of northeast wall of buttress building [14]	67
2.31	North Flat: CF48–58 looking northwest	67
2.32	CF58 Burned Room 2 b1 (c. 2700 BC, after 1976 excavations)	68
3.1	Wares by phase	77
3.2	Number of forms through phases	80
3.3	Number of forms: Late Hissar I (phase F)	82
3.4	Phase F (Late Hissar I)	85
3.5	Number of forms: Late Hissar I–Early Hissar II (phase F-E)	86
3.6	Phase F-E transitional (Late Hissar I–Early Hissar II)	89
3.7	Phase F-E transitional (Late Hissar I–Early Hissar II)	91
3.8	Phase F-E transitional (Late Hissar I–Early Hissar II)	93
3.9	Phase F-E transitional (Late Hissar I–Early Hissar II)	95
3.10	Phase F-E transitional (Late Hissar I–Early Hissar II)	97
3.11	Number of forms: Early Hissar II (phase E)	98
3.12	Phase E (Early Hissar II)	101
3.13	Phase E (Early Hissar II)	103

3.14	Phase E (Early Hissar II)	105
3.15	Phase E (Early Hissar II)	107
3.16	Phase E (Early Hissar II)	109
3.17	Number of forms: Early to Mid-Hissar II (phase E-D)	110
3.18	Phase E-D (Early to Mid-Hissar II)	113
3.19	Phase E-D (Early to Mid-Hissar II)	115
3.20	Phase E-D (Early to Mid-Hissar II)	117
3.21	Phase E-D (Early to Mid-Hissar II)	119
3.22	Phase E-D (Early to Mid-Hissar II)	121
3.23	Phase E-D (Early to Mid-Hissar II)	123
3.24	Phase E-D (Early to Mid-Hissar II)	124
3.25	Number of forms: Mid-Hissar II (phase D)	126
3.26	Phase D (Mid-Hissar II)	129
3.27	Phase D (Mid-Hissar II)	131
3.28	Phase D (Mid-Hissar II)	133
3.29	Phase D (Mid-Hissar II)	135
3.30	Phase D (Mid-Hissar II)	137
3.31	Phase D (Mid-Hissar II)	139
3.32	Phase D (Mid-Hissar II)	141
3.33	Phase D (Mid-Hissar II)	142
3.34	Main Mound: DG01 burial 6	143
3.35	Number of forms: Late Hissar II (D-C transitional phase)	144
3.36	Phase D-C transitional (Hissar II to Early Hissar III)	145
3.37	Phase D-C transitional (Hissar II to Early Hissar III)	147
3.38	Phase D-C transitional (Hissar II to Early Hissar III)	149
3.39	Phase D-C transitional (Hissar II to Early Hissar III)	151
3.40	Phase D-C transitional (Hissar II to Early Hissar III)	153
3.41	Phase D-C transitional (Hissar II to Early Hissar III)	155
3.42	Phase D-C transitional (Hissar II to Early Hissar III)	157
3.43	Number of forms: Mid-Hissar III (phase B)	159
3.44	Phase B (Mid-Hissar III)	161
3.45	Number of forms: Late Hissar IIIC (phase B-A/A)	162
3.46	Phase B-A/A (Late Hissar III)	163
4.1	Distribution of the Main Mound and North Flat burials with contour lines	168
4.2	Work in the Tepe Hissar necropolis on the Main Mound	169
4.3	Main Mound burial: DF09 x1, Warrior II	174
4.4	Main Mound burial: DF09 x52	178
4.5	Main Mound burial: DG00 x14 and x16	178
4.6	Main Mound burial: CG90 x23	183

4.7	Main Mound burial: CG90 x9	183
4.8	Main Mound burial: DF08 x1, The Priest	184
4.9	Three carinated jar forms: H2497, H3989, and H572	198
4.10	Drawing of a unique canteen (H3522) from square CF89	198
4.11	Main Mound burial: DG00 burial 8	202
4.12	Main Mound burial: CG90 B1 and B2	203
4.13	North Flat burial: CF57 x28	211
4.14	North Flat burial: CF57 x40, with grey burnished goblet (H4162)	213
4.15	The lion-gate of a Seljuk Cemetery, near the city of Shiraz, southern Iran	215
5.1	A GIS map of Tepe Hissar showing the distribution of burials on the Main Mound and North Flat areas	218
5.2	Main Mound: DF19 "mass burial"	219
5.3	DG00 "mass burial," 11 burials are recorded	219
5.4	DG00 "mass burial," northeast quadrant	220
5.5	Main Mound: DG11 burials from store room area /18/ of Building 3	220
5.6	A cist burial, CG25 x1	221
5.7	Drawing of burials x4 and x5 from CF89 (both infants) showing the placement and detailed sketches of copper artifacts	223
5.8	Main Mound: DF29 burial chamber, from southwest	224
5.9	CG90 "Mass Burial"	225
5.10	Copper pin with double wire-loop head from DG01 x32, phase D-C	230
5.11	Main Mound DG00 group burial	231
5.12	CG31 x7: H4885, a wand with an agricultural scene	237
5.13	Photographs of early 20th century Iranian agricultural practices	238
5.14	Copper bracelets with multiple coils found in burial group 4	238
5.15	North Flat Burial CF55 x1, the Dancer	239
5.16	Main Mound burial: DF19 x12	242
5.17	Main Mound CF47 x1: Cow effigy vessel of pottery	243
5.18	Main Mound CF47 x2: Female effigy vessel of pottery	243
5.19	Main Mound burial: DF19 x2, Warrior 1	244
5.20	Alabaster animal figurines found in Warrior 2's grave, DF09 x1	245
5.21	Main Mound burial: DF18 x1 Little Girl	247
5.22	Main Mound burial: DF08 x1, the Priest	248
5.23	DF08 x1, Priest: Silver diadem with ram, ibex, and other animals in repoussé technique	249
5.24	DF08 x1, Priest: Human effigy (H482)	249
5.25	DF08 x1, Priest: Fan/mirror (H451), coiled copper with stem	250
5.26	DF08 x1, Priest: Copper wand depicting two seated human figures	251
5.27	Main Mound burial: DF18 x1, Little Girl with prestige burial gifts	251
5.28	Multiple coil copper bracelets from burial CF55 x1, the Dancer, H2379 (33-21-925), H4158 (33-21-632)	251

5.29	CF57 x28: Disarticulated skeletal remains	254
5.30	DF18 x10: "Bone piles in grave"	255
5.31	Thirteen copper figurines from an enigmatic hoard	257
5.32	Period IIIC, Main Mound "hoard," pointed cup: H3312 (33-22-10); figurines: H3271 (33-22-132), H3289 (33-22-134), H3281, H3282, H3283 (33-22-133 a,b,c)	258
5.33	Vessels from the CF99 hoard	259
5.34	Pottery vessels, including braziers, from Main Mound hoard CF99	260
5.35	Silver vessel, H5205 (33-22-148), found with burial CG13 x1	261
5.36	Gold necklace, H2360 (33-22-180), from Period IIIB, North Flat, Burned Building	262
5.37	Alabaster spouted vessel, H4187 (33-22-78), found with Treasure Hill, burial CH87 x1	263
5.38	Period IIIC, North Flat, CF38, alabaster disc and column, H2769 (33-22-82)	263
5.39	Animal figurines carved from alabaster (H750, H748, and H758) from the Warrior 2 burial, DF09 x1	264
5.40	Copper lid or plate (H2252) from Burned Building	265
6.1	Animal figurines: Period IIA, DH06, H2978 (33-21-342); Period IC, DH36, H3656 (33-21-137); H1072 (33-15-51)	270
6.2	Period IIIC, tokens and animal figurines	271
6.3	Period I, ceramic vessel, H1553 (33-15-33)	272
6.4	Grey burnished vessel, H5118 (33-22-517), Period IIB, South Hill, burial DF78 x22	274
6.5	Period II, North Flat, burial CG25 x1, grey burnished pedestal bowl, H1149 (33-15-297)	275
6.6	Period IIB, South Hill, DG53, ceramic vessel, H1822 (33-22-519)	276
6.7	Double scroll pin H5019 (33-21-620)	277
6.8	Period II-III transitional, thin-walled ceramic vessel, H2212 (33-21-807)	278
6.9	Period IIIC, North Flat, burial CF47 x2, hourglass shaped ceramic female figurine, H2790 (33-22-55)	281
6.10	Period IIIC, North Flat, burial CF38 x11, hourglass shaped female figurine crafted from copper, H5178 (33-21-983)	282
6.11	Period IIIC, Treasure Hill "Hoard II", plaster cast of an alabaster hourglass shaped female figurine, H3500 (33-22-92)	283
6.12	Period IIIC, Treasure Hill, ibex: H3578 (33-22-115), dog: H3159 (33-22-136); Period IIIC, Main Mound, burial DF08 x1 "Priest," 3 person wand: H463 (33-15-582); Period IIIB, Treasure Hill, burial CH85 x18, bird wand: H4279 (33-21-920)	284
6.13	Period IIIC, Treasure Hill, copper dog figurine H3159 (33-22-136)	285
6.14	Period IIIC, North Flat, burial CF55 x1 "Dancer," jewelry, H2388 (33-21-1017)	286
6.15	Period IIIC, Treasure Hill, burial CH75 x9, handmade grey ware vessel, H3841 (33-21-836)	287
6.16	Period IIIC, Treasure Hill "Hoard", spouted ceramic vessel, H4296 (33-22-449)	288
6.17	Period IIIC, Main Mound, burial DF16 x15, ceramic vessel, H5047 (33-21-748)	289
6.18	Period IIIC, North Flat, miniature column: H1844 (33-22-189); Period IIIC, Main Mound, Burial DF19 x2, disc: H174 (33-15-718)	290
6.19	Maceheads: Period IIIB-C, North Flat, H2748 (33-22-202); Period IIIC, Main Mound, Burial DF09 x1 "Warrior 2", H771 (33-15-574)	292
6.20	Period IIIC, Treasure Hill, burial CH64 x1, metal weapon, H3582 (33-22-108)	293

Tables

2.1	Vertical sequence of the Main Mound	50
2.2	New stratigraphic phasing of Tepe Hissar sequence and their correlates from 1931–32 and 1976 excavations	69
3.1	Overall percentage frequency of wares by phase (1976)	77
3.2	Dimensions of general form-types including all wares and phases	79
3.3	Percentage frequencies of forms through phases	80
3.4	New ceramic sequence and stratigraphic contexts from the Main Mound and the North Flat according to 1976 stratigraphy	81
4.1	Main Mound: Chronology of dated burials according to the reconstructed stratigraphy and the new ceramic sequence	204
4.2	North Flat: Chronology of dated burials according to the reconstructed stratigraphy and the new ceramic sequence	214
5.1	Group 1: Sex, age, and position of burials	227
5.1a	Group 1: Mortuary gifts	228
5.2	Group 2: Sex, age, and position of burials	228
5.2a	Group 2: Mortuary gifts	229
5.3	Group 3: Sex, age, and position of burials	233
5.3a	Group 3: Mortuary gifts	234
5.4	Group 4: Sex, age, and position of burials	235
5.4a	Group 4: Mortuary gifts	236
5.5	Group 5: Sex, age, and position of burials	240
5.5a	Group 5: Mortuary gifts	241
6.1	Relative chronology	268
A2.1a	Group 1: Low Outliers	319
A2.1b	Group 2: Low Outliers	320
A2.1c	Group 3: Low Outliers	322
A2.1d	Group 4: Low Outliers	331
A2.1e	Group 5: Low Outliers	334
A2.2a	Group 4 North Flat: High Outliers	341
A2.2b	Group 5 Main Mound: High Outliers	342
A4.1	Radiocarbon Dates from the 1976 Restudy Project	372

Sections

(all Pottery Charts appear in Appendix 1)

4.1	DF09 Building 1	172
4.1a	DF09 Pottery Chart	*Appendix 1: 300*
4.2	DF09 Building 1, Building 2 (NW part)	173
4.3	DG00 NE Building 2	177
4.3a	DG00 Pottery Chart	*Appendix 1: 301*
4.4	DG01	179
4.4a	DG01 Pottery Chart	*Appendix 1: 302*
4.5	DF09 Building 1, Building 2 (NW part), DG00 NE Building 2, DG01 N of Building 3	181
4.6	CG90	182
4.6a	CG90 Pottery Chart	*Appendix 1: 303*
4.7	DF08	185
4.7a	DF08 Pottery Chart	*Appendix 1: 304*
4.8	DG10 Building 2	187
4.8a	DG10 Pottery Chart	*Appendix 1: 305*
4.9	DG11 S of Building 3	188
4.9a	DG11 Pottery Chart	*Appendix 1: 306*
4.10	DG11 S of Building 3, DG12, DG13	189
4.11	DF28, DF29, DG20	190
4.11a	DG20 Pottery Chart	*Appendix 1: 307*
4.12	DF29	191
4.12a	DF29 Pottery Chart	*Appendix 1: 308*
4.13	DF18	193
4.13a	DF18 Pottery Chart	*Appendix 1: 309*
4.14	DF19 S of Building 1 and SW corner of Building 2	194
4.14a	DF19 Pottery Chart	*Appendix 1: 310*
4.15	CF88	196
4.15a	CF88 Pottery Chart	*Appendix 1: 311*
4.16	CF89	199
4.16a	CF89 Pottery Chart	*Appendix 1: 312*
4.17	CF88, CF89	200

4.18	CF99	201
4.18a	CF99 Pottery Chart	*Appendix 1: 313*
4.19	CF99, CG90	205
4.20	CF37, CF38	206
4.20a	CF37 Pottery Chart	*Appendix 1: 314*
4.20b	CF38 Pottery Chart	*Appendix 1: 315*
4.21	CF47, CF48	208
4.21a	CF47 Pottery Chart	*Appendix 1: 316*
4.21b	CF48 Pottery Chart	*Appendix 1: 317*
4.22	CF57	210
4.22a	CF57 Pottery Chart	*Appendix 1: 318*
4.23	CF55	212

Maps

(all maps listed below appear in Appendix 3)

Map 1	CF37	351
Map 2	CF38	352
Map 3	CF47	353
Map 4	CF48	354
Map 5	CF55	355
Map 6	CF57	356
Map 7	CF88	357
Map 8	CF89	358
Map 9	CF99	359
Map 10	CG90	360
Map 11	DF08	361
Map 12	DF09	362
Map 13	DF18	363
Map 14	DF19	364
Map 15	DF29	365
Map 16	DG00	366
Map 17	DG01	367
Map 18	DG10	368
Map 19	DG11	369
Map 20	DG20	370

Acknowledgments

It is not possible to name all who have helped me in the course of the research, writing, and rewriting of this monograph; however, several people, friends, and colleagues stand out. First and foremost, my mentor, Robert H. Dyson, opened the door for me to study anthropology and Near Eastern archaeology. He first encouraged and supported my career as an anthropological archaeologist during fieldwork in Turkey and later involved me in the Tepe Hissar project. After the excavation and reassessment study of 1976 was concluded, Dyson proposed that I produce a reliable ceramic chronology for Tepe Hissar by integrating the data he collected in 1976 along with that from Erich F. Schmidt's excavations of 1931 and 1932. Our discussions led me to boxes of documents in the Penn Museum Archives, which included a rich collection of handwritten field registry books, plans, sections, object cards, and albums of black-and-white photographs depicting stages of the excavations. All these documents were pieces of a puzzle that took much longer to sort out and put together than anticipated. I owe Dr. Dyson my special thanks for his enthusiasm and generous help in explaining the 1976 data. These discussions gave me a clearer understanding of the Tepe Hissar settlement in order to address the interpretation of its cultural chronology and regional importance in southwestern Asia.

Unpublished field notes from the 1976 field season by Susan Howard and Dr. Vincent Pigott along with Howard's preliminary analysis on the ceramic assemblage provided useful data for the research. To both I extend my appreciation.

In the course of studying Schmidt's archival materials from Tepe Hissar, I came upon his daily notes and black-and-white images of landscapes and simple life of village inhabitants during his overland travels from İstanbul to Baghdad. Also present were his field notes from excavations at the site of Fara (1931) prior to his work at Tepe Hissar. These documents, interspersed with humorous anecdotes, mirrored a portrait of the person behind the Tepe Hissar project, his detailed thinking process and ambitious personality. These records diverted my attention and inspired me to write a semi-popular book Exploring Iran: The Photography of Erich Schmidt, 1930–1940 (2007). I am indebted to Walda Metcalf, then Assistant Director of Penn Museum Publications, for suggesting the idea of developing this book and to Erika Schmidt, Erich Schmidt's daughter, who provided me with family photos and biographical anecdotes about her father, which are included in the book.

Dr. Christopher Thornton, both friend and colleague, has generously given many hours of his time to discuss some problems of stratigraphy, to make useful suggestions in editing the manuscript at different stages of research and writing, to provide critical information on the Tepe Hissar metallurgy, and to assist the interns working on different aspects of the database at the Penn Museum while I was doing fieldwork at Gordion, Turkey. I would like to extend my sincere gratitude to him, especially for his unwavering good spirits.

My thanks are due to Dr. Fredrik Hiebert, who shared his field research in Turkmenistan, and extensive bibliography. I thank him also for discussions about the Bronze Age connections of the northern Iranian plateau with Turkmenistan and Central Asia.

In 2007, I had the opportunity to give a progress report on the Tepe Hissar research at an international conference organized by Dr. Hassan Fazeli in Damghan, Iran ("7000 Years of Civilization at Tepe Hissar"). I am grateful for his invitation to the conference, which provided an invaluable opportunity to see Tepe Hissar in its present highly eroded state. At the conference, I gained new insights about recent research in Iranian archaeology, especially carried out by Iranian archaeologists. Fruitful discussions with Barbara Helwing, Hassan Fazeli, Christopher Thornton, Michèle Casanova, Kourosh Roustaei, and Raffaele Biscione deepened my understanding of the papers. Ali Mahfroozi kindly invited several of the Damghan conference participants for a tour of the site and archaeological laboratory of Gohar Tepe, Mazandaran, where he is director of excavation. I am grateful to him for his friendship and sharing his knowledge about the region and the site.

At the Penn Museum, Alex Pezzati, the Senior Archivist, has been generous with his time in helping me find my way through the archives and bringing out specific documents and drawings, in his usual good spirits, through the different stages of my research. His then-assistant, Alison Miner, was good-natured about finding documents, making copies, and even working up some simple statistics on pottery. Ray Bednarczyk, a dedicated volunteer, completed with grim determination the task of deciphering Schmidt's field register written in "German" style handwriting, to produce a legible handwritten version. Jana Fisher, as one of the past illustrators at the Penn Museum, did the early pencil drawings of nearly a thousand diagnostic sherds from the 1976 excavation. These drawings were later corrected and digitized by Rie Yamakawa, an architect and a graduate student of conservation at Penn School of Design. I am grateful to them both for the many hours they spent in correcting and re-drawing of the illustrations in this book.

Dr. Brian Rose made comments and bibliographic suggestions; Dr. Naomi F. Miller went through the final draft of the manuscript with a critical and intelligent eye. I appreciate their contributions.

At least a dozen volunteers played an important role at different stages of the research, keeping the database up-to-date, doing bibliographic research, reading part of the manuscript, preparing power-point presentations, and helping to write up progress reports. One of the volunteers, Anne Bomalaski, who worked tirelessly on different aspects of research over several years, supervised the short-term volunteer interns. I am especially thankful to her and the other volunteers for help on many aspects of the research.

Among the long-term volunteers, William (Bill) Gardner and James (Jim) Mueller worked on Schmidt's burial data; Bill deciphered Schmidt's original handwritten burial sheets and then inventoried and organized the large assemblage of burial groups into spreadsheets. This arduous process also revealed unpublished notes by Schmidt. Jim did statistical work on burials, so that more precise descriptions of the context of grave objects and burial rituals could be reconstructed. I am grateful to them.

My thanks go to Dr. William Fitts, then-researcher at the Penn Museum, and David Massey, then a graduate student at Ohio State University, for the initial drafting of the GIS maps that were later revised by Ayşem Kılınç Ünlü and Joseph Torres, both graduate students at Penn School of Design. Invaluable technical support was given by two professionals and close friends. James Rowland helped with preparing the manuscript according to the publication guidelines and Jason Francisco, a documentary photographer, took additional photographs of objects. Katherine Blanchard, keeper of the Near East collection, kindly brought the objects from storage so they could be photographed.

I also appreciate the timely and thought-provoking comments and suggestions by the two anonymous reviewers.

To my husband Laurence I express my gratitude for his continued patience and support. Now I can finally say to him, "The Tepe Hissar manuscript is finished," in response to his intermittent queries, "when will it be completed?"

To my daughter Han who patiently helped me with German translations of articles and, as a talented illustrator and architect, drafted the line drawing of the iconic gold "mouflon" imprinted on the hard cover, which is considered a symbol of sustenance, fertility, and sacred power in ancient Southwest Asia.

Last but not least, my gratitude goes to Erich F. Schmidt, an archaeologist who was trained as an anthropologist under Franz Boas in late 1920s. He undertook a most intellectually and politically challenging project in northern Iran, which, at that time, was an archaeological "terra incognita." Schmidt's systematic and untiring work at Tepe Hissar, which lasted 10 months over two field seasons, revealed a major Bronze Age settlement on the crossroads of southwestern Asia and also brought up many questions, which were addressed forty-five years later by Dyson and, after three more decades, by this author, in light of new excavation data from Tepe Hissar and other sites in Iran and Central Asia.

Major funding for the Tepe Hissar Publication Project came from The Shelby White and Leon Levy Program for Archaeological Publications. I received additional funding from the University of Pennsylvania Museum Research Fund; the American Institute of Iranian Studies paid for my trip to the Damghan Conference; and Erika Schmidt kindly responded to my request for additional funds for illustrations, in memory of her father's excavation at Tepe Hissar. To all I extend my heartfelt thanks.

Tepe Hissar, an Introduction

Tepe Hissar was one of the first systematically excavated Bronze Age settlements in the northern Iranian plateau. Two cycles of excavation were undertaken at the site by the University of Pennsylvania Museum of Archaeology and Anthropology (hereafter Penn Museum). In June 1931, the Penn Museum launched its first archaeological expedition to Iran—then Persia—at Tepe Hissar and the monumental Sassanian palace, near the town of Damghan. Erich Schmidt was appointed to direct the project, which lasted until the end of 1932.[1] Almost five decades later, in 1976, another expedition was initiated at Tepe Hissar by the Penn Museum under Robert H. Dyson Jr.,[2] in collaboration with Maurizio Tosi of the University of Turin, and with the support of the Iranian Center for Archaeological Research in Tehran.

Both cycles of excavation resulted in publications (Schmidt 1931, 1937; Dyson and Howard 1989). While Schmidt's excavations established the historical framework, Dyson and his team presented a stratigraphically clearer sequence for the site with associated radiocarbon dates. Nevertheless, a full study of the ceramic assemblages has not been published to date. In this publication, the new ceramic sequence from the Tepe Hissar settlement is established and linked to the grave assemblages, which should provide ample evidence for the chronology of the site, the nature of the progression and the abandonment of the settlement, and its chronological correlations on the northern Iranian plateau.

A. Site Location and Description

The site of Tepe Hissar ("Castle Hill") is located on the Iranian Plateau, to the southeast of the Caspian Sea (36° 09' N, 59° 22' E), about 1.5 km from the modern city of Damghan (Fig. 0.1). It is situated along the historic east-west trade route between Tehran and Meshed. To its north are the majestic Elburz Mountains that provide the main source of water to the Cheshmeh Ali (Eye of Ali) spring, drained by the Damghan River (Fig. 0.2). To the south are the fringes of the Central Iranian Salt Desert (Dasht-i Kavir).

The site's favorable location must have facilitated the movement of prehistoric inhabitants and provided them with a wide range of natural resources, as evidenced by geomorphological and ecological studies (Meder 1989:7–12). Thus, in terms of subsistence strategy, the ancient populations of Tepe Hissar were able to exploit resources from the desert (*kavir*) to the Elburz range[3] and, perhaps, from the Caspian coastal zone which is about 100 km over the mountain range. Diet would have been varied, for "natural resources are distributed around the [Damghan] basin. Equidistant from Tappeh Hesar are the high valley to the north, rich in flint, lead, wood, fruit, deer, stag, boar, fish and fowl and the arid periphery of the kavir to the south with its known occurrences of copper, gold, turquoise and semi-arid fauna with herds of gazelles and onagers" (Dyson and Tosi 1989:6).

While the principal sustenance of the ancient population derived from different species of domesticated wheat, barley, and lentils, this was combined with a Mediterranean type diet that included wild grape and olive plant foods (Costantini and Dyson 1990).[4] The diet was supplemented by meat mostly from caprines and cattle. The exploitation of aquatic resources is attested to by fish bones excavated during 1976. Mashkour's references to the presence of onager (*Equus hemionus*) and "some cattle principally kept for traction," indicate uses of onager in herding and distance travel and cattle in plowing.[5]

Rising six to eight meters above the surrounding plain, Tepe Hissar comprises seven disconnected mounds and flat settlements. As of the mid-1970s (Fig. 0.3), it measured about 600 meters in diameter; roughly 12 hectares of

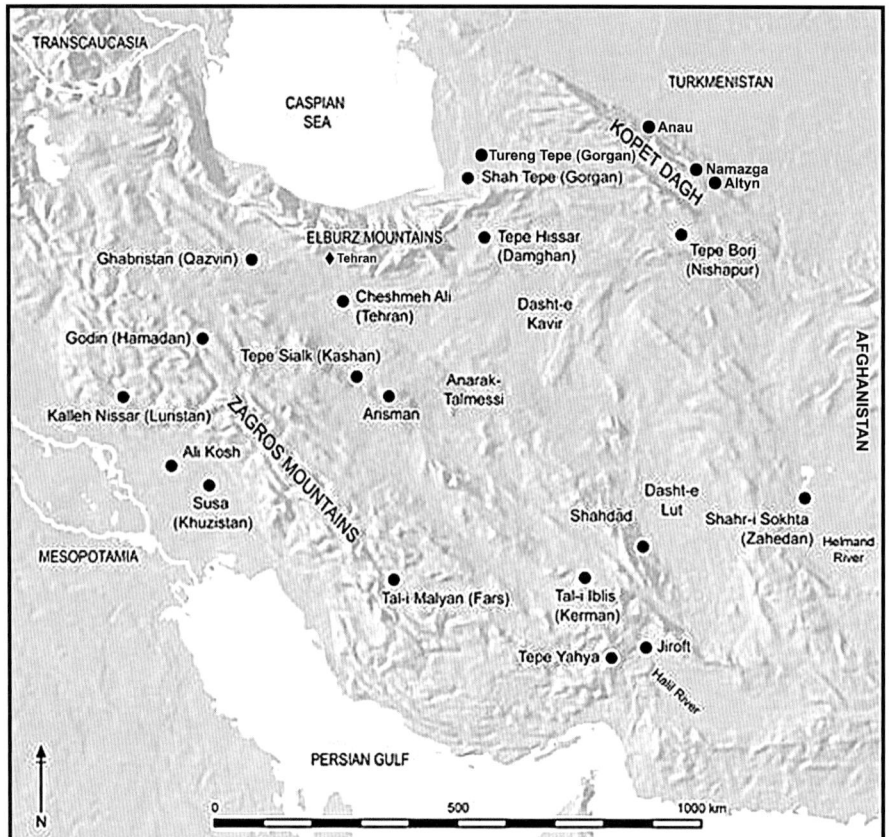

Fig. 0.1 Topographic map of Tepe Hissar and surrounding sites (after Roberts and Thornton, 2014: Fig. 23.1).

visible mounded occupational remains were partly buried in the alluvial fan of the Damghan River (Meder 1989).

Over time, the ancient populations at Tepe Hissar moved around within the settlement complex—possibly for agricultural reasons or for proximity to water resources—leaving behind an abandoned area that subsequently became used as an intramural cemetery until the beginning of another occupation in the same area. Therefore, during each phase of the settlement, part of the mounded area was residential and part of the flat area was burial ground.

In 1976, Dyson and his team attributed the general destruction of the site and its environs to long-term erosion and the result of marginal cultivation, as seen from a 1940s Schmidt aerial photo. They also noted some of the ancient sites shown on Schmidt's map (1933: pl. LXXVI) were most likely ploughed away by the fields surrounding modern villages. Clearly, since the 1970s, the process of destruction has continued under mechanically ploughed irrigated fields[6] and with the railway cutting through the site (Dyson and Tosi 1989:6) (Fig. 0.4). Nevertheless, Dyson (pers. comm.) was surprised to find relatively good state of preservation of some of Schmidt's trenches despite the passing of nearly five decades.

B. Research History

A summary of the research history at Tepe Hissar is a key component of this study as the evidence in reports is limited and scattered. The present summary is an attempt to assemble what is available relating to the depositional stratigraphy as a background to the excavators' reasoning and interpretive conclusions.

In addition to the two cycles of excavation, a cursory salvage excavation was carried out in 1995 by Ehsan Yaghmai on behalf of the Iranian Center for Archaeological Research (ICAR), but this material remains almost entirely unpublished. More recently, in 2006, Kourosh Roustaei and his Iranian team have surveyed the boundaries of the Tepe Hissar settlement[7] and investigated the geomorphology of the site and possible continuity of the settlement into the Iron Age.

B.1 The Penn Museum's Involvement: Erich F. Schmidt Excavations (1931–32)

The earliest mention of the site is found in the notebook of General A. Houtum Schindler (Schindler and

Fig. 0.2 Damghan Plain, ringed by snow-capped Elburz mountains, looking northeast, October 1976.

Fig. 0.3 Aerial view (via Google Earth) of Tepe Hissar with site features marked. The site is surrounded by agricultural fields and the contemporary village.

Fig. 0.4 The Tehran-Meshed Railroad, which cuts through Tepe Hissar.

Fig. 0.5 A view of the modern eroded landscape of Tepe Hissar, as seen from south in 2007.

Schmeltz 1887), an Austrian who served in the Persian army and wrote about the inhabitants of the region looting the site in search of antiquities. The site was later brought to the attention of the archaeological community by Ernst Herzfeld of the German Archaeological Service in Iran. In 1925, he surveyed the Damghan region, cataloged the looted objects mentioned by Schindler (Herzfeld 1988:44), and recommended the site for exploration to Horace F. Jayne, then the director of the Penn Museum.

In 1930, Jayne invited Schmidt, who trained at Columbia University under the renowned anthropologist Franz Boas, to undertake the Damghan Project on behalf of the Penn Museum and the Pennsylvania Museum of Art. Schmidt had come highly recommended to Jayne after his previous field research in Arizona and at the Bronze Age site of Alishar Höyük in central Turkey.

In Jayne's mind, the Damghan Project could provide another link in the chain of cultural connections between

Fig. 0.6 A photograph from Schmidt's first day of excavation at Tepe Hissar on July 19, 1931 (Courtesy of the Penn Museum).

quired a complex network of communications among museum directors, diplomats, scholars, as well as bureaucrats in Reza Shah's government. Among the key consultant-scholars—apart from Herzfeld, who had strong influence on Jayne's decisions—were Frederick Wulsin and Arthur Upham Pope. The latter, a strong advocate of the Tepe Hissar Project, was an art historian, whose connections in Iran would later help establish the American Institute for Persian Art and Archaeology, headquartered in New York City. Wulsin had been sent to Iran by Jayne to carry out his own excavations under the auspices of the Penn Museum.[8] Thus, Wulsin played a key role in getting the Tepe Hissar Project started as he was already familiar with the rules and regulations for foreign archaeologists working in Iran. In June of 1931, the Iranian Antiquities Law[9] was passed. In the same year, Schmidt and his team arrived in Damghan after two months of testing and restudy of the Sumerian site of Fara in southern Mesopotamia. He started excavations at Tepe Hissar on July 19, 1931 (Fig. 0.6).

Mesopotamia and Iran. Further, he hoped that it would produce a wealth of objects for display. Fiske Kimball, then director of the Pennsylvania Museum of Art, was interested in the Sassanian palace near Tepe Hissar because of its many exquisite architectural stuccos (Schmidt 1933:455–56, 1937:327–350). As always, funding the project was a crucial matter, especially during the Great Depression. Despite funding difficulties, $16,000 was raised by both museums from member contributions and, later, additional funds were acquired from private sources over a period of three years. To launch the project re-

The Damghan Project had a full program of excavation at three sites: Tepe Hissar (prehistoric), Damghan town citadel (Late Islamic [Fig. 0.7]), and the nearby Sassanian palace (3rd–7th centuries AD). However, the project's primary focus was the site of Tepe Hissar.

B.2 Robert H. Dyson Jr. Excavations (1976)

The second cycle of excavation in 1976 was aimed in part at correcting the stratigraphic and chronological problems from Schmidt's excavations. In addition, the occupational history of the Main Mound (Buildings 1, 2,

Fig. 0.7 The late Islamic town citadel at Damghan, excavated as part of Schmidt's Damghan Project.

and 3), the North Flat (Burned Building complex), the South Hill (industrial workshop), and the Twins were clarified with stratified levels and radiocarbon dates. Additional investigations included geomorphology and ecology (Meder 1989:7–12), archaeometallurgy investigations (Pigott 1989:25–33), and an archaeological survey of the Damghan Plain (Trinkhaus 1989:135–139).

B.3 Archival Research: Re-excavating the Archives of Schmidt and Dyson[10]

At Dyson's suggestion, I started to examine the Tepe Hissar ceramic assemblages in 1994, as a post-doctoral research topic. In 2004, the research topic evolved into a more comprehensive project to reassess Schmidt's excavations in light of the 1976 campaign, specifically, aimed at generating a comparative ceramic chronology. This required an in-depth analysis of the Schmidt and Dyson et al. excavations, using original archives, three published monographs,[11] and other largely unpublished reports. Previously, I had done similar research in a study of the Bronze Age burial groups and ceramics from Wulsin's excavations at Tureng Tepe, which has chronological parallels with the Tepe Hissar ceramic assemblages (Daher 1968), and a re-assessment of the Bronze Age site of Alaca Höyük in central Turkey (Gürsan-Salzmann 1992), excavated by Hamit Z. Koşay in the 1930s. Hence, my long-term experience in archival research and studies of Bronze Age ceramic assemblages provided a solid background for the Tepe Hissar project.

In the course of analyzing the Tepe Hissar material, I had access to Schmidt's excavated objects and sherds (50% of the total excavated artifacts) and the 1976 project study sherds, all housed at the Penn Museum. Schmidt's archival papers and the 1976 project field notes were used to generate detailed relational databases for the Main Mound and the North Flat from both cycles of excavation. These relational databases provided efficient cross-referencing of the records.

B.3.1 Schmidt Archives

The entire corpus of Schmidt's archives consists of 42 boxes of records grouped into sub-series: field notes, reports from the field, a potsherd catalogue, several boxes of object cards and drawings that were grouped into sub-series, burial sheets, and correspondence between Schmidt, Jayne, and other individuals and institutions involved in the project. The Schmidt archives occupy roughly 25 linear feet of box space and several drawers for large-scale drawings of plans and sections. The photographic collection consists of photos of the excavation and expedition trips. They are referenced in the photographic negative card catalogue, which takes up 10 linear feet. In addition, there are 12 large-sized photo albums containing black-and-white prints of excavation shots, burials, objects, and landscape images taken during Schmidt's reconnaissance trips. All of these records were indispensable to the research undertaken in this restudy. A list of the contents of the Schmidt archives is as follows: general correspondence, reports and publications, field notes, drawings and plans, burial sheets, indexes and catalogs, and financial records. For the most part, the original order has been maintained.

The general correspondence series includes as major correspondents, Jayne, Schmidt, Pope (Director, American Institute for Persian Art and Archaeology), William M. Krogman, (Western Reserve University School of Medicine), Mrs. William Boyce Thompson (the principal patroness of the Iranian Expedition), and Herzfeld. Schmidt's correspondence files appear to be arranged alphabetically by the last name of the writer, but the letters are sometimes signed only with a first name. The content of these include Schmidt's correspondence with colleagues and friends during his association with the Penn Museum. This material is mixed with correspondence and financial records from Alishar Höyük, which Schmidt excavated in the 1920s for the Oriental Institute of the University of Chicago. These records were kept within the correspondence, so as not to disrupt the original order. The field registers/catalogs and architect's notebooks were used together to provide information concerning the provenience of objects. A road diary dated February 1931 describes Schmidt and his staff's visits to sites in the vicinity of Fara and the trip from Baghdad to Damghan.

B.3.2 Dyson Archives

While working with the 1976 materials, I had access to field notes, drawings, study sherds, and above all, personal communication with Dyson. Dyson et al.'s field records clarify and supplement Schmidt's information related to stratigraphy, chronology, architecture, and the overall cultural development at Tepe Hissar. They include field notes, reports, object cards, and a large slide collection. Among those items most relevant to my research were:

(1) a stratified assemblage of about 5100 sherds, excavated from two deep soundings DF09S and CG90P and from horizontally-exposed architecture[12];

(2) architectural information principally from the Main Mound, North Flat, and the South Hill;

(3) radiocarbon dates based on samples from settlement contexts and published results of flotation samples (Dyson and Lawn 1989; Costantini and Dyson 1990:46–68);

(4) Susan Howard's field notes and her unfinished dissertation "The Cultural Chronology of Tepe Hissar: A Reappraisal" (based on her excavations of the Main Mound).

B.3.3 Working with Archives

Two databases were generated from the Schmidt and Dyson assemblages from the Main Mound and the North Flat: (1) pottery and other objects from the Main Mound and the North Flat (as reconstructed and digitized images of 1976 pottery and other objects from settlement levels), (2) burial records from 1931–32 seasons (Fig. 0.8–0.10).

The process of reconstructing Schmidt's analysis of the burial stratigraphy was a difficult task in the absence of clear sections from 1931–32. Moreover, information on burial stratigraphy was mainly reconstructed from multiple lines of evidence, examining archival photographs, field notes, and published plans (Schmidt 1937: figs. 84–86). This is in contrast to Schmidt's method, which was primarily based on meter-depths at which burials were found. An example of the process of reconstruction follows:

(1) Using the plans and sections, wall heights and depths (where available) were measured and indicated on a new section (a schematic section was reconstructed for each square from the Main Mound).

(2) Estimated positions of graves in relation to floor levels were marked using the plans, the architect's notebook (notations for floor levels), and the two generated databases for graves and associated objects (Fig. 0.12).

(3) Ceramics from the graves were plotted by meter-depths in each square and from the settlement (fill/dump—Schmidt's designations from his field register) to check their relation to architectural/floor levels.

(4) The results were compared with the 1976 stratified pottery sequence from the settlement. In some instances, there was a discrepancy between the information given for data in the field register and the corresponding burial sheets or card file entries that were filled out after Schmidt returned from Tepe Hissar. Many of these mistakes are probably copying errors; therefore, I relied on the field registry as the main reference, which also contains categories of information for each data point in separate columns.

C. Research Questions

This research is explicitly descriptive and chronological. It presents the available evidence and, within its limitations, four main objectives are explored:

(1) To establish a ceramic chronology based on combined evidence from occupational levels using 1976 stratified ceramic assemblages.

(2) To correct Schmidt's burial sequence employing results of the new ceramic chronology. Schmidt did not generally trace the burials to the strata from which they originated, but rather recreated the burial stratigraphy using overlying or underlying floors or walls.

(3) To address the "purposes and assumptions lying behind funerary behavior as part the social context" (Shepherd 1999:9). Schmidt's descriptive/quantitative presentation of burial practices based on burial data is limited insofar as it constitutes only an inventory of the individual's body orientation, sex, and mortuary gifts. In describing burial ritual, I use a paradigm that leads to an understanding of the funerary behavior as part of the social and cultural contexts. Use of ethnographic analogy, where applicable, is incorporated to reconstruct underlying funerary behavior.

(4) To address the sociocultural trajectory of the Tepe Hissar settlement and its role in regional and inter-regional connections. Was Tepe Hissar part of the so-called "interaction sphere" of Middle Asia, spanning the early fourth to the beginning of the second millennium BC? This cultural zone covered an extensive area from southern Mesopotamia to the Indus Valley, the Iranian Plateau, Gulf area, and as far as Afghanistan and west Central Asia, in which powerful political and economic systems were established around 3500 BC (Possehl 2007; Ratnagar 2004; Lamberg-Karlovsky and Tosi 1973). At Tepe Hissar, regional/inter-regional "interaction" with Central Asia and Mesopotamia is demonstrated by certain types of material culture, administrative devices (clay counters, blank tablets),[13] and prestige objects, par-

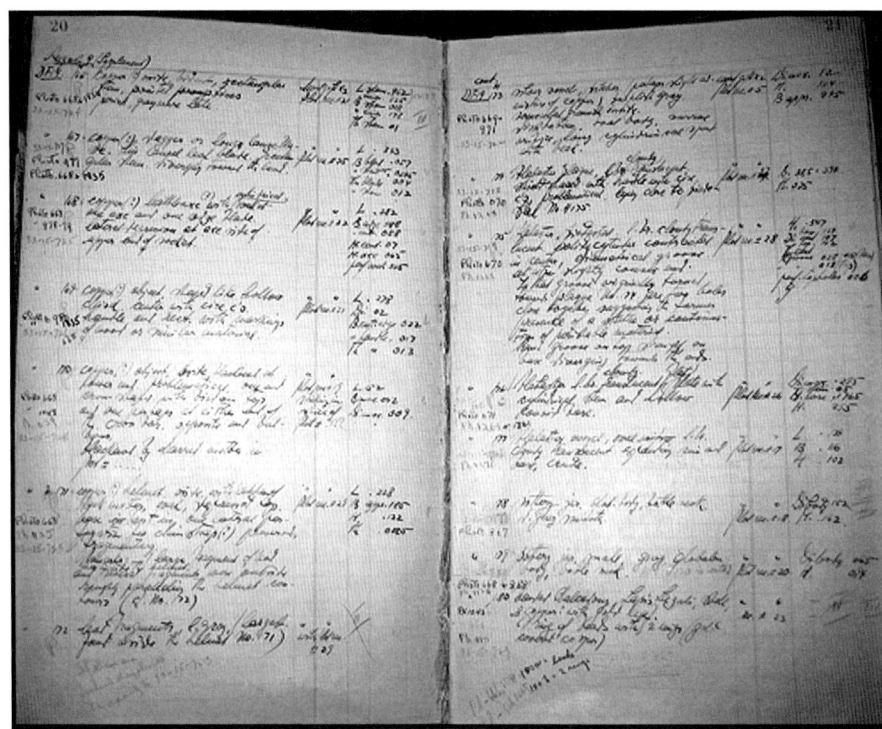

Fig. 0.8 An example of Schmidt's original handwritten registry for Tepe Hissar (Courtesy of the Penn Museum).

reg.	date	square	photo	inv. #	material	artifact type	obj. description	depth (m.)	area (plot rec.)	location	burial #
0	1931 july 26	DG 10	050	H0060	pottery	bowl	dark grey	1.10-1.17			x3
4	1931 july 21	DG 10	1104, 1870	H0022	serpentine	whorl	dark grey biconical	.6 - .8		fill	
4	1931 july 21	DG 10	1055, 1969	H0022	pottery	figurine	light & dark grey	.6 - .9		fill	
4	1931 july 21	DG 10	1017	H0024	metal, gold	fragment	yellow gold frag.	.6 - .8		fill	
5	1931 july 21	DG 10	1104	H0029	pottery	whorl	grey brown	.6 - .8		fill	
6	1931 july 23	DG 10	1056 (not found)	H000	bone	awl	light brownpolish	1.0 - 1.45		fill	
6	1931 july 23	DG 10	1005	H0039	metal	curved obj.	copper oxide			fill	
6	1931 july 25	DG 10	1040	H0042	pottery	figurine	pendant	1.15		fill	
6	1931 july 25	DG 10	1408	H0043	stone	polisher	grey, boconical	1.15		fill	
6	1931 july 25	DG 10	1003	H0044	copper	?	?	1.45		fill	
7	1931 july 26	DG 10	1057	H0051	pottery	figurine, quad	slightly fired	1.65		fill	
7	1931 july 26	DG 10	1060	H0052	pottery	figurine	grey brown	1.65		fill	
7	1931 july 26	DG 10	1057	H0053	clay	figurine	light grey brown	1.65		fill	
7	1931 july 26	DG 10	1106	H0054	stone	bead	br. red, pyramidal	dump heap		fill	
7	1931 july 26	DG 10	1107	H0055	pottery?	bead	light grey	2.25		fill	
7	1931 july 26	DG 10	1020	H0056	pottery	cup	brown on light br.	2.25	P rec 16	fill	
7	1931 july 26	DG 10	1265, 1859	H0057	stone	bowl	gr. White transluc	1.10-1.17			x3
7	1931 july 26	DG 10	1266, 1860	H0058	stone	cup	grey brown	1.10-1.17			x3?
8	1931 july 26	DG 10	857, 1815	H0059	pottery	cup	grey, smooth mug	1.10-1.17			x3?
8	1931 july 26	DG 10	1330	H0061	? Paste?	bead/s	grey white	1.10-1.17			x3
8	1931 july 26	DG 10	1007	H0062	metal	earring, oxide	coiled	1.10-1.17			x3
9	1931 july 27	DF 19	843	H0074	pottery	cup	grey, truncated	0.20 +	P rec 1	?fill?	?
9	1931 july 27	DF 19	844	H0075	pottery	cup	grey	0.15	P rec ?	?fill?	?
9	1931 july 27	DF 19	1162	H0076	pottery	cup	lt. Grey w. Dark	0.15	P rec 3	?fill?	?
9	1931 july 27	DF 19	844	H0077	pottery	cup	lt. Grey w. Dark	0.10		?fill?	?
9	1931 july 27	DF 19	045	H0070	pottery	cup	lt. Grey w. Dark	0.15	P rec 7	?fill?	?
9	1931 july 27	DF 19	1267	H0079	stone	bowl	brownish white	0.20			x1
9	1931 july 27	DF 19	1420	H0080	stone	stone	lt. brown polisher	0.20 - 0.30			x1
9	1931 july 27	DF 19	1421	H0081	stone	stone	grey polisher	0.20 - 0.50		?fill?	?
9	1931 july 27	DF 19	1427	H0082	stone, lime.?	stone	grey globe,sling	0.20 - 0.50			
10	1931 july 28	DG 10	1060	H0083	clay?	figurine, grey	slightly baked	1.0 - 2.50	L.2		
11	1931 july 28	DF 19	1409	H0092	stone, oval	?	light grey	0.50 - 0.60		?fill?	
11	1931 july 28	DF 19	996	H0093	metal	arrowhead	copper oxide	0.50 - 0.60		?fill?	
11	1931 july 28	DF 19	1050	H0094	stone	awl frag.	light brown	0.50 - 0.60		?fill?	
11	1931 july 28	DF 19	1420	H0095	stone	polisher	light brown	0.50 - 0.60		?fill?	
11	1931 july 28	DG 10	1062	H0097	pottery	figurine	light brown	1.8 - 2.5	L.2	?fill?	
12	1931 july 29	DF 18	1109	H0102	stone	bead/s	elliptical	0.0 - 0.10		?fill?	
12	1931 july 29	Df 18	1065	H0103	stone	pin/s	plain, polished	0.0 - 0.10		?fill?	
14	1931 aug 1	DG 10	1301	HH0116	stone	cylinder seal	grey brown	2.45		?fill?	
14	1931 aug 1	DG 10		H0117	pottery	figurine	light red brown	1.8 - 2.6		?fill?	
14	1931 aug 1	DG 10	1064	H0119	clay	biconical	grey brown crude			?fill?	
14	1931 aug 1	DG 10	1064	H0118	clay	globe	grey brown	1.0 - 2.6		?fill?	
14	1931 aug 1	DG 10		h0120	clay	Figural Obj.	grey brown			?fill?	
15	1931 aug 1	DG 10	1056	H0123	pottery	figurine	light grey brown	1.0 - 2.6	L.2 high	?fill?	
16	1931 aug 3	DG 10	1064	H0126	clay	bicone	light grey brown	2.7	L.2	?fill?	
16	1931 aug 3	DG 10	1065	H0127	clay	figurine	red brown	3.45	L.1 ?.1	?fill?	
16	1931 aug 3	DG 10	1066	H0128	clay	fig.,human	grey brown	3.45	S.1	?fill?	
16	1931 aug 3	DG 10	1060	H0129	clay	figurine	grey brown	3.45	S.1	?fill?	

Fig. 0.9 An example of the database created from Schmidt's field register.

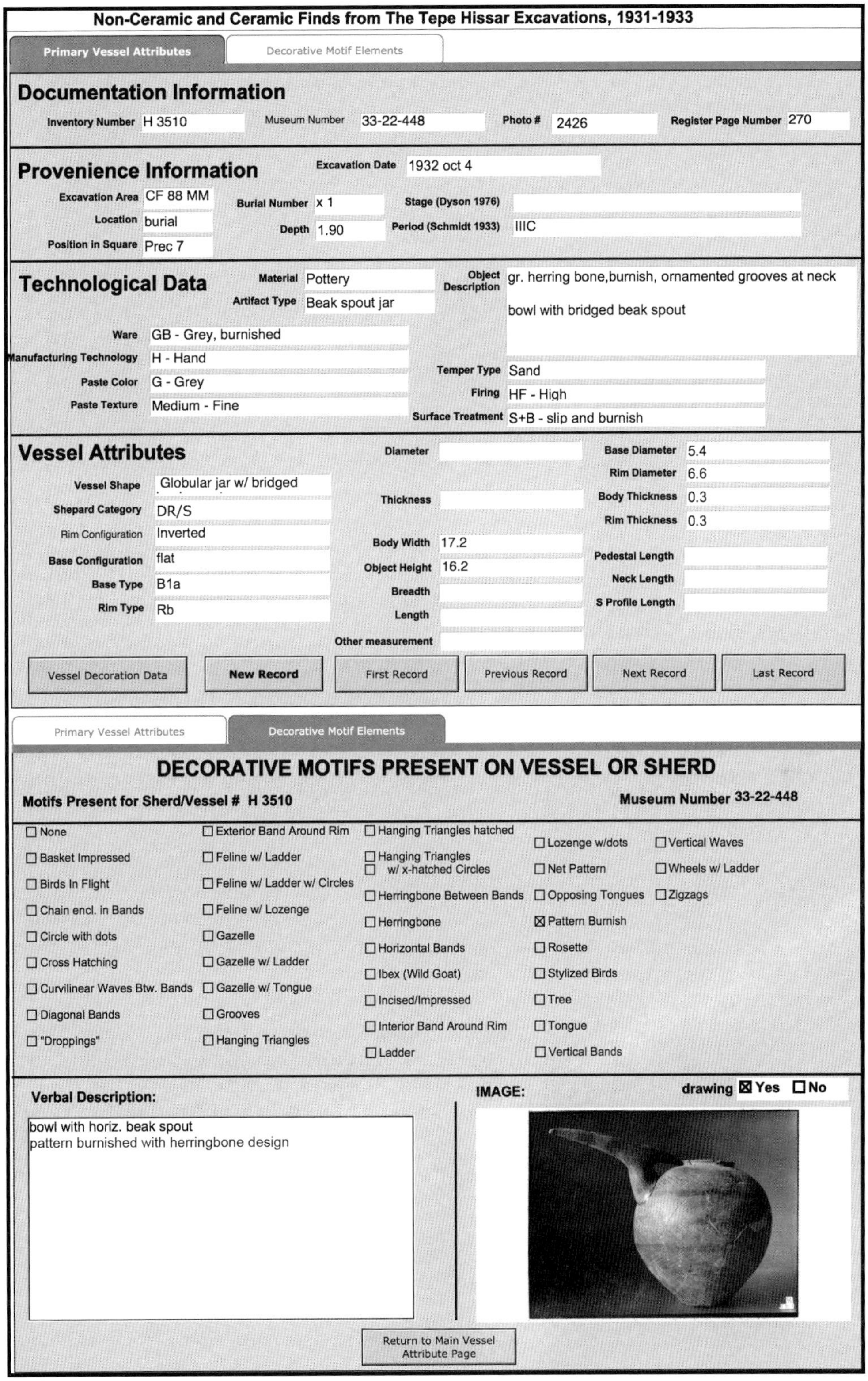

Non-Ceramic and Ceramic Finds from The Tepe Hissar Excavations, 1931-1933

Primary Vessel Attributes | Decorative Motif Elements

Documentation Information

Inventory Number: H 3510
Museum Number: 33-22-448
Photo #: 2426
Register Page Number: 270

Provenience Information

Excavation Date: 1932 oct 4
Excavation Area: CF 88 MM
Location: burial
Position in Square: Prec 7
Burial Number: x 1
Depth: 1.90
Stage (Dyson 1976):
Period (Schmidt 1933): IIIC

Technological Data

Material: Pottery
Artifact Type: Beak spout jar
Object Description: gr. herring bone,burnish, ornamented grooves at neck
bowl with bridged beak spout
Ware: GB - Grey, burnished
Manufacturing Technology: H - Hand
Paste Color: G - Grey
Paste Texture: Medium - Fine
Temper Type: Sand
Firing: HF - High
Surface Treatment: S+B - slip and burnish

Vessel Attributes

Vessel Shape: Globular jar w/ bridged
Shepard Category: DR/S
Rim Configuration: Inverted
Base Configuration: flat
Base Type: B1a
Rim Type: Rb
Diameter:
Thickness:
Body Width: 17.2
Object Height: 16.2
Breadth:
Length:
Other measurement:
Base Diameter: 5.4
Rim Diameter: 6.6
Body Thickness: 0.3
Rim Thickness: 0.3
Pedestal Length:
Neck Length:
S Profile Length:

Vessel Decoration Data | New Record | First Record | Previous Record | Next Record | Last Record

Primary Vessel Attributes | Decorative Motif Elements

DECORATIVE MOTIFS PRESENT ON VESSEL OR SHERD

Motifs Present for Sherd/Vessel # H 3510
Museum Number 33-22-448

☐ None
☐ Basket Impressed
☐ Birds In Flight
☐ Chain encl. in Bands
☐ Circle with dots
☐ Cross Hatching
☐ Curvilinear Waves Btw. Bands
☐ Diagonal Bands
☐ "Droppings"
☐ Exterior Band Around Rim
☐ Feline w/ Ladder
☐ Feline w/ Ladder w/ Circles
☐ Feline w/ Lozenge
☐ Gazelle
☐ Gazelle w/ Ladder
☐ Gazelle w/ Tongue
☐ Grooves
☐ Hanging Triangles
☐ Hanging Triangles hatched
☐ Hanging Triangles ☐ w/ x-hatched Circles
☐ Herringbone Between Bands
☐ Herringbone
☐ Horizontal Bands
☐ Ibex (Wild Goat)
☐ Incised/Impressed
☐ Interior Band Around Rim
☐ Ladder
☐ Lozenge w/dots
☐ Net Pattern
☐ Opposing Tongues
☒ Pattern Burnish
☐ Rosette
☐ Stylized Birds
☐ Tree
☐ Tongue
☐ Vertical Bands
☐ Vertical Waves
☐ Wheels w/ Ladder
☐ Zigzags

Verbal Description:
bowl with horiz. beak spout
pattern burnished with herringbone design

IMAGE: drawing ☒ Yes ☐ No

Return to Main Vessel Attribute Page

Fig. 0.10 An example from the Salzmann database for 1931–32 small finds.

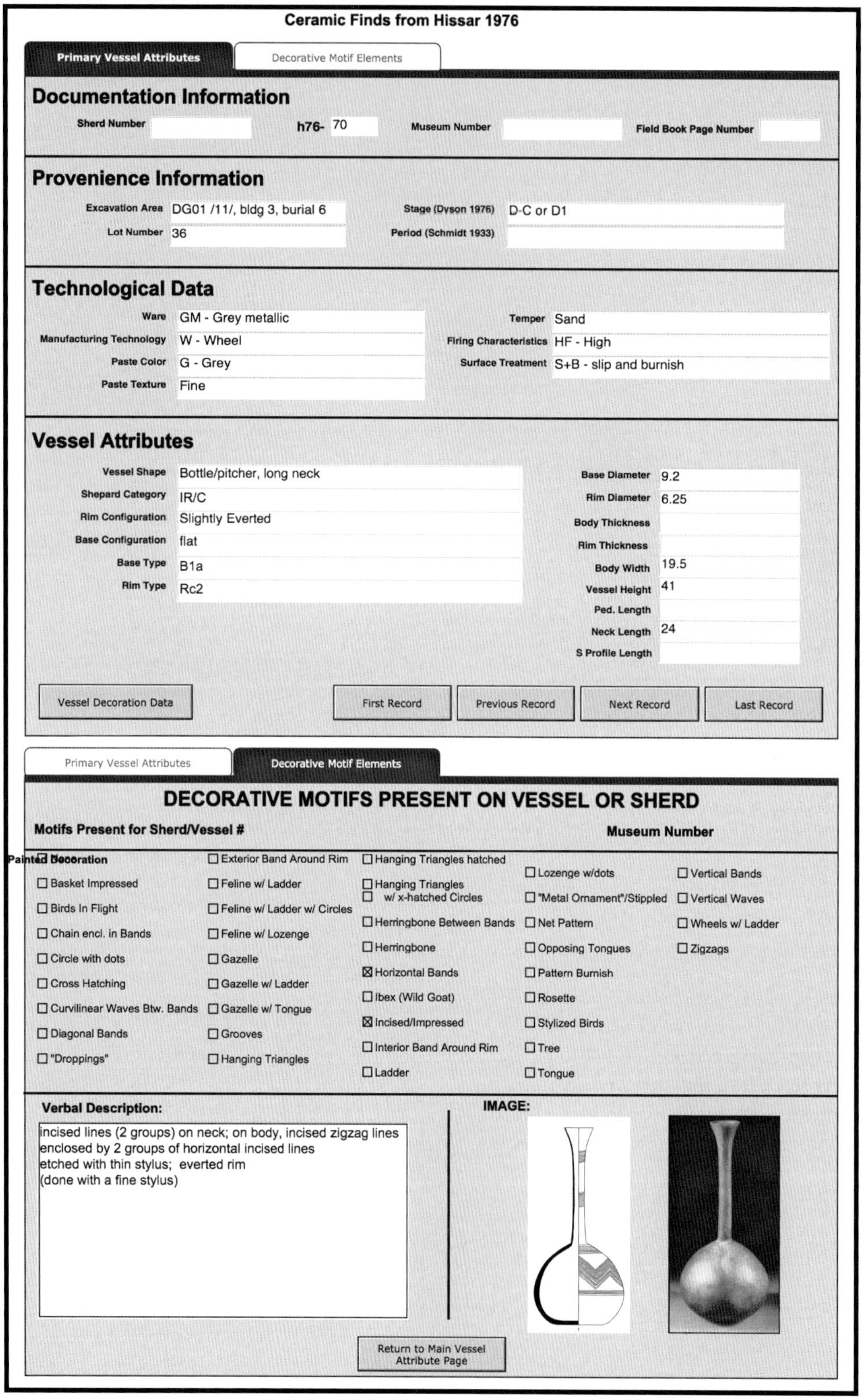

Ceramic Finds from Hissar 1976

Primary Vessel Attributes | Decorative Motif Elements

Documentation Information

Sherd Number | h76- 70 | Museum Number | Field Book Page Number

Provenience Information

Excavation Area	DG01 /11/, bldg 3, burial 6	Stage (Dyson 1976)	D-C or D1
Lot Number	36	Period (Schmidt 1933)	

Technological Data

Ware	GM - Grey metallic	Temper	Sand
Manufacturing Technology	W - Wheel	Firing Characteristics	HF - High
Paste Color	G - Grey	Surface Treatment	S+B - slip and burnish
Paste Texture	Fine		

Vessel Attributes

Vessel Shape	Bottle/pitcher, long neck	Base Diameter	9.2
Shepard Category	IR/C	Rim Diameter	6.25
Rim Configuration	Slightly Everted	Body Thickness	
Base Configuration	flat	Rim Thickness	
Base Type	B1a	Body Width	19.5
Rim Type	Rc2	Vessel Height	41
		Ped. Length	
		Neck Length	24
		S Profile Length	

Vessel Decoration Data | First Record | Previous Record | Next Record | Last Record

Primary Vessel Attributes | Decorative Motif Elements

DECORATIVE MOTIFS PRESENT ON VESSEL OR SHERD

Motifs Present for Sherd/Vessel # **Museum Number**

☐ Painted Decoration
☐ Basket Impressed
☐ Birds In Flight
☐ Chain encl. in Bands
☐ Circle with dots
☐ Cross Hatching
☐ Curvilinear Waves Btw. Bands
☐ Diagonal Bands
☐ "Droppings"
☐ Exterior Band Around Rim
☐ Feline w/ Ladder
☐ Feline w/ Ladder w/ Circles
☐ Feline w/ Lozenge
☐ Gazelle
☐ Gazelle w/ Ladder
☐ Gazelle w/ Tongue
☐ Grooves
☐ Hanging Triangles
☐ Hanging Triangles hatched
☐ Hanging Triangles ☐ w/ x-hatched Circles
☐ Herringbone Between Bands
☐ Herringbone
☒ Horizontal Bands
☐ Ibex (Wild Goat)
☒ Incised/Impressed
☐ Interior Band Around Rim
☐ Ladder
☐ Lozenge w/dots
☐ "Metal Ornament"/Stippled
☐ Net Pattern
☐ Opposing Tongues
☐ Pattern Burnish
☐ Rosette
☐ Stylized Birds
☐ Tree
☐ Tongue
☐ Vertical Bands
☐ Vertical Waves
☐ Wheels w/ Ladder
☐ Zigzags

Verbal Description:

incised lines (2 groups) on neck; on body, incised zigzag lines
enclosed by 2 groups of horizontal incised lines
etched with thin stylus; everted rim
(done with a fine stylus)

IMAGE:

Return to Main Vessel Attribute Page

Fig. 0.11 An example from the Salzmann database for 1931–32 small finds.

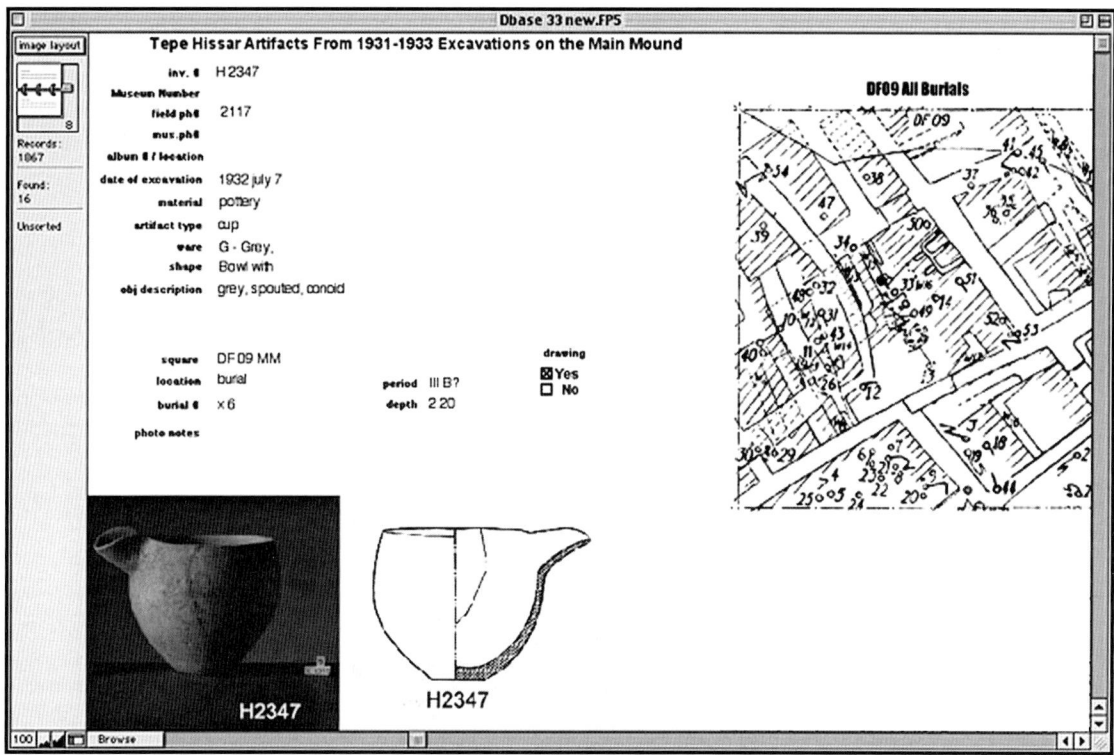

Fig. 0.12 An example from the Salzmann database for 1931–32 burial assemblages.

ticularly from burial evidence on the Main Mound and the Treasure Hill, but also in the settlement levels of the Main Mound, the North Flat, and the South Hill. A full account of Tepe Hissar's participation in the "interaction sphere" is beyond the scope of this monograph.

In this monograph, the Tepe Hissar ceramics from the 1931–32 and 1976 excavations on the Main Mound and the North Flat are juxtaposed with archaeological and burial data in order to address the topics raised above. In Chapter 1, a summary of Schmidt's excavations (1931–32) is presented, including his methodology and chronological sequence that changed at the end of the 1932 season. Chapter 2 provides a detailed description of Dyson et al.'s 1976 excavation, primarily focusing on the revised stratigraphy and architecture from the Main Mound and the North Flat. At the end of Chapter 2, Table 2.2 correlates architectural levels from the Main Mound and the North Flat sequences with Schmidt's periods and range of dates based on radiocarbon dates using 2009 calibration (for radiocarbon dates see Appendix 4).

Chapter 3 is the analysis of ceramic assemblages from the 1976 project that generated a revised ceramic chronology for the settlement sequence at Tepe Hissar, covering periods Hissar I–III (see Table 3.4). The "Ceramic Phases" in the second column is based on the analysis of stratified ceramic assemblages and also compared to Schmidt's ceramic assemblages, largely from burials. Chapters 4 and 5 address the dating of burials excavated by Schmidt (for dated burials, see Tables 4.1 and 4.2) and the analysis of burial practices in social/cultural contexts. The dated burials are grouped in each square (see Tables 4.1a, 4.2a) and plotted horizontally using a GIS measurement method, so that the vertical and horizontal plotting of individual burials and their clusters is no longer "floating" in space and time.

The Concluding Remarks (Chapter 6) focus on the sociocultural development of the Tepe Hissar settlement. The implications of which are observed through the sequence of the new revised chronology, in light of evidence from the Schmidt and Dyson et al. excavations. Tepe Hissar's role in the region and its inter-regional cultural/trade interactions during the fourth through the third millennia BC is explored. Lastly, some future research directions are presented.

NOTES:

0.1 For background information on the initiation of the Tepe Hissar Project in 1931 and Schmidt's nearly a decade of researches in Iran, including archival photographs, see *Exploring Iran* (Gürsan-Salzmann 2007).

0.2 In the early 1960s, Dyson was at the forefront of archaeological field research in Iran, implementing up-to-date methodology and theory. His first major excavation project at the Iron Age site of Hasanlu in northwestern Iran, Azerbaijan and the second at Tepe Hissar in the northeast became field training ground for several generations of accomplished American and Iranian archaeologists.

0.3 Based on archaeological faunal and floral evidence, a range of animal figurines, and painted animal motifs on ceramics (Meder 1989:12).

0.4 The archaeobotanical samples are from Period II, late fourth millennium BC (Costantini 1990:66). Wild grape and olive samples are limited.

0.5 The faunal analysis was done by Marjan Mashkour, based on the 1995 excavations by Ehsan Yaghmai. The faunal remains studied (Mashkour and Yaghmai 1996) are from the Main Mound and the Red Hill, Period IIIB-C, late third millennium BC. Remains of fish and mollusks were also retrieved.

0.6 I visited Tepe Hissar in 2007, three decades after the Dyson team had left, rain and wind erosion had completely destroyed the 1976 Main Mound trenches, so I could not compare my photos with those from 1976.

0.7 Roustaei (2010:614) describes the modern landscape: "the most conspicuous structures are several mudbrick fortresses of middle Islamic period and a small prehistoric mound several hundred meters from the site. In this way, the complex of Tepe Hesar constitutes a terrain [that] measures about 200 ha with several ancient sites."

0.8 In May 1931, Wulsin and his wife began excavations at Tureng Tepe, a Bronze Age site in the Gorgan Plain to the north of Tepe Hissar.

0.9 This law allowed non-French archaeologists to begin excavations in the country.

0.10 To the best of my knowledge, nearly fifty percent of excavated objects from Schmidt's excavations are housed in the National Museum of Iran (Tehran), the other half at the Penn Museum (Philadelphia). There are small collections at the American Museum of Natural History (New York) and the Metropolitan Museum of New York. All original expedition records from the 1931–32 and 1976 excavations are kept in the Penn Museum Archives and at the University of Turin. A large collection of skeletal material from the Schmidt expedition is in the Penn Museum, as are the study sherds and some botanical samples from the 1976 restudy project.

0.11 Erich F. Schmidt 1933, 1937; R. H. Dyson and S. M. Howard, 1989.

0.12 The preliminary results of the ceramic analysis show transitions from the Late Chalcolithic painted pottery levels to the early grey ware horizon (Hissar IC–IIA) and from the mature grey ware period (Hissar II–III) to the end of the Bronze Age settlement. However, the latter study does not provide a full analysis of the ceramic assemblages; specifically, it lacks "form" criteria and drawings of sherds in the classification that are critical for comparing and dating Schmidt's typology (which is based largely on complete vessels).

0.13 To date, no Proto-Elamite tablets have been found at Tepe Hissar, though there are sealings and other bureaucratic devices that "seem to relate to the accounting of local agricultural produce rather than long-distance trade" (Lamberg-Karlovsky and Beale 1986:208–11).

1

Erich F. Schmidt Excavations (1931–32)

A. Introduction

This chapter is as much a descriptive synthesis of Erich F. Schmidt's goals and methodological approach (pp. 1–27) in his two seasons of excavations at Tepe Hissar, as it is a critique of his thought processes in interpreting his data (pp. 28–39) in light of my updated ceramic analysis. As such, I have extracted extensive quotes from his 1937 publication to bring forth the evidence of his architectural levels and to provide a summary of the finds wherein his stratigraphic and chronological framework rest. Additionally, it is hoped that providing Schmidt's original insights as appropriate in this volume will help to make his, often difficult to locate, published work more accessible to current scholars.

Schmidt set up his excavation headquarters in the modern town of Damghan in a spacious building that had previously belonged to the gendarmerie. Of the two long seasons of excavation, the first season took place from July until mid-November 1931 and the second lasted from May through November 1932. At the end of the first season, the staff spent the winter months in Tehran (until May 1932) in order to process finds and divide objects among the three museums (Penn Museum, Pennsylvania Museum of Art, and Tehran Museum). In January 1932, two months after the end of the second field season, Schmidt and the rest of the staff departed Tehran by "Camel" (the expedition car) for their respective destinations, braving the snow-covered passes of the Elburz Mountains.

The Damghan project staff was an international team of seven members in addition to the local Iranian household personnel. While some staff members were replaced after the first season, the original staff included: Schmidt, a German-American archaeologist; Kurt Leitner, an Austrian surveyor; Derwood W. Lockard, an American archaeologist; Erskine L. White, an American architectural assistant; Boris Dubensky, a Russian photographer; Ivan Gerasimoff, a Russian artist; and Stanislas Niedzwiecki, a Polish artist-photographer. Schmidt, as the project director, had multiple roles; in addition to administering funds and reporting to the sponsoring museums, he was in charge of daily supervision of the staff's work and most of the recording of finds and architecture (Fig. 1.1).

From the beginning, it was clear to Schmidt that he had a dual mission. While primarily concerned with re-

Fig. 1.1 Schmidt's excavation staff (1931–32), from left: Derwood W. Lockard, Erskine L. White, Erich F. Schmidt, Kurt Leitner, and their Iraqi guide, standing in front of the Lion Gate on a trip to Babylon.

trieving accurate archaeological information from Tepe Hissar, he also had to provide spectacular objects for the two sponsoring museums in Philadelphia and for Tehran, in accordance with the 50/50 division clause of the revised Iranian Antiquities Law. Schmidt's overall objective was to write a cultural history of the Iranian plateau, which meant documenting and explaining reasons for cultural change. As with many archaeologists of this time, Schmidt attributed cultural change to invasion by foreign "ethnic groups." For example, Schmidt (1937:325) attributed the introduction of "grey wares" (i.e., reduction fired pottery) in his Hissar II period to the immigration of populations from the northern Eurasian steppes.

To accomplish his goals, Schmidt had to learn about Iranian prehistory, which at that time was mostly an archaeological *terra incognita*. In Iran, previous archaeological investigations were mostly confined to the site of Susa in Elam, although the French excavations at this site were of limited scientific value (Le Breton 1957). The site of Tepe Sialk near Kashan was the only other scientific excavation on the central Iranian plateau, carried out by Roman Ghirshman (1938) between 1933 and 1937. It is also important to mention, however, that two of the early expeditions undertaken during the turn of the century and in the early 1930s paved the path for an interest in Irani-an antiquities, specifically, Jacques de Morgan et al.'s *Mission Scientifique en Perse* (1896) and J. Conteneau and R. Ghirshman's *Fouilles du Tepe-Giyan* (1933; see also Conteneau, Ghirshman, and Vallois 1936). Sir Aurel Stein's classic account of his journeys in Western Iran (1936) was published in 1940.

In the course of nearly two years of excavation at Tepe Hissar and other sites in the region, Schmidt familiarized himself with the topography of Damghan and the surrounding areas. With the help of surveyor Kurt Leitner, he documented single and multi-period prehistoric and historic sites and created a series of archaeological maps (Schmidt 1933: pls. LXXV, LXXVI, opp. p. 326). Schmidt noted that, in the Damghan area, the sites were mostly flat prehistoric ruins and a few small mounds, dated to Islamic and earlier historical periods. These archaeological maps became the basis for later systematic surveys in 1976 when Kathryn Maurer Trinkaus recorded 166 sites in an area of 450 to 500 square kilometers in the Damghan region, with settlements dating from the fourth millennium BC to the present (Dyson and Howard 1989:135–139).

Prior to excavations at Tepe Hissar, Schmidt surveyed and briefly tested the Islamic levels at the Damghan citadel (Schmidt 1933:329–331, 1937:11–12, figs. 4, 5). At Tepe

Fig. 1.2 An example of an intramural burial from the Main Mound, DF18 x13, the occupational level is not clear, the deceased might be on floor level or above it (Courtesy of the Penn Museum).

Hissar itself, the mound of the Sassanian palace complex was drawn, its architectural details recorded, and the stucco ornaments of the columns in the colonnaded hall were restored (Schmidt 1933:455–470). In the course of both seasons, the staff was engaged in testing smaller sites nearby, such as Tepe Muman and Tarikh-Khaneh (both historic sites), as well as Shir-e Shian (a Chalcolithic site preceding Hissar IA; see also Ch. 6, Concluding Remarks). The team also made several long-distance reconnaissance trips to southern Iran and Luristan (Penn Museum Archives, box 21).

B. Research Goals and Methodological Problems

Schmidt's main research goal was to excavate Tepe Hissar stratigraphically in order to establish a cultural sequence for the site and the region. He planned to "section the main complex from the highest point to the bottom of the culture deposit, at least in one square" (1933:336). However, the excavation of 1,637 intramural burials had greatly disturbed extensive sections of the original stratification, which, in turn, conflicted with the correct recording of the occupational levels (Fig. 1.2). Schmidt made little attempt to trace the burials to the strata from which they originated, but rather recreated the burial stratigraphy using overlying or underlying floors or walls.

Similarly, superimposed construction phases were not clearly defined. Schmidt frequently identified structures as belonging to "somewhere between" different ceramic periods. A clear example of this problem is his description of Hissar III architectural remains (Buildings 1, 2, and 3) on the Main Mound (Schmidt 1937: figs.84, 86; see also Fig. 1.3). In describing phases ("levels") 1 and 2 of these structures, Schmidt attributed Level 1 to Period IIIC (uppermost level) with incoherent foundations. Of the earlier phase he wrote (Schmidt 1937:155–56): "Level 2 (marked in black) has suffered by the numerous burials of later settlers, and of course, by the subsequent building activities. Most remains of this level belong to Hissar IIIB, but at several spots particularly at the eastern section of the excavation, structures attributed to this level may already have been inhabited during Hissar IIIA….walls which may belong to the slightly later building phase of level 2…may actually have been built during the occupation of level 1, [and] are marked with heavy vertical lines."

With such problems, what building phases could he assign to Levels 1 and 2 and to what periods (IIIA, IIIB, IIIC) could he associate Buildings 1, 2 and 3 on the Main Mound? Schmidt eventually assigned them to Hissar IIIB based on the ceramic types in the graves associated with these strata, but he did so without delineating the sub-phases of construction of each building (for revision of building phases on the Main Mound, see Table 2.1, after Howard 1989a:56–59) and without checking to be sure the graves were, in fact, associated with these levels. This sort of ambiguity has made the Tepe Hissar project difficult to navigate for later scholars and has contributed to the lack of a final publication of this important site.

Similar confusion is encountered when attempting to assign burials to specific chronological or cultural periods (Fig. 1.4). Schmidt based his periodization on his ceramic typology and not necessarily on stratified building phases or objects from building contexts. He argued that Period I burials contained only painted ware, Period III burials contained only burnished grey wares, while Period II burials contained both painted wares and grey wares. Sometimes the same burial was assigned to two different periods (e.g., square DF18 x1), no doubt because the contents of the burial (assigned to the end of Tepe Hissar, his Period IIIC), and the stratigraphic location of the burial (assigned to IIB) did not match up. In fact, his field registry indicates that Schmidt changed the periodization of the graves from the earlier to the later periods only *after* he returned from the field.

Concerning Schmidt's recording methods, his speedy recording of a large number of simultaneously excavated areas make his notes often incomplete or unclear. To his credit, he had several crews numbering over 250 people, each working in different areas of the site, so the fact that we have any usable records is remarkable. Not surprisingly, his staff of four field assistants could not supervise each area of excavation. Schmidt himself notes, "The excavation of 1932 had to be extremely flexible in order to cope with the problems. In the South Hill, Stratum II was being cleared while sections of the Main Mound were carried down to the principal occupational level of Stratum III, and a third unit of the crew started to slice the architectural levels of Stratum I in a test square of the past season, in order to penetrate to virgin soil and thereby determine the earliest traces of the settlement history," (Schmidt's field report, Tepe Hissar Season 1932: Penn Museum Archives, box 41). Schmidt does not clarify the nature of these problems, however, he may be referring to understanding the stratification of building remains.

Schmidt generally registered objects on the same day that they were excavated. This system of recording proved to be useful for later researchers in that unprovenienced objects could be assigned a context (i.e., square, plot record, depth, level) if they were excavated on the same day as other objects that had been registered. In addition to registering the objects, each ceramic vessel was measured (in centimeters) for rim diameter and height, while each small find was measured for length and width.

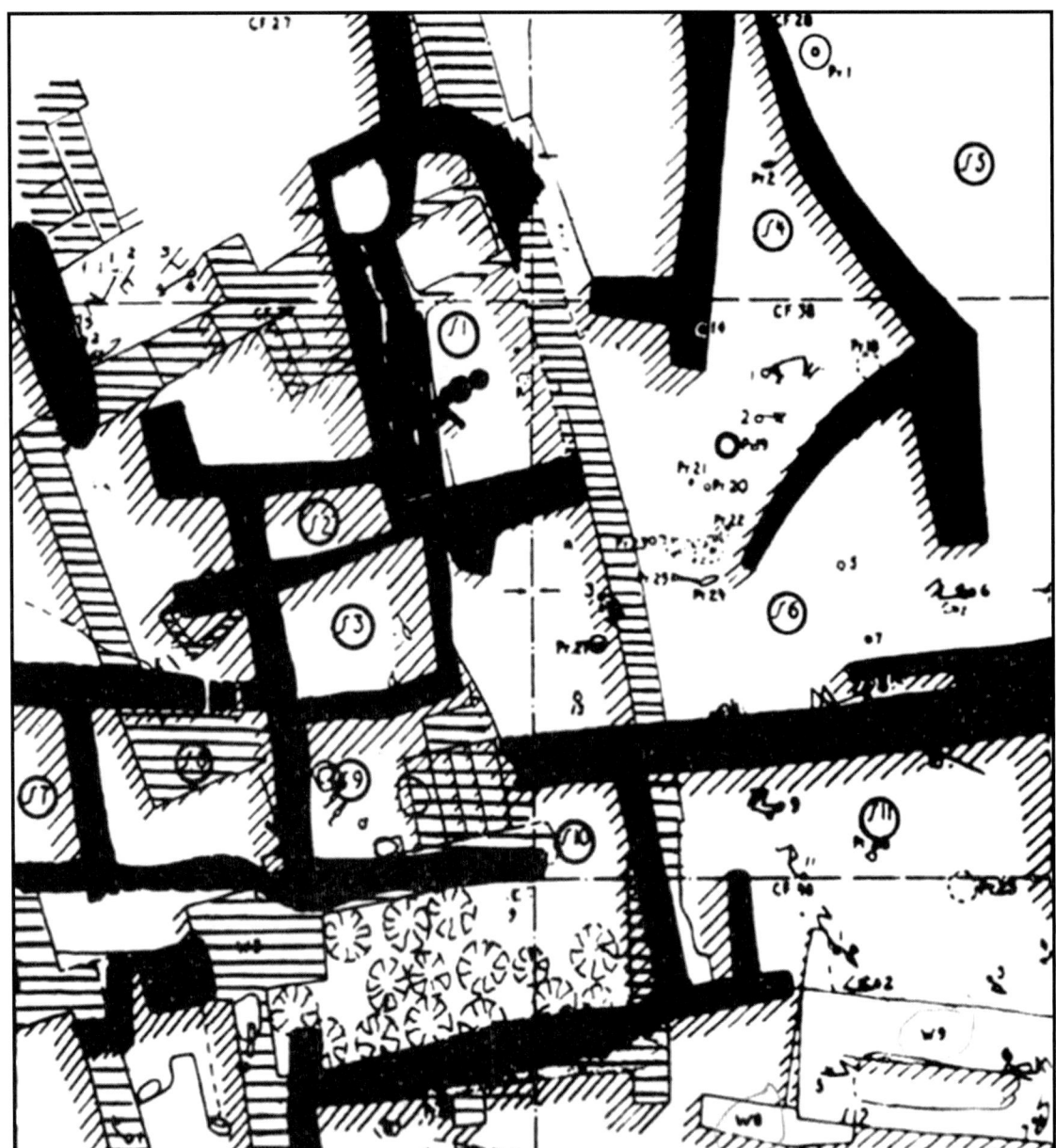

Fig. 1.3 Schmidt's representation of Hissar III architecture with burials and construction phases superimposed. His method of representation obscures stratigraphic definition of each occupational phase, as well as the levels to which the burials belonged.

Although in some cases the field recording was not exemplary, Schmidt's use of the stratigraphic method was a pioneering effort for 1930s excavations. However, he used meter levels to place objects, graves, and structures into arbitrary 'levels'. For example, all objects or burials found between five and seven meters below the surface were grouped together, regardless of soil configuration or the presence of architecture or graves. There was no systematic collection of sherds to serve as typological indices of strata. The sedimentary deposits were not "read" as they are today, making a more accurate description of depositional history impossible. The use of "levels" in Schmidt's terminology meant that finds were recorded in relation to the quadrant and the number of the test square in which they were found. However, their exact position in relation to floors, walls, or other architectural features was not always recorded. In his own words, only "depths of the finds and excavations were measured from the stable 'naught-

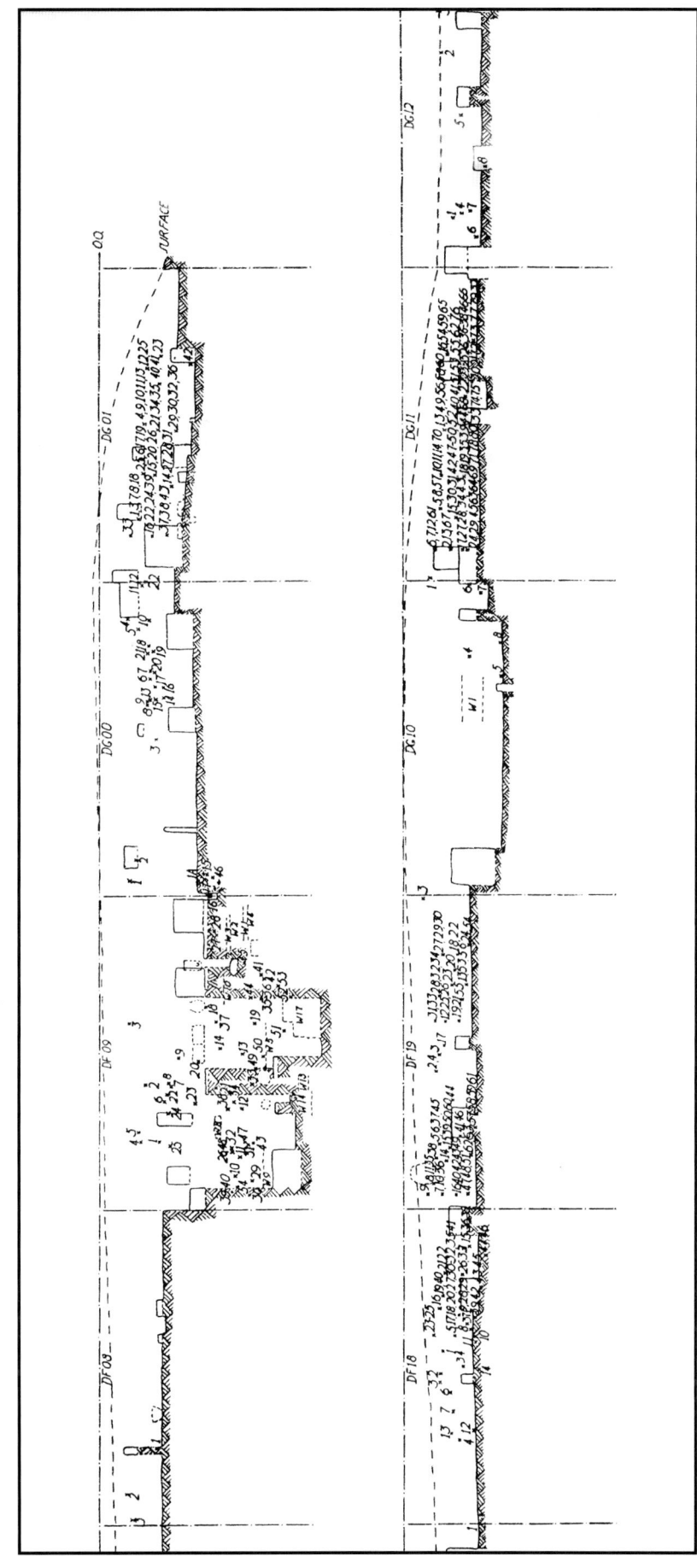

Fig. 1.4 Schmidt's plots of burials from locations on the Main Mound at Tepe Hissar drawn East-West. Note the lack of correlation between building levels and burials (after Schmidt 1937).

naughts,'" (Schmidt 1933:338). Leitner later described the surveying and recording methods as follows:

> The excavation and the system of recording the finds, burials, remaining structures etc. at Tepe Hissar were based on a detailed topographical map with half meter contour intervals, on the survey of which I had to start right away. An arbitrary center point was fixed on the mound and concreted. Through this point lines were run north and south, west and east, which were marked every 100 meters with pegs. Through these pegs, lines were run at right angles and again marked every hundred meters with pegs. Thus the whole area of the mound was covered with 100-meter quadrants. Each row of quadrants was then defined with capital letters: A, B, C, D etc.; starting with "A" at the northwest corner of the map and running along the west-east line and also the north-south line. Each quadrant could be divided into 10-meter squares. These squares were defined with numbers starting at each quadrant with 0, 1, 2…to 9 and running west-east and north-south…. Four quadrant corners were cemented to serve as benchmarks. BM1 was given the elevation of 10.0 meters on which the elevation of the contours was based. Each find was given a 'Field Number' in numerical order. This field number was preceded by the letter "H" (for Hissar). The 10-meter excavation-squares were marked out on the ground, based on the letters and numbers as stated above. The finds were recorded in relation to the quadrant and the number of the test square in which they were found. (Leitner, July 1990, prepared at the request of Robert H. Dyson Jr., Penn Museum Archives)

According to the field notes of Schmidt and Leitner, find-spots of objects (given 'plot record' [pr] numbers) were recorded horizontally, while the strata in which burials were found were indicated by meter-levels below datum point. Although plot-record designations for at least some objects are in the field register, the find-spot data kept in the surveyor's notebooks for each excavated square were unfortunately damaged in a flood and are now unreadable. Thus, the exact horizontal distribution of many objects is unknown. Additionally, on the original burial sheets, the location of burials in relation to building remains (walls, floors, etc.) is often incoherent.

Burials are frequently described as being "slightly below or above" a certain building level, while the building level itself has a depth of 1.0 to 1.5 meters. Thus, burials and objects are literally floating in space, as can be seen in some sections and plans in the 1933 and 1937 publications (Fig. 1.4). This ambiguity in correlating building levels and burials arises partially from the fact that the topographic map of Tepe Hissar was completed *after* the start of the excavations, so that exact find-spots and measurements in relation to the fixed datum point were not accurate.

Over Schmidt's two field seasons at Tepe Hissar, roughly 10,700 square meters were excavated. The distribution of areas tested and excavated from the three periods is uneven, as shown on Schmidt's topographic maps (1937: figs. 21, 61, 83; see also Fig. 1.5). The Hissar I level, the earliest of the three periods, was reached at various places throughout the mounds, but more extensively uncovered on the Painted Pottery Flat (Schmidt 1937: figs. 22–24). Hissar II remains were excavated more extensively than the preceding period on the Main Mound and the North Flat, as well as on the South Hill, the Twins (southernmost), and Treasure Hill (eastern edge of Tepe Hissar) (ibid., figs. 63, 64). For the later Hissar III level, the test areas were the same as Period II, although plans of Period III buildings were uncovered in only three areas: the Main Mound, the North Flat, and Treasure Hill, where horizontal exposures revealed diagonally-oriented, contiguous rectangular buildings (ibid., figs. 84–86, 102–104, 95, 100–101).

Schmidt still managed to test and excavate a large portion of the site and established a chronological sequence based primarily on ceramic typology and the associated grave objects. Two major ceramic stages with subdivisions were identified stratigraphically: painted pottery in the lower levels (Periods IA, IB, IC, IIA, and IIB) and grey burnished pottery in the upper levels (Periods IIA, IIB, IIIA, IIIB, IIIC). Thus, Periods IIA and IIB were defined by the presence of *both* painted wares and burnished grey wares. Schmidt encountered, excavated, and recorded a large number of graves, an activity that, for the most part, occupied his full attention and time. In retrospect, had he spent more time recording building remains and the sequence of episodes/phases relating to them, we would have a more complete picture of the development of the settlement, its functional nature, and, most importantly, a clear stratigraphic sequence independent of graves.

In the 1931 season, as excavation proceeded, Schmidt formulated new research problems. One was the cultural implications of the transition from the painted pottery of the early levels of Hissar I to the grey ware tradition of Hissar II and III. His explanation was based on an invasion theory, with the invaders originating on the Turkoman steppes (Schmidt 1933:325, 367). Another problem was to investigate the circumstances of the end of the Tepe Hissar settlement in Period III. He was almost certain that the end was caused by "catastrophies, epidemics, or the like" (ibid., p. 235). Schmidt changed his mind when he re-dated the

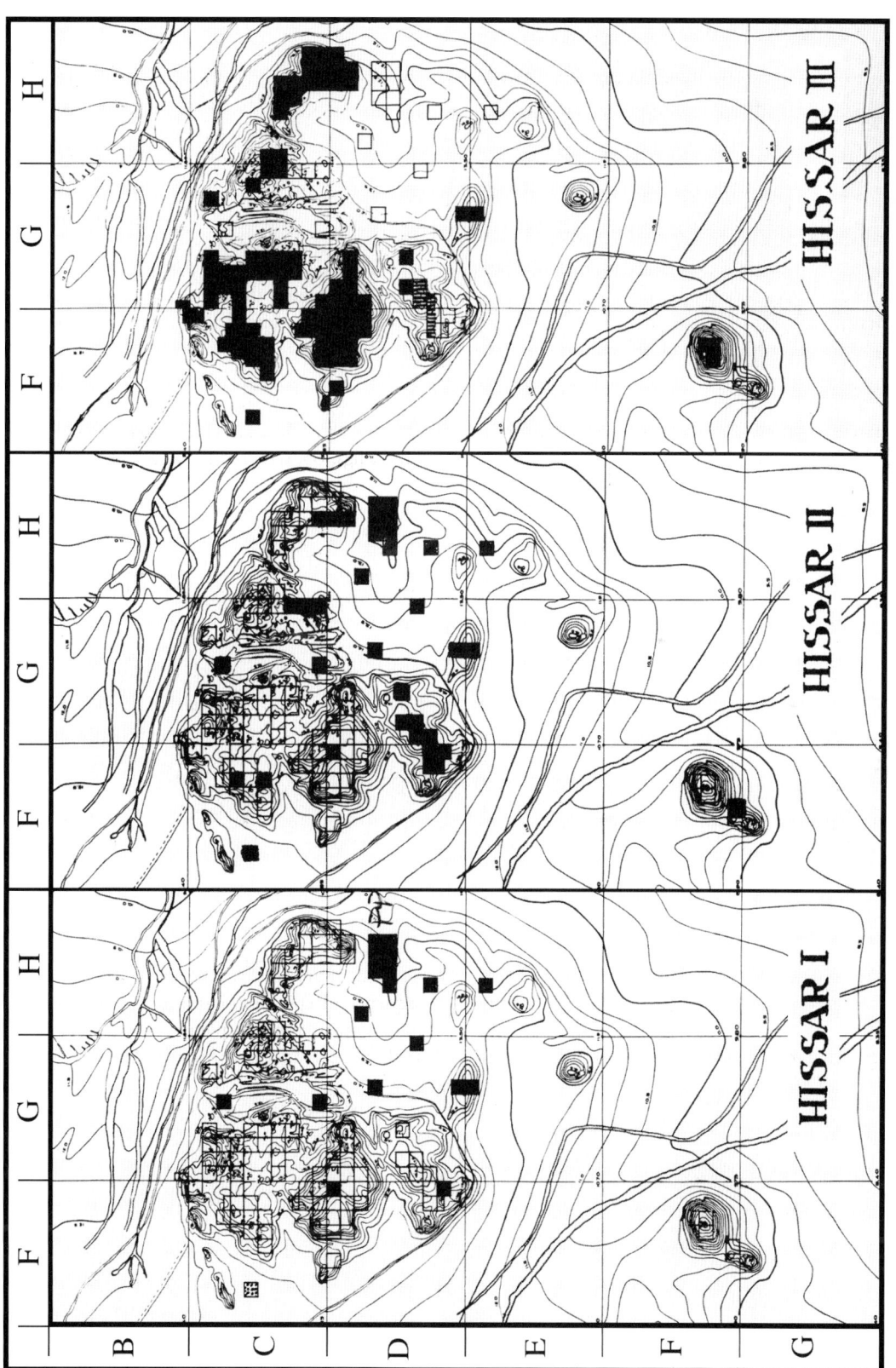

Fig. 1.5 Maps of areas excavated by Schmidt's team for Periods Hissar I–III. Dark areas mark the plots in which Stratum I, II, III remains were uncovered (after Schmidt 1937: figs. 21, 61, 83).

"mass burials" (as the cause of the settlement's end) to Period IIIB instead of IIIC (ibid., pp. 235, 237). As shown in the present study (see Chapter 4), many of those "mass burials" from the Main Mound can be re-dated even earlier to Period II and some to the transitional Period II-III.

C. The 1931 Excavation Season

The first season of excavation at Tepe Hissar, undertaken by Schmidt for the Penn Museum and the Philadelphia Museum of Art, began on July 19 and continued until November 6, 1931 and was partially published in 1933. The contents of this report have generally been ignored and were not republished in 1937. A study of the report and relevant archives is useful in that the assumptions and methods of the work were established in 1931 and elaborated in 1932. A comparison of the documentation of 1931 with that of 1932 identifies many of the problems in using the reports.

In the case of Tepe Hissar, Schmidt's aim was "to illuminate the Dark Age of Persia by means of the prehistoric remains" (Schmidt 1933:323). The remains were expected to include: houses of commoners and rulers, places of worship, works of art, domestic tools and utensils, ornaments and weapons, and human, animal, and floral remains. Such remains collectively "enable the archaeologist to reconstruct a fairly complete picture of the material culture of past people" (ibid.). In stating this aim, Schmidt was drawing on his perspective as an anthropologically-trained archaeologist with the holistic approach to cultural reconstruction he learned from his mentor, Boas.

C.1 Methods

Schmidt wrote, "we divided the tell into 100 x 100 meter quadrants which were subdivided into 10 x 10 meter squares, or excavation units....In one square only... we had time to penetrate to the mound base. However, we shall explain below that even such limited excavation plots can furnish a reliable miniature cross-section of extensive deposits....All test...plots were situated in the main elevation [Main Mound] of the tell....In the twin plots... we penetrated to the original surface...below the northeast corner....The objects were recorded according to their depth below the surface or if possible according to their associations with structural remains and with burials. Thus we obtained...a complete series of superimposed remains reaching from the mound surface to the base of the deposits" (Penn Museum Archives: Schmidt correspondence) (Fig. 1.6).

At Tepe Hissar, they began with this system, however, the team was soon overcome by the sheer quantity of burials and associated objects on the mound. With only four people to do the recording, plot notebooks were soon given up and written notes held to a minimum.

C.2 Maps, Elevations, and Cross-Sections of 1931 Season

Leitner undertook the major mapping tasks, completing a contour map of the site (Schmidt 1933: pl. LXXVIII) in September 1931, a map of Damghan and its environs (ibid., pl. LXXVI) in October 1931, and a regional archaeological map (ibid., pl. LXXV) in Novem-

Fig. 1.6 Shows Tepe Hissar square DF09 where a trench was dug from the top of the mound to the base of the mound, exposing all occupational levels (after Schmidt 1937: fig.27).

ber 1931. The site survey was fixed by the placement of four benchmarks (BM 1–4). Elevations were based on the highest point, BM-1, the elevation of which was arbitrarily set at +10.0 meters, marked as 00, with depths taken down from this line (Schmidt 1937: DF09, fig. 85). A discrepancy may be noted in that the scale used with the mound sections of 1937 (ibid., fig. 19) end at +20 meters which equals the 00 datum. The elevation system allowed the recording of depths of walls and burials below the 00 datum, which, in the absence of depositional stratigraphic recording, was the main recording method. These depths were plotted on "cross-sections" taken across each excavated "plot" (10 m square) along a center west-east line. Each cross-section recorded the actual walls and burials encountered along the section line, plus depths of other walls and burials in the square projected against it. Apparently no north-south cross-sections were drawn as they are absent in both publication and archives. These "cross-sections" are really elevation profiles, and should not be confused with measured, drawn, stratigraphic sections with numbered depositional strata as are currently in general use—a system which post-dates Schmidt by some 20 years (Wheeler 1956).

C.3 Grid System, Quadrants, Plots (Squares), and Plot Record Numbers of 1931 Season

An east-west, north-south grid system was laid out running through the center of the Main Mound (the highest area), plot DF09. The grid consisted of 100 m square quadrants designated by capital letters of the alphabet running west-to-east (e.g., A–D) and north-to-south (e.g., A–F). Each quadrant was then subdivided into "plots" of 10 square meters, numbered 0–9 west-to-east and north-to-south. Thus, 09 is a "plot" number located by east-west (0) and north-south (9) coordinates within quadrant DF (Schmidt 1933: pl. LXXVIII). At the beginning, before the grid system was in place, Schmidt designated plots being worked by lower case letters of the alphabet (e.g., plot "a," "b," etc.). Later the grid coordinates were assigned to these temporary letters in his daily journal: (a=DG10; b=CG60; c=CG61; d=DG96; e=CH95; f=DH05; g=DF19; h=EG06; and i=DF18), a list which also indicates the first squares explored. These plot numbers differ from the "plot record" (pr) numbers that were used to locate artifacts on graphed notebook pages for each 10 meter plot or square in individual "plot books."

These plot-record numbers (e.g., pr 10) often appear in the field catalogue of artifacts, and occasionally on plans (e.g., pr 25 on Schmidt 1933: fig. A). Unfortunately, over the years, many of these notebooks have badly deteriorated or disappeared, so the record is not complete. Aside from burial sheets, these notebooks gave the only horizontal locations for the artifacts found. In 1931, Schmidt used the terms Main Mound and the Painted Pottery Flat as area designations; in 1932 the terms North Flat, Red Hill, Treasure Hill, South Hill and the Twins were added (1937: fig. 16). These designations were added after the fact, on photographic plate LXXIX (Schmidt 1933), but do not appear in the text. An additional term, CG Depression, is used informally in 1933 for an older trench between the North Flat and the Red Hill in the CG quadrant.

C.4 Field Catalogue of 1931 Season

In the daily field catalogue, artifacts were recorded sequentially with H-prefixed numbers on the day of recovery. The depth of the object recorded is usually given. In all cases, the burial number is given; from these, depths can be calculated using their placement on cross-sections. Schmidt (1933:338) notes that the plot books also recorded the daily state of the operations. Architectural records also give dates and depths of excavations. Since the field catalogue provides the date of registration for objects recorded on the same day as excavation, artifacts are grouped by date, which, when correlated with dates and depths recorded elsewhere, orders them in vertical clusters. All burials excavated (180 in the top [Building] Level I of the Main Mound; ibid., pp. 392, 439–440, pls. CXLVII, CXLVIII) had individual burial sheets with a drawing of the skeleton and associated remains (ibid., pl. CLII), where artifacts are drawn but not numbered. These burials were not plotted on the excavation plan of the Main Mound in 1931 (ibid., pl. CXII) but were plotted on the DG36 plan from the Painted Pottery Flat (ibid., fig. A), on the CG25 plan between the Main Mound and Red Hill (ibid., fig. B), and on a plot plan for the Main Mound (ibid., pl. CXLVII). Burial plans are not published in 1933 for the other excavated plots (CG60, CG61, DG96, CH95, DH05, EG06) but appear in the final publication of 1937.

The field catalogue also records the type of object, material, dimensions, and occasionally depth and/or "pr" number. While in Philadelphia, Schmidt assigned objects to his major periods in the margins of his notes. Subsequently, a number of these were changed, showing a shift in his thinking based on his stylistic analysis of the burial ceramics largely in the absence of reference to stratigraphic context. This revision obviated opinions recorded in his daily journal at the time of excavation. Ironically, his original opinions correspond more closely with the results of the 1976 restudy.

In addition to objects recorded in this catalogue, Schmidt published two plates of painted pottery sherd drawings from Hissar I (1933: pls. LXXXVIII, LXXXIX) without regular catalogue numbers; each item is identified by an H followed by a letter of the alphabet and a number. In a separate typed list entitled "Potsherd Catalogue Tepe Hissar 1931" (Penn Museum Archives, Box 9), 96 sherds are listed as H a1, a2, etc., using the alphabetical plot designations that indicate excavation squares prior to the adoption of the grid system (see above under Grid System). These two plates are not reproduced in 1937.

C.5 Plans

Only three plans are provided for squares excavated in 1931 (Schmidt 1933: fig. A: DG36, fig. B: CG25, and pl. CXII: DF07–09, DG00, DF18–19, DG10, and DF29). These plans are somewhat misleading since they plot more than one building level of architecture on the same plan. The plans make it appear as though the architectural remains in different squares lie on the same level (Schmidt 1937: fig. 84), whereas, in the Main Mound plan of 1931, the base of excavation in DF18 and 19, west of Building 2, is over a meter above the floor level of Building 2 in DG00 and DG10 (Schmidt 1933: pl. CXIII). The examination of extant walls in 1976 showed that they were well-built, of regular brick masonry, with standard dimensions. In the case of the first two plans mentioned above, the burials are plotted with the architecture, sometimes directly over walls. The depth relation to the walls is given in an accompanying cross-section.

In the case of the Main Mound DF–DG squares, the architectural plan lacks the burials, which are plotted on a separate plan without reference to walls or depth (ibid., pl. CXLVII). This latter information was subsequently provided (Schmidt 1937: figs. 84, 85). The plans are often obscured by height shadings along the walls and superimposed burial numbers. In addition, plans for most excavated squares were not published in 1933, a fact which makes it difficult to reconcile published photographs with textual description (e.g., CG95 Schmidt 1933: pl. LXXXI, p. 343). Walls on plans sometimes bear sketched-in brick lines that provide the direction of the bricks (usually laid as stretchers), brick size (bricks essentially match text dimensions when sketched), and the number of rows of bricks (two or three rows), which indicates approximate wall widths of 60 or 90 cm. These widths match the wall widths in the cross-sections.

C.6 Periodization

In 1931, the sequence at Tepe Hissar was defined with three periods: I, II, and III. Schmidt points out (1933:364–365) that the most delicate phases of an excavation are those concerned with the top and bottom deposits of a "stratum" (i.e., cultural period), which often contain the clues for the beginning and the end of such periods. At the end of the 1931 season, he speculated that the people of Hissar II came as foreign invaders, while Period II then "faded" into Period III. He thought, on the evidence of mass burials, that Hissar III ended with an epidemic (ibid., p. 365). He recognized the need to deal with the terminology of these transitions, which he did in 1932 (see below).

C.7 Terminology

The overall Tepe Hissar cultural and depositional sequence was divided by Schmidt in 1931 into three prehistoric cultural periods: Hissar I, Hissar II, and Hissar III (1933:355 n5) which he often referred to as Stratum I, II, and III (ibid., pp. 355 n5, 364–367). The use of the term stratum (in lower case) is somewhat confusing when not accompanied by I, II or III since it can refer to a depositional layer as commonly used in present-day reports (e.g., "any prehistoric stratum," [ibid., p. 364]). Although using only Periods I, II, and III in 1931, Schmidt already indicates the need for additional terminology for transitional periods (provided in 1937 as IIA and IIIA), for the transition between Period I and II and between II, and III.

Note that the cultural periods are based primarily on the occurrence of painted pottery and "early" or "late" grey ware. Deposits containing painted ware (such as refuse layers, floors, surfaces, occupational or building levels) are grouped together under the term Stratum[1] (or Period) I, II, or III. Since the term Stratum I, II, or III is ceramically defined, it is applied wherever the painted pottery occurs on the site. As a result, excavated squares may contain Stratum I materials in different areas of the site, but this in no way indicates an identical sequence of structures and deposits from area to area. Each square requires its own description and analysis, addressed in Chapter 4 of this study with the reconstruction of sections for each square.

Regarding recording of architecture, in each excavation square the architectural levels encountered were numbered from the top down: "Level 1," "Level 2," etc. These designations are square specific and, thus, account for local stratigraphic variations.

Schmidt uses a number of terms for actual deposits such as refuse, layer, sub-layer, or occupational level. For architectural remains, he uses terms like building, building complex, floor, wall, and surface. These features are presented on plans, often overlain by burial distributions. The vertical relation of walls is presented in "cross-sections" that plot the heights and sometimes depths of walls against burial depths. Many of these elements are projected onto the cross-section, so that it is necessary to use both plan and section to understand the data plotted. No deposit surfaces or floor levels are traced on them. Also, no north-south cross-sections were drawn. Most walls are unnumbered although occasional sequential numbers within a square occur, e.g., DF09, W-1, W-2. Room areas were confusingly also called "sections" with "S" designations. Although these "S" numbers were assigned in the field (as seen in the archives), they often do not appear on the published plans, even though he refers to them in the text.

C.8 Survey

Surface survey of the site showed sherd distributions on a low raised mound with higher areas of mound above (Schmidt 1933: pl. LXXVIII, topographic plan). Burnished grey sherds covered these higher areas while painted pottery occurred over the lower areas and at a twin mound [the Twins] in quadrant FF southwest of the main site. The high areas came to be called the Main Mound, the South Hill, the North Flat, and the East Hill (ibid., p. 453); in 1937 Red Hill and Treasure Hill were added designations. The lower eastern area was designated as the Painted Pottery Flat (Schmidt 1937: fig. 16, 1933: pl. LXXIX). Schmidt states specifically that the extent of occupation of each period was initially indicated by sherd scatter only (Schmidt 1933:343).

Schmidt's original intention was to excavate from the highest point to virgin soil in DF09 on the Main Mound. This project was deferred due to the presence of many burials (Schmidt 1933: pls. CXLVII, CXLVIII). The approach to establishing the sequence was, thus, switched to "indirect sectioning by examining those points where the earlier deposit cropped out from below later accumulations" (ibid., p. 336). First, the assumption based on survey that the painted pottery lay below the grey ware was tested by digging square CG95 on the Painted Pottery Flat. The test proved the assumption to be correct (ibid., p. 370, pl. LXXXI). Second, CG25 at the north end of the CG Depression was tested, providing a good sample of "early" grey ware above painted pottery (ibid., p. 368). Finally, the Painted Pottery Flat was also sampled in square DG36 (Schmidt 1933: pl. LXXX, fig. A, 1937: fig.22). The task of uncovering coherent building remains was put off until the following season (Schmidt 1933:343).

D. The Twins (FF)

Part of the crew was sent to truncate the higher mound of the Twins (Schmidt 1933:336), but no further mention is made of this operation in the 1933 report.

Squares FF76-77-67 are marked on the northern mound as excavation areas. It is stated that these hillocks "are capped with culture refuse containing grey pottery, but the sub-stratum always seems to contain painted ware" (ibid., p. 333). The 1976 excavations confirmed this sequence on the southern mound (see below).

E. The Main Mound (MM)

Excavation was initiated on the Main Mound in DG10, then expanded to DF19, areas "which proved to be extremely fertile" (Schmidt 1933:336), yielding an excellent sample of the "late" grey ware that was designated Hissar III. The Main Mound excavation (ibid., pp. 390, 392, pls. CXII, CXLVII, CXLVIII), which covered DF07-08-09-DF18-19-DG00-10-DF29, was carried out with 160 laborers. Architectural remains designated "Level 2" (Building 2) were reached in DF19-DG10 (ibid., pl. CXII). The partial plan shows a door to an outside area. DF09 was taken down to Level 1 while DG10 was lowered to Level 2 (Building 2) (ibid., pl. CXII).

F. CG Depression: CG25

Excavation was also undertaken in CG25, a square located at the north end of an old trench separating the North Flat from the Red Hill. This effort produced a large quantity of "early" grey ware, termed Hissar II (ibid., pp. 368, 369). The grey pottery illustrated for Hissar II includes only two goblets (H1149 and H1150 [ibid., pl. XCVIII]) designated as from CG25 x1 (a brick cist tomb [ibid. pl. CXI]). The other vessels are published with H numbers but without plot designations and are absent from the published 1937 field catalogue. Funerary vessels from CG25 (ibid., pls. XCVII, XCVIII, XCIX) include H1660, x3; H1381, x5; H1385, x8; H1517, x8; H1149 and 1150, x11; H1607, x24; H1664, northeast quarter, floor. Three painted jars are also illustrated (ibid., pl. CII): H1154, x15; H1384, x25; and H1153, room 14.

G. CG Depression: CG95

Excavations in CG95 located at the south end of the CG Depression, reached Period I (Schmidt 1933:337). In this sounding, the walls of Period I are described as incoherent and lacking any brick lines suggesting that they were of packed mud. The walls, visible down to about 2 meters (as seen in Schmidt 1937: pl. LXXXI) are clearly of good masonry and may be later than Period I(?). Illustrated vessels (Schmidt 1933: pl. XCVIII) are H1604, x14, grey ware, and (ibid., pl. CII) H1654, x1, and H1655, x1, both painted ware.

H. Chronology

In 1933, Schmidt estimated the chronology of the sequence by comparison with other areas. He estimated the arrival of the Hissar II culture in the second half of the third millennium BC. Pottery played an important role in his assessment. The pottery types found seemed to relate only to the north at Tureng Tepe (Wulsin and Smith 1932). Because of this, Schmidt theorized that grey ware "drifted south" from Turkmenistan along with the migration of people (Schmidt 1933:367).

Further, it was believed that the occupation of Tepe Hissar—definitely a Bronze Age site—ended before the Iron Age.[2] The only definitive clue was the absence of iron in Hissar III (ibid., p. 366). Schmidt estimated that the Iron Age began in the first half of the second millennium BC on the basis of Hittite iron dating from 1500 to 1200 BC in Anatolia (ibid., p. 390). His suggested date for Hissar III was the first half of the second millennium BC (ibid.), based on the presence of Hittite iron in the second half of the millennium.

I. Results of the 1931 Season

During the first season of excavation, in Schmidt's words, he "attacked" the mound with 200 workmen, following a two-week clearing of the Damghan citadel, which was curtailed as modern buildings occupied the historical settlement. Both Schmidt and Leitner noted that, while the topographic map was being drawn (it was not ready until the middle of the first season), pottery collections from the surfaces of elevated and relatively flat areas were used to select test squares and as chronological guide-fossils.

Schmidt (1933:343) wrote: "Our excavations in the Painted Pottery Flat only sounded the stratum of Hissar I [Plate LXXXI] without uncovering coherent building complexes. This task was deferred until the second season." He observed that the walls of these early levels were of *pisé* construction, in contrast to the mudbricks used in the later periods. An undisclosed number of simple pit burials were found, while thousands of painted sherds from Hissar I with elaborate geometric and figurative animal and plant motifs were collected. Schmidt indicates in one of his reports to the museum that the mound was covered with masses of sherds and fragments of other objects suggesting the productiveness of the site.

Regarding the abundance of (mostly clay) animal figurines, Schmidt argued that they had a 'utilitarian' purpose: "They were magic images of domesticated beasts and birds, made to increase their number and the wealth of the owner. Others represented game of the steppe and of the hills, to help the hunter's luck and to protect him against the ferocious species, such as the tigers represented by the alabaster figurines of Stratum III" (Schmidt 1933:357). Clay "stamp seals" with geometric designs of Period I are considered by Schmidt as probably ornaments/buttons as there were no associated seal impressions found. On the other hand, the workers may have missed the balls of clay with impressions during hasty removal of earth. Of significance, however, is one clay "stamp seal" (H20) found in the upper refuse of "Stratum I" [Hissar I], which depicts two human figures, an ibex, and snakes(?) (ibid., p. 357, pl. XCI). Its significance is in the depiction of the human figure as incorporated into the geometric and animal motifs, an unusual stylistic choice for Hissar I period.

Only a small percentage of Period I sherds were registered, most of them painted, and they were sent to the Penn Museum. Fortunately, complete vessels and other objects were carefully recorded in the field register. Only thirteen burials are noted in the first season's 1933 report.

Schmidt noted that Hissar I material extended from the main complex of mounds to the fringes of the plain and covered a larger area than the later settlements, Hissar II and III. There were three superimposed "strata" recorded at the South Hill, at the North Flat's eastern extension, and on the Main Mound. Schmidt's usage of the term "stratum" is meant to connote both a stratigraphic "layer" (with or without architectural remains) and sometimes also a chronological-typological "period." On the Painted Pottery Flat and in other flat areas, "Stratum II" appears as a "thin top layer over Stratum I" (Schmidt 1933:367), marked by the appearance of grey ware pottery types in larger quantities than in Stratum I, although still with an admixture of earlier painted buff vessels.

Thus, Hissar II was reported to follow directly from Hissar I. Hissar II was mainly explored in test squares; larger exposures had to wait until the second season. As in the case of Stratum I, no complete buildings of "Stratum II" were uncovered. However, there was one technological change in Hissar II: the use of straw-tempered mudbricks in contrast to the pisé walls of "Stratum I." On the South Hill, in the North Flat's eastern extension, and on the Main Mound, test squares showed that Stratum II lay directly below Stratum III.

On the eastern extension of the North Flat, 30 burials belonging to Period II were cleared in plot CG25. According to Schmidt, there was a smooth transition from the end of "Stratum II" into "Stratum III." However, he goes on to say, "there are quite a few pottery vessels and other objects which we cannot attribute to one or the other stratum" (Schmidt 1933:389).

"Stratum II" is marked by a large number of copper objects, including weapons (blades of daggers/knives/

spearheads) with mid-ridges that were superior in their craftsmanship to those of "Stratum I." In addition to personal ornaments (such as copper and silver earrings, bracelets, pins, and weapons), objects suggesting markers of ownership and a differentiated social position of the deceased individuals were found, such as an ornamented macehead (H1200) and copper stamp seals with compartmented/cross designs. (ibid., p. 381, H1176, H320, pl. CVII). One of the most frequently occurring category of grave objects in "Stratum II", as in Hissar I, was beads[3] made of semi-precious and exotic stones (alabaster, carnelian, rock crystal, and the earliest appearance of lapis lazuli), while silver and gold pieces appear as personal ornaments.

Some "stamp seals" with geometric designs, such as those encountered in Hissar I burials, are also found in Stratum II burials, and are, again, most likely ornaments/buttons.

The pottery assemblage of "Stratum II" is marked by the appearance of grey wares in larger quantities than in Hissar I; in fact, a somewhat equal admixture of grey and painted buff vessels was deposited in the graves. Nevertheless, some of the Hissar II pottery forms are distinctly different from those found in Hissar I, including goblets and bowls with long stems and wide splayed bases. Additionally, the painted motifs change between Periods I and II.

Concerning Hissar III, Schmidt (1933:389) wrote, "the archaeological situation suggests that Period II faded into Period III." The plans of building remains show walls of several structures, which in the 1976 season were found to enclose three large buildings on the Main Mound (Schmidt 1933: pl. CXII, 1937: fig. 86; Howard 1989a: fig. 1).

On the Main Mound, eight contiguous squares of 10-meters each were tested and an intramural "necropolis" of 180 burials was cleared (Schmidt 1933: pl. CXLVII). In the process, two superimposed occupation levels were recorded: Level 1 (earlier), largely destroyed by erosion and anthropogenic agents and Level 2 (later), which showed evidence of burning and had burials from even later periods dug into it. The intramural "necropolis" of Hissar III was placed over and into the abandoned Level 1. These were simple pit burials in which traces of fabric were often found under some of the bodies.

The burials contained a rich assortment of objects that ranged from grey burnished pottery to copper tools, weapons, copper medallion seals (ibid., pl. CXXIX) and personal adornments, as well as animal figurines, "effigy" vessels, and beads of lapis lazuli, crystal and carnelian. Objects made of alabaster and soapstone are among the rich burial finds, most notably elegant vessels, a stemmed plate, a curious "disc" with handle and an accompanying grooved "column," and a female effigy (ibid., pp. 423–30, pls. CXXXV–CXLI, CLIII, CLIV). Of the 180 burials in this group, Schmidt described four very rich graves in detail, attributing rank and status to the deceased, called by him "warrior 1," "dancer," "little girl," and "priest." These graves were furnished with metal weapons, agricultural tools and/or domestic utensils, including a group of copper "wands"/symbols, stone and copper seals, a unique "fan"/mirror, small sculptures of animals, and female figurines modeled in copper, silver, and alabaster. Gold and silver ornaments (vessels, diadem/belts, figurines) were found in a few of the graves.

The Hissar III pottery assemblage is largely burnished grey ware, often decorated with pattern burnishing and in rare cases with linear incised patterns. New forms are described as "bottle pitcher," "canteen," "stemmed brazier," and vessels with "bird spout," "bill spout," or "long straight spout" (Schmidt 1933: pls. CXIII–CXVII). In addition, there are some "surviving" painted cups and a pot-stand from types related to Hissar I and II. Some simple and beak-spouted silver and copper bowls recall pottery vessels of similar forms.

Regarding glyptic art, the stamp seals and seal-shaped ornaments with simple geometric motifs that closely resemble the clay seals/ornaments of Hissar I and II. The copper "medallion" seals appear to be specifically associated with the Main Mound burials (ibid., p. 414, pls. CXXIX, CXXX); they are "shaped like a pendant with bilateral sealing pattern" with perforated handles (ibid., p. 414). Two cylinder seals in alabaster/calcite and serpentine with human and animal figures on them (ibid., pl. CXXX H116, H892) were found on the Main Mound in the fill of Building 2 (DG10) and in a rich burial (DF19 x60), respectively.

Schmidt and his staff's observations during the first season of work established the framework for subsequent research at Tepe Hissar. Among their main accomplishments were a timely publication of a preliminary report, a final topographic map of the site and the Damghan region, soundings to retrieve occupational strata and burials, and general observations of architecture. Above all, they systematically recorded large quantities of objects from several hundred graves. Schmidt devised a preliminary sequence of occupational strata grouped into Periods I, II, III, based on the ceramic typology from graves. He placed painted pottery in the earliest and grey pottery in the later strata, and defined each group by surface color, technique, shape, and decoration. He recognized the breadth of the divisions of his chronological scheme, so he aimed for a more finely-tuned division of his chronology in the second season of excavation.

J. The 1932 Excavation Season

The main objectives of the second season of excavations at Tepe Hissar[4] were, first, to complete the DF09 area sounding on the Main Mound and second, to open up larger areas of the South Hill, the North Flat, Treasure Hill, and the Painted Pottery Flat to sample the various periods. Schmidt commented (1937:297), "By eliminating in the final report the material obtained during the testing operations and described [in the 1933 report], we gain a much clearer impression of the culture sequences and of the individual culture complexes." Of course this approach eliminates the need for careful reanalysis of the 1931 data and also eliminates a quantity of unique material.

J.1 Methods

The same excavation methods of were used in 1932 as in the 1931 season.

J.1.1 Maps, Elevations and Cross-Sections

The basic maps made in 1931 were not reproduced in 1937 with the exception of the topographic site plan with superimposed grid (Schmidt 1937: fig. 16). The names of general areas, Main Mound, etc., are now included on the plan. The plan with grid system is reproduced for each period with excavated squares filled in with black: Period I (ibid., fig. 21); Period II (ibid., fig. 61); and Period III (ibid., fig. 83). Cross-sections, as in 1931, continue to be provided in an east-west direction for excavated squares. As in 1931, north-south cross-sections are lacking.

J.1.2 Grid System, Quadrants, "Plots," Plot Record Numbers, Sections [Rooms/Areas]

The 1931 system continued largely unchanged. Plot record numbers (pr) do not as a rule appear on the plans, although they are often mentioned in the field catalogue. On the other hand, section "S" (i.e., room) numbers are included in the 1937 report: the Painted Pottery Flat, figs. 24–27 (section numbers listed consecutively); the South Hill, fig. 63; the North Flat Level 1, fig. 102, and Level 2 (Burned Building), fig. 91. No such numbers are added to the plan of the Main Mound, fig. 86 (but are preserved in a separate plan in the archives, see below), or on the Treasure Hill plan, fig. 95.

J.1.3 Field Catalogue

The field catalogue from 1931 was carried forward with sequential H numbers ending with H5278.

J.1.4 Plans

Large plans are provided for the major excavated areas as line drawings by the architect: Painted Pottery Flat, (Schmidt 1937: figs. 22 and 23), South Hill (including Building 4) (ibid., fig. 62), Main Mound (including Buildings 1–3) (ibid., fig. 84), the North Flat Level 1 (ibid., fig. 103), Burned Building Level 2 (ibid., fig. 90), and Treasure Hill (ibid., fig. 101). These are the original records from the field. A second set of these plans is provided with Schmidt's inked-in walls, giving his later interpretation of period and structure. The architectural elements on the plans is obscured by an overload of superimposed burial icons, section (i.e., room), and rarely wall numbers and depth shadings for the walls. The reading of structural plans is made difficult by the inclusion of walls over-riding and underlying the given structures. Furthermore, of great importance but never pointed out, is the fact that although drawn as if on a single excavated level (e.g., the Main Mound, [ibid., fig. 84]), different squares, in fact, lie at different levels (those to the west of Buildings 1 and 2, for example, were 1–2 m higher than the floors of those buildings).

K. Periodization

In 1932, Schmidt (1937: IIA, 106, 299, 303, IIIA, 155, 307) introduced the transitional Periods IIA and IIIA. Their definition is, however, rather vague (Fig. 1.7).

Also, in terms of occupational debris, these two periods are ill-defined. However, these terms are defined ceramically in the 1937 publication:

> Thus the group of vessels attributed to Hissar IC may include specimens of Hissar IB and others of the final phase (IIA) of the painted pottery era, overlapping with the beginning of Period I. (Schmidt 1937:48)

> Nearly all painted vessels described…were found in graves which also contained the typical grey ware of Hissar II. Consequently, there is no doubt that these vessels belong to the last sub-phase of the painted pottery era, overlapping the beginning of the era of grey ceramics. (ibid., p. 108)

> Hissar IB [is] marked by the appearance of the wheel….The final phase of pottery decoration…is marked by extreme conventionalization of certain Hissar IC patterns, the gazelle design offering the most striking example. Felines disintegrate….The ibex and the bird seem to have disappeared entirely….pottery makers turn again to the simple style of decoration used…during Period IA….At times

Schmidt's Levels	Schmidt's Periods
Lev. "1"	IIIC
Lev. bet. "2-1"	IIIB
Lev. "2"	IIIB/IIIA
Lev. "3"	IIA/IIB
Lev. "4"	IC/IIA

Fig. 1.7 Correspondence between Schmidt's defined Levels and Periods.

we could distinguish potsherds only by means of the wheelmarks present on the Hissar II ware [cups and bowls]. (ibid., p. 108)

Vessels and sherds with long-necked gazelles always appear in deposits with an admixture of Hissar II grey ware" (ibid., p. 109); "only such vessels [Hissar IIA grey bowls] are described and pictured as were found associated with painted vessels in the graves….Bowls with exaggerated tall stems [occur] solely in the grey ware vessels of Hissar II[A]. (ibid., p. 112)

We have little doubt that goblets also occur in the transitional IIA layer, though we have not found specimens definitely attributable to this time. (ibid., p. 114)

However, the very facts that the old chalice form persists and that during the first sub-phase of the new culture period [IIA] painted vessels of the last Hissar I sub-period [IC] rest in the same graves beside the grey pots of the new type, indicate that Hissar I did not end in a destructive catastrophe (ibid., p. 302)

Hissar IIIA is the period of transition from Hissar II to Hissar III…a layer containing material with both Hissar II and III characteristics. In several instances, we are sure, individual objects and even entire graves of Hissar IIB or Hissar IIIB were attributed to this transitional layer, due to find conditions….The stemmed vessels of Hissar II type…do not show any distinctive features…surviving painted vessels…resemble the surviving vessels of Hissar II more closely than those of Hissar III…the [grey ware] bottle-pitcher appears for the first time…the brazier…occurs during all sub-phases of Hissar III. (ibid., pp. 178, 180)

The technique, the color scheme and the forms of the painted Hissar IIA vessels are identical with the corresponding features of the Hissar IC ware. Partly conventionalized feline patterns occur towards the end of Hissar IC, as well as in IIA…some very distinct features…of Hissar IIA…do not occur in any of the other sub-periods of Hissar I. The most characteristic…pattern is the long-necked gazelle, in certain cases conventionalized beyond recognition….The disintegration…of the feline pattern is also a typical feature….The leopard is turning into a headless and tailless decorative element. The designs of some Hissar IIA vessels…resemble…the earliest painted ware of Hissar IA…the color scheme is also identical. On sherds the wheelmarks on the later [IIA] ware sometimes have to decide to which sub-period they should be attributed….[Grey ware] neckless jars… tall-stemmed bowls or goblets, unstemmed bowls and jars, in addition to…parallel ridges and stipples, suggesting prototypes of metal, are newly introduced features; still, the main ceramic evidence for distinguishing Hissar II and III is the frequency of the stemmed vessel during the first period of grey ware and the absence of stemmed vessels (except for braziers) in Hissar IB and IC. (ibid., pp. 303–304)

The bottle-pitcher…the guide vessel of Hissar IIIB, appears…for the first time. Other new vessel types are the brazier…and the Hissar III painted cup of surviving type….Cups and goblets of…Hissar II…surviving painted ware are also found as late as Hissar IIIA (ibid., p. 307)

Furthermore, while wheelmarks are usually well pronounced on Hissar II ware, by far the greater part of the Hissar III pottery appears to be made by hand, a puzzling fact. (ibid.)

L. Survey

No survey work at Tepe Hissar is reported for the 1932 season.

M. The 1932 Stratigraphic Sequence

The evidence for the stratigraphic sequence at Tepe Hissar is summarized for 1932 in the 1937 publication (Schmidt 1937: figs. 18 and 19. These cross-sections, north-south and east-west, show the relative depths of the different periods in the various excavated squares. The controlling sequence is in the Main Mound, square DF09, which extends from the surface to below Building 1. The base of the sequence extends a short way, about 1.5 meters, into the top of the earlier painted pottery mound. Slightly less than 2 m above this lies the Period II deposit. At the top is the Period III deposit, about 4 m thick, making a total of about 7.5 m. The projected base of the Period I mound below this column lies a further 2.5 m down, making a sum total of 10 m. At this point, the Period I mound is at its highest, and it is quite possible that its lower core contains an even earlier deposit.

It is notable that no level containing straw-tempered ware was identified, nor was such pottery mentioned at the site, although we now know that it occurs in the period preceding Hissar I at Sang-i Chakhmaq near Shahrud (Dyson 1991). A single sherd of this ware was recovered in 1976 from lot #3 in the deep test on the North Flat in CF57 with sherds of Hissar IC/IIA type (Dyson and Remsen 1989:106), suggesting a possible source lower down.

Period I remains on the cross-section were also reached in the following squares: DF89 (South Hill), CF57 (North Flat), CG25, CG95 (CG Depression), DG96-EH06 (Treasure Hill), and DH43-44 (Painted Pottery Flat).

Period III remains are indicated on the cross-section above Period II levels in: DF79 and DF89 (South Hill), CF42 and CF57 (North Flat), CG95 (CG Depression), CH95-97, DG60, (Treasure Hill), EG06 (Painted Pottery Flat).

Other squares reached these periods as shown on the plans of excavated individual periods:

Period I—DG36, DG96-EG06, DG69, DH21, DH34-36, DH43-46, DH73, EG13 (all from Painted Pottery Flat).

Period II—the same squares as in Period I; DG51, 53, DG60-61, DF78-79-DG70, DF88-89-DG80 (South Hill); CF42, 37, 57 (North Flat); CG25, 95 (CG Depression); CG79-89-99 (Red Hill), CH95-DH05-DH15 (Treasure Hill) (see maps above).

N. South Hill (SH)

The South Hill location includes Building 4 (Sections 15–18), DG60-61 (Schmidt 1937:107, figs. 62, 63) from building Level 2, Period IIB (ibid., p. 106, fig. 63).

> It is possible that this structure was actually constructed during the intermediate Hissar II-III phase, namely Hissar IIIA, as some of the vessels found on the floor of Room 15 have definite Hissar II forms… during the transitional phase some stemmed Hissar II pots still occur….The fireplace (a) is a square elevation with a shallow [round] depression in the center…it is oriented diagonally to the direction of the walls….The walls and the floors…show the effect of conflagration, but one wall (15b) has no markings of fire and must have been added later, suggesting that the building was at least partly re-used after its destruction. (Schmidt 1937:107)

n.b. Schmidt assigns Building 4 from the South Hill to Period III, however, its stratigraphic position and some of its architectural features are comparable to those of Building 2 on the Main Mound, which dates to Period II in the new chronology.

O. Main Mound Buildings

O.1 Building 1 (Sections 1–7,[5] Fig. 1.9)

Information on this structure comes from DF09 (Schmidt 1937: 156, figs. 84, 86). Schmidt assigns Building 1 Level 2 to Period IIIB[6] (ibid., p. 156, fig. 86, no sections marked). "The main livingroom [S1]…apparently the kitchen…is enclosed by mud-plastered walls. The plaster, 15 [cm] in average thickness, consists of many coats, suggesting a rather long occupation of the room. The hearth [d], against the northeast wall] has three rectangular cooking holes; two are on one level, while the third is attached in front of and somewhat below the others [see below]. A doorway at the north corner opens into a narrow room with problematical outlet. A neatly wrought niche, 50 [cm] high, 27 [cm] broad and 19 [cm] deep, is at the side of this doorway. Mud-plastered walls enclose the small divisions of this building" (ibid., p. 155).

The revised archival plan gives the section numbers, which do not occur on figs. 84 and 86 of Schmidt (1937). The plan shows a central room (S1) more or less square that appears to be built against the north wall of Building 2 with no connecting door indicated. This room is about 4 x 4.5 meters square (Schmidt gives no measurements;

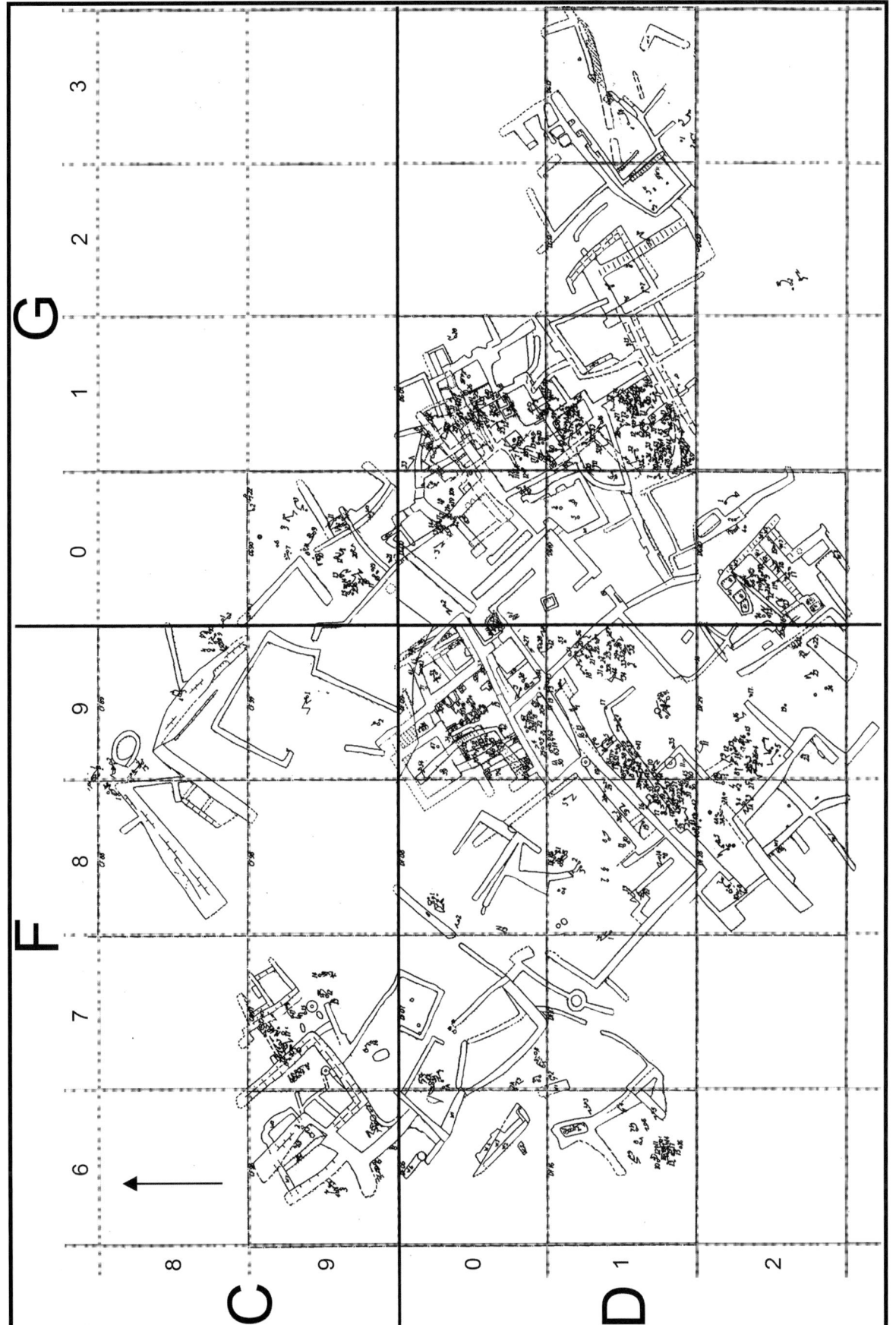

Fig. 1.8 Map of Tepe Hissar's Main Mound showing the grid system for identifying squares along with locations of burials (after Schmidt 1937: fig.84).

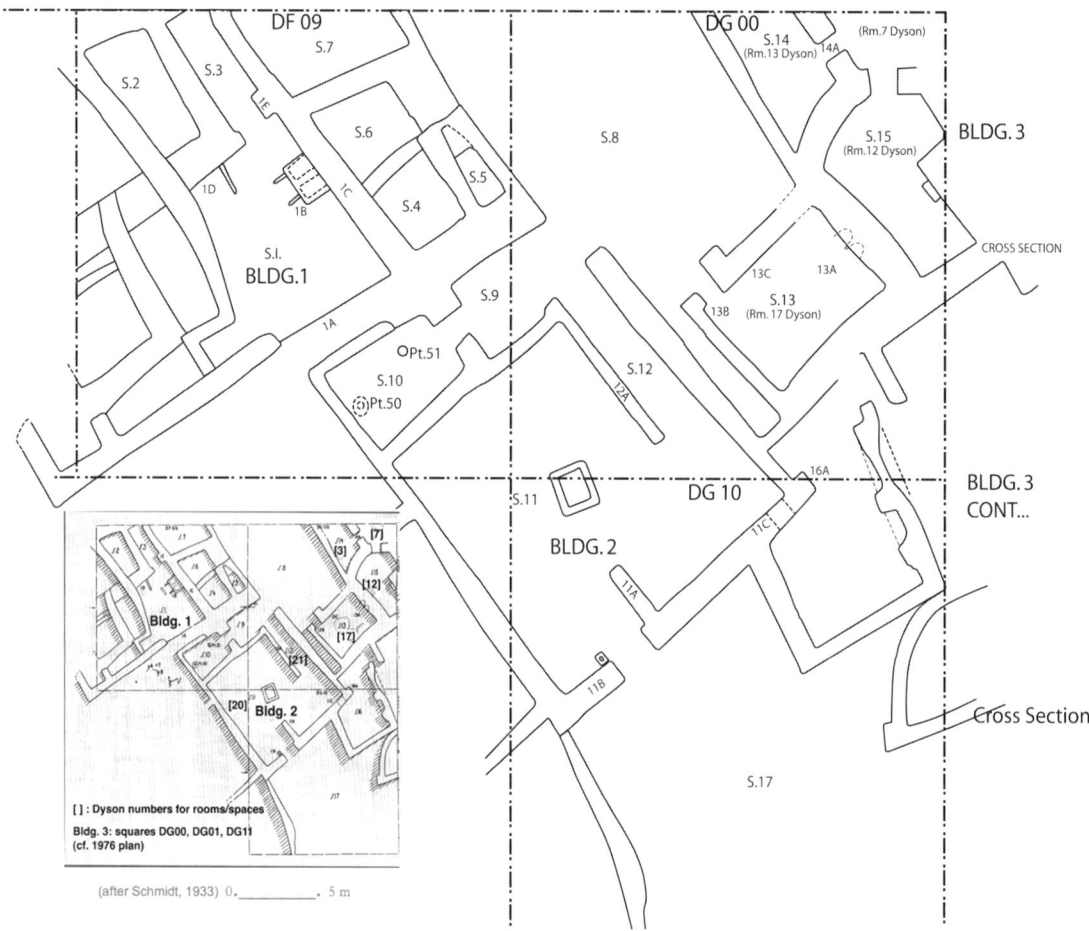

Fig. 1.9 Schmidt's (1933) revised archival plan of Main Mound Buildings 1 and 2; Building 3, partially excavated (original plan inset).

these must be estimated from the plans). The room is overlain by a curved wall of Building Level 1 (see Schmidt 1933: pl. CXII in DF09 center left and in DF09, figs. 84 and 86). A doorway (1E) leads from Room 1 north to Room 3, a long narrow room about 1 meter wide and 2.5 meters long with no outlet. To the left of this door in Room 1 is a short (70 cm) screen-wall (1D) only 10 cm wide. Against the northeast wall, clearly drawn on the archival plan and on fig. 84, is a raised hearth (1B) with two rectangular openings. In front of these, on the floor, is a third chamber formed by two bricks, one on each side, set against the front of the double hearth. To the left of Room 3 are two sides of a projected Room (2). On the northeast side of Room 3 lies the south end of a space designated as Room 7. South of this room, east of Room 1, is a second room divided on the archival plan into three parts: S4–6. S4 and 6 are separated by a wall about 30 cm wide (ibid.), which appears to abut the main outside walls at either end. It is either a secondary addition or is

at a lower level. The wall separating S4 and S5 is similarly unclear. On the plan the southwest wall of Room 1 has a doorway indicated at its north end, probably the main entrance (Schmidt 1937: fig. 84; see also the revised archival plan, Fig. 1.9).

Unmentioned by Schmidt but documented by a field photograph below (Penn Museum Neg. 83727), is a double row of "crescent-shaped" niches located on the west end of the northwest wall of the main room (S1) (Fig. 1.10). This is the same feature found in Building 3 (see below, Ch. 2).

O.2 Building 2 (Sections 9–12)

Information for this structure can be found in DF09-19-DG00-10 (Schmidt 1937:156, figs. 84, 86) and the revised archival plan (Fig. 1.9). Schmidt assigns Building 2 to Hissar IIIB (ibid., p. 156, fig. 86). "It is difficult to say whether Building 2 formed a separate construction or

Fig. 1.10 A field photograph showing a double row of "crescent-shaped" niches located on the west end of the northwest wall of the main room (S1) in Building 1, which Schmidt dated to Hissar IIIB (Courtesy of the Penn Museum, image no. 83727).

whether it was combined with one or both of the other buildings" [1 and 3] (ibid., p. 156). Building 3 is too far away beyond intervening structures to be part of Building 2 (see Fig. 2.11). The south wall of Building 1 is continuous and provides no access to Building 2, which is built against it (see Fig. 1.9 and Schmidt 1937: fig. 84).

The large room [S11]…is supplied with the… rectangular type of fireplace noticed in the main room [S1] of the Burned Building [North Flat] and in a doubtful Hissar IIB-IIIA building [4] on the South Hill….The hearth…is disoriented in the same manner as the other fireplaces…Screen-walls [11A and 12A] extend from the northern and southern doorways, and a hinge stone [door socket] is in situ at [left of] the southern door. Fragments of mullers were scattered about in the two chambers [S9 and 10] adjoining this room to the northwest. (Schmidt 1937:156)

Room 9 is connected by an opening to the narrow (1 meter wide) passage (S12) separated from the main room

(S11) by "screen-wall" 12A. The southwest wall of Room S11 is solid with no openings.

O.3 Building 3

Information on this structure comes from DG00-01-10-11 (Schmidt 1937:156–157, figs. 84, 86). Building Level 2 is assigned to Hissar IIIB (ibid., p. 156, fig. 86). In the revised chronology, Building 3 is dated to Hissar II and transitional Period II-III. "Building 3 was destroyed by a conflagration, as the floor layer of charred debris and the discolored, black and red walls indicate…the rooms… were almost sterile [of objects]" (ibid., p. 156).

The large main room is interesting. The northwest wall (a) is ornamented with crescent-shaped depressions which seem to be filled with a clayey matter [see Dyson and Remsen 1989: fig. 5]. The crescents are 18 [cm] wide by 10 [cm] high, and extend 16 [cm] into the wall. The lowermost of the three rows…is 40 [cm] above the floor. The rectangular platform (90 [cm] square by 15 [cm] high) in the center of the room (b) reminds one of the hearths above described [in Buildings 1 and 2]. However, the central hole is 80 [cm] deep…presumably made to accommodate a central roof support. The original opening was 25 [cm] in diameter. In the western corner of the room (c) marks on the wall suggest the former presence of a storage bin enclosed on two sides by thin walls.

Three mud-plastered terraced fireplaces (d) adjoin the northeast wall. They are 10, 30 and 45 [cm] above the floor respectively. The [south]eastern section (e) of the room is 15 [cm] lower than the rest. A creephole (f), 80 [cm] above the floor, connects the [main] room with a small chamber to the southeast [visible on the fig. 84 plan]. It is the only entrance to this chamber.…A screen-wall (g) is between the creephole and the low section (e) of the main room. (Schmidt 1937:156)

An interesting doorway opens through the southeast wall at the point marked 'h'. It is a rounded rectangle 95 [cm] high by 80 [cm] wide. The jambs and the sill protrude, while the lintel is flush with the wall.

Another doorway connects the main room in the northeast with a granary subdivided by thin, low walls (25 to 35 [cm] high)….An almost semicircular enclosure adjoins the main room on the south. A mud-brick from the central room to the northwest of the main room measured 54 x 26 x 8.5 [cm]. [This room forms a separate structure, see Ch. 2.] The bricks of all walls appear to be staggered. (ibid., p. 157)

n.b. The plan of Building 3 replicates Buildings 1 and 2 in having a main room surrounded by subsidiary rooms, including a storeroom on the northwest side of the main room. It consists of two features, a rectangular platform in the center of the room (hearth?) and three terraced fireplaces/bins. The building was built in three stages according to Howard and Dyson's reconstruction: the earliest 3, then 3a, and lastly 3_1. The second building stage (3a) went through a fire and restoration. After burning, the interior walls were plastered. Two main characteristics are its externally buttressed walls and niches on all four exterior walls of room /16/ which are similar to those in Building 1 (see Fig. 1.10 and Fig. 2.11; Dyson and Remsen 1989:80, fig. 5). According to the New Chronology, Building 3 is dated to Period II, phases E-D/D.

P. The North Flat (NF)

The excavations on the North Flat duplicated the sequence for Hissar II and III as found on the Main Mound.

P.1 CF27-28-37-38-47-48

Level 1 is presented in Schmidt (1937:177–178, figs. 102, 103). Note that figs. 102 and 103 only include the southern half of CF27-28—the northern half of CF26-27 and adjacent CF17 must have been removed since the plan of the Burned Building (ibid., fig. 91) covers these squares. Level 1 is assigned to Hissar IIIC, which is characterized by graves with alabaster objects. "In Level 1 we found rather poorly-defined wall remains" (ibid., pp. 177–178). Three small rectangular rooms (S7–9) run west to east with two more rooms (2, 3) running north from Room S9, the only coherent grouping (ibid., p. 177, fig. 102). In a most likely separate structure (Room S1) were found three alabaster "mini-columns"[7] (H1841–43) and two alabaster discs (H1845, H1846). These finds are noteworthy, as elsewhere these types occur in burials or hoards. They were associated with short-necked grey ware jars (H1848). Recorded brick sizes for adjacent squares are: CF39, Wall 17A, 63/64 x 30 x 11/11.5 cm; and CG30, Wall 21A, 59/60 x 29 x 11 cm (ibid., p. 177).

P.2 CF37-47-57

Level 2 consists of the Burned Building and appears in Schmidt (1937:157–171, figs. 89–94, 102, 103). This structure is fully described by Schmidt since it was well-preserved by fire and contained a rich assortment

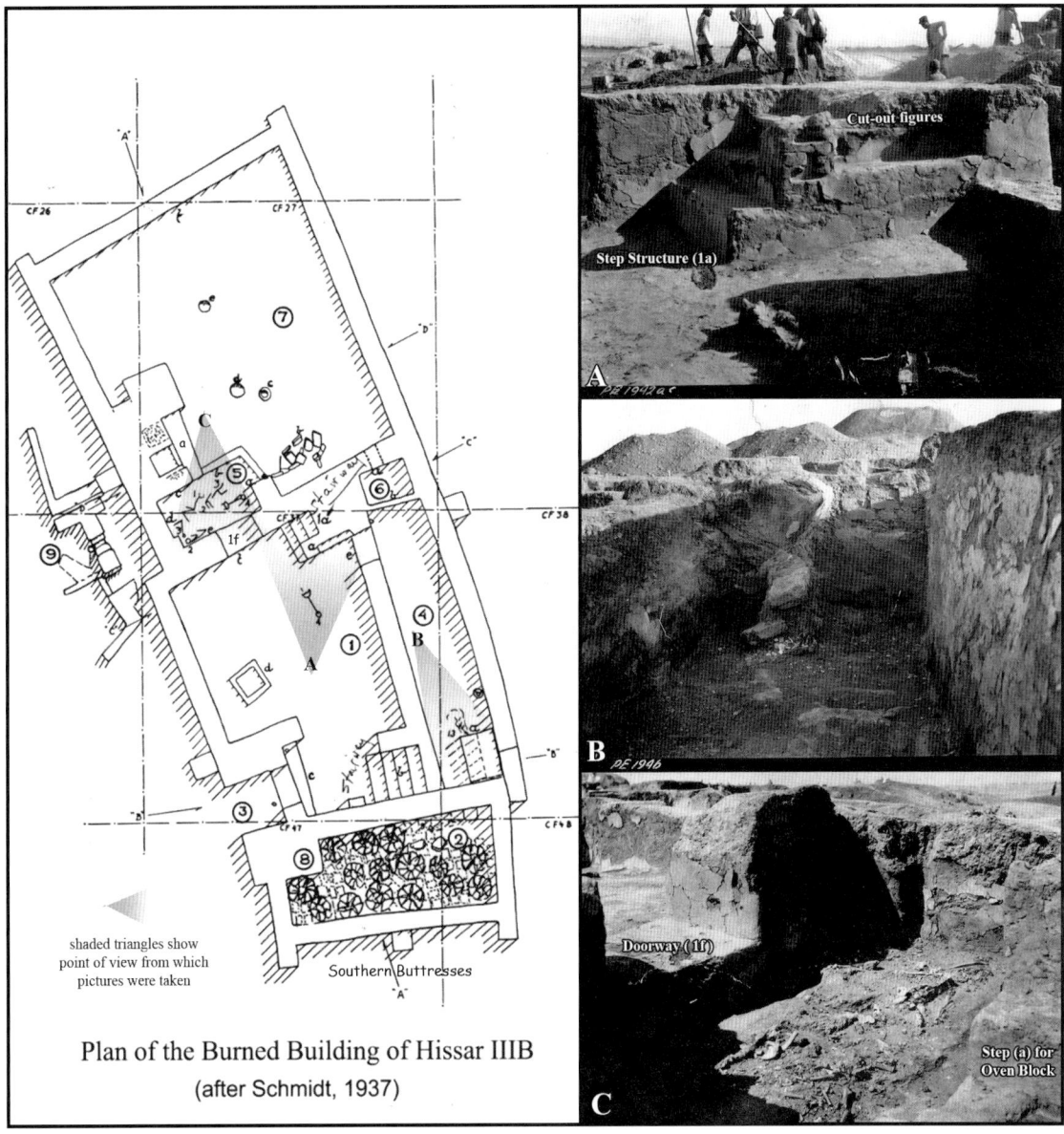

Fig. 1.11 Plan and photographs of the Burned Building on the North Flat. (A) CF37 below the floor of the rectangular main room (1), Period IIIB; view toward north (Courtesy of the Penn Museum, image no. PE1942a). (B) CF37–38 narrow storage area (4); view towards south-southwest (Courtesy of the Penn Museum, image no. PE1946). (C) CF27–37 Charred human skeletons on floor of room 5 with room 1 beyond; view towards south (Courtesy of the Penn Museum).

of objects. The building consisted of a rectangular main room (1) (Fig. 1.11a) with a narrow storage area (4) (Figure 1.11b) entered through a door (1e) on the east side of the room. In the southeast corner a flight of five steps (1b) led upwards to a second level. The upper part (4a) fell on burned debris in Room 4; the fire had also destroyed Room (5), leaving charred human skeletons on the floor (Fig. 1.11c). A stepped structure (1a) with cut-out figures

(a) occupied the northeast corner of Room 1 (ibid., fig. 93). A square hearth (1d) set diagonally to the walls lay on the southwest floor. A doorway (3) set back from the western façade led down one step (c) to floor level. The doorway was flanked on both sides by a block of masonry strengthening the entrance, called Gate Passage 3. The southern block (8) was reconstructed as a "tower" (ibid., fig. 94), an effort that ignored the scale of the plan. Another doorway (1f) led out of the main room to an enclosed courtyard (7), called a kitchen, containing a large brick oven block (7a). This courtyard was defined by trench along the inside of its walls (ibid., fig. 89).

The trench can be seen in Schmidt (1937: fig. 89) along the bottom of the picture where the northern wall is being traced both on the inside and outside. The trench turns south on the right side of the photograph and runs mistakenly into the brick oven block. This error is recorded but not noted on the building plan (ibid., figs. 90, 91). The oven block has a step (a) in front of a square chamber and a square burnt surface on the top. Between the southeast corner of the oven block and a buttress to the left of the door from Room 1 is a low curb enclosing area 5, ending in a posthole. To the right of this, on the courtyard floor, is a pile of collapsed brick (7b). A narrow "creephole" connects the courtyard to a small bin (6) at the north end of storeroom 4. A rectangular storeroom (2) full of pithoi occupied the south end of the building. No entrance to this is shown on the plan. Its floor was "considerably higher than that of Room 1" (ibid., p. 168). At a level 35 cm below the pithoi and the evidence of burning was a brick floor. The south wall is supported by three narrow buttresses. Charred human skeletons were found on the floors of Room 1 and 5 and in 2.

P.3 CF47-48-57

"Level 3" is described in Schmidt (1937:177, figs. 102, 103).

> A third level, most probably of Hissar IIIA origin, is visible south and west of the [Burned Building], while most of the wall remains in Plots CF39 and CG30 [east of the Burned Building] seem to belong to Level 1....In Plot CF57 and inside the Burned Building [in Room 2, the south storeroom] we penetrated through the deposit of Hissar III to Stratum II, where we found house sections and burials of that time. (Schmidt 1937:177–178)

P.4 CG42

This location is a test square on the edge of the North Flat, west of the Burned Building (Schmidt 1937:106, figs. 16 and 18). "A thin film of Hissar I was covered by a rather thick deposit of Hissar II" (ibid., p. 106), indicating that the Period II occupation in this direction extended beyond the Period I mound. Fragmentary walls of Hissar I did not appear in CF42 "which apparently is situated outside the occupation area of that time" (ibid., p. 37).

Q. Red Hill

Q.1 CG79-89-99

"In plots CG79, CG89, and CG99, building remains of Period II (B) cropped out from below deposits of Hissar III....All building remains from this area consist of fragments only, oriented, as usual, diagonally to the main directions. There is no need to illustrate or describe these wall fragments" (Schmidt 1937:108). Bricks from the IIB walls measured 50 x 26 x 7.5 cm, 56.5 x 29 x 8.5 cm, 59 x 31 x 8.0 cm, and 60 x 29.5 x 8.5 cm.

R. Painted Pottery Flat (PPF)

Information on this location can be found in: DH36 (Schmidt 1937:26, 36); DH34-36, 43-46 (ibid., pp. 23, 26–36, figs. 20, 22–27, 28). Four building levels are shown in a stratigraphic diagram (without scale) of DH34 (ibid., fig. 28)

Level 1 is not shown in Schmidt 1937: fig. 28, but appears in black on fig. 24 of that volume. A few vertically hatched wall fragments in DH36 (sections 1 and 2 on fig. 24) are assigned to Level 1A, later than Level 1. The walls were constructed of sun-dried bricks laid as headers. Schmidt also notes walls constructed of *chineh* (packed mud). He dates Level 1 to the transitional I-II phase, Hissar IIA, based on an assemblage of painted wares mixed with early grey ware (Schmidt 1937:26).

Level 2 is indicated by four courses of a buttressed mudbrick wall in Schmidt (1937: fig. 28), assigned in Schmidt (1937: fig. 26) to Level 2. This buttressed structure (Section 69, Complex IV) is assigned to Period IC, (ibid., p. 26). Four "complexes" (I–IV) are identified, each representing a cluster of rooms: I, Sections 42–48, (ibid., p. 32, fig. 26); II, Sections 49, 50, 52–59 (ibid.). Included in this level are buttressed walls: III, Sections 60–67 and 70; IV, Sections 69 (ibid., p. 33), 71 and 72. Schmidt noted buttressed walls altogether in three sections: 69, 71 and 72.

Level 3 on the plan (ibid., figs. 23, 27 in black) is represented by "only individual walls and some rooms are well marked below the structures of Level 2." (ibid., p. 33). n.b. Instead of the expected use of chineh, some walls were constructed with sun-dried bricks (ibid., p. 36). Schmidt tentatively dates this level by buff painted ceramics that are a mixture of IC and IA assemblages, containing geometric and curvilinear designs and ibex, feline, gazelle motifs (ibid,. pls. III–XIII).

> A mixture of IA and IC sherds appeared in Level 3 in addition to fragments of a type not occurring in either sub-phase, but more closely related to IC than

IA. Sherds and vessels of this sub-type we called IB [1937:39ff] and we may tentatively attribute Level 3 to this sub-phase [IB] of Hissar I. (Schmidt 1937:33)

Section 81 of Level 3 has the same appearance as the Chineh-built parts of Level 2. Sooted mud plaster covers the walls. A rectangular doorway with mud plastered Chineh jambs and sill opens through one wall…building fragments of Level 4 in the vicinity of, and below Section 81 are also mud plastered Chine.…Below Section 56 of Level 2 an interrupted single course of bricks [25 cm broad and of unknown length] showed one of these relatively rare instances of the use of such building units, instead of the Chineh type construction more common during the earlier phase of Period I.…Another Level 3 wall, below Section 55 of Level 2, was also constructed of bricks. (ibid., p. 36)

Level 4 appears in Schmidt (1937:33, figs. 23, 27 in black). n.b. It is the earliest phase of Painted Pottery Flat and is recorded below Level 3. The Level 4 wall fragments are largely of chineh with mud plastering (ibid., p. 33). Schmidt also notes traces of brick contours on the face of a wall. So, use of bricks is documented even in the earliest Level 4, Period IA.

S. DG69 – South of the Painted Pottery Flat

Information on this location can be found in Schmidt (1937:37, 39, figs. 30, 31).

Of Level 1, Schmidt (1937:37) says, "The upper level showed incoherent wall sections only. Slight differences of depth suggested two building phases [ibid., fig. 31]. Wall 1b [center left of fig. 31, Level 1] may have been built during the early phase (IIA) of Period II.…Faint brickmarks appeared on Walls 1a and 1b."

"A thick refuse layer separated this wall [1b] from the underlying burials of Hissar IC. In the bottom layer of the excavation of 1931 [below Level 1, marked on fig. 31, cross-section], grey ware was entirely absent. This fact, combined with the occurrence of IC burials in the lower part of the same layer, proves that it had accumulated during Hissar IC" (ibid., p. 39). It is highly probable that the refuse layer had accumulated before Period IC, since the graves were dug into it.

"A small enclosure (2), [not marked on the plan], only contained the typical IIA mixture of grey and late painted ware" (ibid., p. 39).

The Level 2 (upper sub-phase) is described by Schmidt:

During the second season the formerly exposed remains [of Level 1] were removed in order to penetrate to the lower levels, and, finally to the mound base. Below the floor of the [1931] excavation [fig. 31, cross-section]…the rather light colored painted pottery of IC and IB began to be displaced by the grey-on-red ware of Hissar IA. Burials of IC still appeared, imbedded in the earlier refuse, on top of the walls and in the rooms of Level 2, which the sherd contents definitely determined as Hissar IA.…The floors of the [upper sub-phase] Level 2 rooms were about four meters below the surface of the Painted Pottery Flat. The plan shows two sub-levels [upper and lower], but the ceramic situation does not seem to parallel the architectural conditions. There are rather neat, diagonally oriented rooms, regular as a rule, and enclosed by thin walls. These are Chineh walls, as are most of those of the upper level in this plot. Many wall faces were coated with smooth clay layers, which aided in defining the courses, otherwise difficult to trace" (ibid., p. 39)

It is reasonable to designate the lower sub-phase of Level 2 as [Level 3], since its walls are below those of the upper phase, are thicker, and have a different orientation.

Level 3 (Level 2, lower sub-phase) consists of a single square room (3) with thick walls and a double-chambered rectangular hearth set against the southwest wall. Part of a second room lies in the south part of the square (ibid., fig. 31 p. 38). This level consists of a single square room (3) and a double-chambered rectangular hearth set against the southwest wall. Ceramically, it also represents the earliest level of Hissar IA, characterized by grey/black painted designs on red ware.

T. CG Depression

Of CG25, Schmidt notes, "In Plot CG25 a deep stratified and sloping deposit of black refuse dirt, with thousands of Hissar I potsherds [none illustrated], but rarely any wall remains, showed the typical situation encountered at the margin of a settlement, where its trash is deposited" (1937:23). "In Plot CG25…a very few wall remains occurred; these were covered by stratified masses of black refuse dirt. Here the northern edge of the Hissar I settlement seems to have been struck" (ibid., p. 37).

U. Chronology

By the time of the 1937 publication, a number of other sites on the Iranian plateau had yielded relevant comparative data: Tureng Tepe (Gorgan), Cheshmeh Ali

(Rayy), Murteza Gerd (Tehran), and Tepe Sialk (Kashan) as shown on Schmidt's chronology chart (1937: fig. 168). In the chart, the grey ware of Tureng Tepe is correlated with Hissar IC-IIIC; the painted ware of Cheshmeh Ali IA and IB is correlated to Hissar IA and IB; the painted ware of Murteza Gerd IB is correlated to Hissar IB, the grey ware is considered post-Hissar Iron Age; early painted ware at Tepe Sialk [III] is correlated to Hissar IB and IC, the grey ware is considered post-Hissar Iron Age. The key correlation rests on the superimposition of a "Proto-Elamite" stratum [Sialk IV]. The following are Schmidt's assessments of the periodization of Tepe Hissar:

> On a layer containing material identical with that of Hissar IC which, in turn, is superimposed upon the earliest Sialk layer identical to Hissar IB.... Thus we know that the entire era of painted pottery (Hissar IC, IB and IA), precedes the Proto-Elamite period and with it the Jamdet Nasr in Mesopotamia; that is we are not far wrong in assuming that Hissar IC ends about 3500 BC, while Hissar IA may actually extend into the fifth millennium. Our conservative estimates of the date of Hissar I as tentatively expressed in the preliminary report [1933] on Tepe Hissar has totally collapsed.... We do not know whether Hissar IC at Sialk was directly followed by the Proto-Elamite occupation and, therefore, we do not know which grey ware phase of Tepe Hissar was contemporaneous with it. For the moment, we assume that it corresponds in time with Hissar IIA and IIB. (Schmidt 1937:321)
>
> It is too early to correlate the sub-phases of Hissar II and III with definite phases of Mesopotamian history.... We could not disregard the striking resemblances between...Early Dynastic Sumer and Hissar IIIC. We are inclined to attribute the end of Hissar III to...the first half of the second millennium BC, but an earlier age may be indicated. (ibid., p. 325)

It is worthwhile to note that although Schmidt participated in the excavations at Alishar Höyük in Anatolia, he makes no reference to the terminal Chalcolithic grey ware at that site with its striking tall pedestal cups and bowls comparable to at least two found at Tepe Hissar in 1931 (1933: pls. CI, H1648, 1622, both Hissar II). In 1945, it was possible to relate Hissar II to Shah Tepe IIB particularly through parallels with stemmed fruit bowls of the Alishar "Chalcolithic" (von der Osten 1937:52 fig. 62; Dyson 1965:240; Arne 1945). This comparison has never been seriously evaluated. The relevant volume by von der Osten was published in 1937, probably too late for Schmidt's 1937 report.

V. Results of the 1932 Season

During the second season of excavation, the team investigated the extent of the settlement for each period. Schmidt estimated the Hissar I settlement to be as large as 200 meters in diameter, extending from the North Flat to the southernmost tip of the Twins, including the Painted Pottery Flat in the southeast where the main concentration of Hissar I settlement remains were found in the previous season. Test soundings were placed in four locations: the Painted Pottery Flat, east of the North Flat, the Twins, and the Main Mound. At the first three locations, test trenches exposed early Tepe Hissar painted pottery levels; on the Painted Pottery Flat, 700 square meters were uncovered, and in several tests virgin soil was reached (Schmidt 1937: figs. 18, 19).

An extensive clearing on the Painted Pottery Flat (square DH12) yielded a "maze" of structural remains that made up four housing complexes (I–IV) and four superimposed "levels" (1–4), which corresponded to the three sub-phases of Hissar IA, IB, and IC (the earliest being Level 4) (ibid., pp. 23–39). Each building level was defined by its architectural features (such as a well-defined fireplace, a rectangular window, a courtyard, a trapezoidal hearth, a buttressed wall fragment) within a complex of buildings. Unfortunately, the notes contain no clear description of which walls enclose a specific room/complex, nor depths of walls and floors of each room/complex. Therefore, the stratigraphic position of levels and features is unclear, as well as their exact horizontal distribution within each complex. Similar confusion occurs with the burial stratigraphy. When the floor of a building level was not clearly observed, it was erroneously assumed that "the belongings of persons formerly living in the upper settlement had been given to the dead, whose graves extended, of course, [from level 1] into level 2. Needless to say, the same phenomenon was encountered in all levels, and often a level was dated, relatively, by the contents of graves in the level below" (ibid., p. 26).

Cultural/stratigraphic changes in Hissar I were defined largely by pottery types found in grave contexts—i.e., graves containing painted ceramics decorated with geometrical or conventionalized "theriomorphic" patterns. Those graves on the Painted Pottery Flat containing both painted wares and stemmed grey ware vessels were assigned to the transitional phase Hissar I-II or Period IC-IIA. While the IA assemblage is handmade, the later pottery of IB, IC and IIA is described by Schmidt as wheelmade,[8] and differentiated by paint and slip color as well as by design elements (earliest, dark grey paint on brown-red slip; later, dark brown paint on light brown or buff slip) (ibid., p. 40). Vessel shapes (stemmed bowl, jar, goblet, and conical cups) continue through Period I; new design elements (feline, ibex, bird, human) are incorporated into the earlier geometric and linear motifs in later phases (IB, IC and transitional IC/IIA).

Over 144 burials of Hissar I were excavated. These burials were all simple pit graves interred in the mound area. Schmidt commented, "[W]heresoever the excavation penetrated below the surface crust of the mound, burials were uncovered. They appeared below the rooms of the houses, below open courtyards and lanes, and below the former surface levels of then uninhabited areas" (ibid., p. 67). Using a selective sample, Schmidt described the manner of disposal and mortuary remains in such detail as to include age, sex, orientation, find-spots of objects, and even the expression on the face of the deceased in postmortem state. He noted that badly-preserved skeletal material and objects were discarded after recording them, along with most of the sherds, although a few of the latter were recorded in the field register with "D," following the inventory number.

Hissar II was extensively investigated in the second season on the South Hill in nine squares (ibid., figs. 62, 63). Schmidt noted that the Hissar II settlement deposit was "thinner" than that of the preceding and succeeding periods, except on the North Flat. On the South Hill, Hissar IIB is characterized by at least four buildings of rectangular rooms, constructed in a "haphazard fashion" and oriented diagonally to the main directions. Four domestic building complexes were cleared; Schmidt limited description of the architecture to the distribution of a few features found in the rooms: a bin, square fireplaces, sleeping platforms(?), and buttressed walls. Resting above or inside Hissar IIB buildings, on higher elevations of the mound, later structures were found that Schmidt dated to Hissar IIIA. A burnt stratum observed in one of the buildings (4) separated IIB from what Schmidt recorded as IIIA. His definition of transitional II-III was a new floor on which stood a Hissar III-type fireplace(?) built on a square elevation (ibid., p. 107). However, the pottery of this level is typologically similar to that of IIB.

In general, the Hissar II pottery assemblage is categorized as IIA (earlier) and IIB (later), in which an increase in the so-called "monochrome" (i.e., grey burnished) ware is encountered in the later period. Both assemblages are wheel-made according to Schmidt and occur with an admixture of painted buff wares. The IIA assemblage has forms identical to earlier painted pottery, while IIB pottery is differentiated by the appearance of new forms (chalice, spouted bowl, unstemmed jar), and variations of an earlier IIA form (e.g., a long-stemmed bowl with elevated rings). The IIB group is of a dark, polished grey; some of the vessels are ornamented with rows of appliqué knobs and ridges, which is a rare decoration in all Tepe Hissar assemblages. Excavations on the South Hill stopped when painted pottery with animal motifs first appeared, which Schmidt labeled as Hissar IC.

During the 1932 season, a large number of burials (782) were again excavated, with 209 graves attributed to Hissar II. The majority were pit graves, mixed with a small number of mudbrick cist graves. Among the mortuary gifts, there is a significant increase in the number of metal objects, which were superior in their quality of craftsmanship to those of Period I. One of the most frequently occurring categories of funerary objects (continued from Hissar I) was beads made of semi-precious and exotic stones, in combination with rare silver and gold pieces. In addition to gold and silver, rock crystal and turquoise were used to manufacture beads.

Burial assemblages of Period II contained personal ornaments (copper bracelets and earrings, and double spiral pins in copper and silver), weapons (dagger blades or spearheads with medial ridge), clay animal figurines, a large copper seal (H2183 in the South Hill grave DG53 x3), and an ornamented macehead (H1200 in the North Flat burial CG25 x28). Metal types continue with little change into Hissar III, while the copper macehead with incised decoration and the daggers/spearheads continue from Hissar I.

Hissar III was extensively explored during the second season; excavations were undertaken on the Main Mound, the North Flat, and Treasure Hill. On the Main Mound, twenty-four squares (2400 m^2) were cleared; in one square (DF09), a deep sounding exposed the top of the painted pottery stratum (IC). In the previous season, the uppermost levels of the Main Mound (IIIC, IIIB) were found to be the site of a mass burial (cemetery/necropolis?). From this "necropolis" level, 473 burials were retrieved. On the Main Mound, the burials extended down into the top and sides of walls of the earlier Levels 2 and 3 (assigned by Schmidt to Periods IIIB and IIIA). As in the preceding periods, pit burials dominated.

On the Main Mound, three well-defined building complexes (Buildings 1–3) were exposed that Schmidt assigned to Period III (1937: fig. 86) and above (archival plan, Fig. 1.9). In each building complex, there is a central room enclosed by secondary smaller rooms that had several coats of thick plaster, suggesting a lengthy duration of occupation. In two of the buildings, the main rooms had rectangular hearths with a central depression. The main room of Building 3 had architectural features not previously found in Hissar III contexts, such as three plastered and terraced fireplaces and a central hearth on a square raised platform, similar to that found on the South Hill and assigned to "Stratum IIB." Two significant features of construction were discovered on the Main Mound and the North Flat: exterior buttressed walls[9] and "crescent-shaped" niches on one of the walls of a North Flat building, as were noted earlier for Buildings 1 and 2 on the Main Mound (ibid., pp. 47–48).

On the North Flat, which is the northern extension of the Main Mound settlement, in the uppermost "Level 1," a Period IIIC building was excavated, but no clear plan was revealed (ibid., fig.102). Beneath this level, the excavation of a large "Burned Building" with buttressed walls raised several questions concerning continuity of architectural style, functional aspects of the building and individual rooms, as well as its chronological relationship relative to the Main Mound and other parts of the settlement.[10] The Burned Building, which Schmidt attributed to "Level 2" (IIIB), exhibited traces of a violent end; it was filled with debris of charred roof poles and a burnt floor with several re-plasterings as well as a few burned skeletons. The rooms contained very large quantities of domestic utensils, storage vessels, arrowheads, suggesting that a struggle/battle had taken place there prior to the fire. The upper "layer," "Level 1" (IIIC), was rich in calcite/alabaster objects, "miniature columns," "discs," and vessels similar to those found on Treasure Hill (see below) and discussed in Chapters 4 and 5 (e.g., "dancer," "warrior 1," "warrior 2," "priest," and "little girl" [Schmidt 1933:444–446]).

In addition to the North Flat, Hissar III levels were also cleared on Treasure Hill, where two rich "hoards" (I and II) of objects were found in Plots DH and CH, Levels 1 and 2 (Schmidt 1937: figs. 96–99). These hoards included copper tools and weapons, gold and silver ornaments, and more of the alabaster columns, discs, and alabaster vessels found on the North Flat. Pottery vessels were largely grey burnished; fossil-index forms are bottles, pitchers with long, horizontal-spouts or long beak-spouts, and canteens with a bottle-neck and perforated lugs. On one vessel, lugs are in the form of heads of animals. Herringbone patterns rendered as pattern burnishing and incised lines are prevalent on bottles with long necks.

Regarding metal objects, copper metallurgy had reached its zenith during Hissar III. Some copper objects, especially weapons and "wands," are of a remarkable quality (ibid., figs. 116, 117). Subsequent excavations and surface collections in the 1970s provided substantial additional evidence for local metallurgical activity, including slag, furnace linings, and ceramic molds from the South Hill and the Twins (Pigott 1989). The case for local metal production is further strengthened by replicas of early clay and stone vessels in metals. For example, the well-known vessel forms of spouted pitchers (e.g., H2031, H2773), beakers (Schmidt 1937: pl. XXXVIII H2434), and the bottle pitcher (ibid., pl. XXXVI H2164, H1902, H2257) were also produced in metal and calcite/alabaster (ibid., pls. LVII–LX H3497, H4187, H2773). Silver and gold objects were found in both the occupational and burial contexts, including silver and gold beads and pins with double scroll heads (ibid., pl. LIV H4333). Among the rare objects of outstanding craftsmanship is an exquisitely crafted silver diadem with repoussé design of "panels of incised gazelles" (Schmidt 1933: pl. CXXII H449). It was found in the rich "priest" burial on the Main Mound (DF08 x1). Other diadems in copper, also decorated with the repoussé technique, are H4112 and H4128 in North Flat burials CF48 x18 and CF93 x3, respectively (Schmidt 1937: pl. LIV). Among the rare, finely crafted gold objects are five modeled mouflon heads made of gold foil, also decorated with repoussé technique, found as part of Period IIIC from hoard I, at Treasure Hill (ibid., pl. XLVI, figs. 97, 111).

In Hissar III, the same forms of clay animal figurines found throughout the three periods of the settlement are reproduced in lapis, chalcedony, agate, and copper (ibid., pl. XXXIII). Human figurines in copper, alabaster, bone, and clay are found in hoards, and also with burials: on the Main Mound, in squares CF89/99 (ibid., pl. XLVI, H3271, H3272, H3274, H3278, H3281–85, H3288–89; in Treasure Hill Hoard II (ibid., pl. XLVII, fig. 114); in burials found at least in two areas, the North Flat and the South Hill (burial CF47 x2, H2790, ibid., pl. XLVI, fig. 194; burial CF38 x11, H5178, pl. XLII; burial DF89 x4, H5142, pl. XLII). The Main Mound hoard consists of a group of copper figurines, 12 nude males and 1 female. Schmidt describes them, "with gestures of the human figurines definitely suggest that the hoard had a ritualistic character....There are conoid knobs as heads; others have animal form; some seem to wear a conoid headdress, while others have a rather naturalistic human head" (1937:193). Of the female figurine he writes, "The left breast of Figurine H3289 is pronounced" (ibid., p. 194; see also Concluding Remarks).

As mentioned earlier, stamp seals were produced in metal, although some were still made in clay and stone (ibid., pp. 199–201). In the 1932 season, a larger variety of seals made of baked clay, stone (serpentine, calcite), and copper (Schmidt 1937: fig. 118: H2697, H2698, 1933:414, pls. CXXIX, CXXX) was retrieved. The copper stamp seals of this type are attributed to Period IIIB (Burned Building storeroom on the North Flat) and Period IIIC graves from the Main Mound and Treasure Hill (Schmidt 1937:97–201, fig. 118). Of great importance are three seal impressions on clay, (ibid., pl. XLIX H1850–1852,) which "have the appearance of labels for merchandise" (ibid., pl. XLIX, p. 200). It is very likely that at least two of them (H1850 and H1851) were labels as they have cord impressions and a cord hole on the reverse side. These sealings were found in the IIIC refuse of the North Flat below the "alabaster room" of the Burned Building. They represent definitive evidence for commercial transactions in the mid- to late third millennium BC. The iconography of the stamp seals includes humans and animals with horns, other quadrupeds, as well as geometric patterns (ibid., pp. 199–201).

Of importance are the three cylinder seals carved from serpentine, alabaster, and limestone(?) respectively (ibid., fig. 118, H116, H892, H3710). They clearly indicate a Mesopotamian link with the northern plateau. Only one of them (H892) is from a closed burial context (DF19 x 60) and its iconography is of a horse drawn chariot with two standing men (for description, see Schmidt 1937:197–98).

Hissar III is also distinguished by an increase (in the thousands) of beads, mostly made of semi-precious stones. For the first time we find beads of amber, ivory, rock crystal, and banded chalcedony, which are combined with incised and encrusted beads made of carnelian, lapis lazuli, turquoise, gold and silver tubes. Lapis lazuli is used lavishly for well-modeled animal figures such as a turtle (H2387), a ram's head (H2388), and a pair of horns (ibid., fig. 134). The beads were found in a variety of contexts in the burials and the settlement.

W. Summary of Schmidt's Excavations

Schmidt undertook a vast project in an archaeologically little-known region of the northern plateau and excavated a complex site systematically in a relatively short period of ten months. While he was not, for most part, able to excavate stratigraphically due to his limited time and the intrusion of a large number of burials, his systematic recording provides a base for understanding the trajectories of a Bronze Age settlement in this region. With the end of the second season of excavation, Schmidt had completed his objectives.

Forty-five years later, the 1976 campaign was begun, aimed at filling gaps in Schmidt's chronological sequence, refining the stratigraphy and architecture, and obtaining radiocarbon dates from stratigraphic contexts. The chronological sequence that Schmidt had set up in the first season was: Periods I (earliest), II and III. Later, he expressed the need for additional terminology to define transitions between Period I and II and between II and III, thus, his final sequence, IA–IC, IIA–IIB, and IIIA–IIIC. The latter was largely based on pottery sequence found in burial contexts that remained unrelated(?) to the architectural and occupational levels. In addition, the lack of similar assemblages from other sites in the region and absence of chronometric dating methods made it difficult to assign absolute dates to the Tepe Hissar sequence. This absence of fixed anchor points led to the second cycle of explorations at Tepe Hissar.

NOTES:

1.1 The term "Stratum" as used by Schmidt is a ceramically-defined term which has no relation to the term "stratum" used to describe occupational deposits in current excavation reports.

1.2 In 2006, a team supervised by Kourosh Roustaei of Tehran University Institute of Archaeology made soundings at the site to investigate Iron Age levels. He writes, "The Iron Age materials were encountered in several trenches south and west of Tepe Hesar and in two burials, probably belong to a cemetery, few hundreds meters west of the site. As in most of the trenches with Iron Age material we had sherds of this period in mostly secondary context we deal with the two trenches with confident context, one a probably occupational deposits and the other a copper smelting workshop. The Charcoal sample associated with the sherd collection from the burials, 1133±980 BC is Iron Age II in the established cultural sequence for Iranian Plateau" (Roustaei 2010:616). Another set of dates are from the copper workshop, charcoal near a crucible 980± 839 BC (93.1%) and a calibrated date 915± 812 BC from sample OxA-18588 (Roustaei 2010:617).

1.3 For a discussion of local lapidary work at Tepe Hissar, see Tosi (1984, 1989) and Bulgarelli (1974, 1979).

1.4 The staff from 1931 (Schmidt, Lockard, Leitner, and White) continued to direct, with up to 200 workmen. Photographer Niedzwiecki was replaced by Boris Dubensky.

1.5 According to Schmidt, sections are "subdivisions of buildings, such as rooms, passages, or indefinable divisions"(1937:26, footnote 1)

1.6 It should be noted here that Buildings 1–3 on the Main Mound have been redated from Hissar III to Hissar II period on evidence from stratigraphy, ceramics, and radiocarbon dates.

1.7 Schmidt referred to these artifacts as "cult objects." We know them today as critical indicators of the burial rituals associated with the Bactria-Margiana Archaeological Complex (BMAC), which infiltrates the Iranian Plateau around the end of the third millennium BC (Hiebert 1998).

1.8 Contrary to Schmidt's assertion, Christopher Thornton's recent work on Hissar I pottery has shown that "none of it is wheel made…only a bit of wheel-finishing on the rim was found" (pers. comm.).

1.9 In the 1976 excavations, buttressing was found to be an important architectural innovation of the Hissar II period. For a discussion of buttressed buildings in general and the revised chronology of the Main Mound buildings, see Dyson and Remsen (1989:69–85).

1.10 For discussion of the stratigraphy and proposed function of the Burned Building, see Dyson and Remsen (1989:91–97).

2

Stratigraphy and Architecture

A. Excavation in 1976

This chapter presents a detailed description of the excavation methodologies used by Dyson and his team,[1] as well as the re-evaluated stratigraphy and the architectural sequence. It includes data from four areas of the mound excavated by Dyson et al., such that it further disentangles the complex stratigraphy and architectural sequence of Tepe Hissar, which Schmidt's two early publications (1933, 1937) partially accomplished.

Dyson first visited Tepe Hissar in 1956 in search of plain coarse ware pottery that was unrecorded in the collection, archives, or publications of Schmidt's work (1933, 1937, 1940), but which should have existed at the site (Dyson 1957). A second visit was made by Dyson and William M. Sumner in 1971 in order to discuss future work at Tepe Hissar. In 1972, Grazia Bulgarelli made a surface survey of lithic materials and tools at Tepe Hissar to compare them to finds at Shahr-i Sokhta in Seistan (Bulgarelli 1972, 1974). In 1974, Jean Deshayes, director of the French team at Tureng Tepe in the Gorgan region, made a surface survey of Tepe Hissar and collected sherds of painted pottery (1975). In the same year, on a visit to the site, Dyson planned the Tepe Hissar Restudy Project with the participation of Firouz Bagherzadeh, then director of the Iran Center for Archaeological Research, and Maurizio Tosi of the University of Turin. The Restudy Project, which took place in the fall of 1976, was jointly undertaken by the Iranian Center for Archaeological Research (ICAR), the Penn Museum, and Turin University.

A.1 Aims and Methods

The Restudy Project was undertaken for the general purpose of reassessing and clarifying the work of 1931 and 1932. Within this context its various aims were:

(1) the collection of data relevant to the reconstruction of the geomorphological and ecological setting of the site; (2) the study of the changing settlement pattern of the plain through time; (3) the accumulation of evidence relating to the use and organization of various areas of the site and the description of manufacturing techniques relating to specialized activities; (4) the collection of stratified carbon samples for the construction of an absolute chronology for the site and for their use in a relative chronology of various parts of the site…; (5) the more accurate description of architectural forms and masonry techniques…; (6) the collection of stratified samples of artifacts and pottery for comparison with the grave groups, and an assessment of the contents of stratified occupation levels in relation to the described stylistic periodization of the grave groups. An underlying question of great interest was also the nature of the transition from the earlier painted pottery levels to the burnished grey Hissar ware of the Bronze Age. (Dyson and Tosi 1989:1–2)

Various methods for collecting samples are mentioned in the *Reports of the Restudy Project* (Dyson and Howard 1989). Since the focus of this summary is stratigraphy and architecture, the following presentation will deal primarily with those aspects.

The central effort was made on the Main Mound, augmented by work on the North Flat and South Hill (Fig. 2.1). On the Main Mound, the careful stratigraphic excavation of a column of the remaining north baulk of DF09 (the Pinnacle Baulk, P) adjoined Schmidt's main DF09 sequence from the highest remaining point down to the level of painted pottery (Fig. 2.2, 2.3, 2.4). Stratified botanical, ceramic, metallurgical, and radiocarbon samples were collected for analysis from this column. Measured drawings of actual baulks were made for this operation (Howard

1989a: figs. 2, 4), and for baulks examined in other areas. The surface of Schmidt's "Level 2" was then traced from the baulk section across Building 1, Building 2, structure /17/ to Building 3, and the floor of new excavations of kiln /3/ and /7/, to kitchen /1/ (Howard 1989a: fig.1) This surface provided the key linkage for these building plans and the Pinnacle stratigraphy. The detailed cleaning and redrawing of individual structures provided rectified plans and evidence for rebuilding, both horizontally and vertically.

Similar studies were carried out on Building 4 of the South Hill (Dyson and Remsen 1989:82–84, figs. 7, 8) and on the Burned Building of the North Flat (ibid., pp. 89–99, figs. 15, 17–23).

A.2 Excavation Staff

The restudy project of 1976 worked at Tepe Hissar from September 10 to October 26 Staff consisted of Robert H. Dyson, Jr. (director, Penn Museum), W. S. C. Remsen (Philadelphia, surveyor), Haydel Eqbal and Hasan Talai (Tehran, site supervisors), all working on the North Flat; Susan M. Howard and Vincent C. Pigott (Philadelphia, archaeologists) working on the Main Mound, Maurizio Tosi (Turin, co-director), Grazia M. Bulgarelli and Ingrid Reindell (Rome, site supervisors), working on the South Hill, and Raffaelo Biscione (Rome, site supervisor) working at the Twins. Mary Virginia Harris (Philadelphia) was field registrar. Oskar G. Meder (Marburg Geographical Institute) carried out a regional geophysical survey while Kathryn Maurer Trinkhaus (Philadelphia) carried out a regional archaeological survey, which extended through November and December. Mirabedin Kabulli (Tehran) participated as a site supervisor for two weeks.

A.3 Maps, Elevations, Sections

Survey maps were created or enhanced from the Schmidt records by Meder (1989: pls. I, II) and Trinkhaus (1989: pl. 1). Measured Sections were drawn for the first time for the Main Mound (Howard 1989a: figs. 2–5); North Flat (Dyson and Remsen 1989: fig. 13); and South Hill (Tosi 1989: pls. IV–VI).

A.4 Grid System, Quadrants, "Plots" (Squares), Building, Stratum (-), Area/-/, and Feature Numbers

The 1976 restudy used the Schmidt grid system designations (quadrants and squares [plots]) as well as his building numbers (1–4). Depositional stratum numbers, e.g., (4), in sequence in a square (from the top down) replaced Schmidt's building Levels 1–3. Area numbers, e.g., /4/, served as room and area (non-room) numbers, where Schmidt's "section numbers" were lacking. Individual features such as hearths were given feature numbers within each square.

A.5 Field Register

The field register was maintained to record finds with provenance information, listed sequentially by [Hissar] numbers (Harris 1989:145–147). Study material from this list given to the expedition by the Iranian government, was assigned Penn Museum numbers (UPM 77-10-x) back in Philadelphia. Slag samples analyzed at the Institute of Archaeology at the University of London were numbered separately (UPM 76-30-x).

A.6 Plans

Work on the Main Mound, North Flat, and South Hill involved the careful cleaning of the generally still-standing structural remains from Schmidt's 1932 excavations (Fig. 2.5). This effort was followed by clarification of the plans (Howard and Pigott 1989: fig. 1; Dyson and Remsen 1989: figs. 7, 9, 15; Tosi 1989: figs. 1, 9, pl. V; and unpublished 1976 field archives). Leitner's existing plans—made during survey work for Schmidt—were corrected or, if necessary, new plans were drawn. Many brick masonry details and measurements were recorded.

A.7 Periodization

Due to the relative lack of documentation relating Schmidt's periods to occupational deposits, the 1976 restudy decided to reserve his nomenclature of Hissar IC, IIA, IIB, IIIA, IIIB, IIIC for his burial sequence. Further, Dyson and the team decided to use the combined depositional strata, which contained sherdage from the new stratigraphic column cut into the "Pinnacle Baulk P" (in DF09 of the Main Mound) to create a new system for occupational deposits and construction phases (see above Fig. 2.2–2.4). The strata were analyzed into "ceramic phases" (see below) designated A through F (Howard and Pigott 1989). Buildings 1, 2, and 3 were then related to this system for purposes of correlation. The A–F units were termed building stages by Howard (1989a:56–59) and consisted of stages A, B, C1, C2, D1, D2, D3, E1, E2, E3, F1, F2, and F3 (ibid., table 1).

A.8 Survey

A surface survey of the mound documenting various industrial waste material concentrations was plotted on a

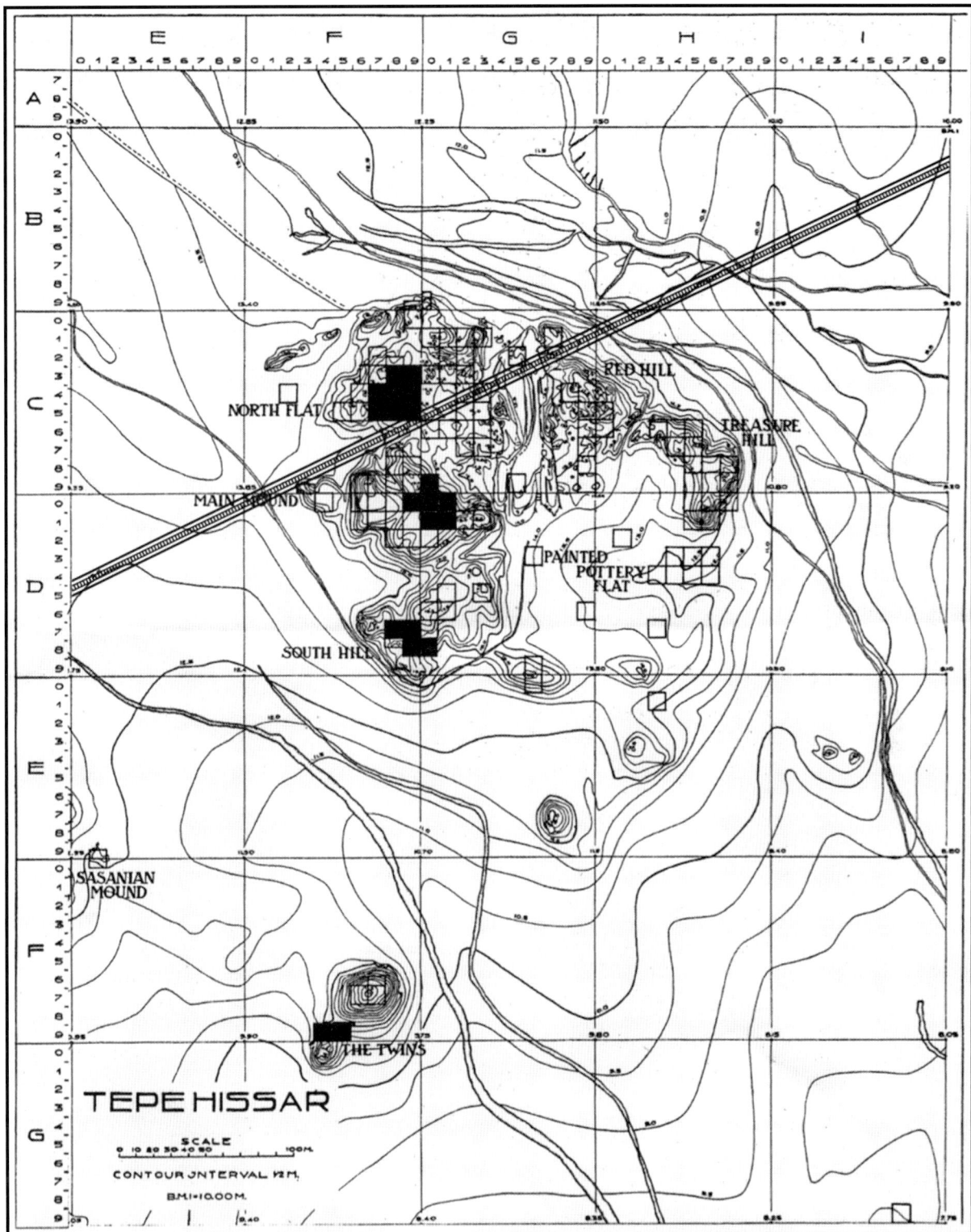

Fig. 2.1 Map of Tepe Hissar, with the 1976 project, superimposed on 1931–32 excavations; clear squares show 1931–32 areas of excavation, black squares are areas of 1976 excavations (after Schmidt 1937, Dyson and Howard 1989).

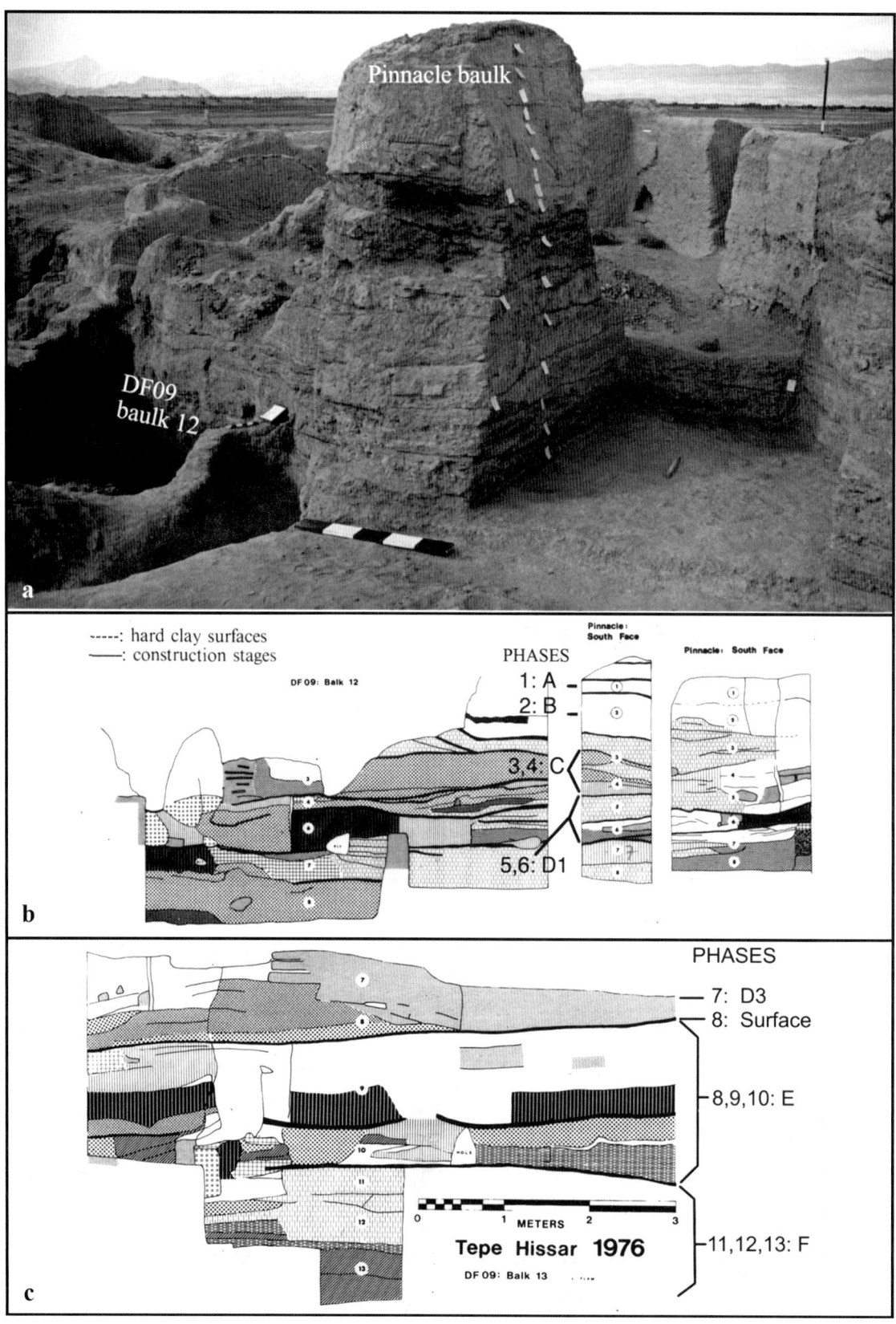

Fig. 2.2 a. Photo of DF09 baulk 12 and the Pinnacle baulk, b. Section showing details of the Pinnacle baulk, c. Section of DF09 baulk 13 (after Howard 1989: figs. 2–4).

Fig. 2.3 Site photograph of the Pinnacle Baulk (right) and DF09 baulk 12 (left). Susan Howard is recording strata (Courtesy of the Penn Museum).

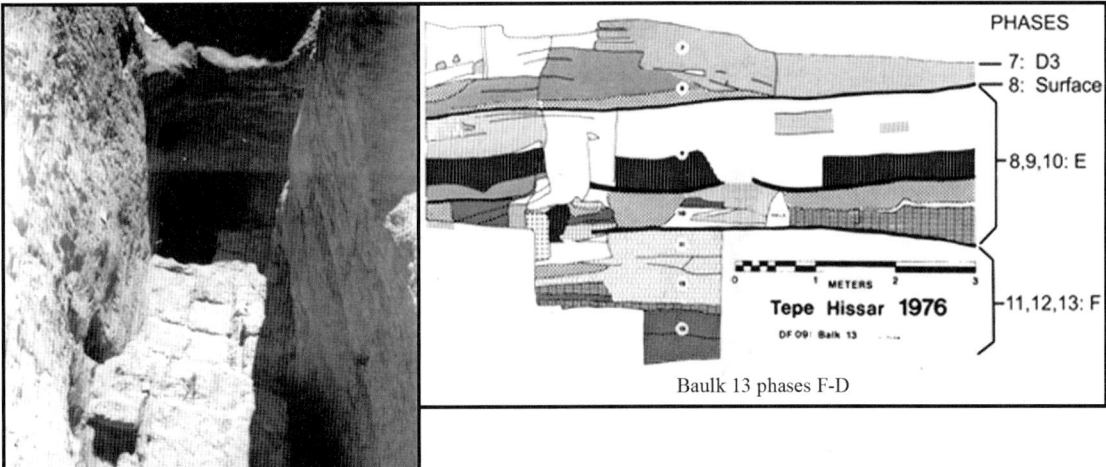

Main Mound Deep pit through DF09 Baulk 13

Baulk 13 phases F-D

Fig. 2.4 Site photograph of DF09 baulk 13 and 1976 section drawing of baulk 13 phases F-D (after Howard, 1989).

Fig. 2.5 Vincent Pigott and Susan Howard cleaning baulks DF09 and CG90 (Courtesy of the Penn Museum).

map of the site (Bulgarelli 1979; Tosi 1989:11–24, pl. III). Metal slag samples (UPM 76-30-x) were also collected for analysis.[2] The Tosi survey plotted vitrified sherds and kiln linings, limestone and soapstone debris, copper/bronze smelting slags in high and low concentrations, lapis lazuli and associated microliths in high and low concentrations, concentrated wasters from the lithic industry, and pottery kilns. A regional geomorphological and ecological survey was carried out by Meder (1989), while Trinkhaus (1989) made a new site survey of the Damghan Plain.

B. The 1976 Tepe Hissar Stratigraphic Sequence

Schmidt excavated DF09 on the Main Mound from the surface to below -3.50 m. This block of remains was attributed in his final publication (1937) to Periods III, II and IC. His periodization (IIIC, IIIB, IIIA, IIB, IIA, IC) is not precise as applied to the architectural levels he excavated. In 1976, the area at the level of the floor of Building 2 (-3.45 m) was expanded, and some 500 additional square meters of horizontal architecture, from DF09 to include DG00, DG01, CG90, DG10, and DG11 was cleared (Howard 1989a: fig. 1).

The section in Howard (ibid., fig. 2) presents the vertical stratigraphy as recorded on baulks 1, P, 12, and 13 (also see, Figures 2.2–2.4). The construction stages have been numbered from the top down, beginning with "A," with "1" being the uppermost building phase within the construction phase. This figure provides a continuous measured section along the north face of DF09-DG00 of some 14.0 m, beginning with Building 1 and extending to Baulk 1 at the east end of Baulk P, which join over the northwest corner of room /3/ (kiln) in CG90, at which point baulk 1 turns north (ibid., fig. 1). The west wall of room /3/ runs into baulk P (ibid.) at its lower right corner, where it is associated with stratum (7). The east wall of room /3/ runs into the lower base of baulk 1 where it appears as a rectangle of brickwork flanked by burned debris on the left and stratum (7) on the right (ibid). Thus, the horizontal complex of kiln (room /3/), kitchen (/1/), and passage (/2/) in CG90 are firmly linked to the vertical section. In the section of the Pinnacle, the surface from the base of the kiln (base of stratum (7)) runs west to baulk 12 above the DF09 deep sounding which lies below Build-

Schmidt's levels 1931-32	Schmidt's Periods	1976 Corr. Periods	1976 Phases and Strata	Location	MASCA Corrected Dates (BC)
Lev. "1"	IIIC	IIIC	A (1) B (2)	Highest preserved stratum	2150-1885
Lev. bet. "2-1"	IIIB	IIIB/IIIA	C1 (3) C2 (4)	DG20 - 3 ovens similar to the one in the North Flat	2640-2390
Lev. "2"	IIIB/IIIA	IIB	D1 (5) D2 (6) D3 (7)	Building 3a Rm 11	3360-2995
				Building 3a Rm 7	3175-2920
				Area /2/	3380-3160
				Kiln /3/	3375-3150
				Kitchen /1/	3385-3165
				Buildings 2, 3	3380-3155
Lev. "3"	IIA/IIB	IC/IIA	E1 (8) E2 (9) E3 (10)	DF09 Baulk 13	4590-4545
Lev. "4"	IC/IIA	IC/?	F1 (11) F2 (12) F3 (13)	DF09 Baulk 13	4345-3515

Fig. 2.6 Correlation of levels, periods, and radiocarbon dates for Tepe Hissar sequence.

ing 1. The east wall of the northeast room S7 of Building 1 (see Ch. 1, p. 28 and Fig. 1.9) appears in baulk 12, two meters west of the south projection of the Pinnacle (Howard 1989: fig. 1). This wall is also associated with the base of stratum (7) that presumably represents Building 1 removed by Schmidt. Thus, the 1976 project established the position of Building "Level 2" in the vertical sequence and provided the linkage horizontally between Buildings 1, 2, and 3. Below this general level, room S7 was cleaned out and a test trench put in at its base. The trench cut into lower building levels designated E1-3 and F1-3, which were associated with sherds of Hissar IC/IIA type.

Terminology

The description of individual depositional layers studied in 1976 uses the term "stratum," often combined with a "lot" number. The latter was used as a means to segregate the associated material found within a stratum or in an area. Schmidt's term "level" was not used, although his Building numbers 1–4 were retained. His "Building Levels" are used only for convenience of cross-reference, since they lack stratigraphic specificity. Areas including rooms were numbered sequentially within squares, e.g., DG00 /1/, /2/, etc. Walls and burials were also so similarly numbered (W1, 2, etc.; B1, 2, etc) within each square. Samples of various kinds, as well as C14 samples were similarly treated (S1, 2, etc.; C14 1, 2, etc.)

C. The Twins (FF)

The Main Mound sequence and dating was in part confirmed by the deep cut made into the Twins that ended in the grey ware Bronze Age and began with a terminal level of Period I painted ware (Biscione 1976, unpublished field notes [Italian], Museum Archives). The painted ware assemblage contains many designs not documented elsewhere, indicating that the period is more complex than presently described. It may be useful to note here that the painted ware occupation ended with a burning, an event *not* noted elsewhere on the site. Schmidt (1933:333) recorded in 1931 that the uppermost material belonged to his "grey ware" period. A radiocarbon date for the burned terminal painted pottery level was 3860–3650 BC

(P2764). The higher grey ware deposit produced 3355–2945 BC, (P2767).

D. The Main Mound: Vertical Sequence DF09

In the case of the Main Mound, a solid meter square column from the highest remaining surface was excavated stratigraphically downward to the extant open horizontal Building Level 2 surface to the south on which stood the well-preserved remains of Building 1. The test was extended downward by a test trench just in front of the baulk (12) west of DF08 inside section 7 of Building 1. This test reached into the terminal levels of painted pottery with the beginning of burnished grey ware (phases F and E), thus, providing a continuous sequence from the end of Schmidt's Period 1 into later Periods II and III (see Figs. 2.2–2.4 and 2.7–2.9). Moving horizontally from the base of the Pinnacle it was possible to trace a continuous surface from under Building 2 eastward to a kiln /3/ (Fig. 2.10), a kitchen /1/, the early version of Building 3 /16/, and other structures (e.g., /17/, /12/), showing that they were all essentially contemporary, belonging to stage D (i.e., Period II, contrary to Schmidt's Period III, as stated in Schmidt 1937). Radiocarbon samples provide an independent chronological framework that confirms this stratigraphic relationship (see Dyson and Lawn 1989; see also endnote 2.4). The most important pottery recovered from this effort was the Main Mound stratified sherd collection, which, for the first time, renders information based on the content of occupational debris rather than on stylistic analysis of grave groups. The differences in conclusions accentuate the problem of the correlation of burials to depositional levels.

The vertical sequence includes the following stages from the top down (after Howard 1989:57, table 1).

E. The Main Mound: Horizontal Level 2—Buildings 1, 2, and 3

(Fig. 2.11, also see comments above in 1976 Stratigraphic Sequence and Main Mound Vertical Sequence).

E.1 Building 1

Building 1 (Howard 1989a: fig. 1) is known to us only from brief notes by Schmidt (1937:156), along with a published (Schmidt 1937: fig. 84) and unpublished archival plan (see Ch. 1, Fig. 1.9).[3] The building was poorly recorded and removed, with few photographs taken. The plans show a central room apparently entered by a door from the west (Schmidt 1937: fig. 84), with a second door leading from the northeast corner into a meter-wide corridor (S3) about 3.0 m long. Just in front of this door against the northeast wall stood a two-chambered hearth (S1B). Slightly west of the passage doorway, a narrow screen-wall projected (S1D). The southeast wall was apparently continuous and contained no opening to Building 2. Although surrounding areas are designated S2–7, no door openings are indicated, and it is not certain how these spaces related to the main room. If they were all rooms, this would make a unique multi-chambered plan. Its position indicates that Building 1 was contemporary with Building 2, which adjoins Building 1 along its southeast wall and dates to stage D3, ca. 3400 BC.

E.2 Building 2

The cleaning of Building 2 (Howard 1989a:59, fig.1; Dyson and Remsen 1989:72, 74–79, table 3) revealed a square main room /20/ (Schmidt's S11, see Ch. 1, p. 30 and Fig. 1.9), 6.3 m square, with the floor level -3.30 m below surface (Figs. 2.12, 2.13). The main room is larger than that of Building 1 (20 square meters), but smaller than that of Building 3 room (31.5 square m); note the centrally located square hearth that is not seen in Figure 2.12a. The main entry was through a door 65 cm wide in the southeast wall that led in from an open court area to the south. The wooden door was mounted originally on a stone door socket to the left inside and opened inward. To the right of the door stood a short screen wall (Schmidt's 11A), 1.5 m long x 40 cm wide x 1.5 m high. Another door led through the back wall into storeroom S9. To the right of this door stood a wall 3.65 m long x 30 cm wide x 1.5 m high, closing off a sort of passage (S12) which was 85 cm wide (Fig. 2.13). This wall, 4.0 m long, of single bricks laid as stretchers (54 x 28 cm), stood to the same height as the screen wall (Niedzwiecki and Dubensky 1937, Museum Archives negs. 83546, 83727, 85066). At its south end, in the room, a low plastered sill 25 cm high is preserved against the exterior wall on the right, indicating that the passage was not closed off at this end, unless by a wooden panel of which there is now no trace.

The northern end of the passage is sufficiently well-preserved to show that it was closed off when it reached the small northeast storeroom (S9) by a 25 cm thick wall (one brick width) pierced by a round porthole 45 cm in diameter, set at floor level (see North Flat: Burned Building, S4 below). Whether there was a thin bin wall inside this end of the passage as in the Burned Building can no longer be determined. The porthole of the passage opens into the northeast storeroom, S9, (erroneously called northwest in Dyson and Remsen 1989:76), the southeastern end wall of which was destroyed by a later wall (Schmidt 1937: fig.

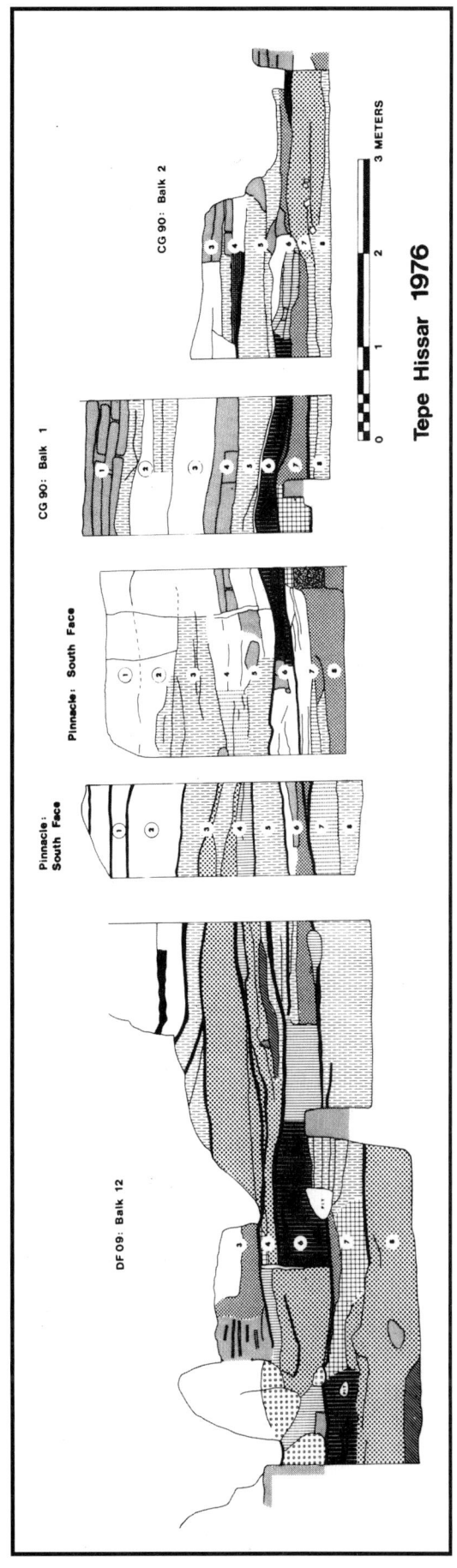

Fig. 2.7 Baulk sections from the 1976 excavations detailing the complete stratigraphic sequence of Tepe Hissar (after Howard 1989: fig 2).

Fig. 2.8 DF09, looking northwest with baulk 12 (center) and the Pinnacle baulk, CG90P (right) (Courtesy of the Penn Museum).

Table 2.1 Vertical sequence of the Main Mound

SCHMIDT'S PERIODS	1976 STAGES	MASCA CORRECTED C 14 DATES	STRATA	DESCRIPTION	BAULKS
IIIC	A	2150-1885 B.C. (P 2620)	(1)	walls and surfaces	1, P
	B		(2)	brick melt and trash	1, P
between C and B	C1		(3)	layered soft trash, wash and fill	1, P, 12
	C2		(4)	walls, fill and trash	1, P, 12
IIIB	D1	3360-2995 B.C. (P 2708)	(5)	trash, burned, brick melt	1, P, 12
	D2	3175-2920 B.C. (P 2710)	(6)	walls, brick melt, trash	1, P, 12
	D3	3355-3165 (P 2711) 3375-3150 (P 2707) 3380 (P 2709) 3380-3160 (P 2621)	(7)	walls, trash, brick melt	1, P, 12, 13
II and I?	E1		(8)	clean fill	12, 13
	E2	4590-4545 B.C. (P 2774)	(9)	brick melt, fill, little trash	13
	E3		(10)	wall, trash, some brick melt	13
	F1		(11)	melted brick and trash	13
	F2	4345-3515 B.C. (P 2622)	(12)	trash lenses	13
	F3		(13)	wall and ash	13

unexcavated cultural deposits below

-----: hard clay surfaces
———: construction stages

Fig. 2.9 Site photograph showing architectural features in squares DG00 and CG90: /3/ kiln; /7/ storeroom; /2/ passage; /4/ open courtyard; /1/ kitchen; and /6/ open courtyard (Courtesy of the Penn Museum).

Fig. 2.10 Site photograph of the remains of Building 2 on the Main Mound (looking north-northwest) showing: /20/ Building 2; /21/ Building 2 alleyway; /12/ storeroom; /3/ kiln; and /1/ kitchen (Courtesy of the Penn Museum).

84, DG00). This storeroom measured about 1.5 x 2.4 m. At its west end, a door with low sill 60 cm wide led into storeroom S10, 1.6 m wide at its east end, 2.1 m wide at its west end, and 2.8 m long. Schmidt (1937:156) notes that both S9 and S10 contained fragments of grain grinding stones appropriate to a grain storage area. North of the western door jamb, at floor level, were two pottery vessels: at -3.30 m a large grey pottery bowl and at -3.50 a red-brown globular storage jar with low everted rim; both apparently discarded without recording. From the underlying fill at -3.75 m, a depth called by Schmidt, building Level 3, came a light grey, short-stemmed bowl (H3925; not in the 1937 catalogue) and a conoid cup (H3929) painted with vertical bands of horizontal stripes (ibid., pl. XXXVI, called "IIIA"). Vessel H3925 may be compared to H3903, a dark grey-brown stemmed goblet (ibid., pl. XXVI, assigned to "IIB"), and H76-81 (Dyson and Remsen 1989: fig. 3) from the North Flat, CF58 (3) /3/, burned room of Period II (ibid., fig. 9).

The exterior façade of the northeast and southeast walls of room /20/ are buttressed. These buttresses or niches are not seen on the plan (Schmidt 1937: fig. 84), which may have been drawn while excavation was at the upper rebuilding stage of the building (2-1)[4] that lacked buttresses. The exterior façade of the northeast and southeast walls remains unexcavated.

The sherds found in the fill of Building 2 from the floor level (-3.45 to -3.65 m) to -2.50 m are described in Schmidt's daily log for August 11th as nearly all grey with some red painted ones. Objects from the fill of the main room included eight baked clay quadruped figurines (H128, H129, H200, H201, H202, H204, H208, and H217), a clay ball (H130), a flat-based bicone (H206), a miniature bowl (H203), and pottery whorls (H131 and H209). None of these objects are illustrated or included in the 1937 catalogue. The ball, bicone, and miniature vessel appear to be Proto-Elamite tokens (Schmandt-Besserat 1992:203, 1. Cones, 206, 2. Spheres, 228, 13. Vessels). Building 2 is assigned to stage D3.

E.3 Building 3

Building 3 (Howard 1989a: fig. 1) originally had buttressed walls on all four sides (Howard 1989a: fig. 11; Dyson and Remsen 1989:fig.5). The original southwestern wall is seen in Schmidt (1937: fig. 84) as an irregu-

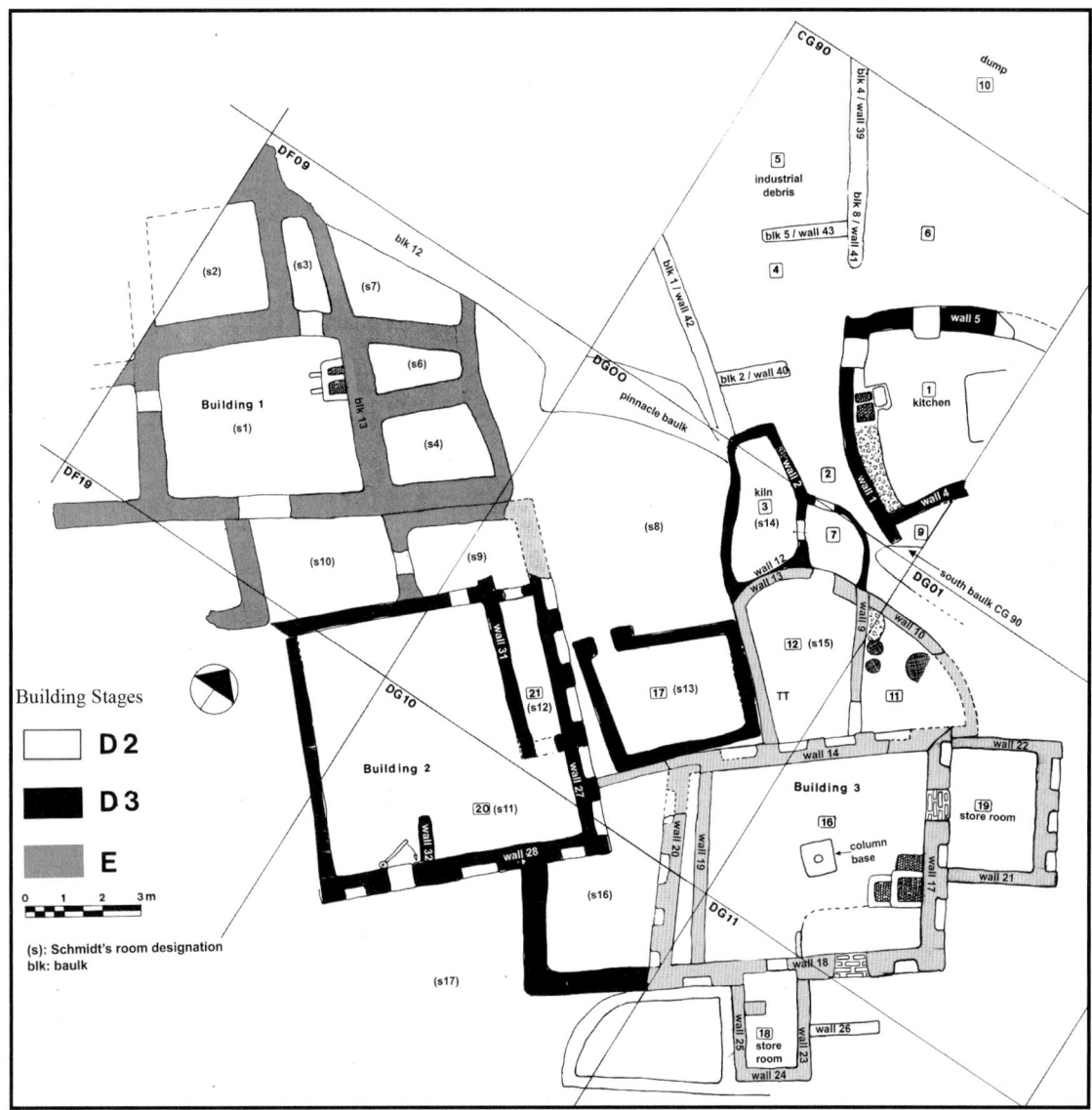

Fig. 2.11 Plan of Buildings 1–3 on the Main Mound during Level 2 (after Howard 1989: fig. 1).

lar wall with three buttresses of the northeast side of S16 across from the east corner of Building 2.

The building was slightly rectangular and initially consisted of a single main room /16/ (Fig. 2.14). At some point, one of the niches was cut through the northeast wall to become a door and a small rectangular storeroom with buttressed outside walls /19/. Prior to construction of the storeroom, this door could have provided access to the main room if it was present. Otherwise, the only door into the room leads through the southeast wall, via a similarly cut-through niche, into a low depressed area flanked on the left by a short screen wall. At the north corner of the depression stood a triple-chambered hearth. In the center of the room lay a square clay base with a deep posthole in the center oriented diagonally to the walls. It is not clear whether this feature was original or added during reconstruction of the building after it burned (Building 3-1). After the initial fire, the exterior niches and the interior rows of "crescent-shaped" niches in the northwest wall (see Fig. 2.14) were filled with ashy debris and plastered over (Building 3-A), an event probably corresponding to the reconstruction of Building 2. At this time, the main room was shortened by the abandonment of the ruined southwest wall by a replacement wall, which was narrower and parallel to the original just inside the room. Perhaps a little later, another small store room without buttresses /18/ was

Fig. 2.12 Two site photographs of a cleaned Building 2 showing the square main room /20/. (A) Schmidt's excavations (Courtesy of the Penn Museum, image no. 85066); (B) Dyson 1976 (Courtesy of the Penn Museum); looking southeast over Main Mound; note the good preservation after four decades.

Fig. 2.13 Upper rebuilding stage of Building 2, DG00–10: looking south over the Main Mound (Courtesy of the Penn Museum).

Fig. 2.14 Site photograph of the remains of Building 3 on the Main Mound with its single main room /16/ (Courtesy of the Penn Museum).

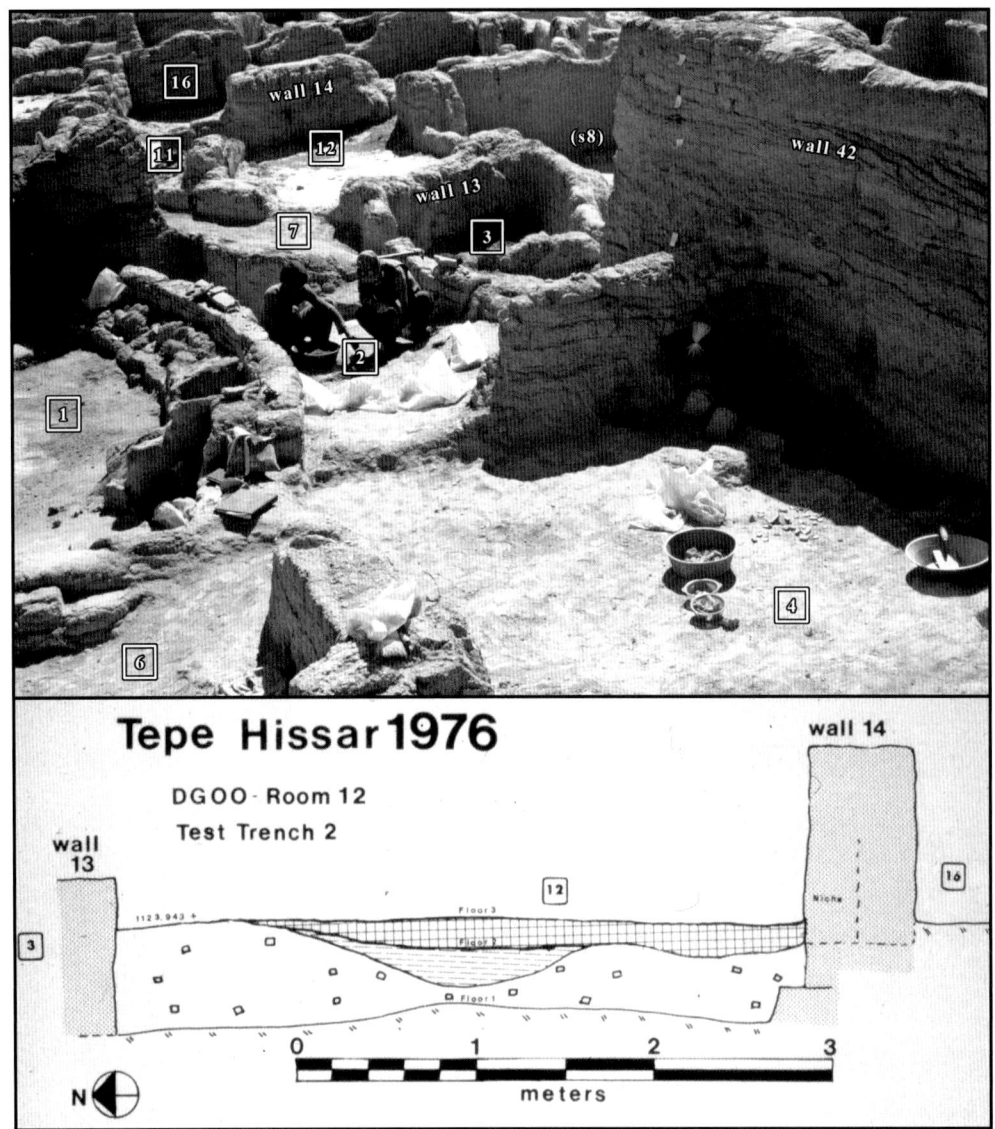

Fig. 2.15 Site photograph looking southeast, overall view from CG90 through DG00 to DG01 (Courtesy of the Penn Museum). Section of DG00 showing floors 1 to 3.

added against the southeast wall with a small door leading into it from room /16/. Later still, a curved outdoor bin was added on the south to the left of room /18/.

E.4 Storerooms /11/ and /12/

On the north side of room /16/, a sub-rectangular storeroom /12/ was constructed on the same level as the fire chamber of kiln /3/ (floor date is 3375–3150 BC, P2707; 3355–3165 BC, P2711), entry to the kiln /7/, the passage /2/ (3380–3160 BC, P2621), and the kitchen /1/ (3380–3155 BC, P2709), all from stage D3 (a test trench on the west side of /12/ showed that floor 1 lay 57 cm below floor 3, the highest floor [Howard 1989a: fig. 5]) (Fig. 2.15, 2.16). Floor 2, 40 cm above floor 1, corresponds to the building of room /16/ in Building 3 (Howard 1989a:63). Finally, floor 3 was built against the burned, filled, and plastered exterior niches of the north wall of Building 3. This places floor 3 in stage D2. At this time, there is a doorway at /12/'s north end leading into the /2/ passageway. A second door on floor 3 led east into an additional storage area /11/ furnished with depressions for two medium-sized pithoi (Fig. 2.17). Into the ruins of this room was dug burial 6, placed within a ring of bricks

Fig. 2.16 Site photograph of a test trench in the west side of room /12/ in DG00, Building 3. Done to resolve the relationship between floor levels in this area (Courtesy of the Penn Museum).

(58 x 28 x 9 cm) and equipped with three grey-black ware vessels (H76-70–72). H76-70 was a very long-necked grey ware vessel, 41 cm high, (Fig. 2.18) as illustrated on the dust jacket of Dyson and Howard (1989). The occupation of room /11/, which is contemporary with /12/ floor 3, stage D1, is dated to ca. 3300–3000 BC.

E.5 The Kiln /3/ and /7/

To the north of storerooms /11/ and /12/ lay the two chambers of the kiln, the entry /7/, and the fire chamber /3/ (Howard 1989a: fig. 7; Fig. 2.18). The kiln stood on the Level 2 surface which joins Building 2, structure /17/, passage /2/, floor 1 of /12/, and the kitchen /1/, (Howard 1989a: fig. 1). As pointed out above (1976 Tepe Hissar Stratigraphic Sequence), the kiln joins the Pinnacle section in phase D3. Carbon dates from the floor of /3/ are: 3375–3150 BC, P2707; 3355–3165 BC, P2711. Floor 2 in entry room /7/ (which abuts the kiln /3/ wall and storeroom /12/) provides an additional date: 3175–2920 BC, P2710. This date overlaps the date (P2708) for the floor of storeroom /11/, thus, confirming a phase D2/1 date for this floor, i.e., floor 3 of /11/–/12/ and the reconstruction of Building 3 (Howard 1989a:61-63).

E.6 The Kitchen /1/

East of the "passage" /2/ next to the kiln lay a large room /1/ called "the kitchen" (Fig. 2.19, see also Figs. 2.10, 2.15). The upper levels had been removed by Schmidt, leaving the outer wall stub with doorways, a three-chambered hearth and bench, and some kind of platform on the floor. The general floor level corresponds to Level 2 that runs west to Building 2. From this room came one radiocarbon date: 3380–3155 BC, P2709, i.e., stage D3 (Howard 1989a:58–60, fig. 1).

E.7 Structure /17/

West of the kiln /3/, between the west corner of Building 3 and the northeast wall of Building 2, stood a one-room structure, /17/ (Howard 1989a: fig. 1; see also Figs. 2.10, 2.15, 2.19). This small rectangular building opened to a northwest outside area through a single door. The building was not attached to other buildings, but was fitted in between the side walls of storeroom /12/ on the northeast and Building 2 on the southwest. Although it stands on the Level 2 surface, it clearly was constructed soon after Buildings 2, 3, and room /12/.

F. The North Flat: The Burned Building and the Vertical Sequence

Information about this location can be found in CF37-38, 47-48, 57-58 (Dyson and Remsen 1989:90, figs. 13, 15; Schmidt 1937: fig.91; Fig. 2.20).

F.1 Building Level 1

This area, above the Burned Building, had been completely removed by Schmidt (1937:177, figs. 102, 103) with minimal recording (Fig. 2.21).

F.2 Building Level 2

The Burned Building, attributed by Schmidt to Period IIIB, was carefully cleaned and its structure studied in detail (Fig. 2.22, 2.23). A short wall foundation, missed in the original excavation, added a small rectangular room at the south edge of the courtyard (7), apparently related to

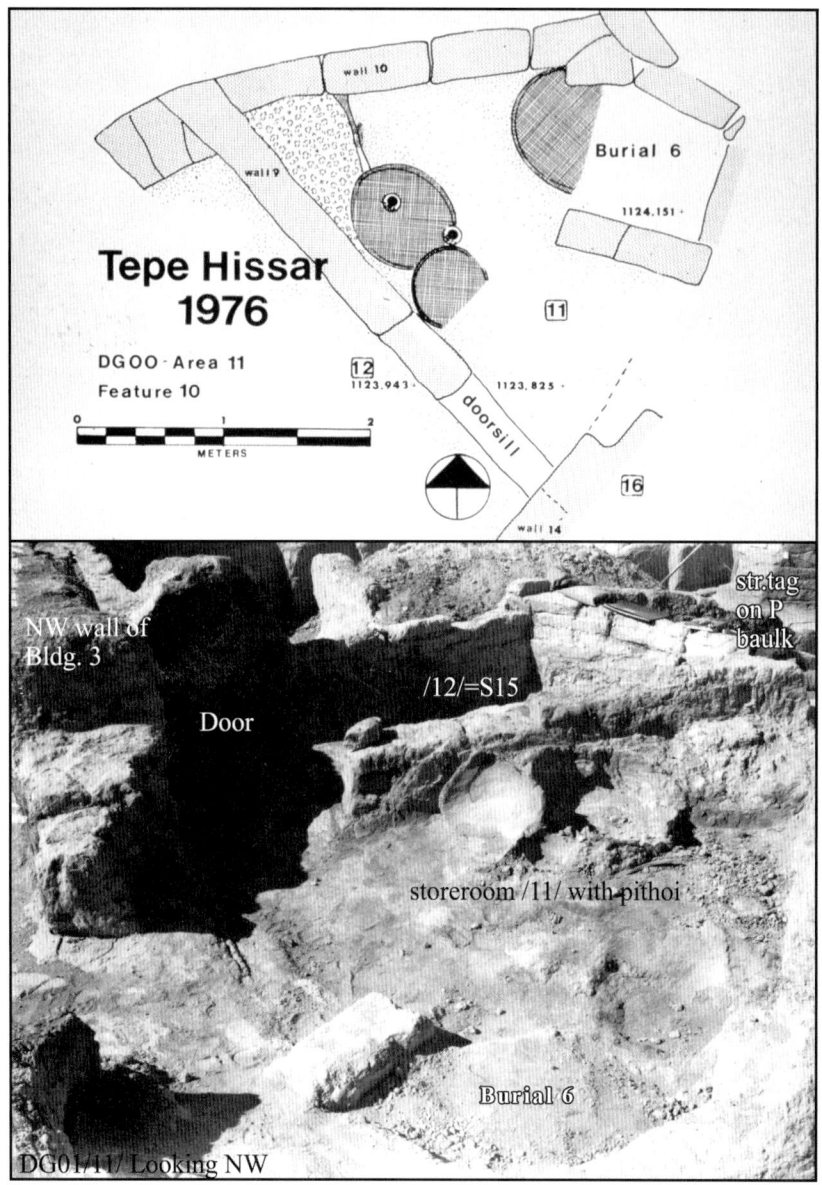

Fig. 2.17 Plan of DG00 storage room /11/. Photo of the same area looking northwest from DG01 to DG00 (Slide # 305137, Courtesy of the Penn Museum).

grain storage (see Schmidt 1937: fig. 91; Dyson and Remsen 1989: fig. 15). The stepped structure in the northeast corner of the main room had never been cleaned down to its original surface at the top (Fig. 2.24; cf. Schmidt 1937: fig. 93 and Dyson and Remsen 1989: figs. 19–22). The cleaning process revealed the presence of a hearth which, combined with the small figurine-shaped niches on the sides, suggests the presence of a small cult altar (Dyson and Remsen 1989: fig. 22; Fig. 2.25, 2.26). The cleaning and measuring of the exterior walls definitively disproved the reconstruction of the Burned Building as a fortress (cf. Dyson and Remsen 1989:93, figs 17 and 18 and Schmidt 1937: figs. 91, 94). The base of the "tower" is only about a meter square and was built in two stages at different times, the second stage providing a reinforcement against a sinking original wall (Fig. 2.27).

From a grey ash level resting against the base of the west wall of the south storeroom /2/ (Fig. 2.28) came a radiocarbon date of 2420–2290 BC, P2701.

F.3 Building Level 3

Test excavations to the south of and below the Burned Building show that it was cut into the preexisting Period

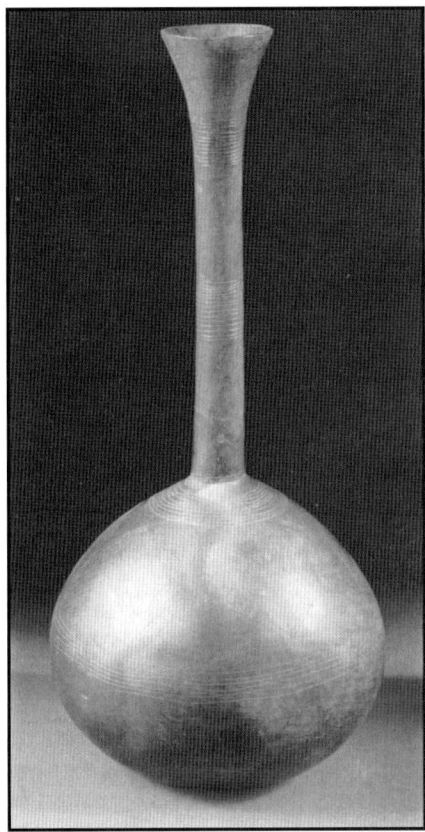

Fig. 2.18 A grey burnished vessel h76-70, Period II (transitional phase D-C).

II mound surface. Radiocarbon dates below the Burned Building in the next building level were: 3030–2875 BC, P2703 and 3355–2955 BC, P2617.

F.4 Buttressed Building CF48 /14/ and CF58 /2/ and /3/

Below the Period II mound surface, southeast of the Burned Building, lay a ruined and partly burned buttressed building, CF48 /14/ (Fig. 2.29). Two burned rooms (CF58 /2/ and /3/), were built as unbuttressed additions on the east side of this structure (Fig. 2.30; Dyson and Remsen 1989:99–105). The buttressed building contained an important collection of grey ware pottery that included tall-stemmed vessels (Dyson and Remsen 1989: figs. 27, 33, 34), small painted and unpainted vessels (ibid., figs. 30–32), a figurine and miniature furniture and bowls (ibid., fig. 29). The radiocarbon dates with 2-sigma cal. BC for the burned rooms are: 3099–2888 (P-2615), 3089–2659 (P-2698), 3135–2884 (P-2700), and 3010–2616 (P-2706)—i.e., they date to D-C phase. Two burials, burial 1 was in CF58 /2/ (ibid., p. 99), and burial 2 in CF58 /3/, each contained burned remains of a child (ibid., p. 102). In burial 1 (Fig. 2.31) there was a dark grey burnished beaker (H76-41) and a dark grey burnished globular bottle (H76-75), which are most likely from first half of the third millennium BC. They both date to phase D-C or soon thereafter (for CF58 burials, refer to Ch. 4 below).

F.5 CF57 Test Trench

A test trench, dug along the inside of the southwest wall of a structure in CF57 (Dyson and Remsen 1989: fig. 13), reached the terminal levels of Period I (ibid., pp.105–107, figs. 35, 36). Among mostly painted sherds, there were only a few grey wares. The sherd assemblage from the upper layer (Lot #3) included classic painted animal motifs (leopards and gazelles). Schmidt (1937:109) dates a similar mixed assemblage to period IC/IIA. Lot #3 is dated 3685–3525 BC (P2619). This test makes the third point at which the earliest horizon was reached on the North Flat, the others being in the deep DF09 sounding on the Main Mound and at the Twins. On the Main Mound, this material was dated in baulk 13 to 4345–3515 BC, P2622 and 4590–4545 BC, P2774. The lowest sample from the southwest corner of CF57 gave a date of 4120–3875 BC, P2623.

G. The South Hill: Horizontal Levels and Building 4

In 1976, on the South Hill (Tosi 1989: figs. 9–12, pls. VI, VII; Dyson and Remsen 1989: fig. 7), an area was cleaned carefully with limited excavation placing lapis lazuli debris and associated flint tools in context as well as identifying metalworking remains slag, prills, furnace linings, etc., none of which had been mentioned by Schmidt. The plan of a long exterior wall with buttresses and a central room with a door on each side was clarified in DF78-79 (Tosi 1989:83). This building is much larger than others excavated—the wall being 8 m long. Work centered on DF89 and extended into DF78, 79, 88, and DG80 (Tosi 1989:35). Dates for the metal and lapis working phase in DF89 were 3650–3370 BC, P2763 and 3895–3765 BC, P2765.

G.1 Building 4

The cleaned up plan shows Building 4 (Dyson and Remsen 1989:82–84, fig. 7) with a square central room /15/, with entrances through both north and south walls. The north entrance from room /16/ into /15/ opens onto a depressed floor area similar to the one in Main Mound Building 3. This is flanked on the east side by a projecting

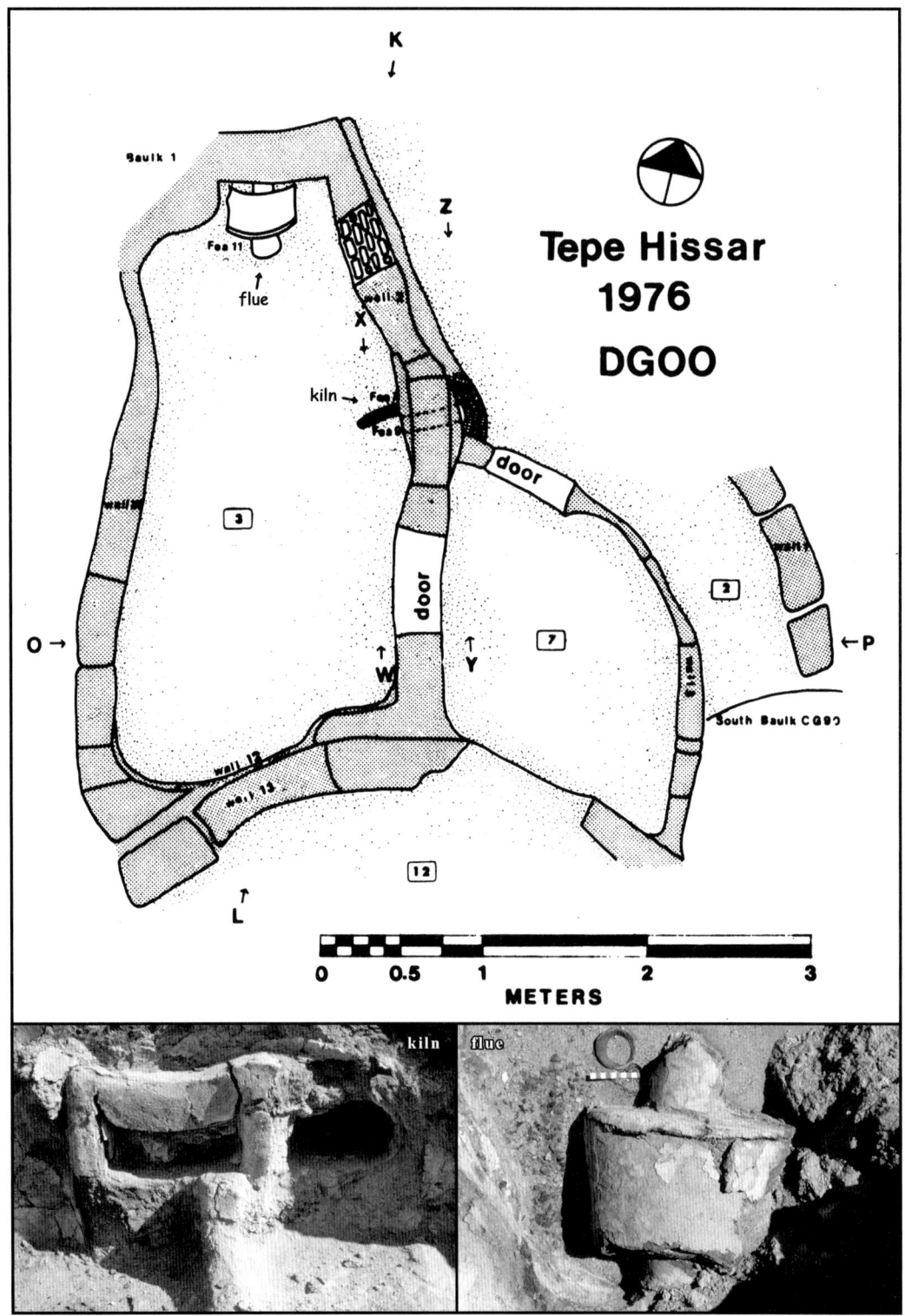

Fig. 2.19 Plan (after Howard 1989: fig 7) and photographs of DG00 from 1976 showing the two-chambered kiln and flue in area /3/ (Courtesy of the Penn Museum).

Fig. 2.20 Site photographs of CG90 showing kitchen /1/: (A) Susan Howard looking southeast; (B) "tripartite dispenser" in foreground, looking southwest (Courtesy of the Penn Museum).

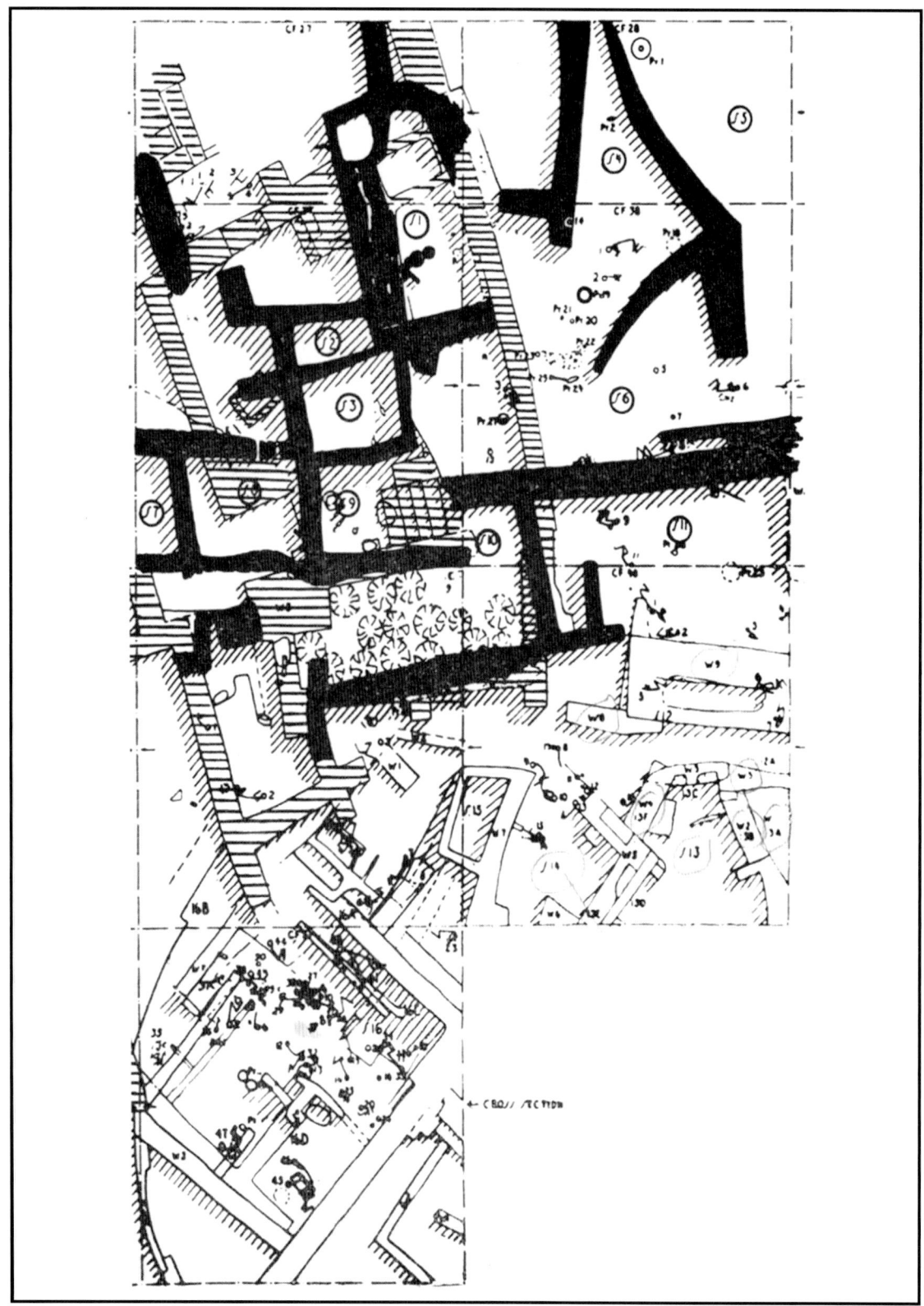

Fig. 2.21 Key plan of architectural remains on the North Flat (after Schmidt 1937: fig 102). Level 1 (IIIC) in black and Level 2 (IIIB) in horizontal hatching.

Fig. 2.22 The North Flat looking southwest over the Burned Building and above it (building level 1) (Courtesy of the Penn Museum).

Fig. 2.23 Two site photographs of the Burned Building on the North Flat (CF37) as cleaned and understood by the 1976 excavation. Features include: a possible grain storage area (7) and a hearth, which may have been associated with a cult altar. W. Remsen is shown documenting this feature (Courtesy of the Penn Museum).

Fig. 2.24 A view looking northwest of the Burned Building remains on the North Flat (CF48–27) showing buttresses (Courtesy of the Penn Museum).

Fig. 2.25 Photograph looking west-southwest of W. Remsen taking measurements of the cleaned stepped structure in the northeast corner of the main room of the Burned Building, CF27 (Courtesy of the Penn Museum).

Fig. 2.26 Photograph of W. Remsen taking measurements of the cleaned stepped structure in the northeast corner of the main room of the Burned Building, CF37–27 (Courtesy of the Penn Museum, image no. 305277), and a reconstructed drawing of the hearth with possible altar.

Fig. 2.27 Two views of the hearth area (CF37): (A) fully cleared with the steps and niches visible; (B) the same area in 1976 (Images courtesy of the Penn Museum).

Fig. 2.28 An area on the North Flat (CF37–47), Burned Building /3/ looking north. Feature /8/ was thought by Schmidt to be a fortified tower. Cleaning in 1976 disproved this finding the base of the "tower" to be only about a meter square (Courtesy of the Penn Museum).

Fig. 2.29 A photograph of CF37–47 on the North Flat, storeroom /2/ which was filled with pithoi (Courtesy of the Penn Museum, image no. PE1947a).

Fig. 2.30 CF48 /14/ a ruined and partly buttressed building found under the Period II mound surface, southeast of the Burned Building (Courtesy of the Penn Museum).

Fig. 2.31 Plan (redrawn after Dyson and Howard 1989: fig 9.) and photograph (Courtesy of the Penn Museum) of CF48 /14/ and CF58 /2/ and /3/. Rooms /2/ and /3/ were constructed as unbuttressed additions to the east side of CF48 /14/.

Fig. 2.32 CF58 Burned Room 2 b1 (c. 2700 BC, after 1976 excavations).

screen-wall. In the center of the main room lies a square clay base with a central hole, as in Building 3. The base is oriented diagonally to the room walls, also as in 3. At the northern end of the east wall of room /15/ is a blocked doorway leading into a rectangular storeroom /18/, which runs along the east side of the building. Along the south wall of the main room /15/, runs a narrow passage about 75 cm wide, ending in a blocked doorway into room /18/ at its south end. This "passage" duplicates the one seen in Building 2. *Thus, a number of features relate this building (which, however, lacks buttresses on its outer walls) to Buildings 1–3 on the Main Mound.* Like those buildings, the in situ pottery is early grey ware (H2151, H2155), and earlier painted wares, including a conical cup painted with gazelles (ibid., p. 84, fig. 8). These items indicate a stage D3 correlation.

H. Chronology

Stratified radiocarbon samples from contexts correlated by ceramics and architectural features from the North Flat, the Main Mound, the South Hill, and the Twins provide a more precise framework for reconstructing the cultural history of the site. Schmidt had it almost right in the field, but gave up his observations in Philadelphia in favor of stylistic dating based on grave goods and the erroneous assumption that structures were to be dated by the graves dug into them. The combined evidence from 1976 indicates that Level 2 with Buildings 1–3 belong to phases D3 to D-C, dated between 3350 and 2900 BC, i.e., the Late Uruk/Jemdet Nasr and Proto-Elamite periods elsewhere. The list of corrected radiocarbon dates are positioned in the main stratigraphic 1976 phases on the Main Mound as follows (after Dyson and Lawn 1989:144; Howard 1989a: table 1). It must be pointed out that some of these dates have been replaced by 2-sigma re-calibrated dates (see Table 2.2 below).

I. Discussion

There is a terminological and stratigraphic lack of integration of interpretation among the four excavators, Schmidt, Dyson, Howard, and Tosi. In terminology, Schmidt's Period is equivalent to Dyson's "phase" and to Howard's "stage." The implication is that Howard's tests

Table 2.2 The new stratigraphic phasing of the Tepe Hissar sequence and their correlates from the 1931–32 and 1976 excavations (after Thornton, Gürsan-Salzmann, and Dyson Jr. 2013)

1976 Stratigraphic Phases	Schmidt Periods	Date Range (BC)	Main Mound (MM)			North Flat (NF)	
			DF09	Context	Howard Stages	Dyson Phases	Context
A	III C	2200–1800	P 1–4		A	A	Schmidt CF39 kiln
B	III B Burials	2500–2200	P 5–8?	DG 20 ovens	B	B	Burned Bldg. CF46–47+56
C*	III A Burials	2900–2500	P 9		C1	C	"diagonal wall" CF58 Burial1
			P 10–11	Walls 40-41	C2		
D-C Trans	Late II B Burials	3100–2900	P 12–14	Building 31		C	CF58 2+3 (burned rooms)
D	II B Burials	3350–3100			D1		
			P 15–17	Buildings 2,3	D2	C	CF48/14 CF57
				Bldg. 1 (upper)	D3		
E-D Trans	Early II B Burials	ca. 3400	Bldg 1(lower)	/10/28+33	E1	D	CF48 'wall9' CF57 TT 'lot 0'
				/14/29+42			
E	II A	ca. 3650–3400	DS 3–8		E3, E2	D	CF57 TT lot 1–3 CF57 /16/
F-E Trans	IC/IIA Burials	ca. 3700	DS 9–14		F1-F2		CF57 Schmidt
F	IC	ca. 3900–3700	DS 15–16		F3		
pre-F	IB and earlier	4300–4000	unexcavated			unexcavated	CF57 SW corner lowest point reached by Schmidt

*"Phase C" is a catch-all phase, meaning later than D-C transitional phase but earlier than phase B." Dyson called the stratigraphic level(s) under the phase B Burned Building "phase C," which included the two burned rooms (CF58 /2–3/) and the buttressed room (CF57 /16/). He noted that the levels in between his "phase C" and "phase B" had been taken away to build the Burned Building. It is this missing phase that is called here "phase C." The missing layer on the North Flat correlates roughly to Howard's "stage C1" on the Main Mound (see also the Ceramic Sequence in Ch. 3, under Early Hissar III). The ceramic assemblage from the Main Mound "stage C1" consists of, in large part, buff painted wares (53%) and grey wares (33%). The "C" assemblage is typologically included in the transitional D-C phase.

in DF09S and CG90P (Pinnacle) are not stratigraphically continuous, although she assumed them to be. That is also apparent in her interpretation of Building 1 stratification:

Schmidt's Building 1 is the "upper" building, which was contiguous with Buildings 2 and 3; whereas Howard's is the "lower" Building 1 which is earlier (also confirmed by pottery). The bottom of the pinnacle is even with floors of Buildings 2 and 3, as well as Schmidt's "upper" Building 1. In fact, the top of the deep sounding DF09S was dug into the floor of Howard's Building 1 (lower) (C. Thornton, pers. comm.).

The new stratigraphic phasing shown on Table 2.2 below integrates and compares the different interpretations as discussed in this chapter. The detailed discussion of ceramics in Chapter 3 builds on the stratigraphic model to generate the ceramic chronology, following Howard's "stage" and Dyson's "phase" terminologies as shown in Table 2.2.[5]

NOTES:

2.1 The stratigraphic and architectural details of the 1976 restudy are largely based on Dyson's synopsis of his field notes, his observations in the field, and my personal communication with him. Also I was able to use Susan Howard's and Vincent Pigott's field notes from the 1976 season. I am grateful to all three.

2.2 For results of slag analyses, the following articles should be consulted: Pigott 1989; Pigott, Howard, and Epstein 1982; Thornton and Rehren 2009; Thornton, Rehren, and Pigott, 2009.

2.3 For Figs. 1.9 and 2.12–2.19, Dyson's numbering system for architectural features as rooms is first the building number, followed by another number between two slashes that designates the feature (for example, Building 3/20/). In Schmidt's notation of rooms and architectural features is a number preceded by 'S', for example, (S10). The notations on the inset plan (Schmidt's revised plan) and the main plan on Fig. 1.9 should correspond.

2.4 The top of the interior wall plaster ended at the level of the top of the screen-wall, with later brickwork above following the same lines. This was a rebuilding phase without the niches, which was designated as Building 2-1. This seems likely to have preceded the rebuilding as the later floor level is above the niches, so this phase was designated as Building 2-A (R. Dyson, pers. comm.).

2.5 These dates are approximate ranges based on two sets of radiocarbon dates: (1) the 1976 restudy project "P" numbers from PENN XXII in Hurst and Lawn (1984); (2) 2-Sigma re-calibrated dates using Calib 5.01 (Reimer et al. 2004). Below the phase E, ceramic correlates with the C14 dated Sialk sequence are used (well dated by Fazeli et al. [C. Thornton, pers. comm.])

3

Analysis of Ceramic Complexes of the Main Mound

The purpose of this chapter is to present a new ceramic chronology for the settlement sequence at Tepe Hissar, Periods I–III[1] ca. 3900–1800 BC, based on ceramic assemblages from the Main Mound and the North Flat. A revised ceramic chronology is established and associated with radiocarbon dates and the architectural stages/phases by using the stratified ceramic assemblages from 1976 deep tests and architectural contexts in comparison with Schmidt's published and unpublished assemblages.

In constructing the ceramic chronology, the new classification system builds on the descriptive and numerical variables of Schmidt and Howard and documents the sequence according to the architectural stratigraphy of the Main Mound and the North Flat.

A. Schmidt's Ceramic Classification

The overall framework of Schmidt's classification of pottery assemblages (Periods I–III) is generally correct and his focus on complete vessels has proven very helpful in reconstructing forms from the 1976 sherds. Nevertheless, there are several important limitations, among which are, lack of systematic description of ceramic attributes, absence of sherd assemblages, and a sampling bias in favor of burial assemblages. Most notably, there is a lack of clear stratigraphic and horizontal provenience for the assemblage, as discussed extensively in the preceding chapters. Furthermore, Schmidt's sequential ordering of pottery is largely based on a stylistic rather than a stratigraphic basis, and is tied to the meter-depths at which the ceramics were found, instead of the building strata with which they might be associated. This resulted in a loss of contextual information about the artifacts. Finally, the pottery records in the archives of the Penn Museum represent an even more selective portion of the total inventory, as Schmidt discarded most of the unpainted and coarse ware sherds and damaged vessels. Thus, Schmidt's reports include selective artifact types, mainly from burials, and ambiguous stratigraphic contexts.

Schmidt grouped the assemblages into two broad categories: he assigned the earlier painted ceramics (red and buff) to Periods I and II, and the monochrome grey wares to Hissar II and III. He described the vessel forms of the early period with nominal categories (e.g., goblet, cup, bowl). The painted motifs include geometric, figurative, and stylized animals described in detail.

Schmidt's categorization was based primarily on characteristic forms and painted designs, but also on technology, manufacturing technique, and surface treatment. He used certain motifs as chronological indicators, although he also admitted that in some graves, the "earlier" vessels were found in the same context as "later" ones. Briefly, he divided Period I into IA (earliest), IB, and IC, with each sub-phase marked by change in technology and painted motifs of a different animal or a stylized version of the same animal. He wrote, "the most decisive difference between the vessels of Hissar IA and IB are the wheel technique and the animal patterns of Hissar IB [gazelle, feline in combination with floral, palmette, and geometric designs], contrasted with the handmade pots of Hissar IA, decorated solely with simple geometrical designs" (Schmidt 1937:42). He assigned the ibex design to the IC sub-phase. However, he later changed his mind about using motifs as sole chronological indicators and stated that "identical designs occur during the transitional Hissar I-II phase (IIA)," also, "the well-executed ibex bowl [Schmidt 1937:42, pl. VII, fig. 37 H4600] is one of the guide patterns of IC, though there are ibexes on IC pots almost identical with those painted on certain Hissar IB vessels. Felines at various stages of conventionalization appear first toward the end of Hissar IC, while gazelles may already occur on IB patterns" (Schmidt 1937:48). On the other hand, Hissar IC decorative elements are distinguished by the appearance of a great variety of wild animal motifs, including ibex, leopard, and bird, signaling the beginning of the succeeding Period IIA. The ensuing chronological confusion could have been eliminated in his ceramic chronology had he correlated forms and wares of vessels in conjunction with decorative motifs, rather than using a motif as a single period indicator.

Schmidt correctly emphasized the continuity of technology and forms throughout Hissar I, and into Early II. In Period II monochrome grey ceramics continue, in addition to the painted buff wares, while the red wares become rare. He subdivided Period II into IIA and IIB, the former distinguished by conventionalized versions of the earlier figurative animals and the latter distinguished largely by geometric patterns. In Hissar IIA, the feline, gazelle, bird, and ibex motifs are reduced to abstract representations. For example, the feline figure becomes a vertical line of stacked triangles with dots (Schmidt 1937: pl. XXI H4460), and the gazelle motif assumes a very long neck, which ends with tiny horns on top (ibid., pls. XX–XXII, XXIV). The earliest grey wares are wheelmade, dark in color, and have a polished/burnished surface; the most characteristic form is the long-stemmed bowl while the earlier short-stemmed goblet form continues (ibid., pls. XXIII, XXV–XXVI). He correctly emphasizes "the continuity of vessel shapes from Period I into Period II with the addition of new decorative motifs, elaborations such as parallel ridges and stipples—suggesting prototypes of metal—are newly introduced features" (ibid., p. 304).

In contrast to the wheelmade pottery of Hissar II and I, Schmidt characterizes Hissar III pottery as an assemblage of predominantly grey wares that are largely handmade. In general, the Hissar III grey wares are lighter in color compared to the grey wares of Hissar II. Pattern burnishing or incised patterns are seldom applied as decorative elements. Schmidt, again, correctly points out that painted wares persist although in very small quantities. The Hissar III assemblage is differentiated from the earlier periods by the addition of new forms: "vase cup" (as Schmidt described it; in this volume it is referred to as a type of beaker) and bottle/pitcher are typical of Period IIIB, while Period IIIC is characterized by beak-spouted bowls and oblong canteens. Another Period III form is the brazier, which is found in all earlier periods.

There are fundamental problems with Schmidt's classification of ceramic types and periods as mentioned above such as: the lack of clear definition of ware, form, and decorative attributes, as well as the absence of relative frequencies of vessel types (if not numbers, at least approximate percentages of each ware type in the assemblage). Most problematic is that the architectural and stratigraphic contexts of the ceramics from the settlement are not verifiable. Furthermore, the transitions between and within periods are blurred. For example, in the transition from Period IIA to IIB, Schmidt observes that painted buff wares display a change from a "naturalistic" to "stylized" version of the leopard and gazelle. In IIB, "the long-necked gazelle, in certain cases [is] conventionalized beyond recognition.... The leopard is turning into a headless and tailless decorative element" (Schmidt 1937:303). Similarly, regarding the Hissar II grey ware assemblage, he writes: "It would be hardly possible to distinguish the gray vessels of Hissar IIA and IIB, were it not for the association of late painted vessels with the early gray pots of Hissar II. At the present state of our knowledge we are not able to say that the gray vessels of Hissar IIB…might not also occur in Hissar IIA, and vice versa" (ibid., p. 116). Schmidt's criteria for subdividing Period II ceramically is as obscure and confusing as his stylistic distinction between Periods I and II: "The designs of some Hissar IIA vessels strikingly resemble the patterns of the earliest painted ware of Hissar IA, and the color scheme is also identical" (ibid., p. 304). In short, Schmidt's methodology was to a great extent based on stylistic criteria, and without the benefit of stratigraphic control, his chronological framework lacked precision.

B. Howard's Ceramic Classification

Susan Howard, in her 1976 restudy, corrected these shortcomings by focusing on a ware-based ceramic typology for ceramics from clear stratigraphic contexts. However, like Schmidt, her typological scheme does not clearly present defined attributes of overall form or compare their correlation with ware types. The present study adds the missing link (vessel form) and correlates wares and form types with decorative motifs in stratigraphic context.

In contrast to the 1931–32 assemblage, which is largely from graves and is stratigraphically unclear, the 1976 ceramic assemblage provides the first stratified ceramic sequence from the settlement of the Main Mound and the North Flat with which to re-interpret the settlement sequence at Tepe Hissar. The 1976 campaign team had as one of its primary goals the chronological revision of the settlement sequence at Tepe Hissar by "the use of the architectural remains to order groups of objects in the strata above and below, and on floors....The problem of dating arises especially for periods of transition when attributes assumed to be characteristic of one period occur alone or mixed with attributes assumed for the following period" (Dyson and Remsen 1989:69; see also Howard 1989b).

The Main Mound was selected as the most appropriate area for the study of the stratigraphic and architectural history of the whole site. As the highest standing point of the site where all the occupation periods had been identified, the Main Mound was also where Schmidt had already uncovered over 2400 square meters of "Period III" (A–C) architecture.

Howard, who was in charge of the Main Mound excavations, explicitly described her method of classification and analysis: "Detailed attributes of provenience, surface treatment, decoration and shape were recorded for each sherd from the two DF09S/CG90P vertical samples. With the aid of a computer and utilizing an SPSS program, frequency distributions, descriptive statistics, and cross tabulation analyses were generated. The goal was to specify synchronic and diachronic statistical variation in particular variables or groups of variables. The wares proved to be overwhelmingly homogenous such that inter-ware rather than intra-ware variation has been more informative," (n.d., II-3).

Indeed, Howard's ware typology has provided a general framework. She collected over 5100 diagnostic and non-diagnostic sherds and classified and quantified them into five distinct wares: red, buff, utility, grey, and coarse. She then documented the frequency distribution of the wares as synchronic and diachronic parameters. However, once again, a key attribute missing from her typology is the description of vessel forms and their correlations with wares and decorative motifs, all of which are critical categories for comparison with the 1931–32 assemblage, which to a large extent, consists of complete vessels. Howard defines vessel forms only in terms of rim and base types and their sub-types, which lack attributes of overall contour, height, and width. The present study resolves that deficiency by careful reconstructions of selected diagnostic sherds.

Regarding decorative motifs, Howard's descriptions are reduced to "geometric," "linear" "animal figures," and "incised/impressed." This is too simple a categorization, especially in view of the fact that the Early Hissar I–II ceramics from Schmidt's excavations are decorated with complex multiple motifs that are described in detail and used as chronological markers. He has coined specific terms for motifs such as, "hanging triangles," "birds in flight," "opposing tongues." I have retained all of Schmidt's descriptive terms for the sake of uniformity.

Furthermore, Howard dismisses Schmidt's nominal form attributes, such as "bowl," "jar," "goblet," possibly in an effort not to confuse form with function. Schmidt's form descriptions are compatible with those of ceramic industries from other sites in the Near East and southwest Asia. Once again, I must underline the importance of form attributes, which are critical for comparing the 1931–32 and 1976 assemblages.

To correct these, I designed a classification system that encompasses categories of both Schmidt and Howard. The new system includes classes of (a) ware types, (b) forms reconstructed from 1976 and 1931–32 assemblages, and (c) the decorative motifs. The typology is derived from a correlation of all three classes of attributes.

C. New Ceramic Classification and Typology

The goals of the new ceramic typology and analysis are descriptive and chronological. "Type" refers to a homogenous class in which attributes cluster with some frequency. The assumption is that similarity and variation within an assemblage can be linked to cultural behavior. Such changes may be an adaptation to different modes of local production, to techniques and stylistic choices, or result from changing physical environments and/or socioeconomic factors. At Tepe Hissar, changes in ceramic production are not due to large-scale migrations of populations as was previously postulated for the introduction of grey wares by Indo-European migrations during Periods Hissar II–III (e.g., Schmidt 1937; Ghirshman 1954, 1977; Deshayes 1968, 1969; Crossland 1971). Rather, it is argued that the Tepe Hissar ceramic assemblages are locally produced due to uniformity in techniques of manufacturing and continuity of forms and some decorative motifs from Late Hissar I through Hissar III.

The primary purpose of the new classification is to bring order to the 1976 assemblage by identifying ware and form groups based on similar attributes. The scheme for the descriptive process is simple and uniform: a sufficient number of attributes were established to provide a total picture rather than an absolute refinement of one criterion. Thus, the scheme provides a basis for comparative study and identification.

In processing the pottery from 1976 and 1931–32, two databases were generated for the purpose of deriving vessel types and their variations along four dimensions: provenience, ware, form, and decorative elements. Each dimension is derived by the clustering of several attributes as determined qualitatively, and they are consistent with Schmidt's published and unpublished types. While provenience, ware, and decoration are recorded in nominal attributes, form is defined descriptively and numerically. The descriptions of form attributes are consistent with Schmidt (1933, 1937).

The cumulative information was entered into Filemaker Pro 9™ database to efficiently sort the ceramics into typological categories and to examine broad variations in vessel form within ware classes.

C.1 Ceramic Samples

This study is based on two large ceramic assemblages of 1976 sherds, and complete vessels from 1931–32 excavations retrieved from the Main Mound and the North Flat. The 1976 sample consists of 5100 stratified sherds derived from six contexts, three from the Main Mound, and three from the North Flat. From the total of 5100 sherds, 3600 (72%) were examined from all phases for ware; of this subsample, 750 diagnostic sherds (20.5%) were used to reconstruct forms. During analysis, it was determined that these samples adequately represented the original selection of sherds. The 1931–32 assemblage comprises nearly 1600 complete vessels and sherds largely from burial contexts and some from the settlement spanning all three periods of the Tepe Hissar sequence. The latter sample is derived from the Penn Museum collection, archival drawings, photographs, and publications.

Contexts, the 1976 Assemblage

The Main Mound sherds, are from: (1) deep soundings (DF09S) and "Pinnacle" (CG90P) and (2) horizontal areas (architectural) across squares CG90, DG00 and DG01 (Buildings 1, 2, 3). The soundings provide about 9 meters of vertical section from the highest surviving point of the Main Mound (stage A) to the lowest point reached by the 1976 team (stage F).

The North Flat sherds are from: (3) a test trench of 1.0 x 2.50 meters by 2.25 meters deep, in square CF57, area /16/ (Dyson and Remsen 1989:105–107), (4) from architectural levels of the Period IIIB Burned Building, and (5) structures of the preceding Period II levels located in squares CF46-48 and CF56-58.

While all of the 1976 sherds were examined for ware classification, only the diagnostic sherds were used for form classification, which constitutes an adequately representative sample.

Contexts, the 1931–32 assemblage

A small number of ceramics from the 1931–32 assemblage were from well-defined floor contexts, while the majority were retrieved from burials, and the rest from "fill"[2] contexts, which are stratigraphically suspect. The assemblage consists of largely complete vessels and a small number of sherds. It was examined for comparison with the 1976 assemblage, with a focus on detecting similarities and differences between the two samples, based on the ware and form attributes, as defined in the following section.

C.2 Ware Classification Attributes

The attributes of ware classes are paste, surface decoration, method of manufacture, and their range of variation. They are comprehensive and in accord with descriptive categories of ceramic assemblages from other Near Eastern and southwest Asian sites. This means that they are easily recognizable and can be reproduced by other researchers. Furthermore, the definitions for ware types proposed by Howard's study of the 1976 sherds are consistent with my analysis, although her "utility ware" has been subsumed under "coarse" ware.

The following attribute classes that define each ware type were examined visually and found to occur in both 1931–32 and 1976 assemblages.

A. Paste – includes properties of clay such as color, texture, and inclusions.

B. Paste color – records the "typical" or original color, as well as irregularities in the color that may be due to incomplete oxidation, carbonization, or reduction (Shepard 1965:104–107).

C. Texture – is described in general terms as coarse, medium, and fine.

D. Inclusions – refers to impurities found in the clay including minerals, natural inclusions, and purposefully added temper. The terms grit and sand are used to refer to unspecified mineral inclusions, while slag was found to be an added temper to a small percentage of the so-called "utility ware" defined by Howard. Chaff refers to vegetal inclusions.

E. Surface color – for immediate identification three colors are selected, red, buff, and grey (dark and light grey). This is a simple and concise method of identification. However, on some surfaces color gradations are observed, such as reddish spots on buff and coarse wares, and light grey spots on dark grey surfaces and vice versa. This may be caused by fluctuations in firing temperature and atmosphere. Tepe Hissar potters fired their wares at relatively high temperatures. Our evidence for firing temperatures comes from refiring experiments, which showed that buff and red sherds were fired at 1100 C° or greater, while grey wares were fired at 800 to 1000 C° (Bouchez 1976:15–16). Bouchez further suggested that "Skilled control of the firing atmosphere is witnessed in the homogeneity of both the oxidizing and reducing processes. A two-storied kiln with a firing chamber separated from the source of heat is suggested as the likely means of achieving such an atmosphere" (ibid., p. 19).

F. Surface treatment – describes treatment of the surface of the vessel, by processes such as scraping, smoothing, and burnishing. Another type of surface treatment is the application of a clay slip/wash that is applied after the process of scraping, smoothing, or polishing the surface. In some instances, the application of a thick slip on the vessel conceals the processes of scraping or smoothing, as well as wheelmarks and traces of coil building. Such is the case with most red and buff painted wares. The surface color is also a function of paint, fire blackening and staining due to exposure to fire, and discoloration by food or other substances, as seen on some coarse cooking wares. Repair holes, which occur frequently on grey burnished wares, may also be considered as part of surface treatment.

G. Method of manufacture[3] – in the assemblages under study, some sherds and vessels were so well finished, smoothed, slipped, and burnished, that it was difficult to decide which manufacturing technique had been used. This was the case especially with small and medium sized grey burnished and buff painted vessels. Nevertheless, there are clues to several types of hand modeling as well as wheel techniques to fashion vessels. Evidence of wheel modeling is generally detected as horizontal striations especially on the interior surfaces of the vessel and uniformity of the thickness of the vessel wall. Hand modeling, on the other hand, is visible if the vessel wall is of irregular thickness, and/or the surface has finger marks.

At Tepe Hissar, three types of hand modeling were employed: coil, slab, and the use of a mold. The coil technique was especially utilized in the production of utilitarian vessels such as plate and wide-based bowl forms (see typology of wares and forms below). The coil technique is visible in section as slightly raised ridges between coils on the interior and outer surfaces. This technique is employed especially in modeling necked jars and conical bowls during Periods Late Hissar I and Hissar II. A mold was used in the manufacture of the wide-based bowl, which is a ubiquitous type.

Two of the frequently occurring vessel forms, the pedestal bowl and the goblet, are generally manufactured by a combination of hand and wheel techniques. The pedestal bowl is made in two or three parts: the stem and base are hand formed from one piece or two separate pieces and the wheelmade bowl is added to it. The joints of the stem to the bowl and to the base are visible and can be felt by hand. Furthermore, base and stem sherds have clean breaks that display the joints. Similarly, goblets with short stem and flaring base are made in two parts, the goblet made by wheel, the stem by hand. An interesting observation from the Bouchez's (1976) xeroradiographic analyses is that the base of buff painted ware goblets are scored for a closer fit with the stem.

H. Surface decoration – the wide range of design motifs are linear, curvilinear, and geometric, as well as animals, bird, and plants. Altogether, I recorded 38 design motifs, of which 35 are painted and three unpainted. Each motif is rendered as a single element or in combination with other design motifs. The painted designs are exclusively applied on buff and red wares, and associated with all vessel forms. The color of the designs on red painted vessels range from dark grey to black on dark red; on buff wares, from brown to dark orange on yellowish to greenish buff. Unpainted designs are few, instead having pattern burnishing, impressed and incised designs, some as thin incised grooves. They are generally associated with grey burnished wares. Plastic decoration is rarely employed; one such design element is the raised band around the stem of the grey ware bowl and on the neck of grey burnished bottle.

In the 1976 assemblage from the settlement, there is a smaller range of painted designs on buff ware vessels than those found among 1931–32 assemblage. While animal motifs seem to end by Early Mid-Hissar II (phase D), the geometric and linear motifs continue from Hissar I into Mid-Hissar III (phase B), a chronological continuity that is also culturally significant in the Tepe Hissar pottery craft tradition.

Painted Motif Elements

The following list comprises the painted motifs identified in the Tepe Hissar ceramic sample:

1. Linear – horizontal or vertical bands; horizontal lines are applied to the exterior and interior of rims and to separate registers of motifs. On small vessels, vertical bands are applied either from the rim to the base, from rim down to shoulder, or to separate panels of motifs on one register or between different registers. Hatched and wavy bands are used as fillers to separate the panels ornamenting the vessel.

2. Curvilinear – these motifs are circles and wavy bands, generally rendered as fillers.

3. Vertical zigzags – generally occur below the rim as one row or from rim to the widest part of the vessel as a

vertical, continuous motif; it is rendered with linear, curvilinear, and geometric motifs, on both the interior and the exterior walls of the vessel.

4. Geometric figures – circle, triangle, and lozenge shapes, are generally rendered as fillers.

5. Animals and plants – felines and gazelles are the most popular animal designs which, together with geometric and linear motifs, form rich patterns such as hatched triangles, zigzags, circles, dots, rosettes, and lozenges. The animals are generally rendered in motion, as in a hunting scene with alternating tree branches.

6. Herringbone – this motif occurs generally along the "belly" (widest portion) of globular vessels and is contained within horizontal bands.

7. Cross-hatched panels – these cover the vessel from below the rim to the midpoint of the vessel.

8. Net pattern – is rendered below the rim and enclosed between two bands.

Unpainted Motifs

These motifs are frequently associated with grey wares:

1. Linear incisions/grooves – generally applied below the rim in several rows or along the midpoint of the vessel in conjunction with incised zigzags.

2. Pattern burnishing – is frequently applied to midpoint of the vessel, either as diagonal dashes or cross hatching.

3. Stippling

C.3 Ware Types

Ware refers to the combination of the ware attributes defined earlier. The attributes display, in general terms, consistent patterns of occurrence in the sample. In examining both the 1976 and 1931–32 assemblages, seven ware types are defined that occur in different proportions throughout the Tepe Hissar sequence. They are: buff (B), buff painted (BP), red (R), coarse (C), grey (G unslipped), grey burnished (GB), and grey stoneware (GS). Table 3.1[4] gives an overall frequency of wares, and Figure 3.1 shows the quantity of vessels associated with wares through all phases.

It should be pointed out that the samples from phases E, E-D, D, and D-C are larger than in the rest of the phases. Therefore, the following generalizations are made considering sample sizes: R ware is prevalent in phase F-E and peaks in phase E, then shows a rapid decline in phase D, while BP peaks in E-D, is steady through phase D, then declines sharply in D-C. Coarse and GB wares rise steadily from phase E through phase D, and both peak at phase D. It is significant that there is a small presence of GB ware in the F-E phase. Both GB and C wares are the most prevalent types from the beginning to the end of Hissar II, (i.e., in phases E-D, D, and D-C). On the other hand, the painted wares (BP and R) start earlier than GB and C wares, and steadily increase until phase E. Buff ware occurs in small percentages from the earliest phase F to phase D, but shows a higher percentage in the transitional phase D-C.

C.3.1 Red Ware (R)

Red ware is characteristic of the earliest periods of occupation at Tepe Hissar. It occurs with and without decorative motifs. The former are much fewer than the latter. In paste, manufacturing technique, and form, R ware is identical to BP ware, but it is distinct in surface treatment and range of painted motifs.

The R painted sherds are generally handmade and are thicker than the BP sherds. The paste usually has gritty inclusions and is not well-levigated. Buff and R wares co-occur in the DF09S assemblage and decrease in quantity after stage E (Period I-II). While the exterior surface of R ware is slipped with a smooth finish, the interior is generally unslipped and not properly smoothed.

Decoration: The motifs are exclusively linear, curvilinear, and geometric. R ware sherds exhibit a more limited range of designs than BP sherds. Their designs are rectilinear with only an occasional curved or slightly undulating line. The designs generally consist of a single element repeated in a continuous band around the vessel. Unlike the BP ware that has a repertory of careful rendition of geometric, animal, and plant motifs, R ware vessels exhibit thicker and less precise lines with overlapping brush strokes.

C.3.2 Buff Ware (B)

In this classification, unpainted B and BP wares are grouped as separate categories; the painted ware differs from its unpainted counterpart with its thicker slipped surfaces, finer paste texture, and painted decorative motifs. Howard, in her preliminary classification of the wares, does not make a distinction between the two B ware types;

Table 3.1 Overall Percentage Frequency of Wares by Phase (1976)

	Late Hissar I (F)	Late Hissar I Early Hissar II (F-E)	Early Hissar II (E)	Early-Mid Hissar II (E-D)	Mid Hissar II (D)	Late Hissar II (D-C)	Mid Hissar III (B)	Late Hissar III (B-A/A)
B	13.3	6.1	4.5	2.5	9	16.1	-	25
BP	66.7	53	42.7	29.9	19.9	6.5	8.3	-
R	13.3	28.6	31.5	10.2	1.5	0.8	-	12.5
C	6.7	10.2	7.9	17.8	19.4	26.6	33.3	37.5
GS	-	-	1.1	8.3	13.9	14.5	25	-
GB	-	2	11.2	31.2	35.8	30.6	33.3	25
G	-	-	1.1	-	0.5	4.8	-	-
Total	n=15	n=49	n=89	n=157	n=201	n=124	n=12	n=8

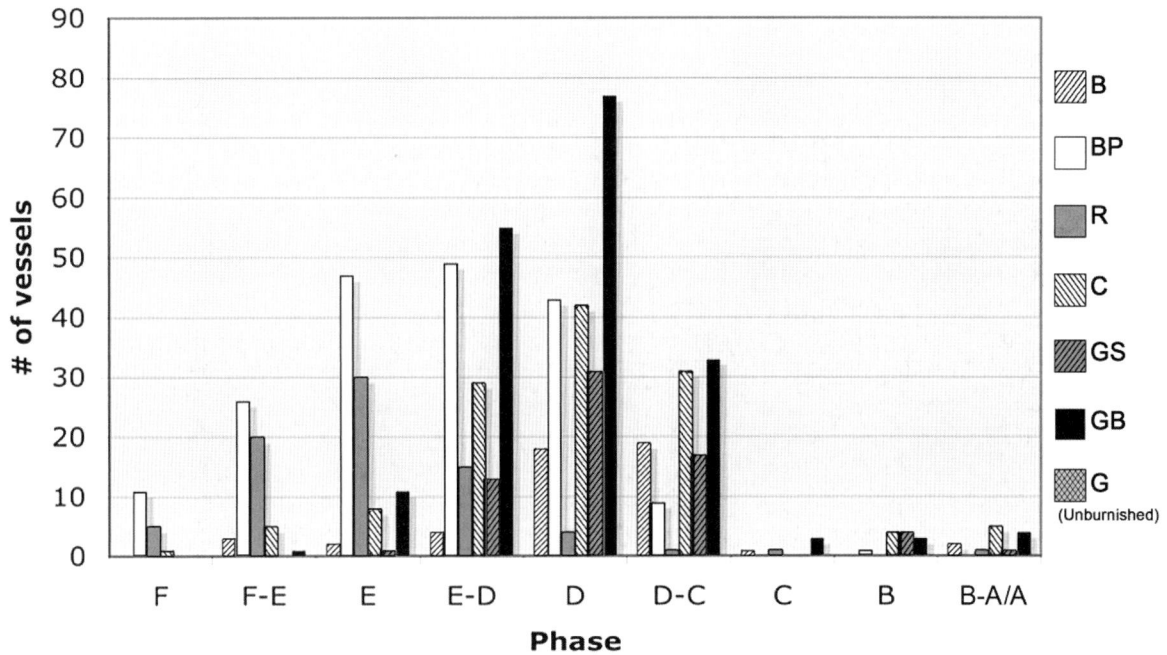

Fig. 3.1 Graph showing the quantity of vessels associated with wares through all phases.

she consolidates all B ware sherds in her descriptive statistics: "they [buff ware sherds] are generally under 1 cm. in width with the majority falling between 0.40 and 0.75 cm. Only 1.9% of the buff ware samples are over 1 cm. thick. The majority of the pottery is fully oxidized, with relatively few partially or incompletely oxidized vessels." (n.d., II-6).

The surface color of B ware ranges from light brown to whitish cream; in a few instances, pink fire marks appear on the surface. The paste is medium well-levigated. While chaff temper is visible in some sherds, gritty inclusions are more frequently observed in the paste. They are also visible on the exterior surface through a binocular microscope of low magnification (20–40x) even though the surface is compacted and smooth to the touch. In both unpainted and painted B wares, the wheel/tournette technique is generally applied. Hand modeling techniques (coil and slab) are discernible in few instances. According to Howard (n.d.), who analyzed the sherds under a binocular microscope, some of the vessels were formed by the addition of coils on a tournette. Hand smoothing and thumb marks are clearly visible, especially on small cups with pointed bases. The unpainted B ware is slipped on both surfaces, the exterior has a smoother surface with a thicker coat of slip intact, while the interior slip tends to peel off. The vessel wall is generally thicker than the rim. An important characteristic of both B and R wares (painted and unpainted) is the high degree of firing, although some vessels have fire marks of uneven color on the exterior surface that indicates lack of control of fire.

C.3.3 Buff Painted Ware (BP)

Three attributes differentiate BP ware from the unpainted B ware: BP has fine paste texture, sand temper, and decorative motifs. Both B wares share similar manufacturing techniques: use of the wheel, especially for smaller cups and bowls and hand plus wheel technique used for larger jars and pedestal bowls. Painted designs are applied on slipped surfaces. The color of the slip is darker than the color of the paste, ranging from dark brown to light brown to tan. The paint is generally grey-black or black-brown and lacks luster. The brush strokes are long and angles are generally not sharp, although some of the designs, executed with thin brushes, are intricate. A small corpus of sherds have faded imprints of designs on the interior which may be due to stacking several vessels together in the kiln.

Decoration: Figurative and geometric/linear designs are used in combination to form a very rich iconography. Motifs are in panels that encircle the vessel wall or they are rendered in several registers from rim to base, each separated by a thick horizontally placed band. The iconography appears to be a dynamic nature represented by plants (trees/branches), flowers (rosette), water (vertical waves), and animal figures in a movement mode (felines hunting gazelles, ibexes with forelegs stretched out to cross through branches, birds in flight) (Schmidt 1937: pl. VII H3366, pl. V H3464, pl. XI H4695, H4742, pl. X H4501).[5] Schmidt describes the stylized rendition of some animals, felines and birds (ibid., pl. VIII H4478, 5130, pl. XIII DH35, 21b) as chronologically significant and places them in later Hissar IIA (ibid., pl. VIII H4478). The linear and geometric motifs are used as "fillers" for the "nature scenes," hanging triangles, herringbone, tongue, ladder, bands, circles, and checkerboard. When they are used without animal figures, the linear and geometric motifs are repeated in vertical or horizontal registers. Generally, they are not drawn with as finely as animal figures (ibid,, pl. X H3052, H4526, H4378, pl. VIII H3359, H4593).

In the 1976 assemblage from the settlement, there is almost the full range of painted designs on BP ware vessels as those found in the 1931–32 assemblage. While animal motifs seem to end by early mid-fourth millennium BC, the geometric motifs continue from Hissar I into Early Hissar III, a chronological continuity that is also culturally significant in the Tepe Hissar pottery craft tradition.

C.3.4 Coarse Ware (C)

The surface color of the C ware ranges from white to pink, although its most common color is greyish white. Frequently, there are soot and stain marks on the surface of large and medium jars and bowls—these marks probably resulted from exposure to fire during use as cooking wares or placement of the vessels near fire. The core is generally the same color as the surface.

Howard makes a distinction between "utility ware" and "coarse ware" based on the "intentional" addition of "slag" temper to "utility" ware: "various combinations of grit, slag, copper prills and lumps of clay can be identified with naked eye." (n.d.). My visual examination shows that both wares have a slightly smoothed surface and paste with gritty inclusions. In general, the inclusions protrude through the surface as large, white and black particles of grit, clay, and slag(?). In this classification, "utility ware" is lumped together with C ware, since it is not certain that "slag" temper was intentionally added to it and that the "utility" ware constitutes very small percentage of the total assemblage.

The C ware sherds are thicker than B and R wares, wall widths on most range from 0.55–1.0 cm, while one-third of them are over 1.05 cm. There are depressions and comb-like striations both on interior and exterior surfaces.

Howard (ibid.) states that "there is no lineation in the thin section so it is not clear whether this pottery is wheel thrown or not." Contrary to her view, a major portion of C wares revealed two hand-building techniques, coiling and use of a mold, based on visual and tactile examination. The coiling technique was employed on most of the large bowls and jars on which junctures between coils is observable. There are thumb marks and depressions on walls of vessels, which result from smoothing to conceal junctures between coils. There is evidence for the use of molds for the manufacture of wide-based bowls and plates.

Decoration: Coarse ware is rarely associated with decoration. Only two vessels, a wide-based bowl and a small bowl, are painted with purplish red paint on interior and exterior, respectively.

C.3.5 Grey Wares (G, GB, GS)

This ware is divided into three classes based on surface finish, firing temperature, decoration, and thickness of vessel wall: grey burnished (GB), grey (G), and grey stoneware (GS). Sand and grit inclusions occur in all three, and the clay is well-levigated as it is for the B, BP, and R wares. Drilled mending holes are seen more frequently on large jars and bowls of GB ware.

Grey burnished ware is distinguished by *slip and burnish* on both the exterior and interior of the vessel wall. Burnishing generally covers the whole surface. The paste has sand temper and is well-levigated. Some vessels are almost black and so highly polished that they have a "metallic" appearance. Wall thickness varies from 0.3–0.5 cm. GB ware is associated with pattern burnishing and motifs such as linear incising, grooves, and stippling.

Grey ware has neither burnish nor slip. It has gritty temper and thicker walls than GB ware.

Grey stoneware is unburnished and generally without slip. It is lighter grey in color, fired at higher temperatures than GB and G unslipped wares. Its wall thickness, 1.0 cm and over, exceeds the wall thickness of GB and G unslipped ware.

The petrographic analysis of grey wares indicates that the mineralogical composition of the clay is richer than those of R and B wares. It consists of magnetite, muscovite, hornblende, quartz, epidote, schorlite, plagioclase, fluorite, and zircon (Howard n.d.). Does that point to a different clay source? This question would require further investigations of clay sources in the region and analyses in the laboratory.

Both GS and GB have decorative motifs, though pattern burnishing incised lines/grooves, and stippling, are more frequently associated with GB ware.

C.4 Form Classification Attributes[6]

The new form classes are built on Schmidt's descriptive and Howard's numerical attributes. I selected two defining attributes for form description. The first is Schmidt's broadly defined 10 nominal types, conventionally described forms that occur throughout the settlement and in grave sequences: bowl, cup, jar, pedestal bowl, goblet, beaker, brazier, bottle, plate/tray, and canteen.[7]

Table 3.2 Dimensions (cm) of General Form Types including all Wares and Phases

	Rim Diameter			Base Diameter			Height		
	Avg.	Max.	Min.	Avg.	Max.	Min.	Avg.	Max.	Min.
Cup	9.1	24	2.7	3.2	5	1.5	7.1	13.5	4
Wide-based bowl	16.5	36	5.4	9	30	3	7.6	25	3.1
Jar	18.7	50	2.7	8.3	22.5	2	22.3	57	5.5
Bowl	20.4	51	3.6	9	27	2	15.5	48	1.9
Pedestal Bowl	21.8	30	3.4	16.8	35	2.4	26.8	40.5	2.7
Goblet	14.3	39	4.4	7.5	20	3.3	14.1	35	3.1
Beaker	13.2	22	8.3	5.5	6	5	12.2	15	8.5
Brazier	16.1	24	12	10.6	12.6	8.5	21.9	25	18.4
Plate/tray	27.8	41.5	11.4	17.2	28.5	7.9	6.2	14.5	2.4

Miniature vessels are appropriately distributed among their general forms (e.g., miniature jars are counted among jars).

Another defining attribute is the quantitative classification of rim and base diameters, and height of the vessel, some of which are estimated ranges of values. Thus, the approach to form classification is both qualitative and quantitative. Each nominal form such as "bowl" is described and defined within a range of numerical values: rim and base diameters, vessel height, as well as other defining attributes, such as height of pedestal or neck height of bottle. These type classes form the basis of comparison with Schmidt's complete vessel types. Finally, descriptive statistics are applied to show percentage frequencies of forms and form and ware co-occurrence through the chronological phases.

Below are three tables related to forms: numerical form attributes (Table 3.2), data in percentage frequencies (Table 3.3),[8] and actual quantities of forms (Fig. 3.2).

In the following section, the 1976 ceramic assemblage is discussed to structure a new ceramic chronology through nine stratigraphic phases of which four are transitional phases.[9] The transitional phases are indicated as F-E, E-D, D-C, and B-A/A. The transitional phases are designated to mark the initial appearance of forms and wares and architectural features that are characteristic of the earlier period and continuing into the succeeding period. Two examples from the transitional phases E-D and D-C illustrate this point.

The first example is from the "lower" and "upper" levels of Building 1 on the Main Mound (for stratigraphy, see Dyson and Remsen 1989:72–74; Thornton 2009b:77–80). The ceramic assemblage of the later "upper" level (phase E-D) shows technical and stylistic innovations in mass-produced pottery, dramatic increases in wheelmade

Table 3.3 Percentage Frequencies of Forms through Phases

	Late Hissar I (F)	Late Hissar I Early Hissar II (F-E)	Early Hissar II (E)	Early-Mid Hissar II (E-D)	Mid Hissar II (D)	Late Hissar II (D-C)	Mid Hissar III (B)	Late Hissar III (B-A/A)
Pedestal bowl	6.7	8.2	1.1	12.7	13.4	10.5	-	-
Wide-based bowl	-	12.2	10.1	10.8	8	10.5	16.7	12.5
Bowl	40	32.7	59.6	31.8	29.4	18.5	16.7	50
Cup	20	18.4	9	15.3	12.9	6.5	16.7	-
Jar	13.3	6.1	10.1	20.4	26.7	25	33.3	37.5
Goblet	20	20.4	6.7	3.8	2.5	8.9	-	-
Beaker	-	2	1.1	3.2	1.5	2.4	-	-
Plate	-	-	2.2	0.6	1	4.8	-	-
Brazier	-	-	-	1.3	1	1.6	-	-
Bottle/pitcher	-	-	-	-	2.5	5.6	8.3	-
Trough-spouted jar	-	-	-	-	1	5.6	-	-
Bridge-beak-sp. jar	-	-	-	-	-	-	8.3	-
Total	n=15	n=49	n=89	n=157	n=201	n=124	n=12	n=8

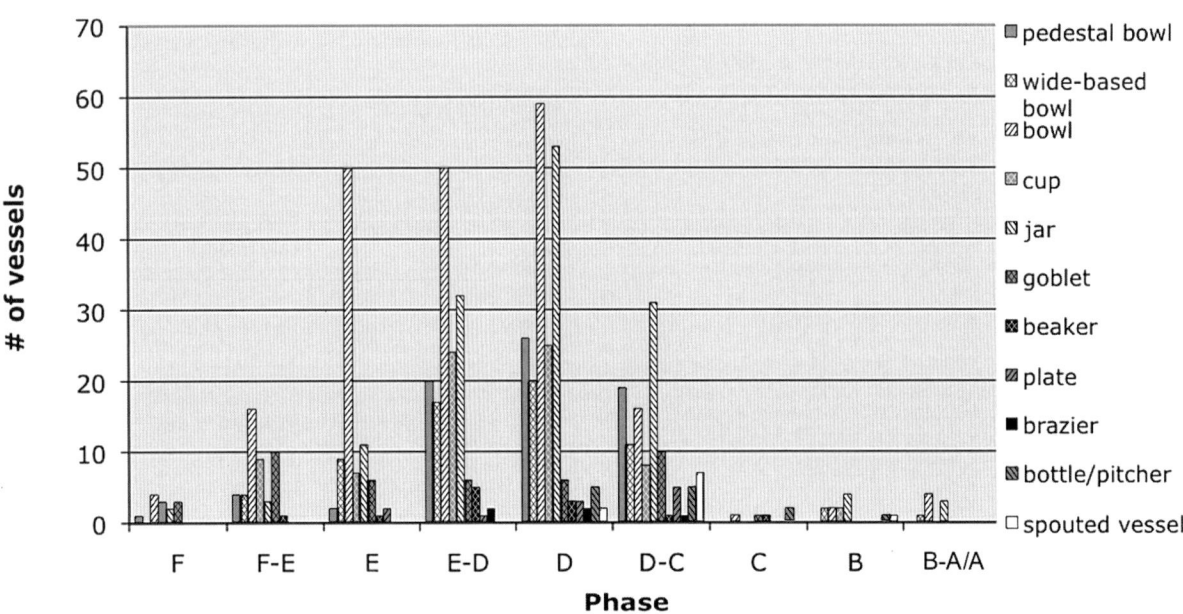

Fig. 3.2 Graph showing the number of vessels present by form across phases.

grey burnished and coarse wares, the appearance of a new coarse ware form (brazier) as compared to the earlier "lower level" (phase E), and a new architectural style of buttressed buildings.[10] The continuity from the earlier phase E into E-D occurs in ceramic forms and motifs: examples are plate/tray and linear and animal figures on BP cups.

Similarly, the transition from Hissar II (phase D) to Early Hissar III (phase D-C) is defined by the continuity of buttressed architecture in both phases and continuity of some phase D ceramic forms into phase D-C. However, in Building 3₁, dated to phase D-C, a new type of masonry is recorded (Dyson and Remsen 1989:79, 81–82).

The descriptive typology is by vessel forms and associated with specifically defined ware types through stratified phases. It is based on two large samples from the Main Mound deep soundings DF09S and the Pinnacle CG90P, the architectural contexts from Buildings 1, 2, and 3, and the North Flat, Burned Building square CF57 test trench, squares CF48 and CF58/2/ and /3/ burned rooms. All ceramic illustrations are from the Main Mound except those with numbers preceded by NF (North Flat).

Table 3.4[11] is a summary of the *revised* ceramic sequence, showing nine phases. It is used as the chronological framework for dating the 1931–32 burials, which is the topic of the following chapter.

D. Ceramic Chronology Through Stratigraphic Phases

D.1 Late Hissar I, Phases F and F-E (3900–3700 BC)

The sherds for this phase were selected from the Main Mound deep sounding (DF09S, lots 16–8); for the range of forms and painted designs, see Schmidt (1933: pls. LXXXII–LXXXIII, LXXXVI, LXXXVII, CI–CII, 1937: pls. III–XIII, XX–XXIII). On the Main Mound, the F-E transitional phase is stratigraphically defined only by two walls (DS lots 8–14); see Schmidt (1933: pls. LXXXII–LXXXIX, CI–CII, 1937: pls. VII–XIII, XX–XXIII).

Table 3.4 The New Ceramic Sequence and Stratigraphic Contexts from the Main Mound (MM) and the North Flat (NF) according to 1976 stratigraphy

Squares	Ceramic Phases	Date Range (BC)	Revised Periods
Pinnacle (lots 4–1) (MM)	B-A/A **Late Bronze Age**	ca. 2200–1800	Late Hissar III
Pinnacle (lots 8–5), DG20 ovens (MM); Burned Bldg. CF46–47 and 56 (NF)	B **Middle Bronze Age**	ca. 2500–2200	Mid-Hissar III
Below Burned Building (phase B) (NF)	C (earlier than phase B in NF; only walls 40–41 in MM)	GAP (NF) 2900–2500 (MM)	
Pinnacle (lots 12–10) Building 3 (upper) (MM); CF58 /2/ and /3/ (burned rooms) (NF)	D-C (Transitional) ↑	ca. 3100–2900	Early Hissar III Late Hissar II
Pinnacle (lots 15–13) and Building 1 upper (MM); CF48/14/, CF57 (NF)	D **Bronze Age** ↑	ca. 3350–3100	Mid-Hissar II
Pinnacle (lots 17,16) (MM); CF57 TT lots 1,2), (NF)	E-D (Transitional) **Transition to Bronze Age**	ca. 3400	Early/Mid-Hissar II
CF57 TT lot 3, (NF) CF57/16, (NF)	E	ca. 3650–3400	Early Hissar II
DF09 deep sounding, lots 9, 14 (MM)	F-E (Transitional) Terminal I	ca. 3700	Late Hissar I–Early Hissar II
DF09 deep sounding lots 16, 15 (MM)	F	ca. 3900–3700	Early Hissar I

Phase F Stratigraphy

The levels corresponding to lots 16 and 15 (phase F) contained only wall fragments, ash, and brick melt, including a plastered wall (wall 6) that was found in "the bottom of two levels of the Deep Sounding (DS lots 15–16)…[and] above Wall 6 was another wall or a platform" (Thornton 2009b:74–75), possibly representing another architectural stage.[12]

Phase F Ceramic Assemblage

The majority of the vessels in phase F are made by hand, though the use of the slow wheel technique is already established to achieve thin-walled vessels, specifically in BP ware, which is fired at high temperatures. There are five known wares: R, B, BP, GB, and C. Most of which are handmade: the most frequent type is BP (66%), followed by B ware (13.3%), C ware is less common (6.7%), and R ware is equal to B ware (13.3%). Some quantity of grey ware is assumed to be present based on Howard's (1976) observations, summarized below. A small percentage of sherds were made on the slow wheel.[13] Buff painted goblets and stemmed vessels have linear and geometric designs, generally ladder and tree motifs. In the following transitional phase F-E, the ibex and feline, as the iconic motifs of this phase, are incorporated to the continuing geometric motifs (see Fig. 3.10). The reconstructed forms are, (1) large storage jar, (2) pedestal bowl/goblet, and (3) bowl/cup.

(1) *Large storage jar*: (Fig. 3.4:1) This vessel with a short splayed base is in BP ware. The exterior surface is slipped. It has four panels of vertical "ladder" motif enclosed between two bands at the rim and belly. The storage jars are handmade by coiling and fired in high temperature (about 800 C°). Schmidt (1937: pls. III–V, VII–IX, pp. 40–53) dates these from Periods IB through IC. According to Schmidt, in the last two sub-periods, IB and IC, figurative motifs (gazelle, ibex, feline) are added to the early repertory of geometric motifs.

(2) *Pedestal bowl/goblet*: (Figs. 3.4:3–5) These forms occur in BP and in R wares. The "tree" motif is popular with branches diverging from a horizontal band at midpoint (Fig. 3.4:3). These vessels are handmade with short and long stems and short splayed bases. The pedestal bowl has a long solid stem, in contrast to the goblet, which has a short and hollow stem. In this early phase, there are also a few vessels made on the slow wheel in BP and R wares.

(3) *Bowl*: (Fig. 3.4:2 with straight rim) These BP vessels have dark brown/black painted band around the rim interior. They are fired in high temperature and have thin walls with sand temper; slow wheel marks are faintly visible on interior surfaces. Painted motifs are linear or a

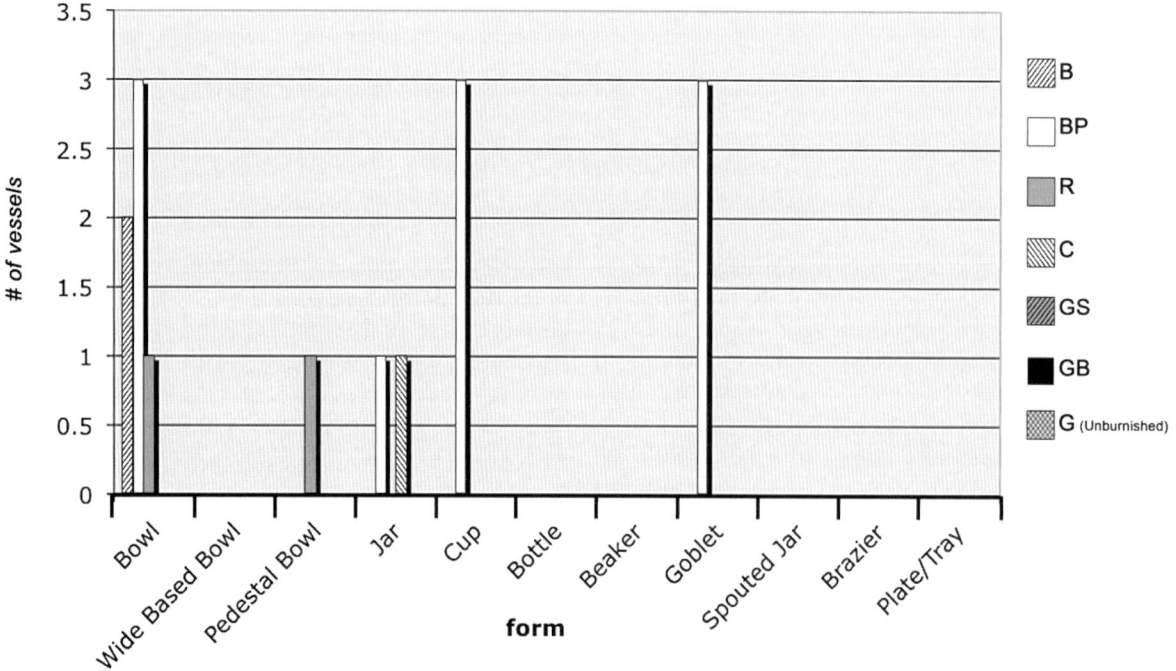

Fig. 3.3 Graph of the number of vessels by ware and form in Late Hissar I (phase F).

figurative series of vertical interlocking zigzags or "birds in flight." The paint is generally dark brown on buff background and covers the entire exterior surface of the vessel.

To summarize, the earliest phase F from the 1976 restudy project is later than Schmidt's earliest level reached at Painted Pottery Flat (Schmidt's sub-period IA), which he reports to include only handmade R and BP wares, mainly jar, bowl, and goblet forms, decorated with zigzag patterns and curvilinear designs. According to Howard (1976), in phase F of the 1976 assemblage from the Main Mound, nearly 30% of the assemblage comprises GB ware sherds, which bears witness to the fact that the unreached earlier levels in 1976 must have had some quantities of G ware assemblages.

Phase F-E Stratigraphy

Main Mound: This phase is stratigraphically defined only by two walls, possibly wall 5 and wall 9, above phase F, wall 6.

Phase F-E Ceramic Assemblage

In the ceramic assemblage, there are two new vessel forms, wide-based bowl and conical cup with pointed base (Figs. 3.9–3.10). These forms occur in B and BP (combined 59%), C (10.2%), and GB ware (2%); the frequency of the latter is considerably lower than expected based on Howard's (1976) notes on the earlier phase F. (Since no diagnostic GB ware sherds of adequate size were found in the assemblage from the Main Mound trench, there is no vessel illustration here). In contrast, there is a decrease of 20% in B and BP wares combined. Red ware, however, more than doubles from phase F (28.6%). So, during this phase F-E, black-on red painted ware has become a substantial component of the assemblage after B and BP wares together.

The technological innovations include frequent use of the wheel to achieve thinner vessel walls, high firing atmosphere, and predominantly sand/grit temper. There are four new vessel forms: (1) conical cup with pointed base in B and BP wares, (2) wide-based bowl in BP, R, and B wares (3) large storage jar with straight or rail rim in C ware and (4) large carinated bowl in BP ware.

(1) *Conical cup*: The vessel is wheelmade, sand tempered, and high fired. It is associated with B and BP wares (Fig. 3.6:1–3). The decorative motifs are well executed in dark brown paint. They consist of geometric elements such as herringbone pattern bordered with registers of lozenges, cross-hatched bands, and spoked wheels rendered in registers. There are detailed renditions of the "ibex" motif (Fig. 3.6:2–3; see also Schmidt 1937: pl. IV H2060, H3066, pl. V H2057, H3464, pl. XII H2990, pl. XXIV H3902, H3913, H5051, H1872, H2147, H2834). Schmidt describes the "ibex" motif as "the favorite motive of Hissar IC" (1937:44, fig. 35). Furthermore, he notes that the ibex "appears here for the first time. One bowl (H2063) and two cups (H2057 and H3463) are ornamented with three or four ibex panels separated by paired branch patterns, perhaps symbolizing the forest. The long, curved horns of the ibexes partly enclose a design which may be sun symbols. Superimposed dots, lines or angles extend from the belly of the animals to the ground" (ibid., p. 44).

Geometric and linear motifs continuing from the earlier phase cover the vessel surfaces, vertical bands extending from rim to base (Fig. 3.6:4–5), of R and BP ware cups. It is not unreasonable to suggest these cups with pointed base and elaborate decoration were used ceremonially with a tripod(?) type stand. In this phase, cup forms comprise 18.4% of the total assemblage.

(2) *Wide-based bowl*: These vessels occur in C, B, and R wares (Figs. 3.6:6–9) and constitute 12.2% of the total assemblage in this phase. They are undecorated, grit tempered, and handmade. On some vessels, the base is slightly convex and thick—it protrudes beyond the angle of the vessel wall, possibly to carry heavy weight (Fig. 3.6:10). They appear to be almost uniform in size, having a base/height ratio of 2:1, which implies that they were standard size vessels, possibly made with a mold, and used as cooking/baking dishes (Figs. 3.6:1, 6, 7, 11). Later in phase D, Hissar II, these vessels are produced also in GB ware.

(3) *Large storage jar*: These vessels (Fig. 3.9:2–5) occur in C and R wares, with flat or short splayed base, making up 6.1% of the phase F-E assemblage. They are usually handmade (some with the coil technique), chaff and grit tempered, and medium to high fired. The lip is rolled and everted from the vessel plane to form a rail rim (Fig. 3.9:4–5). The decorative motif is vertical wavy lines in dark brown on red extending from the rim. Both rim diameter and height range from 20–41 cm. An important attribute of the large storage jars is that rim and height dimensions are very close if not the same (Fig. 3.9:2, 4). See smaller varieties in BP ware in Schmidt (1933: pl. LXXXVI H815).

(4) *Large carinated bowl*: In BP ware (Fig. 3.9:1) is wheelmade has thin walls with sharp carination below the rim. There are two drilled repair holes on both sides of the vessel. This is a rare form in this phase, but it becomes popular in later phases E and D.

The continuing forms are pedestal bowl/goblet and storage jar to which globular bowl is now added.

Globular bowl: These vessels occur in C, R, and B wares, in small, medium, and large sizes (ranging from 6–42 cm in rim diameter, with an average of 22 cm). Only the BP small and medium sized bowls are made by wheel (Fig. 3.7:1–2). The C and BP ware forms are characterized

Item	Inventory	Form	Ware	Description
1	1a–f	Large Storage Jar	BP	hand-coiled; everted rim and short neck; ladder motif
2	20	Bowl	BP	wheelmade; sand temper; zigzag/birds in flight motif
3	23, 154	Pedestal Bowl/Goblet	BP, R	wheelmade; everted rim and carinated belly; sand and grit temper; tree pattern
4	13	Pedestal Bowl/Cup	BP, R	handmade; splayed base; grit and sand temper; irregular vertical lines on splayed base of pedestal
5	190	Pedestal Bowl/Goblet	BP, R	handmade; splayed base; grit temper; irregular lines on base of pedestal

Fig. 3.4 *facing page*, Hissar I – Phase F.

ANALYSIS OF CERAMIC COMPLEXES OF THE MAIN MOUND 85

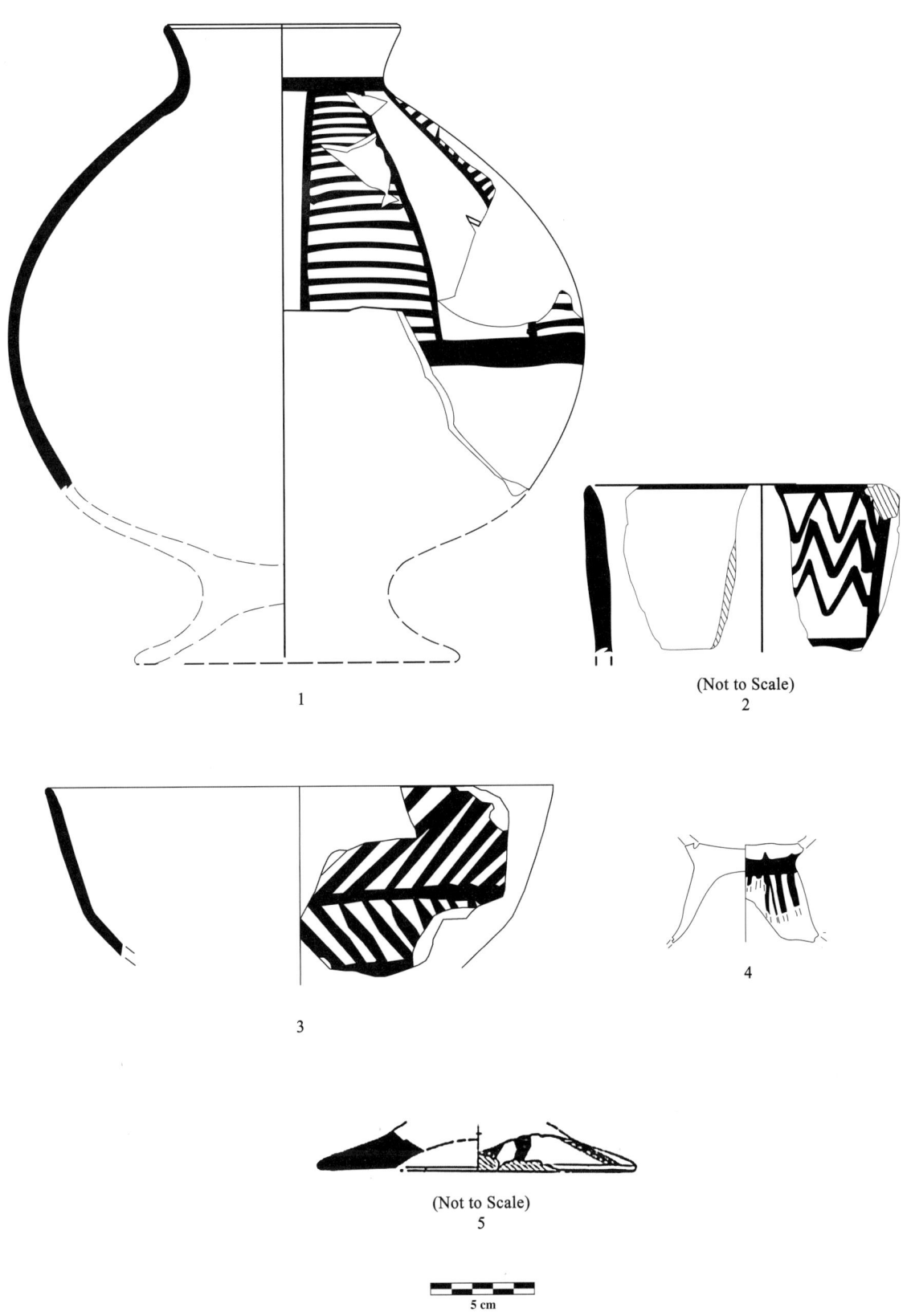

5 cm

by a thin band of paint around the interior and exterior of the rim.

The R ware bowls are generally handmade by coiling, with either sand and chaff or sand and grit temper. Both R and BP wares share thin walls and high firing temperatures. They have scrape marks on the interior of the vessels either from smoothing the vessel wall or from wear (Fig. 3.7:4). These bowls have a thin slip on the exterior.

On BP wares, the decorative motifs are rich and varied: linear (bands/waves) (Figs. 3.7:3, 5–6, 3.8:1–2) and geometric (hatched "hanging triangles" between horizontal bands), herringbone design (Figs. 3.7:4, 7, 3.8:3; see also Schmidt 1937: pl. IV H2092); vertical zigzags alternating with tree pattern (Figs. 3.8:4–6, 3.7:2). Both BP and R wares share the Early Hissar I motif of "birds in flight" (Fig. 3.7:5).

Pedestal Bowl/Goblet:[14] This vessel type is one of the earliest forms associated with R and B wares. In this phase, the pedestal bowl/goblet continues to be produced in GB and BP wares. However, unlike the earlier handmade, chaff or grit tempered form, the later pedestal bowl/goblet vessels are wheelmade, high fired, and have sand temper. Also, the decorative motifs vary from those of the earlier pedestal bowls forms in that, instead of simple linear and geometric motifs, animal motifs are more frequently applied (gazelle, stylized leopard in combination with geometric designs diagonal "ladder" motif, tree alternating with vertical "waves") (Fig. 3.10:1–7; see also Schmidt 1933: pl. LXXXIX, 1937: pls. V DH 44, 22a, IX H2887, H4747). Note that the GB pedestal bowl/goblet has horizontal and vertical polishing marks on its exterior surface (see Dyson and Remsen 1989: fig. 1).

Summary

Regarding vessel forms:
- In this phase there are six of the type forms (pedestal bowl and goblet combined).

- Wide-based bowls appear at low frequency (12.2%) associated with B, R, and C wares.

- Bowl (32.7%) and pedestal bowl/goblet (28.6%) peak, as the most numerous vessels in this phase.

Regarding wares:
- BP and B ware are most frequent (59%) and associated with bowl, pedestal bowl/goblet, cup, jar, and beaker forms.

- GS is missing, as in the earlier phase F.

- GB ware is minimally present (2%, not represented in Figs. 3.4–3.10).

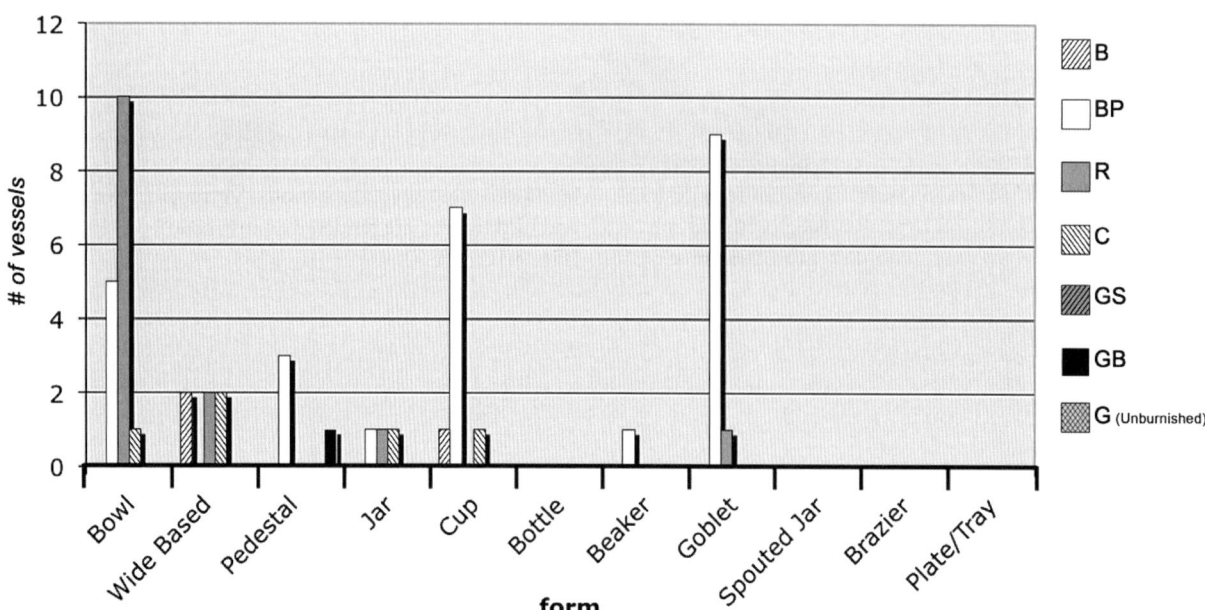

Fig. 3.5 Graph of the number of vessels by ware and form from Late Hissar I to Early Hissar II (phase F-E).

D.2 Early Hissar II, Phase E
(ca. 3650–3400 BC)

Ceramics from this phase are found in DS lots 3–7; NF, CF57 test trench lot (3)[15] (see Schmidt 1933: pl. CI, H1621, H1648, pl. CII H1654, H1365, H515, H1655, 1937: pls. XX–XXIII).

Stratigraphy

Main Mound: Above the F-E transitional phase is the earliest level of phase E that contains evidence of copper slag, steatite, and calcite flakes that testify to copper smelting and stone working (Pigott unpublished field notes, as cited in Thornton 2009b:76). This phase has been divided into two floor levels on the Main Mound by Howard (E3, E2).

North Flat: Dyson's exploration of the earliest levels at the North Flat consisted of a 1 x 2.5 m test trench CF57 "along the southwest baulk of a buttressed (phase D) building" (Thornton 2009b:84). The only stratified ceramic evidence is from below the buttressed building (CF57) in which three lots of sherds were collected and examined; lot #3 contained ceramics similar to those from phase E on the Main Mound, and lots #1 and #2 had ceramics of the later E-D transitional phase (Dyson and Remsen 1989:104–107). Lot #3, gave a C14 date of 4830±60 BP (P-2619) that has a 2-sigma range of 3737–3506 cal. BC, which corresponds to phase E, Early Hissar II. Lots #1 and #2 had later E-D transitional phase ceramics, corresponding to the Main Mound assemblage (Dyson and Remsen 1989:104–107).

Ceramic Assemblage

The earlier floor level (E3) contains similar forms and motifs already identified in phase F-E, including pedestal bowl, wide-based bowl, and large storage jar with rail rim. The pedestal bowl has more complex geometric motifs, such as hanging triangles with hatched circles in horizontal registers. Schmidt's characteristic Period IIA motifs, feline, ibex, and bird figures, are rendered as abstractions on BP vessels (Fig. 3.12:3, 5, 7). The later floor level E2, roughly corresponds to Schmidt's IIB and contains two new vessel forms and two new motifs.

These two new vessel forms are, (1) a shallow plate/tray in C and G wares, and a (2) carinated cup/bowl in BP ware associated with new decorative motifs (see below).

(1) *Plate/tray*: (Fig. 3.12:1) This form is a shallower version of the wide-based bowl, which is a frequently occurring form in the transitional F-E phase (see above). The vessel is found in C and G wares with grit temper. Some vessels have slag inclusions in the temper. They are undecorated, handmade cooking/serving vessels. This supposition is reinforced by their find spots near a kiln at the Main Mound Building 3, square DG00/3/ (Howard 1989a:56, fig 1).

(2) *Carinated cup/bowl*: These vessels are handmade in BP ware (Figs. 3.12:2–8, 3.13:1–6, 3.14:1–3), GB (Fig. 3.14:4) and R wares (Figs. 3.14:5–9, 3.12:4–7). Similar to these vessels is a group of handmade miniature cups with thin walls (Dyson and Remsen 1989:105–107). The decorative motifs on some of the carinated cups/bowls in BP ware are unique, one is a tradition of thin brush strokes of precisely rendered circular motifs below the rim, the other consists of bold, wide strokes of linear motifs (Figs. 3.12:4, 6, 3.13:1–6, 3.14:1–9). These are high fired, small vessels retrieved from the North Flat trench, square CF57, and not documented on the Main Mound. Howard refers to them as "clinky ware."

The animal motifs on BP ware vessels evolve into abstractions of gazelles, felines, and giraffes(?) in motion enclosed by horizontal bands (Fig. 3.12:5). It is a stylistic tradition heretofore not observed, perhaps it should be attributed to the work of a specific potter. Another characteristic of these vessels is the presence of reddish brown painted band on the exterior of the rim and belly of everted bowls (Figs. 3.14:5–9).

From earlier phases, four forms continue:

Conical cup: This form is wheelmade in B ware with very thin walls; it is quite similar to those in phase F-E.

Pedestal bowl/goblet: This ubiquitous, continuing form is produced in thin GB and BP wares, (Figs. 3.15:2, 4–6, 3.10:6–7), in R (Figs. 3.15:3). The vessels are all wheelmade, high fired, and have thin walls. The BP wares are decorated with geometric motifs, hanging triangles with cross hatched circles (Fig. 3.15:1), hatched lozenges, and stylized gazelle horns (Figs. 3.15:5, 3.12:2–3). Schmidt's characteristic Period IIA motifs, feline, ibex, and bird figures, are rendered as abstractions on BP vessels (Fig. 3.12:3, 5, 7).

The GB ware has fine fabric, light grey color, and a metallic sheen (Fig. 3.16:1–3; Schmidt 1937: pl. XXIII "Gray Pottery of Hissar IIA").

Wide-based bowl: This form occurs in R (Fig. 3.16:4), C (not illustrated), and GB wares (Fig. 3.16:5). Only the GB ware is wheelmade. The wheel production of this form, its varied sizes, and its occurrence in multiple wares, contrast with its earlier handmade C ware form in phase F-E (see above).

Jar with rail rim and necked jar: These vessel forms are wheel- and handmade, high fired, and found in C (Fig. 3.16:6), BP (Fig. 3.16:7), and GB wares (Fig. 3.16:8–9; Dyson and Remsen 1989: fig. 36c, d). The C ware vessels

Item	Inventory	Form	Ware	Description
1	627	Conical Cup	B	wheelmade, pointed base; sand temper
2	344A, 347	Conical Cup	BP	wheelmade; pointed base; sand temper; slip; vertical zigzag motif
3	392	Conical Cup	BP	wheelmade; tree, ibex with wheel motif in horizontal panels; sand temper
4	457, 557, 580	Globular Cup/Bowl	R	wheelmade; inverted; sand and grit temper; slip; vertical bands from rim to base
5	1390	Conical Cup	R	wheelmade; exterior burnish; grit temper; slip; vertical bands from rim to base
6	629	Wide-Based Bowl	R	wheelmade; raised base; grit temper; slip
7	933	Wide-Based Bowl	R	wheelmade; raised base; sand temper; slip
8	213	Wide-Based Bowl	B	wheelmade; raised base; grit temper; exterior slip
9	460, 461	Wide-Based Bowl	B	handmade; raised base; grit temper; exterior slip; interior scrape marks
10	1583	Wide-Based Bowl	C	handmade; raised thick base; grit temper; slip
11	628	Wide-Based Bowl	C	handmade; flat base; chaff and grit temper; exterior slip; interior scrape marks

Fig. 3.6 *facing page*, Hissar I, Transitional Phase F-E.

ANALYSIS OF CERAMIC COMPLEXES OF THE MAIN MOUND

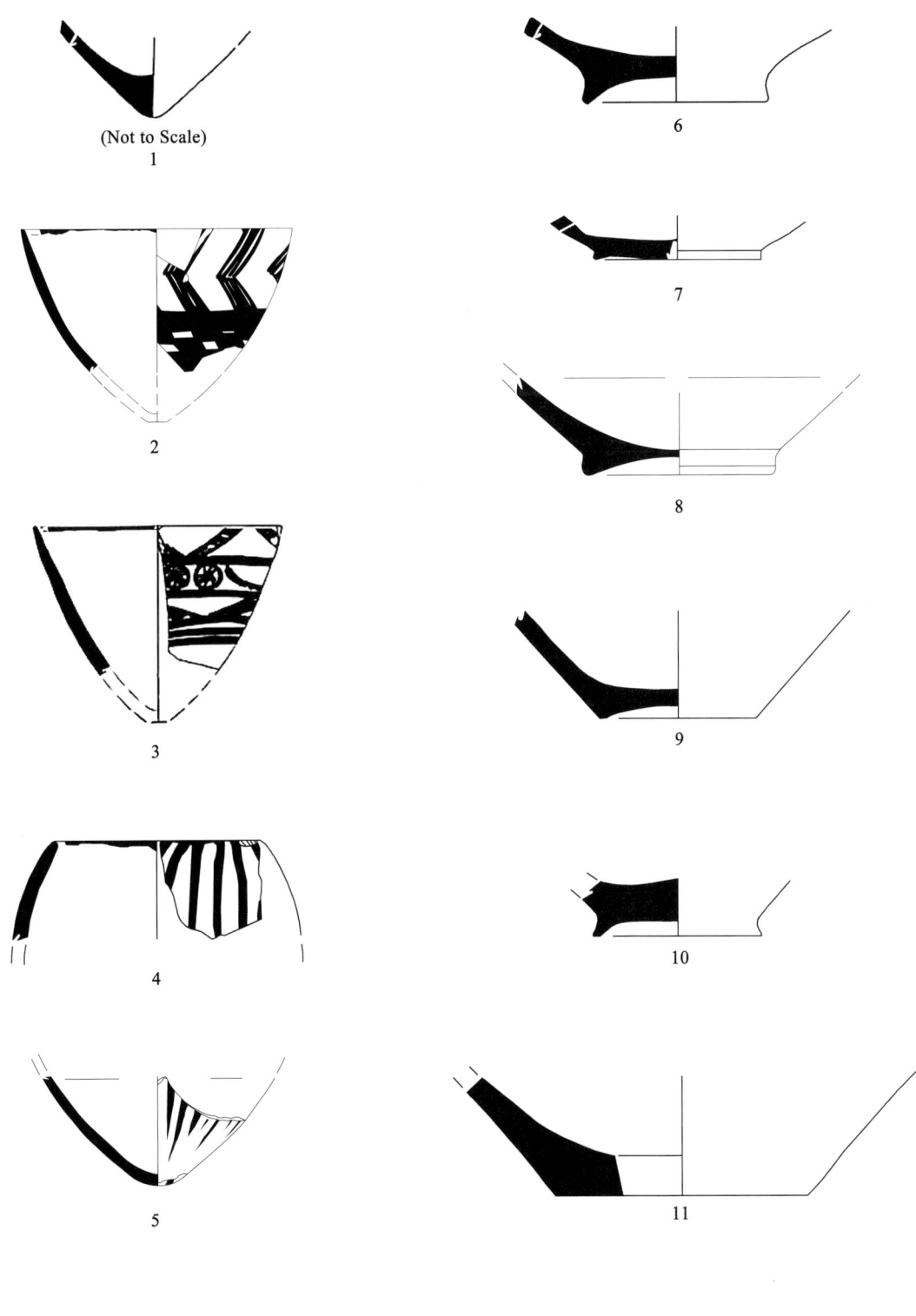

5 cm

Item	Inventory	Form	Ware	Description
1	1397	Beaker	R	wheelmade; globular and carinated; sand and grit temper; slip; drill holes; black painted circular designs
2	1376	Globular Bowl	BP	wheelmade; slightly outcurving rim and globular; sand temper; slip; vertical zigzags and alternating trees
3	1599	Globular Bowl	BP	wheelmade; slightly outcurving rim and globular; sand and grit temper; slip; linear designs
4	394	Globular Bowl	BP	handmade; slightly inverted wall; sand temper; linear filled zigzags alternate with tree design
5	454	Globular Bowl	BP	wheelmade; slightly everted wall; sand temper; slip; vertical strips of birds in flight
6	1021a	Globular Bowl	BP	handmade slab; sand and grit temper; slip; curvilinear designs in vertical strips
7	1195a–c	Globular Bowl	BP	handmade, sand and grit temper; slip; vertical filled zigzags between horizontal bands

Fig. 3.7 *facing page*, Hissar I, Transitional Phase F-E.

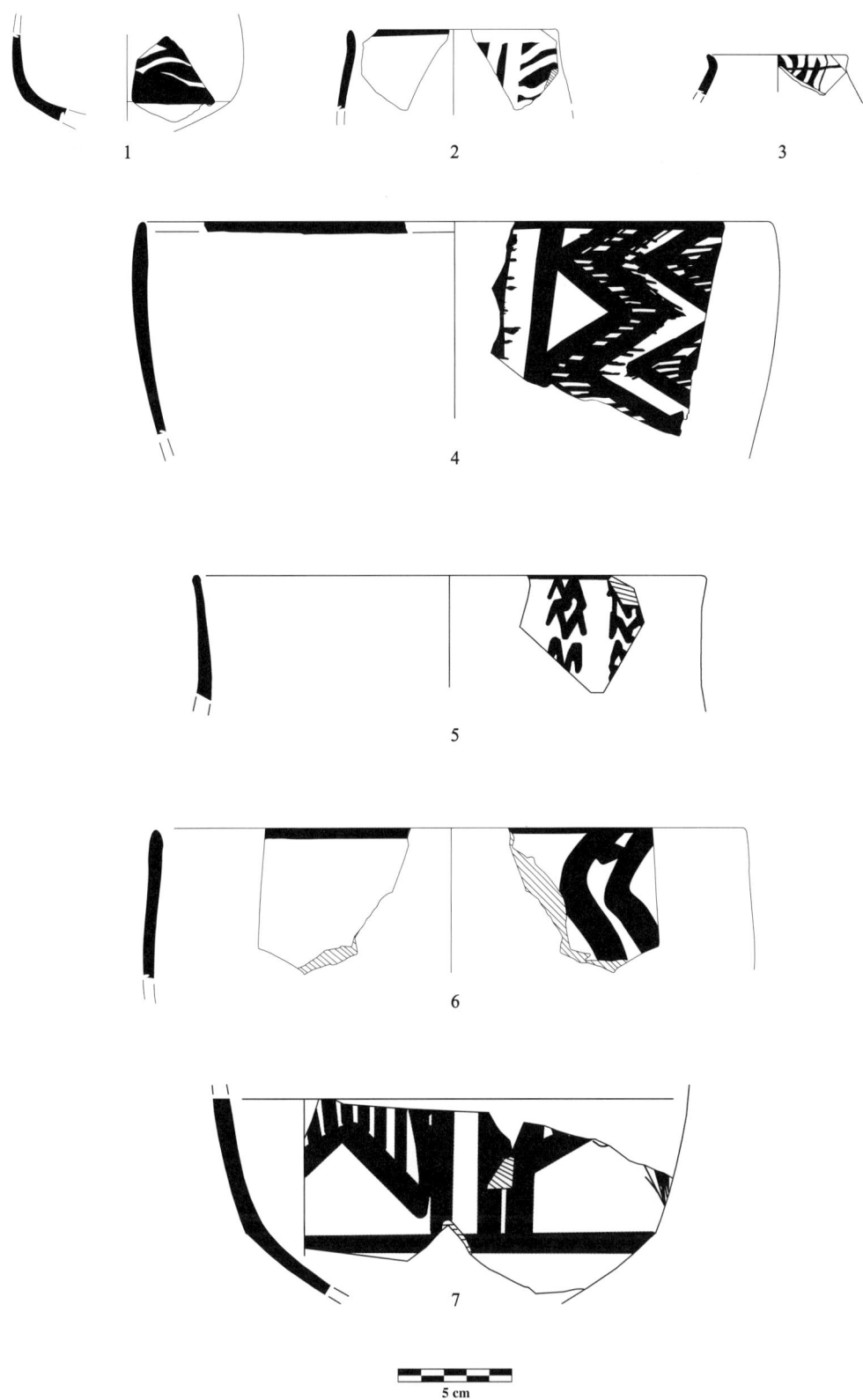

Item	Inventory	Form	Ware	Description
1	836a,b	Globular Bowl	BP	wheelmade; everted wall; sand and grit temper; linear design from rim to base
2	606	Globular Bowl	BP, R	wheelmade; inverted wall; sand temper; linear design from rim to base
3	217	Globular Bowl	BP	wheelmade; everted wall; sand temper; herringbone design
4	396	Globular Bowl	BP	handmade; everted wall; sand and grit temper; vertical zigzags and alternating trees
5	1007a,b, 1067	Globular Bowl	BP	wheelmade; sand temper; vertical zigzags and alternating trees
6	453	Globular Bowl	BP, R	handmade; inverted wall; chaff and grit temper; vertical zigzags and alternating trees

Fig. 3.8 *facing page*, Hissar I, Transitional Phase F-E.

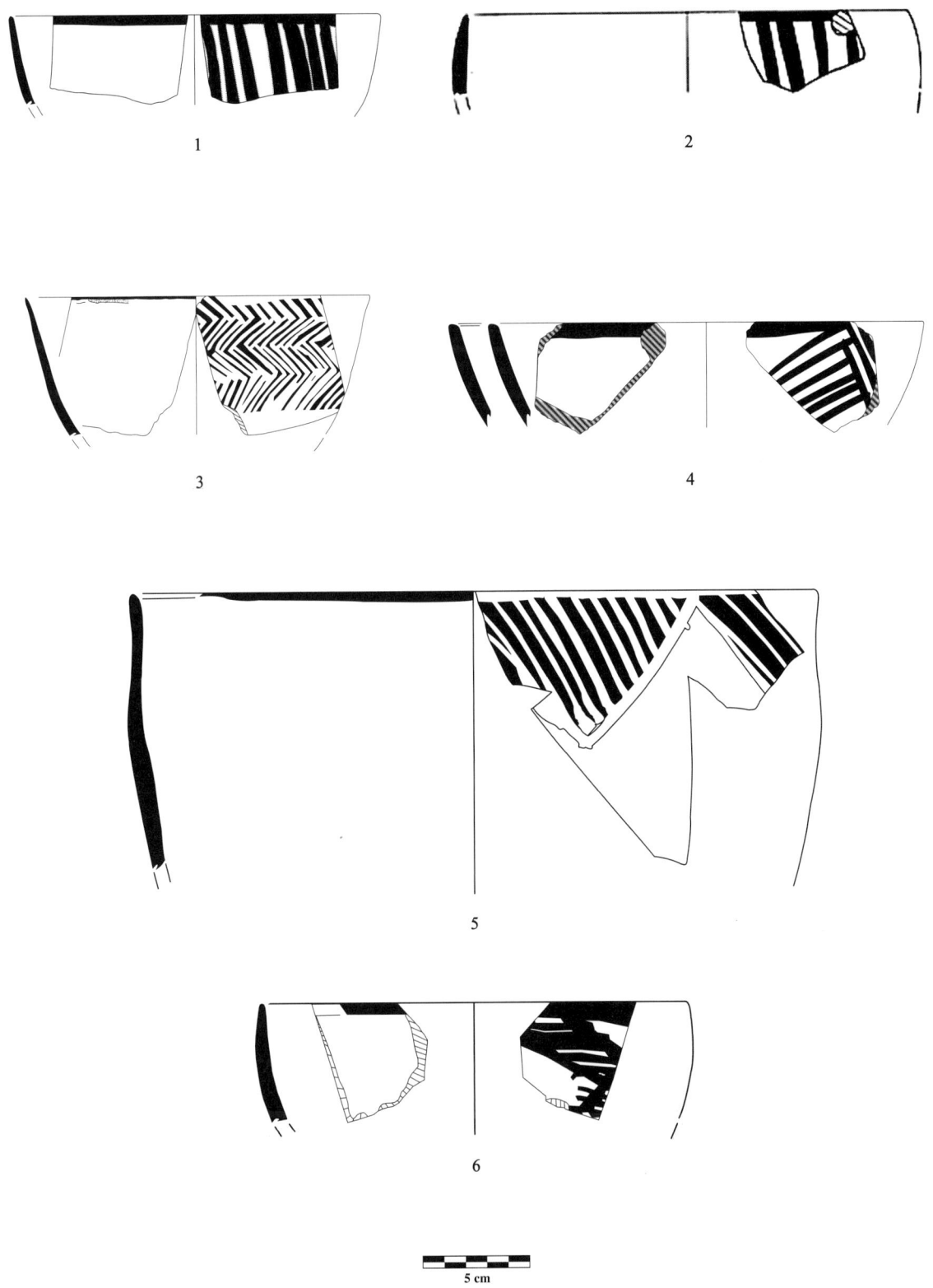

5 cm

Item	Inventory	Form	Ware	Description
1	1923	Bowl	B	wheelmade; carinated belly; grit temper; slip; repair hole
2	521hh	Globular Jar	R	handmade; outcurving rim; sand and grit temper; slip; curvilinear design from rim, ends with a horizontal band
3	522, 343a	Bowl/Jar	BP	handmade slab; chaff and grit temper; filed zigzags in vertical panels; slip
4	17	Jar	C	handmade; outcurving rolled rim; chaff and grit temper
5	216	Globular Jar	C	wheelmade; outcurving rolled rim; grit and chaff temper; slip

Fig. 3.9 *facing page*, Hissar I, Transitional Phase F-E.

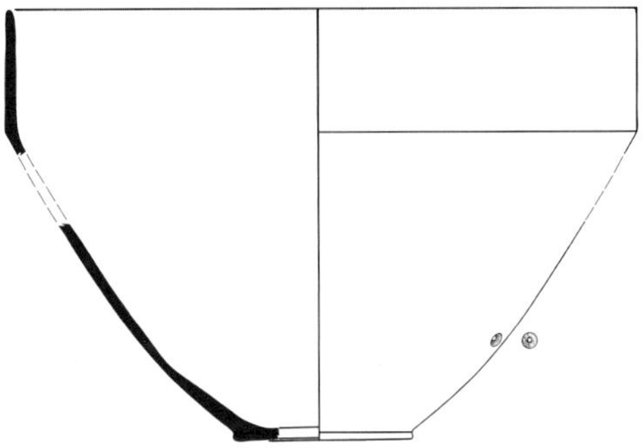

ANALYSIS OF CERAMIC COMPLEXES OF THE MAIN MOUND

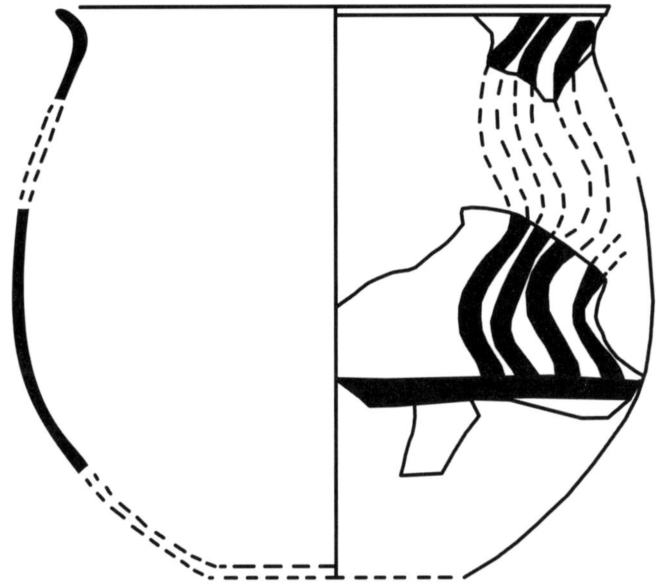

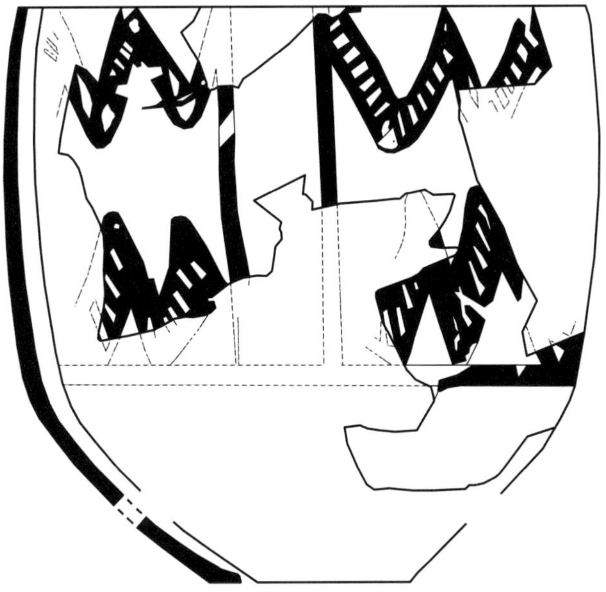

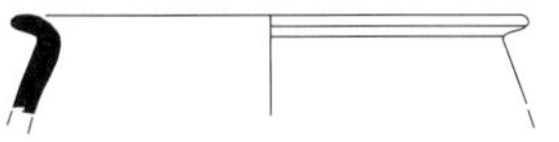

95

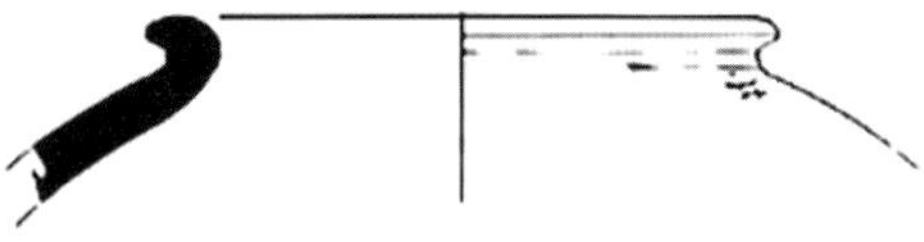

10 cm

Item	Inventory	Form	Ware	Description
1	200, 218	Pedestal Bowl/Goblet	BP	wheelmade; everted wall; sand and grit temper; slip; tree pattern alternate with vertical waves from rim to base
2	302	Pedestal Bowl/Goblet	BP	wheelmade; everted wall; sand temper; slip; ladders in zigzag alternate with leopard in registers, interior circle with dots (droppings)
3	698b,c	Pedestal Bowl/Goblet	BP	wheelmade; carinated belly; sand temper; slip; brown triangles stacked, right side and upside down, filled with dots, stylized leopards
4	626, 668	Pedestal Bowl/Goblet	BP	wheelmade; everted wall; carinated belly; sand temper; slip; panels of dotted triangles alternate with dotted vertical panels
5	1182, 1193a–c	Pedestal Bowl/Goblet	BP	wheelmade; everted wall; sand temper; slip; feline and hatched lozenges in registers
6	746, 623, 660	Pedestal Bowl/Goblet	BP	wheelmade; sand and grit temper; slip; brown stylized gazelles, alternate with tree design
7	1190b, 1127	Pedestal Bowl/Goblet	BP	wheelmade; everted wall; carinated; sand temper; slip; birds in flight in vertical rows; brown bands below

Fig. 3.10 *facing page*, Hissar I, Transitional Phase F-E.

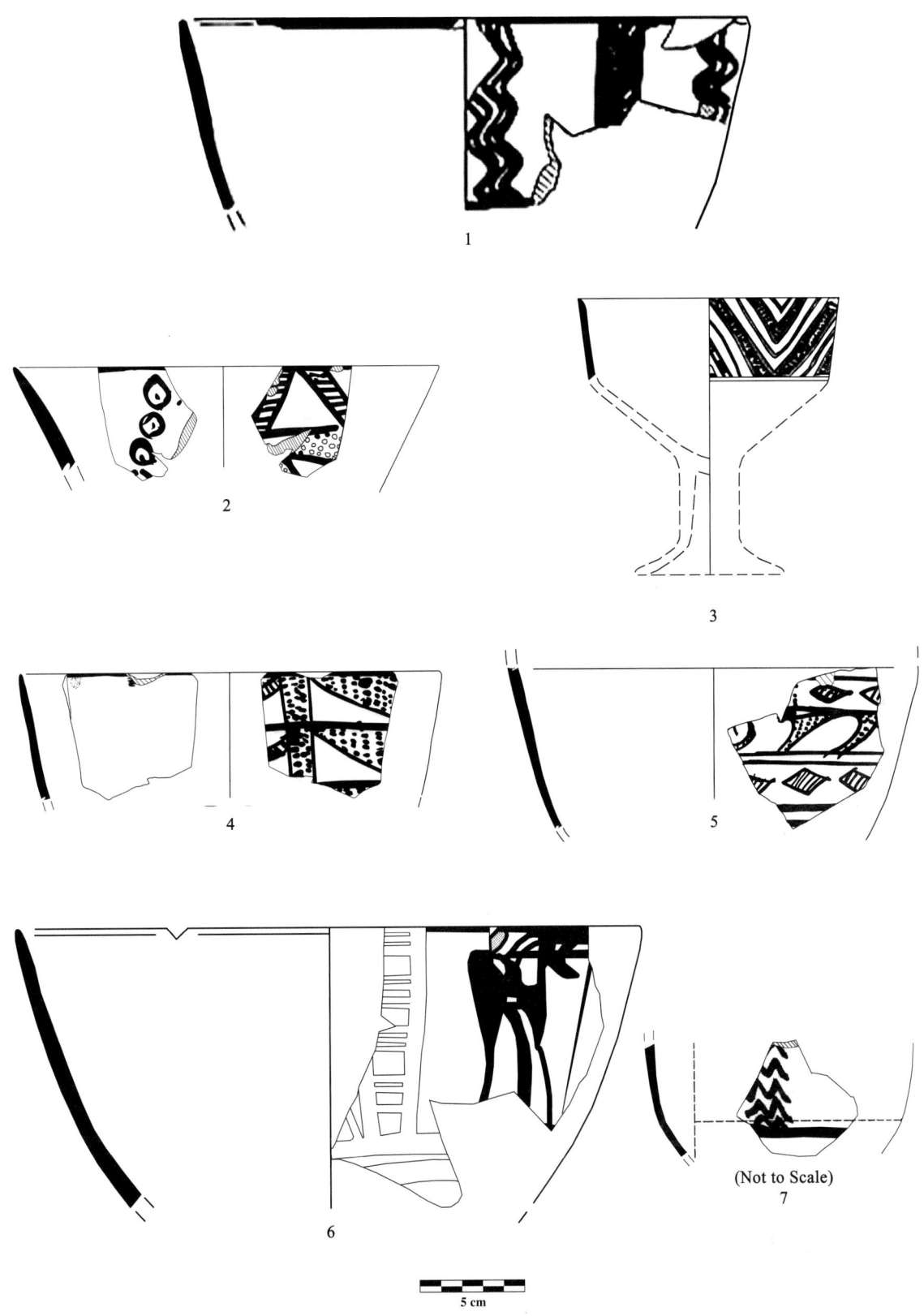

are grit and slag tempered, slipped, and medium fired. The exterior color is pinkish buff and undecorated. There are horizontal striations on the interior vessel walls. The addition of neck and rail rim are features that begin in earlier phases, and continue into the early third millennium BC.

Summary

In this phase, there are two innovations in ceramic production, slag as an inclusion in clay (unknown if intentionally added) and "metallic" (glossy) surface finish on grey ware that resembles metal vessels. Both of these changes may point to increased metallurgical activities and the production of metal objects at Tepe Hissar.

Regarding Forms:
- Bowl is the predominant form (59.6%), associated with BP ware.

- Second in frequency are wide-based bowl (10.1%), jar (each 10.1%), and cup (9%), associated with B, BP, R, C, and GB wares.

- Pedestal bowl, beaker, and plate/tray occur in low frequencies (1.1–2.2%) and are associated with C, BP, and GB wares

Regarding Wares:
- The ceramic assemblage is characterized by a slight decrease in the percentage of B and BP wares (47.2%), as well as in C ware (7.9%). Grey wares encompass 13.4% of the assemblage with the majority being GB ware (11.2%). There is a slight increase in R ware (31.5%).

D. 3 Hissar I-II, Phase E-D, Transition to Bronze Age (ca. 3400 BC)

This part of the ceramic sample originates from the Pinnacle lots 17, 16 (MM); lots 1, 2, (NF); Main Mound Building 1 (lower), Buildings 2 and 3; North Flat CF57 test trench lots 1, 2; also see, Ch. 2, pp. 48–57, 68; and Schmidt (1933: pl. CII, H1154, 1937: pls. XXIV–XXVI).

Stratigraphy

Main Mound: This transitional phase[16] is represented by a structure associated with the earlier phase of Build-

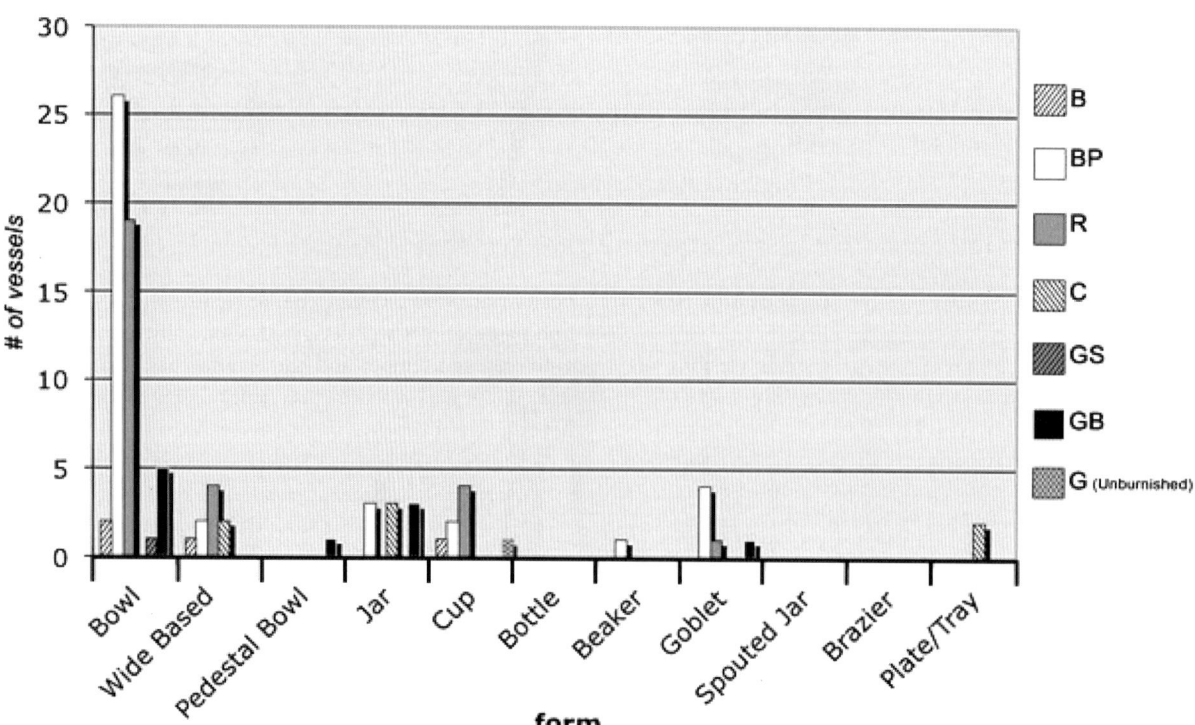

Fig. 3.11 Graph of the number of vessels by ware and form in Early Hissar II (phase E).

ing 1 ("lower"). Another structure belonging to E-D phase was excavated by Schmidt in square CG90[17] (see Ch. 4, reconstructed sections 4.1, 4.2).

North Flat: The stratigraphic evidence for the E-D transitional phase here is elusive. Directly underneath the wall of a phase D buttressed structure, Dyson dug a test trench in square CF57 (lots 1, 2) and CF57/16/, where several levels of the E-D transitional phase and phase E pottery are documented. The pottery types from these trenches are similar to those at the Main Mound, large GB and C ware jars with rolled rims and pedestal bowls with metallic sheens. In the E-D transitional phase assemblage, two new features are noted at the North Flat but not encountered at the Main Mound. They are raised "rings" on the hollow shaft of the pedestal bowl, which may be a decorative addition (Fig. 3.18:9). The other new feature is incised raised ridges on small cups (see below and Fig. 3.24:7), a rare type of decoration that becomes frequent in the later D-C transitional phase through phases B and B-A/A. Also see above, other decorative motifs on North Flat vessels from phase E, not present on Main Mound ceramics.

Ceramic Assemblage

In this period, all ware types occur with significant changes in percentages. Clearly, painted pottery is present only in BP ware, but it is gradually replaced after the mid-fourth millennium BC by GB and C wares, which become prevalent in the succeeding phase D. The only new forms are brazier and miniature jars.

Brazier: is associated with C ware; it has an everted or inverted rim and short stemmed base. The exterior is a pinkish buff color, handmade, with chaff temper, and unslipped. The holes are irregular circles (Fig. 3.18:1–2). In the later phases D through B-A/A, there are a variety of forms resembling the published braziers (Schmidt 1937: pl. XXXVI H5215, pl. XLIII 3300, 3304).

Miniature jar: These vessels are small versions of necked jars and they are only in GB ware (Fig. 3.21:7–9). Miniature vessel forms (jar, bowl, and cup) are included with the corresponding large forms in graphs and tables.

The following forms continue from the earlier phases:
Pedestal bowl/goblet:[18] occurs in GB, BP, and R wares; GB ware is wheelmade and fired at high temperatures. It has a "metallic" sheen (Fig. 3.18:3–12). Some of these vessels have everted rims and thin walls (Dyson and Remsen 1989: fig.1; Schmidt 1937: pl. XXV H2784, H5056). The BP vessels are distinguished by high temperature firing and thin walls. Howard refers to them as "clinky" ware to distinguish it from the earlier BP vessels. A notable characteristic of the GB pedestal bowl is the hollow shaft of the long stem base that has one or two raised ridges (Fig. 3.18:9–12; Schmidt 1937: pl. XXV H5070).

Goblet: This form is associated with BP ware. It is wheelmade and decorated with circular, linear, and animal motifs that characterize the earlier transitional E-D phase of Hissar II (Schmidt's "surviving painted pottery"). The characteristic motifs are composite plant, geometric and linear designs (Figs. 3.10:3, 3.19:1), linear motifs, vertical, horizontal, and diagonal bands (Fig. 3.19:3), vertical zigzags (Fig. 3.19:2), zigzag band with diagonal stripes (Fig. 3.19:4), vertical with horizontal bands (Fig. 3.19:5), "ladder design" (Fig. 3.19:6), registers with diagonal stripes (Fig. 3.19:7–8), "opposing tongues" (Figs. 3.19:9–10), net pattern in circles (Fig. 3.19:11), hanging triangles in registers separated by horizontal bands, a chain between horizontal bands (see Dyson and Remsen 1989: fig.35 [except k, h]), and chain alternating with net pattern circles in registers (Fig. 3.19:12). There are also few animal motifs (Fig. 3.19:13). The same vessel forms with similar motifs occur in R ware, (Fig. 3.19:3, 7–8).

Other continuing forms are storage jar with rail rim, plate/tray, and wide-based bowl; they are produced in different wares. Some of the jars are made on a slow wheel, and possibly smoothed by hand, but plate/tray and wide-based bowl are still handmade with a mold.

Jar with rail rim, jar with short neck: Some of the necked jars are produced with the addition of an everted rail rim. This vessel is handmade, medium to high fired, with grit and chaff temper, and occasionally with slag temper. It occurs in six wares: B ware (Fig. 3.20:1); BP ware (Fig. 3.20:3); R ware (Fig. 3.20:2); C ware (Figs. 3.20:4–6, 3.21:1–6), GB ware (Fig. 3.21:7–9), and GS ware (not illustrated). Some jars in C ware are made with a short neck that rest on carinated shoulders and have plain everted rims (Figs. 3.20:6, 3.21:1, 3).

Wide-based bowl: This vessel is a variation of the earlier C ware form. Unlike the latter, it is high fired, with fine paste, and is well-levigated. Generally, the paste has sand and grit temper and the exterior has cream slip. It is made on a slow wheel. As a rule, this form has everted simple rims and flat or slightly raised bases. As in the earlier phases F-E and E, it is associated with multiple wares: in B (Fig. 3.22:1), C (Fig. 3.22:2–3), and GB wares (Fig. 3.22:4–6). Present but not illustrated for this form are wares BP, R, and GS.

Plate/tray: This vessel type is handmade and medium temperature fired in C ware, with slag and grit temper (Fig. 3.22:7). It is similar to the earlier phase E form in C ware.

Globular bowl: This is the same form as discussed in earlier phase F-E. It occurs in four wares, the C ware is handmade, grit and sand tempered, and slipped on the

Item	Inventory	Form	Ware	Description
1	1746	Plate/Tray	C	handmade; slightly everted; chaff and grit temper
2	1496, 1122	Cup/Bowl	BP	wheelmade; carinated belly; inverted wall; sand temper; cross hatched circles and triangles alternate; slip; impressions of paint on interior wall
3	NF1037	Cup/Bowl	BP	wheelmade; carinated belly; sand temper; slip; long necked gazelles under rim
4	NF44	Beaker	BP	wheelmade; carinated; everted wall; temper?; horizontal band with dots below rim, connected swirls alternate with tree pattern in registers
5	NF47	Cup/Bowl	BP	wheelmade; carinated; sand temper; brown line inside rim, horizontal band around rim, gazelle or feline in motion motif (skidding animal and kid), horizontal lines above and below
6	NF54	Cup/Bowl	BP	handmade; carinated belly; temper and slip??; triangle within a triangle enclosed in wide bands
7	NF67	Cup/Bowl	BP	wheelmade; carinated, ring base; temper?, slip?; wide horizontal band around belly, wide vertical bands below rim to belly
8	NF62	Cup/Bowl	BP	wheelmade; carinated belly; temper?, slip?; bold bands of vertical zigzags below rim, horizontal band at belly

Fig. 3.12 *facing page*, Early Hissar II, Phase E.

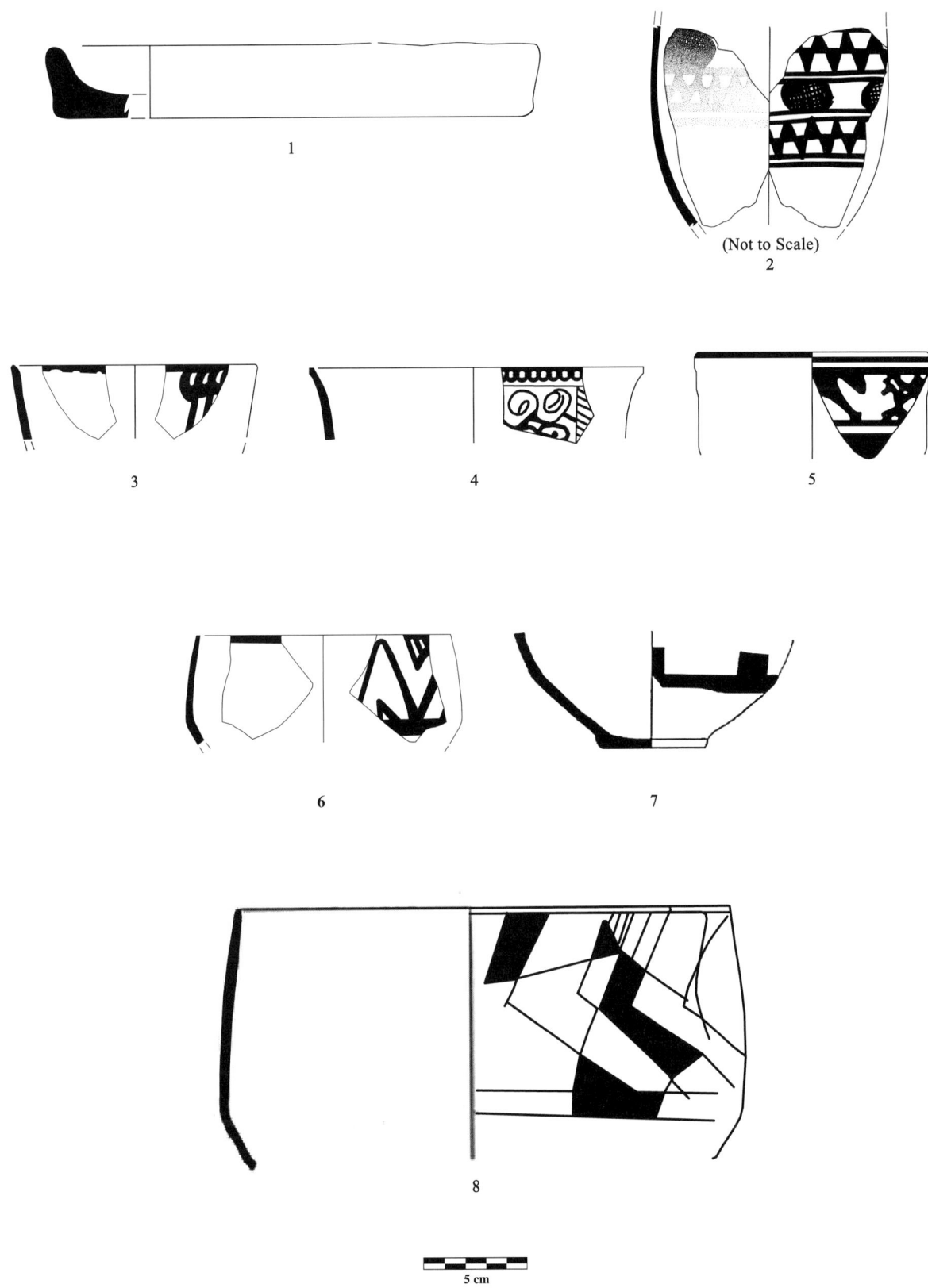

Item	Inventory	Form	Ware	Description
1	NF70	Bowl	BP	wheel- and handmade; inverted wall, carinated belly; temper?; slip?; black, band around rim, animal motif enclosed by horizontal bands
2	NF71	Cup/Bowl	BP	wheel- and handmade; inverted wall, carinated belly; temper?; slip?; brown band around rim, animal motif? enclosed by horizontal bands
3	NF72	Cup/Bowl	BP	wheel- and handmade; carinated belly; temper?; slip?; black herringbone pattern, band around rim
4	NF73	Cup/Bowl	BP	wheel- and handmade; carinated; temper?; slip?; brown band around rim, wide horizontal band below
5	NF80	Cup/Bowl	BP	wheel- and handmade; carinated; brown band around rim, wide vertical bands
6	NF#?	Cup/Bowl	BP	wheel- and handmade; fine paste, fine sand temper; slightly carinated; wide vertical bands on surface; brown band on rim, around exterior and interior

Fig. 3.13 *facing page*, Early Hissar II, Phase E.

ANALYSIS OF CERAMIC COMPLEXES OF THE MAIN MOUND

103

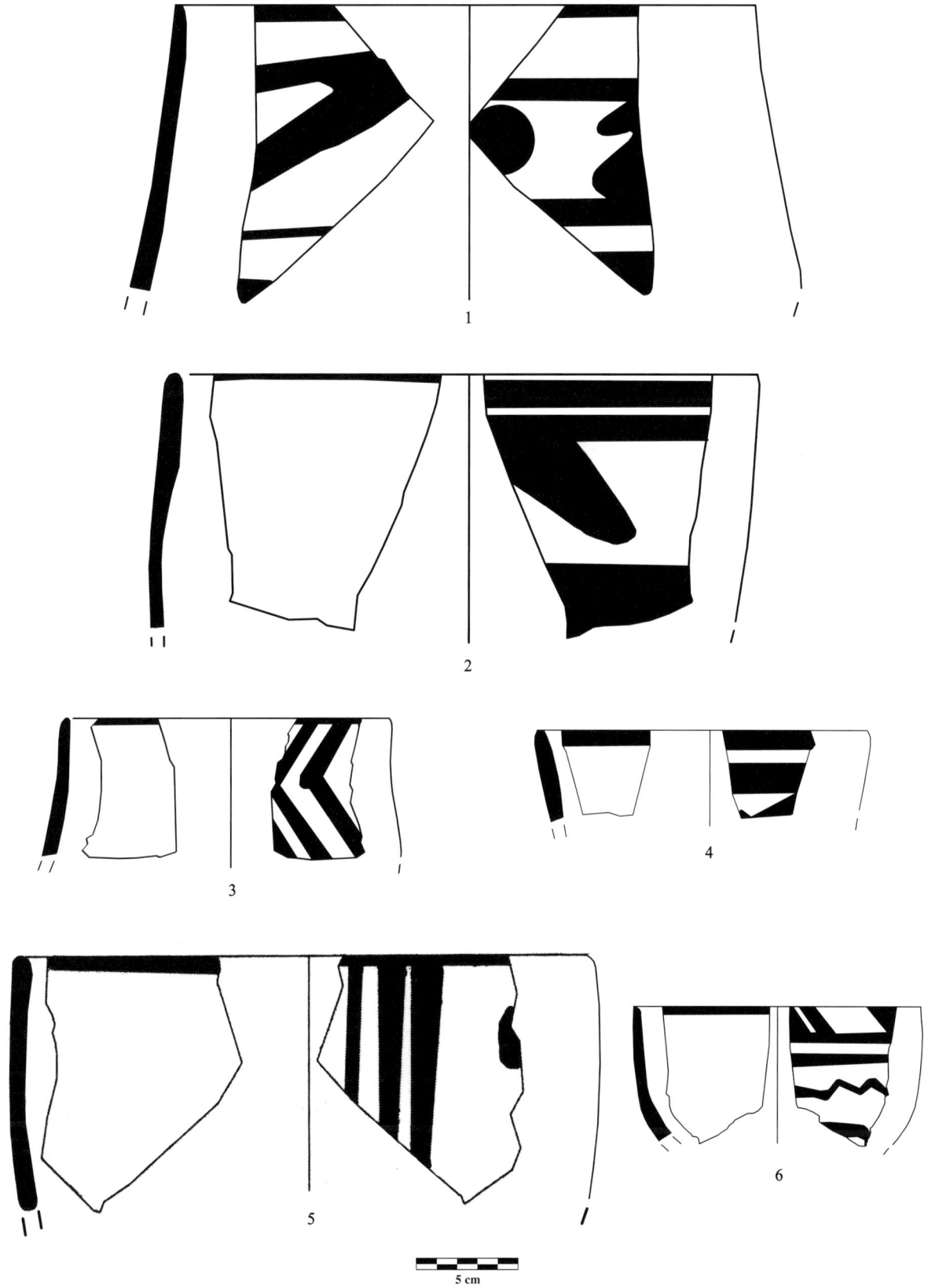

Item	Inventory	Form	Ware	Description
1	NF82	Cup/Bowl	BP	wheel- and handmade; everted wall; temper?; slip?; tow horizontal bands around interior rim, diagonal bands from rim exterior
2	NF85	Cup/Bowl	BP	wheel- and handmade; temper?; slip ?; band around rim interior and exterior; horizontal waves/birds below rim enclosed by bands
3	NF84	Cup/Bowl	BP	wheel- and handmade; temper?; slip ?; band around rim, vertical bands below rim
4	981a,b	Cup/Bowl	G	handmade; inverted wall; grit and chaff temper; slip
5	NF69	Cup/Bowl	R	wheel- and handmade; carinated belly; sand and grit temper; slip; wide horizontal band along belly
6	NF74	Cup/Bowl	R	wheelmade; carinated belly; temper?; slip; band around interior rim, wide vertical bands from rim
7	NF75	Cup/Bowl	R	wheel- and handmade; temper?; slip; band around exterior and interior rim, vertical/diagonal bands
8	NF76	Cup/Bowl	R	wheel- and handmade; carinated belly; temper?; slip; black band around interior rim, diagonal bands exterior
9	NF77	Cup/Bowl	R	wheel- and handmade; inverted wall; temper?; slip?; black band around rim interior and exterior, diagonal bands from rim on exterior

Fig. 3.14 *facing page*, Early Hissar II, Phase E.

Item	Inventory	Form	Ware	Description
1	1497a–e	Pedestal Bowl/Goblet	BP	wheelmade; sand and grit temper; slip; cross-hatched circle sand hanging triangles in registers
2	5159	Pedestal Bowl/Goblet	GB	wheelmade; outcurving rail rim; sand temper; slip
3	NF#?	Pedestal Bowl/Goblet	GB	
4	4718	Pedestal Bowl/Goblet	BP	handmade; chaff and grit temper; slip; wide band below rim
5	1027	Pedestal Bowl/Goblet	BP	wheelmade; sand temper; slip; hatched lozenges in registers between bands
6	3219	Pedestal Bowl/Goblet	GB	handmade; pedestal base; grit temper; slip

Fig. 3.15 *facing page*, Early Hissar II, Phase E.

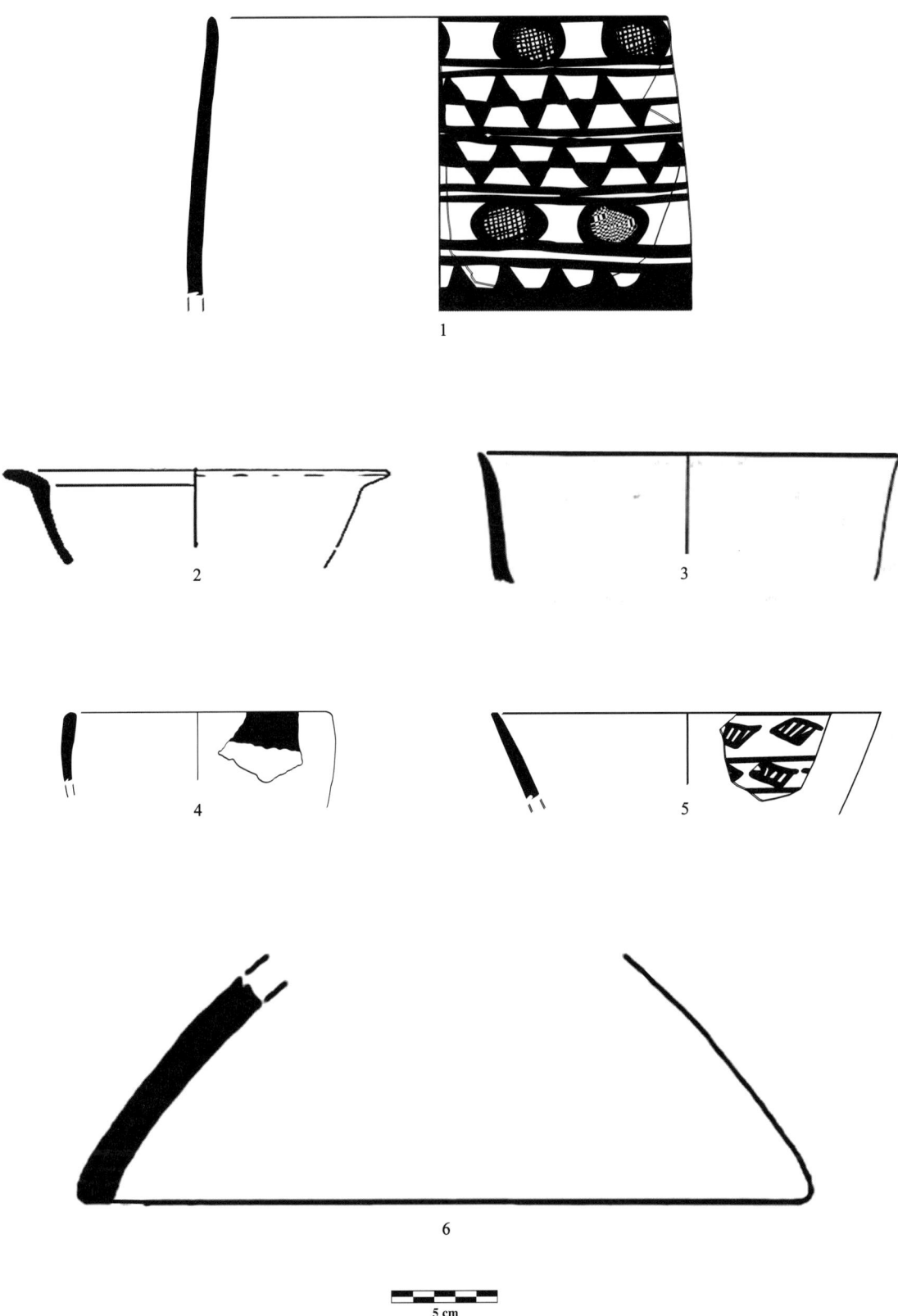

Item	Inventory	Form	Ware	Description
1	NF#?	Pedestal Bowl/Goblet	GB	metallic sheen
2	NF65	Pedestal Bowl/Goblet	GB	wheelmade; temper; slip? metallic sheen
3	4719	Pedestal Bowl/Goblet	GB	handmade; globular; grit temper; slip; metallic sheen
4	8991	Wide-Based Bowl	R	wheelmade; grit temper; slip
5	4397	Wide-Based Bowl	GB	wheelmade; sand temper; slip
6	1498b	Jar	C	wheelmade; outcurving rim, short neck; grit temper; slip
7	NF58	Jar	BP	handmade; outcurving rim, short neck; temper?; slip?; horizontal band on neck; pitted surface
8	NF50	Jar	GB	wheel- and handmade; globular, outcurving rim, short neck; temper?; slip?
9	NF51	Jar	GB	handmade? outcurving rolled rail rim, short neck; mica temper; slip?

Fig. 3.16 *facing page*, Early Hissar II, Phase E.

ANALYSIS OF CERAMIC COMPLEXES OF THE MAIN MOUND

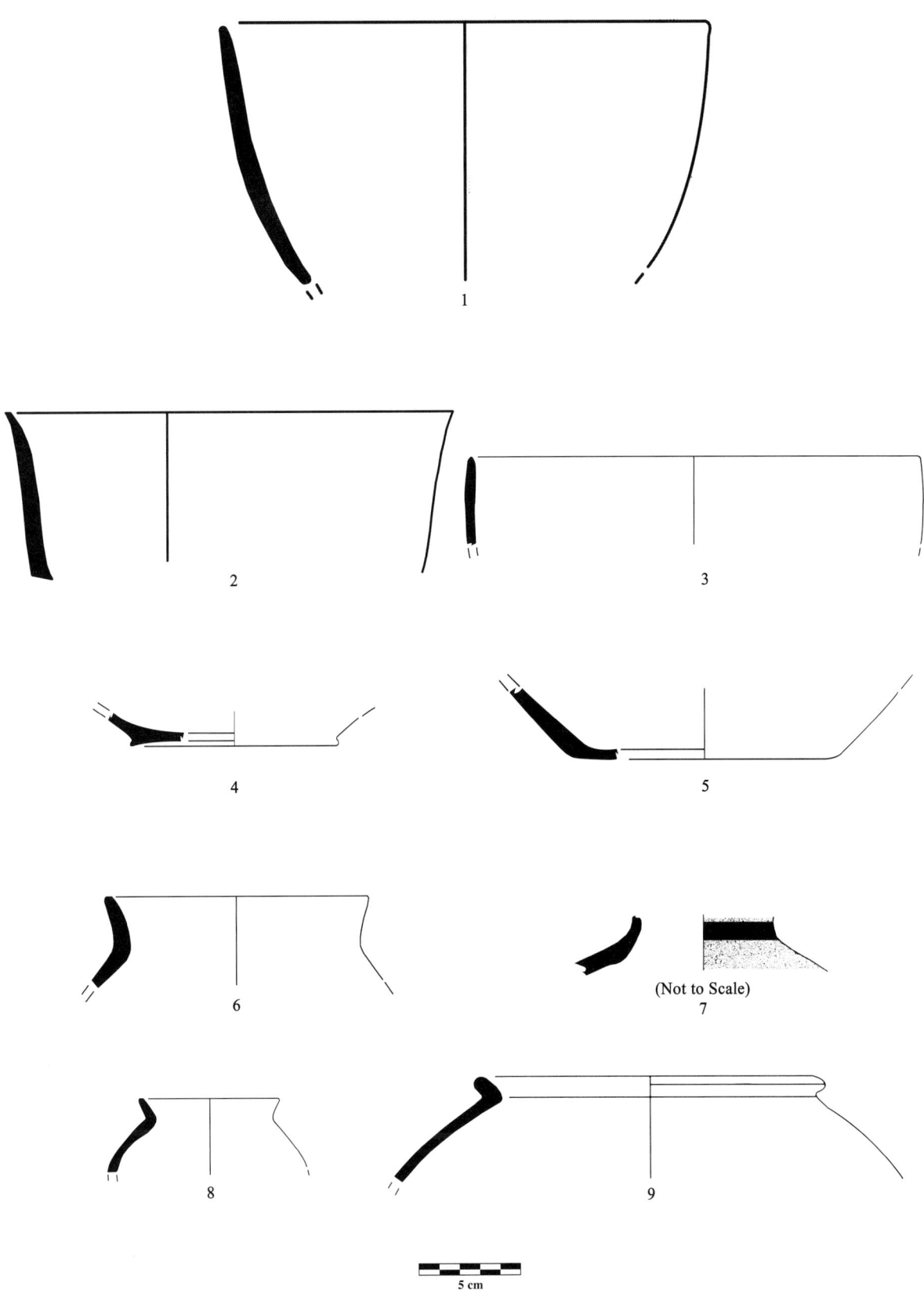

5 cm

exterior (Fig. 3.23:1), in contrast to the BP and the GB (metallic) ware, which is wheelmade, with thin walls, high fired, and without temper. This form also appears in B ware.

A variety of the globular bowl form is an S-shaped vessel, sharply carinated rim (Fig. 3.23:2–4).[19] Although this vessel is generally produced by wheel (Fig. 3.23:5–8), it is also made by hand with thicker walls and grit temper (Figs. 3.22:7, 3.23:9).

Cup/beaker: The vessel is wheelmade with thin walls, and associated with BP, R and GB wares. Geometric, plant, and animal motifs are generally placed around the rim (Fig. 3.24:1–7;[20] see also Dyson and Remsen 1989: fig. 36e, f, g). These motifs are stylized leopard elements (ibid., fig. 36i) and hatched triangles (ibid., fig. 36g)[21] in dark brown paint on a greenish buff background. Other motifs that continue from earlier phases are "opposed tongues," "tree," panels of zigzags, hatched circles, and hanging triangles in succeeding registers. Some vessels/sherds have traces of imprints of the same motif in the interior surface, probably from the way in which they were stacked in the kiln (see above section on Wares).

Also some bowls have the same design painted both on the interior and the exterior (ibid., fig. 36, gazelle motif, on bottom left of sherd drawings).

In this phase, we have the earliest appearance of "knobs" and "ridges" as decorative motifs on GB ware (Schmidt 1937: pl. XXVI H4783) and "ridges" (ibid., pl. XXVI H5118; see also Fig. 3.24:7, n4650). These motifs become more frequently used in later phases D-C through B.

Summary

Regarding vessel forms:
- Bowl (31.8%) is the most frequent form as in phase E and is associated with all wares except for G (unburnished).

- The second most frequent forms are jar (20.4%), cup (15.3%), pedestal bowl/goblet (16.5%), and wide-based bowl (10.8%).

- Brazier (1.3%) and plate (0.6%) in C ware are minimally found.

Regarding wares:
- Much of the GB ware has a "metallic" sheen.

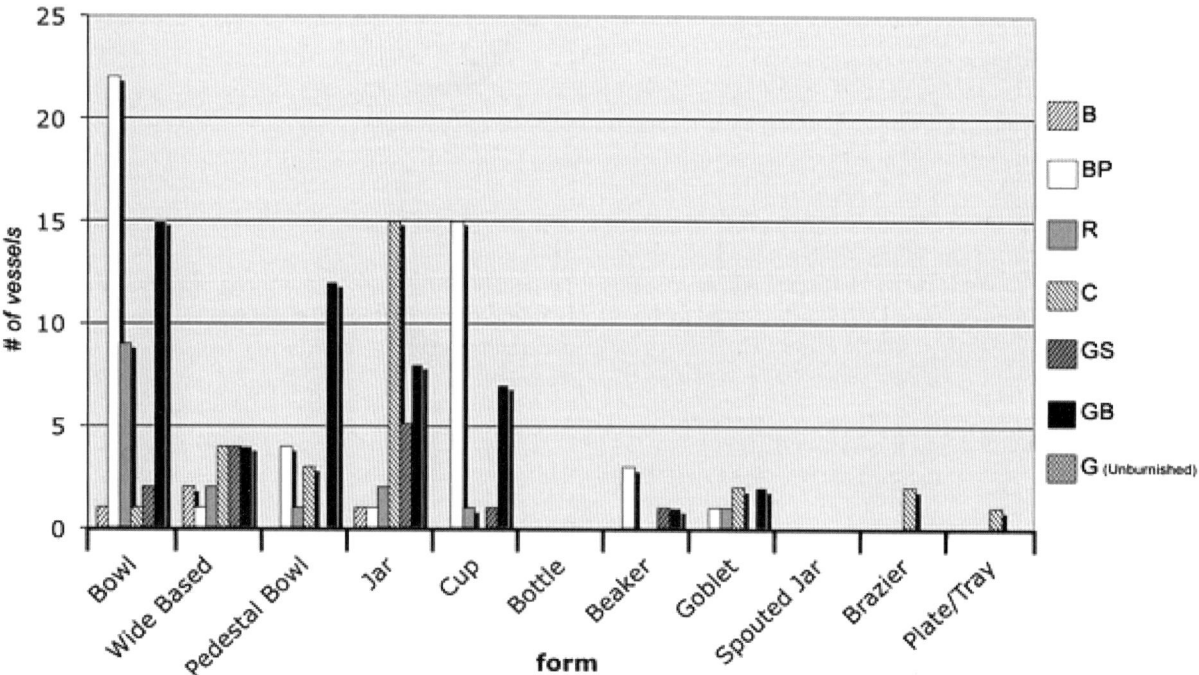

Fig. 3.17 Graph of the number of vessels by ware and form in Early to Mid-Hissar II (phase E-D).

- BP and R wares decline compared with phase E, while GB and C wares increase. GB ware increases to 31.2%, almost triple that of the previous phase E (11.2%) and C ware (17.8%) more than doubles from the previous phase (7.9%). The most drastic decrease is in R ware down to 10.2% from 31.5% in phase E.

D.4 Mid-Hissar II, Phase D, Bronze Age (ca. 3350–3100 BC)

Ceramics from this phase come from Pinnacle lots 17–14; Building 1 ("upper"); Buildings 2, 3; NF CF48/14/, and CF57 TT lots 1, 2.

Stratigraphy

Main Mound: Phase D occurs in three building stages, D3–D1, as recovered from domestic Buildings 1 ("upper"), 2, and 3. The construction stages were documented by the 1976 team during horizontal excavations (for architectural and stratigraphic details of the buildings, see Howard 1989a:57–66; Dyson and Remsen 1989:72–82; Schmidt 1937:155–157; this volume Ch. 1, pp. 28–32; Ch. 2, pp. 48–57, Fig. 1.9). While all three buildings have two depositional sub-phases of Early Period II (D3, D2), Building 3 consists of a later construction stage D1, which is associated with Building 3_1.

All three buildings are planned uniformly and are externally buttressed. Each has a main room with a centrally located hearth, with the exception of Building 1(stage D3). The main room of Building 2 has two construction stages, D3 and D2. The earlier stage D3 is contemporary with Building 1 (upper level excavated by Schmidt) and adjoins Building 1 along its southeast wall. The main room, however, was built during the later stage D2. After the construction stages D3 and D2, the main room of Building 3 was re-floored (stage D1), which is dated to the later D-C transitional phase in Early Period III.

North Flat: Stratigraphically, phases D and D-C in North Flat are placed by Dyson below the "C" mound on which the later "Burned Building" of phase B was built. In other words, under the "C" mound there were two earlier levels; they contained two burned rooms, CF58/2/ and /3/ (Dyson and Remsen 1989:99–103), of which CF58/2/, provided a C14 date of 4350±50 BP (P-2615), which has a 2-sigma range of 3099±2888 cal. BC. This date is within the range of the Main Mound transitional phase D-C. A single burial B1 is dug into one of the burned rooms, on ceramic evidence it is also assigned to phase D-C (see Ch. 2, pp. 58–59). So, phase "C" at the North Flat is ceramically dated to the transitional phase D-C on the Main Mound (see also Dyson and Remsen 1989:105–107, figs. 35, 36).

Ceramic Assemblage

On the Main Mound, phase D is represented by a large sample of ceramics; while the repertory of forms are associated with all of the main ware types, GB is the prevailing ware. Remarkably, all of the ceramic types of phase E-D are included in phase D. The only two new forms are the GB bottle and the trough-spouted jar in GS and GB wares (not illustrated). Bottle continues to the middle of the third millennium BC (phase B) with slight changes in profile (globular, carinated, and ovoid) and pattern burnishing covering the whole vessel (see also phase B below). It is also important to note that the early practices of technological innovations continue regarding control of firing, burnishing, slipped surfaces, and control of the wheel in the production of thin walled vessels. These attributes are especially observable on forms that occur with BP and GB wares. In phase D, GB ware with "metallic" sheen and GS are examples of high fired vessels.

Bottle/pitcher: The ovoid and globular bottle in GB ware has thin walls, with sandy temper, and is high fired; on the exterior there are ridges and horizontal striations left from use of the wheel. It appears that it was made in two pieces—the long neck of the bottle is separately made and attached to the body with a piece of "ring" at the base of the neck possibly to provide support for the long neck, which I refer to as a "metallic ring" (Figs. 3.26:1–2). Schmidt uses the bottle pitcher form as the index fossil of Period III (Schmidt 1937: pl. XXXVI H2164). The stratigraphic evidence, however, firmly dates the appearance of the bottle to Period II.

The continuing forms in phase D are, pedestal bowl, globular bowl, storage jar, wide-based bowl, plate/tray, brazier, beaker, and cup/bowl. Yet the most commonly found forms of this phase are conical cup in BP ware, pedestal bowl, wide-based bowl, globular bowl, and large/small jar.

Conical cup/bowl: This form appears exclusively in BP ware. It is wheelmade with, well-levigated paste, and is high fired. The conical cup/bowl has a rounded base and is painted in light brown/orange with wide or wavy bands extending from rim to midpoint enclosed within horizontal bands, as observed in the earlier E-D phase (Figs. 3.28:1–9). The potters continue to use the early repertory of motifs such as "opposing tongue," hatched circles and hanging triangles between bands, and a net pattern (Figs. 3.28:10–11). In form they are very similar to the conical cup of early phases F-E and E, except they have more a pronounced pointed base. The decorative motifs

Item	Inventory	Form	Ware	Description
1	4433	Brazier	C	handmade; inverted wall; chaff and grit temper; slip; interior rough; circular holes
2	4400	Brazier	C	handmade; everted wall; chaff and grit temper; slip; interior rough; circular holes
3	4713	Pedestal Bowl/Goblet	GB	wheelmade; outcurving rim, carinated; sand temper; slip; metallic sheen
4	4384	Pedestal Bowl/Goblet	GB	wheelmade; outcurving rim; sand and grit temper, slip; faintly pattern burnished metallic sheen
5	4741	Pedestal Bowl/Goblet	GB	wheelmade; splay base; sand temper; slip; metallic sheen
6	4736	Pedestal Bowl/Goblet	GB	wheelmade; outcurving rim; sand temper; slip; metallic sheen
7	4442	Pedestal Bowl/Goblet	GB	wheelmade; outcurving rim; sand and grit temper; slip; metallic sheen
8	4635	Pedestal Bowl/Goblet	GB	wheelmade; outcurving rim; sand temper; slip; metallic sheen
9	4717	Pedestal Bowl/Goblet shaft	GB	wheelmade; grit and sand temper; slip; metallic sheen, relief band on shaft
10	NF22	Pedestal Bowl/Goblet shaft	GB	wheelmade; grit and sand temper; slip; metallic sheen, relief band on shaft
11	4684	Pedestal Bowl/Goblet shaft	GB	wheelmade; grit and sand temper; slip; metallic sheen, relief band on shaft
12	4472	Pedestal Bowl/Goblet	GB	wheelmade; splayed base; grit and sand temper; slip; metallic sheen

Fig. 3.18 *facing page*, Hissar I-II, Transitional Phase E-D.

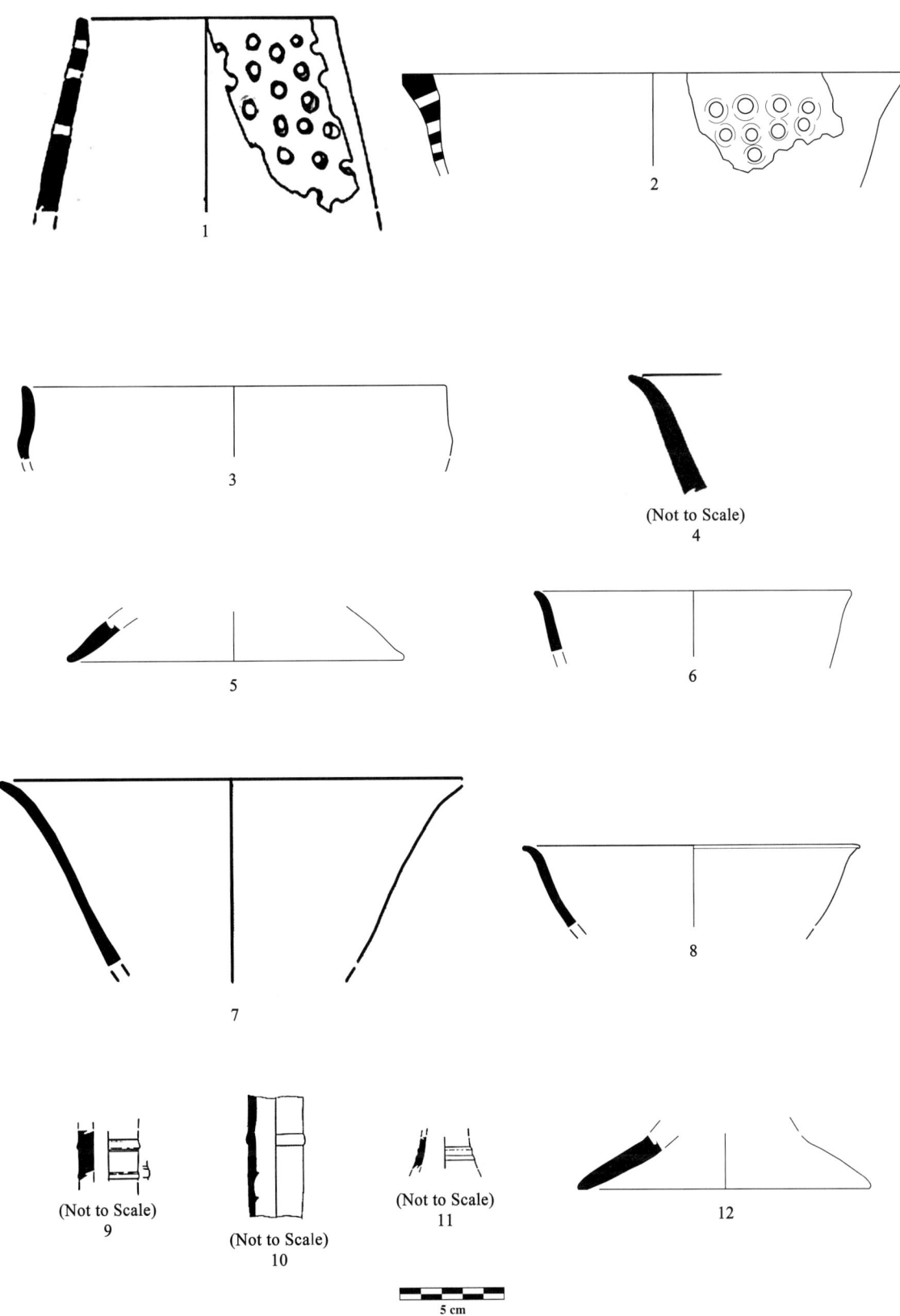

Item	Inventory	Form	Ware	Description
1	no#	Pedestal Bowl/Goblet	BP	plant design motif
2	NF02	Pedestal Bowl/Goblet	BP	wheelmade; sand temper; slip; vertical zigzags
3	4393	Pedestal Bowl/Goblet	R	wheelmade; inverted rim; sand temper; slip; diagonal bands below rim
4	4619	Pedestal Bowl/Goblet	BP	wheelmade; sand and grit temper; slip; zigzag panel of vertical bands
5	no#	Pedestal Bowl/Goblet	BP	
6	NF30	Pedestal Bowl/Goblet	BP	wheelmade; sand temper; slip; ladder design
7	NF04	Pedestal Bowl/Goblet	R	wheelmade; sand temper; slip; registers with diagonal stripes
8	NF#?	Pedestal Bowl/Goblet	R	wheelmade; registers with diagonal stripes
9	4598	Pedestal Bowl/Goblet	BP	wheelmade; sand temper; slip; interior motif impressions; band along interior rim; opposing tongues motif
10	4595	Pedestal Bowl/Goblet	BP	wheelmade; sand and grit temper; slip; paint impression interior; opposing tongues motif
11	4724a	Pedestal Bowl/Goblet	BP	wheelmade; sand temper; slip; hatched circles of net pattern
12	4608	Pedestal Bowl/Goblet	BP	wheelmade; inverted wall; chaff and grit temper; slip; registers of chain alternating with net pattern circles in registers
13	NF16	Pedestal Bowl/Goblet	BP	wheelmade; outcurving rim; sand temper; slip; animal motif, gazelle motif

Fig. 3.19 *facing page*, Hissar I-II, Transitional Phase E-D.

ANALYSIS OF CERAMIC COMPLEXES OF THE MAIN MOUND 115

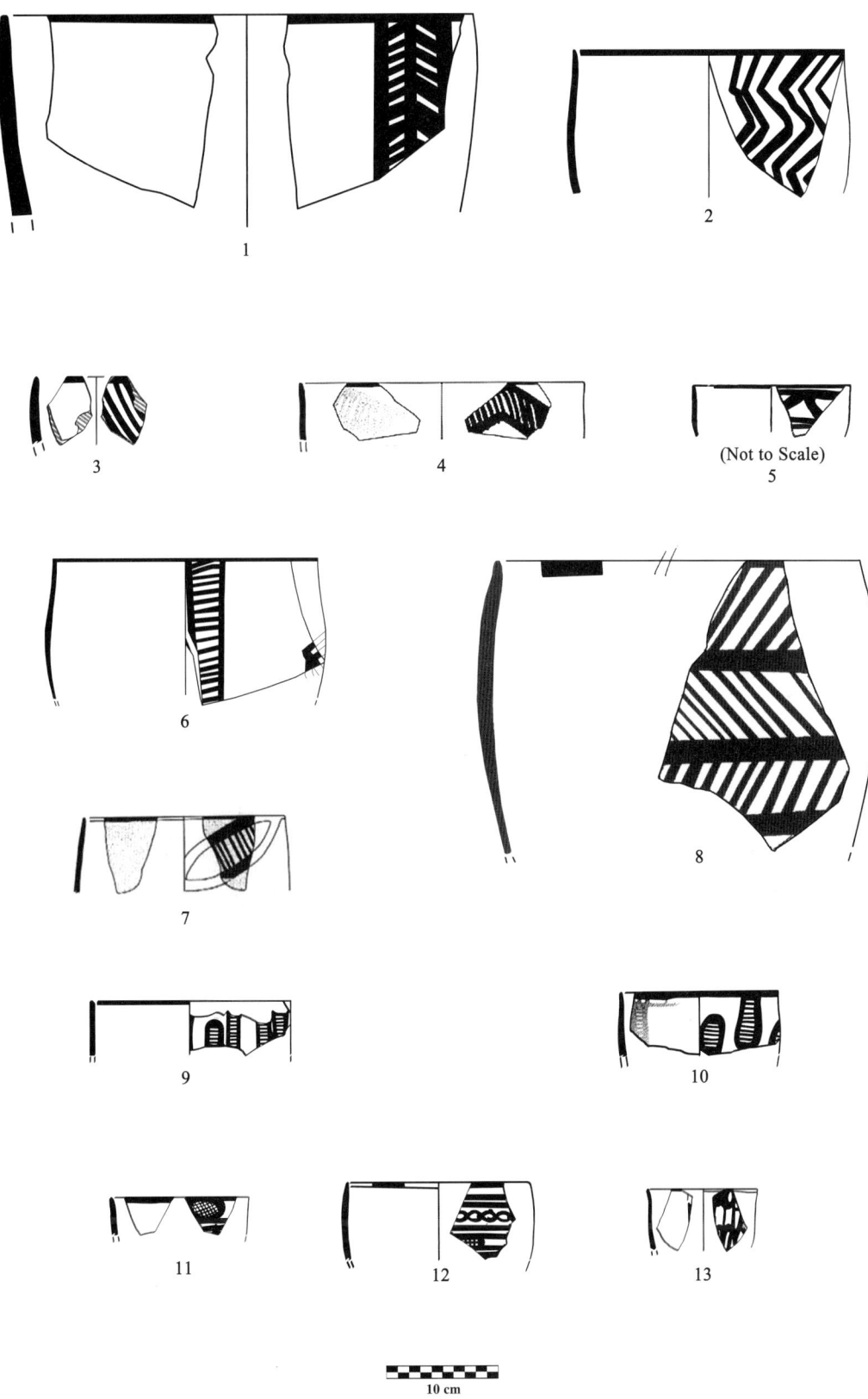

Item	Inventory	Form	Ware	Description
1	4729	Jar	B	handmade; outcurving rim, short neck; sand temper; slip
2	09	Jar	R	handmade; outcurving rim, short neck; sand temper; red slip
3	4821, 4382	Jar	BP	handmade; outcurving rim, short neck, globular; sand temper; slip; interlocking zigzags alternate with horizontal lines in registers
4	4303	Jar	C	wheel- and handmade; outcurving rolled rim; gravel and sand temper; slip
5	4581	Jar	C	wheelmade; outcurving rim; slag temper
6	4668	Jar	C	handmade; outcurving rim, extra clay on interior rim; chaff and grit temper; slip

Fig. 3.20 *facing page*, Hissar I-II, Transitional Phase E-D.

ANALYSIS OF CERAMIC COMPLEXES OF THE MAIN MOUND 117

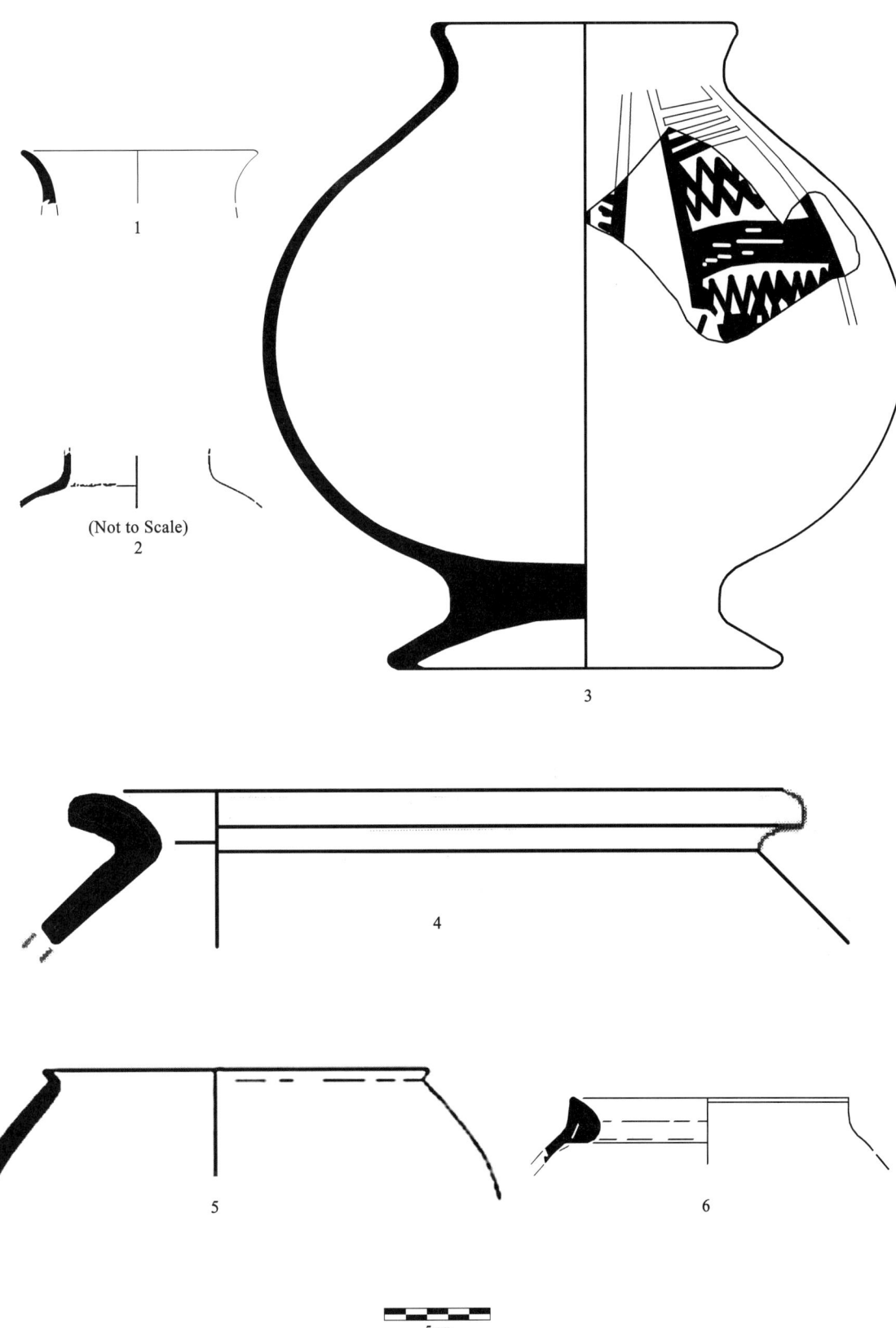

5 cm

Item	Inventory	Form	Ware	Description
1	4445	Jar	C	wheelmade; outcurving rim, short neck, chaff and grit temper; slip
2	4461	Jar	C	wheelmade; grit temper; slip; outcurving rail rim
3	4470	Jar	C	outcurving rim, long neck; grit temper; slip
4	4459	Jar	C	wheelmade; outcurving rolled rim; gravel temper; slip
5	NF#?	Jar	C	outcurving rolled rim
6	NF#?	Jar	C	outcurving rim, short neck
7	4390	Small Jar	GB	wheelmade; outcurving rim, short neck; grit temper; slip
8	6393	Small Jar	GB	wheelmade; outcurving rim, long neck; sand and grit temper; slip
9	no#	Small Jar	GB	wheelmade; outcurving rim, long neck; sand and grit temper; slip

Fig. 3.21 *facing page*, Hissar I-II, Transitional Phase E-D.

ANALYSIS OF CERAMIC COMPLEXES OF THE MAIN MOUND

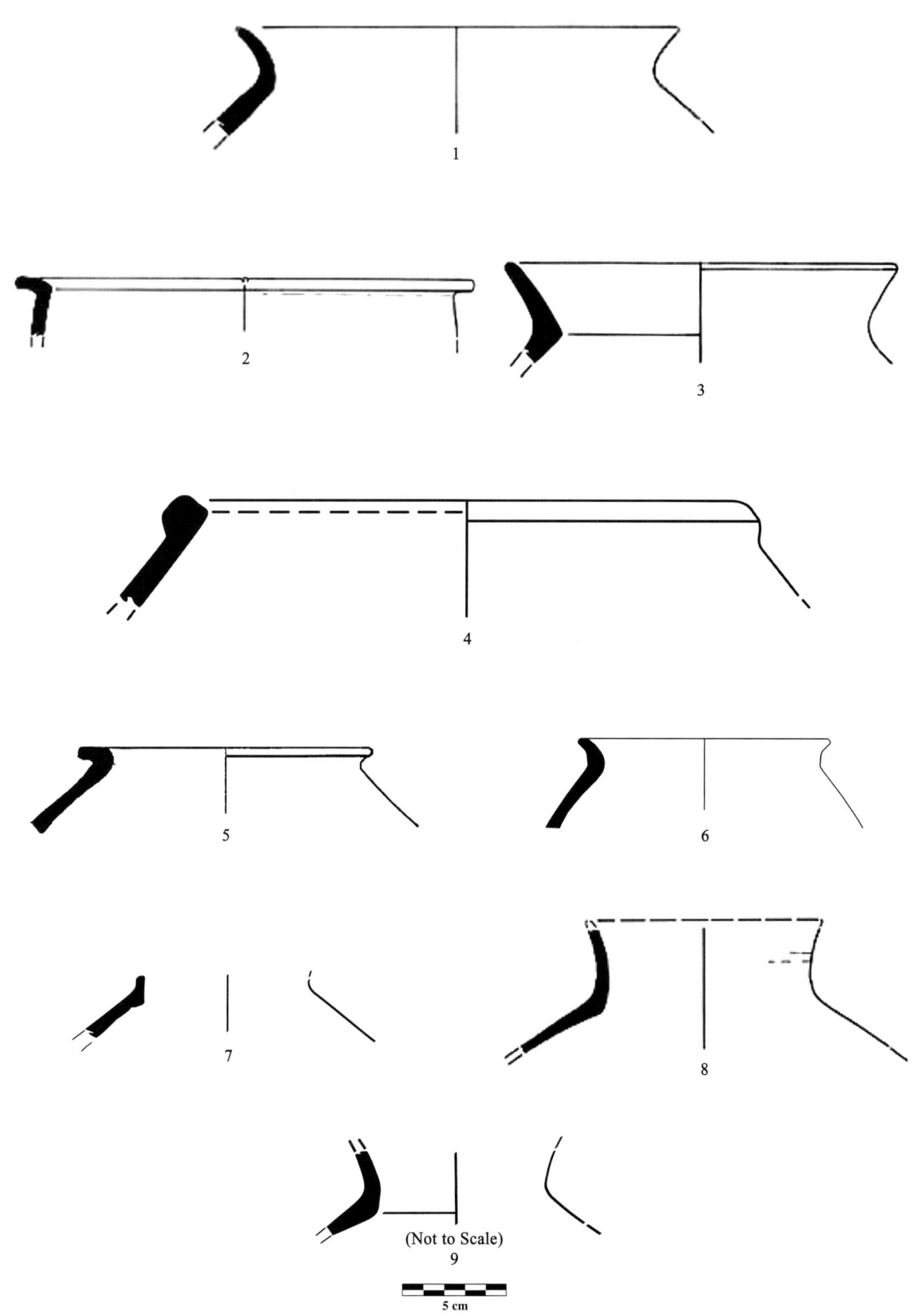

Item	Inventory	Form	Ware	Description
1	4315	Wide-Based Bowl	B	wheelmade; raised base; sand and grit temper; slip
2	4399	Wide-Based Bowl	C	hand-coiled; grit temper; slip
3	4391	Wide-Based Bowl	C	wheelmade; grit temper; slip peeling off
4	NF#?	Wide-Based Bowl	GB	
5	4737	Wide-Based Bowl	GB	handmade; sand temper; slip
6	4667	Wide-Based Bowl	GB	wheelmade; sand and grit temper; slip
7	4709	Plate/Tray	C	handmade; slag and grit temper (showing on surface); slip

Fig. 3.22 *facing page*, Hissar I-II, Transitional Phase E-D.

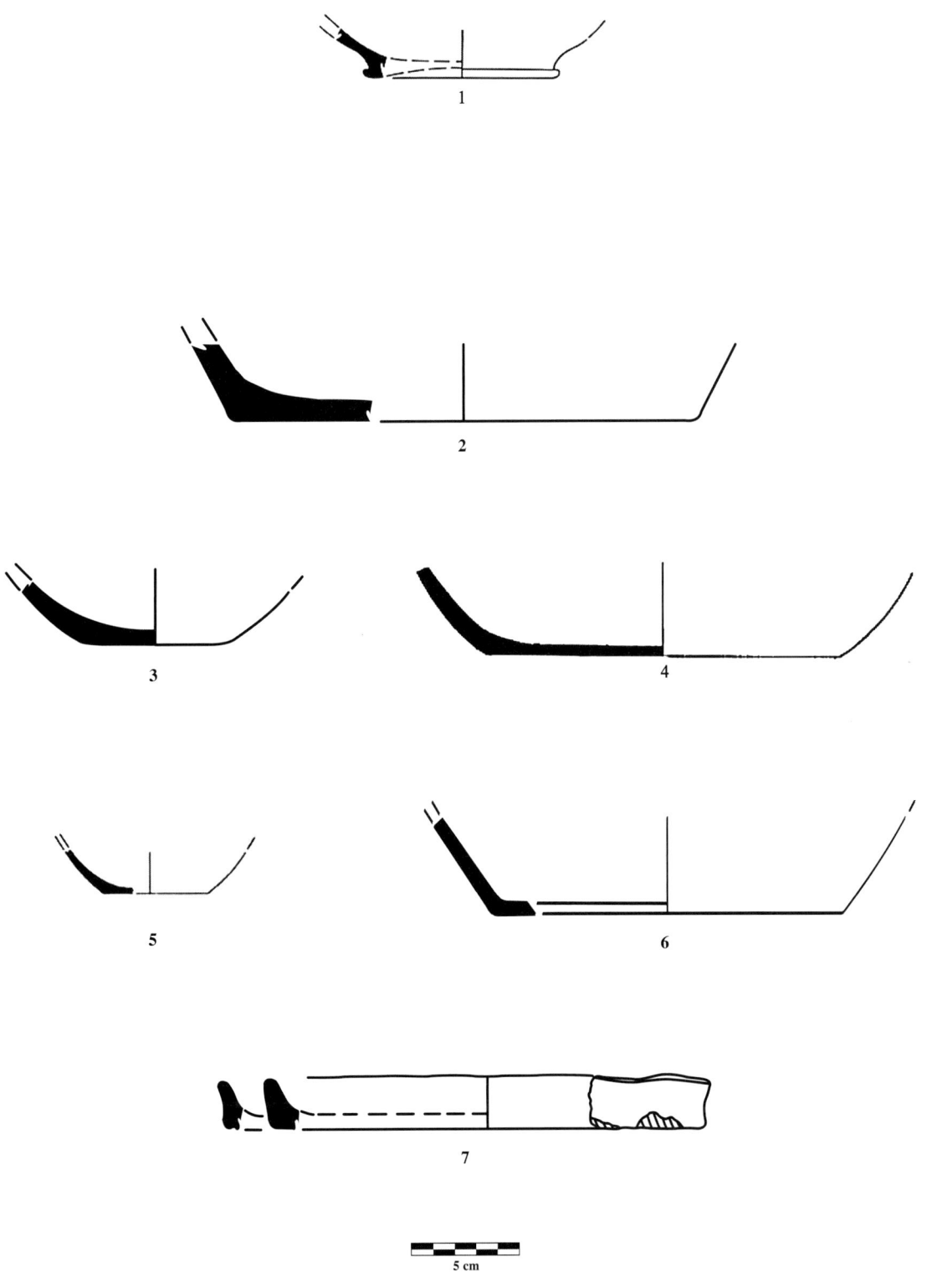

5 cm

Item	Inventory	Form	Ware	Description
1	2389	Globular Bowl	C	handmade; sand and grit temper
2	4607	Bowl	GB	wheelmade; outcurving rim, carinated shoulder; sand and grit temper; slip
3	4313	Globular Bowl	GB	wheelmade; inverted rim sand temper; slip
4	4675	Globular Bowl	GB	wheelmade; outcurving rolled rim, sand temper; slip
5	4734	Globular Bowl	GB	wheelmade; inverted rim; sand temper
6	NF#?	Globular Bowl	GB	straight rim, carinated belly
7	4588	Globular Bowl	GB	wheelmade; slightly everted rim; sand and grit temper; slip
8	4497	Globular Bowl	GB	wheelmade; inverted rolled rim; chaff and grit temper; slip
9	4714	Globular Bowl	GB	handmade; slightly outcurving rim; grit temper; slip

Fig. 3.23 *facing page*, Hissar I-II, Transitional Phase E-D.

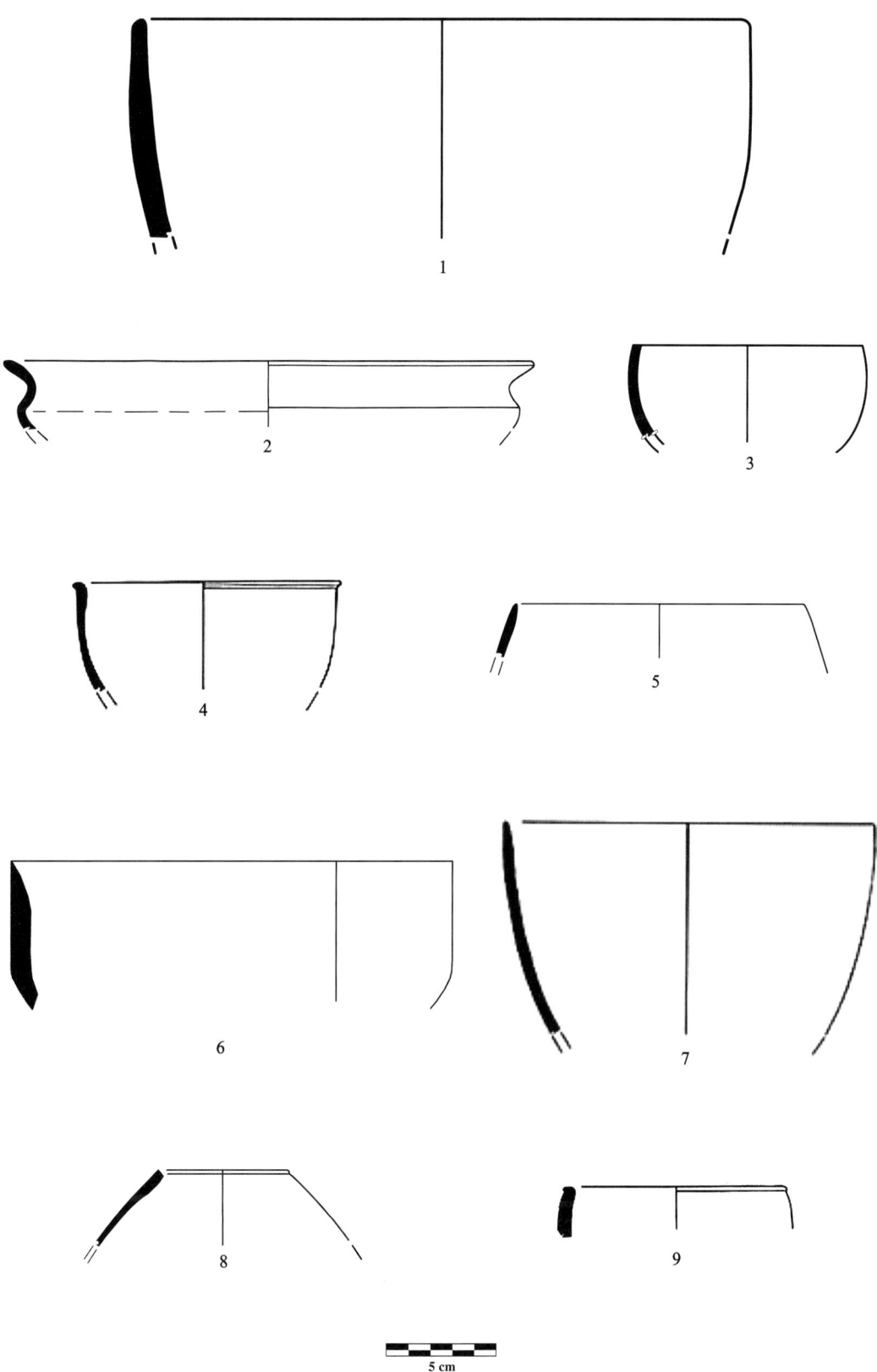

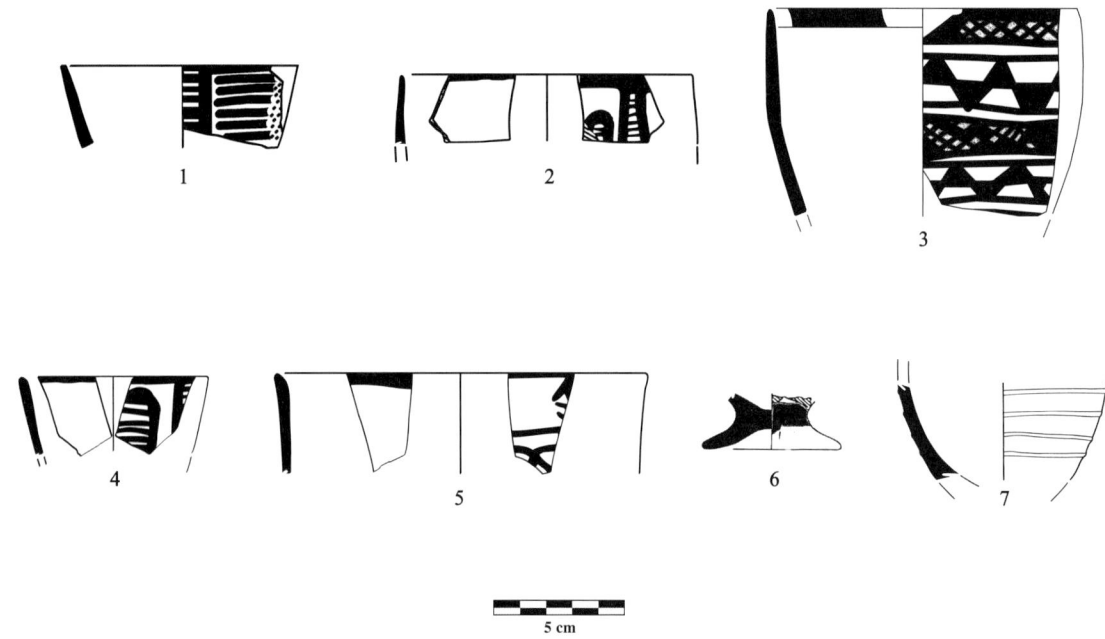

Item	Inventory	Form	Ware	Description
1	NF03	Cup/Beaker	BP	wheelmade; everted wall; sand temper; alternating tree branches
2	4706	Cup/Beaker	BP	wheelmade; slightly inverted; alternating ladders motif; sand temper; slip
3	4604	Cup/Beaker	BP	wheelmade; sand and grit temper; slip; net pattern alternates with hanging triangles in registers
4	4733	Cup/Beaker	BP	wheelmade; everted wall; sand temper; slip; alternating ladders motif
5	4723	Cup/Beaker	BP	wheelmade; slightly everted wall; sand and grit temper; gazelle horn? motif
6	4715	Goblet Base	BP	wheelmade; short splayed; grit temper; slip; wide painted band around base of shaft
7	4650	Cup/Beaker	B	wheelmade; inverted wall; grit and chaff temper; slip; incised raised ridges

Fig. 3.24 Hissar I-II, Transitional Phase E-D.

consist of more stylized versions of animal figures of the early phases E and E-D (ibex, feline), in addition to elaborate geometric and plant motifs that cover most of the exterior surface. Utilitarian vessels in C ware are prevalent. Notable among them are storage vessels with rail rim and wide-based bowls.

Pedestal bowl/goblet: This form is frequently wheel-made, in B (Figs. 3.26:3, 5) or BP wares (Fig. 3.19:4), with a bell shaped (splayed) or straight-angled base (Fig. 3.26:6–8). The GB vessels have a metallic sheen, thin walls, and are high fired with sand temper (Figs. 3.26:9–14, 3.27:1–2). Some pedestal bowls (e.g., Fig. 3.27:2) have drilled repair holes, which are also associated with large globular bowls. They are found in situ with burial #5 at square CG90/4/ in "industrial debris," in Building 3, near the kiln room (DG00/3/), and in CF58/2/ burial #1.

Wide-based bowl: These vessels occur in four wares. Grey burnished ware (metallic) is wheelmade and high fired (Fig. 3.27:3). Coarse ware has a buff slip, hand-smoothed exterior, chaff and grit temper, and is medium fired. Some C ware vessels have a slightly thickened base (Fig. 3.27:4), as well as having a flat base (Fig. 3.27:5–10). There are only a few B ware forms (Fig. 3.27:11–13).

Jar: These large storage vessels (rim dia. 20–42 cm, height 30–45 cm)[22] are associated with R, C, and GB wares (similar jars are in phases F-E and E). The GB ware jars have an everted rail rim and deep grooves on the interior wall. Except for in R ware, they are all wheelmade, high fired with sand temper, slipped, and burnished. The everted rail rim is painted with black/brown vertical wavy lines that extend from the rim (Fig. 3.29:1–3). The vessel (Fig. 3.29:2) has lug handles on each side under the rim, which is a unique feature of the Tepe Hissar ceramic assemblage. The C ware jar occurs in large and smaller dimensions (for large, rim dia. 46 cm; for small, rim dia. 3–8 cm; height 4–7.5 cm) and is associated with chaff and grit temper. Some vessels have short everted necks (Figs. 3.29:4–6, 3.30:1–4). Also, some C ware jars have short necks (Fig. 3.30:5–8).

Globular bowl: These vessels occur in four wares (B, BP, C, GB), and they range from small, medium, to large in rim diameters, 6–27 cm and in height 4–20 cm. Most vessels are in the medium range, (rim diameter, 11–17 cm, height 11–16 cm). The latter are associated with B and BP wares. The B ware vessels are both hand- and wheelmade, high fired, slipped, and with sand temper. They have straight or slightly everted rims. The vessels in BP ware are exclusively wheelmade, with thin walls, and well-levigated paste (Fig. 3.31:3–9). The decorative motifs are similar to those on the conical cup and globular bowl forms of the previous phase E-D—wide vertical/wavy bands, net pattern, "alternating tongues," hatched circles, and "hanging triangles" (Fig. 3.28:11).

The globular bowl in C ware is handmade, medium fired, and with grit and slag temper. The bowls in GB ware generally range in small sizes similar to the B ware vessels (Fig. 3.32:1–10). They are hand- and wheelmade, high fired, and with sand temper. Most have thin walls and metallic sheen. One large vessel has unusually thin walls, and an outcurving rail rim (Fig. 3.32:10). Some bowls have drill holes just below the rim, possibly for suspension from a hook in the absence of a handle.

Bell-shaped beaker: There are few wide rim beakers in this phase; they occur in three wares and are all wheelmade and high fired. The motifs on the BP beakers are all geometric, repeated from the earlier phases, cross hatching, with hanging triangles, circles on registers, and enclosed in horizontal bands (Fig. 3.33:1–3). The vessel has a characteristic painted line around the interior of the rim. The exterior of the C ware beaker is characterized by thumb smoothing and a thin slip (Fig. 3.33:4). Its concave wall profile is *well-defined with carination*. The GB ware beaker has a narrow mouth and some have carinated shoulders.

Brazier: There are two braziers in C ware with slip on the exterior, grit temper, and low fired (Fig. 3.33:5).

Summary

Regarding Forms:
- Bottle (2.5%) and trough-spouted jar (1%) appear for the *first time*, associated with GB and GS wares. Bowl and jar forms peak (29.4% and 26.7%, respectively), primarily associated with GB and C wares. Pedestal bowl/goblet combined are 15.9% and associated with B, BP, GS, and GB wares.

- Cup form peaks (12.9%), associated with BP and GB, and, in smaller quantities, with C, GS, and G wares.

- Wide-based bowl (8%) is associated with four wares: B, C, GS, GB.

- Beaker (1.5%) in BP, C, GB wares.

- Brazier and plate occur in minimal percentages (each 1%) in C ware (plate is not illustrated).

Regarding Wares:
- Wide-based bowl (8%) is associated with four wares: B, C, GS, GB;

- There is a definite increase in GS ware from 8.3% in E-D to 13.9% in D.

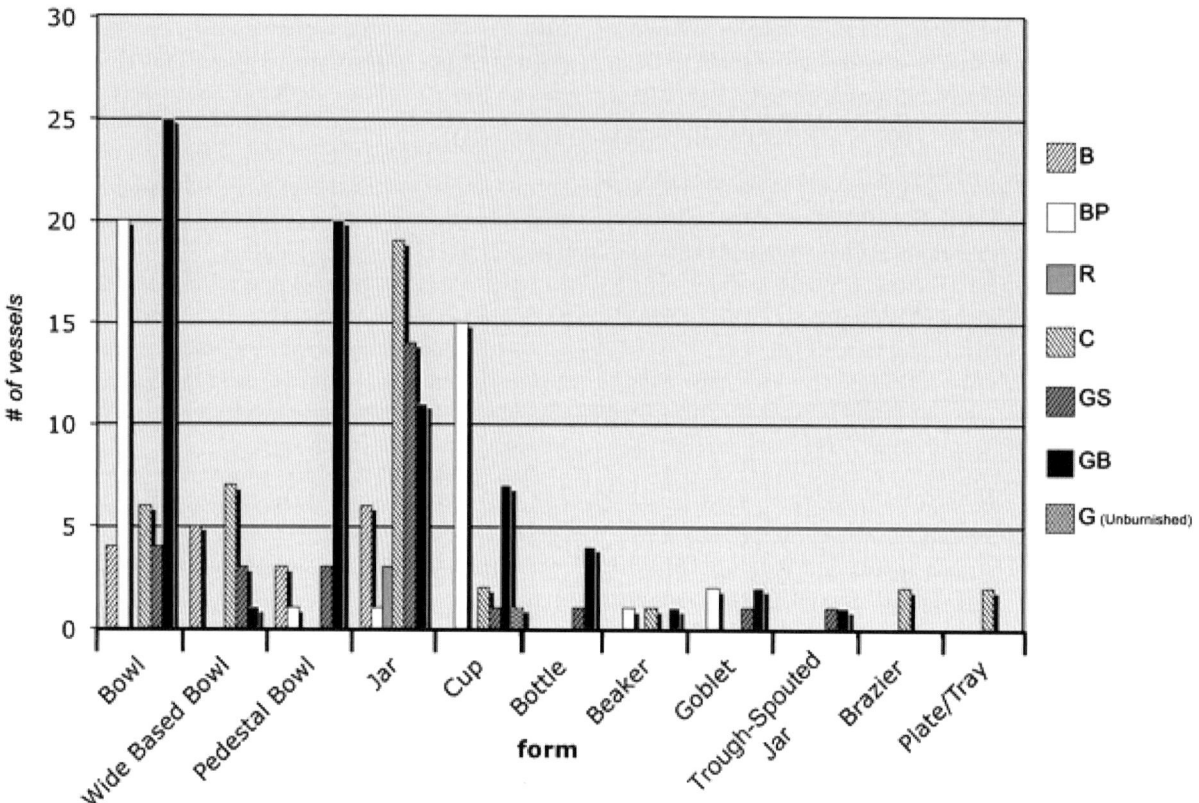

Fig. 3.25 Graph of the number of vessels by ware and form in Mid-Hissar II (phase D).

- B more than triples to 9%.

- BP and C wares make a subtle increase.

- Grey wares (GS, GB, and G) make a substantial increase.

- R ware (1.5%) makes a drastic decrease from E-D (where it was at 10.2%).

D.5 Late Hissar II–Early Hissar III, D-C Transitional Phase (ca. 3100–2900 BC)

Ceramics from this phase come from Pinnacle lots 13–10, Building 3_1 (upper) (see Ch. 2, pp. 48–57); NF CF58/2/ and /3/ (burned rooms) (see Ch. 2, Table 2.2).

Stratigraphy

Main Mound: The CG90 Pinnacle provides the only stratified occupational sequence for the transitional phase D-C and later. "The Pinnacle lots 10–11 consist of an occupational debris containing ashy fill on top of a compact 'bricky fill' (lots 12, 13) (i.e., brick decay with pottery, bone, and other debris). This compact level sits on a hard-packed surface (a floor?) above the earlier phase D. Thus, lots 12–13 represent primary contexts for the D-C transitional phase (ca. 3100–2900 BC), while the later P lots 10–11 are likely to be mixed deposits that also include D-C transitional phase material and dumped fill from later phase C (ca. 2800 BC)" (Thornton 2009b:81–82).

North Flat: For stratigraphy see p. 111 above.

Ceramic Assemblage

The transition from Hissar II (phase D) to Early Hissar III (phase D-C) shows a slight decrease in GB ware (from 35.8% to 30%), an increase in C ware (from 19.4% to 26.6%) and a decrease in R wares (from 1.5% to 0.8%), while B and BP wares combined show a slight decrease (28.9% to 22.6%). In this phase, there are two new forms (1) tulip-shaped beaker (Fig. 3.36:1; also Schmidt 1937: pl. XXXVIII, H2434) and (2) trough-spouted jar (Fig.

3.36:2–5). A rare feature in phases D and D-C is a circular lug handle[23] that is attached to C ware jars or canteens (Fig. 3.36:7–8). As in the previous phase D, all early forms are represented, in addition to miniature vessels of most of the old forms: cup, goblet, jar, pedestal bowl, and long-stemmed pedestal bowls.

Tulip-shaped beaker: This form is found in GB (metallic) ware (Fig. 3.36:1). Schmidt refers to it as "vase-jar", "cup jar," "vase cup," and dates it to IIIB (Schmidt 1937:180, pl. XXXVIII H2540, H3967, H3971, H2540). In the new ceramic chronology, its appearance is firmly dated to the transitional phase D-C. The vessel has an elegant concave shape. It is wheelmade with thin walls, high fired, and sand tempered. These beakers are frequently found as burial gifts in graves (see Ch. 5 and Appendix 2 for burial assemblages). They were also found in a Main Mound context, square DG01/11/, Building 3, burial #6.

Trough-spouted jar: This form is the forerunner of the beak-spouted vessel that appears in later phases B and B-A/A. It is also from firm contexts at the Main Mound, n4991 from CG90/5/ associated with burial #8 (Fig. 3.36:2–4, 6; floor of Building 3), and at the North Flat in square CF58/3/ floor (Fig. 3.36:5).

The continuing forms consist of:

Miniature vessels: These occur in various sizes and forms (bowl/cup, goblet, and jar). They were found in situ in a closed context at the North Flat, in the burned rooms at square CF58/2/ and /3a/ floor with an assemblage of bottles, pedestal bowls, a human figurine, and animal figurines. These vessels (bottles and pedestal bowls) are handmade in B and BP wares (Fig. 3.37:1–12). The painted motif comprises simple vertical bands, cross hatching from rim to shoulder, much like the BP conical cups in the early F-E transitional phase (see above and also Dyson and Remsen 1989:99–105, figs. 26–34). The globular miniature jar with trough spout in GB ware is wheelmade and has two sets of grooves around the rim (Fig. 3.36:5), a motif characteristic of the later Period III (phases B and B-A/A).

Continuing forms are bowl/cup, goblet and pedestal bowl, and jar. They are generally in B, BP, C, and GB wares.

Bowl/cup: The miniature bowl in BP ware is wheelmade with thin walls; it has an inverted rim, and globular body, carinated at mid-point. The painted decoration is simple dark brown bands extending from rim to belly (Fig. 3.37:11–12). Another group is handmade in C ware with grit temper; it has a straight rim and rounded base (Fig. 3.37:5).

Jar: These vessels are handmade by coil or in combination with the wheel; they have rolled rail rim and occur in B, C, and GS wares. The latter ware has a glossy finish (Figs. 3.38:1–6, 3.39:1–2).

Wide-based bowl: This early form has a slightly raised base. It occurs in C, B, and GB wares; the first two wares are handmade by coiling. They have grit and slag temper (Fig. 3.39:1–5, 7). Unlike the C and B wares, the GB variety is wheelmade, high fired, with sand and grit temper (Fig. 3.39:6, 8–9). Its thin wall makes a sharp angle with the flat base (Fig. 3.49, see also Schmidt 1937: pl. XXXVIII H5189). Schmidt assigns this vessel to a much later date to Period IIIB.

Pedestal bowl: As mentioned above, these vessels are part of the assemblage from the North Flat burned rooms at square 58/2/ and /3/. They are wheelmade, high fired with sand temper, and found in B and GB wares. The hollow stem is *longer* than the earlier vessels, and sits on a splayed base (Figs. 3.40:1, 3–7, 3.18:7). All except one vessel (Fig. 3.40:3) is of GB ware; these vessels have rims with triangular section and the rim interiors have a deep groove.

Bottle/pitcher: This relatively new form, which continues from phase D (Hissar II), is not associated with a handle in the 1976 assemblage. Its long neck possibly served that purpose.[24] The vessel is wheelmade in GB ware, high fired, and the paste is well-levigated with sand temper. On some vessels, the intersection between the body and neck is covered with a piece of rolled clay to form a "metal ridge" that serves to cover the connecting seam (Fig. 3.41:1). One of the bottles is unique in having a very long neck (Fig. 3.41:3). It has a smooth, high-gloss finish and incised decoration, a rare motif in the Tepe Hissar assemblage. On its long neck, there are two sets of incised grooves. The globular body has zigzags enclosed by two sets of horizontal lines. The motif is etched with a thin stylus. The vessel was found at the Main Mound, in square DG01/11/, Building 3 associated with burial #6 (Fig. 3.34; see also tulip-shaped beaker in Fig. 3.36:1). Two bottle/pitchers were also found at the North Flat square CF58/3/ floor (Fig. 3.41:2, 4), dated to phase D-C.

Beaker: The bell beakers are in GB ware, handmade, with chaff and grit temper (Fig. 3.42:1), as well as wheelmade with sand temper.

Plate/tray: This is another long-lived vessel form, with the earliest version appearing in phase E. It occurs in C, GB, and GS wares (Fig. 3.42:3–6). It is handmade and medium fired with chaff temper. It has a wide, flat base, and the walls of the vessel are perpendicular to the base or slightly everted. One vessel (Fig. 3.42:3) has basket impressions on its base that suggests the use of a basket as a mold (see jar with basketry impression base in Schmidt 1937: pl. XLII H3493); this latter vessel is from Treasure Hill, Hoard II, dated to IIIC by Schmidt.

Brazier: These vessels are handmade in C ware with chaff temper and are medium fired (Figs. 3.42:7, 3.18:1–

Item	Inventory	Form	Ware	Description
1	N32	Bottle	GB	wheel- and handmade; ovoid/pear shape; sand and grit temper
2	4937	Bottle	GB	wheelmade; ovoid/pear shape; sand temper; slip
3	2197	Pedestal Bowl/Goblet Base	B	wheel- and handmade; splayed base; sand and grit temper; slip
4	5245	Pedestal Bowl/Goblet Base	BP	handmade; grit temper; slip; vertical bands on short legs
5	4233	Pedestal Bowl/Goblet	B	wheelmade; outcurving rolled rim; sand and grit temper; slip; incision under rim
6	2391	Pedestal Bowl/Goblet	GB	wheelmade; splayed base; sand and grit temper; slip;
7	4827	Pedestal Bowl/Goblet Base	GB	wheelmade; splayed base hollow inside; sand and grit temper; slip
8	5313	Pedestal Bowl/Goblet Shaft	GB	wheelmade; sand and grit temper; slip; part of the hollow pedestal base; grooves on interior surface for bowl attachment
9	4184	Pedestal Bowl/Goblet	GB	wheelmade; everted wall, shoulder carinated; sand temper; slip
10	5323	Pedestal Bowl/Goblet	GB	wheelmade; everted wall, shoulder carinated; sand and grit temper; slip
11	5189	Pedestal Bowl/Goblet	GB	wheel- and handmade; sand and grit temper; slip
12	4260	Pedestal Bowl/Goblet Base	GB	wheelmade; splayed base; sand temper; slip
13	5258	Pedestal Bowl/Goblet Shaft	GB	wheelmade; grit temper; slip
14	5310	Globular Bowl	GB	wheelmade; inverted rim; sand temper; slip

Fig. 3.26 *facing page*, Hissar II, Phase D.

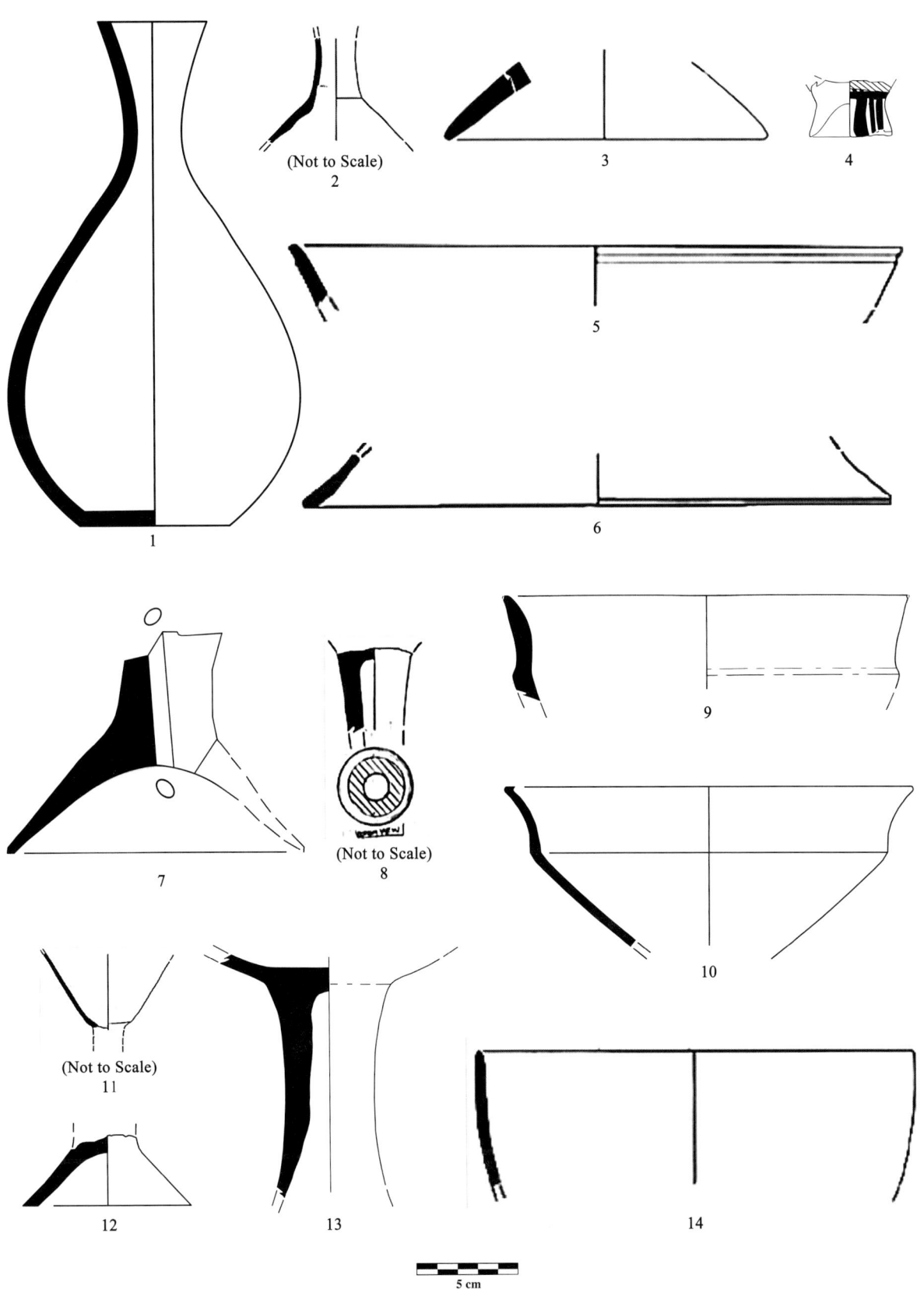

Item	Inventory	Form	Ware	Description
1	4861	Bowl	GB	wheelmade; outcurving slightly rolled rim, interior ridge; sand temper; slip
2	5353	Pedestal Bowl/Goblet	GB	wheelmade; slightly everted wall; drill hole; sand temper; slip
3	4163	Wide-Based Bowl	GB	handmade; sand and grit temper; slip
4	4060a	Wide-Based Bowl	C	wheel- and handmade; raised base; sand and grit temper
5	5249	Wide-Based Bowl	C	handmade; irregular interior of base; gravel temper; slip
6	5250	Wide-Based Bowl	C	handmade; grit temper; slip
8	5267	Wide-Based Bowl	C	hand-coiled; chaff and grit temper; slip
7	4269	Wide-Based Bowl	C	handmade; raised base; slag temper
9	4055	Wide-Based Bowl	C	wheelmade; chaff and grit temper; slip
10	4060a	Wide-Based Bowl	C	wheel- and handmade; sand and grit temper
11	4106	Wide-Based Bowl	B	wheelmade; circular base; gravel temper; orange slip; brown paint on exterior peeling off
12	4097	Wide-Based Bowl	B	wheelmade; sand and grit temper; slip
13	4053	Wide-Based Bowl	B	handmade; chaff and grit temper; slip

Fig. 3.27 *facing page*, Hissar II, Phase D.

ANALYSIS OF CERAMIC COMPLEXES OF THE MAIN MOUND

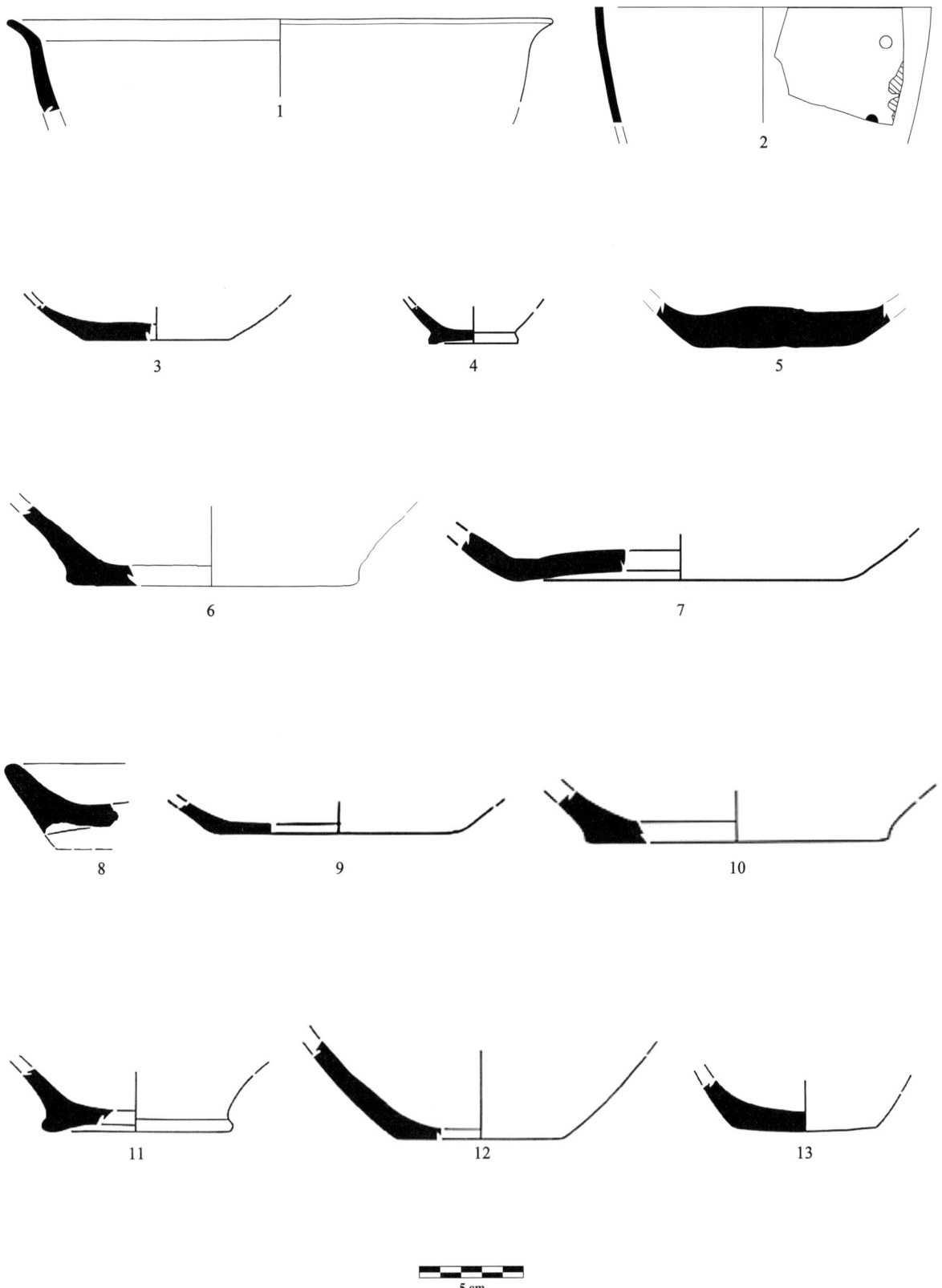

Item	Inventory	Form	Ware	Description
1	2196a	Conical Cup/Bowl	BP	wheelmade; chaff and grit temper; slip; reddish vertical bands below rim; pointed base
2	2447	Conical Cup/Bowl	BP	wheelmade; chaff and grit temper; slip; orange-brown vertical bands below rim, horizontal band near base, pointed base
3	5210, 5224	Conical Cup/Bowl	BP	wheelmade; sand temper; slip flaking; panel of wavy bands below rim, painted band along rim interior; pointed base
4	5262	Conical Cup/Bowl	BP	wheelmade; grit temper; slip; horizontal bands below rim; pointed base
5	5252	Conical Cup/Bowl	BP	inverted wall
6	5283	Conical Cup/Bowl	BP	wheelmade; sand and grit temper; slip; below rim are: circles with cross hatching, horizontal bands, chain motif; pointed base
7	4262	Conical Cup/Bowl	BP	handmade; grit and chaff temper; slip; panel of wavy bands below rim, painted band along rim interior
8	5229	Conical Cup/Bowl	BP	wheel- and handmade; sand temper; slip flaking off; wavy bands below rim; pointed base
9	5292	Conical Cup/Bowl	BP	wheelmade; grit temper; slip; part of ibex horn in orange
10	5273	Conical Cup/Bowl	BP	wheelmade; sand and grit temper; slip; dark brown net in circles and hanging triangles between bands
11	H76-33	Conical Cup/Bowl	BP	wheelmade; chaff and grit temper; below rim registers of motifs: horizontal waves; circles with cross hatching enclosed in bands; another band of cross hatching.

Fig. 3.28 *facing page*, Hissar II, Phase D.

Item	Inventory	Form	Ware	Description
1	4944	Jar	R	handmade; outcurving rail rim; sand and grit temper; slip; brown/black below rim and waves on rail rim
2	2209	Jar	B	wheelmade; outcurving rail rim; grit temper; four painted loop handles with lateral holes
3	MM08	Jar	R	wheelmade; outcurving rim; grit temper; brown/vertical waves on rim and below it
4	5291	Jar	C	wheel- and handmade; grit temper; slip; outcurving rim, short neck
5	4176	Jar	C	wheelmade; grit temper; slip; outcurving rolled rim; large grit on exterior surface
6	4817	Jar	C	handmade; outcurving rolled rim, short neck; gravel temper; slip

Fig. 3.29 *facing page*, Hissar II, Phase D.

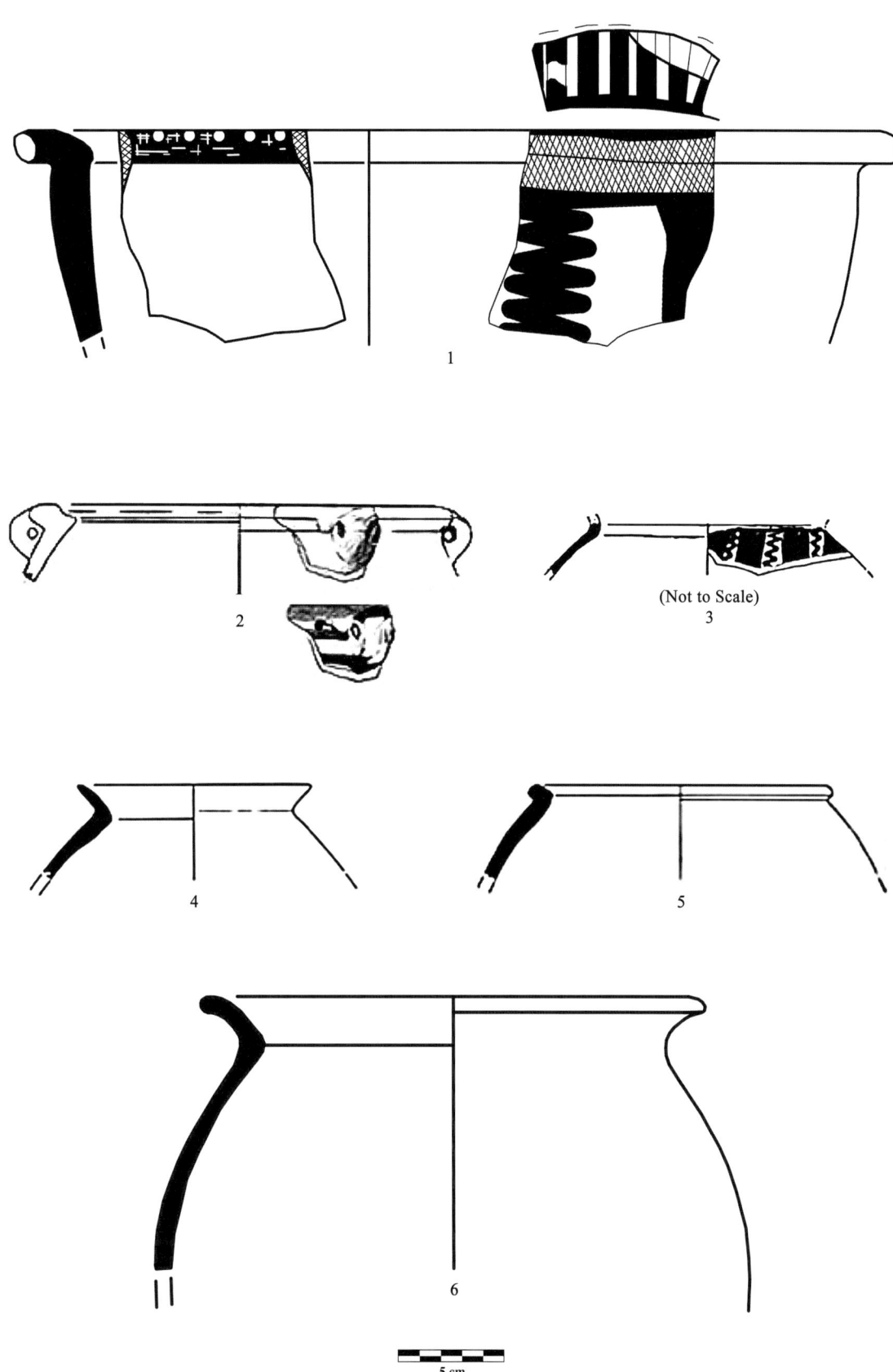

Item	Inventory	Form	Ware	Description
1	2405	Globular Jar	C	handmade; inverted wall, outcurving rim rolled rim; gravel temper
2	4837	Globular Jar (mini)	C	handmade; inverted wall, outcurving rolled rim; chaff and grit temper; slip
3	no#	Globular Jar	GB	wheelmade; outcurving rim, short neck; sand and grit temper; slip
4	2135	Globular Jar	GB	handmade; outcurving rim, short neck; sand and grit temper
5	3995	Jar	GS	wheel- and handmade; outcurving rim; grit temper; slip;
6	4972	Globular Jar	GS	wheelmade; everted rolled rim; sand temper; slip
7	4463	Globular Jar	GB	wheelmade; everted rim, short neck ; sand temper; slip
8	4077	Globular Jar	GB	wheelmade; everted rim, short neck; sand and grit temper

Fig. 3.30 *facing page*, Hissar II, Phase D.

ANALYSIS OF CERAMIC COMPLEXES OF THE MAIN MOUND

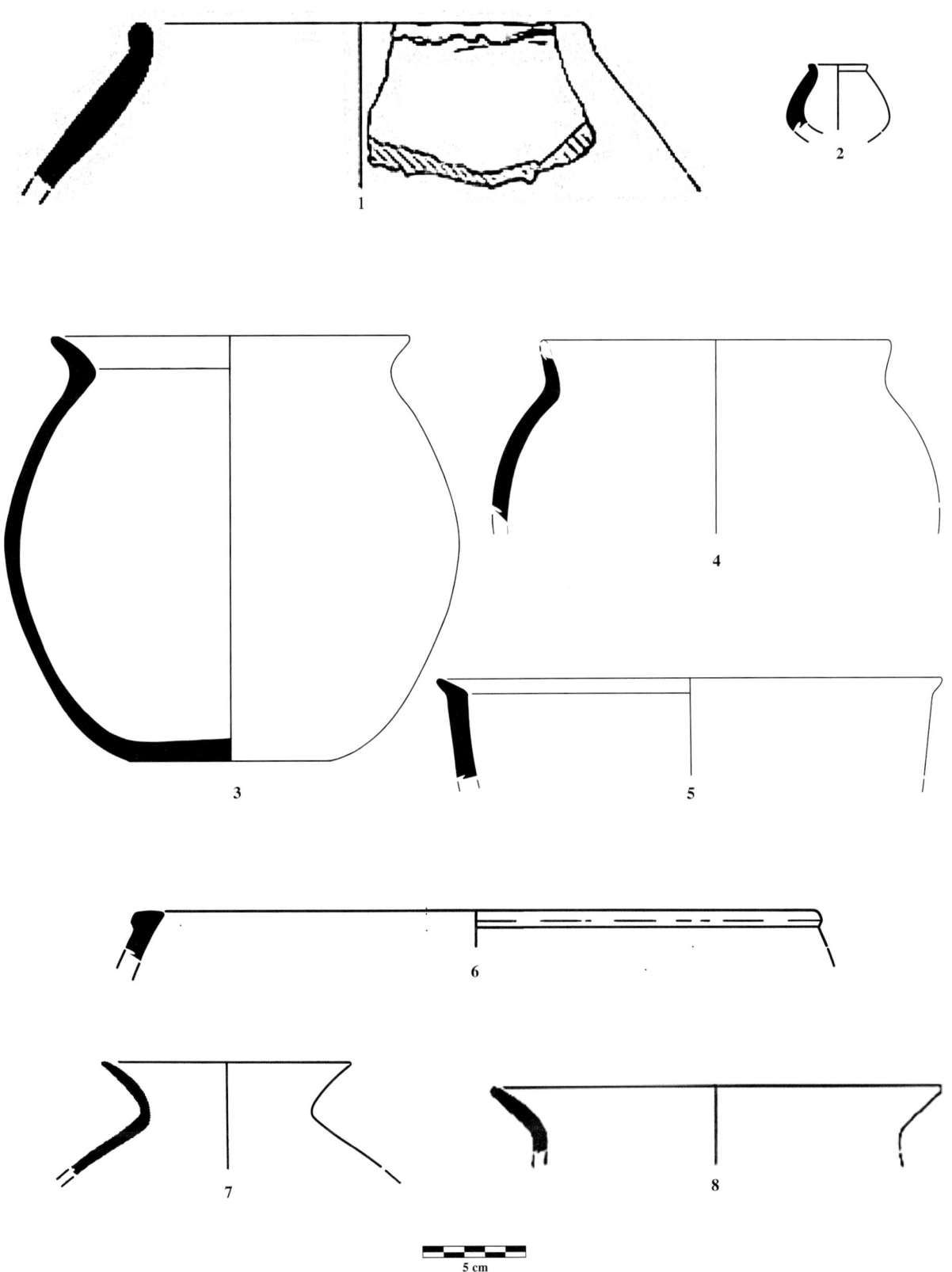

Item	Inventory	Form	Ware	Description
1	5264	Bowl/Cup	BP	wheelmade; rounded base; sand and grit temper; slip
2	4249	Globular Bowl	BP	wheelmade; slightly outcurving rolled rim; chaff and grit temper; slip; net pattern from rim to shoulder
3	NF01	Globular Bowl	BP	wheelmade; slightly everted wall; temper?; below rim, hatched connected diamonds in a panel
4	4104	Globular Bowl	BP	wheelmade; inverted wall; sand temper; slip; horizontal grooves painted, below rim
5	4109	Bowl	BP	wheelmade; outcurving rolled rim; grit temper; slip; wide horizontal and vertical band below rim
6	5247, 5264	Globular Bowl	BP	wheelmade, inverted wall; sand and grit temper; slip; opposing tongue motif, alternate with vertical waves; interior painted with brown sign/signature
7	5265	Globular Bowl	BP	wheelmade; everted wall; sand temper; slip; opposing tongue motif between bands
8	4852	Globular Bowl	BP	wheelmade; sand and grit temper; slip; painted band along interior rim, opposing tongue motif below rim
9	4136	Globular Bowl	BP	wheelmade; sand temper; slip; opposing tongue motif below rim, painted band along interior rim

Fig. 3.31 *facing page*, Hissar II, Phase D.

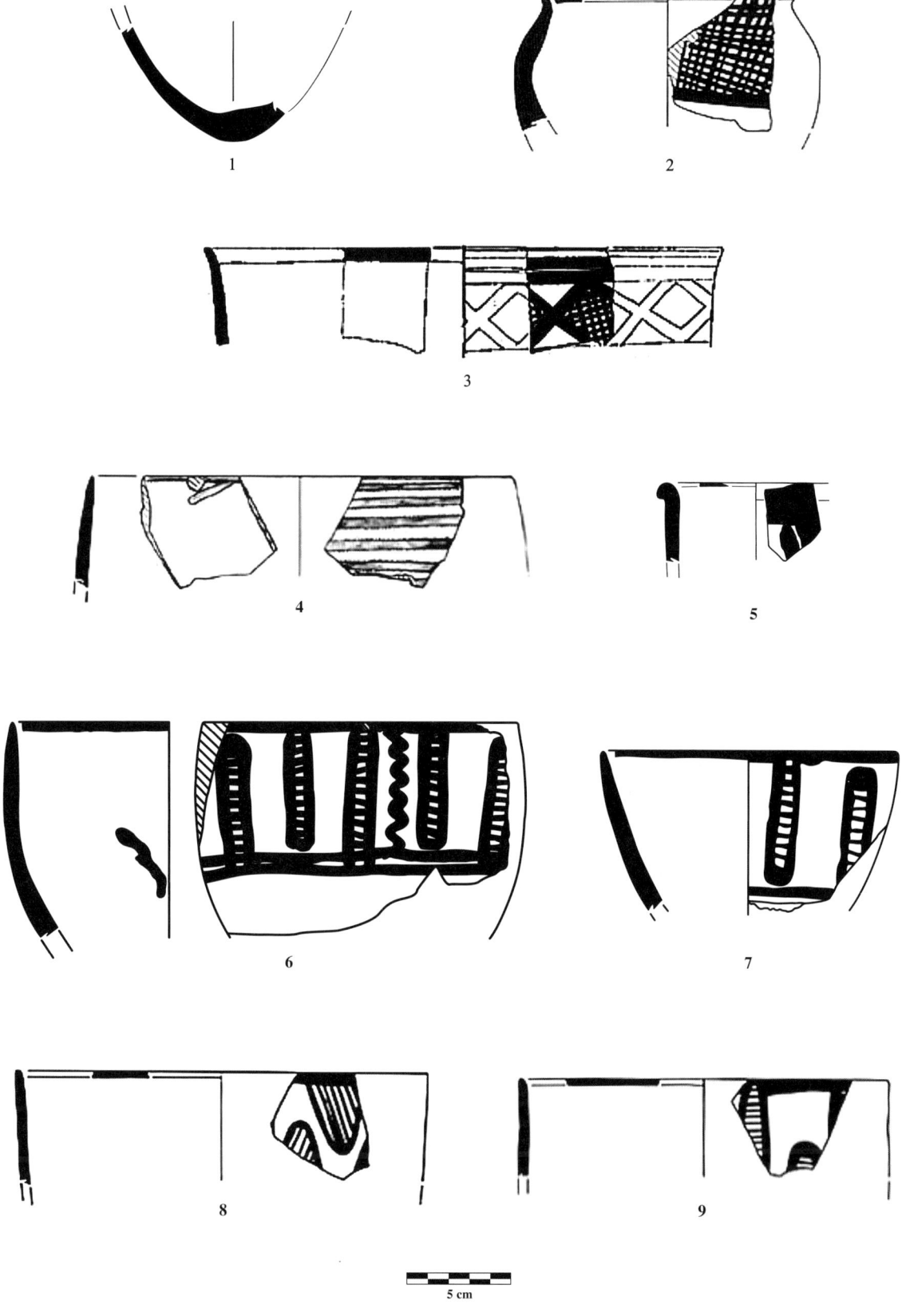

Item	Inventory	Form	Ware	Description
1	2444	Globular Cup (mini)	G	handmade; sand temper; slip
2	4162	Globular Cup (mini)	GB	wheelmade; grit and sand temper; slip
3	4966	Globular Bowl	GB	wheelmade; inverted wall; sand temper; slip; three drill holes
4	5330	Globular Bowl	GB	wheelmade; outcurving rolled rim; sand temper; slip
5	4928	Bowl	GB	wheelmade; sand temper; slip
6	4134	Globular Bowl	GB	wheelmade; sand and grit temper; slip
7	4192	Globular Bowl	GB	wheelmade; outcurving rolled rim; sand and grit temper; slip
8	4781	Globular Bowl	GB	wheelmade; inverted wall; chaff and grit temper; slip
9	4173	Globular Bowl	GB	wheelmade; sand temper; slip; incised below rim
10	4089	Globular Bowl	GB	wheelmade; outcurving rolled rim; sand and grit temper; slip

Fig. 3.32 *facing page*, Hissar II, Phase D.

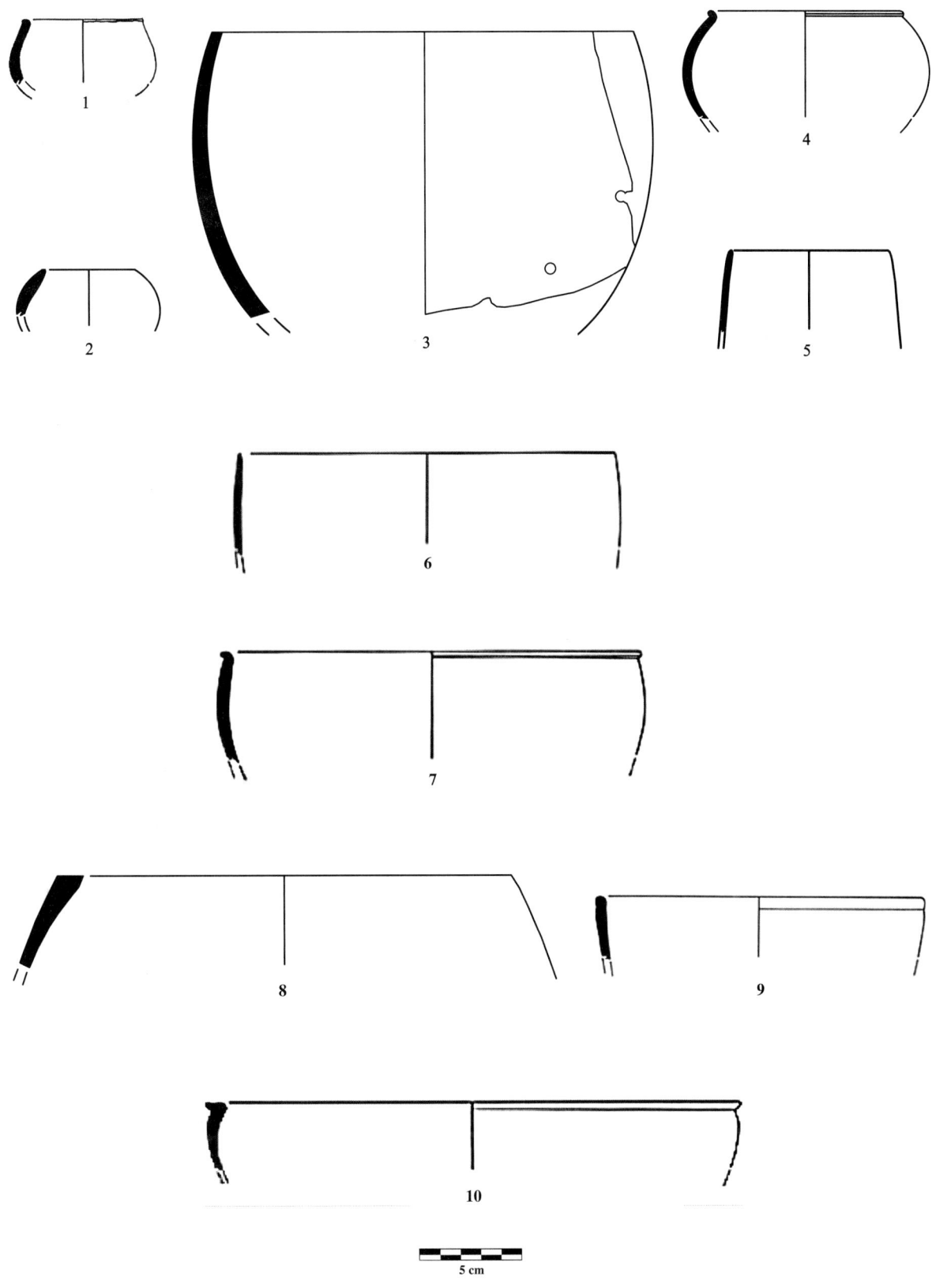

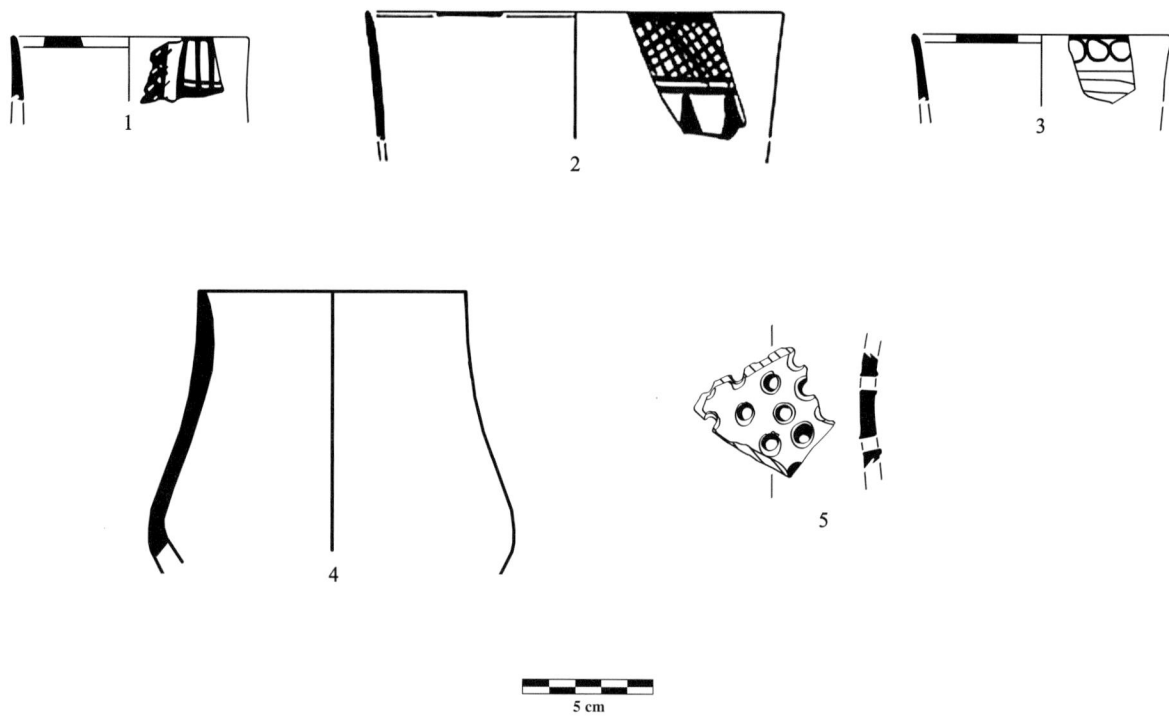

Item	Inventory	Form	Ware	Description
1	4088	Beaker (mini)	BP	wheelmade; grit temper; slip; vertical lines below rim alternate with cross hatching
2	4096	Beaker/Bowl	BP	wheelmade; sand temper; slip; two rows of panels with cross hatching and hanging triangles
3	4110	Beaker	BP	wheelmade; sand temper; slip; band around interior rim, brown circles and incised lines below rim
4	4936	Beaker	C	handmade; grit temper; slip; exterior has thumb smoothing and thin slip
5	2417	Brazier Sherd	C	handmade; grit temper; round holes

Fig. 3.33 Hissar II, Phase D.

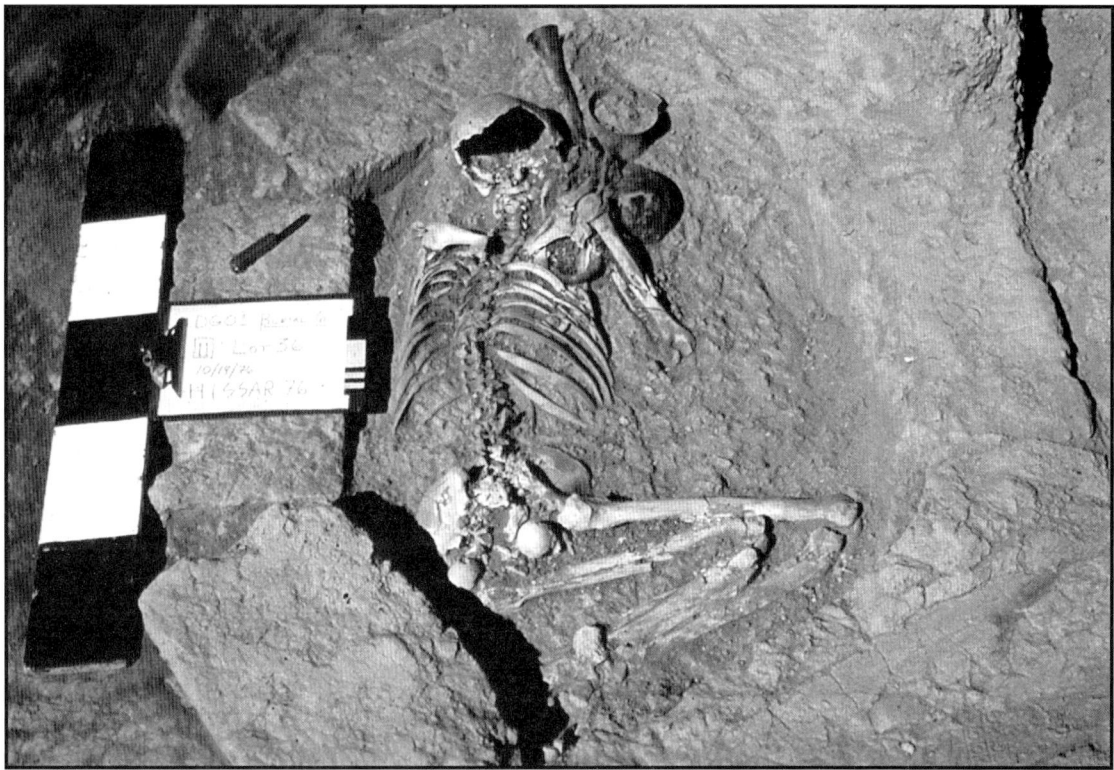

Fig. 3.34 Main Mound DG01, burial 6 (H76-SL243, Courtesy of the Penn Museum)

2). The earliest occurrence is in Early Mid-Hissar II (phase E-D)[25] and it continues through Late Hissar III. It has a short, goblet-like, splayed base; the circular holes are in a straight line or diagonally bored/drilled from the exterior surface when the vessel was still wet, leaving extra pieces of clay clinging on the edges of the holes in the interior. The early braziers, Period III braziers, have square openings in addition to circular holes on the same vessel.

Summary

Regarding Forms:
- New forms are the tulip-shaped beaker and trough-spouted jar (in phase D this form was minimally present but in phase D-C increases to 5.6%).

- All of the previously existing form types are found in the D-C transitional phase.

- Two types of bowls and a jar form are frequent with most bowls in C and GB wares, most pedestal bowls in GB ware, and most jars in C ware.

- Bottle form increases substantially (2.5% to 5.6%).

- Beakers (including tulip-shape beaker) appear, with the beaker form in general increasing from 1.5% to 2.4%.

- Wide-based bowl increases from 8% to 10.5% from the previous phase and is produced more frequently in GS ware.

- Trough-spouted jar continues in GB, GS, and C, as in phase D.

- Goblet increases from 2.5% in phase D to 8.9% in phase D-C, occurring in three wares (B, GS, and GB) in phase D and four wares (B, BP, C, and GB) in Phase D-C.

- Plate/tray increases (1% to 4.8%) and is produced in five different wares (R, C, GS, GB, and G) combining both phases D and D-C.

Regarding Wares:
- Only four of the seven wares occur frequently: GB, GS, B, and C wares. GB and C wares peak while painted wares, G, BP, and R occur in smaller percentages.

D.6 Early Hissar III, Phase C (ca. 2900–2500 BC)

Ceramic material from this phase comes from Pinnacle lots 11–9 (gap); North Flat two burned rooms, CF58 /2/ and /3/; the buttressed room (CF48 /14/) below phase B (see Ch. 2, p. 58 and Table 2.2).

Stratigraphy

Main Mound: Building stage C is clearly missing on the Main Mound. It may be considered a stage of abandonment during which the area was used as a burial ground.

North Flat: See p. 111 in this chapter; also see Dyson and Remsen 1989:99–105.

Ceramic Assemblage

The ceramics of the North Flat assemblage are similar to the assemblage of the D-C transitional phase from the Main Mound, both containing the same forms and wares. The North Flat assemblage from the two burned rooms (CF58/2/and /3/) contained GB and C ware vessels, including pedestal bowl with metallic sheen, bottle with metal ridge, wide-based bowl, and dark grey burnished tulip-shaped beaker. The assemblage also consists of large unpainted jars in GS, replicas of these vessels in C ware. The motifs include predominantly incised, grooved, and repoussé, as in the earlier phases. A new form, the bridge-beak-spouted jar, is added to the repertoire and is characteristic of later phases B and B-A/A. The trough-spouted jar, which continues to occur, is its forerunner.

D.7 Hissar III, Phase B, Middle Bronze Age (ca. 2500–2200 BC)

Ceramics from this phase come from Pinnacle (lots 8–5); North Flat Burned Building CF46-47 and CF-56.[26]

Stratigraphy

Main Mound: The Main Mound levels of the later phases B and A can only be surmised from the baulks of the 1976 excavations and Schmidt's notes. Schmidt defines the building "stage C" as "walls which may belong to the slightly later building phase of level 2, (phase B) or which may actually have been built during the occupation of level 1" (in Schmidt's terms, Level 1 corresponds to phase A, Period IIIC) (Schmidt 1937:155–156). Howard (1989a:56–58, figs. 1–4) documents these walls and

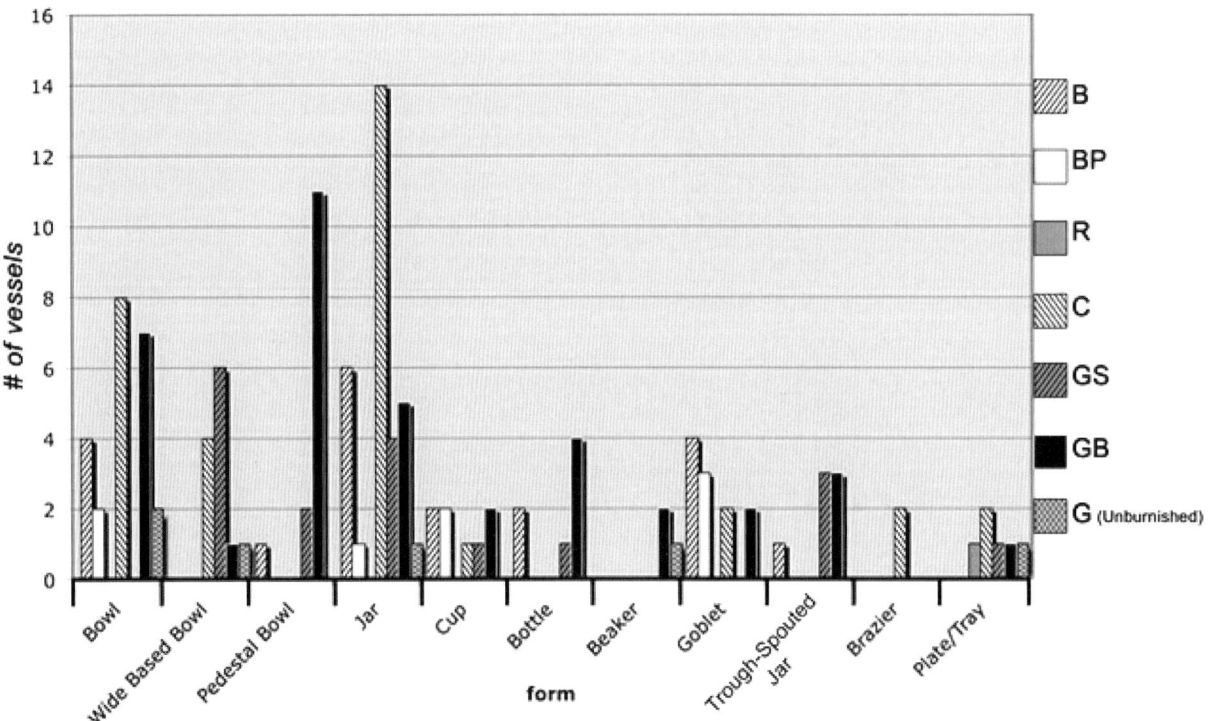

Fig. 3.35 Graph of the number of vessels by ware and form in Late Hissar II (transitional phase D-C).

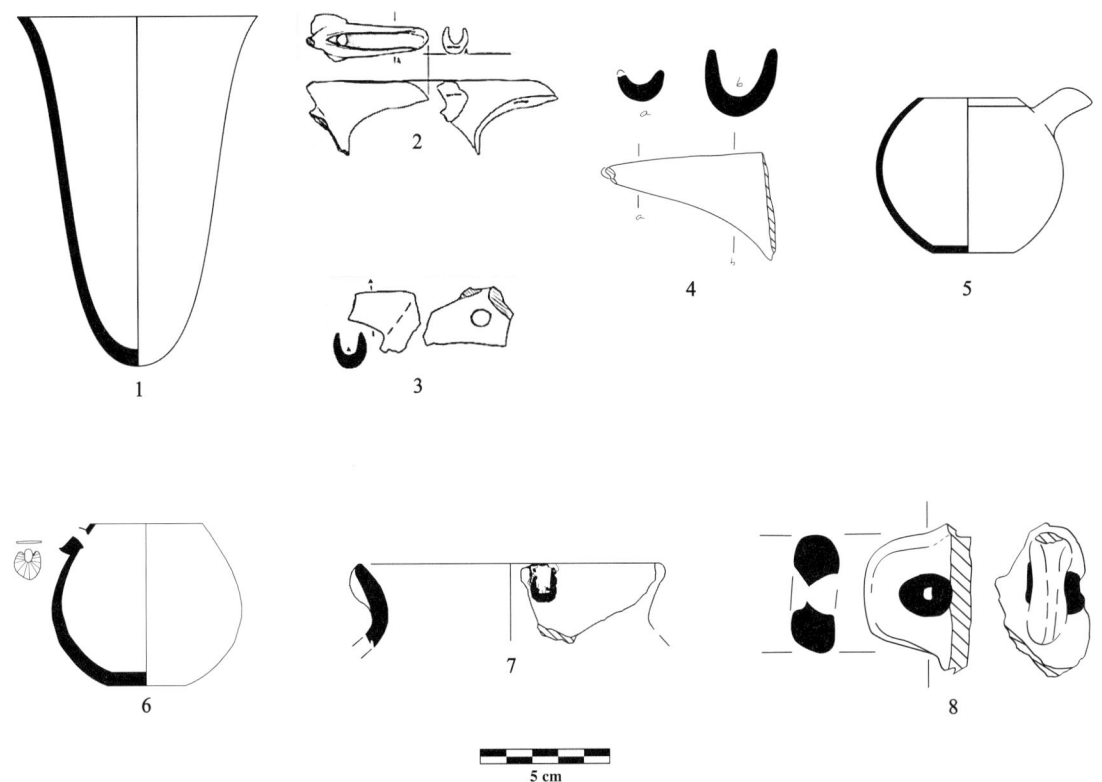

Item	Inventory	Form	Ware	Description
1	72	Tulip-Shaped Beaker	GB	wheelmade; sand temper; slip
2	2803	Trough-Spouted Jar	G	sand and grit temper; slip
3	4991	Trough-Spouted Jar	G	grit and sand temper; slip
4	2894	Trough-Spouted Jar	GB	grit and sand temper; slip
5	NF55	Trough-Spouted Jar (mini)	GB	wheelmade; sand and grit temper; slip
6	NF116	Trough-Spouted Jar (mini)	B	handmade; grit temper; slip
7	3061	Jar	C	handmade; grit temper; slip; two ledge handles attached to jar
8	2869	Jar/Canteen Lug Handle	C	circular lug handle attached to jar

Fig. 3.36 Hissar II-III, Transitional Phase D-C.

Item	Inventory	Form	Ware	Description
1	NF88	Goblet (mini)	B	handmade; outcurving rim; splayed base; temper?; slip
2	NF103	Goblet (mini)	B	handmade; outcurving rim, splayed base; grit temper
3	NF78	Goblet (mini)	B	wheel- and handmade; outcurving rim, splayed base; grit temper; slip
4	NF129	Goblet	B	wheel- and handmade; outcurving rim, splayed base; grit temper; slip
5	NF102	Cup (mini)	B	handmade; sand temper; slip
6	NF108	Goblet (mini)	GB	wheelmade; splayed base; sand temper; slip
7	N77	Goblet (mini)	BP	wheel- and handmade; splayed base; grit temper; slip; vertical bands from rim to shoulder
8	NF58	Goblet (mini)	BP	wheel- and handmade; splayed base; chaff and grit temper; vertical and horizontal hatching from rim to shoulder
9	NF111	Goblet (mini)	BP	wheelmade; sand temper; slip; vertical and horizontal hatching from rim to shoulder
10	NF89	Bowl	BP	wheelmade; high neck; sand temper; slip; vertical and horizontal hatching from rim to shoulder
11	N59	Bowl/Cup	BP	wheelmade; sand temper; slip; carinated, globular; vertical bands from rim to shoulder
12	N59a	Bowl/Cup	BP	wheelmade; temper?; slip; carinated, globular; vertical bands from rim to shoulder

Fig. 3.37 *facing page*, Hissar II-III, Transitional Phase D-C.

ANALYSIS OF CERAMIC COMPLEXES OF THE MAIN MOUND

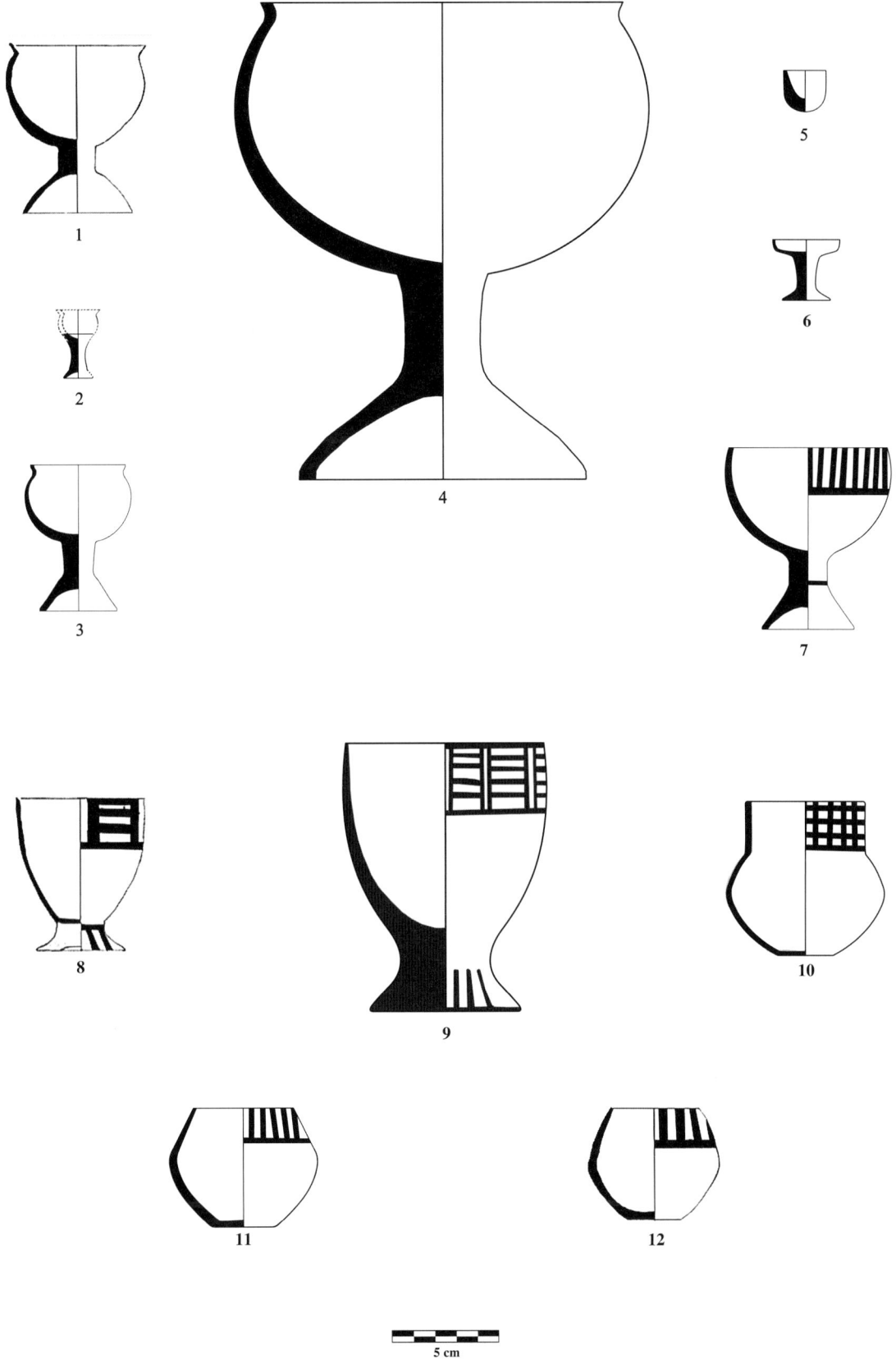

5 cm

Item	Inventory	Form	Ware	Description
1	5123	Jar	C	wheelmade; inverted rim; grit temper; slip
2	2808	Jar	C	wheelmade; outcurving rolled rim; grit temper; slip
3	5011	Jar	C	wheelmade; inverted wall; outcurving rolled rim; grit and chaff temper; slip
4	4576	Jar	GS	wheelmade; chaff and grit temper; slip; inverted wall, outcurving rolled rim
5	2817	Jar	GB	wheelmade; inverted wall, outcurving rail rim; grit and chaff temper; slip
6	2781	Jar	GS	wheelmade; outcurving rolled rim; grit temper; slip

Fig. 3.38 *facing page*, Hissar II-III, Transitional Phase D-C.

ANALYSIS OF CERAMIC COMPLEXES OF THE MAIN MOUND 149

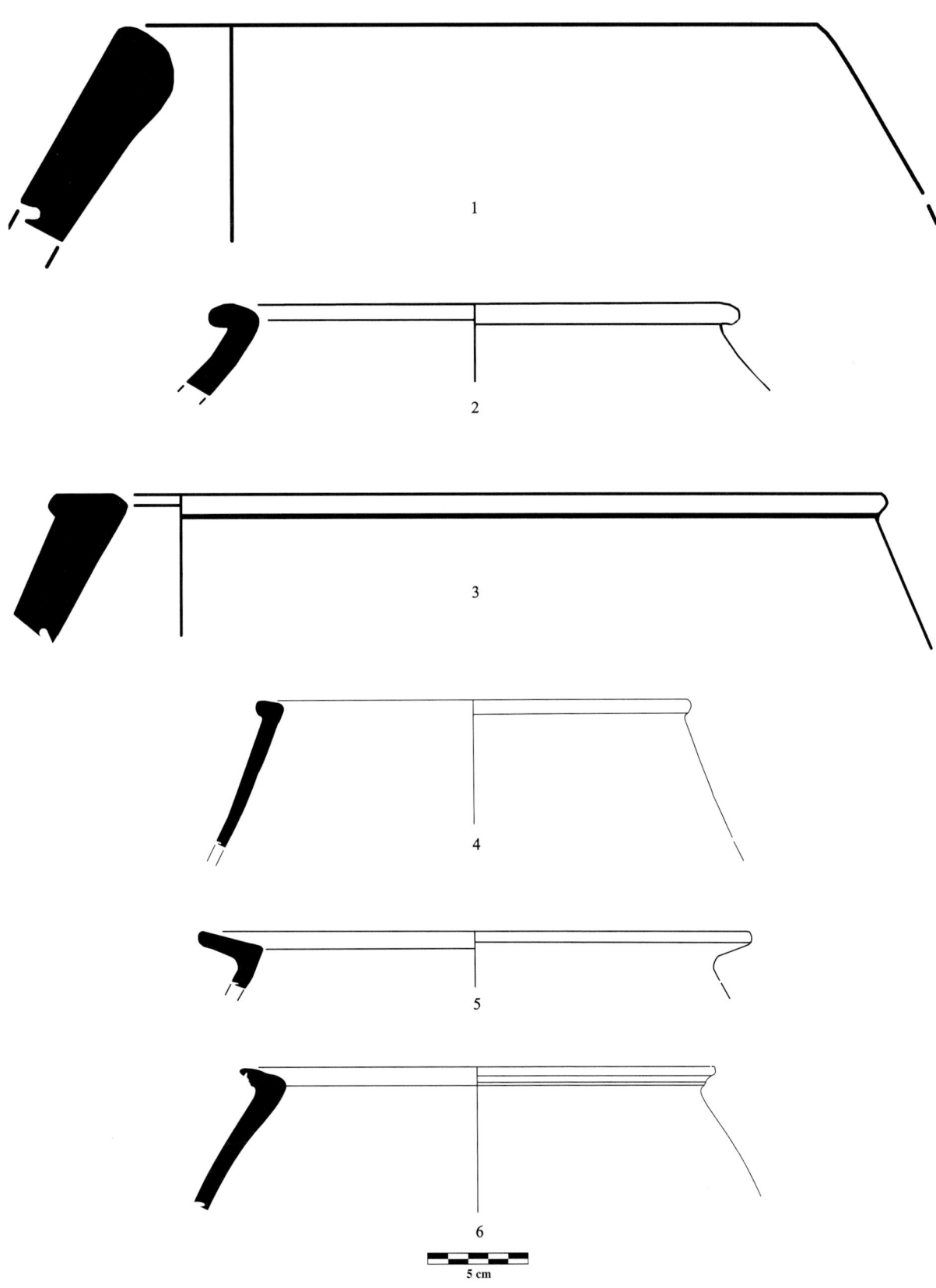

Item	Inventory	Form	Ware	Description
1	5188	Jar	GB	wheelmade; outcurving rolled rim; sand and grit temper; slip
2	3452	Jar	G	wheelmade; outcurving rolled rim, short neck; grit and chaff temper; slip; painted band under rim
3	NF79	Wide-Based Bowl	C	handmade; chaff and grit temper; two repair/suspension holes
4	NF139	Wide-Based Bowl	B	handmade; grit temper; two repair/suspension holes
5	3444	Wide-Based Bowl	C	handcoiled; gravel temper; slip; interior ridges
6	NF112	Wide-Based Bowl/Vase	GB	handmade; outcurving bevel rim; chaff temper; slip
7	5050	Wide-Based Bowl	C	wheelmade; grit temper; slip
8	3371	Wide-Based Bowl	G	wheel- and handmade; sand temper; slip
9	4326	Wide-Based Bowl	GS	wheelmade; sand and grit temper; slip

Fig. 3.39 *facing page*, Hissar II-III, Transitional Phase D-C.

ANALYSIS OF CERAMIC COMPLEXES OF THE MAIN MOUND

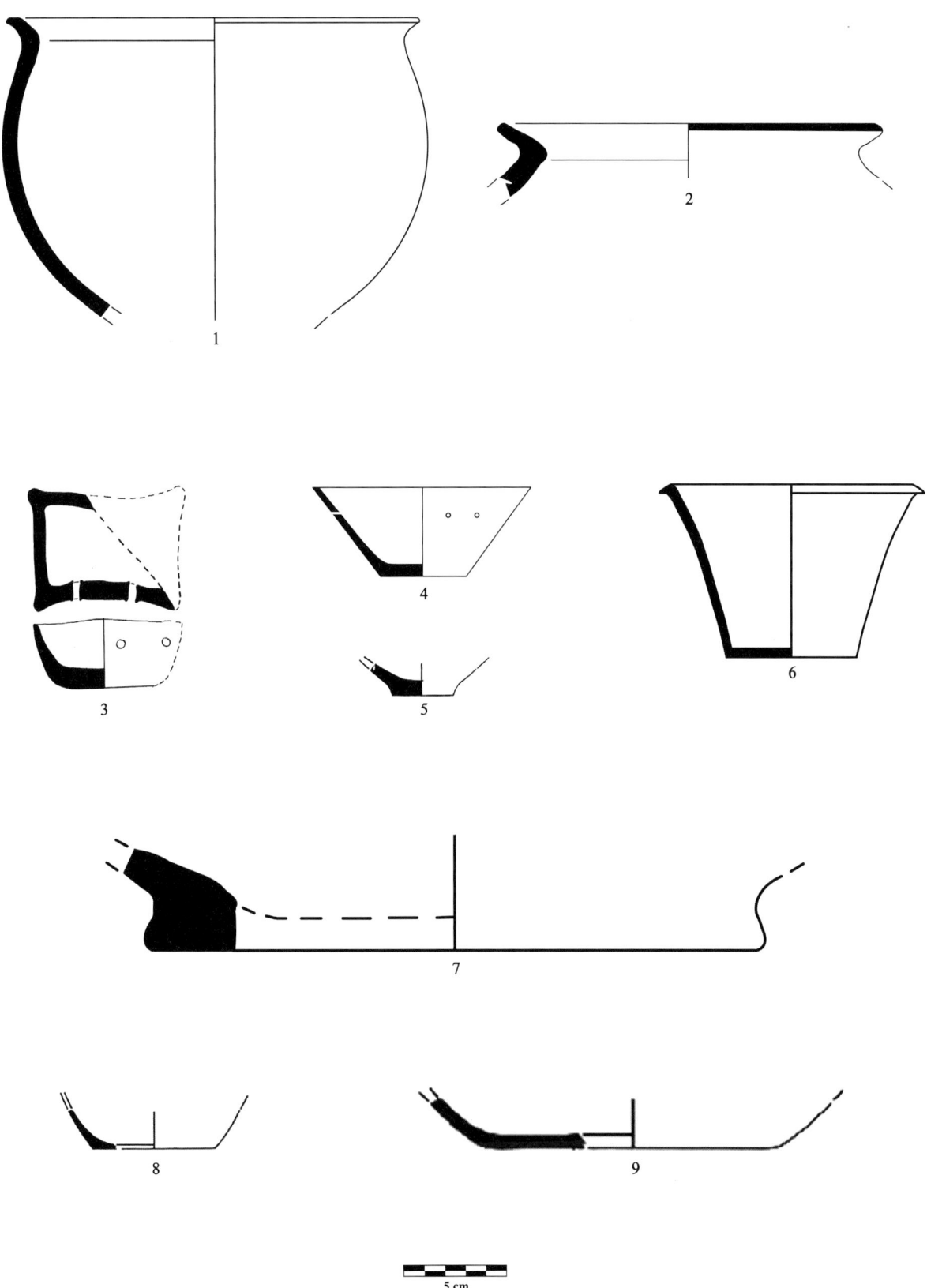

Item	Inventory	Form	Ware	Description
1	2804	Pedestal Bowl	GB	wheelmade; outcurving triangular rim; sand temper; slip
2	5158	Pedestal Bowl	GB	wheelmade; outcurving rolled rim; sand and grit temper; slip
3	NF61	Bowl	C	handmade; chaff and grit temper; slip; two repair/suspension holes
4	4259	Pedestal Bowl Base	GB	wheelmade; splayed base; grit temper; slip
5	NF84	Pedestal Bowl	B	wheelmade; long shaft; grit temper; slip
6	NF141	Goblet	GB	wheel- and handmade; outcurving rim, splayed base; sand and grit temper; slip
7	NF82	Goblet	GB	wheel- and handmade; outcurving rim, splayed base; grit temper; slip

Fig. 3.40 *facing page*, Hissar II-III, Transitional Phase D-C.

ANALYSIS OF CERAMIC COMPLEXES OF THE MAIN MOUND

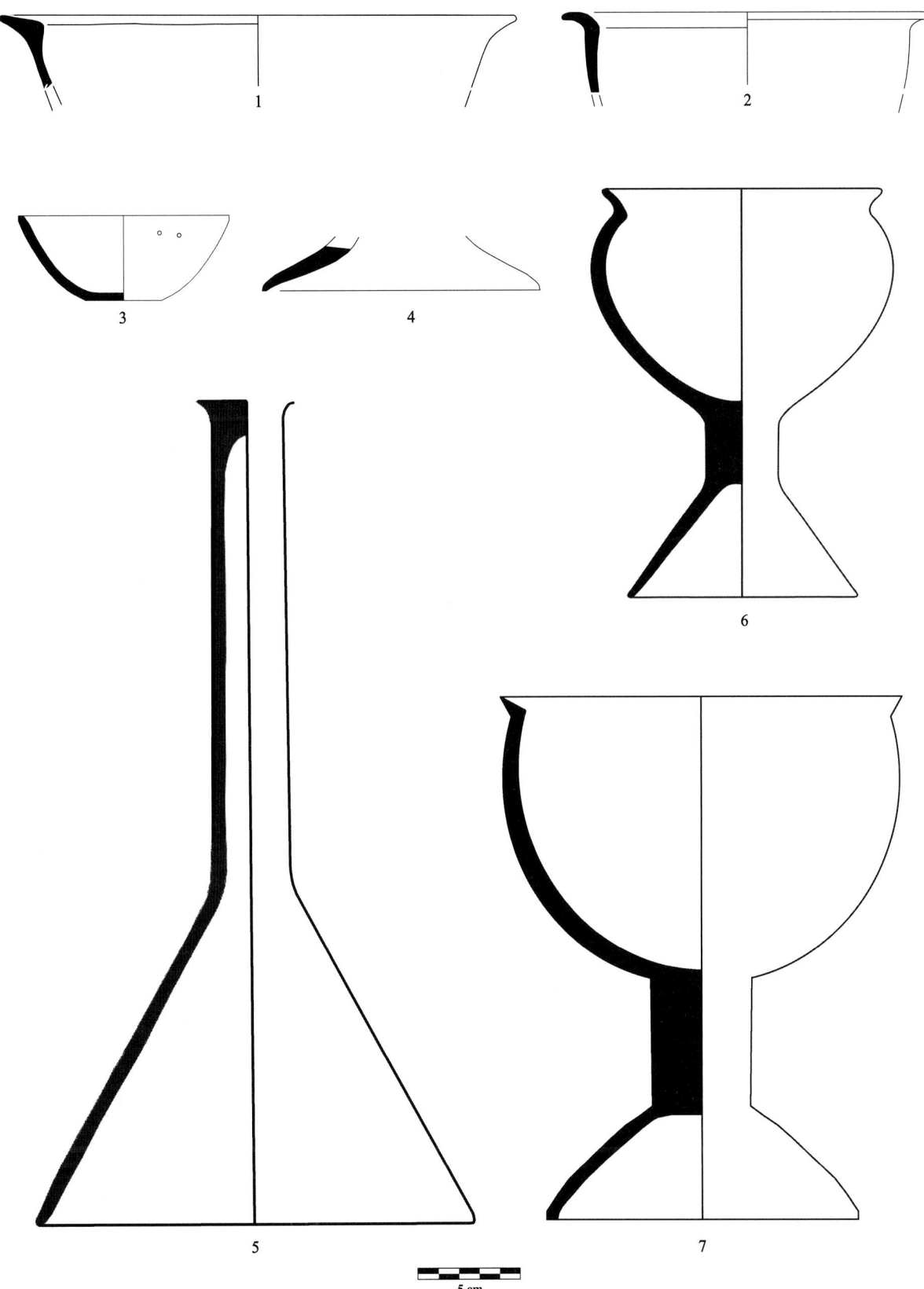

Item	Inventory	Form	Ware	Description
1	NF140	Bottle/Pitcher	GB	wheelmade; sand and grit temper; slip; long neck; "ring" around base of neck
2	NF83	Bottle/Pitcher	GB	wheelmade; sand temper; slip; long neck
3	N70	Bottle/Pitcher	GB	wheelmade; sand temper; "metallic" (high gloss), long neck, incised decoration—two sets of incised lines on neck; panel of horizontal incised lines enclosing zigzag incised lines
4	3215	Bottle/Pitcher	GB	wheelmade, sand and grit temper; outcurving rolled rim, short neck

Fig. 3.41 *facing page*, Hissar II-III, Transitional Phase D-C.

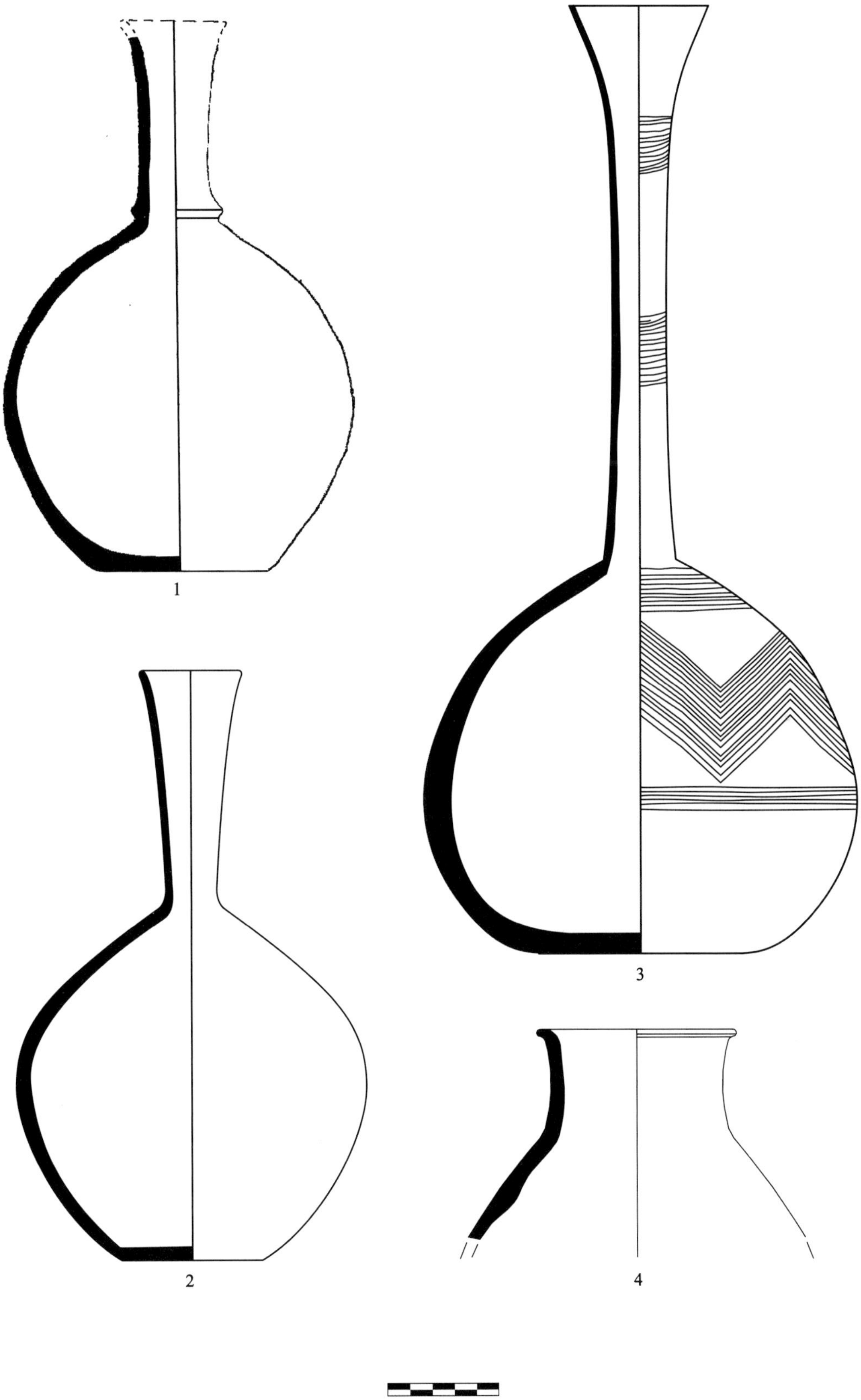

ANALYSIS OF CERAMIC COMPLEXES OF THE MAIN MOUND

5 cm

Item	Inventory	Form	Ware	Description
1	NF41	Bell Beaker	GB	wheelmade; sand and grit temper; slip
2	71	Bell Beaker	G	handmade; carinated belly; sand and grit temper; slip
3	3440, 3437	Plate/Tray	C	handmade; vertical wall; chaff and grit temper; basket impression on exterior of base
4	NF118	Plate/Tray	C	handmade; everted wall; chaff temper; slip
5	2794	Plate/Tray (mini)	G	handmade; vertical wall; grit temper; slip
6	3207	Plate/Tray	GB	handmade; vertical wall; grit temper; slip
7	NF66	Brazier	C	handmade; inverted wall, long shaft, splayed base; chaff temper; slip

Fig. 3.42 *facing page*, Hissar II-III, Transitional Phase D-C.

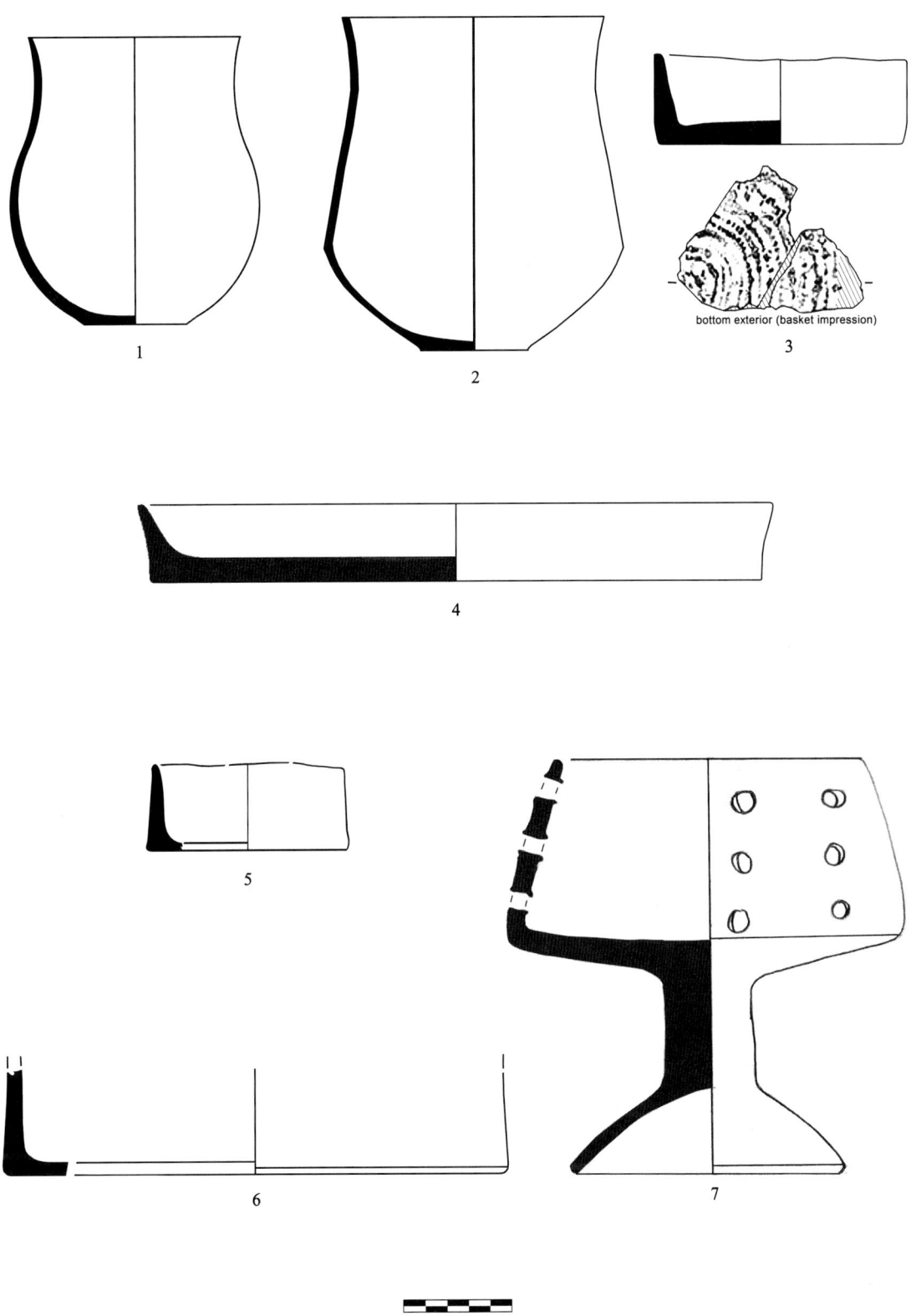

melted bricks as seen in baulks 2, 4, 5, 8 of the Pinnacle in square CG90 corresponding to a series of plaster floors with thin archaeological deposits. According to Howard's speculation, these floors may be representing stages C(?) through B.

In the absence of clear architectural and stratigraphic information for the final building stages, phases B and B-A/A of Period IIIB and IIIC on the Main Mound can be ceramically defined from the limited assemblages retrieved from Pinnacle lots 1–8, as well as Schmidt's burials that are grouped according to the new ceramic sequence (see Ch. 4).

North Flat: On the North Flat the stratigraphic situation for the latest levels is complex. Dyson used the Burned Building (Schmidt's Period "IIIB"), below the topmost level 1, "as a major stratigraphic element…to place other deposits above and below that structure" (Dyson and Remsen 1989:89–90, figs. 13, 15). So, the Burned Building is attributed to level 2, between the topmost level 1 and level 3 of the Buttressed Building CF48/14/ and CF58/2/ and /3/ burned rooms.

Dyson and Remsen (1989:108, see figs. 26–34) describe succinctly the occupational stages, A to D (Period IIIC to II) on the North Flat: "that the uppermost level covered the whole area at the end of the third millennium (phase A, Schmidt's 'IIIC'); that the Burned Building, and, in its late stage, the enclosure walls extending to the west, was built into the slope of a preexisting mound. This construction, phase B, appears to date to the third quarter of the third millennium BC (Schmidt's 'IIIB'). Directly underlying the phase A remains east and south of the Burned Building, and under the Building itself and its western enclosure walls, is the complex older mound of phase C ('Schmidt's IIB') remains, which date to the end of the fourth millennium B.C.…The two burned rooms excavated at the top of this sequence [CF58/2/ and /3/, see above, phase D-C] provide a unique collection of associated artifacts from an occupational context for comparison with the grave groups. Below the phase C mound lies a deep deposit of trash and ash, phase D, containing lapis lazuli debris and a mixture of painted buff and red ware with some classic grey burnished ware" (see also Figs. 3.30, 3.36–3.42 for phase D-C ceramics).

Ceramic Assemblage

In this phase, GB and C wares are the most common both at 33.3%, including miniature vessels. There is increased use of slag temper in C ware. The only new form is the bridge-beak-spouted jar.

Bridge-beak-spouted jar: This form is associated with GB ware; the jar is wheelmade and the spout is hand formed, with well-levigated sand temper, and is high fired. Below the rolled rim are thin grooves surrounding it (Fig. 3.44:1; see also Schmidt 1937: fig.107, pl. XLI H3511). "Spouted pitchers of pleasing shapes are frequent in Hissar IIIC [phase B-A/A]. The globular vessel (H3511) with burnished herringbone pattern and long beak-spout is typical of the layer under consideration" (Schmidt 1937:182). On the contrary, pattern burnishing on GB vessels starts earlier, in phase B (Period IIIB), as indicated by the present ceramic analysis. It is generally applied as herringbone pattern to bottle/pitcher and to trough-spouted jar forms (ibid., pl. XXXVII H3841, H3987) and continues through phase B-A/A. Trough-spouted vessels are already manufactured in the phase D and transitional D-C ceramic assemblage. The continuing early forms are wide-based bowl, bottle, jar, and cup.

Wide-based bowl: These vessels are in C ware (Fig. 3.44:2, 4, 6) and GS ware (Fig. 3.44:3, 5). They are handmade with slag temper and are high fired. The exterior is pitted and they have smoke/fire marks on both the interior and exterior; a miniature size wide-based bowl, (rim dia. 7.6 cm, ht. 5 cm, base dia. 3.5 cm) has fire marks only on the exterior (Fig. 3.44:4). In the C ware vessels, the interior of the base is thickened with an extra layer of clay. Also, there is evidence of the use of a mold to produce a large vessel (Fig. 3.44:6), a C ware vessel with a rim dia. 45–50 cm, base dia. 22 cm. It has a layer of white plaster pieces stuck to its base, which may be part of a mold. Similar to phase D-C, use of basketry as a mold for the plate form is suggested.

Bottle: This vessel type has a short neck and flaring rolled rim in GB ware; it is possibly handmade, with sand temper, and is medium fired (Fig. 3.44:9). It should be noted that Schmidt's publications contain a larger inventory of ovoid ("pear shaped") globular bottles, than is available in the 1976 assemblage. He dates these bottles to Period IIIB, which roughly corresponds to phase B, dated to mid- to late third millennium BC (Schmidt 1933: pl. CXIV H1025, H651, H614, 1937: pl. XXXVII). The ("pear shaped") bottles are grey burnished with long necks and are partly wheelmade with fine incised and pattern burnished motifs. An unusual type is H3820, which sits on a narrow and short flaring base (Schmidt 1937: fig. 106). This vessel is an almost exactly like one from the site of Gohar Tepe in the Mazandaran region (Mahfroozi and Piller 2009:181, fig. 5). Both vessels have pattern burnished decoration. Mahfroozi dates the Gohar Tepe vessel to the late third millennium BC, which corresponds to phase B-A/A, according to the Tepe Hissar ceramic chronology. Also, at Tureng Tepe III, there are close parallels to "pear shaped"/ovoid bottle forms with pattern burnishing. The latter have short or longer necks with a "metallic ridge" around the neck (Daher 1968).

Jar: The vessels are generally wheelmade in GB ware. They vary in size from 5.5 to 9 cm rim diameter and 8 to 11 cm in height (Fig. 3.44:7–8). One jar (Fig. 3.44:8) has a high neck and rail rim decorated with a burnished "loop" pattern along the base of its neck.

Cup: This form has a thin wall, is wheelmade with sand temper, and is high fired. It is associated with BP ware. The vessel, is decorated with vertically placed continuous hatched "hanging triangles" below the rim (Fig. 3.44:10). There are faint traces of the design on the interior, possibly left from stacking multiple numbers of vessels with the same painted design. Stacking multiple vessels, specifically cups and bowls, is a practice that appears early in E-D phase, which is a clear indication of mass production of these cups.

Summary

Due to the small sample size of the phase B[27] assemblage, percentage frequencies of vessel forms and wares are skewed. In addition to the bridge-beak-spouted jar, most of the early forms appeared to continue in this phase.

Regarding wares, GS and GB wares combined account for 58.3% of the sample, while C ware is present at 33.3%, and BP ware remains low (8.3%). Both B and R wares are absent, however, both reappear in the later phase B-A/A.

D.8 Late Hissar IIIC, Phases B-A/A, Late Bronze Age (2200–1800 BC)

Stratigraphy

Main Mound: The stratigraphy of the later levels of the phases B and B-A/A can only be surmised from the baulks of the 1976 excavations and Schmidt's notes (as described above). Howard also notes, "The architecture of the last occupations, levels A and B, were still visible in the western and southern portions of the Main Mound" (as quoted in Dyson and Remsen, 1989:66, see also Howard 1989a: 56–57).

North Flat: Schmidt's excavations of the topmost levels revealed a mixed deposit of mudbrick remains probably belonging to level 1, Period IIIC. This level is assigned to phase B-A/A on the basis of correlations of small finds from the Main Mound, North Flat, and the upper stratum of Treasure Hill.

In the absence of clear architectural and stratigraphic information for the final building stage B-A/A of Period

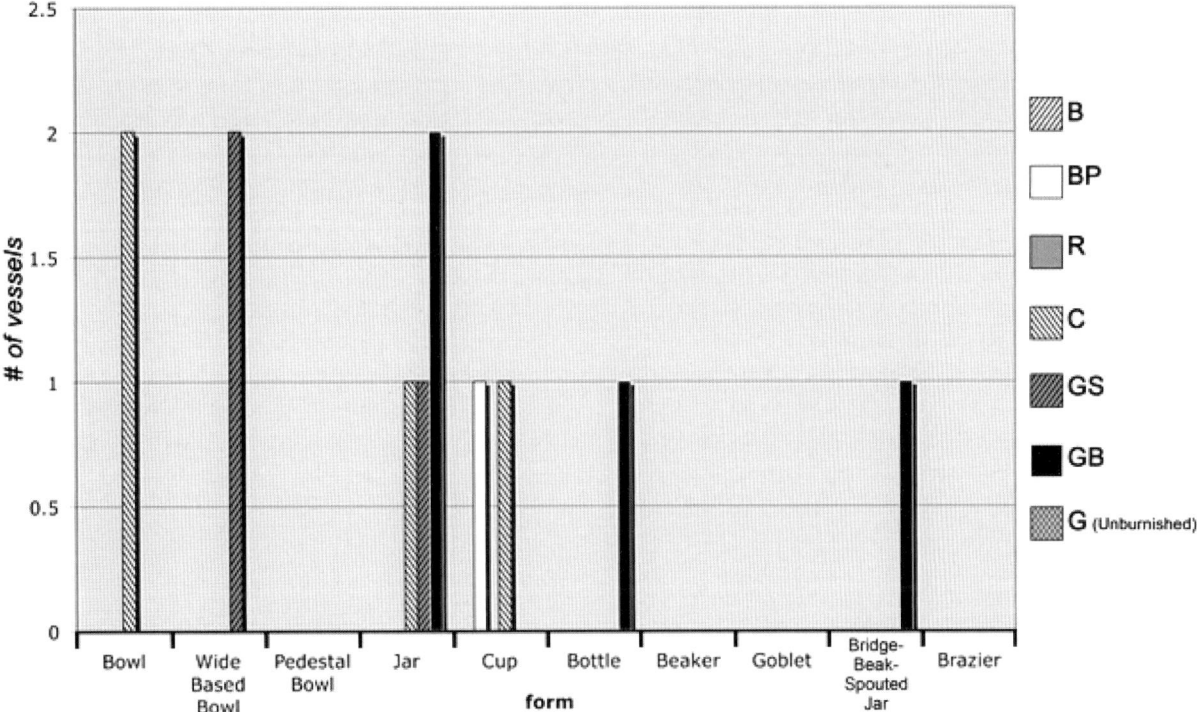

Fig. 3.43 Graph of the number of vessels by ware and form in Mid-Hissar III (phase B).

Item	Inventory	Form	Ware	Description
1	3698, 3706a	Bridge-Beak-Spouted Jar	GB	wheel- and handmade; sand temper; slip; thin grooves below rim
2	3839	Wide-Based Bowl	C	handmade; slag temper; slip
3	3863	Wide-Based Bowl	GS	wheelmade; sand and grit temper; slip
4	3612	Wide-Based Bowl (mini)	C	handmade; sand temper; slip
5	3614	Wide-Based Bowl	GS	handmade; sand and grit temper; slip
6	3672a–c	Wide-Based Bowl Mold	C	handmade; gravel and slag temper; pitted exterior, interior has thick white plaster molding
7	3699b	Jar	GS	wheelmade; outcurving rim, short neck; slag temper; slip
8	3670a	Bottle	GB	wheelmade; swirl pattern burnish below neck; slag temper; slip
9	5194	Bottle	GB	wheelmade; everted rim, short neck; sand temper; slip
10	3589	Cup	BP	wheelmade; sand temper; slip; hanging triangles vertically placed in panels

Fig. 3.44 *facing page*, Hissar III, Phase B.

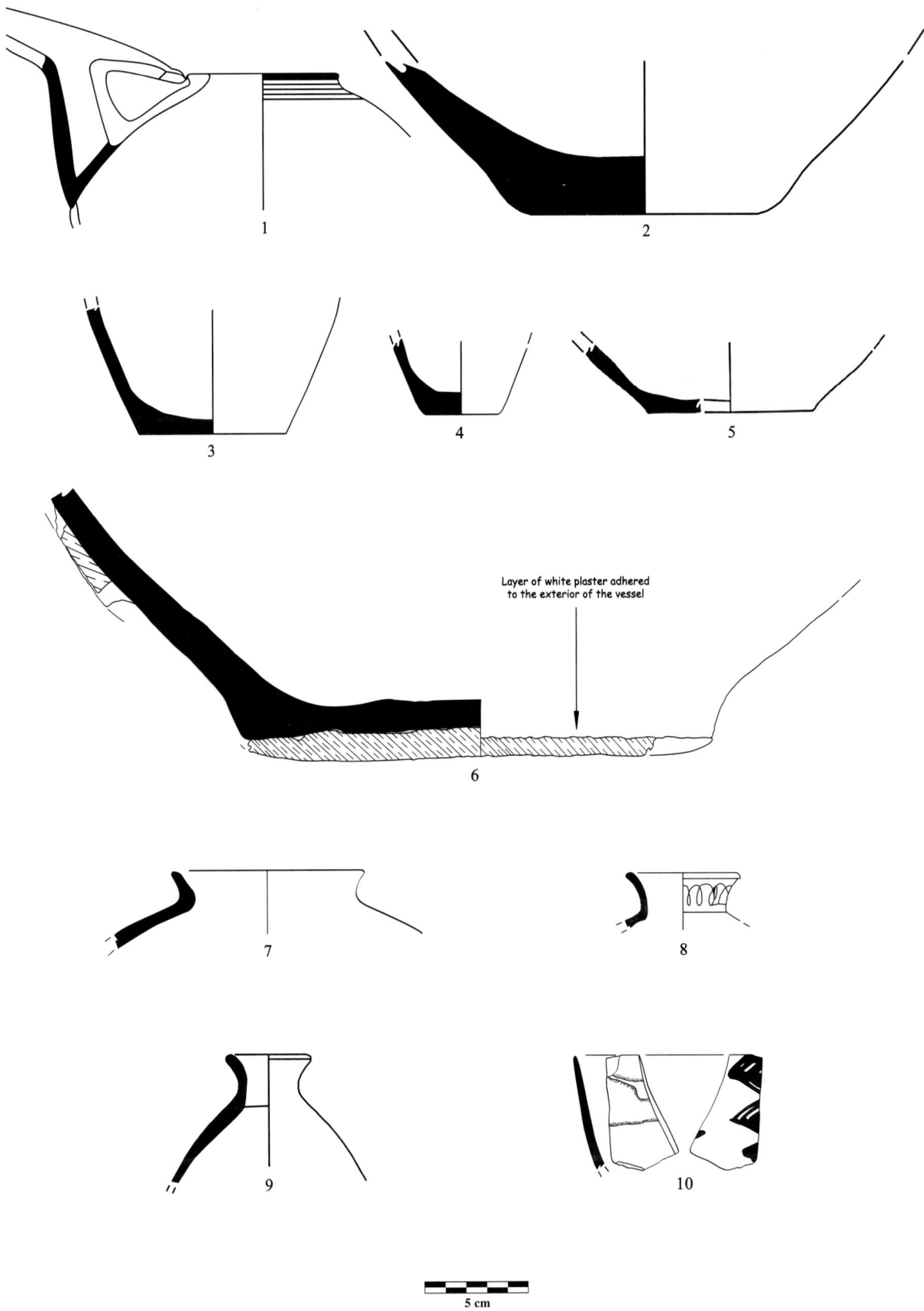

IIIC on the Main Mound and the North Flat, these phases can be ceramically defined from the limited assemblages retrieved from Pinnacle lots 1–8 and more clearly from Schmidt's burials that have been grouped according to the new ceramic sequence in Chapters 4 and 5 (see also Dyson and Remsen 1989:90–91).

Ceramic Assemblage

The 1976 assemblage from Hissar IIIC Main Mound and North Flat settlement levels is extremely small. Therefore, it does not provide a representative sample (Schmidt 1937:178–184, pls. XXXVII–XLIII). The range of forms is limited and there are no new forms encountered in the assemblage.

In the transitional and final phase B-A/A, all wares except BP, G, and GS are represented. As in phase B, GB and C wares predominate. There is an increase in B ware and a small percentage of R ware is present. The continuing forms are:

Miniature jar: This GB form with high neck, is very similar to the GB miniature jar in phase B. It is high fired with grit temper (Fig. 3.46:1).

Large globular jar: This jar type is made on a fast wheel with ridges visible in the interior. On the exterior, there are pieces of white limestone. It has slag and grit temper (see forms in other phases F-E through B-A/A).

Bowl: These vessels are associated with B (Fig. 3.46:4) and GB wares (Fig. 3.46:2). The large vessels have an average rim diameter of 27 cm; they are wheelmade with slag and grit temper, and are high fired.

Another bowl in R ware has thin walls, is wheelmade and high fired, and has wheel marks (horizontal ridges) visible on the interior and exterior. It has brownish red vertical and diagonal bands extending from the rim (Fig. 3.46:3).

Lug handle (not illustrated): Lug handles are mainly associated with G pattern burnished canteens in phase B, (see Schmidt 1937: pl. XL H5140, H4219, H3541, H3533, H4009). From this small assemblage there is only one sherd with pattern burnishing, possibly from a canteen.

Summary

Regarding wares:
- Four out of seven wares are present.

- Pattern burnishing continues from the earlier phases D through D-C.

- Note that B and R wares are present at this latest phase.

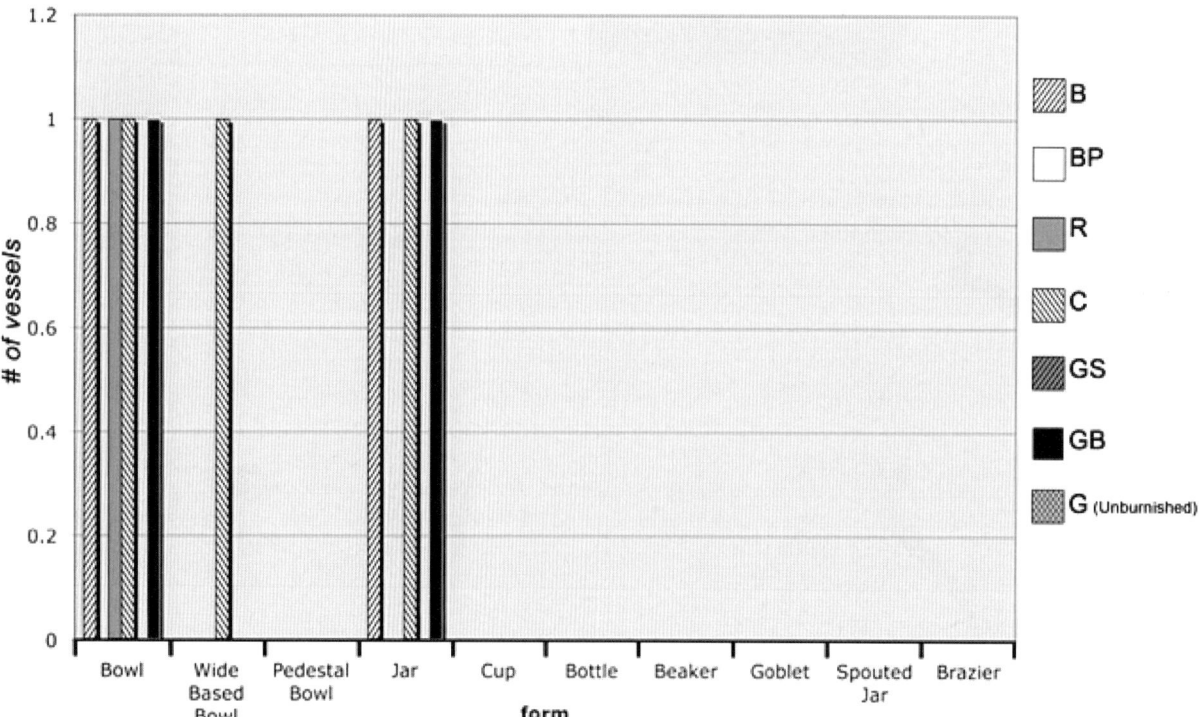

Fig. 3.45 Graph of the number of vessels by ware and form in Late Hissar III (phase B-A/A).

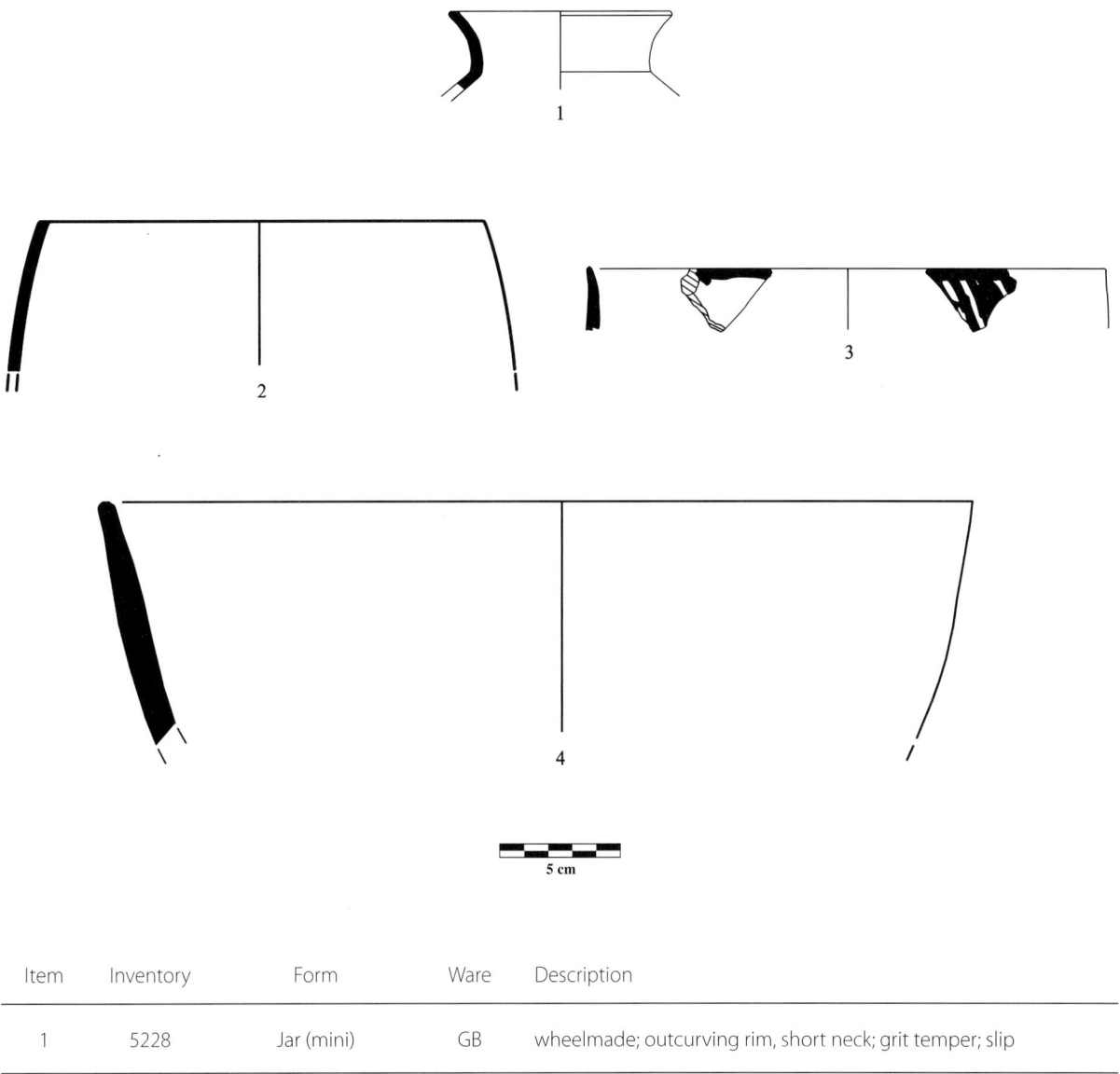

Item	Inventory	Form	Ware	Description
1	5228	Jar (mini)	GB	wheelmade; outcurving rim, short neck; grit temper; slip
2	5217	Bowl	GB	wheelmade; inverted wall; grit temper; slip
3	3731	Bowl	R	wheelmade, everted wall; sand temper; slip; brown vertical and diagonal bands below rim, horizontal ridges interior and exterior
4	3708	Pedestal Bowl	B	wheelmade; grit temper; slip

Fig. 3.46 Hissar III, Transitional Phases B-A/A.

Regarding forms:
- Only bowl and jar forms are represented, although in a larger sample we would expect more of the earlier phase B vessel types, such as canteen and bottle.

E. Conclusion

In this chapter, the *new* ceramic chronology of the Tepe Hissar settlement is built to correspond with stratigraphic phasing and architectural contexts (see Ch. 2, Table 2.2). The ceramic typology on which the chronology rests is defined by the co-occurrence of seven wares and 12 form types in each phase and throughout the settlement.[28]

By the early fourth millennium BC, the Tepe Hissar ceramic assemblages are already well-developed. The potters were clearly skilled in the use of hand and wheel techniques, frequently combining both of these techniques on individual vessels. By the beginning of Hissar II (phases E and E-D), we note two innovations in ceramic production: one is the intentional use of copper slag in C ware as an inclusion in the clay, which is clearly related to increased metallurgical activities during this period. The second is a controlled firing atmosphere (reduction of oxygen in the kiln) that explains the production of grey wares.

Most wares occur throughout the sequence, however, GS ware first appears in Periods II and Early III (phases E and E-D) Also, Periods II and Early III (phases E through D-C) usher in new form types from mid-fourth to the beginning of the third millennium BC. These types are trough-spouted jar and bottle in GB and GS wares, tulip-shaped and bell beaker in GB ware, and brazier and plate/tray in C ware. The bottle appears in phase D, continues in phases D-C and B, and occurs in a variety of short and long necked vessels with fine pattern burnishing. The bridge-beak-spouted jar and canteen (not illustrated) in GB ware are late forms, frequently associated with pattern burnishing. They occur in phases B and B-A/A in periods IIIB and IIIC. The overall decline of wares in later phases (C, B, B-A/A), is, undoubtedly, a factor of excavation procedure.

One of the shortcomings of the 1931–32 excavations was Schmidt's "creation" of a burial stratigraphy based only on the contents of the graves without tracing them to the strata from which they originated, that is to say, without the certainty that the graves were associated with specific construction phases of the settlement. The new ceramic chronology corrects this deficiency by dating a representative sample of burials in stratified phases and contexts, as discussed in Chapters 4 and 5.

NOTES:

3.1 Phases Early Hissar I and Late Hissar III (phase B-A/A) were not explored by Howard, Dyson, and Remsen, so the ceramic assemblages that correspond to those phases can only be reconstructed from Schmidt's ceramic assemblages.

3.2 "Fill" terminology is not contextual. Schmidt uses this term to refer to a settlement level, but he offers no further description of the level to which he refers.

3.3 Howard states that the results of mineralogical analysis of thin sections from 1976 confirmed the conclusion drawn from similar analyses on Tepe Hissar ceramics published in 1937; that there is a basic uniformity of minerals in buff, red, and grey wares (Schmidt 1937:358ff.) Quartz, calcite, hematite, plagioclase, and muscovite were identified in both studies. The more recent analyses [Howard's] identified additionally "sandstone, shell, chert, and other microscopic rock fragments. In both red and buff wares the clay is well levigated….The clay minerals show distinct lineation in the thin sections suggesting that the vessel was turned during its shaping. Coil and hand modeling are the methods of manufacture suggested by the striations, finger impressions and breaks" (Howard n.d.).

3.4 The percentage in each cell reflects the frequency of each ware in each phase and is based on the *total* number of 655 reconstructed vessels of known ware in the assemblage. Table 3.1 reflects *wares* of the reconstructed forms of vessels from the Main Mound and the North Flat.

3.5 Schmidt describes the stylized rendition of some animals, felines and birds (1937: pl. VIII H4478 5130, pl. XIII DH35, 21b) as chronologically significant and places them in later Hissar IIA (ibid., pl. VIII H4478).

3.6 In the 1976 assemblage, the paucity of reconstructable sherds limited the range of vessel types illustrated in each phase. Therefore, the 1976 illustrated forms should be supplemented by those referenced in Schmidt's publications.

3.7 The canteen form could not be reconstructed with the available sherd assemblage.

3.8 The percentage in each cell reflects the frequency of each form in each phase; it is based on the *total* frequency of 655 reconstructed vessel forms and decorative motifs from the 1976 excavations and restudy. For a full range of forms, especially in red, buff painted, and coarse wares in IB-IC, roughly contemporary with stage F, see Schmidt (1937:39–53, pls. III–XII, 1933:345, 353, pls. LXXXII, LXXXIV–LXXXVII).

3.9 In 1976, the earliest strata reached from the Main Mound were in baulks 12, 13, and P (see Ch. 2). "The lowest stage exposed, F, (Schmidt's IC), incorporates strata (11), (12), and (13)" (Howard 1989a:57). On the other hand, Schmidt's excavations struck Hissar "IA" and "IB" that were four meters *below* the surface of Painted Pottery Flat (for ceramics see Schmidt 1937: pls. III–VI). Hissar IA and IB (Schmidt 1937:37–39) correspond to the earliest phases of Period I, predating Howard's stage F.

3.10 The buttressed architectural style continues into phases D and D-C in Buildings 2 and 3.

3.11 Ceramic samples from B and B-A/A phases are small since there were only three lots from the Pinnacle sounding.

3.12 In the reconstructed section 4.1 in this monograph, there are three earlier walls (W13, W14, W17) marked by Schmidt near the bottom level in his deep trench.

3.13 The percentage frequencies are based on total number of sherds for each ware divided by total number from each phase, retrieved from the Deep Sounding (DS) and Pinnacle (P). In this calculation, utility ware which constitutes a very small percentage of the total is combined with coarse ware. In Howard's scheme, buff and red wares also include buff painted and red painted wares. Her two categories, "Blank" and "Weird," are not counted in my calculations.

3.14 These two forms are very similar except for the shape of the base; generally, the pedestal bowl has a long, tubular stem (shaft) on a small circular base, while the goblet sits on a short, splayed base. Since the bowl and the base are found separately, it is difficult to assign the correct base to these vessels.

3.15 The 1976 stratigraphic phase "E" is contemporary with North Flat "D" phase, based on test trench sequence excavated in square CF57 (see also Table 3.4). There are 915 sherds from the North Flat deep test that are divided into three excavation lots, all from below Dyson's C phase, (i.e., Early and Mid-Hissar II Period). Buff:Red ratios are 1:1, 2:1, and 4:1 from the latest stratum 3 to the earliest 1. Thin burnished G and C wares occur in all lots with similar frequency. The only change is in BP decorative motifs from linear and dot patterns in stratum 3 to figurative animal and geometric patterns (for details see Dyson and Remsen 1989:105–107).

3.16 On the North Flat, the E-D transitional phase ceramic assemblage is from the earliest Buttressed Building 1, stage pre-D3 (see phase D, p. 111).

3.17 A detailed description of the stratigraphy of transitional phase E-D is in Thornton's dissertation, 2009b:77–79.

3.18 Since these vessels lack bases, except for one (Fig. 3.10:3) it was not possible to differentiate pedestal bowl from goblet. Schmidt (1937: pls. XXII–XXIV, XXVI, figs. 64–66) provides an excellent comparanda for these forms. Schmidt places these vessel types in Period "IIA," based on his association of one vessel (H4549) with a IIA burial (ibid., p. 89). According to the new stratified ceramic sequence, however, it is dated slightly later, to phase E-D, contemporary with Schmidt's Period "IIB."

3.19 Vessel is decorated with incised horizontal lines from rim to mid-point.

3.20 Vessel is decorated with raised ridges from rim down to the base.

3.21 Sherd drawings from CF57 deep test at the North Flat are not numbered, but they have letter designations (see Dyson and Remsen 1989: figs. 35, 36)

3.22 Refer to dimensions shown on scaled drawings.

3.23 Schmidt notes the scarcity of vessels with handles in Period IIIC. He mentions only two pitchers, at least one found in a grave context (H2871) and the other (H5235) associated with a horse skull (Schmidt 1937:182, pl. XXXVII). No specific find location for these vessels is given.

3.24 For bottle pitcher with handles, see Schmidt (1937: pl. XLI H5235, H2871) dated to Late Hissar III (IIIC).

3.25 Compare with Schmidt (1937: pl. XXXVI H5215, 1933: pl. CXV H1032) dated to Early Hissar III.

3.26 Ceramic samples from phases B and A are small since there were only 3 lots from the Pinnacle sounding.

3.27 For a larger sample of types from phases B and B-A/A, see Ch. 4 and Appendix 1.

3.28 The inventory of complete vessels and the range of forms constitute a larger assemblage from the early excavations; it should be kept in mind, however, that same or similar vessel forms are found in the 1976 assemblage as those retrieved from the 1931–32 excavations.

4

Burial Stratigraphy: The Main Mound and the North Flat, 1931–32 and 1976

Introduction

A major part of Schmidt's fieldwork involved excavating burials, especially during the first season (1933: pl. CXLVII). Of the more than 1,637 burials recorded during two seasons, Schmidt's statistics are based on 782 burials retrieved in the second season: 144 (Hissar I), 209 (Hissar IIA, IIB), and 429 from (IIIA, IIB, IIIC). Nearly 37% of all burials came from the Main Mound and the North Flat (ca. 600 out of 1,637 burials). The Main Mound concentration includes almost 31% of the total. This may be due in part to the Main Mound being the largest area of excavation, totaling ca. 2400 square meters, or that the Main Mound was in fact selected as a preferred cemetery site for its location situated on higher ground.

In the first season, Schmidt chose to excavate the centrally located high ground on the Main Mound, which, to his good fortune and delight, proved to be the richest area for burials. In the second season, the Main Mound and the North Flat, as well as the South Hill and Treasure Hill, produced a large number of burials. Hissar I burials appeared to be poorly preserved; they were retrieved from small trenches at Painted Pottery Flat (PPF), in the northern extension of the Main Mound, the Red Hill (east of North Flat), and the South Hill. For Hissar II and III larger samples were recorded, 209 and 609 respectively, from the Main Mound, the North Flat, the South Hill, and the Treasure Hill. At this latter location, "well-equipped" burials with alabaster objects were attributed to Hissar IIIC, but they were also mixed with earlier IIB or IIIA deposits of wall remains (see Schmidt 1937:171–175, figs 96–99).[1]

My primary source for the burials was Schmidt's burial sheets recorded in the field. Despite nearly illegible handwriting and unclear stratigraphic information, the sheets provide ample descriptive evidence for burial square, level, position of the deceased, sex, age, and burial gifts.

A. The Burial Site (Map 1)

The Tepe Hissar burial site can be described as several intramural cemeteries where the preferred mortuary practice was simple inhumation of individual or multiple burials. Schmidt writes:

"The dead of all Hissar periods [I–III] were buried in the mound area. We do not know whether any extra-mural burial grounds exist. We doubt it.[2] At any rate, wherever the excavation penetrated below the surface crust of the mound, burials were uncovered. They appeared below the rooms of houses, below open courtyards and lanes, and below the former surface levels of then uninhabited areas. There were graves everywhere" (1937:67).

It appears that there was no special area set aside as a burial site. Schmidt, however, does not overlook the possibility of the existence of an extramural cemetery, though he was not able to find it. The elevated areas appear to be formed by the remains of abandoned buildings reused as burial grounds, as discussed elsewhere (Ch. 2). Consequently, each hillock became a necropolis in the course of its existence for a living community that was not far from it. The raised central area of the Main Mound, however, has the highest density of burials that span the duration of the settlement (Schmidt 1937: figs. 84, 85; see also Fig. 4.1 below). The estimated size of the Main Mound cemetery is about 0.2 hectares, which includes all of the 24 excavated squares (Fig. 4.2, see also Fig. 1.8 in Ch. 1). Burial grounds on the other hillocks are as follows: south of the Burned Building on the North Flat, in squares CF55-57 (Schmidt 1937: figs. 103–104); on the South Hill in squares DF78-79, 88-89, and DG60-70 (ibid., fig. 62); on the Painted Pottery Flat in squares DH34-36, DH43-46 (ibid., p. 24, fig. 22); and on Treasure Hill in squares CH64-65, 74-75, CH85, CH95-96, DH05-06 (ibid., p. 176, figs.100–101).

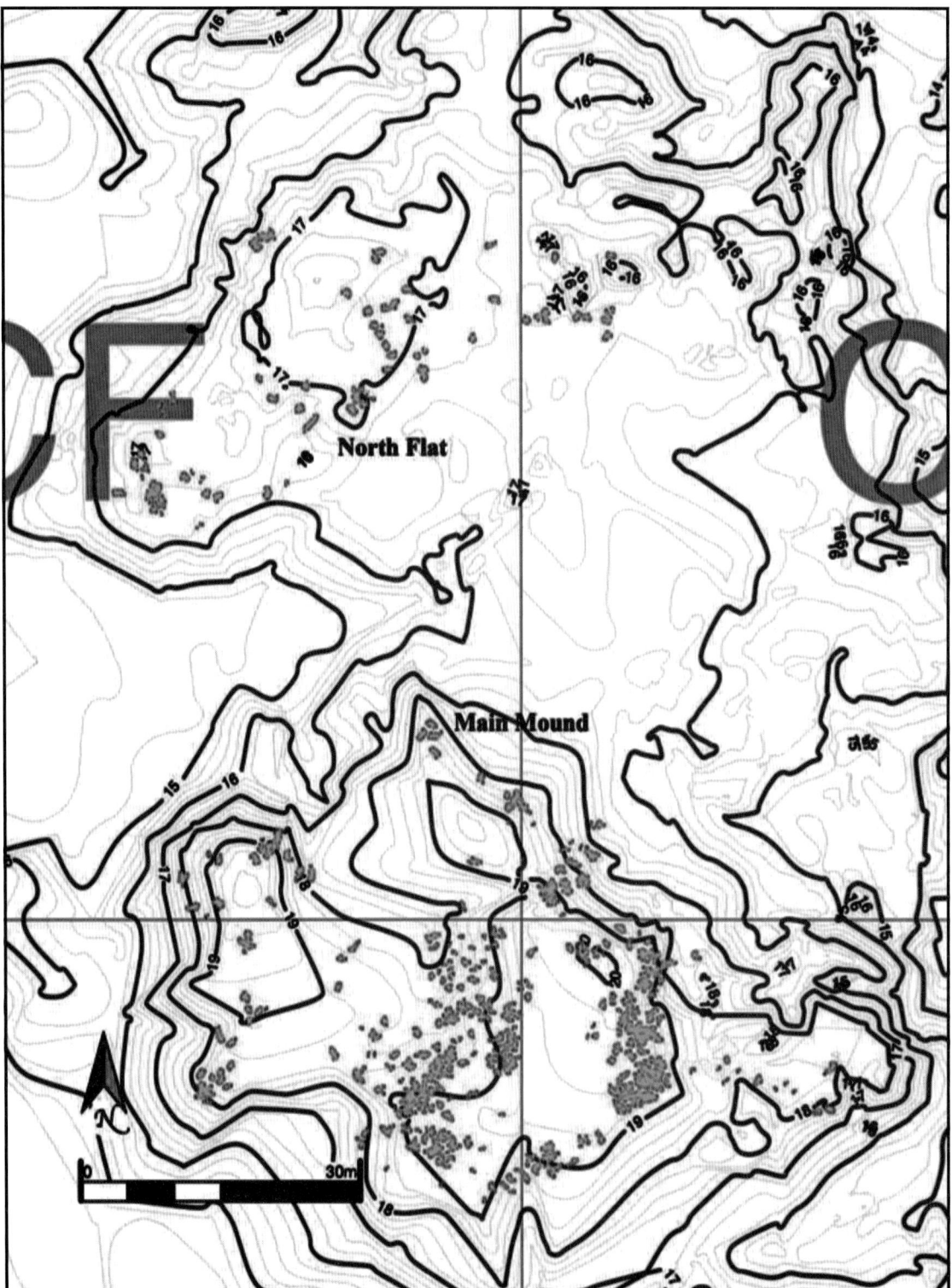

Fig. 4.1 Map of Tepe Hissar with contour lines showing the distribution of burials on the Main Mound and North Flat (Fitts 2008).

Fig. 4.2 Work in the Tepe Hissar necropolis on the Main Mound (Courtesy of Penn Museum).

B. Limitations of the Evidence

Generally speaking, Schmidt's periodization was based on his burial stratigraphy. In his recording system, the burials were assigned to the same "levels" as structures and walls, even though he asserts that the burials were found immediately below the associated surfaces (Schmidt 1937:67). So, his burial stratigraphy is generally *not* in accord with the actual building phases in which they occurred. In fact, a close examination of 1931–32 sections and the results of the 1976 field study (see Ch. 2), make it clear that, in most cases, the burials were dug *into structures* from above following each episode of abandonment of the settlement. Therefore, in most instances, the burials are later than the structures with which they are associated. Indeed, at this time, the question of the length of time between abandonment and rebuilding is still open to speculation.

Another limitation is related to sampling. Schmidt's analysis is derived from burials uncovered only during the 1932 season. Of the 1,637 burials he recorded, he analyzed 40% (664) for statistical purposes, from *all* excavated areas (144 burials are attributed to Hissar I, 91 to Hissar II, and 429 to Hissar III) (Schmidt 1937:301–302), but only 100 burials (ca. 6%) were published in detail from all excavated areas in his second monograph (Schmidt 1937), which represents a considerably small number in proportion to the total excavated.

Method of Reconstructing Sections

In order to revise and reconstruct Schmidt's burial stratigraphy, multiple sources of archival data were used. Archival documents on the location of burials, heights and depths of walls, floor depths, and "Levels" (1–4) were examined, as well as surveyor's sketch plans with depth notations. Schmidt's sections had limited usefulness,[3] as depths of walls or floors were not indicated on them. Furthermore, the burials were lumped together in such close proximity that their horizontal and vertical positions were blurred. The plans were equally problematic. Thus, the process of reconstructing the section for each square was detailed and time-consuming; it involved tracing the burials to the strata from which they originated (where possible) and pinpointing their relative position to structures. Also, the section for each square was reconstructed separately, as depths of building stages shown by meter-level varied for each square because of topographic differences. For example, "Level 1" was within 1.0–1.5 m in square DF09, while in the adjoining square DF19, "Level 1" was within 0.50–2.0 m, a difference of 0.5–1.0 meters.

Having confirmed that Schmidt's architect had taken his sections in east-west direction from the mid-point of each of the 10 x 10m squares, I plotted the estimated position of the burials on schematic sections in relation to building levels for each square excavated on the Main Mound and the North Flat. The placement of the burials utilizes Schmidt's designated meter-levels as well as the available "plot records" for their *estimated* horizontal position. These reconstructed sections are the basis for interpreting Schmidt's burial stratigraphy. They show (a) the relative positioning of burials at different depths and (b) the relation of burials to floors and structural remains. This revised framework was then compared and correlated with the 1976 sequence of building stages from the Main Mound, specifically with Buildings 1, 2, and 3 in squares DF09, DF19, DG00, DG10, DG01, DG11, and CG90 (see Table 4.1).[4] The North Flat burials and structures were processed similarly in relation to the Burned Building, which was also the focus of 1976 campaign.

After unraveling the position of the burials from Schmidt's excavations, they were placed in the reconstructed section of each square in stratigraphic relation to the building remains such that the burials are *dated* according to the stratigraphic building stages and correlated with the new ceramic chronology. Significant chronological corrections were accomplished by the 1976 campaign as Schmidt's Period III on the Main Mound was amended to Period II or transitional between Periods II and III and his Periods IIA/IIB to the earlier Period IC/IIA. These corrections are supported, in most cases, by the new ceramic chronology and radiocarbon dates (see Ch. 2, Table 2.2).

In addition to the temporal distribution of the dated burials, the latter are plotted horizontally for spatial distribution on GIS maps, which are discussed in Ch. 5. Finally, the combined evidence reveals patterns of settlement use alternating between occupational and burial functions on the Main Mound and the North Flat.

Tables 4.1 and 4.2, showing the dated burials from the Main Mound and the North Flat, follow the discussion of each area.

C. The Archaeological Context

This section presents a reconstruction of 1931–32 burial stratigraphy correlated with the 1976 stratigraphy: Main Mound Buildings 1, 2, 3 and the North Flat, including the Burned Building (BB). The burials are presented in schematic sections based on the 1976 building "stages" in relation to Schmidt's "Levels" (below the 00 point). Hence we are able to present a corrected stratigraphic sequence and re-dating of the burial assemblages associated with the occupational sequence. The distribution of artifacts in the burials and their position in relation to the deceased are, in part, derived from Schmidt's publications, but more detailed data is compiled from his archival burial sheets.

The revised burial stratigraphy starts with a correlation of Schmidt's "Levels" with 1976 stages, as the latter is stratigraphically reliable. It must be kept in mind that this correlation is based on the 1976 analysis of building stages and supported by the ceramic chronology. Where possible, the architectural features recorded by Schmidt in each square on the Main Mound are correlated with Buildings 1, 2, or 3 and architectural features from the North Flat squares were associated with the Burned Building. These include: Main Mound, correlated squares DF09, DG00, DG01, CG90 and North Flat, correlated squares CF37-38, CF47-48, CF57.

Burials from both areas were dated using combined evidence from the dated ceramics and small finds and stratigraphic approximations based on Schmidt's sections. Those burials in the Main Mound squares that were neither associated with Buildings 1–3, nor examined in 1976, are dated based upon their artifacts, architectural features, and Schmidt's approximate "Levels". The uncorrelated squares include: Main Mound CF79, CF88-89 and CF99, DF08, DF18-19, DG10, DG11, DF29 and North Flat CF55.

The correlated and uncorrelated squares, when viewed together, comprise the "core" of both the Main Mound and the North Flat and should help future scholars to decipher Schmidt's field notes in other areas of the site.

For a more detailed reference and comparison with the 1976 ceramic assemblages, ceramics from the 1931–32 burials are organized in pottery charts in Appendix 1.

D. The Main Mound

On the Main Mound (see Figure 2.5 in Ch. 2, after Howard 1989a, fig.1), the majority of Buildings 1, 2, and 3 lie within squares DF09, DG00 and DG01. A single room /1/ in square CG90 ("the kitchen") was not connected to these buildings, but was also included in the 1976 correlations. Chapter 2 provides a more in-depth discussion of the 1976 restudy of these buildings not repeated here. The reader is reminded, however, that the walls of Building 1, extant in 1976, were almost one meter lower than the walls of Buildings 2 and 3 and likely date to the earlier E-D transitional phase (as defined in Ch. 3). A later Building 1 that was contemporary with Buildings 2 and 3 (i.e., phase D) and which was built using the E-D transitional phase walls as foundations, was fully excavated by Schmidt and removed. Thus, this volume uses the terms "Building 1 (upper)" and "Building 1 (lower)" to differentiate these two phases.

D.1 Building 1 (upper and lower): Square DF09

Square DF09 encloses most of Building 1 (upper and lower) and the northwestern part of Building 2 (see Fig. 2.11 this volume).[5] According to Schmidt's framework, "Level 1" burials are found directly below the existing mound surface, between 0.70–2.4 m, and they are intermixed with wall remains. After examining Schmidt's sections and the surveyor's notebook, it is clear that the topmost burials were dug from *above* the current surface, probably from a later occupational level that had been demolished prior to the 1931–32 excavations. Below "Level 1," Schmidt designated a transitional level "between Levels 2-1." In this study, the latter is divided between "Level 1" or "Level 2" as there is no stratigraphic or artifactual evidence to support his transitional level.

Stratigraphy and Architecture

In DF09, no architecture was found higher than at 2.0 m depth (Schmidt's "Level 1"). As mentioned above, Building 1 (upper) was built using the walls of Building 1 (lower) as foundations (see Howard 1989a: fig.2). The reconstructed sections of individual squares *with* the burials as correlated with the 1976 stratified building stages[6] are shown in Section 4.1.

The floor of Building 2, seen on the eastern side of the section (under SE wall of Building 1 at ~3.5 m depth), is most likely the floor of building stage D3 (early phase D), based upon the depth of the early phase D floor in Building 2 (see below). The floor at about 3.0 m depth associated with the base of unspecified walls of Level 2 in the west of the section probably correlates to the upper floor of stage D (phase D2-D1). Thus, Schmidt's "Level 2" can be associated with ceramic phase D, which is equivalent to Building 1 (upper).

The earlier floor of Building 1 shown in the section as "L.3 floor" at ~3.8 m depth is most likely a later floor level of the E-D phase (or lower Building 1). Schmidt's "W1–4," "W8," and "W10" likely represent walls of an earlier building stage of the same transitional phase E-D.[7]

Below the "Level 3" floor, Schmidt recorded several walls (W 5, 9, 13, 14, 17) in his deep sounding; these he called "Level 4." Such walls likely date to ceramic phases F through E, as they are of similar depth to the various walls and architectural stages found by Howard and Pigott in the 1976 deep sounding (see Ch. 2, Figs. 2.3, 2.4). In DF09, there are three major burial episodes: "Level 1," between "Levels 2 and 3," and below "Level 3."

Burials

Of the 56 burials that Schmidt found in square DF09, only 28 had ceramics that could be correlated with the 1976 sherds to reconstruct the ceramic phasing presented in Ch. 3 (for the pottery chart from 1931–32 burials, see Section 4.1a in Appendix 1).[8] In "Level 1," the graves are randomly distributed over the square. Burials x1, x2, and x5 contain ceramics of phases B through A (late Hissar III). The ceramic assemblage consists of largely grey burnished wares, mainly Period III forms, including a pattern burnished canteen and a trough-spouted jar (a continuing form from Period II).

One of the notable burials in this group is x1, which Schmidt named the "second warrior" (Schmidt 1933:440, pl. CXLVII). The burial was located within "Level 1" at the corner of an unspecified wall. The individual was buried with artifacts that probably denote his status (Fig. 4.3): a macehead (Schmidt 1937: pl. LII H771); a cache of stone arrowheads (chalcedony, flint, etc.); copper objects, a spearhead, and several bidents (similar to that found with the "first warrior" in square DF19 x2); miniature tokens; and painted animal figurines carved of alabaster, among them, several birds, a tiger, a bear, and a horse (see Ch. 5 for a detailed description of the burial).

Continuing with burials in square DF09, x6, x9, x24, and x25 in "Level 1" contain ceramic types from phases D-C through B (Early Hissar III through Mid-Hissar III). These burials are located in the southwestern part of the square. The ceramic assemblage is clearly mixed, including mainly grey burnished wares, trough-spouted jar, bell-shaped and wide rim carinated beakers, and a bottle (with short neck). Many of these appear first in the early D-C transitional phase (Early Hissar III).

The DF09 burials from below "Level 1" can be subdivided into three clusters. Burials DF09 x15, x17, x23, x46, and x48 appear to be later than the other burials in this group, with ceramic assemblages attributed to phases D through C (grey burnished bell-shaped beaker, globular pitcher, wide rim carinated beaker). Burials x13, x29–31, x33, x35–36, x41, x42, x42a, x43, x45 and x54 contain earlier ceramics of phases E through D (Early Mid-Hissar II). The assemblage is largely wheelmade, monochrome, burnished grey wares of open and closed forms, cups and

172 THE NEW CHRONOLOGY OF THE BRONZE AGE SETTLEMENT OF TEPE HISSAR, IRAN

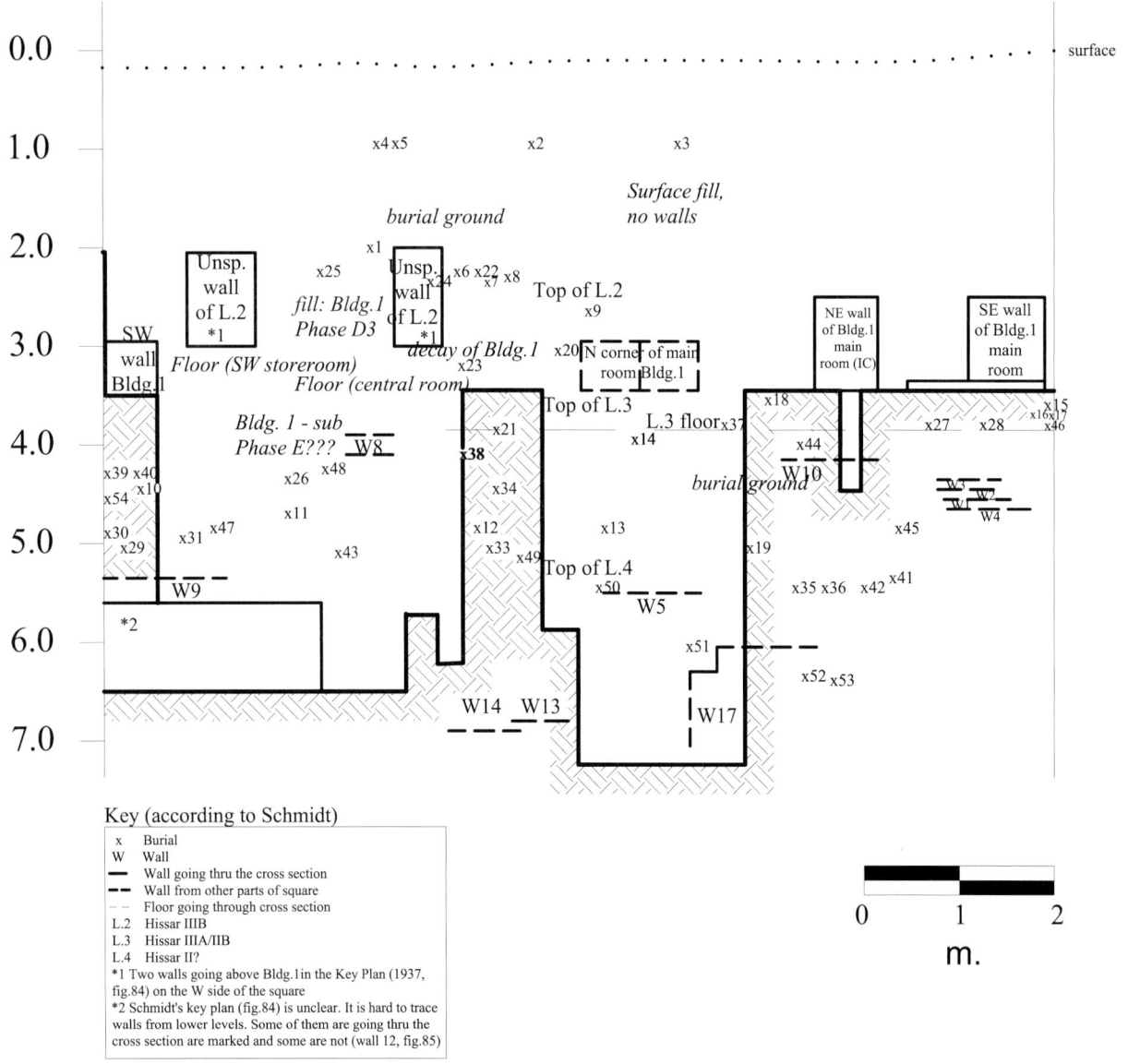

Section 4.1

BURIAL STRATIGRAPHY

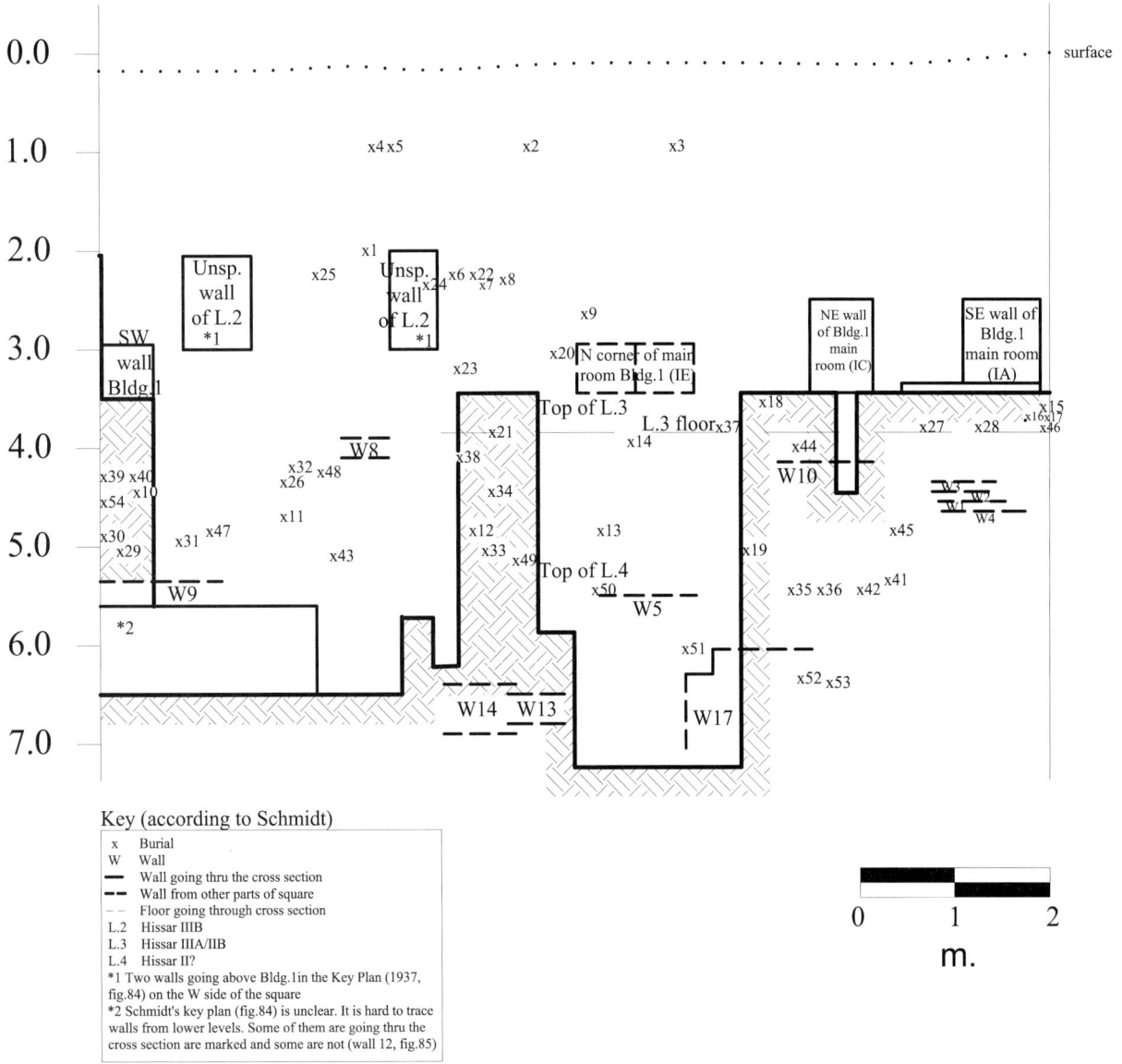

Section 4.2

Fig. 4.3 Burial x1 from DF09 termed "Warrior II," notable for his more elaborate burial offerings: a macehead, a cache of stone arrowheads, several bidents, miniature tokens, and painted animal figurines (Courtesy of Penn Museum).

bowls, with a few handmade vessels with chaff temper and linear and wavy designs rendered in dark brown on buff background (e.g., cup with pointed base, H3902) (Schmidt 1937: pl. XXIV).

Only one burial, x52 (Fig. 4.4), can be firmly assigned to ceramic phase F-E (Late Hissar I-Early Hissar II); it contains a grey burnished, wheelmade, pedestal bowl that has a unique decorative pattern of two raised ridges on its base (H5035; see pottery chart). Burials x51 and x53 have no ceramics, but they could also be attributed to the same phase or even an earlier one on evidence of their stratigraphic position.

D.2 Building 2

Although the majority of Building 2 is contained in DG10, there were very few burials found in that square, making relative dating of the levels difficult. Instead, the section from DG00 shows Dyson's notes from 1976, as well as Schmidt's 22 burials for comparison.

Stratigraphy and Architecture

In 1976, Dyson divided Building 2 into three building stages. He assigned the construction stage D3 to the earliest sub-phase which also had the buttressed wall construction (Dyson and Remsen 1989:75).

A slightly later renovation stage was labeled "Building 2a" and was assigned to stage D3-D2 (early phase D). For the latest phase of Building 2, when the buttress niches had been bricked up to allow for reconstruction of the main structure (Dyson and Remsen 1989:77), Dyson called this "Building 2_1" and assigned it to stage D2-D1 (late phase D).

Under Dyson's reconstruction, Building 2_1 went from 1.8–2.5 m deep in Schmidt's section, while Buildings 2/2a went from the floor of Building 2_1 (at 2.5 m depth, preserved on the east side of Schmidt's section) down to the lower floor located between 3.2 and 3.45 m depth (the surface seen on Schmidt's section associated with the walls of S12 and S13). This followed Schmidt in assigning all

Fig. 4.4 Burial x52 from DF09, which is the only one from this square firmly dated to ceramic phase F-E (late Hissar I to Early Hissar II) (Courtesy of Penn Museum).

sub-phases of Building 2 to one level ("Level 2").

There are two problems with this reconstruction. Most of the stratigraphic building stages (correlating with a single ceramic "phase") were rarely more than 80–100 cm in depth, including phase/stage D as seen in the CG90 Pinnacle baulk just north of Building 2 (lots 17–14). Thus, the idea of stage/phase D straddling almost 1.7 meters (from 1.8–3.45 m) seems unlikely. Second, the finds from these two major building stages (i.e., 2/2a and 2_1) are distinct and somewhat diagnostic. Near or on the floor of Building 2_1, Schmidt found a buff painted conical cup with pointed base (H56). This vessel type occurs first in E-D phase and continues into phases D and D-C transitional phase. Additionally, an imported Proto-Elamite cylinder seal (H116) is documented in the fill of Building 2 (Dyson and Remsen 1989:77).[9] Both suggest a date in the Late Hissar II Period (ca. 3050–2750 BC) or the transitional phase D-C. In contrast, the finds of Buildings 2/2a were of phase D, such as the miniature bowl (H203) and miniature jar (H205)—both discarded. These date earlier, to the Mid-Hissar II Period (ca. 3350–3100 BC).

It should be the noted that Dyson and Howard did not recognize the transitional phase D-C as a distinct building stage, given that it continues rather seamlessly from stage/phase D (e.g., in the burned rooms on the North Flat in CF58 and in the CG90 Pinnacle lots 14–10). Similarly, they did not recognize the transitional phase E-D underneath the phase D structures. However, two of the objects found below the lower floor of Building 2 (between 3.45–3.65 m depth) were a painted cup with "alternating tongue" motif (H3929) and a stemmed grey ware bowl (H3925). Both could be assigned to the mid-fourth millennium BC, either the transitional phase E-D or early phase D3. Both vessels are typical of the ceramics seen in the upper levels of Howard's test trench in CG90 (/10/ lot 28), which were directly underneath the stage D3 surface.

Following the final abandonment of Building 2_1, the fill was used as a cemetery, particularly on the eastern side of the square, where the burials were deposited from the top of Schmidt's "Level 2." There was only one more architectural stage in Schmidt's "Level 1," although the exact date of these walls is difficult to surmise.

Burials

Of the 22 burials in square DG00, only 11 contained datable ceramics (for the pottery chart, see Section 4.3a in Appendix 1). Burials x1, x4, and x5 contained ceramics of phases B through A (Hissar IIIC): a pattern burnished canteen (H610) (cf. Schmidt 1933: pl. CXIII H537), a beak-spouted jar (H501), and a pear shaped bottle (H558). It is also worth noting that another beak-spouted vessel was found in the fill at a lower level (1.75 m depth) associated with black-on-buff painted cups and bowls of the transitional phase D-C, although that may have been retrieved from a later burial not found by Schmidt.

Burials x6, x10, x19, and x22 had ceramic assemblages dated to phases D through C or slightly later, dating to the late fourth millennium BC. Burials x14 and x16 (Fig. 4.5), found dug into the upper fill of the stage D structures, had ceramics typical of the transitional phase D-C, particularly the tulip-shaped beaker and carinated jar that could be dated to the early third millennium BC. These two vessel types are long-lived, as they continue into phase B.

E.3 Building 3: Square DG01

Stratigraphy and Architecture

Building 3 lies within squares DG00, DG01, DG10, and DG11, with DG01 containing the majority of the structure. Dyson notes that "the structure went through three stages: the original building (stage 3), a fire and restoration (stage 3a), and a total reconstruction (stage 3_1)" (Dyson and Remsen 1989:79–81). He dated the building to stages D3-D2 and D2-D1, which correspond to ceramic phase D. The last reconstruction stage, post-D, that correlates with the transitional phase D-C, is approximately dated to ca. 3100–2900 BC. The building stage D walls are shown in the section as "NW wall of Main Room Bldg. 3," and "NE wall of Main Room, Bldg. 3," and "SE wall of store room, Building 3," where "Main Room" is Howard's area /16/ and "store room" is Howard's /19/.

The surface seen in Schmidt's section (below) on the eastern-most and western-most side of the square at ~2.5 m depth likely correlates with the transitional phase D-C as seen in DG00. The "floor of (bldg. 3_1)," noted by Dyson at 2.0 meters, is probably a later floor of the transitional phase D-C. The deeper surface seen between the "NE wall of the main room of Bldg. 3" and the "SE wall of store room Bldg. 3" at ~3.0 m depth likely correlates with the stage D3 floor. The higher floor level marked in the section from Dyson's notes ("floor [bldg. 3/3a]") at ~3.0 m depth probably relates to a later stage at the very end of phase D (stage D2-D1) as seen in DG00.

Above this surface (Schmidt's "Level 2"), other structures were built, possibly dating to the Late Hissar III Period (building stage B-A/A; Schmidt's "Level 1"). Unfortunately, Schmidt records no ceramics associated with these "Level 1 walls," but given their stratigraphic position

BURIAL STRATIGRAPHY

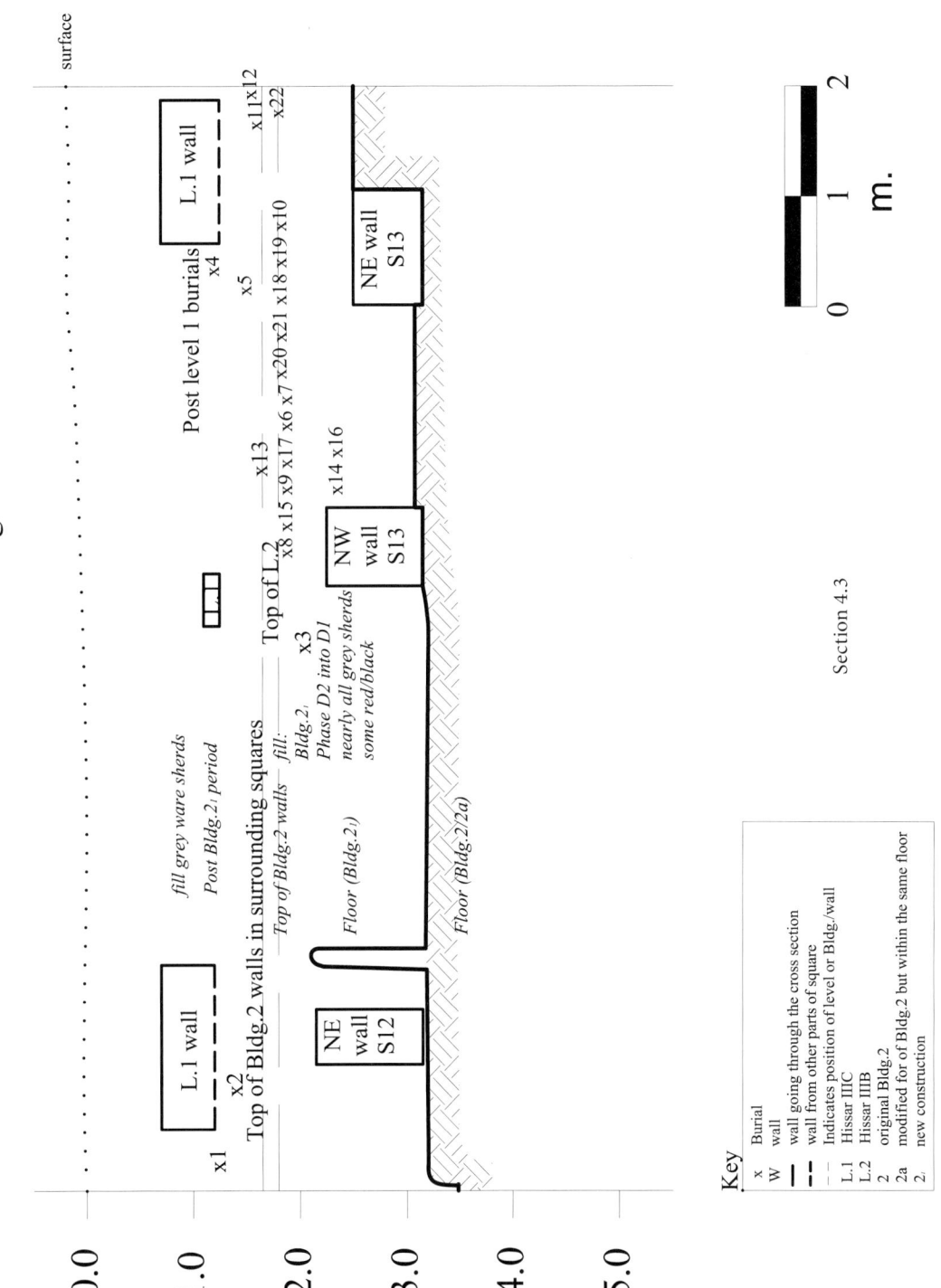

Section 4.3

Fig. 4.5 Burials x14 and x16 from square DG00 were found with ceramics associated with the transitional phase D-C (Courtesy of Penn Museum).

(between 0.5–1.5 m depth) and relation to other "Level 1" structures in DG00, we can hypothesize that the upper architectural stage belongs to ceramic phase B (Hissar IIIB). Given the strong evidence for a late phase B cemetery located in this square between the two building levels (see below), the "Level1 walls" may in fact date to the end of phase B or a transition to phase A.

Burials

Of the 44 burials recorded by Schmidt in DG01, only 14 contained ceramics that could be used for relative dating (for the pottery chart, see Section 4.4a in Appendix 1): two from phases B or B-A/A, mid- to late third millennium BC (x1, x6, x9, x15, x16, x17, x18, x21, x22, x38, x39, x41). The evidence for the strong similarity in ceramic types found in these graves (pear shaped bottles, short necked globular bottle, carinated jar, and wide rim beaker in grey burnished monochrome wares) points to the group burials as being contemporary with the rest of the assemblage. Only two vessels—a trough-spouted jar from burial x32, and a grey burnished beaker with incised zigzag decoration from burial x36—could be dated to late phase D or the transitional phase D-C. Four individuals (x1, x6, x9, x18) formed a group burial. They were found concentrated on the floor and in the fill of Building 3_1.

D.4 CG90 (Room /1/, Areas /4/ and /6/)

Stratigraphy and Architecture

For the area north of Buildings 1–3, Howard (1989a:59) noted, "the earliest horizontally exposed standing architecture present in this area was that in square CG90, at the base of baulks 1 and [Pinnacle baulk]. This architecture corresponds to [stage] D3." She describes room /1/ as a "kitchen" surrounded by walls 1, 4, and 5 on the 1976 plan (after Howard 1989: fig. 1). Howard's "wall 1" (i.e., the SW wall of /1/) is equivalent to Schmidt's "w2" in the section, while his "w3" correlates to the "bench" abutting the SW wall of /1/. Howard's "wall 5" is most likely represented by the area underneath w*2, which represents the small wall extending northward

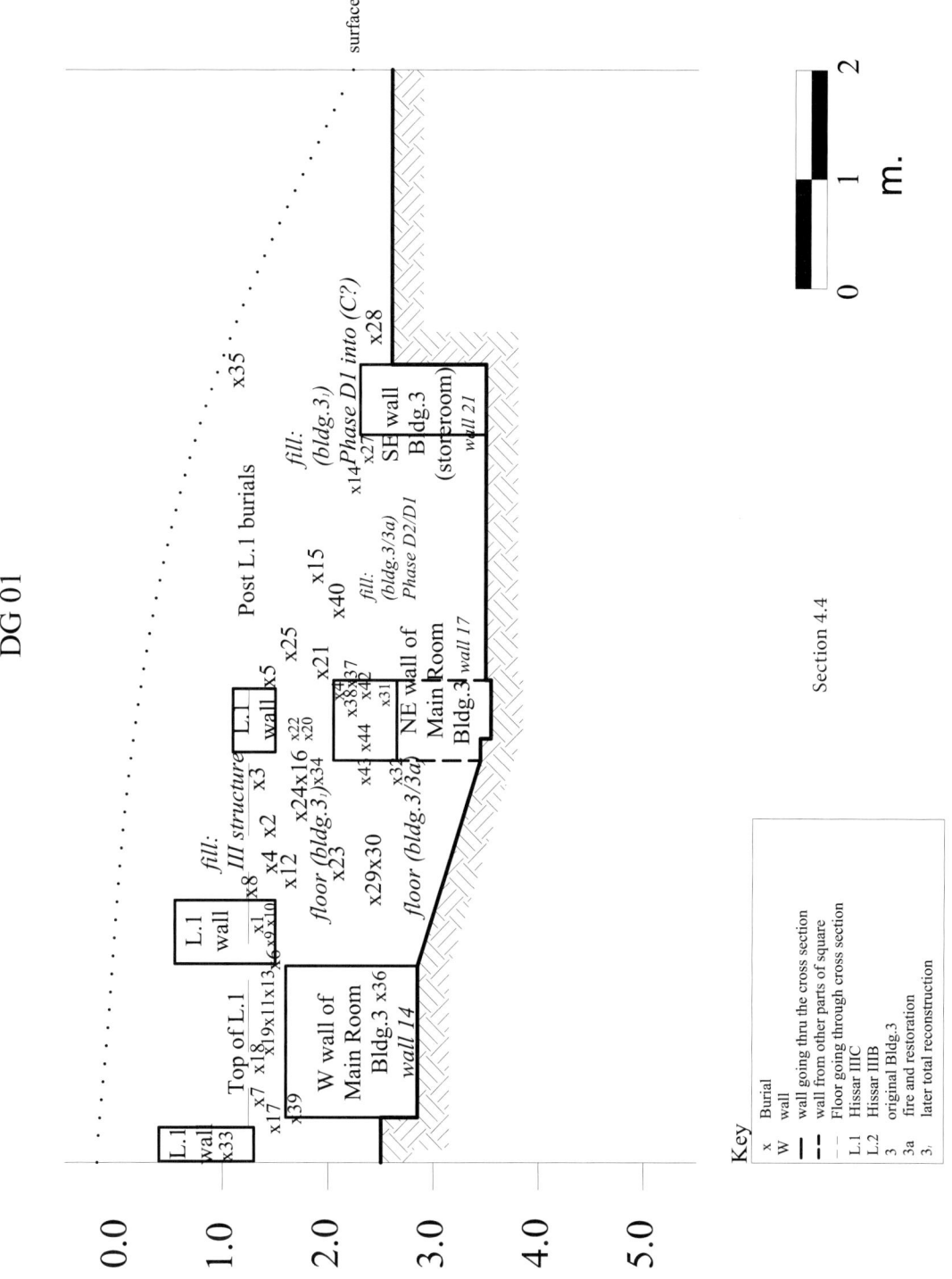

from the west corner of area /1/ in Schmidt's plan (see square CG90 on Schmidt 1937: fig. 84 and Fig. 2.11 this volume).

Howard's "wall 43" between /4/ and /5/ is represented by the "*1" wall in Schmidt's section, while her "wall 42" is depicted as the "*3" wall in the western side of Schmidt's section. This latter wall represents a possible "Level 1" wall as seen in DG00 and DG01, both of which likely correlate to building stage B-A/A and ceramic phase B (Hissar IIIB). It is unclear what Schmidt's "w1" represents.

The lower surface seen in the east side of Schmidt's section that correlates with the stage D3 floor of room /1/. Ceramic phase D likely includes all walls between 2.0 and 3.0 m depth. Thus, walls 41 and 43 (on section, "*1" and "*2") probably represent later additions to the stage D3 kitchen, but are still within phase D, although wall 41/*1 may be an unrecognized transitional phase D-C structure based on its depth. Following the abandonment of these structures, areas /4/ and /6/ were used as a burial ground in the transitional phase D-C (see below) before the much later construction of the stage B-A/A structure indicated by wall 42 (*3).

Burials

Altogether there were 24 burials concentrated in areas /4/ and /6/, of which 16 contained diagnostic ceramic vessels (for pottery chart, see Section 4.6a in Appendix 1) attributed to different periods (x1, x3, x7–10, x13–16, x18–19, x20, x22, x23, and x25). Burial x1 contained a grey pattern burnished canteen (H5090), which is clearly dated to ceramic phases B through A (Hissar IIIC). Burials x9, x10, and x23 (Fig. 4.6) are possibly from phases C through B or B in the first half of the third millennium BC. The rest of the burials are of the transitional phase D-C. In Burial x9, there is a unique teapot (H5094 unpublished) with tube spout, a rare form in all of the Hissar III assemblage; it is grey burnished and handmade (Fig. 4.7). Schmidt describes it as grey bottle pitcher with elevated tube spout (Schmidt 1937:180–182). It corresponds closely to another vessel (ibid., pl. XLI H4296) that has pattern burnished herringbone and zigzag decoration. Both vessels are erroneously dated to Period IIIC by Schmidt.

Classic ceramic indicators of the transitional phase D-C burials include the trough-spouted jar in burial x19 (H5105); wide rim beakers in x8 (H4122) and x14 (H5097); and two varieties of bottles in x14, x15, and x25 respectively, (pear shape and carinated H5096, H5099 and H5108 [with drilled repair holes]). The buff painted cup with vertical bands in x22 (H4125) is identical to those found by Dyson in the transitional phase D-C burned rooms on the North Flat (Dyson and Remsen 1989:102, fig.31–3). An identical vessel is dated to Period IIA (i.e., phase E) by Schmidt (1937: pl. XXXVI H4755).

The inventory of objects found in Schmidt's late "fill" and "refuse" levels can be assigned to Periods IIIB and IIIC. They include a different set of artifacts than those in the earlier building stages D and D-C (Period II, early Period III). They comprise artifacts in metal and semi-precious beads characteristic of IIIB/C burial objects; some depict symbols such as a copper female figurine (well modeled), copper wands, several copper pins (one with double scroll), alabaster and serpentine(?) beads, and "hematite ore" (H3147). These artifacts might have been retrieved from the stage B-A/A structure as indicated by wall 42 (*3) in section 4. The artifact inventory from the D3-D1 stages in CG90 areas /1/, /4/, and /6/ largely contain tools (polishing and grinding stones, spindle whorl, bone awl, flint blades, alabaster, and jar seal fragments), as well as a cache of animal figurines. Of note for its early date (Period II D3 stage) is a finely crafted silver spindle whorl (N40) from area /6/.

To summarize, it appears that the area including squares DF09, DG00, DG01, and CG90 served as a small burial ground during mid- to end of the fourth millennium BC. The analysis of the correlated burial data from the Main Mound Buildings 1, 2, and 3 reveals that from stages F and F-E (Late Hissar I) through Late Hissar II Early III (stage D-C), multiple burial episodes alternated with settlements during 3600–3000 BC. The latest burials from Early to Late Hissar III are found mainly in a mixed fill associated with Schmidt's "Level 1" and above it.

If we consider the possible existence of early burials from unexcavated sections of DF09, (i.e., below phase F) the chronology of the cemetery would then be extended to early fifth millennium BC.

We now turn to the rest of the Main Mound squares where more burials were recorded by Schmidt. Since, in 1976, there were no excavations/assessments done in these areas, the sections are not correlated with the 1976 stratigraphy. Instead, the author's revised sections of Schmidt's burial stratigraphy are presented using his meter-depths below the 00 point and his "levels" as benchmarks to place the burials relative to burial groups. The burial ceramics are then dated according to the ceramic chronology presented in Chapter 3.

E. 1931–32 Burial Squares, uncorrelated with the 1976 sequence

Main Mound squares DF08, DF18–19, DG10, DG11, DF29–DG20, CF88–89, and CF99.

Section 4.5

Section of Schmidt's Burial Stratigraphy
(reconstructed by Salzmann)

CG 90

Section 4.6

Key (according to Schmidt)

- x   Burial
- W   wall
- —   wall going through the cross section
- – – wall from other parts of square
- *1   Between L.1 and L.2
- *2   Unspecified wall of L.2 going S of burials
- *3   wall of L.1 in SW of square

Fig. 4.6 Burial x23 from square CG90 that may date to phases C through B or B in the first half of the third millennium BC (Courtesy of Penn Museum).

Fig. 4.7 Burial x9 from square CG90, found with a unique teapot (H5094 unpublished) with tube spout (Courtesy of Penn Museum).

E.1 DF08

Stratigraphy and Architecture

The westernmost part of Building 1 is visible on the east side of the plan of DF08, although Schmidt does not show this in the section. Instead, he shows the walls in the center of the square that were between 0.5–2.0 m deep. The "L.1 wall," around 0.5–1.0 m in depth, most likely corresponds to the "L.1" walls in DG00 and DG01 (i.e., building stage B through A). The wall marked "L.2" in the section of DF08 is probably the top of a wall emerging from the floor of the square, which would suggest that it is most likely equivalent to the upper Building 1 (i.e., building stage D). The wall "between L.2 and 1" may be one of the elusive transitional phase D-C walls.

Burials

Altogether there are three burials, of which only x1 contained a datable ceramic item (for pottery chart, see Section 4.7a in Appendix 1), a classic phase B through A (late Hissar III) grey canteen (H484) with "lateral string handles" and patterned burnishing (cf. a similar vessel, H537, in DF09 x2).

Schmidt refers to the deceased person in burial x1 as "the priest," whose mortuary gifts comprise one of the richest Main Mound burials (see Ch. 5): weapons/tools, alabaster objects, finely crafted silver and copper objects, vessels, a silver diadem, and female figurines (Fig. 4.8). Two copper stamp seals (Schmidt 1937: pl. CXXX H458, H459) cut with animal figures, and a copper wand terminating with three human figures (ibid., fig.117 H463) were also associated with this burial. According to Bennett (1989:129), the seals can be assigned to Period III, which supports its Late Hissar III date.

E.2 DG10-DG11: South of Buildings 2 and 3

Stratigraphy and Architecture

The area of DG10-11 can be partially correlated due to the presence of the southwest corner of Building 2 in

Fig. 4.8 Burial x1, "the priest" from DF08, one of the richest Main Mound burial assemblages, with: weapons/tools, alabaster objects, finely crafted silver and copper objects, vessels, a silver diadem, and female figurines (Courtesy of Penn Museum).

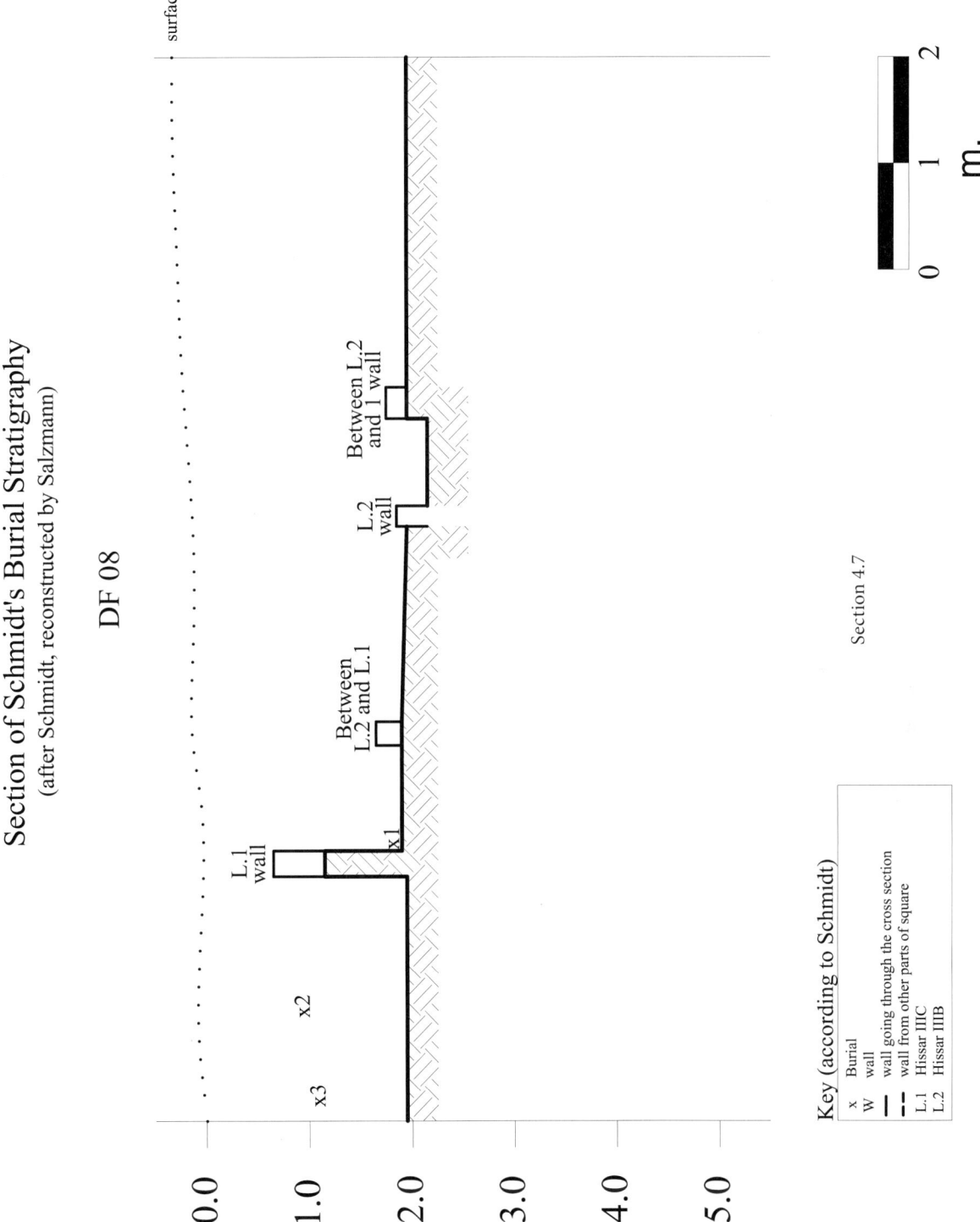

Section 4.7

the DG10 section (marked "L.2 wall" on west side). This wall, which straddles almost two meters, likely documents both the upper "Building 2_1" of the transitional phase D-C (discussed above) and the lower "Building 2/2a" of phase D. Schmidt's indication on the DG10 section of "Top of L.2" at around 1.90 m depth probably signifies the floor between 1976 stages D and D-C; the ceramics found in the fill at around this depth in DG11 (H3999–H4002) are of the transitional phase D-C.

Below the stage D walls in DG10, Schmidt came down onto the tops of earlier walls (marked "*1" in Schmidt's section) of either stage E or E-D. Above the stage D walls are a number of thick but poorly-defined walls that appear only in DG11 as "L.1" walls. These walls sit directly on top of the stage D walls in some cases, suggesting either that they are from the transitional phase D-C or, more likely, that later walls (of phase B?) used the earlier walls as foundations after significant clearing (as under the Burned Building on the North Flat, see below). Given the significant cluster of phase B burials on the western side of DG11 (see below), it is possible that these "L.1" walls date to stage/phase B, as they seem to in DG00 and DG01.

DG10 Burials

Schmidt recorded eight burials from square DG10 (for pottery chart, see Section 4.8a in Appendix 1); of these, only three were datable (x3, x6, and x7). The vast majority clustered on the west side of DG11 where 80 burials were recorded.

In DG10 x3, a grey unburnished tripod container (see Schmidt 1933: pl. CXVI H59) and dark burnished conical bowl are found with two alabaster bowls (ibid., pls. CXXXIX, CXL, CXLI H57, H58). The pottery is dated to phase B through A. The two burials, x6 and x7, contain a buff painted small bowl with linear bands from rim (H611) and a small grey beaker (H557). Both of these vessel types endure from, early phase D to transitional phase D-C.

DG11 Burials

Schmidt recorded 80 burials, but not all are shown on his cross section. Only 19 of the burials contain datable ceramics (for pottery chart, see Section 4.9a in Appendix 1). The largest concentration of burials was just south of the storeroom, area /18/ of Building 3 (see square DG11 on Schmidt 1937: fig. 84 and Figure 2.11 this volume) (x1–9; x10, x11, x13–16, x54, x56, x58–62, x67), as well as the storeroom which Schmidt called a "burial room" (x12, x17–26, x32–34, x36–38, x40, x41 x43, x44, x46, x47, x52, x63–66, x68–75, x77–80).

Two ceramic assemblages from the above mentioned burials are from Schmidt's "Level 1" and "Level 2"; they are typologically indistinguishable. In the revised ceramic sequence, they are dated to transitional phase D-C (Late Hissar II–Early III). The datable ceramic types in grey burnished ware are beakers: bell-shaped, wide rimmed, and tulip-shape, in x9 (H3944), x17 (H3950), x36 (H3970), x48 (H3971), x52 (H3980), x54 (H3983), and x68 (H3991); globular and pear shape bottles in x33 (H3969), x48 (3973), and x74 (H3994); carinated jar in x5 (H3943) and x66 (H3989); and trough-spouted jar in x24, x25 (H3963) and in x20 (H3956—with three pairs of repair holes).

The later vessel types in this assemblage, globular and oblong bottle, are dated to ceramic phase B and are associated with five burials: x16 (H3946—repair hole at neck), x18, x32 (H3968—with "metal" ridge at neck base), and x62 (H398—herringbone pattern burnish).

The vessels that Schmidt refers to as "surviving" types, phase E-D from early fourth millennium BC through the early third millennium BC are: buff painted miniature cup with vertical bands, in x21 (H3990) and a similar cup in x47 (3960), but in coarse ware. They continue into phases D and D-C (see above DG10 burial x6).

E.3 DF29 and DG20: South of Building 2

Stratigraphy and Architecture

Squares DF29 and DG20 seem to have a sequence similar to that of the "Burned Building" squares on the North Flat (see below). That is, a well-constructed building likely associated with stage B ("W1" "W2" "W3" and "W4" in the plan and section for DG20), with somewhat undefined walls of stage A overlying them ("L.1 walls" in the sections of both DF29 and DG20). Beneath the possible stage B level, there are a number of disassociated walls "between L.2 and 1" in DF29 and DG20; also, "unspecified wall of L.1" in DG20, at ca. 1.5m depth that are likely related to the transitional phase D-C or late phase D.

DG20 Burials

There are 21 burials, of which 7 contain datable ceramic vessels (for pottery chart, see Section 4.11a in Appendix 1). A cluster of burials (x6, x9, x18, x19, and x21) in the center of DG20 underneath the well-constructed possible stage B structure contains pear shaped bottles and bell beakers, both of which are long-lived vessel forms from transitional phase D-C and continue into phase C through B. In this context, they most likely date to the transitional phase D-C.

BURIAL STRATIGRAPHY

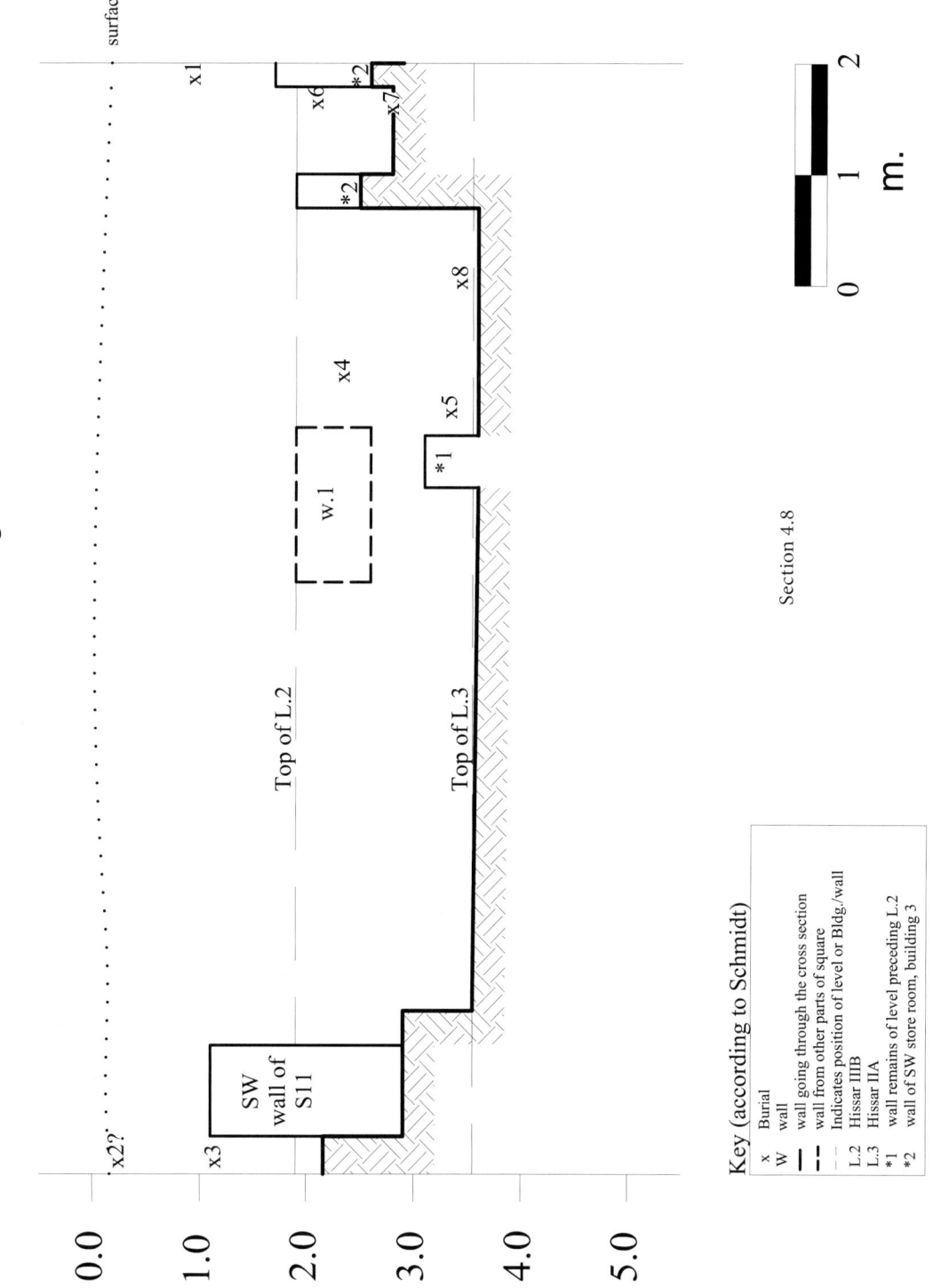

Section 4.8

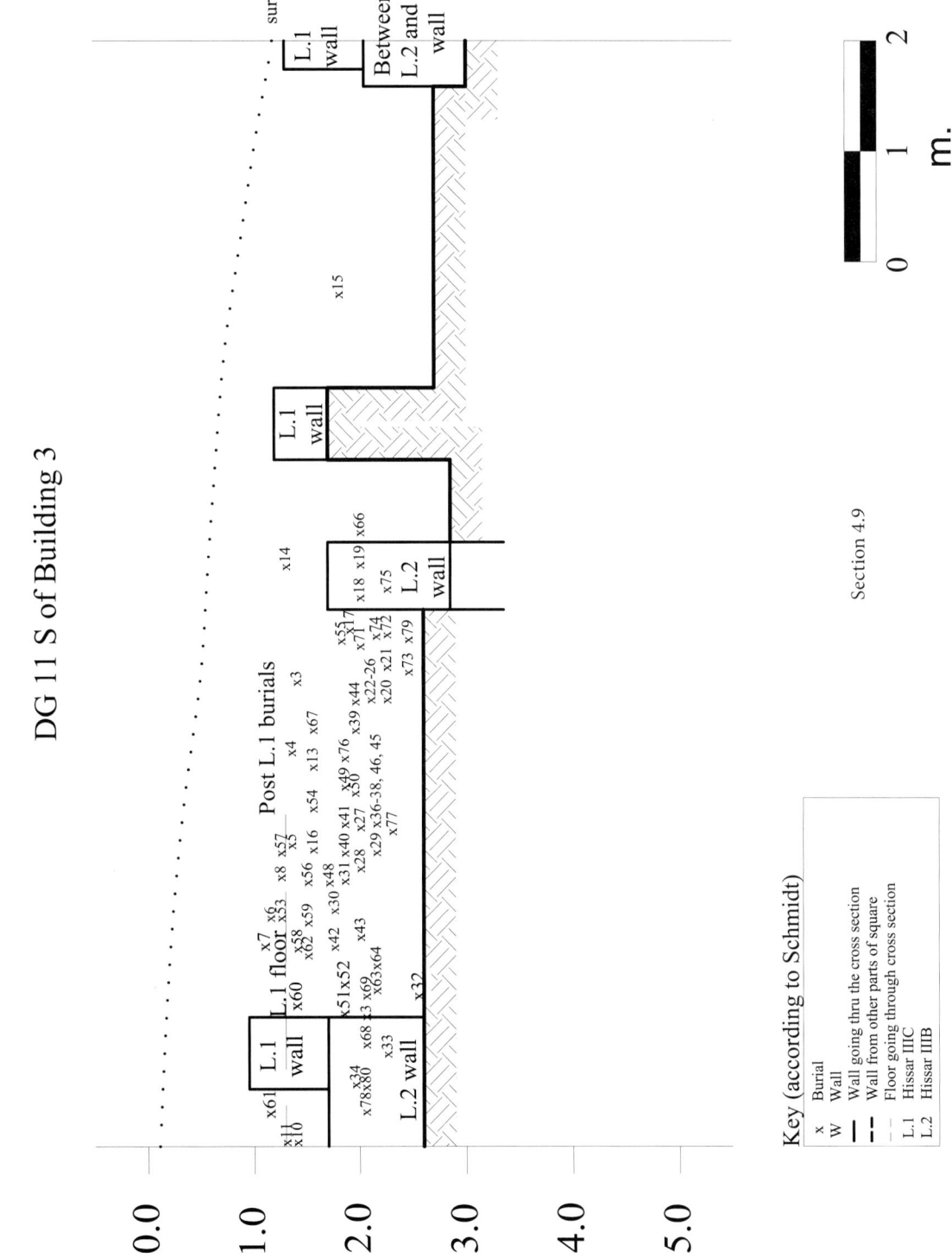

Section 4.9

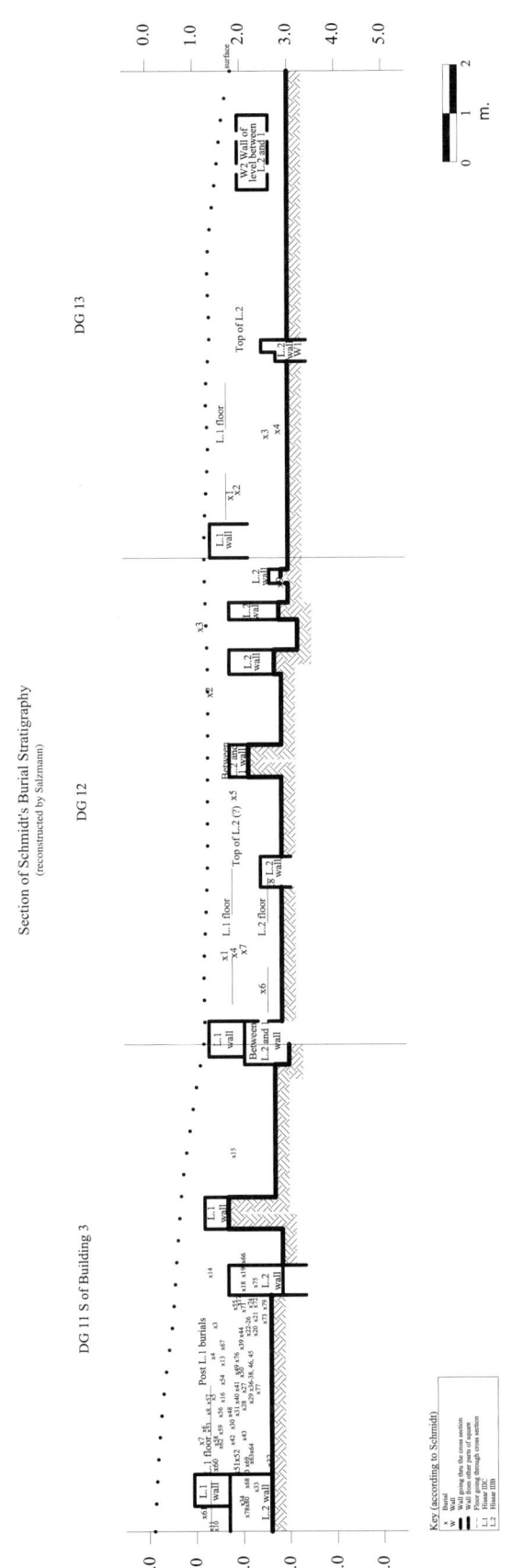

Section 4.10

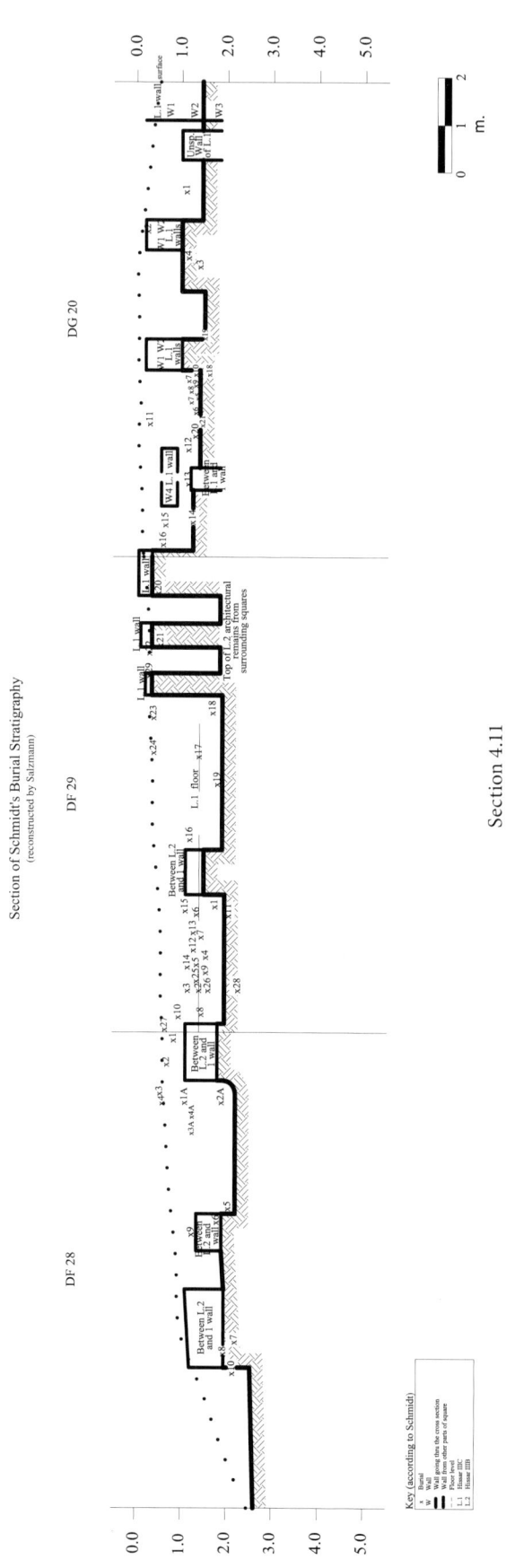

Section 4.11

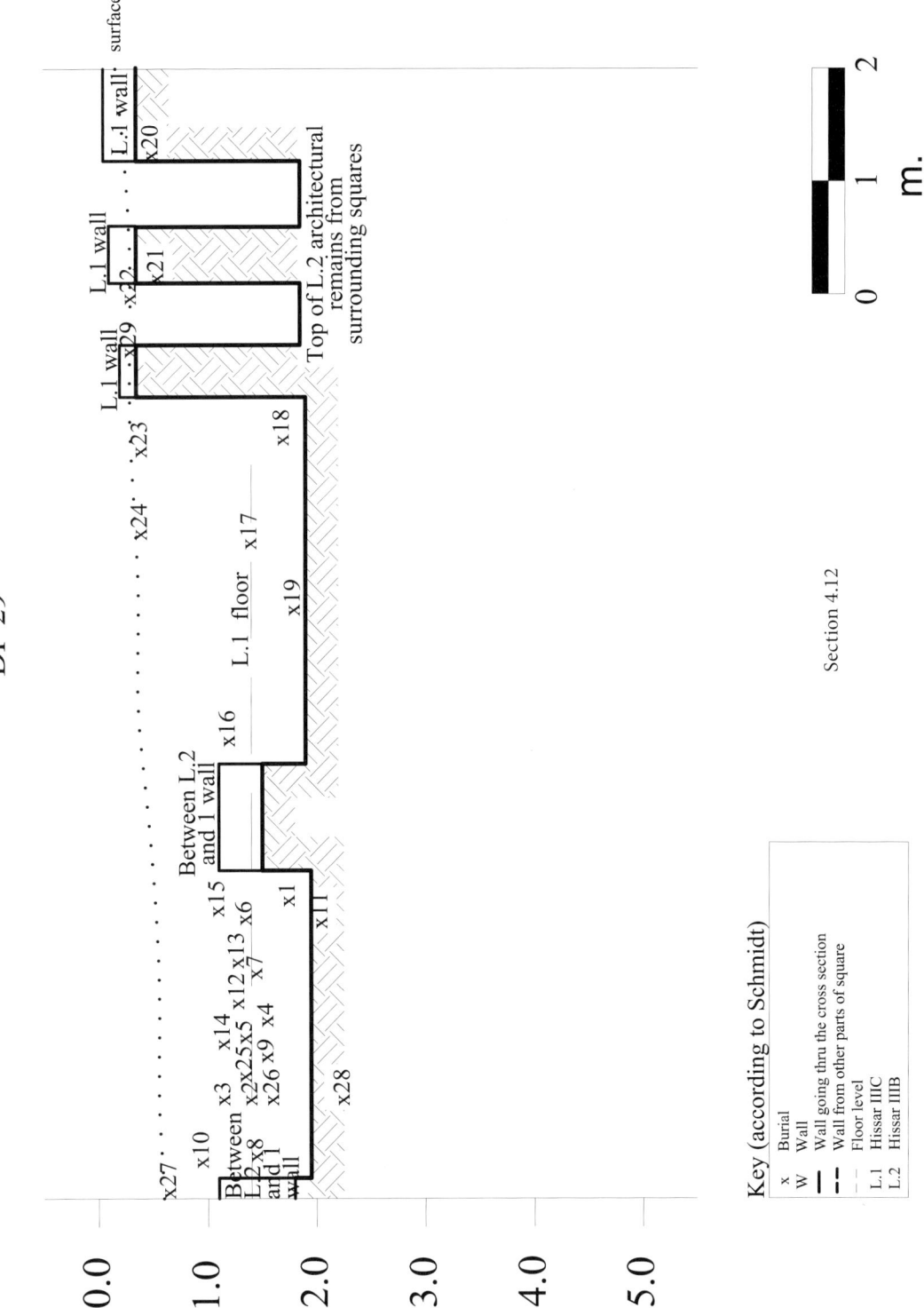

Section 4.12

Burials x13 and x17 are dated to ceramic phase B through A; the teapot with tube spout (H4033) in x17 is a handmade, coarse vessel, similar to the one in square CF88 burial x1 (H3508), also dated to phase B-A/A.

DF29 Burials

There are 29 burials in DF29, mostly concentrated in the northwestern and southeastern parts of the square, and 13 burials are datable (for pottery chart, see Section 4.12a in Appendix 1). In the northeast cluster, burials x1, x2, x5–8, x17, and x28 can be dated to the transitional phase D-C based on an assemblage of largely grey burnished beakers (one tulip-shaped beaker, H635, is pattern burnished) and one buff painted cup with red bands (H642). Schmidt refers to the six burials x1, x2, x5–8 as a "group burial," at 1.50 m depth (see Ch. 5, pp. 221–222).

The southeast cluster (x20, x22, x24 and x29) appears to be stratigraphically higher than the northwest group, which can also be observed in the grave goods. Burial x24 has a rare form, straight-sided plate/tray (H1018); a similar vessel (H4227) is dated to Period IIIB by Schmidt (1937: pl. XXXVIII). However, these handmade plate/trays occur in grey burnished and coarse wares and are also dated to the transitional phase D-C in the ceramic sequence of the 1976 stratified assemblage (H3437, H3440, H2794, and H3207, see Ch. 3, Figs. 3.42, 3.43, 3.45, and 3.46). The pear shaped bottle is an anomaly in this phase; it may be intrusive as it is rarely found in the transitional phase D-C. It occurs most commonly in phase B.

E.4 DF18-DF19 = S and SW of Building 1 and W of Building 2

Stratigraphy and Architecture

The only architecture in DF18-19 that can be correlated is in DF19, where the western corner of Building 2 and the southern extension of Building 1 (lower) can be seen (see squares DG00 and DG10 on Fig 2.11 this volume). Unfortunately, these features are not noted by Schmidt in his section of DF19. Indeed, given that the walls of Building 1 (lower) were located around 3.5–4.5 m below datum and that Schmidt's section of DF19 is no lower than 2.0–2.5 m below datum, it seems clear that the northern part of DF19 was excavated from DF09 and was not on an even level with the rest of the square.

Similarly, the walls of Building 2 in DG00 were located between 2.5–3.5 m below datum. Schmidt's indication on his section of DF19 of "top of Bldg. 2 walls in other squares" no doubt refers to what Dyson called Building 2_1, or the transitional phase D-C walls. However, the discovery of three painted cups of the transitional phase D-C around 1.0 m below datum in DF19 may suggest that the fill of this phase was slightly higher than in DG00. If so, then the walls shown in the sections of DF18 and DF19 may correspond to later stage D or early D-C.

DF18 Burials

Even though there are only 46 burials shown on Schmidt's section in DF18, he recorded 52 burials in his field register. Of the 52 burials, 21 (x1, x4, x5, x13, x15, x17, x19–22, x24, x25, x31, x36, x38, x39, x39a, x41, x43, x46, and x52) contain datable ceramics (for pottery chart, see Section 4.13a in Appendix 1). The majority of the burials cluster in the SE corner of DF18 and form an extension of the burial site as seen in the SW corner of DF19 (see section).

Two of the earliest burials with ceramics are x43 and x46 found in the cluster in the SE corner of DF18. Both are transitional phase D-C vessels; the one from burial x43 is a buff painted cup with "fence pattern" (H1010) identical to those from the burned rooms excavated by Dyson on the North Flat (Dyson and Howard 1989: fig. 31 H76-89; see also Ch. 3, Fig. 3.37:11). The other, from burial x46, is a bottle pitcher decorated with series of incised zigzag lines that was reused as a canteen with four suspension holes at the neck (H1007—unpublished). The rest of the eight burials from the SE cluster are also dated to transitional phase D-C.

The later ceramic assemblage has vessels that are metal inspired, including dark grey burnished bottles with a "metal ridge" around the neck. Also included are pear shape bottles, all types of beakers from wide mouth to bell shaped and tulip-shape ("vase jar") (see burials x25, x36, and x41 on pottery chart). These would all be dated to phase B (first half to late third millennium BC). Also included in the same group are burials (x4, x5, x15, x38, x39, x39a, and x52) located in and outside of "Level 2" walls.

The only late burial is x1, referred to as "little girl" (Schmidt 1933: pls. CLII, CLV H440, H446). The inventory of objects in this grave is rich and includes silver cups and amulets, alabaster vessels, and a large number of semi-precious stones. One of the more diagnostic ceramic vessels is an oval bottle with narrow neck that is pattern burnished in a way similar to the canteens of the phase B through A. The assemblage of associated artifacts with the ceramic vessels is also datable to phases B through A, late third millennium BC (for details of this burial, see Ch. 5, p. 247).

BURIAL STRATIGRAPHY 193

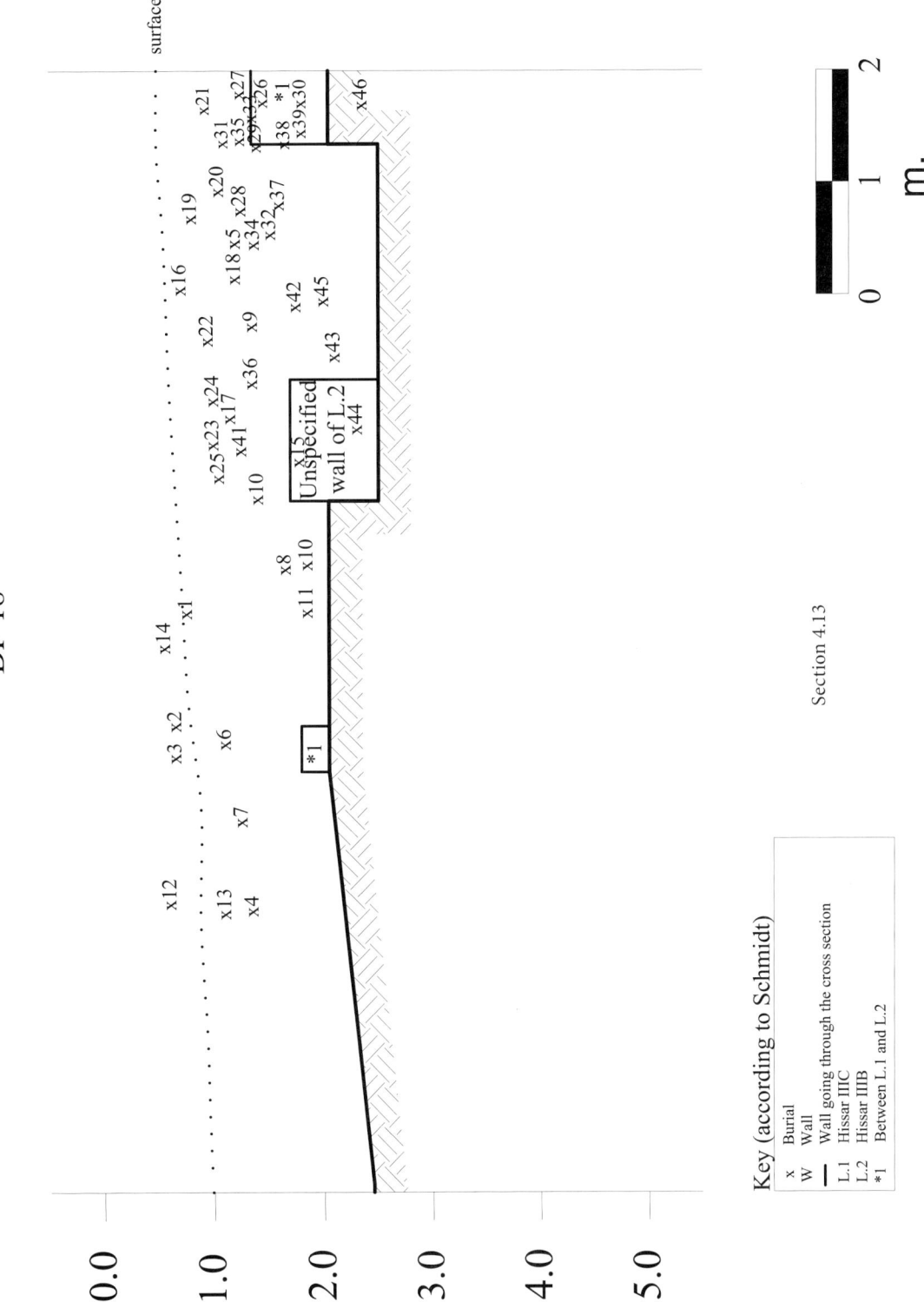

Section 4.13

Section of Schmidt's Burial Stratigraphy
(reconstructed by Salzmann)

DF 19 S of Building 1 and SW corner of Building 2

Section 4.14

Key (according to Schmidt)

- x — Burial
- W — wall
- — wall going through the cross section
- - - - Indicates position of level or Bldg./wall
- L.1 — Hissar IIIC
- L.2 — Hissar IIIB
- *1 — Between L.1 and L.2
- *2 — Unspecified wall of L.2 going through w community plot

DF19 Burials

Of the 63 burials recorded in this square, 21 contained ceramic vessels (for pottery chart, see Section 4.14a in Appendix 1) from later levels at depths ca. 0.50–2.05 m (x2, x3, x4, x7, x8, x11, x12, x13, x17, x18, x19, x21, x23, x24, x27, x29, x30, x40, x43, x55, and x 60). There are no burials recorded from the earliest stages excavated in the northern part of the square.

The majority of the burials exist in two concentrations on the east and west sides of the square, dated to phase B and B through A, mid-third to early second millennium BC. The burials with the earlier ceramic assemblage includes: finely burnished globular bottles with short necks (x13, H1000); bottles with "metal ridge" (x21, H876); an unburnished grey bowl with raised beak spout (x19, H1029), also lateral beak spout (x40, H896); two varieties of grey burnished beakers wide rim (x43, H885 and x55, 1638) and bell shape (x2, H1112); and a grey burnished bottle pitcher (x21, H875). An early type of grey burnished goblet (H1636) was found together with a grey plate (x24, H1637). The latter vessel displays the ceramicist's ingenuity as it was fashioned from a stemmed bowl of which the broken base was reground for use as a plate (Schmidt 1933: pl. CXVII).

The later burials (x2, x3, x4, x7, x8, x11, x12, x17, x23, x27, x29, x30, and x60) date ceramically to phase B-A/A. They contain: long-neck bottles with a "ring" in relief around the neck (x4, H186), as well as a coarse ware brazier in x30 (H1032—footed), pattern burnished canteens and three new types, which I refer as wide-based bowls (Schmidt's terminology is "bowl with expanding rim"), in x30 and in x7 (H1026 and H1031, H873), in x60 (H891), "cylindrical bowl" in x8 (H228), and a grey pattern burnished jar in x17 (H874). Continuing from phase C through B are two vessel types, grey burnished bottle with a "ring" in relief around its neck and a globular bottle with short neck.

One of the outstanding burials from the phase B through A assemblage is DF19 x2, which Schmidt named as the "first warrior" due to the presence of a cache of military equipment (weaponry, helmet) and copper figurine symbols (H550—wand with double headed ram) (Schmidt 1933: pl. CXXXI). The weapons are similar to those found in the grave of the "second warrior" (DF09 x1) (see Ch. 5, Burial Groups, p. 226). The assemblages from the graves of both "warriors," including the alabaster vessels, columns and discs (generally compared to the BMAC [Bactria-Margiana Archaeological Complex in Turkmenistan]), are similar to those found on the Main Mound (CF99), the Treasure Hill (Hoard I), and the North Flat. All are from the latest building stage (B-A/A), ceramic phase B through A, and dated to the late third to early second millennium BC.

It should be mentioned that burials *uncorrelated* with the 1976 sequence in squares CF88, CF89, CF99, to the north of Building 1, are also ceramically dated to phase B-A/A. The "Hoard" from squares CF89-99 (below) provides clear evidence for the latest chronological context for the artifacts in the "hoard" on the Main Mound (see also Ch. 5, Burial Rituals, p. 252).

E.5 CF88-CF89 and CF99: Northwest of CG90/1/

Stratigraphy and Architecture

There are at least two architectural levels apparent in this part of the Main Mound. The lower walls, indicated as "L.2" walls in Schmidt's sections, have no associated pottery, so their dates are uncertain. However, given the depth at which they were found, they may belong to stage D or D-C. Alternatively, they may correspond to the "Burned Building" stage B on the North Flat. Above this ambiguous level are a series of large walls assigned to "L.1" by Schmidt. These walls seem to be associated stratigraphically with the important hoard of fenestrated braziers, copper figurines, and small pointed cups that straddle CF89 and CF99. Schmidt (1937:156, 193) describes the hoard as "below the floor of Level 1" (see detailed plan, Schmidt 1937: figs. 87 and 88). The date of this hoard is estimated to be in phase B-A/A, late third to early second millennium BC.

CF88–CF89 Burials

The only burial found in square CF88 is x1, situated on the border of square CF89, below "L.1 wall." The associated pottery is a classic assemblage of grey burnished vessels (for pottery chart, see Sections 4.15a and 4.16a in Appendix 1) dated to ca. 2200 BC, phases B-A/A: bridge-beak-spouted jar (H3510), pattern burnished bottle, disc based bowl (H3503, H3507), and trough-spouted jar. A red ware, wheelmade vessel (H3509) has "corrugated" patterning on the exterior, which is a rare surface finish (Schmidt 1937: fig.109).

There are eight burials clustered at the corner of three squares: CF88 x1, CF89 x2, x3, x4, x5, x7, x10, and CF79 x1, north of square CF99. All were found just below the level of the "L1" walls. They contain a classic assemblage of grey burnished vessels, from Late Period III, phases B through A. The largest group is from CF88 x1 and includes: two beak-spouted jars with glossy pattern bur-

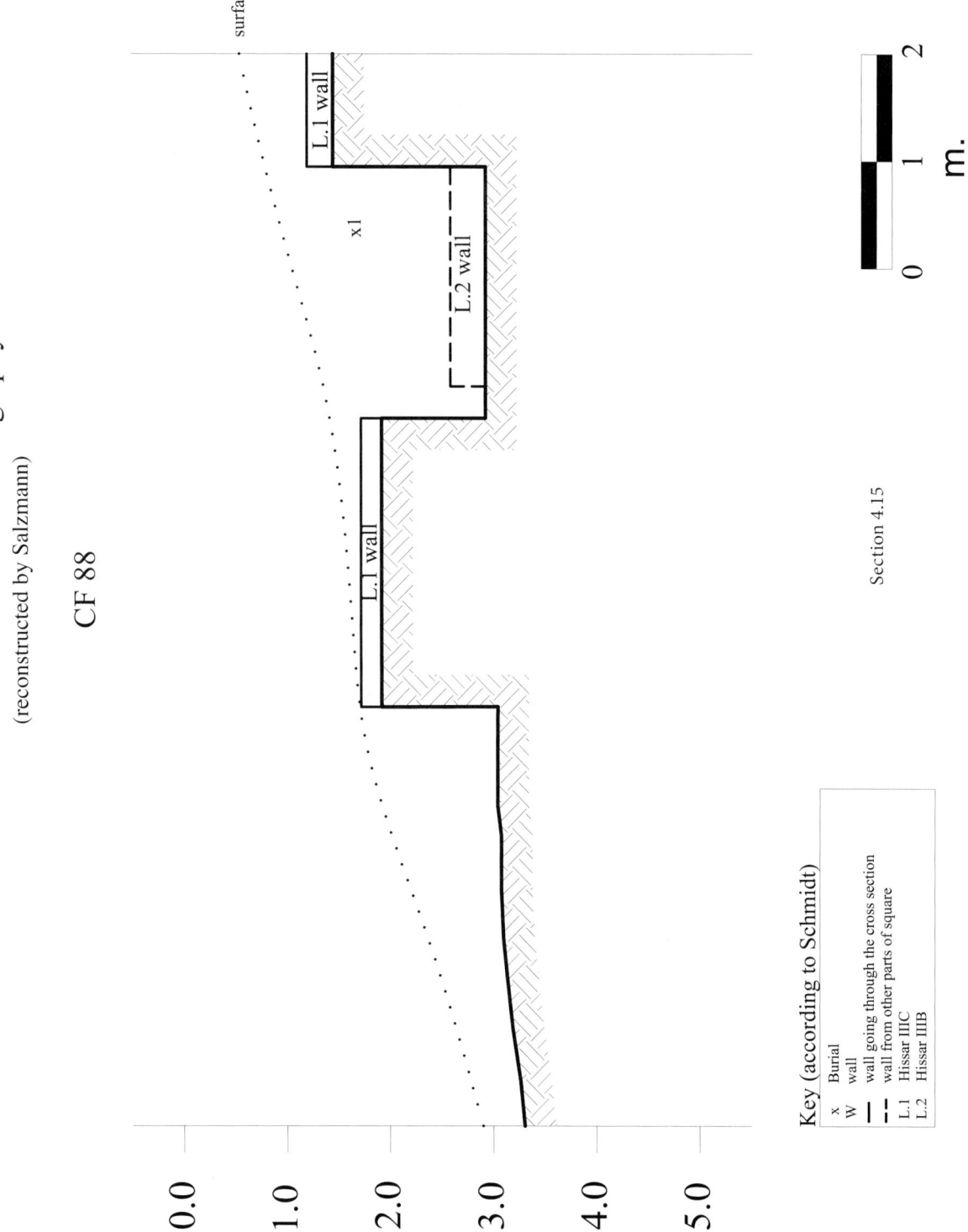

nish with herringbone pattern (H3510–11; see Schmidt 1937:181, fig 107 and p. 254, fig 160) which display exceptional craftsmanship; a zigzag pattern burnished bottle (H3504); two disc based bowls in red ware (H3505, H3507) both are wheelmade with "corrugated" patterning on the exterior, and another vessel with a rare surface finish (H3509) (Schmidt 1937:fig. 109). An early form, tube-spouted teapot, reoccurs in coarse ware (H3508). Also from square CF79 x1, there are two buff ware canteens with lug handles (H3932, H3941; see Schmidt 1937: fig. 107). Two different forms of grey burnished jars have unusual decorative patterns: H5231is tall, with broad mouth, and burnished zigzags, herringbone and triangles in five registers; another is a carinated jar, H3933, that has a pattern of two cross hatchings and two ridges around its neck (ibid., pl. XL). The pattern is a new decorative motif applied to this early carinated jar form that continues from Late Hissar II through Early Hissar III to Late Hissar IIIC (cf. H2497, from burial CF57 x20; H3989, from burial DG11 x66; H572, from burial DG00 x16). These unpublished vessels are retrieved from archival pottery sheets (Fig. 4.9). The wheelmade, coarse ware jar in CF89 x7 (H5144) is most likely from phases B through A, as is the coarse jar from CF99 x1 (H5138). Also dated to Late Hissar IIIC are a coarse ware spouted pitcher, a grey burnished canteen (H3516), and a miniature brazier (H3087).

The burials from phase B-A/A also contain alabaster vessels such as H3506 in CF88 (ibid., pl. LIX). Similar alabaster stemmed plates came from DF19 x2, x3, and DF19 fill (ibid., pl. CXXXVI H1666, pl. CXXXVII H176, pl. CXL H182). In CF89 x2 and CF89 x3 there are more alabaster vessels, two finely crafted stemmed plates with grooves around the rim (H5199, H3517; cf. similar vessels in Schmidt 1937: pl. LIX H3506, H2769).

A unique find is a canteen (H3522) from CF89 "refuse" with two handles of quadruped heads and two serpents in relief (Fig. 4.10; see also Schmidt 1937: pl. XL H3522). Unfortunately, its context is unknown, but Schmidt states it was found in the "refuse" of "Level 1, high" (Schmidt 1937:182, pl. XL). It is the only vessel of this type, most likely it is from *above* Schmidt's level IIIC and dates to the early second millennium BC.

CF99 Burials

The burials x1 and x2 are clearly below Level 1. Burial x2 might be slightly earlier than x1 (for pottery chart, see Section 4.18a in Appendix 1). The evidence from the both burials dates them to phase B-A/A. Burial x2 contains a pattern burnished canteen with 2 cord handles and vertical lines on neck (H5140).

CF89 and CF99: "The Hoard"

On the Main Mound, between plots CF89 and CF99, Schmidt documents a hoard of: "copper figurines of men and pottery vessels were…found below the base level of a Hissar IIIC wall," (Schmidt 1937:157, figs. 87 and 88). Schmidt places this hoard in a doubtful context called "fill" below "L.1 wall", at 1.0–1.50 m depth, which would place them in the early second millennium BC (see Sections 4.16 and 4.18; for pottery chart, see Section 4.16a, 4.18a; cf. Schmidt plan, 1937: fig. 86; also Fig. 1.8 this volume). Although this hoard is not recorded in association with any burials, it is very likely that it may have been part of the burial assemblages in squares CF89 and CF99 based on similar finds (conical cups and braziers) from burial contexts elsewhere (cf. DF07 x3).

The hoard contained culturally and chronologically significant assemblages. The most remarkable is a cache of 13 male and female copper figurines depicted almost in a state of motion (Schmidt 1937:191–194, pl. XLII). Among the associated artifacts are several mini braziers, a dozen coarse ware drinking cups of varying sizes with pointed bases, alabaster plates and vessels, and two herringbone design pattern burnished canteens (ibid., pl. XL H5140, H3522). The latter canteen has a unique handle in the form of a quadruped and 2 serpents in relief. Other artifacts are three copper ingots (ibid., figs. 87, 88 H3273, H3275, H3277) described by Schmidt as "mini bowls," a lump of "iron ore" (H3323), and two pieces of hematite (H3158, H3280). The stratigraphic position of the burials and the artifact types clearly support an early second millennium BC date according to Schmidt (1937:191–194, pl. XLII; see also Ch. 5, Burial Rituals).

F. 1976 Burials

During the 1976 campaign, 11 burials (see Ch. 2, Fig. 2.5) were excavated from the Main Mound (n=8) and the North Flat (n=3). The burial numbers and their contexts are not always clear in the 1989 publication (Dyson and Howard 1989). Of the eight burials cited from the Main Mound, five are from square CG90 (B1–5); two are from square DG00 (B7, B8; Fig. 4.11); and one is from DG01 (B6; see Fig 3.27). On the North Flat, three burials were excavated, one from the Burned Building in square CF48 and two in the burned rooms in square CF58 /2/ and /3/.

Two of the burials from square CG90 (B1, B2) contained scattered human bones—a child and an adult (Fig. 4.12)—from incompletely excavated graves located to the northwest of room 1. The human bones were associated with some animal bones (unidentified), ceramic sherds,

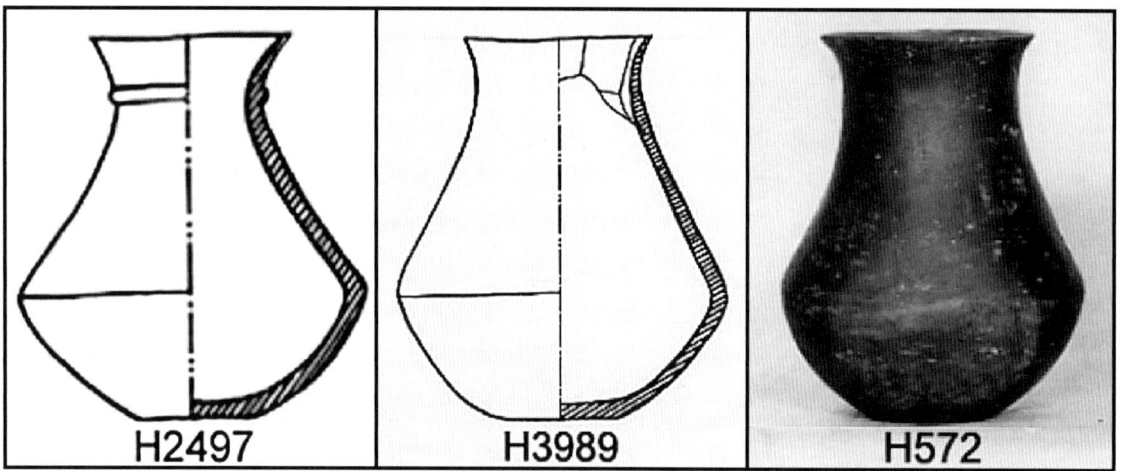

Fig. 4.9 Three unpublished examples of the carinated jar form which is found from Late Hissar II until Late Hissar IIIC: H2497, from burial CF57 x20; H3989, from burial DG11 x66; H572, from burial DG00 x16.

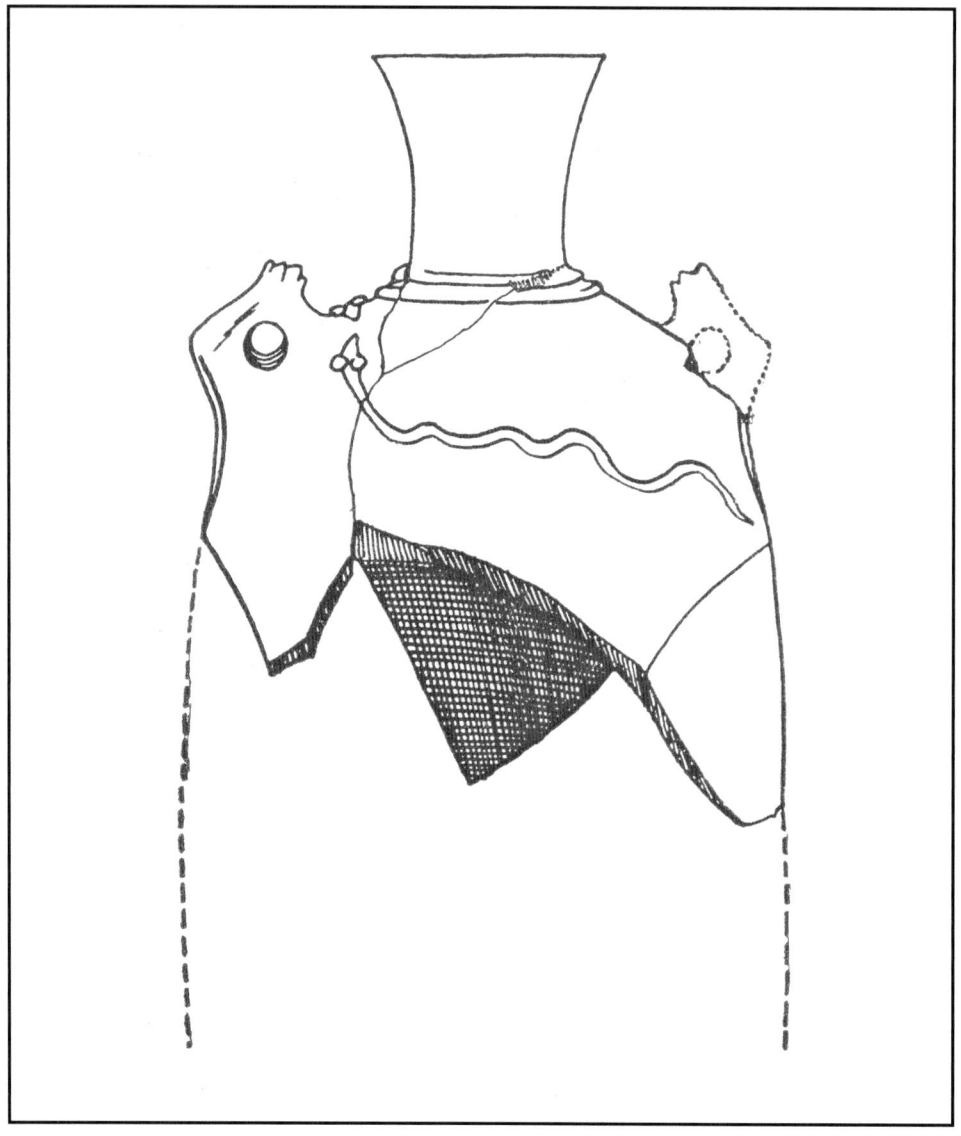

Fig. 4.10 Drawing of a unique canteen (H3522) from square CF89 "refuse" with two handles of quadruped heads and two serpents in relief.

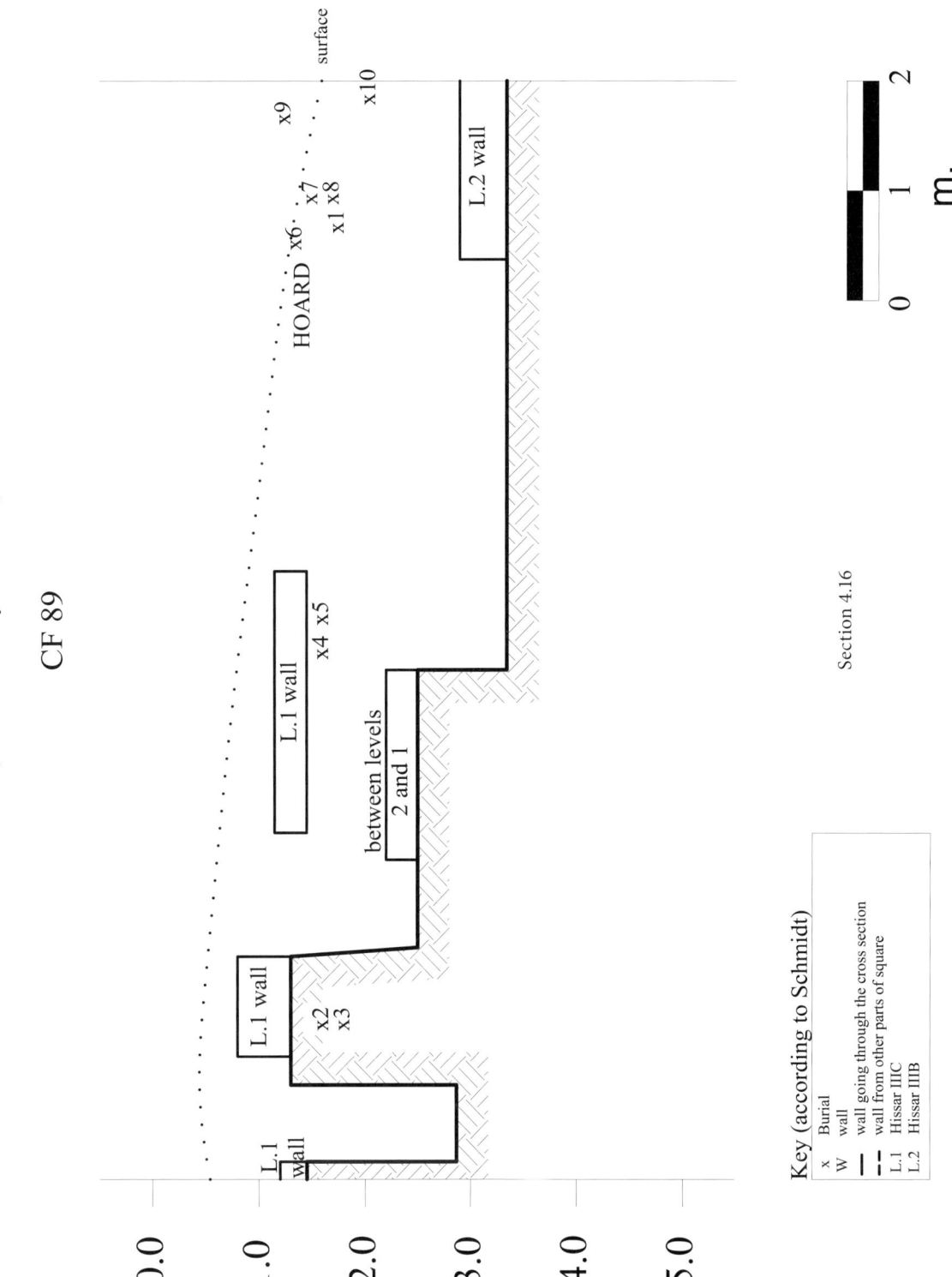

Section 4.16

BURIAL STRATIGRAPHY

Section of Schmidt's Burial Stratigraphy
(reconstructed by Salzmann)

CF 99

Section 4.18

Key (according to Schmidt)

x   Burial
W   wall
—   wall going through the cross section
- - wall from other parts of square
L.1 Hissar IIIC
L.2 Hissar IIIB

Fig. 4.11 Photograph of burial 8 from square DG00 in situ (Courtesy of Penn Museum, image no. H76-SL222).

a figurine, alabaster fragments, and other refuse from Schmidt's fill (Howard 1989a:61).

Also from square CG90, burial B3 contained an infant burial dug into Howard's wall 41 (baulk 8) in /6/ with no associated finds; burial B5 was found in stage D3 refuse in /4/, although the small grey burnished bottle (H76-32) suggests the grave may have been dug from a later level. In the floor of a room dated to phase E-D, two more child burials were found (B4, B6). The child in B4 had a bead necklace (H76-38); B6 was associated with a grey burnished beaker (H76-115). Since the beaker is handmade using the slab technique, the ceramic dating cannot be later than phase D, which correlates well with its stratigraphic position. In square DG00/12/, directly on top of the stage D3 floor, B7 was buried with a handmade wide-based bowl in coarse ware. Its context suggests a date in early phase D. At least six of the Main Mound burials are assigned to phases E-D and D, Early Mid-Hissar II.

G. North Flat

As mentioned at the beginning of Chapter 4, the North Flat burials comprise only 8% of the total number of burials (n=1637) as indicated by Schmidt. How-

Fig. 4.12 Two photographs showing burials 1 and 2 from CG90 located northwest of room 1 (Courtesy of Penn Museum).

ever, the exact number of the total number of burials is unknown because Schmidt's burial sheets in the archives have different numbers for some of the squares than those mentioned in his two publications (Schmidt 1931, 1937).

The stratigraphic sequence of the North Flat was defined during the 1976 restudy of the Burned Building (Dyson and Remsen 1989:89–93). As discussed in detail in Chapter 2, the most important stratigraphic information deduced was that the foundations of the Burned Building were placed on a cleared area (a "foundation trench" of sorts). Thus, the phase B Burned Building of Hissar III sits directly on top of transitional phase D-C layers equivalent to the Late Hissar II. The entire early third millennium BC layers (the elusive "Period IIIA" or phases C through B) were removed from squares CF37-38 and surrounding areas associated with the Burned Building.

Thanks to careful excavations in 1976, Schmidt's sections and plans of CF37-38, CF47-48, and CF57-58 that contain burials below the Burned Building (level 3), can now be correlated with stratigraphic building stages and placed chronologically by radiocarbon dates.[10]

G.1 The Burned Building

For information on the Burned Building see: Chapter 1, pp. 30–34 and Chapter 2, pp. 57–59.

Stratigraphy and Architecture

There are two building stages visible in Schmidt's sections for CF37-38. The Burned Building, called by Schmidt "Level 2" (or "L.2"), is shown in section by two walls ("L.2 R.1 E wall" and "L.2 E wall of R.4") and indicated by two staircases that were not in the actual section, but which are, nevertheless, marked. The walls of the "level 1" structure, which sat above the Burned Building (Dyson's "phase A" [Dyson and Remsen 1989:89–93]) are indicated in CF37 by "L.1 S3 N wall" and "L.1 S3 E wall." Since the Burned Building provides the very definition of "phase B" or Period IIIB, the later walls of the "Level 1" structure essentially define the "phase A" or Period IIIC at Tepe Hissar.

We know from Schmidt's field notes that he excavated below the Burned Building in square CF37 ("Level 3"), although he did not record any depths. The section indicates the floor of "L.2" at ca. 1.2–1.5 m depth and the "Top of Level 3" at ca. 3.0 m depth. At 3.15 m depth (i.e., within "Level 3"), a buff painted goblet with checkerboard pattern (Schmidt 1937: pl. XXXVI H4070) was found; it can be dated to the transitional phase D-C based on comparison with the burned rooms excavated by Dyson in CF58. Similarly, two vessels of the transitional phase D-C H4075 and H2784 (ibid., pl. XXV, fig.74) were found under the floors of R.1 and R.4, the Main Rooms of the Burned Building at 1.60 m depth.

CF37 Burials

In this square, Schmidt recorded 12 burials, although his section shows only four: x1–4 (1937: fig. 104). Of the 12 burials, only two (x1 and x9) contained ceramics (for pottery chart, see Section 4.20a in Appendix 1). Burial

Table 4.1 MAIN MOUND: Chronology of Dated Burials According to the Reconstructed Stratigraphy and the New Ceramic Sequence

Squares and total # of excavated burials	Dated Burials	New Ceramic Phases	Revised Period according to 1976 sequence
DF09 (56)	1, 2, 5	B-A/A	Late Hissar IIIC
	6, 9, 24, 25	B	Mid-Hissar IIIB
	15, 17, 23, 46, 48	D, D-C	Late Hissar II–Early Hissar III
	13, 29, 30, 31, 33, 35, 36, 41, 42, 42a, 43, 45, 54	E-D	Early/Mid-Hissar II
	50, 51, 52	F, F-E	Late Hissar I–Early Hissar II
DF08 (3)	1	B-A/A	Late Hissar IIIC
DG00 (22)	1, 4, 5	B-A/A	Late Hissar IIIC
	7	B	Mid-Hissar IIIB
	6, 10, 14, 16, 19, 22	D, D-C	Late Hissar II–Early Hissar III
DG01 (44)	1, 6, 9, 15, 16, 17, 18, 21, 22, 38, 39, 41	B-A/A	Late Hissar IIIC
	32, 36	D, D-C	Late Hissar II –Early Hissar III
CG90 (24)	1	B-A/A	Late Hissar IIIC
	9, 10, 23	B	Mid-Hissar IIIB
	3, 7, 8, 13, 14, 15, 16, 18, 19, 20, 22, 25	D, D-C	Late Hissar II–Early Hissar III
DG10 (8)	3	B-A/A	Late Hissar IIIC
	6, 7	D, D-C	Late Hissar II–Early Hissar III
DG11 (80)	16, 18, 32, 62	B	Mid-Hissar IIIB
	5, 9, 17, 20, 24, 25, 33, 36, 48, 52, 54, 66, 68, 74	D, D-C	Late Hissar II–Early Hissar III
	21, 47	E-D	Early/Mid-Hissar II
DF29 (29)	1, 2, 5, 6, 7, 8, 17, 20, 22, 23, 24, 28, 29	D, D-C	Late Hissar II–Early Hissar III
DG20 (21)	13, 17	B-A/A	Late Hissar IIIC
	6, 9, 18, 19, 21	D, D-C	Late Hissar II–Early Hissar III
DF18 (52)	1	B-A/A	Late Hissar IIIC
	4, 5, 15, 25, 36, 38, 39, 39a, 41, 52	B	Mid–Hissar III
	13, 17, 20, 21, 22, 24, 31, 43, 46	D, D-C	Late Hissar II–Early Hissar III
DF19 (63)	2, 3, 4, 7, 8, 11, 12, 17, 23, 27, 29, 30, 60	B-A/A	Late Hissar IIIC
	13, 18, 19, 21, 24, 40, 43, 55	B	Mid-Hissar IIIB
CF88 (4)	1	B-A/A	Late Hissar IIIC
CF79 (1)	1	B-A/A	Late Hissar IIIC
CF89 (10)	2, 3, 7, 10	B-A/A	Late Hissar IIIC
CF99 (2)	1, 2	B-A/A	Late Hissar IIIC

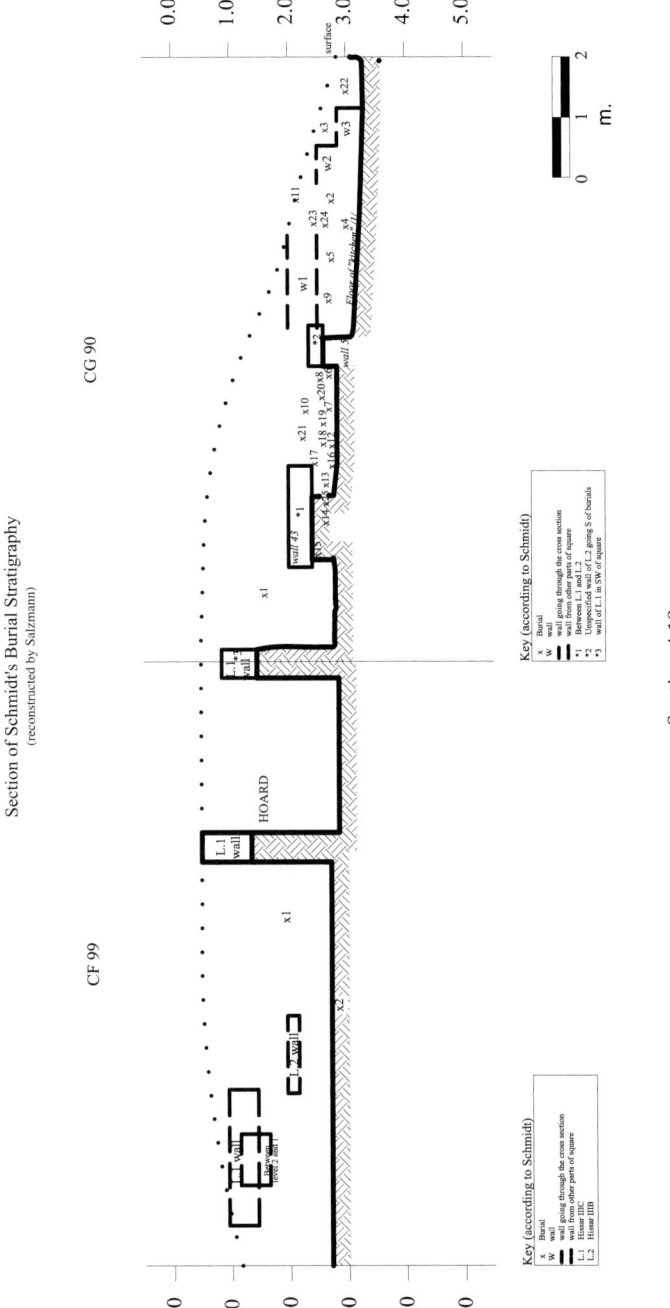

Section 4.19

Section of Schmidt's Burial Stratigraphy
(reconstructed by Salzmann)

CF 37
R.1, 4 and Gate Passage (3) of Burned Building

CF 38
E and SE part of R.4 Burned Building

Section 4.20

Key (according to Schmidt)
- x   Burial
- W   wall
- ▬   wall going through the cross section
- ▭   wall from other parts of square
- L.1   Hissar IIC
- L.2   Hissar IIIB
- L.3   Hissar IIIA/IIB

x1 is above the floor level of the Burned Building; two vessels (H2356, H2357) found in burial x1 can be dated to phase B-A/A. One vessel is a dark grey polished globular bottle with narrow/short neck and disc rim characteristic of the Late Period III bottles (H2357). It is similar to those found at CF99 fill, also dated to phase B-A/A (H3317, H3318). In the fill above the L.1 structure over the Burned Building (Schmidt's "upper sub level"), there is an assemblage of alabaster discs and columns that he dates to Late Period IIIC.

In burial x9, a handmade buff painted goblet (H4070) was found below the Burned building at 3.15 m. The vessel, buff painted with dark brown cross hatching and checkered squares around the rim, can be dated to phase E-D, so earlier than the Burned Building.

CF38 Burials

Of the 18 burials in this square (Schmidt recorded only 15 on his section), six (x6, x9, x11, x15, x16, and x18) contained ceramic vessels (for pottery chart, see Section 4.20b in Appendix 1). The earliest burial, x15, at 3.60 m depth has two grey burnished vessels—a stemmed goblet and carinated jar (H4076, H4077)—and is dated to phase E-D. Burials x11, x16, and x18 are described as below "R4" of the Burned Building at depths 2.0–3.60 m. They contain vessels dated to the early third millennium BC, transitional phase D-C. The later burials, x6 and x9, have ceramics dated to phase B, including highly burnished globular bottles (H2842 and H2855).

G.2 CF47-48 "Enclosure" and Buttressed Room

Stratigraphy and Architecture

To the southwest of the Burned Building and on the same level, Schmidt excavated what he called the "Enclosure," a large open structure that Dyson attributes to phase B. This structure appears in the section for CF47 as "L.2 wall enclosure" walls. Schmidt's purported "tower" bastion associated with the Burned Building was not in the actual section, although it is drawn in dashed lines as "W3 L.2" wall "Tower (8)." The later "phase A" structures are indicated by "Level 1" or "L.1" walls in both the CF47 and CF48 sections.

In the eastern part of CF47 and throughout most of CF48, Schmidt excavated below the Burned Building level and uncovered a number of structures. These are designated as "Level 3" ("L.3") walls in the CF47 section and as the walls of "S.14" and "S.13" on the eastern side of CF48. Unfortunately, Schmidt's section of square CF48 ran right down the middle of a street, so all the walls have been drawn in schematically. Room "S.14" was restudied by Dyson in 1976 and determined to be a buttressed structure typical of building stage D on the Main Mound (ceramic phase D). The area demarcated "S.13" by Schmidt is, thus, likely also of this period. In contrast, the "L.3" walls shown in CF47-48 may in fact date to the transitional phase D-C, as they are stratigraphically comparable to the burned rooms excavated by Dyson in square CF58 that date to this period (Dyson and Remsen 1989:99–104).

CF47 Burials

There are, altogether, nine burials in this square, although only five (x1, x2, x4, x6, and x7) contain datable ceramic vessels (for pottery chart, see Section 4.21a in Appendix 1). Burials x4, x6, and x7 are the earliest and date to ceramic phase E-D, represented by grey burnished, wide-rim beakers (these vessel types continue into phase D-C). An exception is the pear shape bottle offset with a "ring" at the base of the neck (Schmidt 1937: pl. XXXVII H2227); this bottle dates to the later ceramic phase B or B-A/A (this vessel is probably mixed from elsewhere).

The later burials x1 and x2 include: a grey, highly polished bottle pitcher with "metal" ring around neck (H2791, x2), globular jar, alabaster cup (Schmidt 1937:256, fig. 161, CF47 x2, H2792) and finely modeled and painted effigy vessels of bovine with curled horns (ibid., p. 191, fig. 113, CF47 x1, H2785), and a headless female with pronounced breasts (ibid., 193, pl. XLVI, fig. 115, CF47 x2, H2790). They are all dated to ceramic phase B-A/A. For a wide range of vessels from later burials of phase B-A/A, see Schmidt (1937:181–184, pls. XL–XLIII).

CF48 Burials

Out of the 22 burials in this square, only 17 are shown on Schmidt's section, and only 13 of those burials (x1, x3, x4, x5, x7, x11, x12, x16–19, x21, and x22) contained datable ceramics (for pottery chart, see Section 4.21b in Appendix 1). The burials were found in two stratigraphic groups: at depths 0.35–1.10 m and 1.30–1.60 m. Clearly, both groups can be dated to the transitional phase D-C, represented by grey burnished tulip beaker, bell shaped, and wide rim beakers (H2811, H2812, H2820, H2823, H2827, H2828); bottles (H2819, 2826); cup with short beak spout (H4104); highly burnished carinated jars (H2805, H4102); and buff painted "surviving" cup with vertical bands extend-

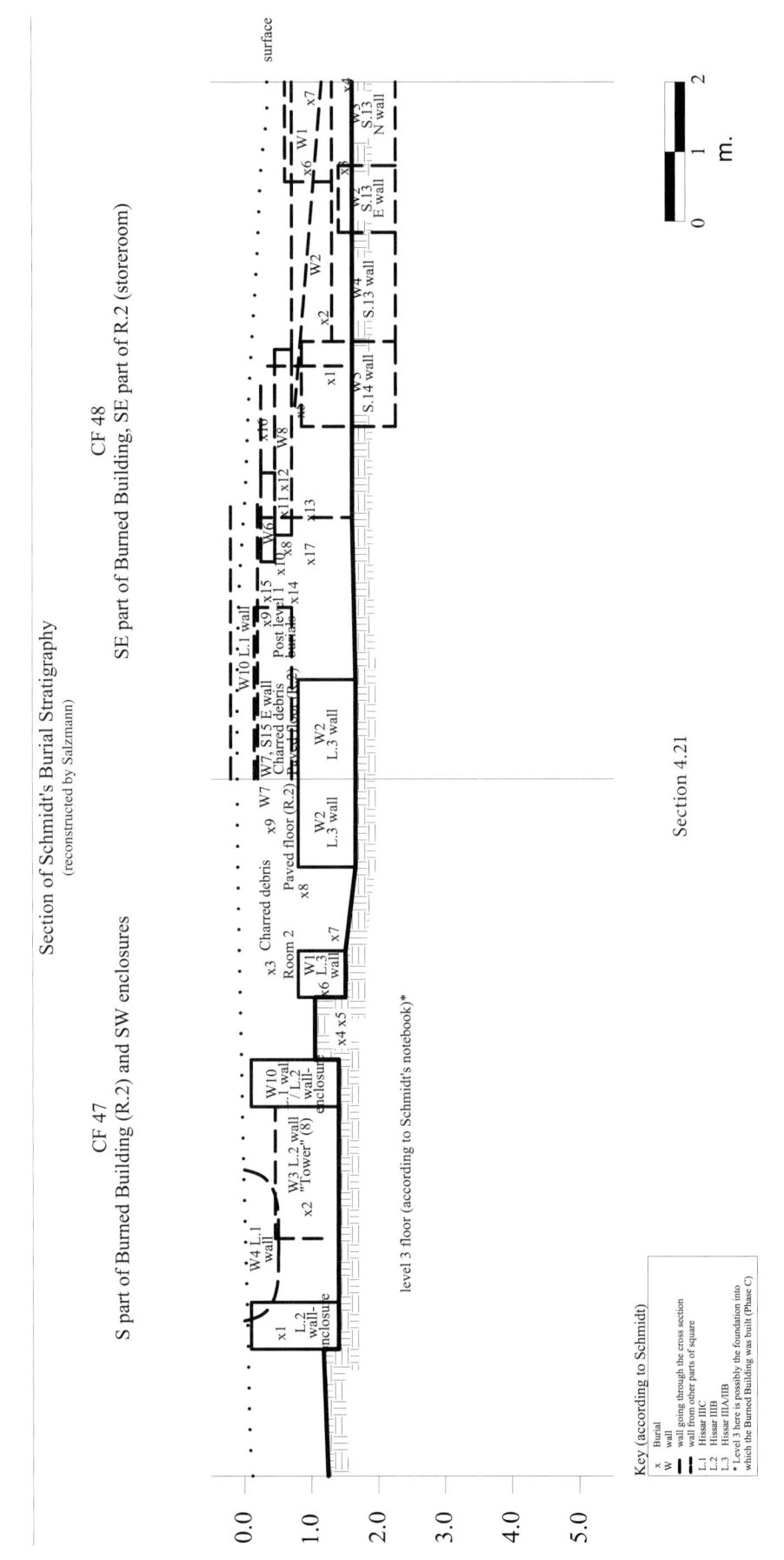

ing from rim to pointed base (H2825). The last vessel as well as the wide rim beaker are continuing vessel types from earlier phase E through D and continue even into the transitional phase D-C.[11]

G.3 CF57 Room 16 (S.16)

Stratigraphy and Architecture

Square CF57 is important for a number of reasons. First, it was one of the few squares on the North Flat where Schmidt went below the Burned Building level. In fact, the deep trench in the southwest corner of CF57 may be one of the deepest points reached by Schmidt across the entire site (excluding the deep trenches on the Main Mound and Painted Pottery Flat). Second, in CF57 Schmidt found a nearly complete structure ("S.16") dating to the level equivalent to building stage D and ceramic phase D on the Main Mound, as opposed to scattered walls of this period as in CF48 or under the Burned Building in CF37-38. Third, in addition to the Burned Building itself, Dyson made CF57 a focus of his restudy in 1976, even placing his test trench into the trench floor left by Schmidt, about a meter below the base of the walls of room 16. It was in CF57 that Dyson was able to deduce the full sequence of the North Flat from his stage A to his stage D, ceramic phase B-A/A to ceramic phase E-D.

In Schmidt's section of CF57 (1937: fig. 104), the southeast wall of the phase B "Enclosure" is marked as the "L.2 wall" on the west side of the section. The walls of "room 16" are marked as "S.16" walls. It is likely that these walls straddle both ceramic phase D and the foundations of the transitional phase D-C (rebuilding phase) marked by the burned rooms in CF58 (see Dyson and Remsen 1989: 85, 86, 99–105). Schmidt's "top of Level 4" at roughly 80 cm below the base of the walls of room 16 should correlate to the lapis-working lens found by Dyson in Schmidt's trench before beginning his test trench (Dyson and Remsen 1989:105–107). This lens is most likely from the transitional phase E-D (2.0–2.8 m in Schmidt's section), which is probably contemporary with the lapis workshops on the South Hill.

Dyson's test trench was begun a meter below the base of the walls of room 16 (S.16) and went down to about 2.25 meters below the base of the walls (roughly 4.25m in Schmidt's section). In "lot 3," Dyson found sherds of the F through E ceramic phases and got a radiocarbon date with a 2-sigma range of 3740–3500 cal. BC. Metallurgical slag and a unique steatite-based crucible were also found in "lot 3" (Thornton and Rehren 2009).

CF57 Burials

Of the 47 burials in CF57, only 14 (x6, x11, x14, x20, x21, x23, x27, x28, x29, x33, x35, x38, x40, and x43) had ceramics that could be used for relative dating purposes (for pottery chart, see Section 4.22a in Appendix 1).

The ceramics can be analyzed in two groups. As mentioned above, the earliest ceramic assemblage from Dyson's deep trench in square CF57 had painted sherds mixed with a few thin, burnished, grey sherds that are assigned to phase F through E (Dyson and Remsen 1989: figs. 35, 36). In the same trench, the lowest SW corner gave an even earlier radiocarbon date with a 2-sigma range of 4237–3918 BC. Schmidt's earliest group starts later at ca. 3.10–2.75 m depth, containing vessel types from ceramic phases E through D dated to 3700–3500 BC: necked jar in coarse buff ware (x33, H4148) and bowl with pointed base and "ladder design" (x33, H4149).

The second group of ceramics is included in Schmidt's "top of Level 3" to the top of "Level 3" room S16 wall at ca. 2.50–1.40 m depth. The burials are within and between the walls of room S16. It consists of a mixed assemblage of transitional phase D-C: dark grey burnished jar in x43 (H4169) "ornamented with four stippled rectangular patterns on the upper body resembling metal ornamentation" (Schmidt 1937:180); bowl with thin walls in x28 (H2465) (Fig. 4.13); wide rim beaker in x23 (H2506) and x29 (H2508); a zigzag incised beaker in x14 (H2447); a miniature grey bowl and bell beaker in x38 (H4156, H4155); a tulip beaker in x11 (H2443); carinated jars in x20 (H2457, H2466—with a ridge below the rim). The two dark burnished goblets in x35 (H4152) and x40 (H4162), a stemmed goblet in x40 (H4161) (Fig. 4.14), and two globular bottles in x21 (H2460) and x6 (H2477) are similar to vessels excavated in 1976 from the North Flat square CF58/2/ and CF58/3/ burned rooms (see Dyson and Remsen 1989:99, figs. 26 H76-75, H76-41, H76-113, 33, H76-140, H76-127). They are also dated to the transitional phase D-C (cf. squares DF18 and CF47 for the same vessel forms).

Some of these forms continue into phase B, such as dark burnished pear shape bottle (H2483); globular bottle with long neck (H2477, H2460); tulip beaker (H2434); and carinated jar with "metal" ridge. Three radiocarbon dates from CF58 /2/ and /3/ and the NW corner of the square CF57 provide a 2-sigma range of 3000–2700 BC (close to transitional phase D-C). In this part of the North Flat, the long continuous sequence of almost 700 years, before the Burned Building, is confirmed by the ceramic chronology and supported by radiocarbon dates.

There is no architectural information for CF55. Ac-

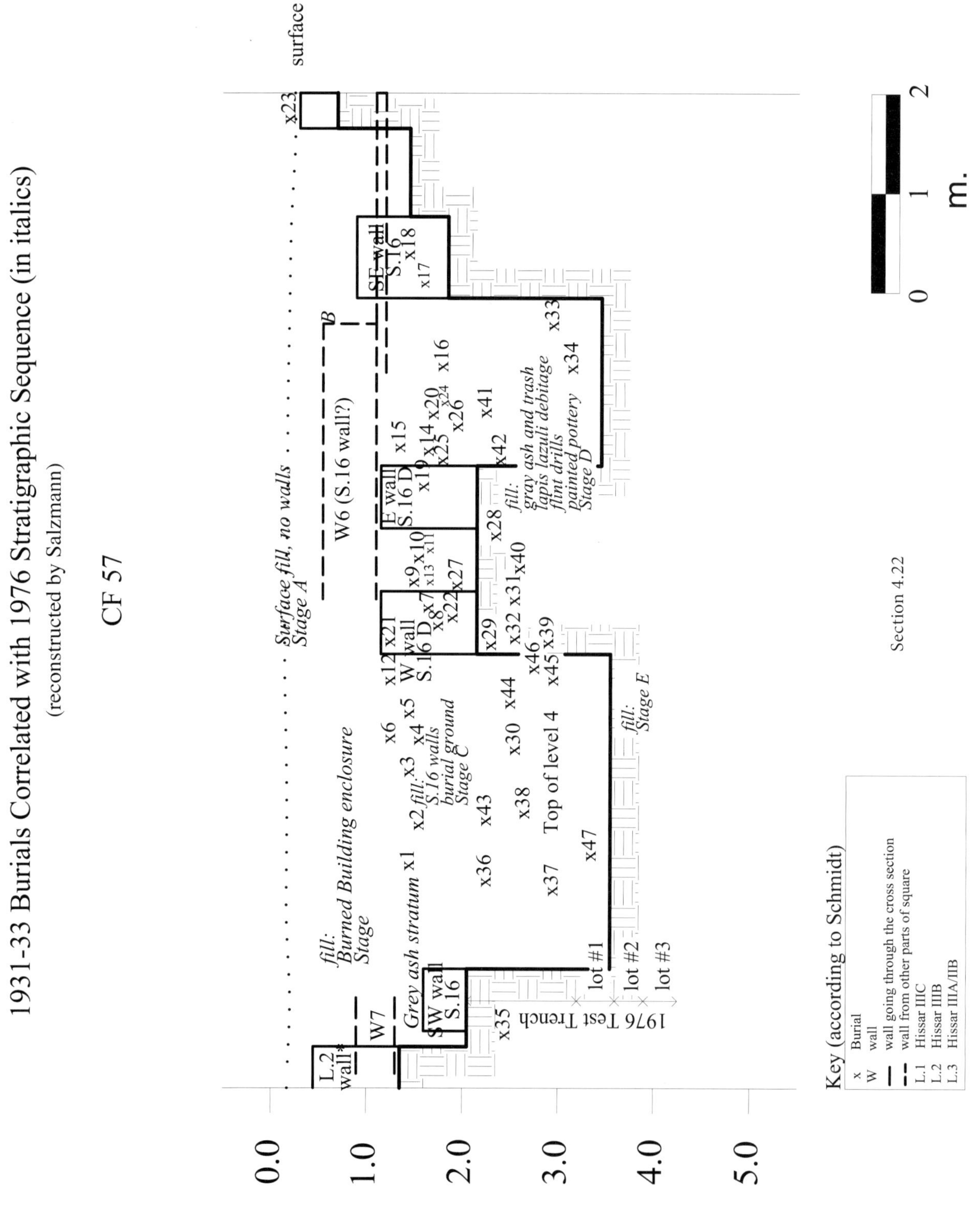

210 THE NEW CHRONOLOGY OF THE BRONZE AGE SETTLEMENT OF TEPE HISSAR, IRAN

Section 4.22

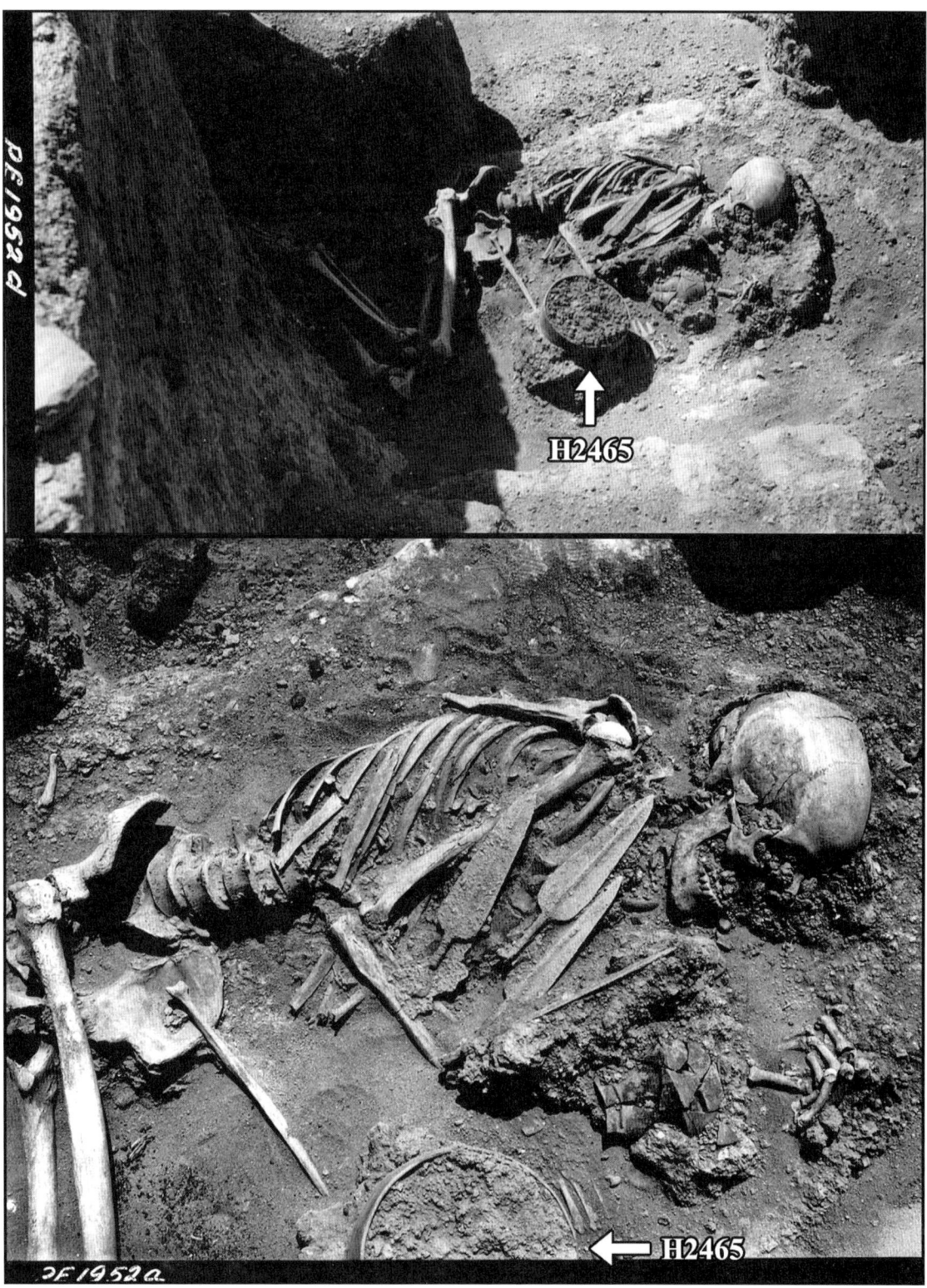

Fig. 4.13 Burial x28 from CF57, which contained a thin-walled grey burnished bowl (H2465) characteristic of transitional phase D-C (Courtesy of Penn Museum).

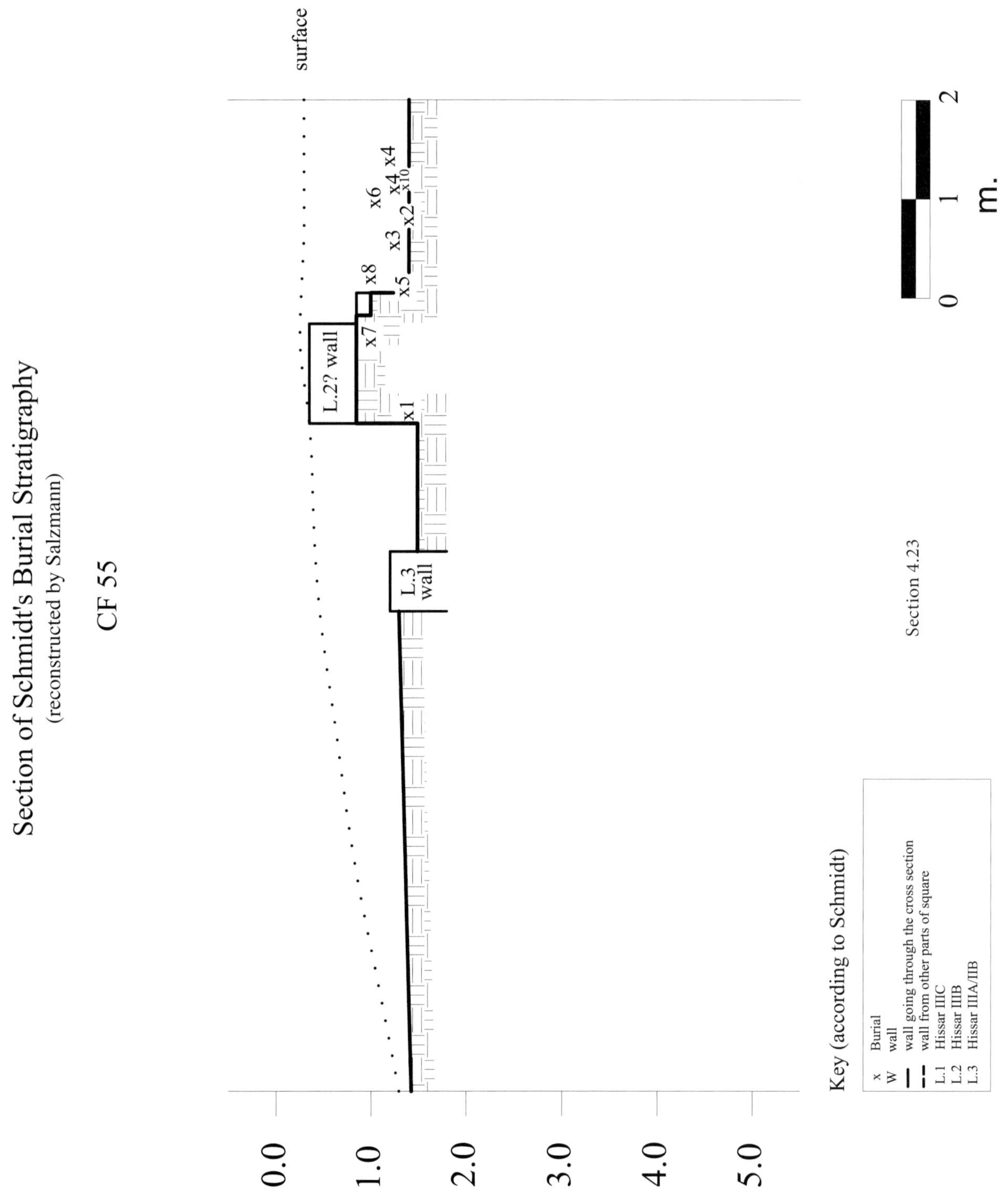

212 THE NEW CHRONOLOGY OF THE BRONZE AGE SETTLEMENT OF TEPE HISSAR, IRAN

Section 4.23

Fig. 4.14 A dark burnished globular goblet (H4162) from burial x40 in square CF57 (Courtesy of Penn Museum).

cording to the North Flat plan (Schmidt 1937: fig.102), it appears that the building in CF55 belongs to Schmidt's "Level 1," *above* the Burned Building.

CF55 Burials

Of the ten burials recorded, five contained datable ceramics. Schmidt notes on burial sheets that x1–9 are found on the floor of "Level 1" and burial x10 on the floor of "Level 2"(?). The ambiguous context leads us to date these burials ceramically and by comparison with other mortuary assemblages that contain similar rare artifacts of high craftsmanship.

Five burials (x1, x5, x5a, x8, x10) can be assigned to phase B on ceramic evidence, which includes: grey burnished vessels; a carinated jar with "ring" at neck, x10 (H2396); a bell-shaped beaker, x8 (H2394); a pattern burnished canteen, x2 (H537); a bottle pitcher and a carinated jar, x5a (H2390, H2391). Vessel H2391 has a long everted neck and pattern burnish on the body. These vessel types continue into phases B and B-A/A from the earlier phase D-C, as noted above. Burial CF55 x1 is dated on evidence from rare gifts of high craftsmanship, as compared with other dated burials. The assemblage of burial gifts comprise several bracelets in copper with 8-coils (H2379), copper cups filled with lapis and turquoise beads, a silver jar, silver ornaments, and a copper diadem crafted with repoussé technique. In addition, there is a simple grey burnished bowl (H2385) that is not datable (see Ch. 5, Burials with Outstanding Gifts: High Outliers).

H. The 1976 North Flat Burials

From the North Flat, three burials are documented: one in the Burned Building in square CF48 and one in each of the rooms in square CF58 (rooms /2/ and /3/).

Square CF48 Burial #1 (B1): This burial was dug into the top of the debris of the foundation trench of the Burned Building. The upper levels of this trench date to transitional phase D-C, 3100–2900 BC. Sex and position of the deceased are unknown. The mortuary gifts consist of a coiled copper bracelet (H76-27) (see Schmidt 1937: pl. XXVIIIB, H2170), and a grey burnished bowl (H76-28; Dyson and Remsen 1989: fig.16, p.91).

Square CF58/2/, Burial #1: Dyson describes the context of this burial as: "cut into the burned debris of CF58/2/ [ca. 3000–2800 BC], at a slightly later date, was a grave (CF58 B1) which contained a short necked black bottle (H76-75) and a grey beaker (H76-41) (Dyson and Remsen 1989: fig.26). The two forms may be compared to generalized bottle pitchers and a beaker of "IIIB" type (Schmidt 1937: pl. XXXVII bottle forms; pl. XXXVIII H3967, a beaker). This grave, intrusive into the dated context of the room, may well belong to Early Period "III" when the abandoned area appears to have been used as a burying ground," (Dyson and Remsen 1989:99). Thus, this burial may be considered contemporary with CF48 burial 1, dated to phase C. Ceramically, however, the two vessel forms, grey bottle and beaker, are also found in the earlier phase D from the Main Mound in square CG90/4/ (H76-32).

CF58/3/ B1: This burial was found in the context of burned room #3 with broken pottery vessels and burned reeds from the collapsed roof. "The burned and scattered bones of a small child (5 years or younger) were found mixed in the fill of the southeast corner of the room" (ibid., p. 102). Dyson compares the inventory of grey burnished vessel types (bottle pitcher, pedestal based bowl, buff painted pedestal based cup, and globular jar) that he retrieved from a closed context of the room, with those from Schmidt's similar vessel types. Dyson dates these types by radiocarbon to 3170–2880 BC (transitional phase D-C). He notes that Schmidt places them in three different Periods, IIB, IIIA, IIIB (ibid., p. 102–105), which is about 300 years later than the 1976 dates.

Using the Burned Building as our fixed point of reference at the North Flat, we observe at least three burial episodes: (1) immediately above the Burned Building, in the "L.1" walls in square CF37; (2) under the floor of Burned Building squares 3CF37-38: and (3) an earlier episode above Dyson's deep trench, below the base of the walls of "room 16." There might be an even earlier fourth episode in the southwest corner of CF57 which was the lowest point reached by Schmidt. Chronologically, these burial episodes display a continuous sequence from Late Hissar I through Late Hissar II (phases F through transitional D-C), with a possible gap of some hundred years between Late Hissar II (phase C) and Mid-Hissar III (phase B), and continue through Late Hissar III (phase B-A/A).

The cultural and behavioral dimensions of the Tepe Hissar communities are topics of discussion in the following Chapter 5 that aims to interpret funerary practices as part of the social and cultural order.

Table 4.2 NORTH FLAT: Chronology of Dated Burials According to the Reconstructed Stratigraphy and the New Ceramic Sequence

Square and total # of burials excavated	Burials	New Ceramic Phases	Revised Periods according to 1976 sequence
CF37 (12)	1	B-A/A	Late Hissar IIIC
	9	E-D	Early/Mid-Hissar II
CF38 (18)	6, 9	B	Mid-Hissar IIIB
	11, 16, 18	D, D-C	Late Hissar II–Early Hissar III
	15	E-D	Early/Mid-Hissar II
CF47 (9)	1, 2	B-A/A	Late Hissar IIIC
	4, 6, 7	E-D	Early/Mid-Hissar II
CF48 (22)	1, 3, 4, 5, 7, 11, 12, 16, 17, 18, 19, 21, 22	D, D-C	Late Hissar II–Early Hissar III
CF57 (47)	6, 11, 14, 20, 21, 23, 27, 28, 29, 35, 38, 40, 43	D, D-C	Late Hissar II–Early Hissar III
	33	E-D	Early/Mid-Hissar II
CF55 (10)	1, 5, 5a, 8, 10	B	Mid-Hissar IIIB

Fig. 4.15 The lion-gate of a Seljuk Cemetery, near the city of Shiraz, southern Iran, dated ca. 10th century CE. March 1932 (Courtesy of Penn Museum, image no. 83452).

Notes:

4.1 The Treasure Hill excavations revealed two hoards (I and II) in squares DH05-07 containing prestige objects such as alabaster vessels, columns and discs, copper weapons and tools, and ornaments of silver and gold. Hoard I included five mouflon head ornaments made of sheet gold of spectacular workmanship (Schmidt 1937: pl. XLVI H3210). Similar columns and discs were also found in a Main Mound burial DF19 x1 (Schmidt 1933: pl. CXXXVI) and on the North Flat building Level 1 (CF37) (Schmidt 1937: fig.132).

4.2 It is not unreasonable to assume the existence of another burial site, possibly an extramural one, considering that the number of burials found by Schmidt could be higher in proportion to the size of the settlement (especially Period I) and its duration. Recent soundings at Tepe Hissar indicate the existence of an Iron Age cemetery several hundred meters west of the main settlement (Roustaei 2010). According to Roustaei, the burials are dated to the Iron Age and Sassanid periods (ibid., pp. 616–17). I would argue only on the basis of the illustrated associated pottery that the "Iron Age" burials in trenches 24 and 25 could be dated to the Late Bronze Age (Hissar IIIC) (ibid., figs. 17, 18).

4.3 Some of the archival burial records had missing information. Additionally, the published and unpublished plans and sections are mostly unreadable, especially in the case of a large group of burials described as "bone piles" and "mass burials" where the skeletal material and the funerary objects are mixed together. Similarly, in the published plans and sections the burials are plotted in such close clusters that individual burials are indistinguishable and burials from different levels merge. Generally, it was most difficult to associate mortuary gifts with individual burials, especially in the case of a large group where the skeletal material is mixed together with artifacts and organic remains.

4.4 The remaining squares on the Main Mound and North Flat excavated by Schmidt but not examined in the field by the Dyson team cannot be correlated accurately with the 1976 stratigraphic sequence. Some of the burials from uncorrelated squares are dated using the new ceramic sequence as a guideline.

4.5 The depth at which the topmost Level 1 was recorded varies at the Main Mound due to the natural topography of the site and the continued erosion that changed the topography over the millennia.

4.6 In this discussion, terms "phase" and "stage" are used interchangeably: Howard's term "stage" denotes a construction level and phase is the term for chronological sequence.

4.7 Two phases of construction were also found in the test trench excavated by Howard underneath the phase D floor to the northeast of the "kitchen" in CG90. Both building stages fall under Schmidt's "Level 3" (3.5–5.0 m depth); however, with two meters of deposit, "Level 3" likely represents two ceramic phases E and E-D, although that is not clear in the section.

4.8 Ceramics from the burials of 1931–32 excavations in the Main Mound squares are organized into pottery charts for reference and comparison.

4.9 In the fill of Building 2_1, below burials x4 and x6, a serpentine cylinder seal was found at a depth of 2.45 m. Therefore, Dyson dates the context to Jemdet Nasr-Proto Elamite period. Additional confirmation for a late fourth or early third millennium BC date comes from animal figurines and counters (for a discussion of Building 2 architecture, stratification, and artifacts from the 1933 campaign, refer to Dyson and Remsen 1989:74–79).

4.10 Schmidt did not excavate in square CF58, although we can use Dyson's burned rooms from this square to correlate CF57 and CF48. The most important square for understanding the lower levels of the North Flat is square CF57, where both Schmidt and Dyson placed deep trenches. However, as with square DF09 on the Main Mound, correlating these lower levels with Dyson's excavations is often difficult.

4.11 Burials x18, x19, x21, and x22 are not indicated on Schmidt's section, thus, dating of the burials is based on ceramic typology. These burials are also not marked on the GIS burial map.

5

Death and Burial Culture of Tepe Hissar

A. Introduction

This chapter follows from Chapter 4, the reconstruction of burial stratigraphy and dating of the burials from the Main Mound and North Flat according to the newly established ceramic sequence. The burials that are stratigraphically verified, even if not ceramically dated, are included in the analysis.

This chapter is organized into four parts. Section B outlines the burial data and its analysis. This includes the location of the cemetery and the horizontal distribution of the burials (GIS map[1]), grave types, and some recent studies of skeletal remains to gain further insight into the diet, disease, and marks of physical disabilities. In section C, the burial groups are contextualized in cultural and chronological units. Section D addresses Tepe Hissar burial culture within a framework promoted by Fahlander and Oestigaard (2008) in their work *The Materiality of Death*. Their analytical method uses the material manifestations of death, bodies, burials, and rituals as the social and cultural order of the surviving communities shared by the deceased individuals. Essentially, this method replaces a strict theological analysis of the meaning of death with an archaeological focus on materialities (ibid., p. 5). This part of the discussion includes remarks on the practice of burial ritual as commemorative performance with examples from Tepe Hissar burials. In that context, references are made to interdisciplinary approaches from social and cultural anthropology, sociology, and history (Williams 2003:5–19; Laneri 2007:1–10; Brady 1999:243–48; Bloch 1974, 1994; Parker Pearson 1982; Van Gennep 1960). Finally, section E presents a diachronic overview of the funerary culture of Tepe Hissar.

B. Burial Data and Analysis

The primary source for the burial analysis is Schmidt's archival burial sheets and field records that list age, sex, body position, and types of funerary objects for all burials (1937:62–63).[2] In this analysis five of his age categories are employed, infant, juvenile, adult, mature, and senile (older than mature). As for body position, Schmidt's terms, dorsal and ventral are replaced by supine and prone, respectively. Body orientation is not used in the analysis, as Schmidt gives complicated and confusing descriptions that are cumbersome to use. Generally, there is no uniform pattern in the orientation of the body within burial groups in relation to sex, age, and through time. Despite missing information for some burials and no information at all for others, the burial sheets provide ample evidence to support re-dating burials using the 1976 stratigraphic re-assessment and the new ceramic chronology discussed in Chs. 3 and 4.

The second source of data generated for this study are the twenty GIS Burial Maps[3] showing the horizontal distribution of the dated burial groups in each square and from different periods. The maps are used to show (a) the relationship of the cemetery to the existing settlements, (b) an association of grave locations with elite individuals (especially for the High Outlier Group) marked by precious funerary offerings, and (c) a possible relationship of burials as members of a kin or a larger social group indicated by proximity of graves. The last two are incorporated into the section on Burial Groups below (pp. 226–251).

The Cemetery

The GIS Map in Fig. 5.1 shows the distribution of the burials on the Main Mound and North Flat. With few exceptions, the burials are on *flat* areas near the slopes surrounding the settlement. The slopes mark the edges of the primary occupation areas on the Main Mound throughout the duration of the settlement. Hence, the evidence supports the observations of Dyson and this author (see Chapters 2 and 4) that the burials were interred in uninhabited areas of the settlement and not through the living floors.

The Main Mound is the primary "cemetery" area where the "mass burials" were encountered in squares DF18, DF19, DF29, DG00, and DG11 (Schmidt 1933: pl. C).[4] It is doubtful that *all* of these burials were interred "en masse" contemporaneously (Fig. 5.2). In fact, Schmidt himself questions their contemporaneity, "We may mention…that the sequence of deposits in all sections of the mound was thoroughly disturbed by numerous burials of the upper occupations dug into the underlying levels" (1933:440–442). For example, questions of contemporaneity are raised in the northeast corner of square DG00, where 11 burials were recorded (Fig. 5.3). Interestingly, the chronological differences of these disturbed burials is also implied by Schmidt as he notes that the bones belonging to the skeleton DG00 x10 are mixed up with the remains of nine more persons. The presence of some articulated skeletal parts indicates that the bodies had not entirely disintegrated before they were buried. In some instances larger parts of the skeletons (i.e., the skull) were disconnected and formed bone piles. They would be considered secondary burials

In the present study, DG00 burials are assigned to three phases, D, D-C, B and B-A/A, from Late Hissar II to Late Hissar IIIC (Fig. 5.4), spanning nearly one thousand years. The later burials from phases B and B-A/A would have disturbed the earlier phase D-C burials, thus, forming the appearance of a mass burial in square DG00.

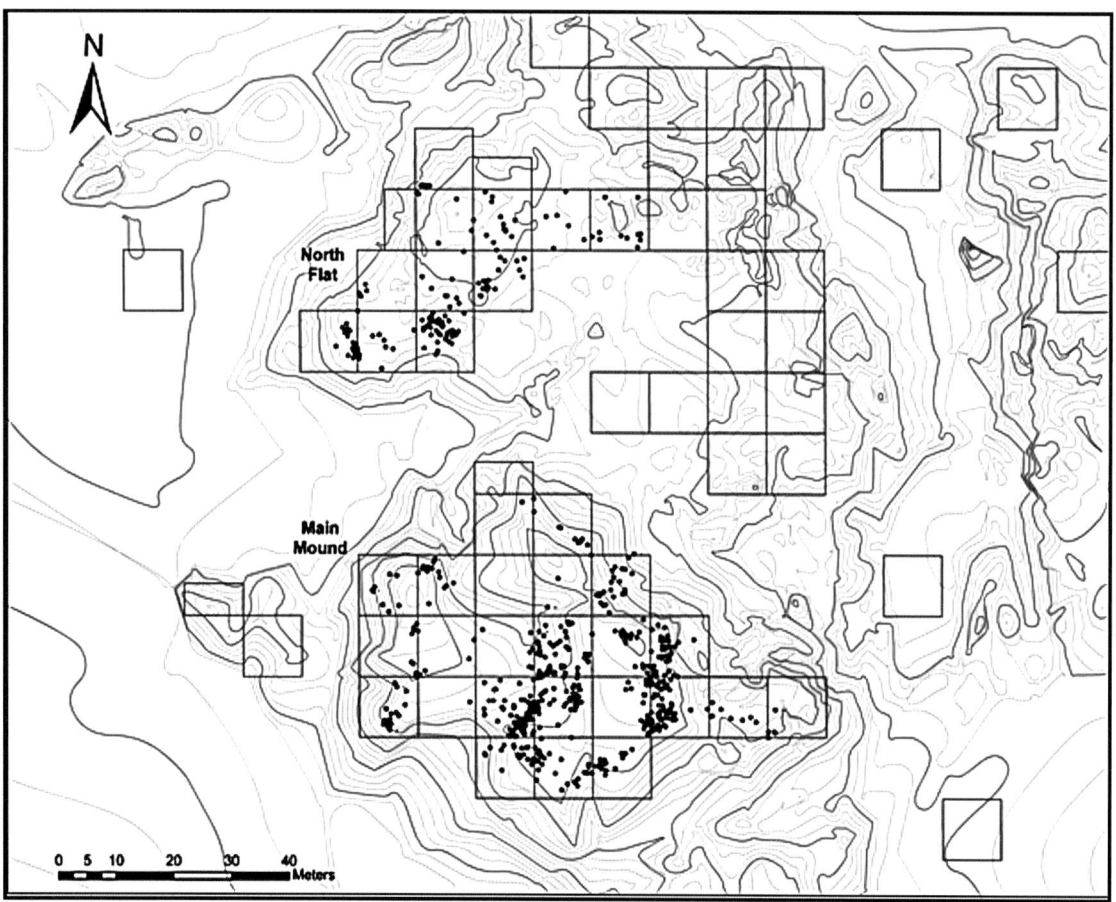

Fig. 5.1 A GIS map of Tepe Hissar showing the distribution of burials on the Main Mound and North Flat areas; architecture is not shown (after Kılınç Ünlü and Torres, 2010).

DEATH AND BURIAL CULTURE OF TEPE HISSAR 219

Fig. 5.2 Group of burials from the Main Mound DF19, deemed "mass burials" by Schmidt, but more likely they were interred gradually over time rather than all at once (Courtesy of Penn Museum).

Fig. 5.3 Photograph of the northwest corner of square DG00, where 11 burials were recorded (Courtesy of Penn Museum).

Fig. 5.4 Burials from the northeast quadrant of DG00, which range in age from Late Hissar II through Late Hissar IIIC (Courtesy of Penn Museum).

Fig. 5.5 Schmidt's "burial room" from DG11, storeroom /18/ of Building 3, where 38 burials were excavated (Courtesy of Penn Museum).

Similarly, in DG11, Schmidt's "burial room" interments in storeroom area /18/, of Building 3, where 38 burials are clustered (Fig. 5.5), belong to two different chronological groups, dated to the transitional phase D-C and B, early and late phases of the Bronze Age.

Grave Types: Pit, Cist, Communal Chamber, and Vault

Pit

Most of the bodies were interred in a "pit" (i.e., in plain earth) and wrapped in woolen garments, a practice that continued throughout the settlement in all types of graves. The other three grave types are few and far between at Tepe Hissar, though it is highly probable that these burial types might not have been observed and recovered archaeologically. Also, they might have been in unexplored locations at the site, for example, east of the North Flat and south of the Treasure Hill.

Cist grave

In his first excavation season, Schmidt found faint traces of a burial with an enclosure from Period I, "in one case only, a thin mudbrick wall bordered a burial" (1933:364). As work continued in the first and second seasons, five more cist graves were excavated with thin-walled mudbrick enclosures. Two of which Schmidt dated to Hissar II, burial CG25 x1 (ibid., pl. CXI; Fig. 5.6, east of North Flat) and DH36 x5 (Schmidt 1937:131, fig. 77, south of Treasure Hill). The cist graves are as unique[5] as the funerary gifts they contained. Burial CG25 x1 is an adult male whose grave is surrounded by six simple graves that are located at a distance from it. The deceased had a large copper stamp seal (Schmidt 1933: pl. CVII H1176, pp. 385, 389) hung from his pelvic bone, a mace head, along with an abundance of copper jewelry, earrings and multiple-coil bracelets near his head and on his arm (H1166, H1173), copper pins with double scroll heads (ibid., pls.

CIV, CV H1168–1171) on his chest, a silver head band, and lapis lazuli, carnelian, turquoise beads scattered on his chest. He was gifted with two grey burnished stemmed cups and bowls (H1149, H1150).

Burial DH36 x5 is a cist grave from Painted Pottery Flat belonging to an infant who is modestly gifted with two grey burnished short-stemmed bowls and a buff painted bowl (Schmidt 1937: fig. 77, pl. XXII H4349, H4350). The infant's beads consist of gypsum, shell and bitumen disks, and a silver loop. According to the new ceramic chronology, these graves should be dated Mid- to Late Hissar II (phases E-D, D). The practice of burying in

Fig. 5.6 Drawing of burial x1 from square CG25, a cist grave dated by Schmidt to Hissar II (after Schmidt 1933: pl. CXI).

cist graves continues into Late Hissar IIIC. Two additional cist graves on the Main Mound, DF18 x10 and DF09 x1 are dated to Late Hissar IIIC, phase B-A/A.

Still another cist grave excavated in 1976, was found in the storeroom of Building 3, on the Main Mound. Howard (1989b) notes the burial is clearly intrusive as it cuts into one of the circular plaster areas in room /11/. The floor was burned and covered with burnt sherds and animal bones in a black ashy deposit. "The body is surrounded by a series of bricks laid around it unevenly, they measure 0.58 x 28.09 m. A fragment of textile was still visible and was recovered." A radiocarbon date of 3360–2995 BC (P-2708) was obtained from the deposit. The ceramic assemblage of phase D-C, Late Hissar II/Early Hissar III, independently confirms the date.

Communal Chamber Burials

Schmidt referred to multiple burials as "communal." One such burial was DG11 x10 and x11 on the Main Mound. It belonged to an infant next to an adult female in a pit burial. Schmidt interpreted these burials as double burials, a child interred with his/her mother. The infant was in the prone position directly in front of the adult female, who was in "sitting" position, "hands extended toward the infant." Neither had funerary gifts, therefore they are not datable. Another double burial belongs to "two infants", CF89 x4, x5, in which the individuals have two copper artifacts with symbolic meaning: a double-headed ram (Schmidt 1937:259, fig 162, pl. XLVI H5141) and a pendant of a female figurine with birds on her shoulder (ibid., pl. XLVII H5142; Fig. 5.7). The double-headed ram must have been the finial of a wand, which is a replica of a wand in the second Warrior's grave (see below, Burial Groups), and is dated to Late Hissar IIIC, phase B-A/A.

Still another double burial belongs to two children (DG11 x2, x3). Burial x2 is an infant, contracted and lying on its right side; x3 is a juvenile in supine position also contracted. The left arm of x2 is leaning over x3. Schmidt (n.d.) describes this as a "double burial, probably close relatives…the younger child pressing toward the older one and hiding its face behind x2's [sic] neck." (Note that it is actually the younger individual x2 who is hiding behind the neck of the older individual x3.)

The largest communal chamber contained 28 burials, only fifteen of which were recorded: DF29 x1–x9; x12–x16; and x26 (Fig. 5.8). Schmidt noted that [these individuals] "were interred below floor level, but not necessarily during the occupation of the building. The room was actually used as a communal burial place but several xs [burials] are above the floor level suggesting that refuse had accumulated within, the wall(?) protruding above the surface during the time of the disposal" (burial sheets, IX.22.31, Penn Museum Archives).

The chamber contained: 10 adult/mature males (x1–5, x7–9, x12 and x16), four infants (x6, x13–15), and one adult female (x26). Of the male burials, x1, x2, x7 were gifted with ornaments: bracelets placed near arms (H628, H629, H637), copper earrings (H638), and beads of lapis lazuli, frit, and alabaster (H640, H643) were distributed near the head of the deceased individuals. Burial x1 also had a copper mattock with traces of a wooden handle (H631) and a copper knife (H630) (carving tool?) near his elbow. Burial x6 has unusually rich gifts for an infant, including copper bracelet and earrings (H644, H645) and a string of frit beads (H643) on his/her arms and near the head. Whereas with the other three infants, DF29 x13 has no gifts, x14 has one tulip beaker (H655), and x15 is gifted with an eight-wire copper bracelet (H658). The female burial has two silver earrings near her face (H1021) and two coarse grey vessels, a jar (H659) and a globular bowl (H660). All of the burials in this group are dated to Late Hissar II and Early Hissar III (phase D-C).

It is not unreasonable to consider the group burial practice as a significant characteristic of Late Hissar II and Early Hissar III Periods. The skeletal material of these individuals was intact, not disarticulated, so they must have been intentionally interred as a group—perhaps members of a family or a social group such as a clan. This practice is clearly different from mass burials that are characterized by disarticulated bone piles. In the latter instance, the funerary gifts are also scattered, as mentioned earlier in the DG00 communal burials.

Vault

Only one vault burial is recorded in CF89 x10; it is on the Main Mound, and described as having a "grave vault" (a semi-circular structure around the superior part of the body) 0.60 m broad and 0.50 m high (from Schmidt's burial notes). It is assumed that the grave is made of mud bricks although Schmidt does not specify the material and details of its construction. The deceased is a mature female, in supine position, with her legs contracted. She has only two alabaster vessels, a cup placed on her chest (H3521) and a jar (H5145) near her leg (Schmidt 1937:259, fig. 162). The burial can be dated to Late Hissar III on stratigraphic and stylistic evidence of alabaster vessels.

Studies of Human Remains

Following Schmidt's preliminary description of the skeletal material in the field, Wilton Krogman classified 250 individuals into "racial/physical types" based on cranial

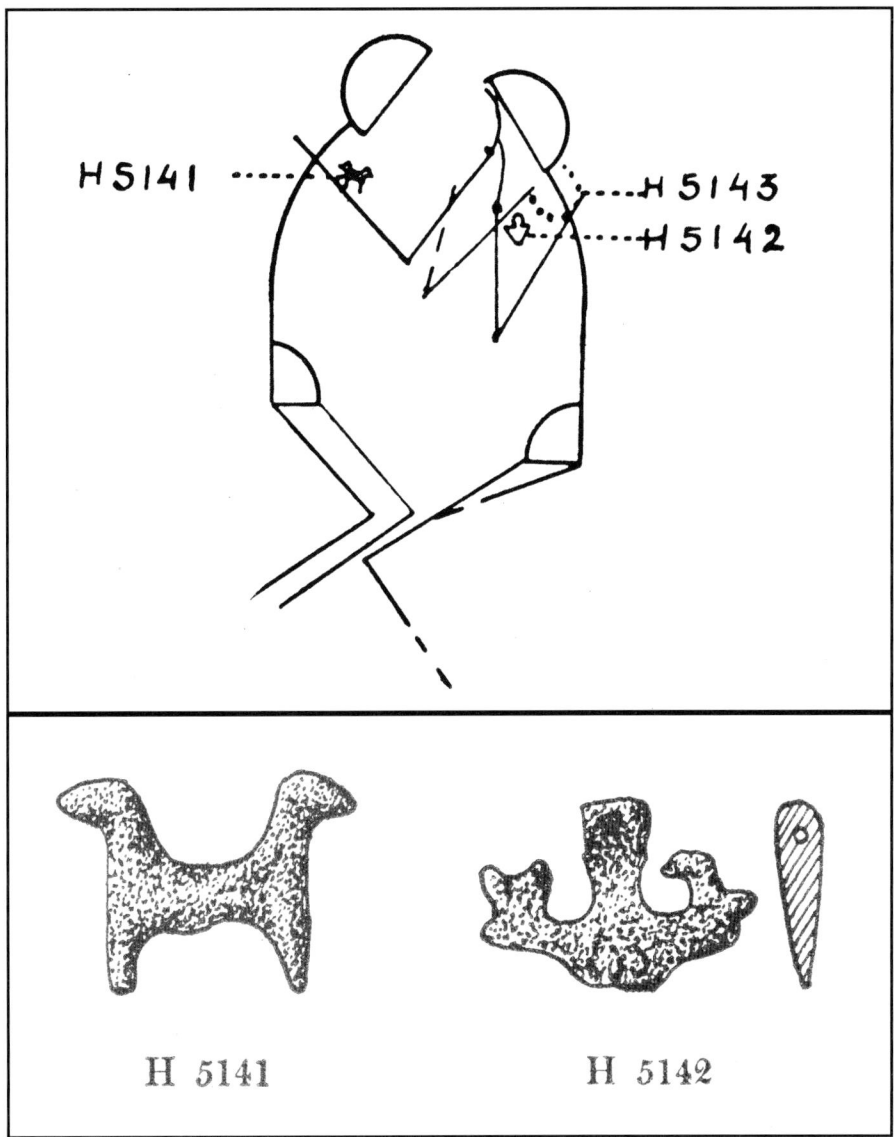

Fig. 5.7 Drawing of burials x4 and x5 from CF89 (both infants) showing the placement and detailed sketches of copper artifacts (after Yule 1982): a double-headed ram (H5141) and a pendant of a female figure with birds on her shoulders (H5142).

characteristics and studied the skeletal and dental pathologies (1940a,b,c). More recent examinations of the material were done by Rathbun (1989), Nowell (1978, 1989), and Ravin-Haque (1992). After commenting on the unrepresentative nature of the sample for the whole population, Rathbun states that the study of cranial traits showed the males to be localized, while the females were more regionally homogeneous (1989:33). Rathbun's comment regarding cranial traits grouping more closely among males than those among females can be interpreted as differences in marriage rules within the population (i.e., males being locally based,

marrying females outside their group). He also detected one particular pathological condition: "Four individuals from period III at Hissar may have suffered from some form of short limb dwarfism. These individuals (one male, one female, and two sexes undetermined) all have strikingly short limb bones. The muscle attachment areas are significantly larger than other individuals, especially on the humerus. The humeri also exhibit classic changes of the humeral head deflected dorsally and downward. Based on Krogman's data, however, the stature of males at Tappeh Hesar was 170 cm and females 157 cm to 154 cm" (Rathbun:133).

Fig. 5.8 A photograph from the southwest of a communal burial chamber from DF29, which included 28 burials (Courtesy of Penn Museum).

Nowell's study evaluated aging using the Tepe Hissar collection's dental sample by using the Miles method based on molar wear. Both Krogman's and Nowell's findings indicate the average age of the population to be 27.5 years; for the adults Nowell found the average age at death to be slightly later, between 29 to 32 years. He also observed skeletal stress markers, due to nutrition, accident, and possible genetic factors. In comparing his results with Schmidt's figures, Nowell points to a great disparity in the number of juveniles (0–6 years of age) and in the number of older individuals (45+ years of age) at the time of death, based on evidence from the sample. Nowell also notes the sample was biased with respect to age and sex due to the small number of individuals brought back from the field relative to the total number excavated.

Ravin-Haque, in a more recent study of dental paleopathology of the Tepe Hissar population, uses 91 individuals from all periods—their complete cranial remains and fragmentary remains of maxilla and mandibles—to test for various types of dental pathology and their relations to diet and general health status of the population (1992). Her thesis postulates that dental diseases are caused by complex interactions between the diet and the microorganisms, which normally inhabit the oral cavity. Further, she comments, "the skeletal population represents the end result of a lifetime of interactions between the individuals and their environments….by noting the presence or absence of certain dental pathologies we can generate a number of hypotheses about the people of Tepe Hissar—the composition of their diet, the methods with which they used to process food and the diseases which they encountered" (for more evidence on diet, see also Introduction p. 1).

According to Ravin-Haque's analysis, there is a high incidence of (a) dental wear that suggests rough diet or lots of "grit" mixed into food from using stone grinders to process cereals, (b) abscess, and (c) antemortem tooth loss. Additionally, hypoplasia (enamel defects) and caries are indicated as low to moderate (Ravin-Haque 1992:34). These pathologies point to some degree of dietary or general health stress, confirming Nowell's findings. She also suggests a cultural factor that may have played a role in

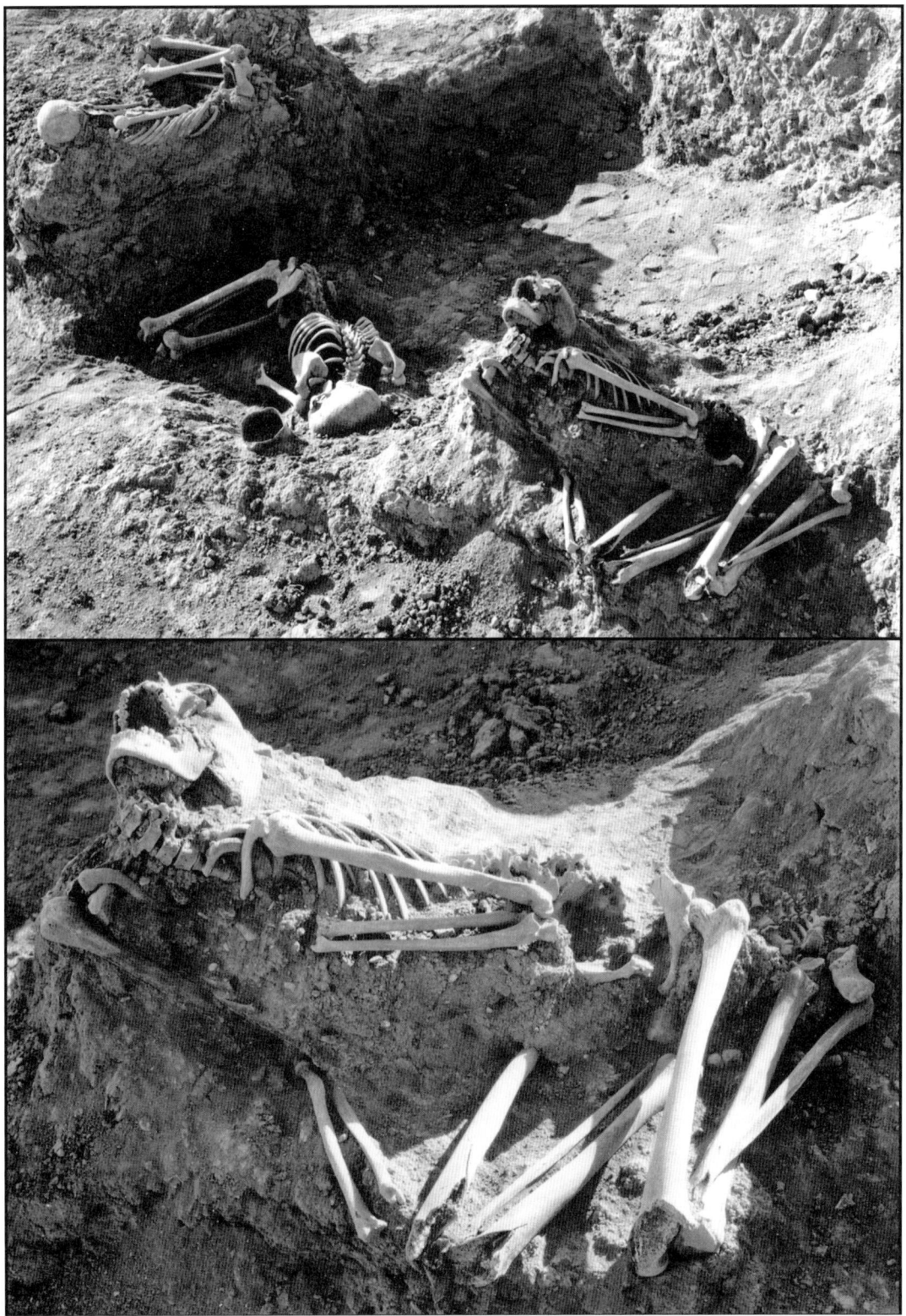

Fig. 5.9 Overview of "mass burial" from CG90 and close-up photographs of burial x5 (Courtesy of Penn Museum, image no. 83801).

early tooth loss, for instance, people using their teeth as tools to soften fibers or work hides (Fig. 5.9).

Following up on previous skeletal analysis, Zahra Afshar's (2014) thesis addresses aspects of health and diet in the Tepe Hissar population using skeletal and dental traits in combination with stable carbon and nitrogen isotope analysis.

Another line of inquiry is based on evidence from Computerized Axial Tomography (CT) scans of the Tepe Hissar skeletal collection, undertaken jointly by the Penn Museum and Indiana University. The goal is to reconstruct in more detail physical and cultural aspects of the Bronze Age population of Tepe Hissar, by detecting individual variations (for example, sexual dimorphism), as well as to arrive at a mathematically modeled 'generic' human skull that can serve as a comparison with a known ethnic group. The scans allow for the precise quantification of linear dimensions, surface area, and volume of the remains, which are useful in studies of variation, pathology, functional morphology, and for answering questions not easily answered by examination of the physical specimens. This on-going study should shed new light on the question of identifying physically different groups within the population that may also explain cultural changes. An additional piece of information that the CT scan technology could provide is accurate renditions of not only the external surfaces of a bone, but also of the internal bone structure and morphology, that is, bones that are not visible externally on the skull (J. Monge, pers. comm. 2013). For more information on the CT scan Project visit: http://plum.museum.upenn.edu/~orsa/Search_The_Archive.html.

C. Burial Groups: Data Presentation and Analysis

The total number of burials excavated in 1931–32 from the Main Mound and the North Flat was 537. This analysis includes 204 dated and stratigraphically verified burials from all periods. Admittedly, it is a small sample in proportion to the total number of burials excavated (n=1637), but it represents a substantial percentage (45%) of the burials in the two areas examined placed in their corrected chronological and stratigraphic contexts.

The dated burials are classified into five chronological groups, to correspond to the revised ceramic phases, as shown below and in Tables 4.1 and 4.2 in Chapter 4: group 1 (phase F, F-E), group 2 (phase E-D), group 3 (phase D-C), group 4 (phase B), and group 5 (phase B-A/A). The hyphenated phase designations are employed for transitional phases indicating the overlapping of ceramic types from earlier into later phases. Some burials containing only non-ceramic assemblages are also included in the groups as they are found in association with stratigraphically confirmed objects, such as alabaster vessels, metal weapons and tools, or ornaments and figurines.

Group 1 (Main Mound, phase F-E) contains only three burials dated to Late Hissar I. Schmidt's main source of Period I burials was excavated from multiple quadrants of the Painted Pottery Flat (1937:22–38, figs. 32–43, pls. III–XIII, Periods IA-IC).[6] The largest number of burials comes from groups 3 and 5 from the Main Mound and North Flat phases D-C and B-A/A. The increase in the number of burials in groups 3 and 5 is partially attributed to an increase in the number of squares excavated by Schmidt on the Main Mound and the North Flat.

For methodological convenience each burial group is listed in two sets of inventory tables: Tables 5.1–5.5, which list categories of sex, age, and burial positions of the deceased individuals and Tables 5.1a–5.5a, which list funerary gifts of each burial along with stylistic and material attributes. Hence these 10 inventory tables represent an aggregate of burials within each square. Each burial group is described along several physical and cultural dimensions in an attempt to infer meaningful patterns of variation within each group and between groups: (a) physical remains (condition of skeletal parts); (b) sex and age, (c) funerary gifts, (d) position of the body and parts of the body, and (e) placement of artifacts in relation to the body of the deceased.[7]

Besides these ten tables, there are two tables referred to as "Low Outliers" and "High Outliers." The first contains burials with artifacts commonly associated with all burials, such as ceramics and beads (see Table A2.1a–e in Appendix 2) while "High Outliers" includes five burials with additional gifts that are characterized as objects with a high level of craftsmanship, such as ornaments and jewelry in precious stones and metals (see Table A2.2a–b in Appendix 2). The rationale for the division into High and Low Outliers is that the counts between them are so divergent numerically that meaningful statistical results are generally not possible. Furthermore, these two groups are used separately to address questions such as sex differentiation in the use of ornaments or the association of funerary gifts with social identity. As an example, the High Outliers had few ceramics and many identity related artifacts and ornaments, while the Low Outliers were just the opposite—many ceramics and few or no symbols of identity markers and ornaments with semi-precious stones. The former category is included in groups 4 and 5, the latter, in groups 1 through 3.

In the High Outliers group, the inventory contained: beads of precious stones (lapis lazuli, carnelian, turquoise, alabaster) that continue to be used in jewelry while amber and chalcedony appear in Late Hissar III, phase B-A/A. Another use of alabaster, serpentine and chalcedony is in carvings of animal figurines (ibid., pl. XXXIII). The precious metals, gold and silver, are not only incorporated to precious stones in the manufacture of jewelry, but they are used in crafting vessels, figurines, wands, as well as decorative elements on weaponry, on shafts of daggers and lance-blades (ibid., pls. L, LI, XXXIV H2023, H2024, H3243). Copper and lead continue to be used largely for weaponry, seals, and symbolic figurines.

Burial Group I: Late Hissar I to Early Hissar II (Phase F-E)

In this group there are only three dated burials from the Main Mound square DF09 x50, x51, and x52 (Tables 5.1, 5.1a, A2.1a, see also GIS Maps in Appendix 3). Burials x50 and x51 are infants of unknown sex. Both are in lateral position with flexed legs. The third burial, x52, is a mature female in supine position. All three have arms flexed in front of chest and hands near the face.

The funerary gifts are sparse: while each of the two infants has a necklace of gypsum stone placed near the neck, the female individual (x52) has a grey burnished, wheel-made pedestal bowl near her head. As explained earlier, group 1 is a small, unrepresentative sample (see Sections 4.1, 4.2, and Pottery Chart 4.1a in Appendix 1). The average number of objects is one per burial.

Burial Group 2: Early to Mid-Hissar II (Phases E, E-D)

Burial group 2 has 20 burials from the Main Mound and North Flat (Tables 5.2, 5.2a, A2.1b, see also GIS Maps in Appendix 3). Some of them appear to have been disturbed either in antiquity or during excavation. The male to female ratio is nearly 4:3 in favor of male individuals. That ratio, however, does not account for a third of the individuals whose sex is unknown.[8]

Abbreviations for Ch. 5 Tables

M	is	male	Inf	is	infant	Su	is	supine
F	is	female	Juv	is	juvenile	Pro	is	prone
Un	is	unknown	Adu	is	adult	L	is	left lateral
Tot	is	total	Mat	is	mature	R	is	right lateral
Bur	is	burial	Sen	is	senile	Sit	is	sitting
Ves	is	vessel	cer	is	ceramic	Orn	is	ornament
Cu	is	copper	Wp	is	weapon	ala	is	alabaster
Tol	is	tool	sto	is	stone	sea	is	seal
Ag	is	silver	Fig	is	figurine	Pb	is	lead
Au	is	gold	bo	is	bone			

Table 5.1 Group 1: Sex, Age, and Position of Burials

Square	SEX				AGE							BURIAL POSITION					
	M	F	Un	Tot	Inf	Juv	Adu	Mat	Sen	Un	Tot	Su	Pro	L	R	Un	Tot
NORTH FLAT																	
MAIN MOUND																	
DF09		1	2	3	2			1			3				3		3
Group 1 Total		1	2	3	2			1			3				3		3

Table 5.1a Group 1: Funerary Gifts

Square	OBJECT CLASS							MATERIAL									Artifacts per burial
	Ves	Orn	Wp	Tol	Sea	Fig	Tot	cer	Cu	ala	sto	Ag	Pb	Au	bon	Tot	
NORTH FLAT																	
MAIN MOUND																	
DF09	1	2					3	1		2						3	1
Group 1 Total	**1**	**2**					**3**	**1**		**2**						**3**	**1**

Table 5.2 Group 2: Sex, Age, and Position of Burials

Square	SEX				AGE							BURIAL POSITION					
	M	F	Un	Tot	Inf	Juv	Adu	Mat	Sen	Un	Tot	Su	Pro	L	R	Un	Tot
NORTH FLAT																	
CF37	1			1				1			1			1			1
CF38	1			1					1		1				1		1
CF47		1	2	3	2		1				3	1			2		3
CF57	1			1			1				1				1		1
NF Tot	3	1	2	6	2		2	1	1		6	1		1	4		6
MAIN MOUND																	
DF09	5	4	3	12	1	1	4	4		2	12	2		4	2	4	12
DG11			2	2	2						2			1	1		2
MM Tot	5	4	5	14	3	1	4	4		2	14	2		5	3	4	14
Group 2 Total	**8**	**5**	**7**	**20**	**5**	**1**	**6**	**5**	**1**	**2**	**20**	**3**		**6**	**7**	**4**	**20**

Of the 13 individuals whose sex was determined, twelve reached adult or mature age at the time of death and one female died as a juvenile. As is the case with the earliest group, the most common position of interment is lateral, turned either to the left or right side, with no uniform preference for one side or the other, and legs flexed.

The most common type of grave good is the ceramic vessel, which is often found near the head of the burials (DF09 x13, x30, x36, x43; CF37 x9; CF38 x15), and less frequently in the back of the body (DF09 x33, x41). Other locations are near the leg or at the knee (DG11 x21). In burial DF09 x45, a cup inside a jar is behind the shoulder of the body. In several burials, we observe multiple ceramic vessels, one inside the other, in association with female burials: in DF09 x42, a small cup is found inside of a small cup, both placed inside a large cup. The pattern continues into later phases for both sexes.

With few exceptions, the very young and very old individuals, are sparsely gifted; they have one or two ceramic vessels (CF37 x9; CF38 x15; CF47 x6, x7; DG11 x21, x47).

Toward the end of this phase, the expansion of the lapidary craft is particularly striking in the production of lapis lazuli, carnelian, and crystal beads that occur in oblong, bicone, and disc shapes (Schmidt 1937: pl. XXXII).[9] The bead jewelry is exclusively associated with female burials whose ornaments appear to be intentionally placed on parts of the body where they would be worn. In later periods, jewelry is no longer sex specific.

In this group, we note the appearance of silver combined with semi-precious stones. Other types of silver jewelry are earrings and finger rings. In DF09 x35, copper rings and large quantities of lapis lazuli and crystal beads were placed in a cup (H3909) "which was held by the deceased female between her arms flexed in front of her chest" (Schmidt's unpublished notes). The woman wore two six-coiled copper rings on the right middle finger (H3911, H3912). In addition to the cup of beads, a necklace of semi-precious stones, carnelian, lapis lazuli, frit, and crystal in tubular, disc, and spherical shapes, was placed on her neck (H3910). The placement of the necklace appears to be intentionally done, as in the case

Table 5.2a Group 2: Funerary Gifts

Square	OBJECT CLASS							MATERIAL									Artifacts per burial
	Ves	Orn	Wp	Tol	Sea	Fig	Tot	cer	Cu	ala	sto	Ag	Pb	Au	bon	Tot	
NORTH FLAT																	
CF37	2						2	2								2	
CF38	3						3	3								3	
CF47	4	1					5	4		1						5	
CF57	2						2	2								2	
NF Tot	11	1					12	11		1						12	2
MAIN MOUND																	
DF09	21	6					27	21	3		1	1	1			27	
DG11	3						3	3								3	
MM Tot	24	6					30	24	3		1	1	1			30	2.14
Group 2 Total	37	7					42	37	3	1	2	1				42	2.1

with the other female individuals. Another adult female wears a carnelian pendant on her neck (CF47 x4) and a male individual (DF09 x33) has a polishing stone on his hand, which is placed inside a bowl. Ceramically, this is a transitional phase from painted pottery to grey burnished and coarse wares; the brazier makes its appearance as a new ceramic form.

In this group the average number of objects per burial is 2.2; the average for North Flat is less than the Main Mound. In later groups 3 through 5 on the North Flat, however, the average number of objects increase substantially compared to those on the Main Mound.

Burial Group 3: Late Hissar II to Early Hissar III (Phases D and D-C)

This is the largest dated group containing a total of 97 burials (Tables 5.3, 5.3a, A2.1c, see also GIS Maps in Appendix 3). The male-female ratio is nearly 2:1. There is also a higher mortality among infants. The most common position of interment continues to be lateral with legs flexed. Supine and prone positions are generally associated with adult and mature males, while female burials have no uniform position. Arms/hands in male, infant, and juvenile burials is frequently flexed in front of the chest or face.

In a few cases, Schmidt noted signs of pathologies on skeletal remains. One such instance is a young adult male (DG11 x52), who is recorded as having "left humerus pathological...atrophied." This young man must have had some kind of trauma, disease, or congenital condition that left his arm visibly diminished.

Schmidt reports large numbers of disarticulated "bone piles," most likely secondary burials in squares DF29 and DG00. He describes the DG00 burials as follows: "in the northeast corner the remains of ten persons were found within a small area. Most of the bones were disturbed, [disarticulated] and mixed up, but a few sections of vertebral columns, arms or legs, pelvic bones and femora, were still articulated. [Those] skeletal parts still articulated indicated that the persons had not entirely disintegrated before they were here disposed of in a communal pit, not immediately but prior to total decomposition" (1933:440, 447, pl. CLI; see also Fig. 5.2–5.5).

In comparison with group 2, the burials in group 3 more than quadruple the population sample and the average number of burial gifts is higher at 2.57 per burial from both the Main Mound and North Flat (as mentioned above, the North Flat has more gifts in this group than before, averaging 3.14 per burial). Although the average number of gifts is not in great numbers in this population, there are several individuals with greater quantity and variety of objects of superior craftsmanship (silver ornaments, figurines, and weapons).

Regarding the types of gifts and their association with age and sex, ceramic vessels are still the preferred objects for all ages and sexes. The majority of the vessels are for pouring liquids, grey burnished spouted bowls and bottle pitchers. The practice of putting an object inside of an object is often done with ceramic vessels as is the practice of placing ornaments in vessels—also observed in group 2. An adult male (DG01 x36) has a jar (H2526) inside a bowl placed in front of his chest; in burial DG11 x20, an adult female's ornaments are all in copper, placed inside a spouted bowl in front of her chest (Schmidt 1937: pl. XXXVIII H3956). Similarly, one adult female burial (CF38 x11) has large quantities of jewelry placed in a grey burnished carinated jar (ibid., pl. XXXVIII H5172). Other gifts include a decorated copper headband (H5175), a copper hourglass shaped female figurine pendant (ibid., pl. XLVII H5178), a necklace made of lapis lazuli beads combined with silver tubes, and various copper earrings. Her bracelets are the only pieces of jewelry placed on her arm. Another mature female burial (DG01 x32) has a more modest assemblage of jewelry that includes only three copper pins (H2518, H2521, H2522, see Fig. 5.10). Her lapis lazuli and crystal bead necklace (H2525) lies near her jaw. There is a notable increase in the jewelry worn and also kept in ceramic vessels placed near the

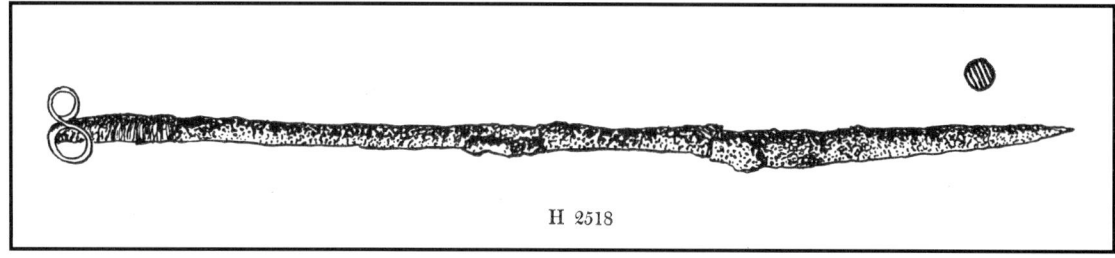

Fig. 5.10 One of three copper pins (H2518, H2521, H2522) found with burial x32 from DG01. This one has a double wire-loop head and dates to phase D-C (Schmidt 1933: pl. LIII).

Fig. 5.11 Photograph of a group burial, DG00 x14 (left, male) and x16 (right, female); x15 (an infant with x16) was badly damaged and discarded according to Schmidt's field notes (Courtesy of Penn Museum).

deceased individuals of both sexes, but more so in female burials. It should be noted that the difference in numbers of elite objects offered to some and not to other individuals implies social differentiation among the deceased.

In general, the social identity related artifacts are on the increase such as copper ornaments, semi-precious stones, wand/macehead,[10] and figurines; they occur across all sex and age groups. Weapons and tools are exclusively associated with male burials. Each of the three male burials in (CF48 x1, x5, x22) is gifted with one copper dagger with medial ridge, a knife, a copper spear point, and another spear point with a wooden handle. Another male burial (DF29 x1) has two tools/weapons, a mattock and a knife placed near his elbow. On the other hand, one male burial (DG00 x16) lacks weapons and tools, but has more beads and symbolic objects than is typically found in a male burial: alabaster beads with copper tubes, copper bracelets, and five grey burnished vessels. A small, copper, hourglass-shaped female figurine (Schmidt 1933:417, pl. CXXXII, H576) found in a male burial is very similar to the figurine pendant associated with a female burial (CF38 x11; Schmidt 1937: pl. XLVII, H5178). In both cases, the figurines were placed on the hands of the individuals. It appears that such stylized female figurines were not gender specific, which implies that they might have represented a universal cult/fertility symbol as suggested by Schmidt (1933:417).

Unlike in the earlier period, in group 3 there is an increase in the numbers and types of gifts for infant burials; while one has one or two cups and a bead (DG10 x6), others contain multiple numbers of copper jewelry and vessels. For example, an infant burial, CF57 x2 contains silver and copper earrings in addition to four grey burnished vessels. In burial DG00 x6, the infant has three grey burnished vessels and three copper ornaments (H560–565), one of which is an unusual v-shaped copper pendant (H563). Another burial, CF48 x18, located under the Burned Building (room 2) of the North Flat, has a copper diadem/bracelet with zigzag repoussé stipples (Schmidt 1937: pl. LIV H4112), which is a highly developed skill requiring special tools and precision in the use of a hammer to create the embossed designs. Additionally, a grey burnished carinated jar is among the offerings (H4102). In the double burial of a female and an infant, DG00 x15, x16, while the accompanying adult female is gifted with five ceramic vessels, three copper ornaments, and an alabaster bead (Fig. 5.11), the infant has only one ceramic vessel.

In this transitional group 3, the funerary gifts are more diversified, especially in the bead and weapon category. Semi-precious beads continue to be manufactured for necklaces that are placed in both adult male and female burials and a few infants are gifted with silver jewelry (DG11 x17, x48; CG90 x20; CF57 x21). Copper objects continue to occur in great quantities as weapons, tools, jewelry, and figurines, and are found in one-third of burials.

An unusual burial belongs to an adult male (DF29 x2) who has, inside his mandible, two items, a copper tube (H639) and an earring (H638) that were stained green. Other associated objects include a copper bracelet at his arm (H637) and copper fragments on his head.

In group 3, silver is a favored precious metal for jewelry and other ornaments (necklace, ring, earring, and band [possibly headband/diadem]) compared with group 2, although only few individuals from all age groups and sexes are gifted with silver ornaments. Another striking characteristic of this group is new decorative elements applied to popular vessel forms, including a glossy, "metallic" grey ware bottle with herringbone pattern burnishing. In selected burials, grey burnished bell beaker and tulip beaker, bottle pitcher, and carinated jar forms co-occur with silver jewelry. The two latter vessels have a "ring" in relief around the neck (CF57, x11, x14, x43; CF48 x5, x12). The male individual in burial DF29 x7 has a grey burnished, glossy, "metallic" beaker at his pelvis (H649), and a bottle pitcher (H650), re-formed from a canteen, placed at his feet. In group 4, there is a similar practice of enclosing re-used vessels as burial gifts.

Burial Group 4: Hissar IIIB (Phase B)

In this group of 40 dated burials, almost one-third of the population is unidentified by sex (Tables 5.4, 5.4a, A2.1d, A2.2a, see also GIS Maps in Appendix 3). These are typically infants and juveniles whose fragile skeletal material was crushed and disarticulated such that no identification could be made.

On the Main Mound the sex ratio of males to females is 3:1, while on the North Flat it is 3:2. Male and female populations lived to adult and mature ages, and, even beyond, to senile stage. Hence, in the context of this population sample, there is high infant mortality rate, but for those who lived beyond infancy there is an equally high longevity rate. This pattern is similar to that of group 3.

The predominant body position for males is supine. For females the most common burial position is lateral with head turned to the left or right, irrespective of age. The only prone position in this group is attributed to the "Dancer" (CF55 x1), who is described below in the section High Outliers.

Some burials are exceptions to the norm in the unusual positions of the deceased and find-spots of ceramic vessels. Among them are three burials, DF19 x21, x19, and x24. Burial x21 is a mature adult male who displays supine position with legs flexed behind and to the right, right arm flexed across chest, and left arm down and bent at a right angle. His ceramic assemblage is arranged along the left side of his body instead of the usual cluster of vessels placed near the head. Similarly, in burial x19, an adult (sex unknown) in lateral position has a short beak-spouted bowl (H1029) into which the coccyx was apparently inserted. The third burial x24 is a female in supine position, with her legs flexed behind, her right arm flexed across chest, and left arm down and bent at a right angle. She is gifted with an array of ceramic vessels placed in different locations around her body: on left side of her cranium a bottle-pitcher (discarded), fragmented bowl (discarded), a goblet (H1636), a bowl (discarded), and a plate (H1637) at her left elbow, and a "terrine" or jar (discarded) behind the right os coxae. On left hand side, at her right elbow, she has a large oval bowl (H1028), a pitcher (H1027), and a grinding stone at right shoulder (H1113).

A few skeletal parts display signs of pathology, as was encountered in group 3. For example, an adult male (DF09 x9) has a cut mark on his occipital bone, which may be the result of an accident, surgery, or even an intentional mark (it is the only one observed by the excavator). Another adult male has a strip of copper wire attached to his lower jaw, which may have been part of his dental repair (DG11 x62).

As in the earlier groups, ceramic vessels constitute the majority of the assemblage (57%), jewelry/ornaments are second (31%), followed by tools and weapons (4%), figurines (4%), and non-ceramic vessels in metal and stone (4%). Tools and weapons are still exclusively found with male burials. Jewelry/ornaments are not sex-specific as in group 3. The ceramic assemblage contains largely grey burnished wares.[11] Four of the frequently occurring forms are generally associated with adult male burials (13 out of 17 males):[12] carinated jar (DG00 x7; DF18 x25), tulip and bell beaker (DG11 x16), and bottle pitcher (CG90 x23, x9; CF38 x6, x9; DF09 x9; DF18 x15, x38; DF19 x21; DG11 x16, x32, x62). On the other hand, spouted cup/bowl with short horizontal beak is associated with both sexes as well as infant burials: (DF19 x19, x40, and x60 H1029, H896, H891; spouted bowl is similar to Schmidt 1937: pls. XXXVIII, XLI H4104 and H3315).

In contrast to wide ranging gifts for adult burials, juveniles and infants have relatively fewer gifts; one or two ceramic vessels accompany the young. For instance, in two infant burials, DF19 x40 and DF19 x43, a small grey burnished spouted pitcher (H0896) and a grey burnished ceramic cup (H0885) are noted. There are, however, a few exceptions to the rule. Copper symbols are gifted generously to adults as well as juveniles: two burials have wands with double scroll placed near their foreheads. One belongs to a mature female burial in CG90 x10 (H4123 unpublished). The other belongs to an infant burial, DG11 x18 (ibid., pl. XLVI H3954). Also, one juvenile female burial, CG31 x7, is distinguished by a large inventory of silver and alabaster vessels and ornaments, in addition to three identity markers: two wands and one stamp seal. One of the wands is a realistic representation of an agricultural scene (ibid., pp. 257, 258, pl. XLVIII H4885; Fig. 5.12, 5.13). Perhaps to celebrate agricultural productivity, thus to memorialize the individual as member of a farming community. The second is a lead figurine of a woman with birds on her shoulder (Schmidt 1937:257, H4887) and the third is a copper stamp seal that depicts a complex hunting scene with a hunter intertwined with a serpent, ibex, and feline (ibid., p. 258, H4886 not drawn)

Table 5.3 Group 3: Sex, Age, and Position of Burials

	SEX				AGE							BURIAL POSITION					
Square	M	F	Un	Tot	Inf	Juv	Adu	Mat	Sen	Un	Tot	Su	Pro	L	R	Un	Tot
NORTH FLAT																	
CF38	1	2		3			2	1			3	1			1	1	3
CF48	5	3	5	13	4	1	8				13	3		3	4	3	13
CF57	6	4	2	12	1	2	7	2			12	1	1	5	2	3	12
NF Tot	12	9	7	28	5	3	17	3			28	5	1	8	7	7	28
MAIN MOUND																	
CG90	5	5	2	12	2	1	5	4			12	3	1	5	2	1	12
DF09	1	1	3	5	3	1	1				5			2	1	2	5
DF18	4	2	3	9	1	1	4	3			9	3		1	2	3	9
DF29	6	2	5	13	5		5	3			13	2	1	6	3	1	13
DG00	4		2	6	1		4		1		6			2	2	2	6
DG01	1	1		2				2			2			2			2
DG10	1		1	2	1		1				2			2			2
DG11	6	4	3	13	3	1	7	2			13	2		6	4	1	13
DG20	3	1	2	6	1	1	3			1	6	1		2	1	2	6
MM Tot	31	16	21	68	17	5	30	14	1	1	68	11	2	28	15	12	68
Group 3 Total	43	25	28	96	22	8	47	17	1	1	96	16	3	36	22	19	96

Table 5.3a Group 3: Funerary Gifts

Square	OBJECT CLASS							MATERIAL								Artifacts per burial
	Ves	Orn	Wp	Tol	Sea	Fig	Tot	cer	Cu	ala	sto	Ag	Pb	Au	bon	Tot	
NORTH FLAT																	
CF38	5	6				1	12	5	5		1	1				12	
CF48	18	17	3				38	18	18		1	1				38	
CF57	30	7	1				38	30	5	1	1	1				38	
NF Tot	53	30	4			1	88	53	28	1	3	3				88	3.14
MAIN MOUND																	
CG90	16	7					23	16	6		1					23	
DF09	7	1					8	7			1					8	
DF18	11	4	1				16	11	4	4						16	
DF29	16	12	2				30	16	11	1	1	1				30	
DG00	15	7				1	23	15	6	2						23	
DG01	3	10					13	3	8		1	1				13	
DG10	2						2	2								2	
DG11	19	6					25	19	4		2					25	
DG20	13	5		1			19	13	2	1	3					19	
MM Tot	102	52	3	1		1	159	102	41	5	9	2				159	2.34
Group 3 Total	155	82	7	1		2	247	155	69	6	12	5				247	2.57

Table 5.4 Group 4: Sex, Age, and Position of Burials

Square	SEX				AGE							BURIAL POSITION					
	M	F	Un	Tot	Inf	Juv	Adu	Mat	Sen	Un	Tot	Su	Pro	L	R	Un	Tot
NORTH FLAT																	
CF38	1	1		2			2				2				2		2
CF55ᵃ	2	1	2	5			5				5	3		1		1	5
NF Tot	3	2	2	7			7				7	3		1	2	1	7
MAIN MOUND																	
CG90	1	2		3			2	1			3			2	1		3
DF09	1	1	2	4	2		1		1		4	3				1	4
DF18	6		4	10	2	2	6				10	3		4	2	1	10
DF19	2	2	4	8	3		5				8	3		3	1	1	8
DG00	1			1			1				1					1	1
DG11	3		1	4	1		3				4			3	1		4
MM Tot	14	5	11	30	8	2	18	1	1		30	9		12	5	4	30
Group 4 Total	17	7	13	37	8	2	25	1	1		37	12		13	7	5	37

ᵃThe Dancer

Beginning in the mid-third millennium BC, copper and silver are widely used in the manufacture of artistically crafted ornaments. Two silver diadem/headbands (H2846, H2850 unpublished) in burial CF38 x6 are replicas of the one found in the Priest's burial in group 5. (A modest version of the silver diadem is the copper one offered to female burials in group 3). Toward the end of the third millennium BC, the jewelry assemblage comprises a large variety of beads: alabaster, lapis lazuli, rock crystal, turquoise, and chalcedony. Copper rings and bracelets of multiple coils are popular, especially in female burials (Fig. 5.14). In general, the distribution of jewelry/ornaments follows the same random pattern of placement as vessels: near chest, head, arms, "vertex" (crown of the head), or near the leg of the deceased. Some male burials have beads and single bracelets scattered near the chest and, in few instances, both sexes have alabaster and lapis lazuli necklaces placed near the neck (CF38 x9; DG11 x16) or behind the shoulder of the deceased (DF19 x 21, x24).

The average number of objects in this group is 2.81 per grave, which is higher than in groups 2 and 3. Most of the gifts are from the North Flat, with an average of 4.86 objects per burial, which includes the rich burial of the "Dancer" (see High Outliers, Table A2.2).

Table 5.4a Group 4: Funerary Gifts

Square	OBJECT CLASS							MATERIAL								Artifacts per burial
	Ves	Orn	Wp	Tol	Sea	Fig	Tot	cer	Cu	ala	sto	Ag	Pb	Au	bon	Tot	
NORTH FLAT																	
CF38	3	9					12	3	5		2	2				12	
CF55[a]	12	10					22	8	8		4	1	1			22	
NF Tot	15	19					34	11	13		6	3	1			34	4.86
MAIN MOUND																	
CG90	4					1	5	4	1							5	
DF09	5	2					7	5	1		1					7	
DF18	17	2		3			22	17	4		1					22	
DF19	17	3	1			2	23	16	6	1						23	
DG00	1						1	1								1	
DG11	5	6				1	12	5	6	1						12	
MM Tot	49	13	1	3		4	70	48	18	2	2					70	2.33
Group 4 Total	64	32	1	3		4	104	59	31	2	8	3	1			104	2.81

[a]The Dancer

A Burial with an Outstanding Set of Gifts in Group 4

The "Dancer" is a richly gifted female burial (Table A2.2a, see also GIS map in Appendix 3), named by Schmidt after the position of her arms and legs, which gave her the appearance of a "dancer" (Fig. 5.15). Her funerary gifts are limited in number, but they surpass in materials and craftsmanship the other burials in group 4, notably in the number of beads of lapis lazuli, banded carnelian, and crystal. Among the most attractive and unique objects is a necklace that combines animal figures carved from semi-precious stones with copper and silver pieces: a copper crescent, with lapis lazuli beads in the shape of rams' heads, a copper lion, and a silver bird and turtle (Schmidt 1937:244–45, figs. 133–35 H2386, H2387, H2388; Yule 1982: Abb. 13, 1). The burial offerings include multiple coiled copper bracelets (H2379) and earrings, silver finger rings, and a silver double scroll pendant strewn on her chest (Schmidt 1937:234, 235, 244, 245, figs. 141, 142; Yule 1982: Abb. 11, 12). One of her copper headbands is crafted with the long-standing tradition of repoussé technique (H2382) along with her silver jewelry and bead ornaments and silver containers (Schmidt 1937: pl. LVII H2381, H2383). The superior quality of her ornaments and her silver vessels foreshadow the gifts of the four individuals in the High Outliers category in group 5 (Table A2.2).

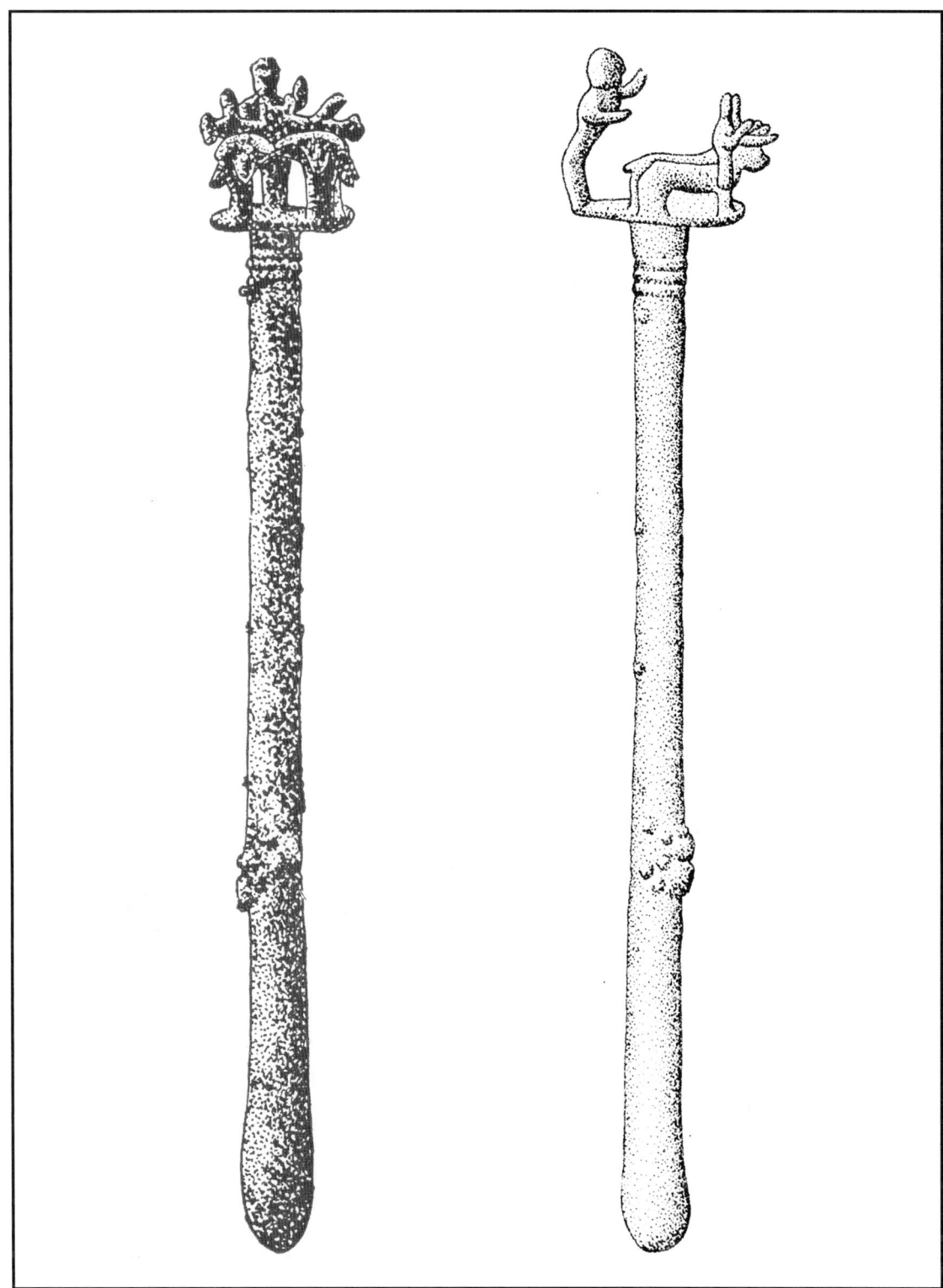

Fig. 5.12 Identity marker from a juvenile female burial, x7 CG31, which is a wand (H4885) depicting a realistic agricultural scene (after Yule 1982).

Fig. 5.13 Photographs of early 20th century Iranian agricultural practices similar to those depicted on the wand (H4885) from burial x7 CG31: a) Harvesting wheat manually, with a sickle; b) Threshing wheat with poles

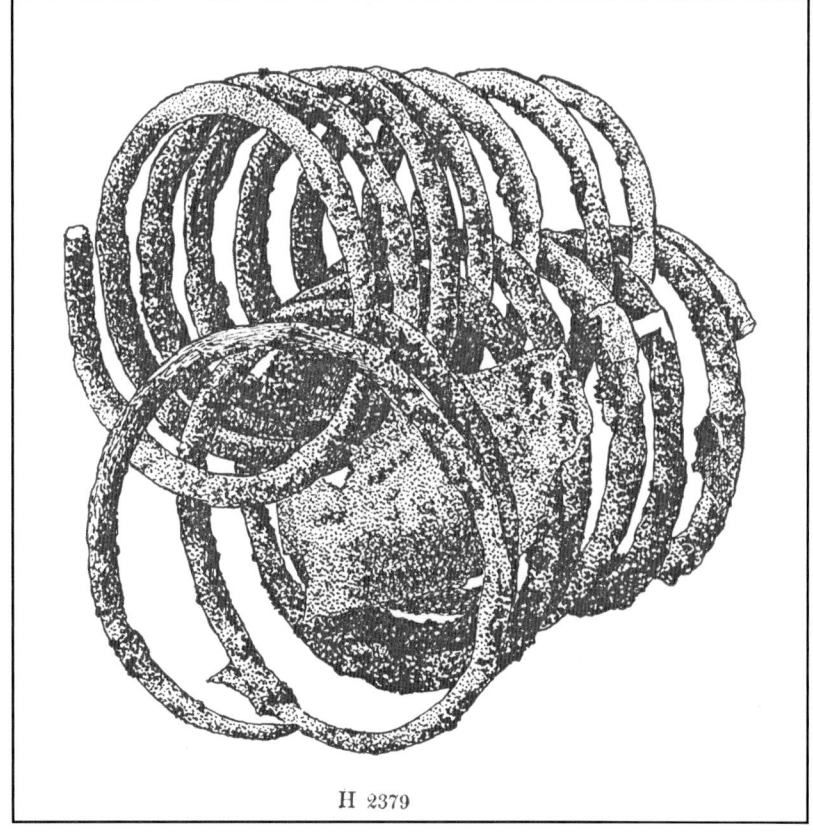

Fig. 5.14 An example of copper bracelets (H2379) with multiple coils found in burial group 4, ca. 2500 BC (after Yule 1982).

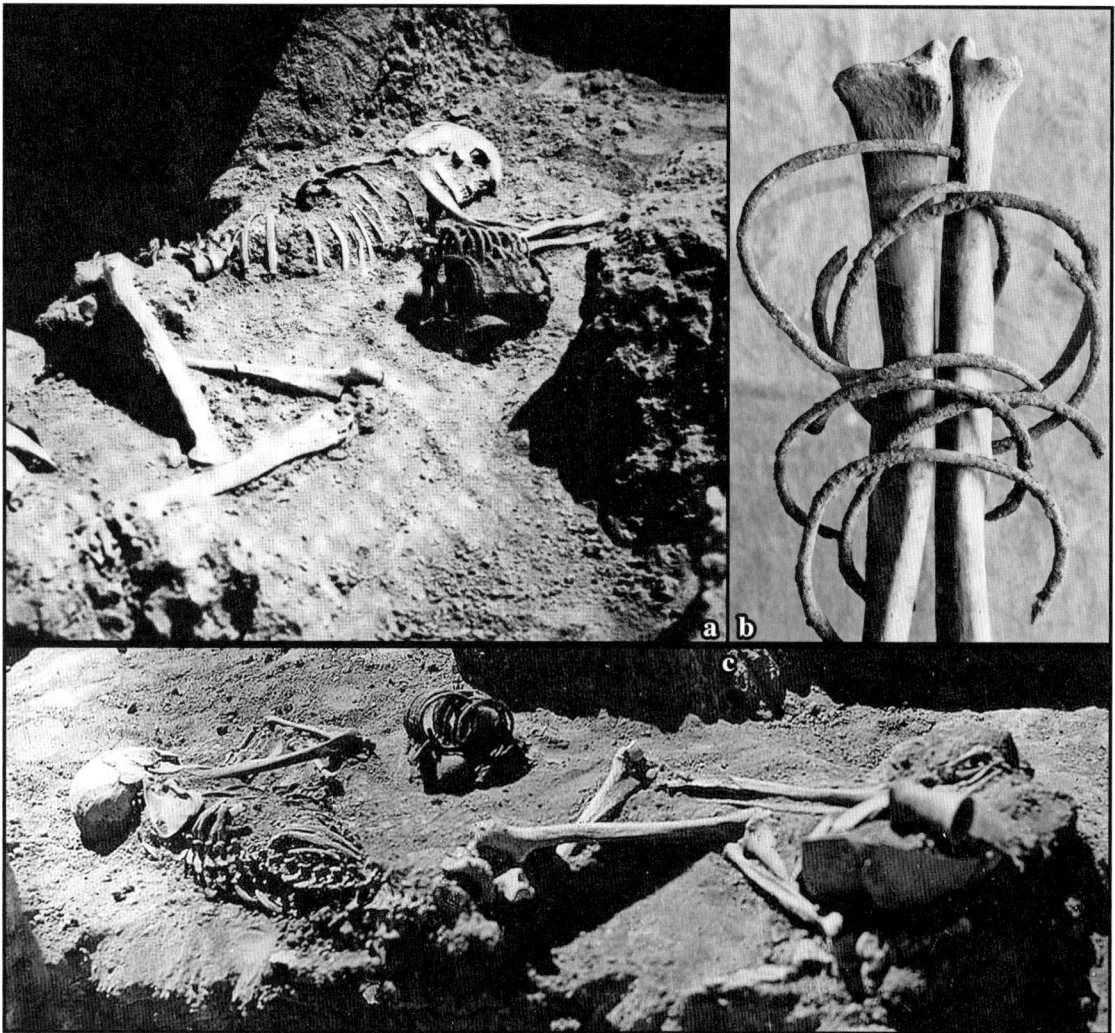

Fig. 5.15 Photographs of the richly gifted burial Schmidt termed the "Dancer," x1 CF55: a,c) After Schmidt (1937: fig 142); b) Copper bracelets still in place on her arms (Courtesy of Penn Museum).

Burial Group 5: Late Hissar IIIC (Phase B-A/A)

Group 5 is the second largest after group 4, containing a total of 49 burials (Tables 5.5, 5.5a, A2.1e, A2.2b, see also GIS maps in Appendix 3). While the male to female ratio is 1:1 in the North Flat, on the Main Mound it is 4:1 with male individuals remaining more frequent, as is the case in all previous groups. Also as previously, one-third of the population is not identified by sex. The predominant burial position is lateral as in the earlier groups. A few adult males, juveniles, and infants are in prone or supine positions. Aside from three cists and one "grave vault," CF89 x10 (described above), all are simple pit burials. The vault burial also has the characteristic white patches of textile/matting underneath and around the bones as observed in the early burials.

In contrast to group 4, the ceramic and stone vessels in group 5 are generally placed near the head, a practice that is consistent with other earlier groups. Some ornaments are placed in positions where they would be worn: for example, a copper ear pendant is found near the "right auditory region" in (DF 19 x7); three alabaster vessels "at head-end of skeleton" in (DF 19 x3) (Schmidt 1933: pls. CXXXVIII, CXL H181, H182, H184). Yet there is very little consistency in the placement of other artifacts. Social identity symbols (figurine, rod/wand, seal) are placed near or in the hand or on the pelvis. The next most common placement of objects is on the dorsal side of the body: on the spinal column or between the scapulae, on the pelvic vault or between the knee or the crouched legs (for Low Outliers, see Table A2.1 in Appendix 2).

In group 5 burials (DF19 x3, x7, x12), two males

Table 5.5 Group 5: Sex, Age, and Position of Burials

Square	SEX				AGE							BURIAL POSITION					
	M	F	Un	Tot	Inf	Juv	Adu	Mat	Sen	Un	Tot	Su	Pro	L	R	Un	Tot
NORTH FLAT																	
CF37		1		1			1				1	1					1
CF47	1		1	2	1		1				2				2		2
NF Tot	1	1	1	3	1		2				3	1			2		3
MAIN MOUND																	
CF79	1			1			1				1			1			1
CF88	1			1		1					1	1					1
CF89	2	1	1	4	1			3			4	2	1		1		4
CF99		1		1		1					1			1			1
CG90	1			1			1				1			1			1
DF08[a]	1			1			1				1		1				1
DF09[b]	3			3			1	2			3		1		2		3
DF18[c]		1		1	1						1				1		1
DF19[d]	8	1	4	13	3		9	1			13	4	1		6	2	13
DG00	2	1		3			2		1		3	1		1	1		3
DG01	9	1	2	12	2	1	7	1	1		12	2	1	2	4	3	12
DG10		1		1					1		1				1		1
DG20	1		1	2	1		1				2				1	1	2
MM Tot	29	7	8	44	8	3	23	7	3		44	10	5	6	17	6	44
Group 5 Total	30	8	9	47	9	3	25	7	3		47	10	6	6	19	6	47

[a] DF08 x1 is the Priest, adult male prone
[b] DF09 xi is Warrior 2, adult male prone
[c] DF18 x1 is the so-called Little Girl, R lateral, and infant, questionably identified by Schmidt as female due only to burial items.
[d] DF19 x2 is Warrior 1, adult male supine

Table 5.5a Group 5: Funerary Gifts

Square	OBJECT CLASS							MATERIAL									Artifacts per burial
	Ves	Orn	Wp	Tol	Sea	Fig	Tot	cer	Cu	ala	sto	Ag	Pb	Au	bon	Tot	
NORTH FLAT																	
CF37	2						2	2								2	
CF47	3	4		4		2	13	4	1	3	2			3		13	
NF Tot	5	4		4		2	15	6	1	3	2					15	5
MAIN MOUND																	
CF79	7	4					11	4	1	4	2					11	
CF88	8						8	7		1						8	
CF89	8	2			1		11	4	1	4	2					11	
CF99	1						1	1								1	
CG90	1						1	1								1	
DF08[a]	19	19	2	1	1	5	47	1	21	11	8	2	4			47	
DF09[b]	17	5	25	2	1	27	77	11	18	26	19		1	2		77	
DF18[c]	25	7		4		2	38	6	5	8	4	11		1	3	38	
DF19[d]	29	9	5	2	1	4	50	22	14	11		1	1	1		50	
DG00	6						6	5		1						6	
DG01	21	4					25	21	3	1						25	
DG10	4	2					6	2	1	2	1					6	
DG20	2	1					3	2			1					3	
MM Tot	148	53	32	9	4	38	284	87	64	69	37	14	6	4	3	284	6.45
Group 5 Total	153	57	32	13	4	40	299	85	65	80	39	14	6	4	6	299	3.36

[a] DF08 x1 is the Priest, adult male prone
[b] DF09 xi is Warrior 2, adult male prone
[c] DF18 x1 is the so-called Little Girl, R lateral, and infant, questionably identified by Schmidt as female due only to burial items.
[d] DF19 x2 is Warrior 1, adult male supine

and one individual of undetermined sex stand out as having unusual body positions as well as an array of prestige objects, especially in copper and alabaster. Burial DF19 x3 is of unknown sex, laterally placed, and all of his/her gifts are alabaster and ceramic vessels and alabaster beads (including unworked chips). A stemmed plate in a brown translucent alabaster (ibid., pl. CXL H182) is a replica of the one gifted to Warrior 1 in burial DF09 x1 (ibid., pl. CXXXVII H176) (see High Outliers below).

Burial DF19 x7, classified as "juvenile-adult," is also interred laterally on the right side. Of particular interest are his legs, which were colored or stained green: "the upper parts of the lower legs are stained green; but no copper object was found there, though it certainly was present originally" (Schmidt's unpublished notes). We cannot dismiss the notion that this green coloring may be some sort of copper oxide left by material that was not recovered or that some copper carbonate was applied to bones for decoration. Lying in front of his chest is a two-lobed copper spatula (H224).

Group 5 burials are characterized by prestige items that are found with most of the individuals, especially seals and alabaster vessels. For example, burial DF19 x12, an adult male, had few gifts but mostly prestige items, some of which are found in the High Outlier category (Fig. 5.16). Placed near his forehead is an alabaster cylindrical cup (Schmidt 1933: pl. CXXXVIII H549), which is an exact replica of the one found in the Little Girl's grave (H388), and a copper seal/pendant (ibid., pl. CXXIX H553) placed at the "hollow of right knee." This seal-pendant or "medallion seal" is also similar to the one found with the Priest's burial (ibid., pl. CXXIX H459). Next to the seal/pendant is another copper square stamp seal and a figurine of a quadruped. The burial also includes three simple gifts: a typical Hissar III grey canteen with two handles and pattern burnishing (ibid., H548), a copper ear pendant of coiled wire (H551) found near the left parietal bone, and a copper "point" (H552) found by the left elbow.

Another notable adult male burial, DF19 x60, has one (H892)[13] of the three cylinder seals excavated at the site (Schmidt 1937:197–199, fig. 118). Schmidt dates all three seals to Hissar IIIB. The seal, H892, is cut from alabaster and is the only one from a documented context. Based on the associated ceramic evidence, it is dated to Mid- to Late Hissar III, ca. 2500–2200 BC (see also Dyson and Remsen 1989:78). According to Schmidt, the other two cylinder seals, H3710 and H116, are slightly later, from fill contexts. The former from Treasure Hill is from the fill of the IIIC buildings and probably contemporary with H892. The latter seal H116 (Schmidt 1933: pl. CXXX H116) is cut from serpentine and is associated with fill of Building 2 on the Main Mound. A possible date for the serpentine seal is earlier than the others, ca. 2900–2500 BC.

Fig. 5.16 Photograph of burial x12 from DF19, an adult male buried with few gifts but those included were mostly prestige items (Courtesy of Penn Museum).

In group 5 burials, effigy vessels are offered to an infant and a mature male in burials CF47 x1 and CF47 x2 respectively. The infant's gift is a vessel in the shape of a cow with pronounced horns and muzzle. This stylized figurine is placed in front of the infant's face (Schmidt 1937:191, fig. 113 H2785; Fig. 5.17). The male individual's gift is a female effigy figure with large breasts, stub arms, and cylindrical neck. This highly symbolic fertility figure is found on his pubic bone (ibid., pp. 193–94, fig. 115, pl. XLVI H2790; Fig. 5.18).

Group 5 represents the highest average offerings for both the Main Mound and North Flat in all groups. The overall average number of objects per burial is 6.36; for the North Flat it is 5 and for the Main Mound it is 6.45. The drastic increase in the average is clearly due to the abundance of objects included in the four burials with outstanding gifts (one of the High Outliers is assigned to Group 4).

Burials with Outstanding Gifts: High Outliers

In the High Outlier category, there are five individuals: "Dancer" from group 4 (CF55 x1) and four from group 5, "Warrior 1" (DF19 x2); "Warrior 2" (DF09 x1); "Priest" (DF08 x1); and "Little Girl" (DF18 x1) (Schmidt 1933: pls. CLII–CLV). Clearly, the variety of precious stones and metals, the superior technical proficiency, and the aesthetic quality of the objects reflect the differential status of these individuals.

Of the three male burials, two are prone and one supine in position. The two females are in lateral position. The distinguishing aspects of these individuals

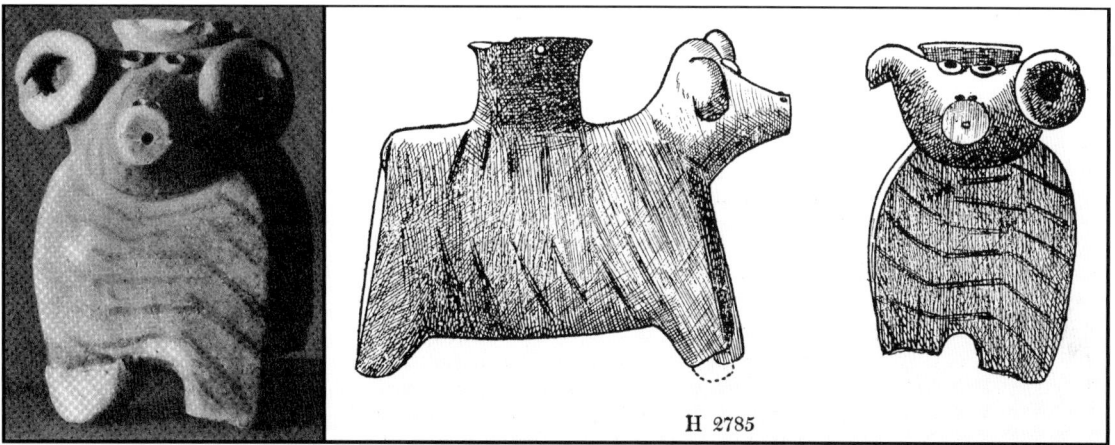

Fig. 5.17 Cow effigy vessel (H2785) included with an infant burial, CF47 x1 (photograph after Schmidt 1937: fig. 113; drawing after Yule 1982).

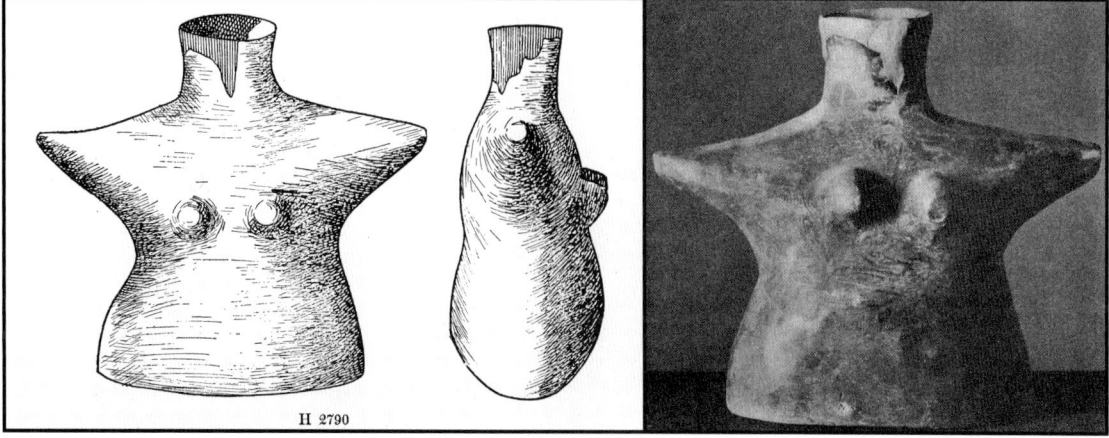

Fig. 5.18 Female effigy vessel found with an adult male burial, CF47 x2 (photograph after Schmidt 1937: fig. 115; drawing after Yule 1982).

from the rest of the burials is, in part, the location of their graves, which are at some distance from the rest of the burials in the group (see GIS maps in Appendix 3), and not just the differences in grave types.[14] The burials have in common a rich assemblage of identity defining symbols (wand/macehead) in copper, silver, lead, and gold/electrum, vessels, and animal and human figurines in alabaster. Among beaded ornaments amber and chalcedony are new additions to the usual bead repertory.

The two "Warriors" and the "Priest" are the only individuals who are gifted with weapons and tools (bident and trident).[15] However, only the "Warrior 2" and the "Priest" have stamp seals. The "Little Girl" and the "Dancer," both females, lack weapons and seals.

Warrior 1 and Warrior 2. Warrior 1 in DF19 x2 (Fig. 5.19) is interred in an awkward supine position, with legs flexed to right, right arm flexed to the left, left arm flexed across chest, and head turned to the right. Warrior 2 in DF09 x1 is in prone position with legs contracted to the left. In comparing their gifts, Schmidt states that Warrior 2 is "more martially equipped."

Warrior 2 is buried in one of the rare cist graves (see Fig. 4.3 this volume) with a few mud bricks at the foot and southwest corner of the grave pit. As observed in the earlier burials, there are white patches on the earth and on his bones, suggesting remains of textile/reed matting. He has the highest number of gifts (n=68) in the High Outlier category, over 30 of which are animal figurines. On Schmidt's burial sheet, the objects are listed and organized by find spots or by functional categories, such as: near the skull, on and beside the skeleton, or weapons bundled up. The bundle contains his weapons, which are his signature possessions. They consist of copper daggers (Schmidt 1933: pls. CXVIII and CXIX, H768, H769) and spearheads placed near animal figurines of quadrupeds crafted in alabaster (n=17) and clay (n=7) (H738–H744 and H746–H762, see Schmidt 1933: pl. CXXXIII, and for H740, H744, H748, H750, H757, H758, see Schmidt 1937: pl. XXXIII; Fig. 5.20). Other weapons are all oriented alike (Schmidt 1933: pl. CXLIII): a copper spearhead "with offset stem" (ibid., pl. CXIX H767), a dagger or knife (ibid., pl. CXIX, H770), and 15 chalcedony arrow-

Fig. 5.19 Photograph of Schmidt's "Warrior 1" burial, DF19 x2 (Courtesy of Penn Museum).

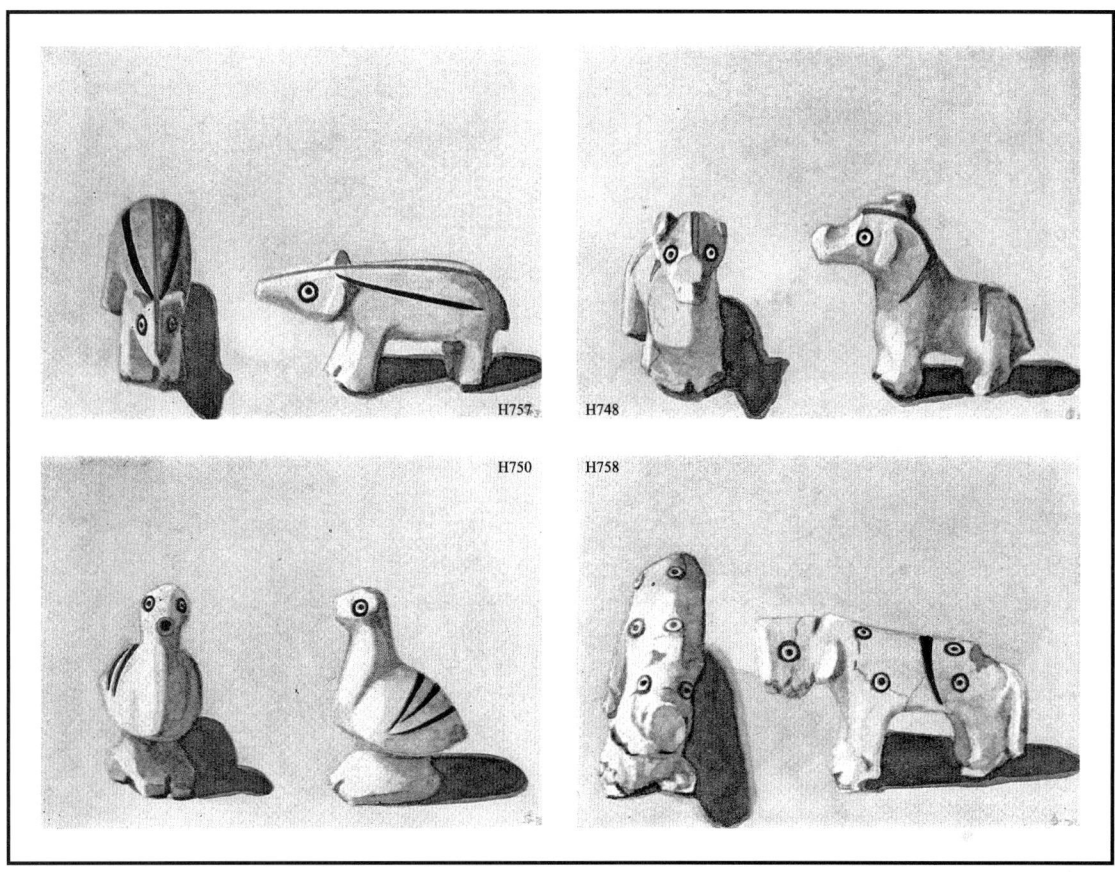

Fig. 5.20 Drawings of painted alabaster animal figurines (H757, H748, H750, H758) that accompanied the burial of Schmidt's "Warrior 2" (DF09 x1). The painted details are restored (after Schmidt 1937: pl. XXXIII).

heads with simple stem (in addition to two in quartz and jasper) (ibid., pl. CXLIII H721, H722, H724–H726, H606). Besides weapons, an impressive collection of identity markers and tools are included in his grave: a copper "mace head" (Schmidt 1933: pl. CXVIII H771); a wood working tool described as "a hollow chisel of copper with parts of wooden shaft preserved" (ibid., pl. CXIX H766); and a copper bident 'killed'[16] "by bending tines" (ibid., pl. CXX H775). There is a pile of many lapis lazuli and onyx beads combined with gold/electrum and copper tubes "touching fingers of [his] left hand and spreading below his right radius" (Schmidt's unpublished notes).

The absence of ceramic vessels in his assemblage of gift offerings is noteworthy (only one jar lid was found, H781). It is, however, compensated by several vessels in copper and alabaster: copper bowls (ibid., pl. CXXVII H772, H774, H776, H777); alabaster jars, bowls, and cups (ibid., pl. CXXXIX H778, H779, H780, H782, H783, H785, pl. CXXXV H536). A number of copper vessels are crushed, either intentionally as part of a ritual practice or by the weight of the body over them (ibid., p.444, pl. CXXIII H453, pl. CXXVIII H454, H455). His bead ornaments are placed inside a copper vessel and his gold-sheathed copper earrings are placed near his jawbone (ibid., pl. CXXII H765, H784). His copper wand has a double-headed horse figure(?) with its rider as its finial (ibid., pl. CXXXI H718) and his copper stamp seal has interlocking opposed animals (ibid., pl. CXXIX H720).

Warrior 2 is one of the two burials associated with charred animal bones (also found in the Priest's burial). Schmidt notes the bones belong to a quadruped, possibly a sheep or a dog (ibid., p. 444). A copper rod with double-headed ram finial is placed on the bones of the sacrificial(?) animal near to the bundle of animal figurines. The latter are fairly well modeled animals, including a horse(?); they are carved from alabaster and clay (Schmidt 1937: pl. XXXIII, 186, 188–189, 1933: pls. CXXXIII, CXXXIV). There is a powerful association between the animal figurines and a sacrificed animal whose bones are probably remainders of a ritual feast that took place prior to or following the burial ceremony.[17] It is very likely that Warrior 2 was a prominent figure, perhaps the head of an agricultural community or tribal chief with political power, who must have been held in high esteem to be honored by such an elaborate array of gifts. His weapons may simply be intended to honor him, rather than identify him as only a "Warrior." The inclusion of figurines of 'wild animals,' his cache of arrowheads, and his seal strengthen the notion of the "Warrior's" multiple identities as a hunter/farmer/shepherd/tribal chief.

Warrior 1, in burial DF19 x2, is in supine position like Warrior 2, with legs flexed and turned to the right. He has the smallest assemblage of gifts (15) in the High Outlier category, but his funerary gifts are similar in type and craftsmanship to those belonging to Warrior 2, except for his silver and alabaster vessels, which are of superior quality. His weapons and tools consist of battle axe/mattock (Schmidt 1933: pl. CXVIII H168), dagger (ibid., pl. CXIX H167), and bident (ibid., pl. CXX H166). The silver and alabaster vessels are exceptionally well crafted, they replicate forms of ceramic vessels. One silver globular bowl has an unusually long elevated beak spout (ibid., pl. CXXIV H173). An alabaster plate is described by Schmidt as an "elegant fruit plate" (1933: pls. CXXXVII, CXL H176). It may have been used as an offering plate to the deceased. Its form is reminiscent of the Hissar I/II pedestal bowls (cf. Schmidt 1933: pl. XXIII H2998). The ubiquitous wand is shaped as a cross with animal/bird figurines on its finial. It is placed "in a small [ceramic] jar filled with black powdered matter" (ibid., p. 414, pl. CXXXI H170).

Warrior 1 has one pair of enigmatic objects, not included in the other burials of the High Outlier group, a set of alabaster columns and discs.[18] Similar objects are also found in the context of the Burned Building, dated ca. 2500–2200 BC (Schmidt's IIIB), in hoards I and II of Treasure Hill, and as part of a large cache of artifacts (Schmidt 1933:216, 218–219, pls. LXI, LXII; fig.132, pl. CXXXVI, 1937:216–219). The function and symbolism of these objects are vague; the disc has been referred as a "weight," and, together with column, as a "cult object." Other interpretations of the disc are a "shield" or an offering plate supported by the column. Schmidt's description of the pair is as follows: "a groove encircles the side of the shallow, discoid top resting on a tall stem with hollow, conoid base" (1937:423). Aside from their ambiguity of origin and function, the distribution of these objects is extensive: to the north of Tepe Hissar, across the Elburz Mountains to the contemporary site, Tureng Tepe; extending to the northeast, Namazga IV sites in Central Asia (see Casanova 1991, Masson 1988); to southern and southeastern Iran at the Bronze age sites of Shahdad (Hakemi 1978, 1997; Salvatori and Vidale 1982), and at Tepe Ya-hya (Lamberg-Karlovsky, 1970; Dyson and Voigt 1989). It has been pointed out that the long-distance distribution of these objects could suggest a "cult" practice that linked northern and southern Iran to south Central Asia.

The Priest and the Little Girl. These two burials represent the most richly endowed individuals after Warrior 1 in the High Outlier category in group 5 (Figs. 5.21, 5.22, 4.8, see also GIS maps in Appendix 3). The Little Girl in burial DF18 x1 is interred with 38 objects and the Priest in burial DF08 x1 has 47. Schmidt notes that the priest is isolated from the rest of all other Low Outlier burials, the closest one being at least one meter away. This treatment is similar to Warrior 2 and the Little Girl, whose graves are also set apart.

The Priest is distinguished by a curious prone position with legs flexed behind him; he is almost doubled up, so that the left ankle is touching the posterior end of the sacrum. There is another unusual aspect to his skeletal remains: the left hand is curved around an alabaster cup (H450) with the bones of his right hand piled inside the cup. It is open to speculation whether the hand is disarticulated as part of a "burial ritual" then placed inside the cup during burial, or if the decomposition over time led to this appearance. Four large copper nails (Schmidt 1933: pl. CXXI H468–71) over the skeleton have traces of wrappings—perhaps a textile.

The Priest's gifts cover practically his whole body. He is gifted with objects similar to the other four in the group, including objects ranging from a copper dagger and trident, copper seals (ibid., pl. CXXIX H458, H459), a lead cup, alabaster vessels, a canteen of grey ware, and serpentine animal figures (ibid., pl. CXXXIII H486–89). He has five outstanding gifts the first three of which found exclusively in *his* grave and not in the other four High Outlier graves. A silver diadem (Fig. 5.23) lies on his forehead with exquisitely rendered animals in panels (stag, mouflon, ibex, and others) in raised repoussé technique (ibid., pl. CXXII H449; Yule 1982: Abb. 14, 2). An alabaster effigy female figurine is crafted in hourglass shape with one globular breast in the center of her chest (Schmidt 1933: pl. CXXXII H482; Fig. 5.24). A copper fan/mirror ornamented with circles stippled in repoussé—a long-lived tradition of decorative motifs (Schmidt 1933: pl. CXXIII H451; Fig. 5.25; Yule 1982: Abb. 14, 1).[19] One of his outstanding gifts is a copper wand depicting two seated human figures, one "holding a child" (Schmidt 1933: pl. CXXXI H463; Fig. 5.26). His copper pendant of a female figure combined with bird figures (Schmidt 1933: pls. CXLV H490a), recalls the figurative finials on copper wands. Both the Priest and the Little Girl have many beautifully cut beads (lapis lazuli, onyx, serpentine, and amber) incorporated to shells and silver and gold/electrum pieces.

The Little Girl is in lateral position with her head turned to the right. Unlike the rest of the High Outlier group, she has the largest assemblage of silver artifacts. In fact, nearly all of her gifts are crafted in silver and alabaster (vessels, ornaments, and animal figurines). Her bead ornaments are very similar to the Priest's ornaments, having large quantities of beads of semi-precious stones incorporated to precious metals, including her copper earrings with gold lining.

Among the Little Girl's unique gifts (Fig. 5.27) are decorated 'cosmetic jars' in frit(?) and a green stone (Schmidt 1933: pls. CXXV, CXXVI H373–383, CXLI, CXXXIX H386, H387, H391). Schmidt interprets the wealth of such a young child's gifts to reflect the status and wealth of her family, rather than her personal accomplishments: "an extraordinarily large number of objects not in proportion with the age of the child....that the character of the equipment proves almost certainly that the child was a girl. At the same time the gifts suggest that the people of the Gray Pottery Age believed that a child would continue growing after death and become an adult person, then needing the gifts an adult person would use [in life thereafter]" (unpubl. notes).

Schmidt's description of her gifts conveys a picturesque scene of ritual performance: "Six small cups and pitchers of silver were grouped around the little girl's head and chest. A large beautiful chalcedony pendant...had dropped into the silver cup in front of her forehead...a stippled silver pendant in the form of the stereotyped silver effigy of Hissar III....in front of the chest a copper wand with a ram as head, a little cow, a sheep of silver and two silver pins" (1933:452). He continues to cite objects near her head and chest: four cups with jars of alabaster and 'cosmetic jars' behind her, surrounded by copper and lead bowls, large pottery jars and bowls (ibid.). The same number of cups and pitchers, cups and jars in silver and alabaster, in addition to her wand with ram's head, female effigy pendant, and animal figurines compose a deliberate placement of an assemblage befitting a ritual celebration.

All of the five deceased individuals in groups 4 and 5 shared similar types of gifts; however, there are discernible variations in the quantities and materials of which the artifacts are crafted. The silver objects belong to the Priest and the Little Girl, but the Priest has most of the silver

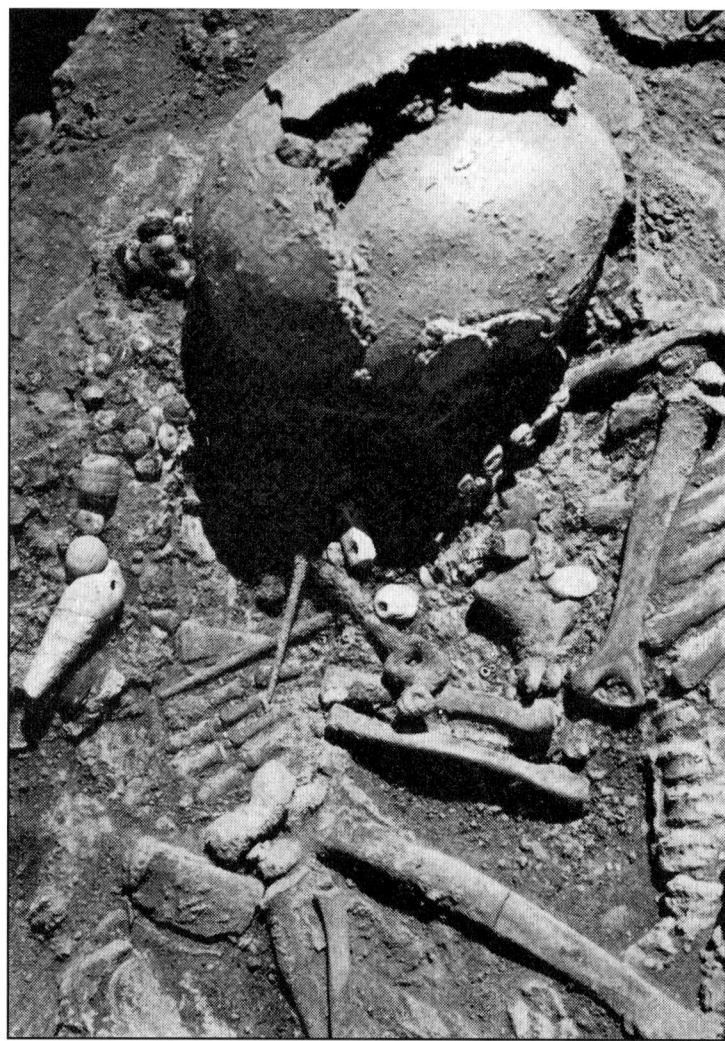

Fig. 5.21 Schmidt's "Little Girl" burial, DF18 x1, richly endowed with 38 objects (Courtesy of Penn Museum).

ornaments, in addition to alabaster, serpentine, and gold, while the little girl's are in onyx, silver, alabaster, carnelian, and lapis lazuli. Her animal figurines are fewer than those belonging to Warrior 2, who has the distinction of having the largest quantity (n=25) of animal figurines in alabaster and clay (Schmidt 1933: pls. CXXXIII H738–762, H740, H744, H748, H750, H757, H758, 1937: pl. XXXIII H747, H748, H757, H758). The Little Girl's animal figurines are crafted in precious silver (Schmidt 1933: pl. CXXXIV H370, H371) and the Priest's are carved in serpentine (ibid., pl. CXXXIII H486, H488, H489).

In terms of the funerary gifts, group 5 has by far the highest average number of gifts per burial (n=6.42) compared to the other groups. Furthermore, the quality of objects is characterized as outstanding in craftsman-

Fig. 5.22 Schmidt's "Priest" burial, DF08 x1, who was accompanied by 47 objects (Courtesy of Penn Museum).

ship, particularly in the use of hammering, chasing, and repoussé techniques of precious metals—silver and gold/electrum—as well as the lavish use of precious stones (amber, alabaster, carnelian, turquoise) in jewelry. While the ceramic vessel is the most common gift, it is represented less frequently, although in the overall distribution of artifacts ceramic vessels comprise 51% of the total artifacts, followed by ornaments and jewelry (26%), alabaster vessels (7%), figurines (human and animal) (5%), metal vessels (4%), tools (3%), and personal symbols, including seals (3%).

The most frequently shared gifts by all four individuals of group 5 are the symbols of copper wand with animal and human finials; small animal and human figurines in semi-precious stones, beads of lapis lazuli, alabaster and other semi-precious stones, and alabaster vessels. Precious ornaments comprise earrings sheathed with gold, as well as multiple-coiled bracelets in copper (Fig. 5.28). Lead and silver vessels occur as frequently as copper vessels. Even within the High Outliers category, variations in craftsmanship of the objects and their materials is highly suggestive of individual status distinctions within the elite community. The distinction may also have been assigned to these individuals by the living community, as manifest in their extraordinary funerary gifts. It is significant that some of the high quality gifts of the five High Outlier individuals are also found in more modest burials, though crafted in non-precious materials, such as clay prototypes of zoomorphic figurines.

What distinguishes these individuals from the rest of the burials is not only the location of their graves, or differences in grave types (see GIS maps in Appendix 3), rather, it is the quantity of unusually rich prestige gifts, combined with their remarkable artistic sophistication. This level of craftsmanship would have required a high investment in the expenditure of labor in production. Hence these individuals had differential social/political status in life or such status was attributed at death by the surviving kin and/or attendants.

In sum, the iconography and the craftsmanship of the funerary gifts convey multiple messages in interpreting the Tepe Hissar burial culture: they display stylistic and technical proliferation of craft production through time which, above all, implies an organized, cooperative network of craftsmen. In turn, the funerary goods serve to reinforce the social memories of the living in regards to the "living" histories of the deceased as members of a social group, family, clan, or an association/guild of craftsmen.

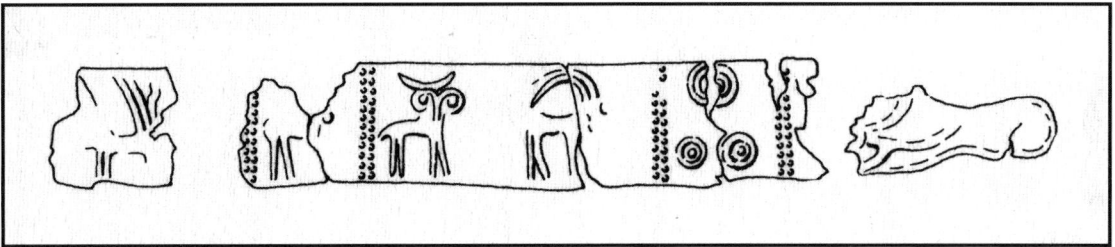

Fig. 5.23 A silver diadem (H449) found on the forehead of the "Priest" burial (DF08 x1) with repoussé ram, ibex, and other animal figures (after Yule 1982).

Fig. 5.24 Also from the "Priest" burial (DF08 x1), an alabaster effigy female figurine crafted in an hourglass shape with one globular breast in the center of her chest (H482) (Courtesy of Penn Museum).

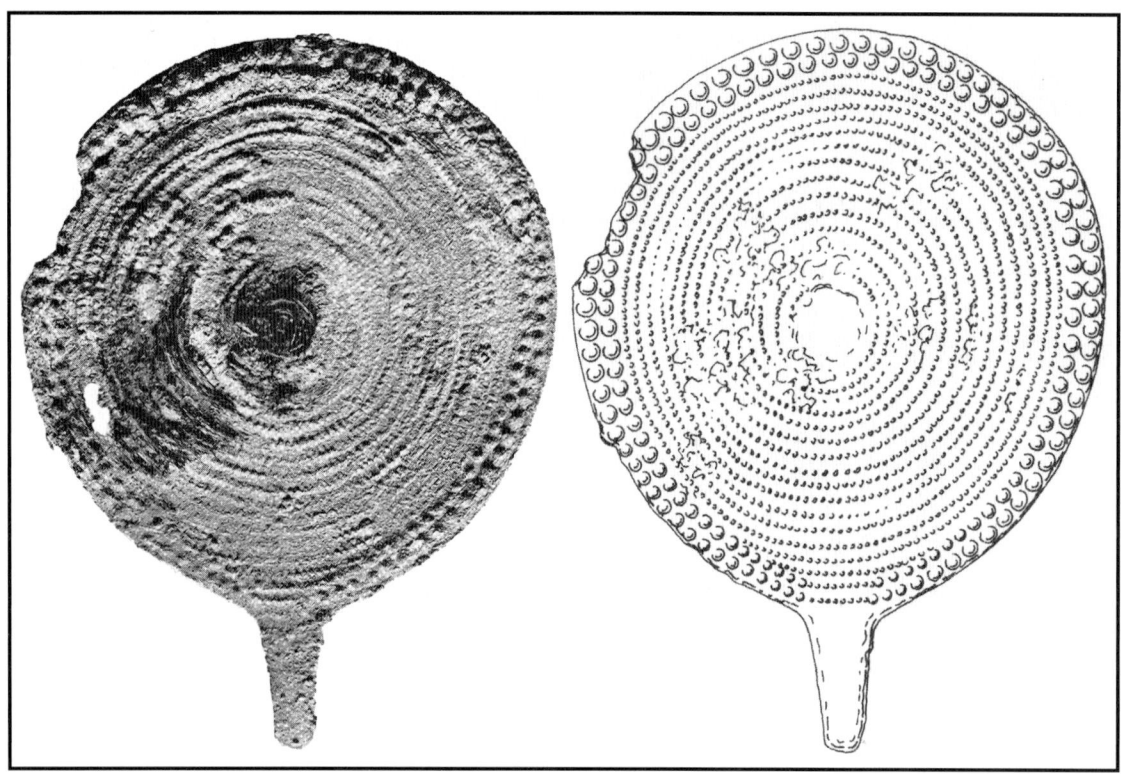

Fig. 5.25 A copper fan/mirror with repoussé circles (H451) from the "Priest" burial (DF08 x1). Made of coiled copper with stem and with traces of fabric on both sides (after Schmidt 1933; after Yule 1982)

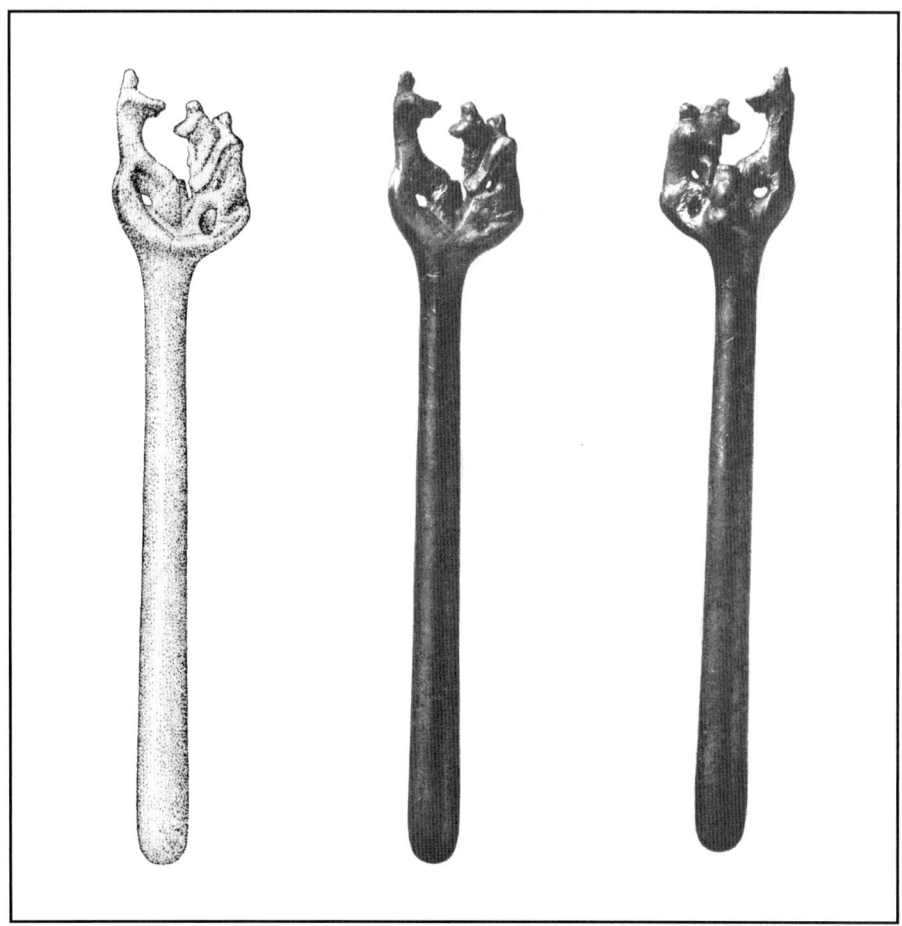

Fig. 5.26 An outstanding artifact from the "Priest's" grave gifts, a copper wand (H463) with two seated human figures, one "holding a child" (after Schmidt 1937: fig. 117; after Yule, 1982).

Fig. 5.27 Photographs showing the context and detail of two unique decorated 'cosmetic jars' (H386, H387) that accompanied the burials of the "little Girl" (DF18 x1) (Courtesy of Penn Museum; inset, Schmidt 1933: pl. CXXXIX).

Fig. 5.28 Multiple coil bracelets made from copper: (left) Period IIIB, North Flat, burial CF55 x1 "Dancer", H2379 (Penn Museum, object no. 33-21-925); (right) H4158 (Penn Museum, object no. 33-21-632) (Photo by Jason Francisco).

D. Burial Rituals

It is universally believed that death is the end of biological life and one's life cycle, after which it is believed that a transition is made to the next stage, the world of the spirit, for spiritual incorporation within one's community. The studies of types of rituals, their function, and the role of the social sphere/community in "performing" the rituals in past societies have made use of interdisciplinary approaches, borrowed from social and cultural anthropology, sociology, and history in the last three decades (Williams 2003:5–19). Anthropological studies of death address the social domain, as in collective memory of the living, or the role of monumentality of tombstones in "reading/misreading" the identity of the deceased (Bloch 1971; Bloch and Parry 1982; Metcalf and Huntington 1991). Concerning the role of ritual performance, Williams writes, "In many societies, the construction, perception and interaction is very much one mediated by ritual performance involving mobile artifacts. For example, Weiss has addressed the active role of material culture in the process of transforming the body and the way it is remembered, focusing particularly on the use of shrouds in wrapping the body" (2003:7).

In his introduction to *Performing Death*, Laneri (2007:3) outlines aspects of funerary ritual as a *rite de passage*, quoting from the anthropologist Van Gennep's (1960) sociocultural model of tripartite division of separation, transition, and incorporation. As a purely inferential illustration of such a transition, I refer to Katz's (2007:173–74) description of the Sumerian funerary ritual involving the passage from the grave to the gate of the next world: "Presumably, the full funerary ritual was the magic power that could turn a grave from a mere pit in the ground into a gate to the world of the dead." Typically, the ritual includes public performances in order to ease the spirit of the deceased through his/her final passage from the grave to the next world. During the process of transition from life to death, therefore, it is the obligation of the living family members and the local community (tribe, clan, etc.) to perform according to socially and culturally accepted rituals. During this process, "the social cohesion of the living community and/or household is reinforced, [while] the physical remains of this act, for example the tomb, stand as a focal point in the social and mnemonic landscape of the society"(Laneri 2007:2–5).

The performance highlights not only the manner in which the deceased individual should be *remembered by the mourners* but also how the *deceased wished to be remembered* or both. Thus, funerals provide a forum "where social roles [of individuals] are manipulated, acquired and discarded" (Parker Pearson 1999:32). These practices, however, need to be contextualized according to social, cultural, and chronological dimensions so that "distinctive elements of individuals' lives and actions" (ibid., p. 7) are construed, as suggested in the concept of the "biography of death" (Robb 2007:288–90; see also Kopytoff 1986:64–94).

The foregoing theoretical remarks are largely drawn from anthropological/ethnographic and historical concepts that are useful in archaeological re-construction. Following the idea of performance of burial rituals as a rite of passage for the dead, it has been argued that "goods associated with a burial represents only the final stage of what may have been a much longer rite of passage" (Campbell 1995:29; see also Bradley 1990:94). To envision such phenomena archaeologically, we may turn to ethnographic case studies as models to test with the archaeological data. Here I present a model of burial performance from the Trobriand Island tribal group (Malinowski 1929) that suggests a perceptible demonstration of a "living" act of secondary burial that reinforces the concept of the social and spiritual continuity through the medium of material culture. This socially meaningful communal performance is played out in stages of the initial burial followed by secondary burial when the relatives manipulate the bones of the deceased.

In the Trobriand Islands, the impending death of the person is marked shortly before the moment of death by the wailing and singing of close kin. This ritual activity is followed by the washing, anointing, and wrapping of the body, during which time gift giving and feasting take place. The attending people touch different parts of the body affectionately before the initial interment. Several days later, the deceased individual is exhumed during another ceremony that continues over a period of time, to ensure that the body is still intact, that there are no signs of sorcery, and that it is not taken away by harmful spirits. In addition, exhumation is a way by which some of the bones of the deceased are removed and carved as relics or ornaments to be worn by the close kin till the day they die. Moreover, the underlying sentiment of exhumation, touching the bones, and wearing the bone ornaments is to evoke communal emotion; in the words of the indigenous people, "the relic brings the departed back to our mind and makes our inside tender" (ibid., p. 156). So, with another round of songs, animal sacrifice, more feasting, and the placement of 'magic' in the pit grave to honor the departed, the rest of the bones are reburied" (ibid., pp. 152–63). This marks the secondary burial process.

Undoubtedly, this ethnographic case study provides only a possible model. The description of the ritual performance brings forth the staging of a burial in a small tribal community. It also highlights the complexity of the meaning of crafting and wearing artifacts carved from the bones of the deceased as part of the secondary burial ritual among some small-scale societies (see also Hertz 1960, describing rituals of secondary deposition of the Dayak people of Borneo). Indeed, the material evidence of food remains (feasting), animal sacrifice, and placement of objects with the dead are commonly observed archaeological evidence interpreted as burial rituals, even though the performance aspect is missing. At Tepe Hissar, the postmortem manipulation of the body in arranging the gestures of the dead can be considered as part of a secondary burial ritual performance by the living. Furthermore, the placement of objects and symbols on *specific* parts of the body must signify the inherent symbolism of the objects shared by the deceased and the survivors.

In discussing burial rituals at Tepe Hissar, we can extrapolate social and cultural practices from the material manifestations of the burials that have already been discussed archaeologically as part of the funerary culture. It is against this background that the burial rituals at Tepe Hissar are considered as structured performances whereby the social persona of the deceased is re-constructed and memorialized by the living community.

It is generally accepted that the fundamental aspect of funerary behavior is ritual and symbolism; at the core of commemorative ritual is a "repetitive and structured sequence of actions" (Chesson 2007:116) performed by the living. At Tepe Hissar, the recurring actions throughout the existence of the settlement are practices of inhumation of individuals and groups in pit graves and the wrapping of bodies in textile or plant material such as reeds. There are also clues about some of the deceased being buried with garments on which are sewn beads and seal-like ornaments or buttons. The key elements of burial rituals, however, can be derived from the following archaeological evidence: (1) long-term continuity of the cemetery; (2) secondary burials and postmortem manipulation of body parts; (3) articulation of objects on skeletal parts; (4) feasting with the inclusion of animal bones and food and drinking vessels, and (5) a ritual performance of what appears to be a drinking ceremony associated with its material correlates.

The Cemetery and Its Long-Term Continuity

At Tepe Hissar, the settlements shifted to different locations from late Chalcolithic through the Bronze Age, from ca. 4000 to 1800 BC. Insofar as we know, during this long period, two distinct areas were used as the cemetery. One is the raised central area of the Main Mound and the other is the Painted Pottery Flat; both are located in abandoned parts of the settled areas. They appear to have been used repeatedly by the inhabitants of successive settlements. Selection of the same burial locations and their long-term intensive use are significant factors in preserving memories of the deceased ancestors. At the large Bronze Age cemetery of Shahr-i Sokhta in southeastern Iran, there is a thousand year continuity of pit and catacomb burial traditions. The excavators explain the phenomenon: "The only reasonable answer is probably to be found in ritual/ideological manifestations and traditions" (Sajjadi 2003:37). Along the same lines, Ellen-Jane Pader argues, "By form and content, rituals symbolize a continuity with the ideal past and with the ancestors who are linked to that past" (1982:39, as quoted in Shepherd 1999:11).

Glenn M. Schwartz (2007:45) interprets monumental tombs of the third millennium BC elite burials at Umm el-Marra in Syria as a visually strong reminder to the surviving families to continue veneration whereby the surviving elite gain prestige. This concept can be applied to the elite burials at Tepe Hissar. Although lacking in monumental tomb structures, the special locations of the High Outlier graves are clear markers for visitors.[20]

It is important to note that, at Tepe Hissar, a striking change occurs in burial assemblages in the late third millennium BC; there is a pattern of including a few prestige objects in otherwise modest burials. This phenomenon may be an indicator of high-value gifts as inherited objects by the heirs of the deceased. Cultraro (2007:87), in his discussion of the Early Helladic cemeteries in Mainland Greece touches on this point, suggesting that the gifts were presumably a combination of the "personal possessions of the deceased and goods accumulated by the survivors," perhaps implying the heirs.

Secondary Burials and Postmortem Manipulation of Body Parts

Schmidt's reference to "human bone piles" is likely to be indicative of secondary burials, as discussed earlier for interments in squares DG00 and DG11 (Fig. 5.29, 5.30, see also p. 230). The sequence of burial events, however, cannot be reconstructed. At the large cemetery of the Bronze Age site Shahr-i Sokhta in southeastern Iran, the excavators attempted to reconstruct the sequence of practices used for secondary burials in collective graves: "The remains and bones of one group of this grave type [multiple graves] were damaged by the newly dug graves.... skeletons were mutilated [in the process of secondary inhumations] and grave goods were broken. Among these burials there are other graves containing only parts of human skeletons, or only a skull with a complete set of grave goods" (Sajjadi 2003:41). Sajjadi's description of the processing of secondary burials suggests enactment of a repetitive and sequential ritual: after the initial burial re-opening the grave pit, moving skeletal parts of the original burials in a pile (perhaps to make space for the new skeletons), collection of disintegrated body parts of the earlier burials, and depositing the new burial. We can conceive these acts performed by the living to be accompanied by commemorative rites in offerings of gifts and foodstuffs.

In examining the skeletal remains in situ, Schmidt suggests part of the burial ritual can be observed in the positions of arms and hands. He attributes the gestures to arrangements made by the living attendants, as they wished to remember the deceased on the journey to the next

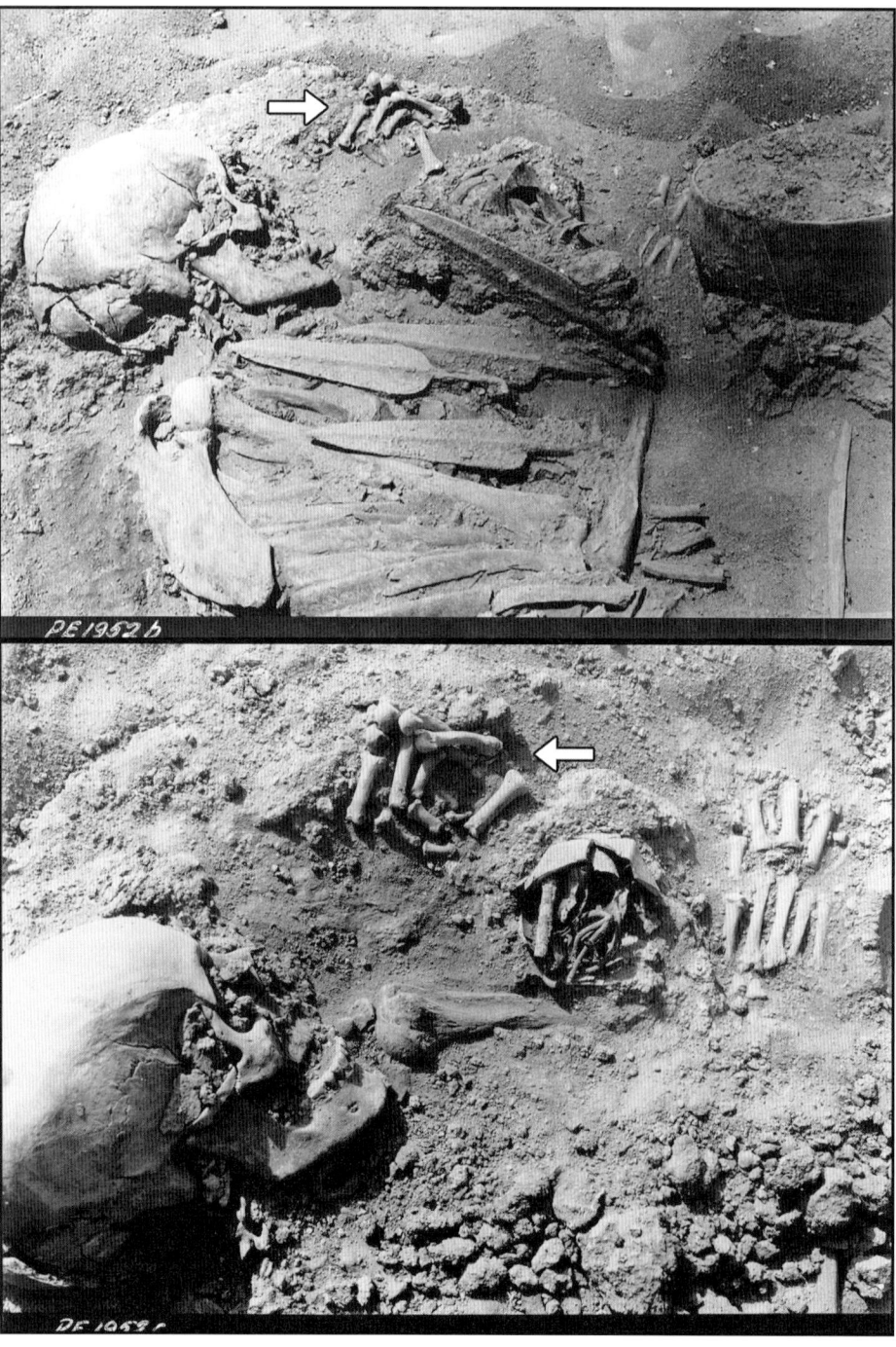

Fig. 5.29 The hand of CF57 x28 is an example of disarticulated skeletal remains. (Courtesy of Penn Museum).

Fig. 5.30 Another example of what Schmidt termed "human bone piles" from DF18 x10 (Courtesy of Penn Museum).

world. Accordingly, he states that in the double burials of a female and infant, two young children, and two infants there is deliberate arrangement of extended arms by the female to the infant, or the younger child hiding his face behind the other one. In another burial, CG31 x7, the excavator remarks that the individual's hands were holding an alabaster cup, which had been placed shortly after death, and that such corpses must have been buried in that arranged position before [or after] rigor mortis (Schmidt 1937:313, 316, pl. LXXI). A puzzling manipulation is the placement of the Priest's disarticulated hand bones inside a cup. While it is difficult to assess the meanings of these bodily expressions, it is conceivable that the gestures/positions were arranged by the survivors and, therefore, must be considered part of the ritual performance.

Articulation of Objects on Skeletal Parts

The placement of personal belongings on specific parts of the body may influence the separation of the spirit and the body (Brown 1981). In most of the Tepe Hissar burials, there is a patterned placement of certain types of objects, such as pottery vessels placed near the head and ornaments near the part of the body where they would be worn or carried: jewelry, diadem, and amulets near the neck, forehead and elbows; identity markers and symbolic objects such as seals, wands, amulets, animal and female effigy figurines near the hand. Weapons and tools are generally placed close to lower part of the body, but not on it. One curious practice is the bending/crushing of metal tools and vessels, the ritual "killing" of the utensils along with death of the owner—especially in elite burials. Also in the elite burials, there are large numbers of varied species of animal figurines crafted in different materials. In the grave of Warrior 2, the figurines are placed next to his spearheads and dagger. Assuming that the weapons are the Warrior's identity marker as a hunter of the animals represented by the figurines, it is likely that their placement is based on the belief in the magical powers of these animals to drive away dangerous spirits and also to provide comfort to the living. The frequent occurrence of individual ram/sheep and bull figurines, their use as parts of precious jewelry and finials on wands corroborates their symbolic meaning (Schmidt 1937: figs. 111, 113, 133, 134, 1933: pls. CXXXIII, CXXXIV; see also Verhoeven 2010:16, 17 for complex animal rituals depicted by the iconography of animal sculptures combined with human images at the pre-Neolithic site of Göbekli Tepe in southeastern Anatolia). Similarly, the female effigy as pendants and as individual figurines brings to mind its universal symbolism as a source of life and fertility (see p. 243 above, for a female effigy figurine placed on pubic bone of adult male in burial CF47 x2). At Tepe Hissar, these figurines were not only offered to the privileged minority of the dead, but they were also placed with people irrespective of rank, age, and sex (see p. 243 above for cow effigy vessel in child's burial CF46 x1). Therefore, we can assume it was part of the shared ideology of the Tepe Hissar population.

Feasting: Inclusion of Animal Bones, Food, and Drinking Vessels

In societies where animals have social and economic significance and magical qualities of bringing fertility to land and people or keeping away evil, their sacrifice would represent a ritually transformative act in which the spirit of the animal is believed to communicate with the deceased to guide him in the next world. In the graves of the Priest and Warrior 2, in association with large number of figurines of quadrupeds, we have evidence of charred sheep/dog bones that might be the remainders of a fire ritual or feasting near the grave. Representations of bird figures as well as the double-headed ram figure appear frequently on finials of wands: a copper rod of a female figurine with two birds on her shoulders or a double headed ram symbol in the burial of two infants, CF89 x4, x5 (Schmidt 1937 pl. XLVI H5141). As part of the assemblage with Warrior 1, another cross-shaped copper wand with two birds or other animals as finials is stuck in a vessel filled with charred organic material (Schmidt 1933:444, pl. CXXXI H170; unpubl. notes). Clearly, these examples support the hypothesis that a link exists between the anthropomorphic and zoomorphic symbols and the spirit of the live animals in the ideology of the living community and, by extension, the deceased in his/her life.

In all periods of the Tepe Hissar burials, the biggest component of the burial assemblage is ceramic and metal vessels: serving bowls, cups, plates, and bottles for liquids. They are generally placed near the head or the upper part of the body and seldom near the hands. While a variety of vessel types are represented in the burials, the most prominent are wide-based bowls and jars, possibly used as food containers; others are bottle pitcher, tulip beaker, and small conical cups that were, undoubtedly, used as drinking vessels. In addition, there are "heirloom" vessels which are repaired or re-formed and subsequently used as burial gifts rather than disposed of, as in burials DG11 x16 (H3946) and DF19 x24 (H1637). In general, the burials have many containers that must have been placed for the nourishment of the spirits of the deceased or for funerary meals eaten by the attending group. The only evidence for food is derived from two jars containing charred grain in burial CF58 x1 on the North Flat and plot DG53 from the South Hill settlement dated to early third millennium BC. Although the grain has not been identified, it is likely to be a type of cereal.

A Ritual "Performance"

An enigmatic hoard was found in a non-burial "fill" context in square CF99 on the Main Mound; it is associated with the latest (Level 1) architecture and dated to the late third millennium BC (Schmidt 1937: figs. 87, 88). The hoard undoubtedly represents a ceremonial assemblage, possibly associated with burials CF89 x1, CF99 x1 or CF99 (see Ch. 4 and Schmidt 1937:193–194; in fig. 86 cf. squares CF89 and CF99). The assemblage consists of a set of unique artifacts that convey a "staged" performance for a celebratory act: 13 male and one female nude copper figurines are displayed almost in motion, some in open-arm positions, others with arms crossed over chest or extended, and legs apart. One male is holding an animal on his shoulder. These are crudely formed figurines measuring about 2.5 inches (Schmidt 1937:193–194, pls. XLIII, XLVII; Yule 1982 Abb. 15; Fig. 5.31). They are associated with 17 conical drinking cups of almost the same size, with pointed base (Fig. 5.32), six fenestrated braziers (Fig. 5.33), small copper bowls, and small jars (Fig. 5.34). The drinking cups are handmade, in coarse buff ware, probably used as daily utensils. Other objects include more of the usual inventory of drinking vessels, bottle pitcher and beak-spouted vessel, tools (stone celt, pestle, spindle whorl, copper point, and a lump of hematite/iron ore(?), and an alabaster pendant, in addition to a well modeled copper duck (Schmidt 1937: pl. XLVI H3279). These almost life-like figurines appear to be communicating with one another and possibly with the spirit of the deceased by means of their gestures, their drinking cups and pouring vessels, and cooking and ceremonial utensils such as braziers, which contained a deposit of ash (Schmidt unpubl. notes). The figurines, in association with the rest of the objects, provide a tableau of a celebratory act, either in a funerary ritual associated with a deceased person or as a cenotaph that stands to memorialize a missing individual/individuals. It may also represent a non-burial feasting and drinking banquet held by members of the community.

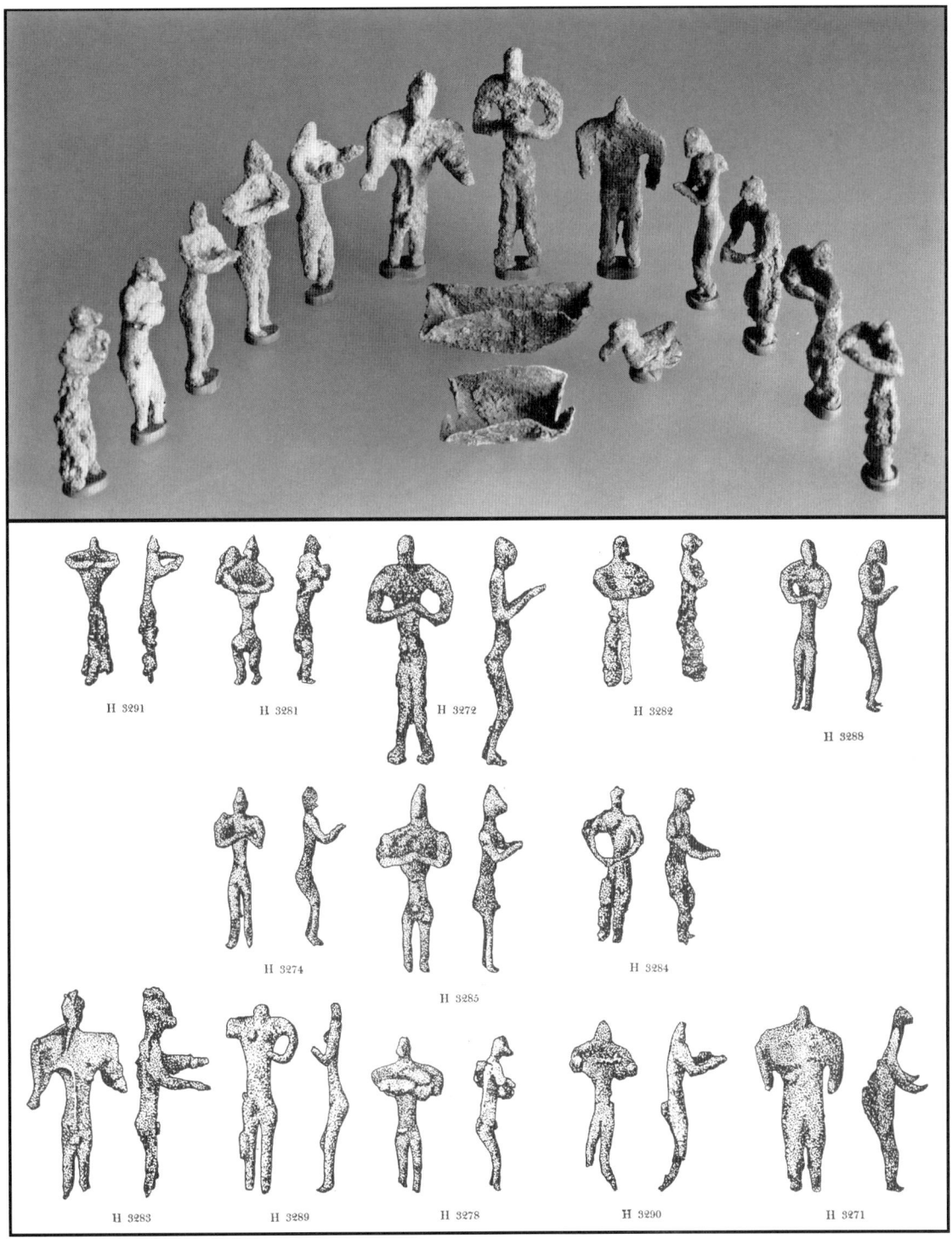

Fig. 5.31 Thirteen copper figurines from an enigmatic hoard found in a non-burial "fill" context in square CF99 on the Main Mound. The figures appear almost in motion and are about 2.5 inches tall.

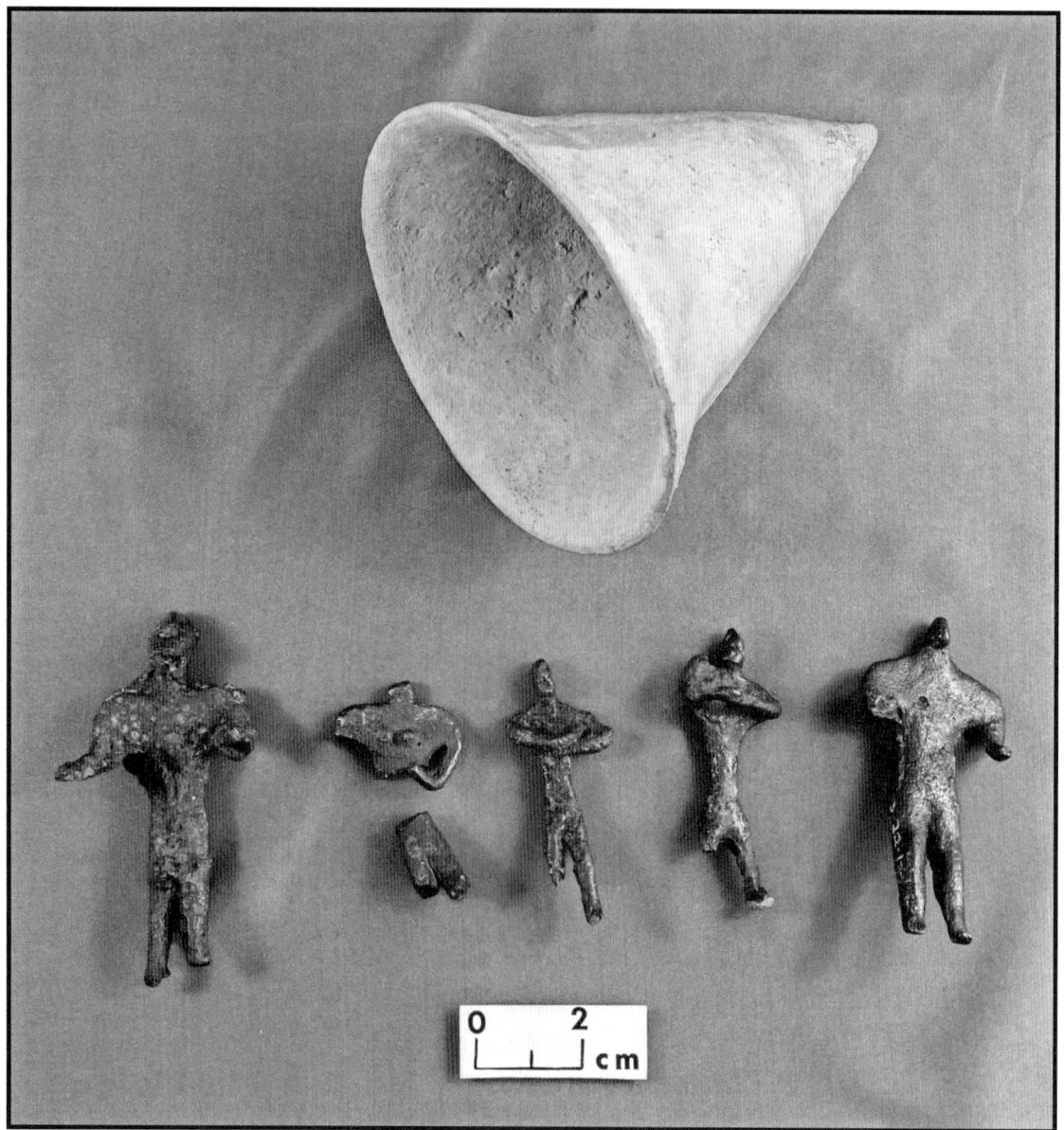

Fig. 5.32 The figurines from the hoard in CF99, H3271 (Penn Museum, object no. 33-22-132), H3289 (Penn Museum, object no. 33-22-134), H3281, H3282, H3283 (Penn Museum, object nos. 33-22-133 a,b,c), are associated with conical drinking cups with a pointed base, H3312 (Penn Museum, object no. 33-22-10) (Photo by Jason Francisco).

E. Discussion: A Diachronic Overview of Burial Culture and Ritual at Tepe Hissar

From the Middle Chalcolithic through the Bronze Age levels, ca. 4000–1800 (phases F to B-A/A), the population of Tepe Hissar was buried intramurally, in the uninhabited areas of the mound.

There are 144 graves, dating to Late Hissar I comprising roughly 9% of the total burials excavated (n=1637).[21] According to Schmidt's records, most of the skeletal material had poor preservation, some of the skulls were decayed and long bones were disarticulated. If uniformity in orientation, body position, burial type, and equally diversified gifts across sexes are used as indicators, we can assert that in this period there was little or no social diversity within the population.

Fig. 5.33 Also found in the CF99 hoard are fenestrated braziers (left to right): unknown; Period III, H3087 (Penn Museum, object no. 33-22-52); Period IIIC, Main Mound hoard, H3300 (Penn Museum, object no. 33-22-53) (Photo by Jason Francisco).

As a general rule, the dead of Late Hissar I are wrapped in some kind of textile or reed matting and interred in single simple pit burials—a long-lived tradition that continues to the end of the settlement. Most of the funerary gifts include handmade buff painted wares, brown on buff with geometric and figurative patterns of plants and animals on stemmed bowl and conical cups. Black-on-red wares have similar forms with linear and circular motifs. The grey burnished ware is already a component of the ceramic assemblage (see Ch. 3 above and Schmidt 1937: pls. III–XIII). Vessels are placed near the head or the chest.

Among the large number of seal-shaped ornaments[22] in gypsum or limestone, there are a few stamp seals (Schmidt 1937: pl. XV) and two or three baked clay counters as administrative tools (ibid., pls. XIV H1806, H3804, H3727). Schmidt identifies them as weight and pestles, respectively. Copper bracelets, rings, and copper pins with pyramidal heads are generally placed in a cup near the hands of the deceased (ibid., pl. XVI). Remarkably, there is little sex and age differentiation in types of funerary gifts, except for copper weapons (e.g., dagger and knife), which are exclusively male gifts.

During Early Hissar II, ca. 3600–3400 BC (phases E, E-D) the tradition of simple pit graves and lateral body orientation (to either right or left) continues. In addition to the individual pit graves as in Hissar I, there are a few cist graves and communal/multiple burials. The latter might represent members of a family/clan or a craft association.

This period marks the beginning of florescence of forms and materials in artifact production; notably in the production of copper ornaments, such as multi-coiled copper bracelets (ibid., pl. XXVIII B), and jewelry of semi-precious stones, alabaster, lapis lazuli, carnelian, and crystal are incorporated to silver beads. Similarly, there is a visible increase in animal figurines in baked clay and administrative devices, seals and seal-shaped ornaments (ibid., pl. XXVIII A).

In the following period, ca. 3100–2900 BC (phase D-C), a large copper stamp seal, two decorated mace-heads, as well as the characteristic double scroll pin are among the outstanding identity markers (ibid., pl. XXVIII H2183, H1200, pl. XXIX H2021, H4856). Copper constitutes 52% of the ornaments and jewelry category, followed by 35% in lapis lazuli, carnelian, and crystal beads, and 12% in silver. Alabaster does not prevail in

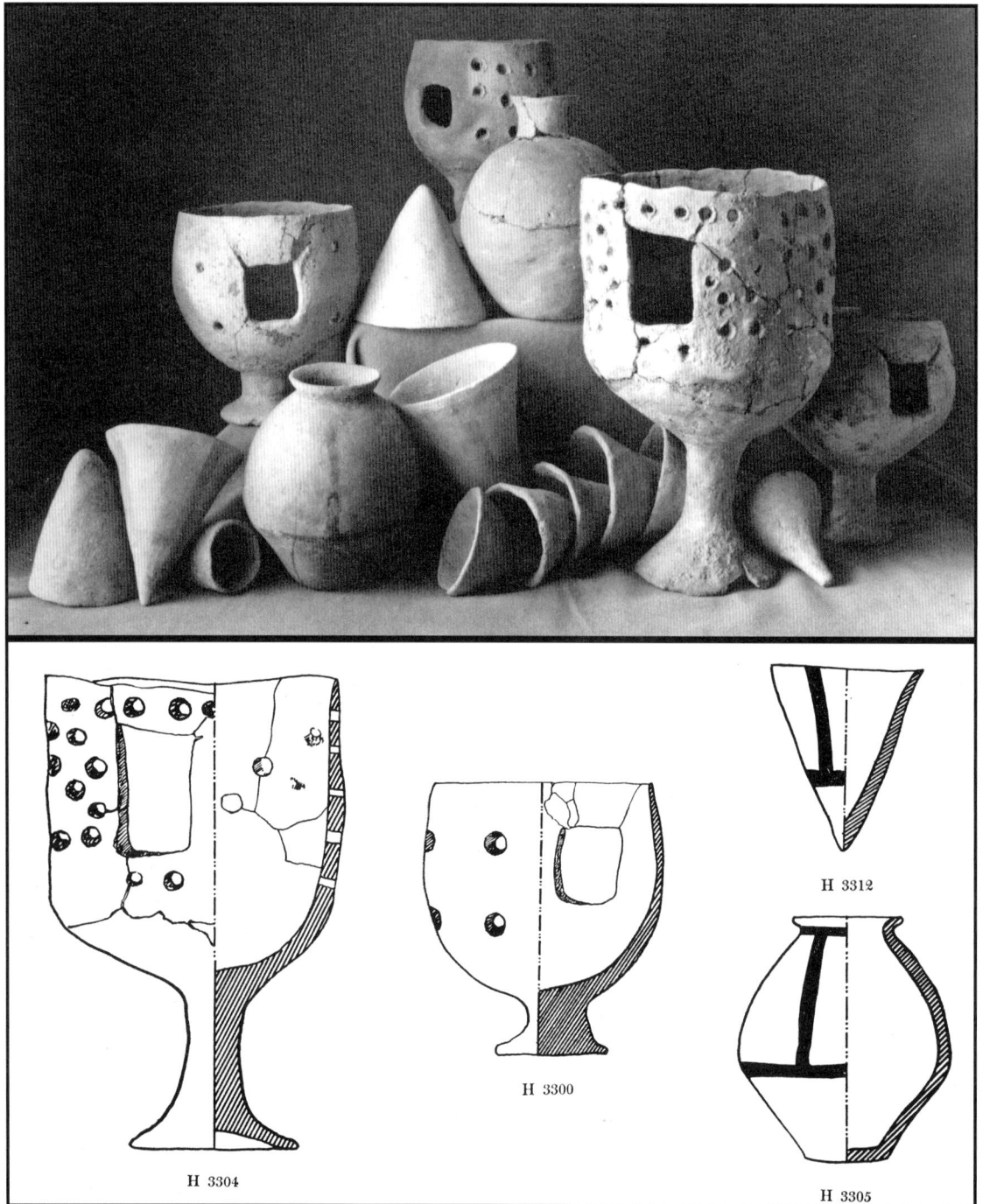

Fig. 5.34 Photograph and drawings of ceramic vessels found with hoard CF99 (Courtesy of Penn Museum; drawing after Schmidt 1937: pl. XLIII).

high quantities until Early Hissar III. Ceramic vessels still make up the largest assemblage in all burials, notably the grey burnished wares.

Toward the later part of the period, frequently occurring symbols of identity markers imply social differentiation among individuals. Weapons (copper dagger, mattock, and spear point) are, as usual, exclusively placed with males, whereas figurines and wands are offered to both sexes, as is jewelry. Infants are buried with relatively few gifts. As mentioned above, in the group 3 burials, the deceased individuals are associated with many items of jewelry both on their bodies and placed in ceramic and copper vessels. Necklaces with lapis lazuli beads combined with silver tubes are especially abundant. Ceramic vessels continue to be placed near the head of the deceased. The majority of the vessel types are utilitarian, such as containers for food and liquids (wide-based bowl, bottle pitcher, short-beaked bowl, and beaker). In this period, there is evidence for secondary burials in the form of disturbed bone piles that are wrapped in some type of animal hide or textile (excavator's notebook).

During Period Hissar IIIB, ca. 2500–2200 BC, social, cultural, and ritualistic elements can be interpreted more fully than before based on burial evidence. Social differentiation is marked by location of pit graves and their prestige goods. One of the best preserved and well-documented structures, the Burned Building on the North Flat, provides ample material evidence for social differentiation. The most outstanding change in this period is the opulence of identity defining symbols of female figurines and wands with animal, bird, or human finials, reflecting a new level of social differentiation. Nevertheless, some early traditions persist throughout the course of the settlement: pit burials and shrouding of the body with fabric or reed matting, irrespective of the burial type or the number and quality of the individual's gifts.

The Late Hissar IIIC Period, ca. 2200–1800 BC (phase B-A/A), is culturally a continuation of the previous period. The occurrence of cist and vault burials is present, but rare on the North Flat and on the Main Mound. It is clearly a period of a different level of social differentiation marked by an increasing quantity of social identity defining objects. In this period, there is wide variability in the quantity of funerary offerings, especially those of high quality craftsmanship such as artifacts crafted in silver (Fig. 5.35), copper, gold (Fig. 5.36), and stone (alabaster and semi-precious stones). Alabaster is a prized commodity used in crafting a variety of artifacts; among them are vessels (Fig. 5.37), "cult" objects (Fig. 5.38), figurines (Fig. 5.39), jewelry, and seals.

Fig. 5.35 Silver vessel, H5205 (Penn Museum, object no. 33-22-148), of high quality craftsmanship characteristic of Hissar IIIC Period found with burial CG13 x1 on the North Flat (Photo by Jason Francisco).

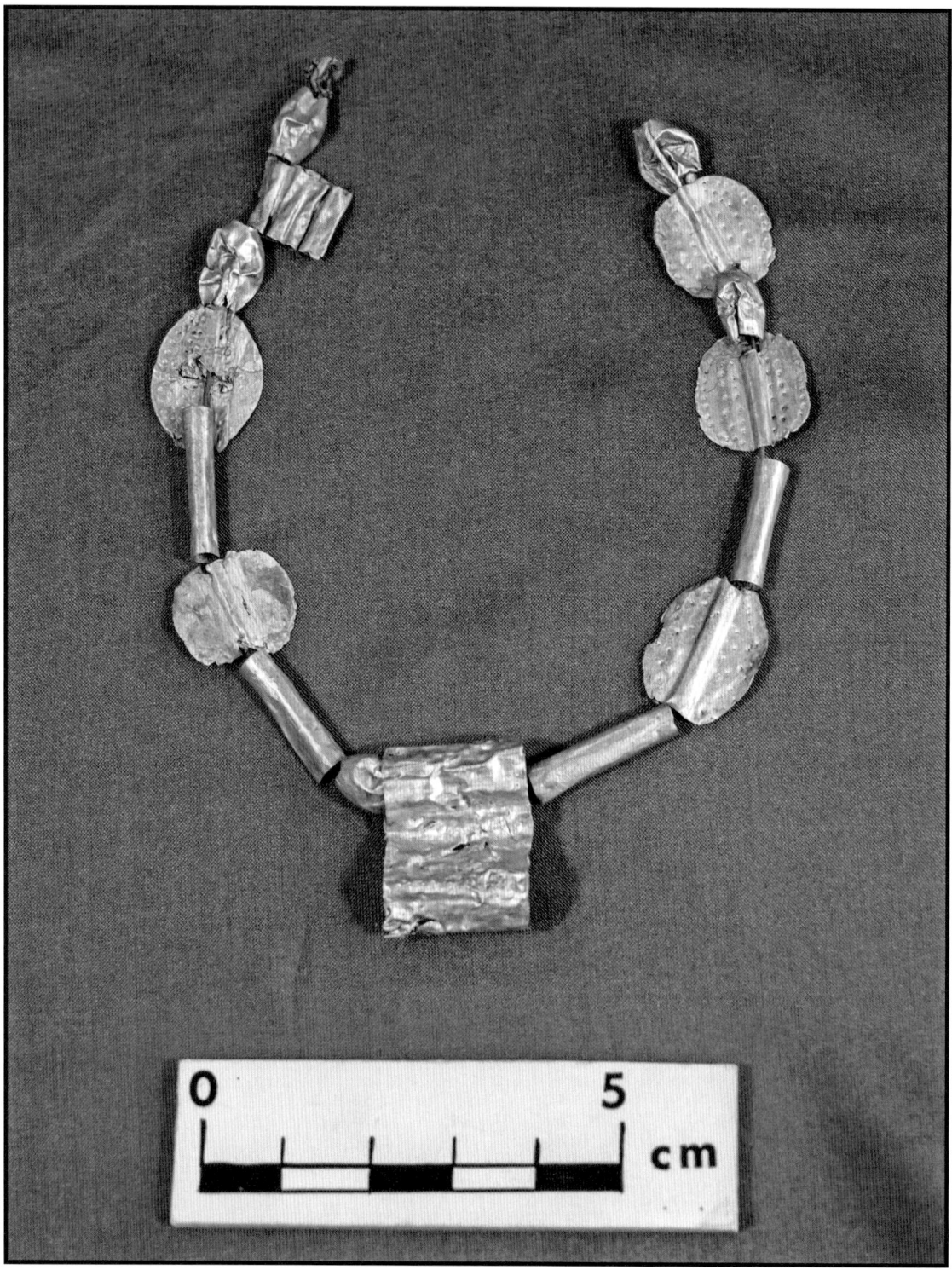

Fig. 5.36 Gold necklace, H2360 (Penn Museum, object no. 33-22-180), Hissar IIIC Period, found in the North Flat Burned Building (Photo by Jason Francisco).

Fig. 5.37 Beautifully carved alabaster spouted vessel, H4187 (Penn Museum, object no. 33-22-78), found with Treasure Hill burial CH87 x1 and dating to the Hissar IIIC Period (Photo by Jason Francisco).

Fig. 5.38 "Cult" object, "disc" and "column," made of alabaster, H2769 (Penn Museum, object no. 33-22-82), dating to Hissar IIIC Period from the North Flat, CF38 (Photo by Jason Francisco).

Fig. 5.39 Animal figurines carved from alabaster (H750, H748, and H758) from the "Warrior 2" burial, DF09 x1. The figures date to Hissar IIIC Period (Penn Museum, object nos. 33-15-526, 33-15-525, 33-15-524) (Photo by Jason Francisco).

The Tepe Hissar artisans of Period III left a legacy of finely crafted artifacts in both burial and settlement contexts. The Burned Building on the North Flat dated to ca. 2500 BC, provides an excellent context of wide-ranging artifacts in precious materials—not unlike those from the burials—from domestic utensils, ceramic vessels, and tools, to luxury goods, banded carnelian beads, and luminous alabaster vessels (Schmidt 1937:157–169; 177–178). One remarkable example of objects with repoussé decoration is rendered on a copper lid with a representation of a bull attacked by a lion (ibid., p. 191, figure 112 H2252; Fig. 5.40). Another expertly crafted object is a silver diadem, a funerary offering of the Priest (Schmidt 1933: pl. CXXII H449). (See also Ch. 6 for discussion of the Burned Building; Fig. 5.23 and the Priest burial in High Outliers category above).

The turning point in the emergence of social differentiation and complexity is during Early Mid-Hissar II (phase E-D), ca. 3400 BC. Archaeologically, there is ample material evidence for differential wealth and status that developed in the mid-fourth millennium and continued until the beginning of the second millennium BC, which coincides with an increasingly prolific local economy attested to by the acquisition of raw materials in the production of prestige objects. By ca. 3100 BC, the stage was set for the emergence of an elite group of Tepe Hissar administrators who served as middlemen to acquire and distribute resources to the local craftspeople's workshops. The administrators would also negotiate and exchange/trade articles, for example raw lapis lazuli for copper wands, through a network of regional and long-distance partners. Locally, the craftsmen, farmers and herders, and the elite administrators would be members of a socially hierarchical but economically interconnected community whose basic sustenance depended upon a prosperous agricultural economy.

In the following chapter, Concluding Remarks, a diachronic survey brings further insight into the levels of sociocultural complexity at the settlement, with an overview of Tepe Hissar's emergence as a craft center on the northern Iranian plateau in the fourth millennium BC.

NOTES:

5.1 Using a geographic information system (GIS) method, 20 burial maps were created based on previously generated architectural CAD drawings to plot the horizontal distribution of the dated burials.
5.2 Schmidt's identification of some skeletons' age and sex were subsequently corrected by Krogman and later by Nowell (see section C in this chapter). In this discussion the corrected versions are used.
5.3 William Fitts, a former researcher at Penn Museum, David Massey, a graduate student at Ohio State Univ. and formerly of Milner Associates, and Ayşem Kılınç Ünlü with Joseph Torres formerly graduate students in Architecture at the University of Pennsylvania generated different parts of the maps. 5.4 It is not possible to assign context, sex, age, and burial type to deceased individuals whose disarticulated body parts are described as "bone piles" and "mass burials." They might be either secondary

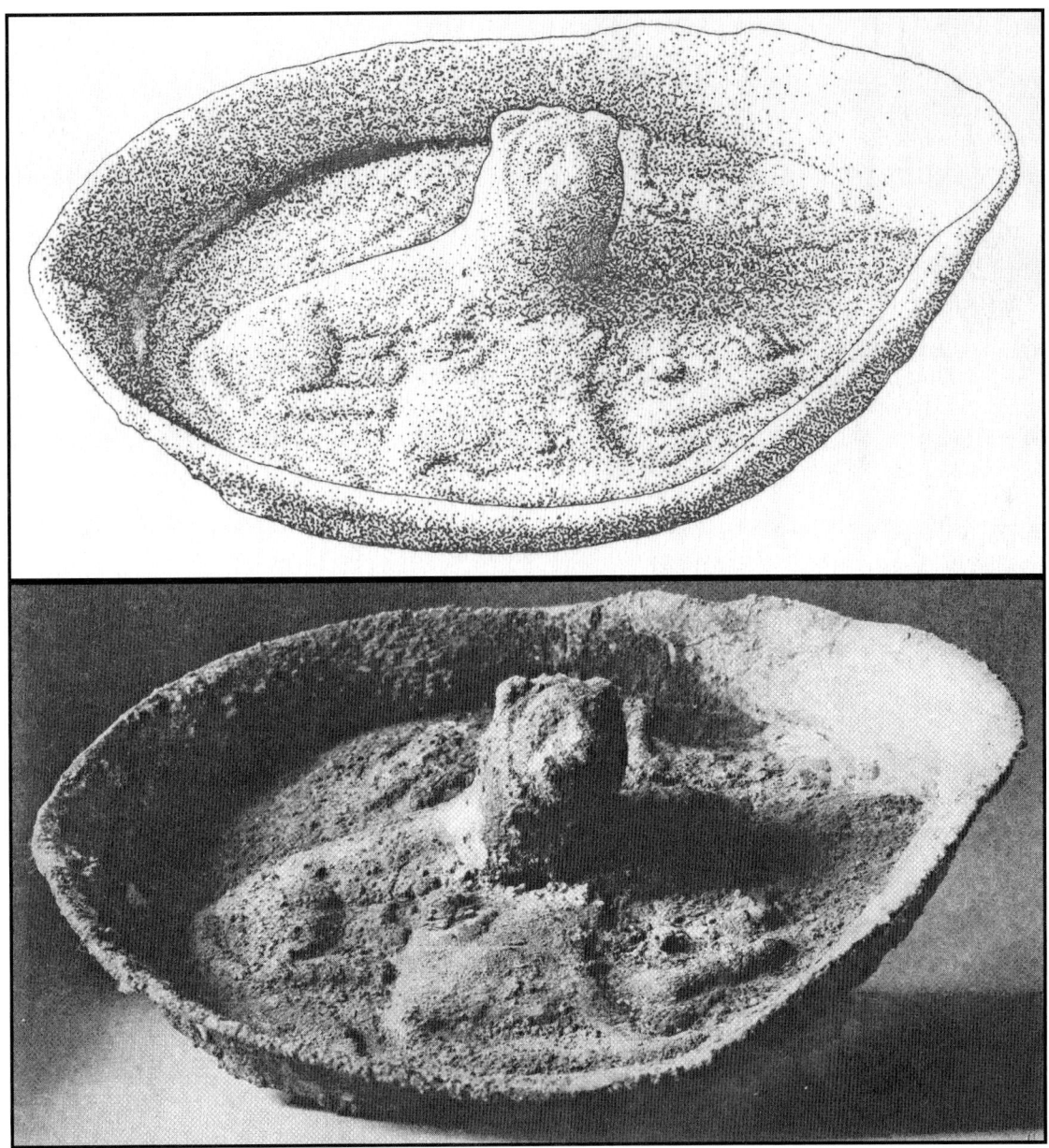

Fig. 5.40 An outstanding example of repoussé decoration is rendered on a copper lid or plate (H2252) from the Burned Building with a representation of a bull attacked by a lion (photograph after Schmidt 1937: fig. 112; drawing after Yule, 1982).

inhumations or intrusive burials.

5.5 That is to say, it is a type rarely found at Tepe Hissar.

5.6 For square DF09 ceramic assemblages from 1931–32 see Section 4.1a, pottery chart, in Appendix 1.

5.7 As noted in Ch. 4, a reconstructed section for each square in a burial group and a table of pottery illustrations from the 1931–32 assemblage listed in meter-depths from the same square appears in the appendices. For example, 5.1 is for the section, 5.1a is for the pottery assemblage.

5.8 Most of the "unknown" are infants, whose skeleton cannot be sexed accurately.

5.9 There is evidence of much debitage from lapis production at the South Hill, along with flint flakes and tools (Tosi 1989:15, 16).

5.10 Schmidt (1933:414, 416) discusses these wands briefly in the first publication, "The funerary equipment of prominent persons always included a curious device which we call 'wand' or 'symbol'. It is a copper rod usually ending in a bulbous base" (ibid., p. 414). He concludes that we may assign a range of possible functions and significance to these wands: "Someday we may find proof whether these wands are personal, family, or group symbols, badges of office, or the like" (ibid., p. 416)

5.11 Repaired or re-formed ceramic vessels are used as burial gifts, rather than disposed of, in DG11 x16 H3946 and DF19 x24 H1637, and also in burial groups 3 and 5.

5.12 This may be accidental, due to the high proportion of males in the population, or possibly, it is a culturally preferred form for male burials.

5.13 Description from Schmidt's burial notes in the Penn Museum Archives, "light brown translucent seal cylinder, chariot? [and] horse, 2 men, zigzag border lengthwise perforated, off-center. The pattern shows, from right to left: a person, probably a man, 1 arm suspended, the other perhaps raised? in front of a horse? (mule?) four legs, tail curved horizontal, long neck, ears pointed backward and upward, muzzle above head of man. From the back of the neck extends a horizontal 'S', probably chariot body? with shaft on the posterior concave part of the 'S', ? [on] chariot body proper, stands a second person, certainly a man, 1 arm suspended, the other one raised forward. The chariot body touches the 'wheel', an irregular circle with four -? spikes. Above the wheel and behind the driver is a problematic angular device, which may actually be part of the zigzag border repeated at the lower margin."

5.14 Schmidt makes a point that these four prominent individual burials were intentionally set apart from the rest of the burials to emphasize their higher rank. He writes, "the environs of the graves of the three outstanding persons, the 'priest' (DF08 x1), the second warrior (DF09 x1), and the little girl (DF18 x1), are rather deserted, while the grave of the first warrior (DF09 x2) is partly enclosed by a crescent of crowded burials, kept, however, in respectful distance. This arrangement suggests definitely that this warrior was a person of high rank or at least highly esteemed by his contemporaries whose loyalty or desire for some advantage in the other world induced survivors to bury their dead close to him" (1933:140, pl. CXLVII).

5.15 The funerary gifts suggest at once that these graves belonged to individuals who in life could have been warriors, in addition to their other roles in the community, such as farmers, fishermen, etc. For, in addition to their weapons, among their gifts, bident and trident could be used as agricultural tools for harvesting and digging and the lance head could be used for fishing. Hence the titles "Warrior" and "Priest" could be misnomers.

5.16 Whatever the function of the bident, its broken, useless state (if intentionally broken) may be paralleled with the lifeless state of the dead Warrior.

5.17 At Gohar Tepe, in the northern province of Mazandaran, a unique jar burial of a dog was discovered in the grave of a male individual dated to the first millennium BC. Daggers, arrowheads, and precious ornaments indicated the higher social/economic rank of the deceased man. Such evidence attests to a special ritual involved in the burial (A. Mahfroozi, pers. comm. 2007). It is unlikely that there is a direct cultural link between the two populations, but the burial of an animal in association with a presumably higher ranked individual underlines importance of the relationship of the man and "the dog" in a ritual context.

5.18 Schmidt notes that these discs also occur in limestone(?) and "grey stone" (H3261, H2798) at Tepe Hissar (1937:219). Therefore, it is a well-known form reproduced in different stones.

5.19 The technique is already known from Early Hissar II ceramics.

5.20 There is, however, archaeological and ethnographic evidence to the contrary: that social ranking of the living may be disguised in death as in graves with few simple gifts or those devoid of objects or without monumental tombstones. An ethnographic case in point is the Islamic emphasis on death as a "leveling" force. Therefore, bodies are to be wrapped in a simple shroud, without the accompaniment of funerary gifts.

5.21 The possibility of an extramural cemetery outside the excavated areas was not explored by Schmidt or Dyson, nor a separate graveyard for different social groups having separate burial places. Therefore, it must be assumed at present, that the only cemetery was in the abandoned areas of the settlement.

5.22 Schmidt refers to these objects as ornaments since there were no seal impressions found. Their numerous quantities in burials also leads him to that conclusion (Schmidt 1937:54–56, pl. XV).

6

Concluding Remarks

Introduction

This monograph brings to final publication the new stratigraphically based ceramic chronology of the Bronze Age settlement at Tepe Hissar in the Damghan region. It is based on a full study of ceramic assemblages from occupational phases excavated in 1976 by a team under Robert H. Dyson and linked to Erich Schmidt's earlier ceramic sequence based on a large corpus of grave contents. The new chronological framework combines evidence from Schmidt's and Dyson's ceramic assemblages, stratigraphy, architecture, and 1976 radiocarbon dates from settlement levels. Additionally, it benefits from the extensive resources of the Penn Museum Archives from the previous explorations.

The new ceramic sequence fills a crucial gap in our knowledge of cultural and chronological developments at Tepe Hissar and more generally in the northeastern region of Iran during the fourth through the late third millennium BC. It provides firm evidence for development of the settlement as an urban craft center in this period and for cycles of abandonment when parts of the site came into use as a cemetery. In sum, the new ceramic chronology anchors our understanding and reinterpretation of the cultural developments of the Tepe Hissar settlement and their inferred social and cultural implications within the framework of material culture from settlement and burial contexts.

This chapter has three parts: the first section summarizes the social and cultural changes at Tepe Hissar from the fourth into the early second millennium BC as detailed in the preceding chapters. The second section focuses Tepe Hissar's role as a partner in regional and long-distance networks of cultural and trade connections (see Table 6.1). In the third section, I propose two projects for future research on Tepe Hissar to be undertaken by archaeologists doing fieldwork in Iran and specialists interested in doing bioarchaeological analyses on the human skeletal remains at Penn Museum.

Social and Cultural Development of the Tepe Hissar Settlement

The interpretative framework for the development of the settlement is based on the premise expounded by Shanks and Tilley, that the production of material culture based on evidence from archaeological data should be viewed as a result of social practices. These practices are a set of social interactions among people and, as such, products of individuals and groups who constitute the sociocultural milieu. In other words, a sociocultural milieu is formed through "the structuring of social practices." Thus, "Material culture is…implicated in the structuring of social practices…[as it] forms a set of resources, a symbolic order within practice, drawn upon in political relations, activated and manipulated in ideology" (Shanks and Tilley 1993:122–134).

To start with, what information can be drawn from the material culture about the nature of basic subsistence and associated social practices of the Tepe Hissar population? Tepe Hissar's favorable geographic location between the Dasht-i Kavir and the Elburz mountain range undoubtedly provided ample resources for subsistence agriculture supplemented by hunting and fishing. Water, the most fundamental resource for an agricultural/herding economy, was provided by the Cheshmeh Ali River and its tributaries, bringing alluvial deposits that enriched the soil. Botanical, faunal, and material evidence attest to Tepe Hissar as a thriving, mixed agricultural/pastoral, highland community along the northern edge of the salt desert.

The Tepe Hissar farmers practiced a wide range of subsistence activities, from cereal agriculture—including various species of wheat and millet—to herding caprines,

Table 6.1 Relative Chronology

Estimated Absolute Dates of Tepe Hissar	1976 Stratigraphic Phase	Revised Ceramic Phase	Schmidt Hissar Periods	Tureng Tepe	Shah Tepe	Mesopotamia	Sialk (South Mound)	Arisman	Shahdad	Tepe Yahya	Shahr-i Sokhta	Anau and Namazga
				IIIC2								
1800–2200	A	B-A/A Late Hissar III **Late Bronze Age**	(IIIC)	IIIC1	IIa					IVA		Namazga VI
2200–2500	B	Mid-Hissar III	(IIIB) Burials	IIIB		Akkadian			Shahdad	IVB	IV / III	Namazga V
2500–2900	C (North Flat)		(IIIA) Burials	IIIA	IIb	Early Dynastic I–II / II–III					II	Namazga IV
2900–3100	D-C	Late Hissar II–Early Hissar III	(Late II B) Burials	IIB		Jemdet Nasr	IV.2	A/D		IVC		Anau IIB Namazga III
3100–3350	D	Late Hissar II **Bronze Age** "Proto-Elamite" (tools, seals, counters)	(IIB) Burials	IIB	←	←	IV.1 Proto-Elamite tablets	C		←	I	←

Date										
		←			←	←			←	←
3400	E-D	Early/Mid-Hissar II **Transition to Bronze Age** "Proto-Elamite" Transition	(IIB) Burials	IIB Grey ware; few Buff painted ware; few semi-precious stones	III-IIb	Late Uruk				Anau IIA Namazga II
3400–3650	E	Early Hissar II	(IIA)	IIA					VB-VA	
3700	F-E Termin. Hissar I	Late Hissar I– (40% burnished Grey) (40% painted)	(IC/IIA) Chalco. 6	IIA Late Chalco.; painted wares; early Grey ware; corr. to Yarim II WM Grey;	III Grey Ware (fully developed)	Middle Uruk	III.6–7	B		
3700–3900	F		IB Chalco. 5 (L. Chalco.)	Earliest Mixed zone Red painted mix w/ coarse, few Grey wheelmade; Red is handmade	Similar to Tureng assemblage	Early Uruk	III.4–5			Anau IIB Namazga I
4000–4300	Pre-F		IB–IA Chalco. 4				III.1–3		VC	IB1 IA (ends)

Fig. 6.1 Ceramic animal figurines, possibly administrative tools (left to right): Period IIA, DH06, H2978 (Penn Museum, object no. 33-21-342); Period IC, DH36, H3656 (Penn Museum, object no. 33-21-137); H1072 (Penn Museum, object no. 33-15-51) (Photo by Jason Francisco).

fishing, and hunting and gathering. It is reasonable to infer that a "symbiotic" relationship existed between the farmers and herdsmen. This relationship alludes to Khazanov's (1994:23) description: " a situation in which the majority of the population leads a sedentary life and is occupied for the most part with agriculture, while the livestock or, more often some of it, is maintained all year round on pastures…tended by herdsmen especially assigned to this task." These herdsmen may not be necessarily pastoral nomads,[1] "not even separate groups, but integrated to the larger agrarian-urban societies" (Khazanov 2009:125).

The material culture bears witness to the ancient settlement as a component of an actively developed agrarian society, whose population engaged in daily tasks of subsistence and household production of tools and crafts, which, in the late fourth millennium BC, developed into mass production in workshop contexts. The tools and other artifacts of the early settlement are manifold: storage bins, stone mortars, pestles, cutting and scraping tools, weights, spindle whorls, and administrative devices (animal figurines, tokens/counters) (Figs. 6.1, 6.2). The chipped stone flint blades were apparently put to use in "non-specialized activities such as agriculture and miscellaneous cutting, scraping, etc.…none related to specialized crafts known to have been practiced at the site….[some] blade fragments exhibit…'sickle sheen' [which] arguably indicates that this was a more common use for the Hesar blades" (Rosenberg 1989:117).

The material evidence brings to the fore a social milieu that encompassed households of farmers and herders whose survival mechanism depended on organizing groups to share labor for agricultural activities, animal husbandry, building irrigation canals, preparation of fields and harvesting, and possibly even sharing labor for building houses. In the early fourth millennium BC, each household was engaged in producing its own utensils for daily use. In the late fourth and third millennia BC, there is an increase in the manufactured craft items that were produced by specialized craftspeople in workshops with raw materials obtained from near and distant sources. The exponential growth, particularly in the production of prestige goods, required marketing of the manufactured crafts and possibly using surplus agricultural produce for exchange in the region and beyond. Accordingly, these processes required a complex social networking of agents[2] to regulate trade/exchange in the region and across the northern east-west route, often called the "high road" or the Great Khorasan trade road, on which Tepe Hissar was located.

The following discussion addresses the trajectories of the Tepe Hissar settlement and the social and cultural implications of expanding craft production in contexts of material culture from the late fifth to early second millennia BC.

Early Hissar I (Pre-F) ca. 4300–3900 BC

The earliest settlement phases at Tepe Hissar (IA, IB) were explored by Schmidt but not by the 1976 study. Therefore, here I rely on Schmidt's explorations and ob-

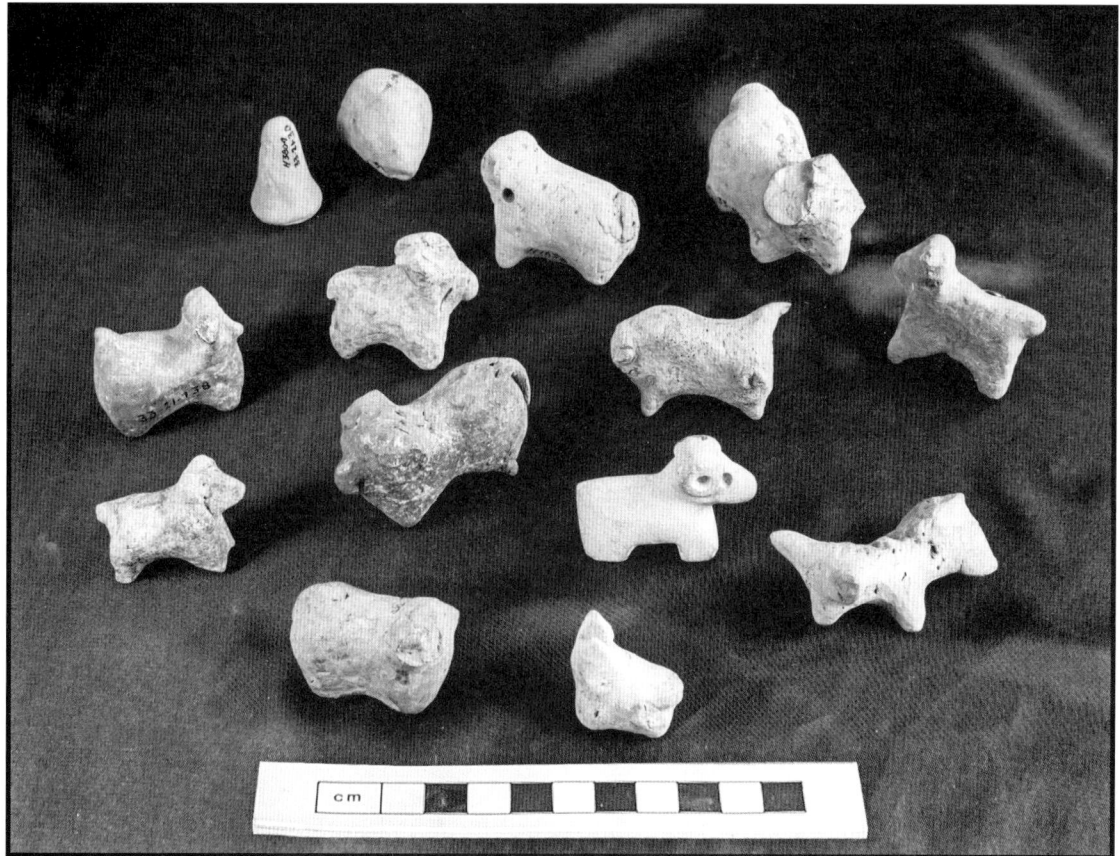

Fig. 6.2 A variety of ceramic animal figurines and tokens (two at the top left), possibly administrative tools from Period IIIC (clockwise from top left, Penn Museum, object nos. 33-21-30, 33-21-31, 33-22-248, 33-21-510, 33-21-135, 33-15-47, 33-21-144, 33-22-59, 33-22-237, 33-15-46, 33-21-139, 33-22-254, 33-15-50, 33-21-138) (Photo by Jason Francisco).

servations. Schmidt only reached virgin soil in several tests near the Painted pottery Flat. However, his excavations at the nearby site of Shir-e Shian revealed a settlement possibly contemporary with Hissar IA levels, preceded by pre-IA settlement. From this context, pottery similar to Anau I black-on-red ceramic type was found dated ca. 4500–4200 BC (Hiebert and Dyson 2002:77; Fig. 6.3). Subsequently, Dyson and Thornton's (2009) comparative study of sherds and small finds from Tepe Hissar, Shir-e Shian, and Tepe Sialk led the authors to date Hissar IA, IB ca. 4300–3900 BC. Their conclusions were based on ceramic comparisons with the central plateau settlements at Sialk III1-3, and Sialk III3-4. Hence, Schmidt's soundings at Shir-e Shian and later studies based on pottery comparisons suggest the existence of the earliest settlement at Tepe Hissar, phase (IA), and its contacts with the central plateau settlements.

In this monograph, the discussion of the first settlement period begins with the later IC and IC/IIA, based on evidence from the 1976 stratigraphic reassessments in the field and comprehensive archival reports (see Chapters 1, 2 and Table 2.2). These levels were observed in test trenches in all areas of the site, from the North Flat to the Twins Hillock, the southernmost point of the settlement in Quadrant FF, which yielded random walls, painted pottery, and simple pit burials (cf. Schmidt1937, fig. 16; see also Biscione 1976).

Late Hissar I/Early Hissar II (Phases F, F-E) ca. 3900–3700 BC

During the first part of the fourth millennium BC, Schmidt verified that the occupation area of Period I, nearly 200 m in diameter, was the largest of the three main periods. Our knowledge of the Late Hissar I settlement comes from the Painted Pottery Flat where Schmidt excavated planned house complexes with several rooms that are diagonally oriented around a courtyard (1937:26, 34, fig. 27). The early building technology involves "chineh" (pisé) wall construction, but later in this period it chang-

Fig. 6.3 A Period I ceramic vessel from Tepe Hissar (H1558, Penn Museum, object no. 33-15-33) similar to Anau I black-on-red ceramic type dated ca. 4500–4200 BC from Schmidt's explorations of the site of Shir-e Shian. (Photo by Jason Francisco)

es in favor of four-course plastered walls built of sun dried mud bricks—although some walls are still built of "chineh." The walls are covered with multiple layers of mud plaster that reflect long-term use of the buildings. Moreover, most of the early architectural features continue into later periods, such as house plans with diagonal orientations, rooms built around a courtyard, and the presence of a central room with fireplace and hearth surrounded by subsidiary rooms. The continuity of these features render strong support to the practice of a long-lived building tradition that evolved over time with minor changes, as is also observed in the pottery and other craft traditions.

The potters of Late Hissar I used the slow wheel and the same type of clay to produce red and buff painted as well as grey wares. The grey ware sherds constitute nearly 40% of the 1976 assemblage, roughly equal to the combined proportion of buff and red painted sherds. Geometric, floral, and animal motifs, specifically ibex, are depicted on the early buff painted ceramics on footed goblets and small cups with pointed base. These motifs are also found on globular storage jars, linking Tepe Hissar to Sialk6-7 (Figs. 3.4 and 3.6–3.10).[3] Most of the grey ware forms are footed goblets, simple bowls and cups, and large, wide-based bowls in coarse ware.

The early fourth millennium settlement can be characterized as occupied by a fairly large population engaged in household-level craft production, as we have no knowledge of production areas from this period at the site. Trinkhaus' 1976 survey of smaller satellite sites did not yield evidence for kilns or metal workshops in the immediate vicinity.[4] One possible explanation for the absence of evidence might be the excavator's lack of precision in his recording methods of the building complexes from Painted Pottery Flat (Schmidt 1937: figs. 25, 26).

Early Mid-Hissar II (Phases E, E-D) Transition to Bronze Age ca. 3650–3400 BC

Toward Mid-Hissar II, technical and stylistic innovations occur in ceramic assemblages: the addition of slag temper to coarse ware, a high gloss burnishing on grey wares with "metallic" sheen, and the frequent use of the wheel, especially on small vessels. The majority of the assemblage in phase E is buff painted and red wares, while in phase E-D, grey burnished ware is the most frequent with buff painted close behind it. Red ware becomes rare in phase E-D. Coarse ware is minimally present. In this period, four new forms appear: carinated bowl/jar with characteristic brown band on the exterior of the rim, large storage jars with rail rim, brazier, and plate/tray (for phase E see Figs. 3.12–3.16, for phase E-D see Figs. 3.18–3.24). All four vessel types are crafted in buff, buff painted, grey, and coarse wares. The wide-based bowl is probably a utilitarian serving dish and it continues with some frequency into Early Period III. There are also several new motif elements and painting styles: bold/wide linear bands in black-brown paint on buff large jars and geometric and circular motifs on small carinated bowls (Figs. 3.12–3.14). Some of the latter motifs are carefully applied with a thin brush. For the first time, incised ridges and knobs are applied on grey burnished pedestal bowls (Figs. 3.18:9–11, 6.4, 6.5, 6.6; Schmidt 1937: pl. XXVI H5118, H1822).

By the mid-fourth millennium BC, the production of craft activities is contextualized at the "industrial" craft workshop at the South Hill, evidenced by pottery kilns, copper smelting furnaces, furnace linings as well as large lapis debitage, and slag from copper smelting (Tosi 1989:13–24; Pigott 1989:25–34; Tosi and Bulgarelli 1989:35–54; see also below pp. 279, 290). As early as the first quarter of the fourth millennium BC, lapis blanks were produced in massive quantities on-site to be crafted into beads and ornaments. The early bead production, which displayed simple forms, continued to evolve into a wider variety of forms manufactured with superior craftsmanship in the third millennium BC.

The burial pattern is consistent with the earlier tradition in the majority of the graves; the deceased was interred in a pit burial, wrapped in a textile. Personal ornaments include double scroll pins (Fig. 6.7; Schmidt 1937: pl. XXIX H4856), copper bracelets, lapis lazuli, and carnelian beads. The most remarkable ornaments that display diversity of forms and materials are "button-seals" and beads of varied shapes: tubular, oblong, disc, and bicone. They are made of clay, gypsum, alabaster, serpentine, red jasper, carnelian, and rarely in shell[5] (Schmidt 1937: pl. XXXII).

Ceramic vessels are regularly placed near the head or upper part of the body and "button-seal" ornaments are randomly distributed on the deceased individuals. It is likely that these ornaments were identity markers of the individuals or their membership in a social group, family, or tribe/clan. While ordinary beads are for all ages and sexes, semi-precious beads—carnelian, crystal, and lapis lazuli—are placed on the neck of only a few females. In some cases, a ceramic cup filled with beads is "held" between the hands of the deceased individual (Schmidt 1937: pls. XV, XIX).

Toward the latter half of the fourth millennium BC there is a major increase in metallurgical activities. Copper daggers and flat axes are cast in copper-arsenic alloy.[6] Silver is obtained through cupellation; it is mainly used to craft beads and small ornaments. Only a few individuals have the distinction of having ornaments in precious silver, notably those buried in cist graves. Among the frequently gifted copper artifacts are pyramidal pins, double scroll pins, bracelets, and earrings (Schmidt 1937: pls. XXVIII, XXIX, XXX). Seals are not commonly gifted. One male burial, however, has an unusually large copper stamp seal[7] placed on his pelvic bone (Schmidt 1933: pl. CVII H1176; see also Ch. 5, p. 221).

Late Hissar II to Early Hissar III, Bronze Age (Phases D and D-C) ca. 3350–2900 BC

During this period, we witness a new era in social and cultural developments. Especially noticeable are advances in the procurement of a broad range of resources for manufacturing goods in workshops and the acquisition of new skills in metallurgy, ceramics, and in ornaments of semi-precious stones. It is highly plausible that this period of labor-intensive craft production and increased importation of raw materials from distant sources implies the

Fig. 6.4 Grey burnished vessel with incised decoration, H5118 (Penn Museum, object no. 33-22-517), Period IIB, South Hill, burial DF78 x22 (Photo by Jason Francisco).

Fig. 6.5 Grey burnished pedestal bowl, H1149 (Penn Museum, object no. 33-15-297), Period II, North Flat, burial CG25 x1 (Photo by Jason Francisco).

Fig. 6.6 Ceramic vessel with circular ridges, H1822 (Penn Museum, object no. 33-22-519), Period IIB, South Hill, DG53 (Photo by Jason Francisco).

Fig. 6.7 Double scroll pin, H5019 (Penn Museum, object no. 33-21-620), a characteristic grave offering for Early Mid-Hissar II (Photo by Jason Francisco).

emergence of a more complex social organization, which includes a hierarchical group of expert artisans along with supervisors/administrators, who were supported by a surplus agricultural economy.

Crafts

In late fourth and early third millennium BC, ceramic production at Tepe Hissar gained new momentum. This period is characterized by grey, highly burnished ceremonial vessels with metallic gloss, in addition to a few simple buff painted bowls (Fig. 6.8). In the production of new forms, especially in grey burnished ware, the potters used hand and wheel techniques, well-levigated, sandy clay, and controlled firing conditions. Among the new forms are several types of bottles, including a long-necked form with incised decoration (Fig. 3.41:2), others with pattern burnishing and a raised "ring" around the neck that recalls metal vessels (Fig. 3.41:1). Another new form is the "tulip" beaker with "metallic" sheen (Fig. 3.36:1). The latter vessel highlights the potter's sophisticated technical skill in the use of the wheel to create a thin-walled elegant form that is also replicated in silver and alabaster.

The innovations in technical and stylistic variations in ceramics co-occurred with shifts in metal and stone technology. In metallurgy, the focus is on production of copper alloys, silver, and lead. Stamp seals are crafted in copper, lead, and silver. Gold beads are frequently incorporated into lapis lazuli and carnelian beads. Metallurgists have much better control of the alloys so that objects of pure copper, pure arsenic, and pure lead are produced, even though some weapons (dagger with medial ridge, blade, and sword) are still manufactured in arsenical copper (Pigott 1989: fig. 4.7e). The parallel transformations in different crafts could be a result of social and technical interdependence among the local specialist craftspeople, who pooled their knowledge.[8] It is conceivable that the potters continued the legacy of the early ceramic traditions and, as they worked in collaboration with metal and stone craftspeople, all three developed an advanced knowledge of the properties of their materials. Technical progress emerged from sharing sets of knowledge from different specialists. We have examples of such collaboration in the earlier phases E and E-D in the use of slag as tempering material for clay to improve the durability of vessels (also some sherds are reported to contain copper prills [Pigott, Howard, and Epstein, 1982]). Another example of knowledge shared by potters and metalsmiths is the reduction of firing atmosphere, a skill that both types of craftspeople practiced in the production of grey wares

Fig. 6.8 A skillfully made thin-walled ceramic vessel, H2212 (Penn Museum, object no. 33-21-807), done in a form replicated in silver and alabaster from Period II–III transitional (Photo by Jason Francisco).

and copper smelting. Thornton (2009b) argues convincingly that multi-craft production processes at Tepe Hissar are intertwined and one strong case is the refractory technical ceramics that are used for copper smelting (see also Pigott [1989: figs. 4–8] for ceramic shaft-hole axe mold and double channel mold). Clearly, the shared technical knowledge among different craftspeople led to parallel transformations in craft production, best illustrated by activities that took place in the industrial workshop area at the South Hill (for details, see Tosi 1989:13–24).

The workshop area is described as a "multi-functional industrial workshop" where lapis blanks were processed and intensive metallurgical activity took place. Heaps of lapis debitage were spread over the whole site in association with chipped stone tools (microliths) that were used in the preparation of the blanks (Rosenberg 1989:117).[9] The by-products of the metallurgical activity were a large scatter of slag, smelting furnaces, and copper ingots (Pigott 1999:85, fig. 4.7b, H76-138; Schmidt 1937: pl. LIV H2256), as well as pans and molds for open-face casting (Schmidt 1937: pl. XLIV H3577, H1727, H2940; Tosi and Bulgarelli 1989: 35–54), slag and furnace linings (Pigott 1989: figs. 1–9). The workshop functioned during three consecutive construction phases of Period II (D3–D1) from ca. 3400 to 3100 BC. In one phase of the workshop building, there was a ceramic kiln and two smelting furnaces with a scatter of lapis lazuli chips and metallurgical debris. Thornton describes the artifactual context of the workshop levels as, "notable for a sizable fill of (20–25 centimeters deep) containing lapis flakes, flint flakes and metallurgical debris, as well as administrative items such as pillow shaped tablet blanks and clay tokens" (2009b:94; see also Tosi and Bulgarelli 1989: fig. 5; Dyson 1987:659).

Architecture

Our most detailed knowledge of domestic architecture in this period is from the three Main Mound buildings and the South Hill building 4 (see Ch. 2, pp. 48–57; Howard 1989a:55–68; Dyson and Remsen 1989:72–84). Two structural and stylistic innovations appear to be characteristic in the architecture of the end of the fourth and early third millennium BC. One is exterior buttressing of walls and the other is "crescent-shaped" niches applied to exterior walls. Exterior buttressing is observed in nine structures on four areas of the settlement: the Main Mound on Buildings 2 and 3; the South Hill building complex (Tosi and Bulgarelli 1989:35–37, fig. 1; Dyson and Remsen 1989:82–84); the Painted Pottery Flat (Schmidt 1933: fig. A), and the North Flat structure, CF 48/14/ (Dyson and Remsen 1989:84–89). The "crescent-shaped" niches occur as a series along the exterior wall of Building 3 on the Main Mound (Howard 1989a:63–64, fig. 11; Dyson and Remsen 1989:74–82). The Main Mound buildings are residential compounds with domestic installations.[10] They have similar plans and common interior features including a centrally placed hearth. Each building is composed of a square or rectangular main room, a reed roof, and several smaller adjacent rooms. Evidently portions of these structures were utilized simultaneously. Among the three buildings, Building 3 appears to be a multi-functional structure with long duration. It is the largest of the three with four storerooms that were built at different stages, a two-chambered updraft open kiln, and a platform, which was possibly used for small-scale ceramic production. One of the storerooms has a depression for two large pithoi for grain storage. The main room has a square clay base in the center and a triple chambered hearth. It is likely that this building is one of the structures belonging to a large extended family or multiple households. Alternatively, it could be a community house for grain storage.

According to the excavators, after the late fourth millennium BC, the quality of masonry declined "as seen in the abandonment of the complex buttress tradition and the reconstruction of walls with plain facades. Brick sizes gradually changed in the direction of longer rectangular forms. The remaining walls of period 'III', with the exception of the Burned Building…seem to form less regular plans" (Dyson and Remsen 1989:89).

Early Hissar III (IIIA) (Phase C) ca. 2900–2500 BC

On the Main Mound, phase C is a "catch-all" phase meaning later than transitional phase D-C, but earlier than phase B. The 1976 ceramic assemblage is typologically included in the transitional phase D-C. In Schmidt's sequence, it corresponds to IIIA burials. (For the North Flat phase C, see explanation in Ch. 2)

Mid-Hissar III (IIIB) (Phase B) Middle Bronze ca. 2500–2200 BC

By the mid-third millennium BC, the population of Tepe Hissar had shifted from several areas of the Main Mound and the North Flat to the east on the Red Hill and the Treasure Hill. A portion of the area on the Main Mound, over Building 3_1 became a burial ground.[11] The extent of the occupied area suggests a decrease in population, possibly as a result of local factors, such as drought or disease that would increase mortality rate or competition among households for economic leadership, eventually leading to displacement of some of the population. Burial evidence of high infant mortality and cranial pathologies may explain a decrease in population during this period. Some of the adult males display pathological marks on their crania and mandibles, even though both sexes lived to mature ages (Rathbun 1989; Schmidt's archival notes on burials; J. Monge, pers. comm).

During the mid-late third millennium BC, metal and stone artifacts reached their zenith in the quality of craftsmanship while retaining early forms. Animal figurines are modeled in alabaster and painted as prestige artifacts (see Figs. 5.21, 5.40). There is a dramatic increase in pure copper, pure silver, and pure lead artifacts, especially the high status objects such as mace heads, wands, and semi-precious jewelry. Silver and gold diadems and wide copper bracelets are decorated with repoussé technique (Schmidt 1937: pl. LIV H4112, H4128). This same technique is also applied to figurines and vessels in copper and precious metals. In the production of jewelry, silver and gold/electrum beads and gold foil are used in combination with semi-precious stones. The only gold vessel is the spectacular tulip-shaped beaker (ibid., fig. 123, pl. LVIII H2257). It was retrieved from the floor of the main room of the notable Burned Building on the North Flat.

The Burned Building on the North Flat

This important building was excavated and published in great detail by Schmidt (1937:157–169) and later studied by Dyson (1972) and Dyson and Remsen (1989:89–99). Stratigraphically it is above phase C and "below the upper [most] layers of mixed building remains and graves" (ibid., p. 89). The only radiocarbon date for the building is a 2-sigma range of 2476–2153 cal. BC (P2711). The building was completely burned down; its contents of hundreds of arrow points, daggers, and charred skeletons were retrieved from the thick ash deposit on the floor. Schmidt attributes the haphazard distribution of the objects to serious fighting inside the building.

The Burned Building is unique in size, plan, brick masonry, and architectural details, in contrast to other buildings known from the settlement. As a formal, long, rectangular structure, it covers an area of more than 300 square meters. Its thick walls are made from mold-made bricks, measuring 60 x 32 x 10 cm, with several layers of plaster on the exterior. Dyson and Remsen describe the built masonry in detail: "The bricks were laid up as headers, each course lapped one-half brick over the one below and bonded at the corners as alternating headers and stretchers" (1989:92). Two of its outstanding features are a formal buttressed entrance hall and a stepped "platform hearth." In Schmidt's reconstruction, the entrance hall included a tower construction built upon a brick foundation and incorporated into a high wall around the interior courtyard (1937: fig. 94). As such, he visualized the building as a fortified mansion, contrary to Dyson and Remsen's conclusion that the foundation could not support such a construction based on measurements (1989:93).

The second important feature is the "platform hearth" situated in the corner of the main room. It was decorated with cut-out motifs, which Schmidt interpreted as female symbols representing deities of the Tepe Hissar population. His suggestion is reasonable as several contemporary burials contained abstract hourglass shape female figurines with pronounced breasts. This iconic female form, conceivably a symbol of deity, is crafted in ceramic (Fig. 6.9; Schmidt 1937: pl. XLVI H2790), copper (Fig. 6.10), precious metals and alabaster (Fig. 6.11; Schmidt 1937: pl. XLVII H5142, H5178, H3500), and it also occurs as an effigy vessel in ceramic (see Ch. 5, Fig. 5.18; Schmidt 1937: pl. XLVI H2785). According to Dyson and Remsen, the "platform hearth" is placed on a high plastered floor that "had been fired red" (1989:94–95, figs. 19–23); therefore, it may be interpreted as a fire altar/shrine. Moreover, the existence of symbolic objects that were strewn around the floor near the platform-hearth—copper wands with human and animal finials (Figs. 6.12, 6.13), a female effigy vessel, heirloom pieces such as a gold diadem and silver vessels, and lance blades ornamented with silver bands—suggests some type of ceremonial activities had taken place close to the hearth, which the residents and/or members of the community used to worship their deities.

The rich assortment of prestige objects in the Burned Building provides an excellent in situ context for the artifacts from the rest of the contemporary settlement and burials. Altogether, the building contained 86 objects, many of which are valuable personal ornaments. The main room (#1) with a square hearth contained weapons (daggers and spearheads), a gold diadem, gold beads, hundreds of semi-precious stones, silver and copper vessels, and a gold/electrum beaker. Storeroom #2 contained large, lidded storage jars filled with grain near copper stamp seals (H2697, H2698) and ingots. In addition, three labels with stamp impressions were found in the fill (Schmidt 1937: pl. XLIX H1850–H1852). The association of the administrative devices with copper ingots and jars of grain strengthens the suggestion that these items were for sale or trade. For a detailed description of the contents of the Burned Building, see Dyson (1972) and Schmidt (1937:164–168).

Also on the floor of storeroom #4 there was charred grain, a stone weight, mullers, a fancy copper lid with repoussé design of a lion attacking a bovine (see Fig. 5.41), and two additional copper ingots. The latter room appears

Fig. 6.9 Iconic hourglass shaped ceramic female figurine, H2790 (Penn Museum, object no. 33-22-55), from Period IIIC, North Flat, burial CF47 x2 (Photo by Jason Francisco).

to have served as an *entrepôt* for trade goods and also for domestic activities related to food preparation in the nearby kitchen. In the kitchen area and the fill outside it, two more stamp seals were found (Schmidt 1937: pl. XLIX H1853, H1854). This cache of seals may have belonged to the owner of the building.

The combined evidence of the plan, architectural features, and contents of the Burned Building reveals its multi-functional nature, as the private residence of a wealthy, sizable household, and possibly a trading post where large amounts of grain and locally manufactured prestige objects were stored and exported. Undoubtedly, the grain must have been stored for household consumption and, the surplus, as a trade item in exchange for imported materials. It is conceivable that at least one of the permanent residents of the building was an individual who had high status in the community, a social and political elite, who acted as the administrator of the commercial transactions.

The demise of the Burned Building created a hiatus of unknown duration, followed by the final period (IIIC) of the Tepe Hissar settlement interpreted as the transition to the Late Bronze Age.

Late Hissar III (IIIC) (Phase B-A/A) Transition to Late Bronze ca. 2000–1800 BC

The end of the Tepe Hissar settlement is stratigraphically ambiguous. Overlying the Period IIIB Burned Building, there are at least two structures on the topmost levels. Dyson referred to these levels as "phase A," which is equivalent to Period IIIC, in Schmidt's terminology. These lev-

Fig. 6.10 Hourglass shaped female figurine crafted from copper, H5178 (Penn Museum, object no. 33-21-983), Period IIIC, North Flat, burial CF38 x11 (Photo by Jason Francisco).

CONCLUDING REMARKS 283

Fig. 6.11 A plaster cast of an alabaster hourglass shaped female figurine, H3500 (Penn Museum, object no. 33-22-92), Period IIIC, Treasure Hill "Hoard II" (Photo by Jason Francisco).

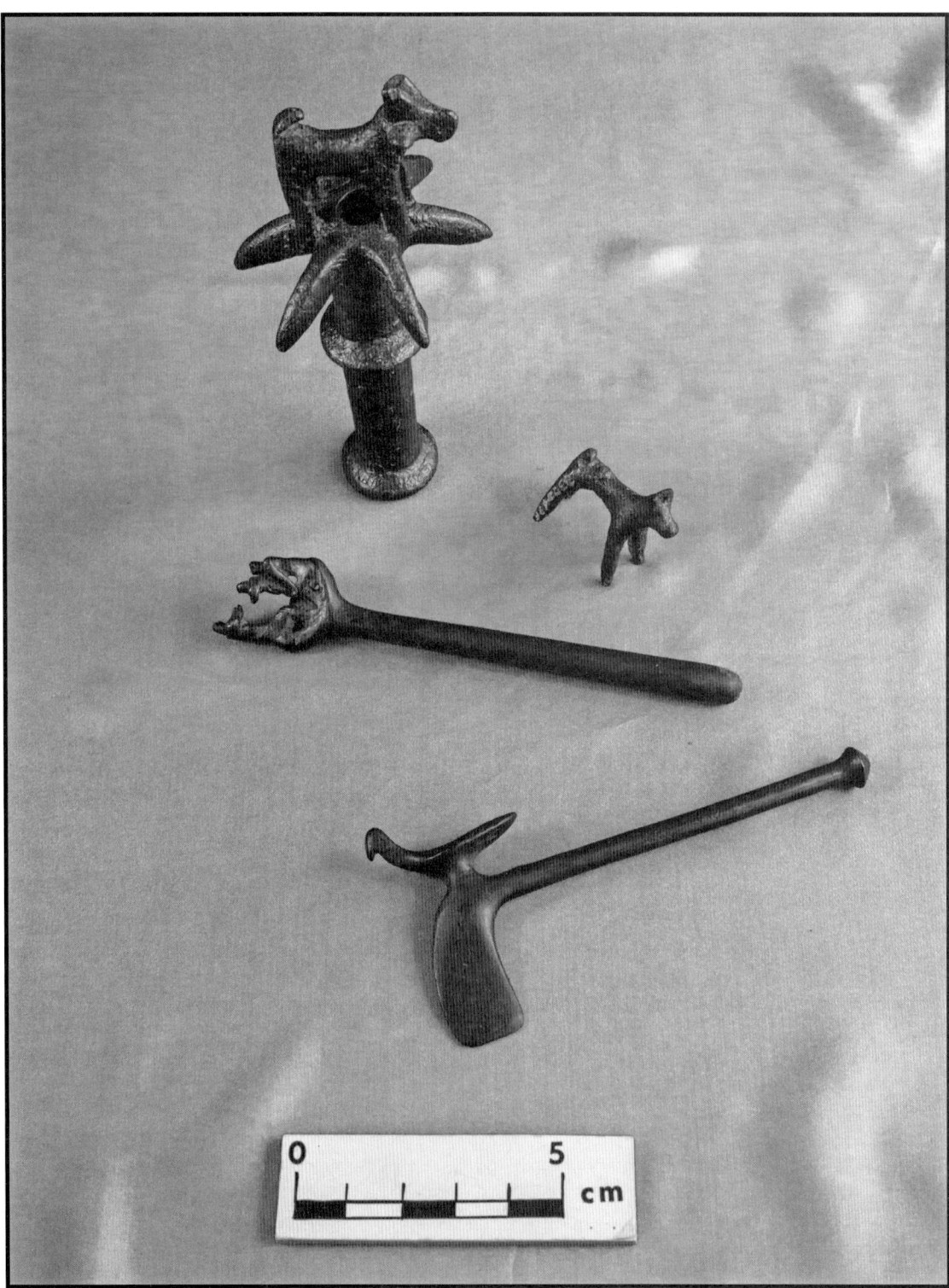

Fig. 6.12 Top to bottom: Period IIIC, Treasure Hill, ibex: H3578 (Penn Museum, object no. 33-22-115), dog: H3159 (Penn Museum, object no. 33-22-136); Period IIIC, Main Mound, burial DF08 x1 "Priest", 3 person wand: H463 (Penn Museum, object no. 33-15-582); Period IIIB, Treasure Hill, burial CH85 x18, bird wand: H4279 (Penn Museum, object no. 33-21-920) (Photo by Jason Francisco).

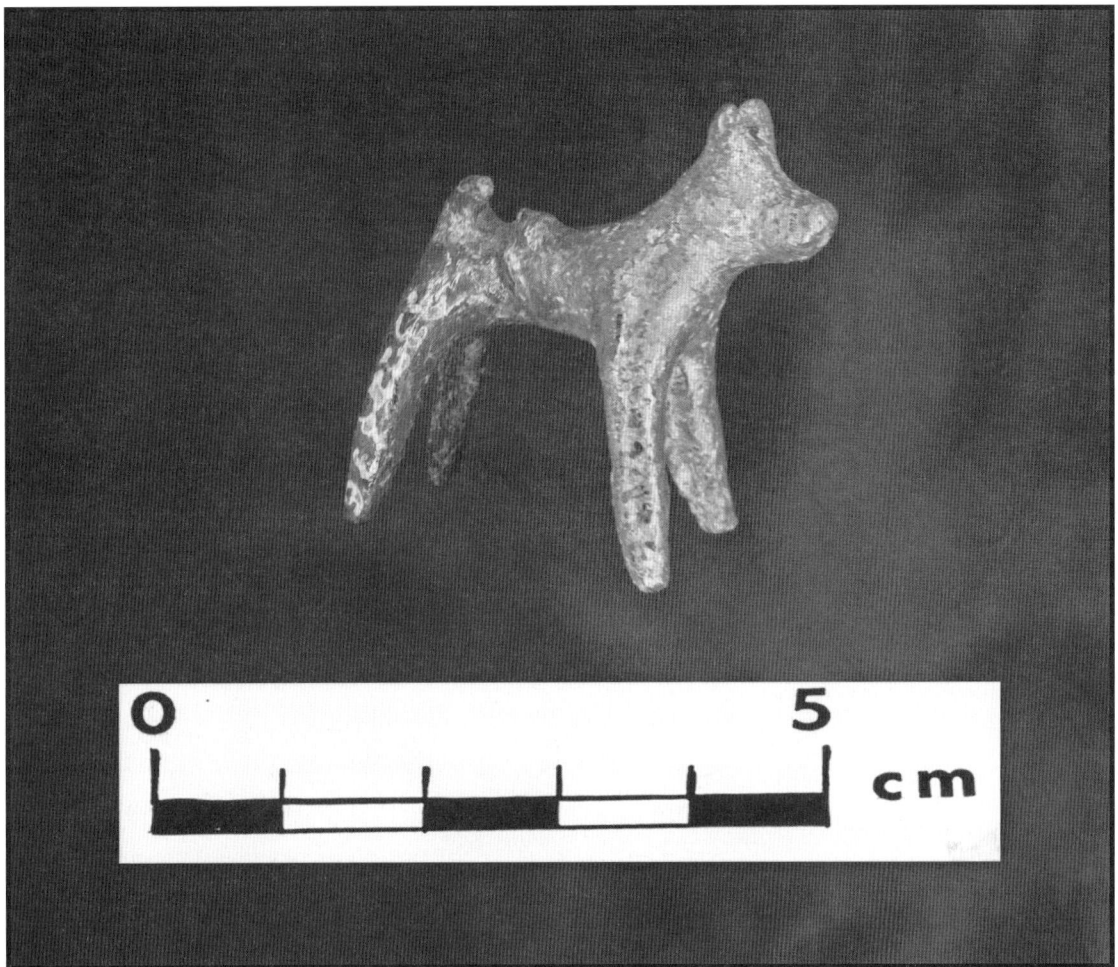

Fig. 6.13 A copper dog figurine with tail and ears raised (Schmidt 1937:188 pl. XLVI); Period IIIC, Treasure Hill, H3159 (Penn Museum, object no. 33-22-136) (Photo by Jason Francisco).

els were also excavated at Treasure Hill "where [Schmidt] found the two famous BMAC cenotaphs ("Hoard I" and "Hoard II") that were probably contemporary with the one from the North Flat" (Thornton 2009b:88; for the North Flat hoard of alabaster objects, columns and discs, and weapons of precious metals see Schmidt 1937:171, figs. 96–99). On the Main Mound and above the "IIIB" graves, Schmidt found incoherent foundations and wall remains with little definition (level 1). In 1976, Schmidt's "incoherent foundations" were translated to a series of plaster floors that were documented on "The Pinnacle" (a three meter high vertical sequence in plot DF09—for details, see Ch. 2, p. 48). While the stratigraphic definition of the final Tepe Hissar settlement remains elusive and open to further investigation, the radiocarbon date for the highest preserved stratum on the Main Mound has a 2-sigma range of 2153–1761 cal. BC; at Treasure Hill,

the radiocarbon date below the two top building levels is 1960–1645 cal. BC. Therefore, the end of the Tepe Hissar settlement at Treasure Hill, sometime between 1750–1600 BC, was later than that at the Main Mound.

The Late Hissar IIIC period is largely defined by grave objects and pottery associations. The Main Mound and the North Flat burials from Level 1 contain splendid prestige objects; there is an abundance of jewelry in precious metals and semi-precious stones (Fig. 6.14), weaponry, and other status-defining objects (see Chs. 4,and 5). Two burial hoards from the uppermost layers of the Treasure Hill contained similarly rich, expertly crafted assemblages, including five spectacular mouflon heads of gold foil (see cover art), with coiled horns and well-defined features. The perforations on the mouflon horns indicate that they were ornaments sewn on fabric (Schmidt 1937: fig. 111 H3210).

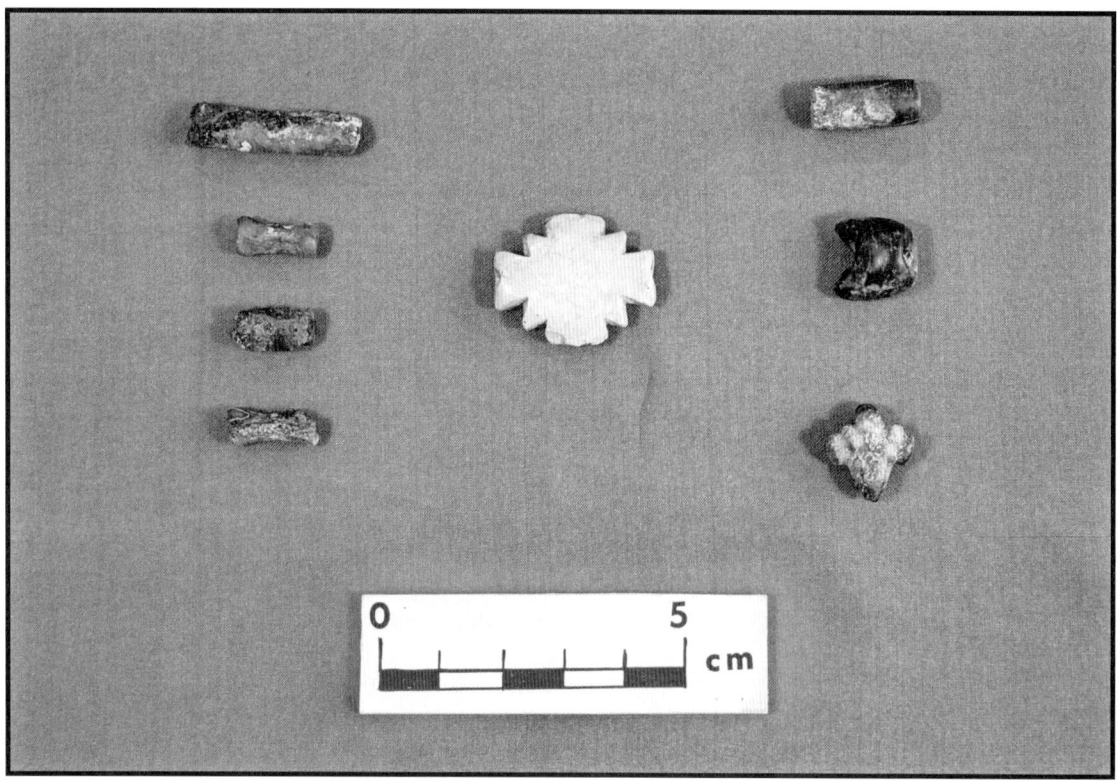

Fig. 6.14 Items of jewelry, H2388 (Penn Museum, object no. 33-21-1017), from Period IIIC, North Flat, burial CF55 x1 "Dancer" (Photo by Jason Francisco).

The large grey ware vessels are handmade, pattern burnished with herringbone or zigzag designs (Fig. 6.15); the forms are restricted to bottles with short neck and bridge-beak-spouted jars (Fig. 3.44, 1; Schmidt 1937: fig. 107 H3511). Among the small forms, the spouted vessels are numerous in contrast with earlier periods (Fig. 6.16; Schmidt 1937: figs. 107–110, pls. XL–XLIII). The large canteen with lug handles and herringbone design appears as an index fossil for this period (Schmidt 1937: fig. 108 H4219). Several ceramic vessel forms that are characteristic of the Bronze Age (Fig. 6.17)—bottle, beaker, trough-spouted and bridge-beak-spouted jars—are replicated in copper, silver, and rarely in gold (Schmidt 1937: pl. LVII).

The highlights of craft production include large alabaster vessels that replicate ceramic forms; elegant stemmed bowls, plates, and trough-spouted vessels (see Ch. 5, Fig. 5.38) are crafted in translucent alabaster and one is made of banded alabaster (Schmidt 1937: fig. 127 H3595). Schmidt describes the latter vessel as "a unique vase of alabaster with a beautiful natural pattern of bands in grayish white and light brown shades. The oblong vessel has a high, hollow base" (ibid., p. 216). A similar vessel was found in the hoard of a "Young Warrior" at Treasure Hill (see above reference to cenotaph). Two forms of the noteworthy alabaster vessels are similar to their ceramic counterparts: trough-spouted jar and long stemmed offering plate; the latter is a replica of the grey burnished long stemmed bowl of Hissar II (phase E-D). Among the wide-ranging prestige objects in alabaster, "discs" and "columns" (Fig. 6.18, see also Ch. 5, Fig. 5.39) represent functionally and symbolically elusive artifacts (Schmidt 1937: pls. LIX–LXII).

Toward the end of the third millennium BC, the quality of craftsmanship and the range of crafted articles had reached their zenith. This brings up two interrelated issues: (1) the relationship between technical and stylistic innovations in crafts and social complexity at Tepe Hissar[12] and (2) the role of Tepe Hissar in a regional/long-distance exchange network. Addressing these issues rests, in part, upon the chronological clarity of the excavated data and its dissemination, which this research project has largely accomplished. Furthermore, technical sophistication and diversity in craft production at Tepe Hissar allow us to make reasonable assumptions about the existence of critical factors underlying social complexity and changes

Fig. 6.15 Large handmade grey ware vessel, H3841 (Penn Museum, object no. 33-21-836), pattern burnished with herringbone or zigzag designs, Period IIIC, Treasure Hill, burial CH75 x9 (Photo by Jason Francisco).

Fig. 6.16 A spouted ceramic vessel form, H4296 (Penn Museum, object no. 33-22-449), Period IIIC, Treasure Hill "hoard" (Photo by Jason Francisco).

Fig. 6.17 A tulip-shaped, grey burnished, ceramic vessel, H5047 (Penn Museum, object no. 33-21-748), Period IIIC, Main Mound, burial DF16 x15 (Photo by Jason Francisco).

Fig. 6.18 Left to right: Period IIIC, North Flat, miniature column: H1844 (Penn Museum, object no. 33-22-189); Period IIIC, Main Mound, burial DF19 x2, disc: H174 (Penn Museum, object no. 33-15-718) (Photo by Jason Francisco).

in social organization: one, organization of labor through a web of hierarchical social relations; two, emergence of an administrative body that supervised pooling of knowledge among craftspeople; and three, trade/exchange connections that motivated production to meet the increased demand for high-value commodities through inter-regional exchanges and east-west trade/cultural connections across several thousand kilometers. These assumptions are supported by archaeological data.

Changes in Social Organization

The transition to the Bronze Age in the mid-fourth to early third millennium BC marked a turning point in the development of specialized craft production at Tepe Hissar. During this period, the scale and diversity of craft production expanded considerably as a result of the procurement of wide-ranging resources, technological innovations, and organizational changes that had powerful impacts on social and cultural change and, consequently, on the emergence of social complexity. Arnold defines this development in terms of 'chiefdom like organization' in which "household labor or products are transferred from head-of household management to individuals outside family units…[and those individuals] begin to manipulate these resources…for political advantage" (1992:62, as cited in Chapman 2003:86). At Tepe Hissar, there is little direct evidence of chiefdom or any other type of social organization, but the material evidence indicates a progressively sophisticated craft economy based on the use of increasingly complex technology and continued flow of imported materials. We can, therefore, infer during the early fourth millennium BC, a technological shift from low-level craft production based on household labor and a socially undifferentiated population to extra-household production that promoted social and organizational changes.

By the mid-fourth millennium BC, the craftspeople were working with technologically effective tools and pooling their expertise in workshop contexts that enabled them to increase production and refine the quality of their crafts. An example of this technological innovation and collaborative effort is observed in metallurgical production, including the use of bi-valve molds for metal, jewelry, and figurines (see above Fig. 6.2) instead of single valve molds.¹³ Collaborative effort is displayed also in replicating forms in different materials; for example, ceramic vessel forms were replicated in copper and stone vessels. Moreover, certain motifs that are frequently used on ceramic vessels also appear on objects in precious metals (Schmidt 1937: figs. 111, 112, 122; pl. LII H771, pl. LIV H4112, H4128). Another example is industrial ceramics such as refractory clay crucibles used by metallurgists for smelting copper (Thornton and Rehren 2009). These are part of the tool assemblage of the Tepe Hissar metalsmiths, which continue until early second millennium BC. Undoubtedly, such an interaction among craftspeople would enable them to share ideas for stylistic and technical innovations and to generate knowledge of new materials and tools. For example, the application of highly polished "metallic" surface finish to grey burnished vessels. It is that kind of dynamic interaction among the craftspeople that ultimately led to internal structural changes and the formation of a management team, which promoted a higher level of social complexity. The most concrete context for the emergence of such structural changes and organization at Tepe Hissar is the craft center at the South Hill industrial quarter.

The proliferation of commodities and labor expenditure at Tepe Hissar workshops entailed an administrator/manager team capable of "multi-stage" planning for production, from workshop management to acquisition of raw materials and trade of manufactured goods. Administrative devices in both settlement and burial contexts attest to the presence of such individuals, so-called agents, who were able to carry out those activities. Hence, during the mid-late fourth millennium BC, a shift to a management team is manifested in a far-reaching level of craft production. Increased numbers of sophisticated artifacts are produced in specialized workshop contexts made from imported semi-precious stones. In addition, social differentiation is attested by the higher quality and quantity of prestige articles, as well as a new group of symbolic/ritual objects that denote social identities of individuals. These objects reveal a new ideological order and status differentiation within the community, as manifested in the burials of individuals gifted with identity related objects in copper and precious metals, including wands (Fig. 6.12), macehead (Fig. 6.19), weapons (Fig. 6.20), and other prestige objects (see also Ch. 5, pp. 221–222).¹⁴

In sum, the internal structural changes in craft management were sustained under the supervision of a hierarchically ranked team of administrator/managers. The administrators were likely to have held political positions that enabled them to structure and organize the economic and social welfare of the population; to establish social networks in marketing the commodities on local and regional levels, not unlike the activities of commercial agents of the contemporary urban sites in Early Dynastic Mesopotamia.

These organizational changes are social processes, the driving forces behind Tepe Hissar's participation as a cultural and trading partner in the wider regional and inter-regional networks that began in the mid-fourth millennium and continued until early second millennium BC.

Regional and Long-Distance Connections

The new chronological framework has broader implications for understanding Tepe Hissar's cultural connections with other Bronze Age settlements in the region and beyond. On a regional level, Tepe Hissar is linked to northern and southern plateau sites. Its location on the Great Khorasan trade route, its proximity to mineral rich sources, and the quantity and elaborateness of its excavated artifacts and funerary customs rank the site prominently on the northern Iranian plateau. These favorable positions render the site critical as a cultural bridge between southern Mesopotamia and Syria on the one hand, and Afghanistan and west Central Asia, on the other.

Over this broad geographical zone we witness evidence of shared craft and organizational practices, such as production of semi-precious beads from imported carnelian, lapis lazuli, turquoise, and amber, as well as, the use of accounting/administrative devices, tokens, seals, including cylinder seals, sealings, and tablet blanks. These cultural links imply diffusion of materials and ideas through trade and individuals who were informed of these cultural practices and acted as agents of change in the region and across the greater Middle East.¹⁵ At Tepe Hissar, we have no textual evidence or even a cursory account of the distribution of objects traded/exchanged to and from the site, but there is reasonably firm archaeological and chronological evidence in support of Tepe Hissar as a major player in an inter-regional exchange circuit in the fourth and the third millennia BC.

During the early fourth millennium BC, regional contacts are indicated by the identification of Late Hissar I painted pottery at thirteen small sites within the Damghan River alluvial fan (Trinkhaus 1989). A few centuries later, Tepe Hissar's interaction is evidenced with the northern Gorgan Plain settlements, Tureng Tepe, Shah Tepe, and Yarım Tepe, located north of the Elburz range, and with Tepe Sialk on the central plateau. The first three sites share Caspian red wares as well as the grey burnished wares. Despite similarities, there are differences in forms and decorative elements of grey burnished wares that indicate local adaptations of "foreign" pottery types in each region (Daher 1968; Cleuziou 1986:231; Dyson 1992:270). Similar-

Fig. 6.19 Maceheads (left to right): Period IIIB-C, North Flat, H2748 (Penn Museum, object no. 33-22-202); Period IIIC, Main Mound, burial DF09 x1 "Warrior 2", H771 (Penn Museum, object no. 33-15-574).

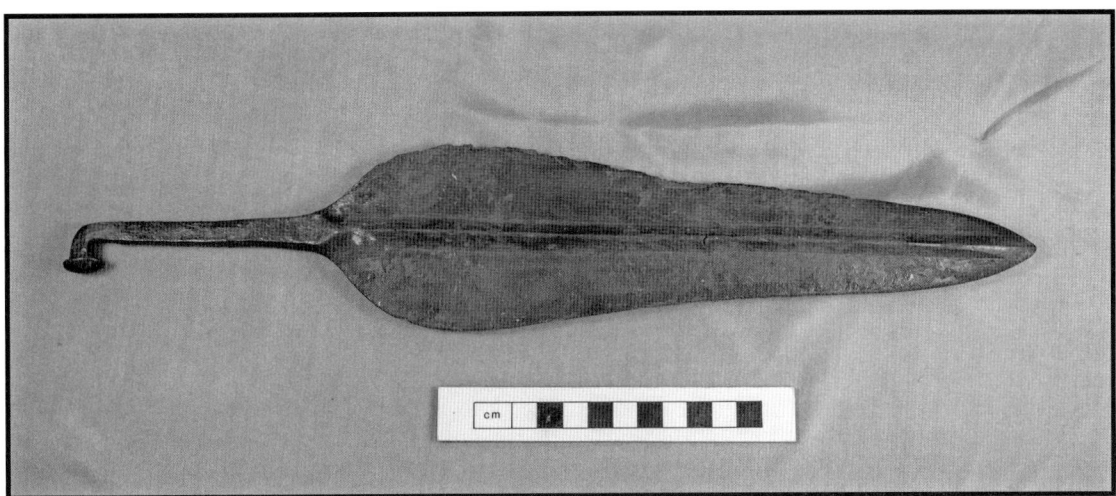

Fig. 6.20 Metal weapon, spearhead, H3582 (Penn Museum, object no. 33-22-108), Period IIIC, Treasure Hill, burial CH64 x1.

ly, Sialk III painted wares are compared with Tepe Hissar buff painted wares, both of which display regional differences. Tepe Hissar's cultural connections with the northern region continue into the late third millennium BC as evidenced by pottery assemblages at Tureng Tepe and Gohar Tepe in the Mazandaran region (for Tureng Tepe, see Daher [1968, UPM inventory # 473]; for Mazandaran, see Mahfroozi [2009:177–205]; for grey pattern burnished bottle pitchers, to compare, see Schmidt [1937: fig. 106 H3820]).

In the first quarter of the fourth millennium BC, Tepe Hissar metalsmiths were already producers of copper and silver artifacts that the Gorgan sites lacked. Artifacts from Tepe Hissar and probably from Tepe Sialk and Arisman, the two other production sites on the central plateau, found markets for their metal goods at Gorgan sites, lending further credence and evidence to the role of central plateau sites as members of an early regional network of producers in the trade/exchange of goods and ideas. Even though these three metal producing centers are some distance from one another, (Arisman is a ca. 60 km southeast of Tepe Sialk and Tepe Hissar is over 300 km northeast of Tepe Sialk/Arisman), they shared the knowledge of copper smelting and silver processing (Nokandeh and Nezafati 2003; Pernicka 2004). In the second half of the fourth millennium BC, the craftspeople at Arisman C and Tepe Hissar had developed common trends in smelting copper in proper furnaces, obtaining silver by cupellation, and using sophisticated kilns for mass production of pottery. Tepe Hissar coppersmiths, however, in comparison to those at Tepe Sialk/Arisman, practiced a different metallurgical technology which resulted in a higher output of metal than at the other central plateau sites (Thornton 2014:686).[16]

During the mid-fourth millennium BC, recording devices, cones, bicones, balls, and clay animal figurines, suggest the earliest contacts with Mesopotamia. At Tepe Sialk III6–7 and Arisman B, cultural contacts with southern Mesopotamia were established several hundred years earlier, as evidenced by Uruk type objects such as bevel rim bowls and administrative devices (Helwing 2013:93–100). Concurrently at Tepe Hissar, the transition to the Bronze Age in the mid-fourth millennium witnesses an expansion of local copper and silver production that is concurrent with the preparation of a massive amount of lapis blanks, carnelian, and turquoise beads. It also corresponds to an increased production of wheelmade glossy grey ware with incised decoration and the earliest occurrence of pattern burnishing. Insofar as we know, most of these craft activities took place in the industrial quarter of the South Hill settlement. The beads were kept for export in the storerooms with label blanks and counters. The administrative technology was so well established that the individual merchant's labels/sealing was imprinted on the product (see above, p. 291).[17]

Tepe Hissar's two-pronged cultural and trade connections included the Mesopotamian Proto-Elamite[18] cultural sphere in the west and southern Turkmenistan in the east. The acquisition of raw materials from a distance of several thousand kilometers required setting up agreements with interim suppliers. Turquoise was obtained from Nishapur ca. 400 km distance, lapis lazuli from Badakshan nearly 2,000 km away, and carnelian from the Hindu Kush, an even greater distance from Tepe Hissar.

Undoubtedly, Tepe Hissar was one of those intermediary trading posts for semi-precious stones along the Great Khorasan Road, thus, linking the southern Mesopotamian lowlands to the Iranian highland plateau sites and further east, to western Central Asia through the Nishapur plain (Hiebert and Dyson 2002:116). The merchandise was transported overland by donkeys. Helwing maintains that lapis blanks were delivered to Mesopotamian workshops/households at Sumer via Tepe Sialk, through networks of Elamite merchants, and that the high-value beads were traded directly to merchants as finished products (2012a:209–211).[19]

During third millennium BC, Tepe Hissar's cultural and trade connection with the Mesopotamian world continued, as evidenced by three cylinder seals, H892, H116, and H3710. The first two are retrieved from burial contexts on the Main Mound, DF19 x19 and DF19 x60 (Schmidt 1937:197–99, fig. 118) and are firmly dated to the last building phase on the Main Mound, B-A/A, the last quarter of the third millennium BC. The third cylinder seal (H3710) is from Treasure Hill, dated to Period IIB, which corresponds to the earlier phases D and D-C according to the new chronology. Thus, the combined evidence of chronological and cultural markers confirms Tepe Hissar's long-term participation in the Proto-Elamite cultural communication and trade network, from the late fourth to the end of the third millennium BC.

By the early third millennium BC, the specialized craft centers of the southern highland sites on the fringes of Dasht-i Lut desert, were also producing and trading commodities in response to the increasing demands of Mesopotamian merchants for highly prized minerals, semi-precious stones, and, possibly, experienced craftspeople. Shahdad's long-distance trade with Mesopotamia is evidenced by exports in copper, locally available chlorite, and spectacular artifacts in silver and semi-precious stones. At Shahdad, metalworking had reached such a level of sophistication that the craftspeople had the knowledge to add arsenic in later stages of smelting in order to strengthen large objects such as weapons (Vidale 2005). Such advanced knowledge and skill, also demonstrated by Arisman metalsmiths, was gained through repeated experimentation and with the use of high quality tools. At Tepe Yahya and Jiroft, stone workshops specialized in intricate carvings on chlorite and steatite vessels and other objects from local supplies of chlorite. The iconic carvings on these chlorite objects depict stylized animals—lion, zebu, birds, snakes—geometric patterns, and architectural structures which have parallels in Mesopotamia (Kohl 1975:19–31).[20]

During the mid-third millennium BC, Shahr-i Sokhta, the easternmost site in the southern highland, transformed into one of the largest urban settlements, covering over 100 hectares. The site is marked by an administrative building (Burnt Building) and a cemetery that is estimated to hold about 200,000 people (Sajjadi 2003:21–47). In the multiple industrial workshops of Shahr-i Sokhta, large vessels and countless beads in alabaster, lapis lazuli, and carnelian were manufactured by specialist craftspeople (Tosi 1974; Kohl 1977:111–127; Vidale 2005). At both Shahr-i Sokhta and Tepe Yahya, Mesopotamian seals and Proto-Elamite tablets attest to their long-distance connections with the Mesopotamian cultural sphere until the last quarter of the third millennium BC.

As the craft centers on the Iranian highlands continued to respond to the increasing demands of the Mesopotamian world, new markets opened up in Central Asia for cultural/commercial exchanges. Tepe Hissar and the other craft centers on the Iranian highland acted as intermediary markets for Central Asian products. At Tepe Hissar, the interconnection with the eastern cultural sphere is manifested by two copper stamp seals deposited in the storage room of the Burned Building, one of which features a distinctive compartmented style, "terraced square pattern" (H2697) and another a "scorpion shape" (H2698), possibly depicting a Central Asian motif of animal figural design. Cultural affiliations are further documented at the site of Altyn Tepe, Turkmenistan, dated to Namazga Tepe IV in terms of similarities in metal technology, artifacts, and building construction techniques and features such as an external buttressed wall system and stepped niches inside the walls of buildings (Dyson and Remsen 1989:80, fig. 5; Masson 1988 [English translation from the original in Russian]).

In the mid-third millennium BC, an assemblage of large and small alabaster objects are introduced at Tepe Hissar comprising elegant replicas of metal and ceramic vessels, animal figurines and abstract female figurines, and "columns" and "discs" (see Ch. 5, Fig. 5.39). The latter are unique objects at Tepe Hissar.[21] Similar "columns" and disc-shaped "weights" are also documented at Altyn Tepe and dated to Namazga IV, V periods (Masson 1988 pl. XXXV 1–4, 6, 7). It is questionable whether the large alabaster vessels and other alabaster artifacts were crafted at Tepe Hissar,[22] as we have no evidence of an alabaster workshop or heaps of chips of waste material. However, in view of the fact that Tepe Hissar had a sophisticated ground stone industry for the production of stone vessels and beads (Horne 1989:121–123), the alabaster objects were probably locally produced and the lack of workshop evidence might be tied to recovery procedure.

Tepe Hissar's connections with the Mesopotamian cultural sphere continued until the end of the third millennium BC. The Tepe Hissar craftspeople and traders procured copper from central plateau sources and semi-precious stones from Badakshan and other sources for the production of jewelry to combine them with gold and silver beads. The alabaster vessels were possibly crafted from unfinished traded objects for local consumption as well as exports to foreign elite households in the Mesopotamian world. In this period of increased production and demand for metals and jewelry with semi-precious stones, it is not unreasonable to suggest that the east-west trade network for such prestige goods could extend as far as north Central Anatolia by overland routes. The rich burial assemblages in precious stones and metals at Alaca Höyük, Eskiyapar, and İkiztepe Bronze Age settlements support this proposition (Rose 2014:17; Bilgi 1984, 1990, 1999, 2005; Gürsan-Salzmann 1992; Özgüç and Temizer 1993; Koşay 1951).

To sum up, during the mid-fourth through the third millennium BC, the breadth of the long-distance trade connections of the highland Iranian sites with the Mesopotamian world is attested to by the volume and elaborate craftsmanship of artifacts produced at the northern and southern plateau sites, along with numerous cylinder seals, sealings, labels, and label blanks. In addition to long-distance connections, each site acted in its capacity as a regional redistribution center beginning in the mid-fourth millennium BC, thereby establishing a solid inter-regional network of cultural and economic relations between the northern and southern plateau settlements that flourished until the late third millennium BC. The decline and eventual abandonment of these settlements in the early second millennium BC has been attributed to different external and internal factors. One theory is the east-west overland trade route was superseded by the maritime routes to reach southern Mesopotamia via the Arabian Peninsula. Another is a disruption in the "global" social and economic order, which effectively lowered demand for prestige goods from the settlements. The collapse of the highland Iranian sites, of course, may have been brought about by multiple factors.[23] Clearly, future studies should predicate the validity of these propositions in the context of each settlement.

Future Research

The new chronology and the analysis of the assemblages from the settlement and burial contexts in this monograph provide critical data for further research. Therefore, I suggest two topics that can be pursued by specialists interested in either doing further fieldwork at the site and in the region of Tepe Hissar or undertaking analyses on the excavated human remains at the Penn Museum.

The first concerns the clarification of the transition from the Late Bronze and Iron Age at Tepe Hissar. Evidence for the continuity of an Iron Age settlement at Tepe Hissar comes from recent explorations at the site by Roustaei (2010). He and his team conducted a number of soundings and environmental surveys in the immediate vicinity of the Tepe Hissar settlement complex, which led him to argue for the existence of an Iron Age occupation, cemetery, and copper workshop near the site. The calibrated radiocarbon dates from charcoal are 980–839 BC, 915–812 BC. This promising evidence could be corroborated by examining the depositional levels overlying the Period IIIC burials and the building remains at three areas of the settlement, the North Flat, the Main Mound, and the Treasure Hill.

The second research topic is an integrated bioarchaeological study of the Tepe Hissar human skeletal remains from the Penn Museum. The principle goal would be to investigate markers of health/disease, longevity, and generalized stress that could determine levels of socioeconomic change (social differentiation, rank, and status). This could be done by a systematic comparative study of firmly dated burials designated as "Low Outliers" and "High Outliers" (see Ch. 5, pp. 226–248). This new research combined with earlier studies of skeletal remains, the on-going CT scan analyses (see Ch. 5, pp. 222–226) and the previously collected environmental, floral, and faunal data would provide a more balanced understanding of the cultural and socioeconomic aspects of the Tepe Hissar populations throughout the Bronze Age.

NOTES:

6.1 D.T. Potts, in his comprehensive book, *Nomadism in Iran* (2014), presents clear evidence to support his conclusion that prehistoric nomadism was non-existent in Iran until the Achaemenid period in the mid-fifth century BC. His work is largely based on Greek and Latin sources (Potts 2014:88–119). He gives a thorough review of the arguments made by the proponents of the nomadic pastoralist sites at: the Neolithic site Tepe Tula'i (Hole 1974); the Neolithic and Bronze Age sites in southwestern, south central Iran, Choga Bonut (Alizadeh 2003, 2008); sites in the Bakhtiyari Mountains (Zagarell 1989) in southwestern and south central Iran; sites from the Central Zagros Mountains (Abdi 2002, 2003), as well as the Chalcolithic and Bronze Age settlements at Tal-e Malyan in Fars (Sumner 1986, 1988; as cited in Potts 2014:27–29) and Khuzistan. Potts' argument rests on (a) lack of critical data and/or examination of the cultural evidence left at sites by the "nomads", (b) the assessment of faunal analysis at Neolithic site (Tula'i campsite) that points to a non-nomadic population as the composition of herds consisted of fallow animals instead of lactating females from whose milk cheese, yogurt, etc. would be produced, as in the case of modern pastoral nomad herds (Wheeler Pires-Ferreira 1975–77),

(c) the appropriateness of 19th and 20th century ethnographic analogies based on Lur or Bakhtiyari pastoral nomadic tribal societies, (d) that there is insufficient faunal evidence even from contemporary sites in the region (see Mashkour [2003] for the Bakhtiyari tribe in the Zagros region), and (e) the sparseness of domesticated equid bones that would be expected in association with a nomadic population, based on genetic and morphological analysis (Mashkour 2009).

6.2 My usage of the term "agent" is linked to practice theory ("praxis") that is still in use as an explanatory framework in social archaeology. The concept is coined by works of Bourdieu (1977, 1990), revised by Giddens (1984) and Finlayson (2010). According to Finlayson, "agency allows us to avoid having to rely on abstract processes as the driving forces of change. Climate may lead to change, but it is humans who select responses, using their existing world to make the new one" (2010:141–145). Accordingly, I use the term "agent" or "agency", specifically in regard to the fourth to early second millennium BC Tepe Hissar populations, as individuals/groups engaged in the practice of interpersonal relations and networking within a social system in order to produce material culture—artifacts, tools, building materials, structures for specific use such as storage areas, and so forth. Indeed, it is a community of people as social groups who play essential roles to produce an artifact; to organize and perform burial rites for the dead; to act as administrators in commerce within local or long-distance exchange/trade and other activities.

6.3 For detailed descriptions of individual vessel types see Chapter 3.

6.4 In 1976, Kathryn M. Trinkhaus conducted a survey of the valley and the alluvial fan of the Damghan River. Out of 166 sites, Tepe Hissar is the largest mounded site. She documented 13 related pottery-bearing sites that are within walking distance of Tepe Hissar. These are small satellite village sites, some located near a major streambed—as Tepe Hissar had been—while others were along an alluvial fan. Only three were small mounds (Trinkhaus 1989:135–141, fig. 1). She found no evidence of kiln sites, pottery, or wasters associated with ceramic production.

6.5 This shell pendant (Schmidt 1937: pl. XIX H3444a) is dated to IA by Schmidt, as the earliest ornament of its kind found in a Tepe Hissar burial, CG95 x20. It is part of a necklace that "includes gypsum tubes and disks, discs of bitumen, red jasper (?) and alabaster, and a light brown shell pendant" (ibid., p.61).

6.6 It has been suggested that at Tepe Hissar, until the middle of the fourth millennium BC, both metal and ceramic technologies have affinities with the western central plateau sites. Accordingly, the copper pins and copper-base daggers are assigned to ca. 4000 BC on the basis of similarities to those at Sialk III4-5 (Thornton 2009a:48; Ghirshman 1938: pl. LXXXIV). The locations of copper and silver ore mines for the Tepe Hissar metallurgists is a continuing question which is still open to speculation. Based on evidence from archaeological and geological investigations, scholars strongly agree that the lead mines of Nakhlak on the central plateau provided silver to the metalsmiths of Sialk III and Arisman IB, IC (Momenzadeh and Nezafati 2000; Nokandeh and Nezafati 2003; Pernicka 2004; Azarnoush and Helwing 2005; Helwing 2011). For Tepe Hissar, the Anaru mine, which is about 100 km south of Damghan, is a potential candidate for the source of argentiferous lead (Roustaei 2004; Momenzadeh 2004; Stöllner et al. 2004). Other more distant arsenical copper ore sources with the same combination of elements seen in Tepe Hissar artifacts are Talmessi and Meskani in the Anarak mining district in Qom-Kashan area, at a distance of 300 km, south of Tepe Hissar. In light of the fact that lapis lazuli was brought in from Badakshan, a distance of almost 2,000 km from Tepe Hissar, we should not regard distance as a constraining factor to the Tepe Hissar metallurgists. Consequently, the Anarak mining district could be a potential candidate, although more extensive investigation and documentation of ancient mining areas in the northeastern region are in order.

6.7 An Early Period II copper stamp seal was found in a female burial whose gifts also included several clay stamp seals (Schmidt 1937: pl. XXVIII H2183).

6.8 See, "A Dynamic Systems Framework for Studying Technological Change" by Roux (2003).

6.9 In addition to finding extensive heaps of stone-working debris on the surface of the site and at the South Hill, the 1976 project members located such debris near the Main Mound, the North Flat, and the Twins. "The surface survey regarded as true clusters only in which lapis lazuli chips occurred in hundreds in 10 square meter, along with flint microliths, larger tools and debitage" (Tosi 1989:15).

6.10 Howard (1976) notes, "total area of each of the buildings is 43/44, 53 and 38 square meters, respectively….the sizes of the dwelling space are comparable with ethnographic information from a contemporary village in north central Iran where preliminary estimates suggest an average of 41 square meters of roofed dwelling space per household" (the ethnographic information is based on her communication with Lee Horne).

6.11 At the Main Mound, the existence of substantial buildings that may have belonged to phases C or early B are recorded in Howard's notes. They consist of walls 40 and 41, in square CG90, visible in baulks, with uniform size bricks that point to the presence of substantial buildings. Howard describes wall 40, in Main Mound square CG90, as "three courses of bricks measuring 60x25x10 cm….As with other walls of this building it was no longer possible to say what this wall was associated with nor exactly in which direction it ran." Of Wall 41, she writes, "a single course of bricks remained (52x25x10 cm.) into which a child burial had been cut….the uppermost bricks contemporary with Wall 41 measured 52x28x12 cm. and were fairly uniform in size." Also at the Main Mound, there is a series of three square ovens/hearths excavated in square DG20 that belong to phase "C".

6.12 In their article "Craft Specialization and Cultural Complexity," Clark and Parry (1990:321) maintain that "patronized specialization is consistently associated with less complex societies than is full time specialization.…patronized craft specialization correlates with agrarian rank, and chiefdom societies; and full-time craft specialization correlates best with complex, highly stratified states, urban centers and intense agriculture. These patterns confirm our expectations that conspicuous production should be associated with rank and chiefdom societies, and full-time production of implements, with more complex societies."

6.13 According to analytical studies, technological conservatism characterizes metal artifacts and ceramics. Changes in Tepe Hissar craft tradition are largely built on traditional techniques.

6.14 The archaeological evidence comes from the Main Mound and North Flat settlements, especially from the burial groups 3, 4, and 5, the Burned Building and its contents, and the industrial workshop activities at South Hill.

6.15 Trade/exchange dynamics have long been a major topic of research in the archaeology of the Near East and Southwest Asia and much has been discussed and written about it (e.g., Beale 1973; Bulgarelli 1974; Kohl 1978; Alden 1982; Pigott, Howard, and Epstein 1982; Tosi 1984, 1989; Potts 1993; Algaze 1993; Ratnagar 2001; Matthews 2003; Lamberg-Karlovsky 2009; Thornton 2009b, 2012; Helwing 2012b).

6.16 The Central Iranian plateau has been suggested, "based on the present level of knowledge, as the birthplace of the silver extraction by cupellation [from lead] and the first supplier of the ore concerned" (Nezafati and Pernicka 2012:37–44).

6.17 On the South Hill, from the storeroom structure in square DF88 and contiguous areas DF89 and DG80, two stamp seals (H76-35, H76-39) and "one inscribed tablet or label" in clay (H76-122) were recovered. They are associated with eight clay "counters" (H76-91, H76-63, H76-94–96, H76-125), two jar sealings/bullae (H76-92, H76-98), and figurines, dating to the mid-fourth millennium BC. The area where they were found "was littered with copper smelting slag" (Tosi and Bulgarelli 1989:38–43, figs. 5, 6, i and m, H76-122; fig. 16). The association of the stamp seals, counters, and anthropomorphic figurines, within a copper smelting slag area, strongly implies storage and transaction of goods under the control of an administrative structure.

6.18 The new ceramic chronology on analysis of the material evidence from the settlement and the burials confirms Voigt and Dyson's (1992) chronological correlations. According to the new chronology: Late Hissar II to Early Hissar III ca. 3040–2900 BC, phase D-C, corresponds to Proto-Elamite I and Sialk IV: 2; L. Hiss. II = 3350–3140 BC, phase D-C corr. to Proto-Elamite Transition and Sialk IV: 1; "Although there is no present evidence of Proto-Elamite script at [Tepe] Hissar, it is evident from both relative and absolute chronology that the site was occupied and prosperous as a production and trading center in both the Proto-Elamite Transitional (Terminal Late Uruk) and Proto-Elamite I horizons. There is no evidence of an interruption between these 2 horizons at [Tepe] Hissar (nor between them and Hissar III for that matter). At Sialk the available record breaks off after Proto-Elamite I (Sialk IV: 2) But that does not mean necessarily that the occupation of Sialk ended" (Voigt 1987).

6.19 See Majidzadeh (1982:59–69) for contra argument of Tepe Hissar and Sialk as intermediary trading posts to Mesopotamian markets.

6.20 Jiroft's connections with the Indus civilization is also demonstrated by characteristic weights, seals, and carnelian beads.

6.21 The sources of alabaster in northern Iran are not known, according to Michele Casanova (1992), there are a large number of possible sources, which adds to the complexity of the guesswork. Some of the alabaster might have been obtained from local supplies of calcium-based stones in northern Iran or further east in the mountainous zones of Central Asia, including the Kopet Dag. Nevertheless, the distribution of these objects constitutes important evidence for a cultural/trade link with the eastern Iranian and Central Asian sources of alabaster and producers of its artifacts in the third millennium BC.

6.22 It is possible that the larger alabaster artifacts (vessels, discs, and columns) are imported prestige objects manufactured in Central Asian workshops and transmitted to the local elites at Tepe Hissar as tribute or political gifts. On the other hand, the workshops at Shahr-i Sokhta and Shahdad—sites on the southern rim of the desert—could also be considered as Tepe Hissar's trading partners in such alabaster artifacts (Carter 1993). Alternatively, the unfinished traded alabaster objects could be finished and given shape by the Tepe Hissar stone craftspeople who had the tools and skills to manufacture similar objects in "common stone" (for discs and columns in alabaster and common stone see Schmidt (1937:216–222, pls. LIX–LXIV).

6.23 Mousavi (2008) proposes an intriguing alternative model for the transition from the Late Bronze Age (Hissar IIIC, (phases B-A/A) to Iron Age in northeast Iran, involving a combination of factors: "disequilibrium in the network of trade", and "over-exploitation" of resources due to an increase in Late Bronze Age sites in the region. Finally, the Late Bronze Age cultures, specifically grey ware cultures, "transformed into what is known as the early Iron Age in adjacent areas" (ibid., p. 117). Using Tepe Hissar as a case study, the transition to the Iron Age in the region can be tested and documented.

6.24. The second research topic ties in closely with a recent dissertation by Dr. Zahra Afshar (2014), who has done extensive bioarchaeological research on Tepe Hissar burials to illuminate dietary patterns, biological affinity, and stress markers through the Bronze Age sequence of the settlement. Her methodology includes metric and non-metric analyses in combination with carbon and nitrogen stable isotope analysis study diet. Her work provides an important baseline for future bioarchaeological research on the collection.

Appendix 1

Pottery Charts

This appendix presents pottery charts to accompany the stratigraphic sections that appear in Chapter 4: Burial Stratigraphy. This includes pottery charts for the Main Mound and North Flat areas of Tepe Hissar. The creation of the pottery charts was done by the author, but the images and vessel drawings are taken from Schmidt (1933, 1937).

Main Mound Pottery Charts:

- Section 4.1a   DF09
- Section 4.3a   DG00
- Section 4.4a   DG01
- Section 4.6a   CG90
- Section 4.7a   DF08
- Section 4.8a   DG10
- Section 4.9a   DG11
- Section 4.11a   DG20
- Section 4.12a   CF29
- Section 4.13a   DF18
- Section 4.14a   DF19
- Section 4.15a   CF88
- Section 4.16a   CF89
- Section 4.18a   CF99

North Flat Pottery Charts:

- Section 4.20a   CF37
- Section 4.20b   CF38
- Section 4.21a   CF47
- Section 4.21b   CF48
- Section 4.22a   CF57

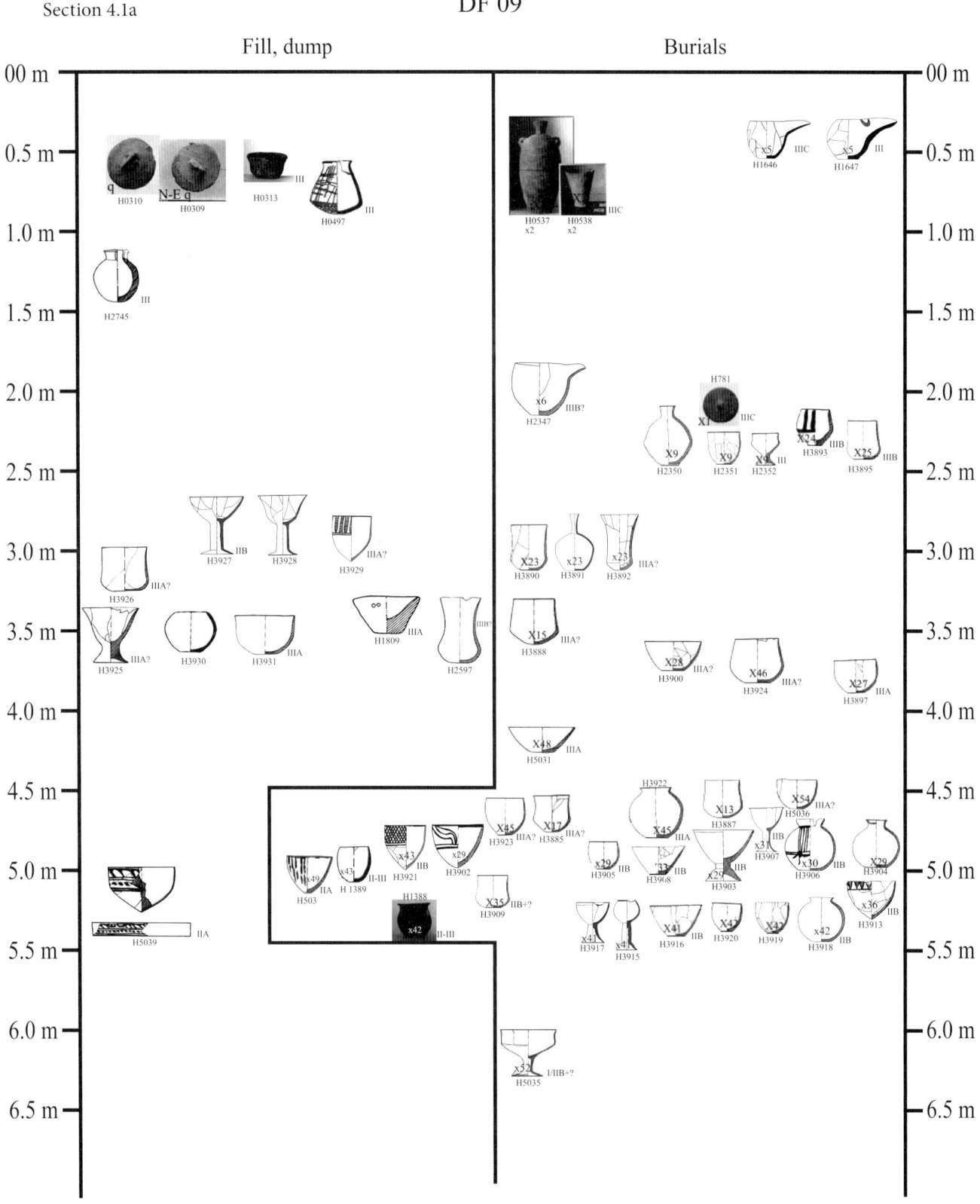

APPENDIX 1: POTTERY CHARTS 301

DG 00

Section 4.3a

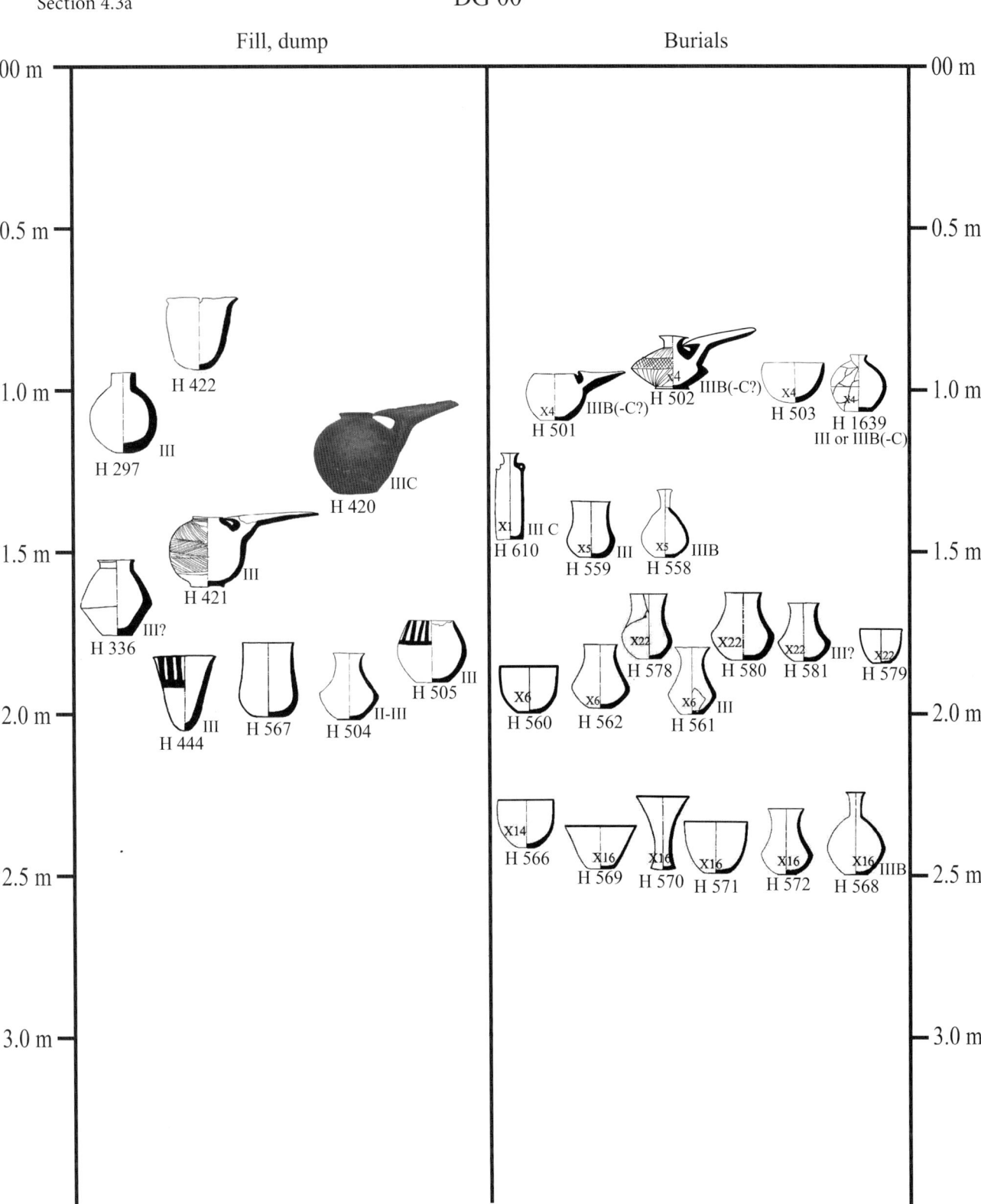

Note: Base of vessels correspond approx. to Schmidt's meter levels

not to scale

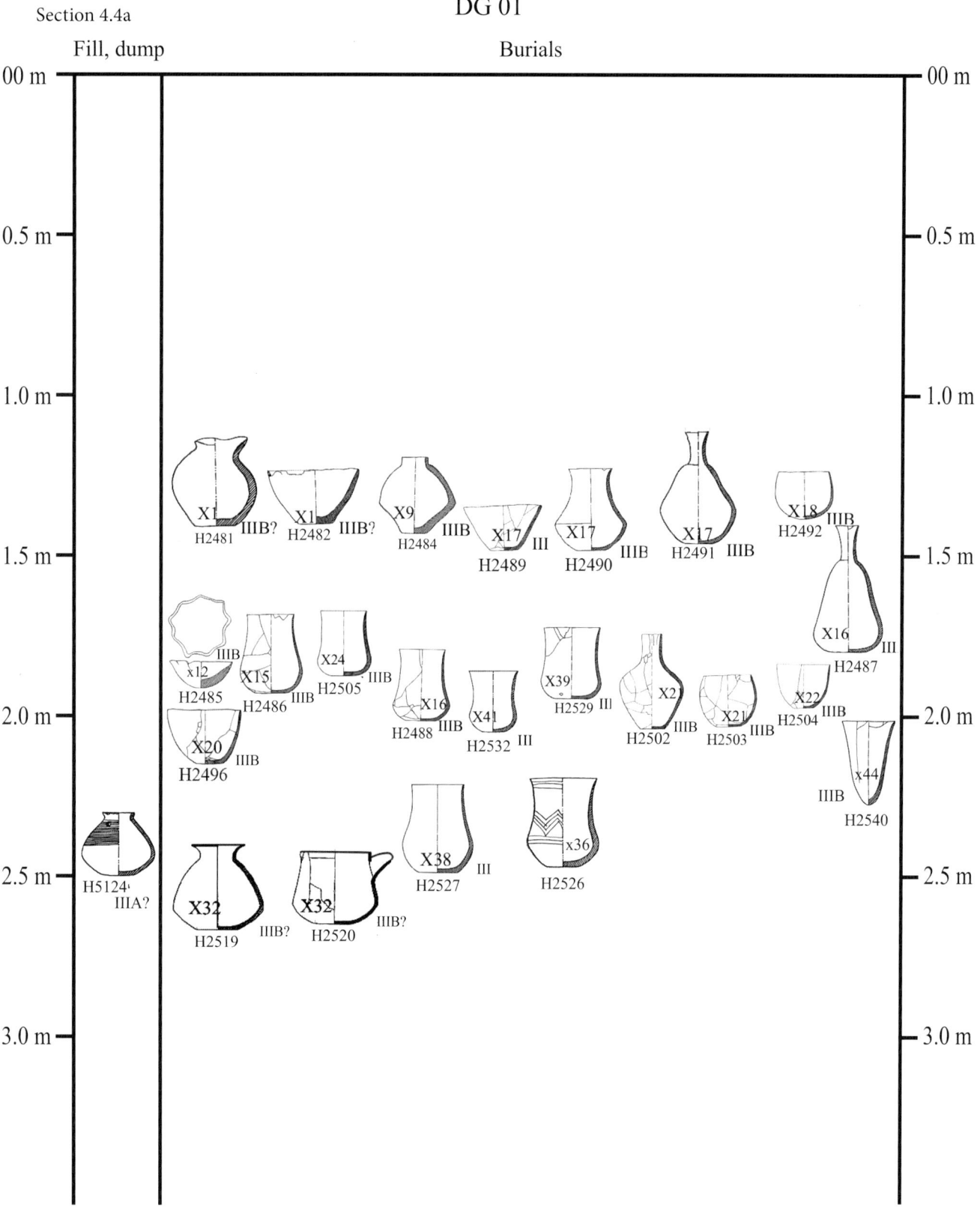

Note: Base of vessels correspond approx. to Schmidt's meter levels

not to scale

APPENDIX 1: POTTERY CHARTS 303

CG 90

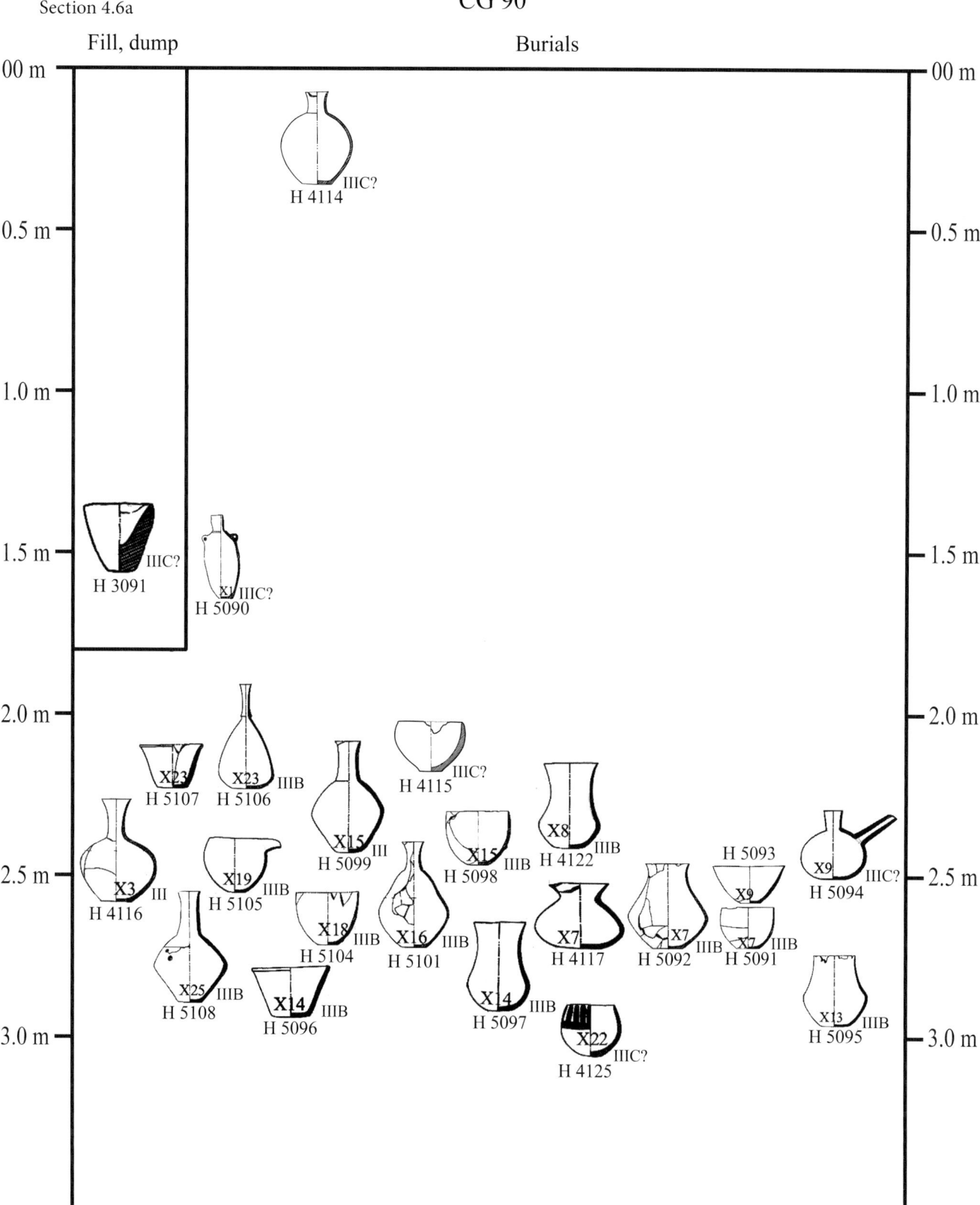

Note: Base of vessels correspond approx. to Schmidt's meter levels

not to scale

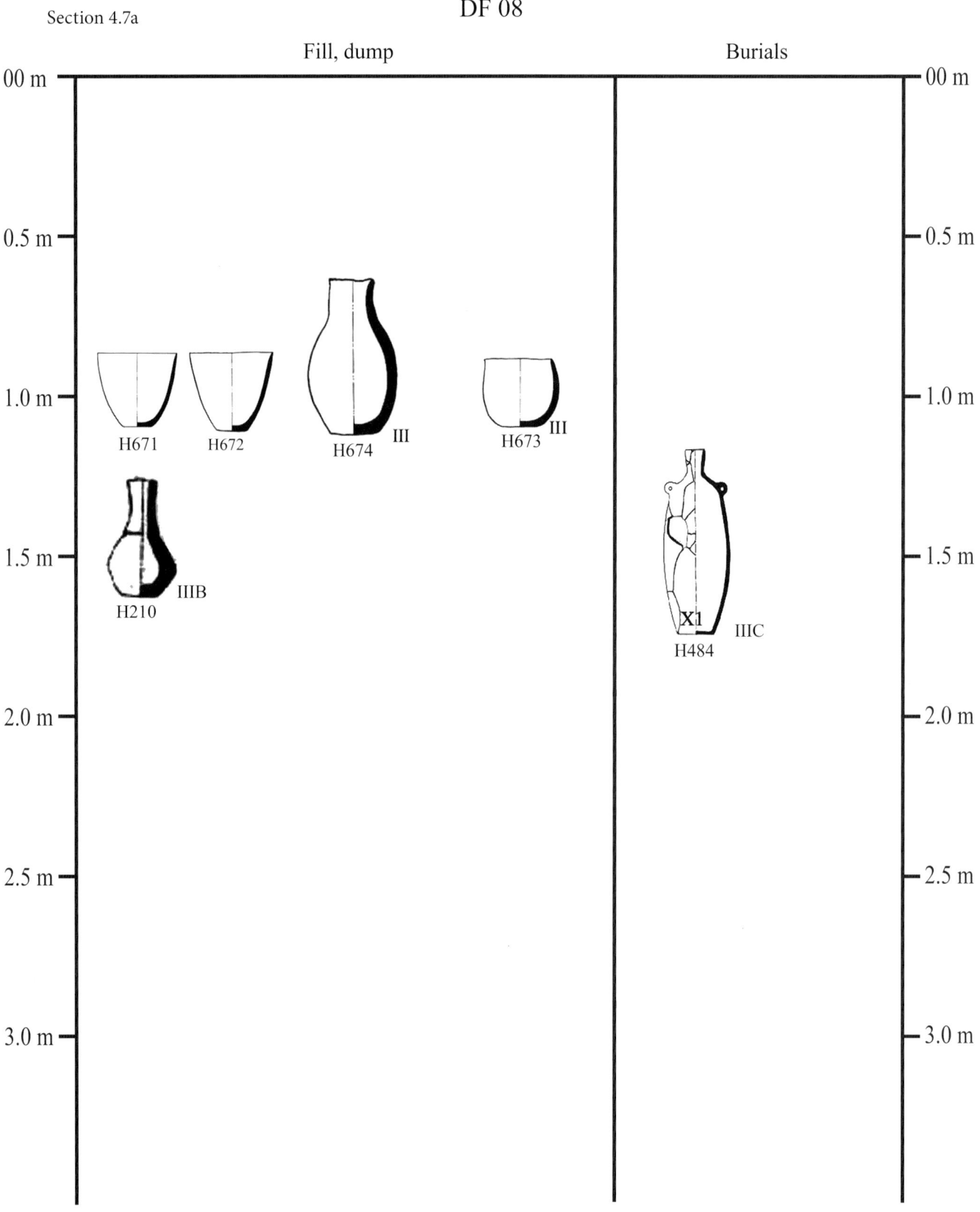

APPENDIX 1: POTTERY CHARTS

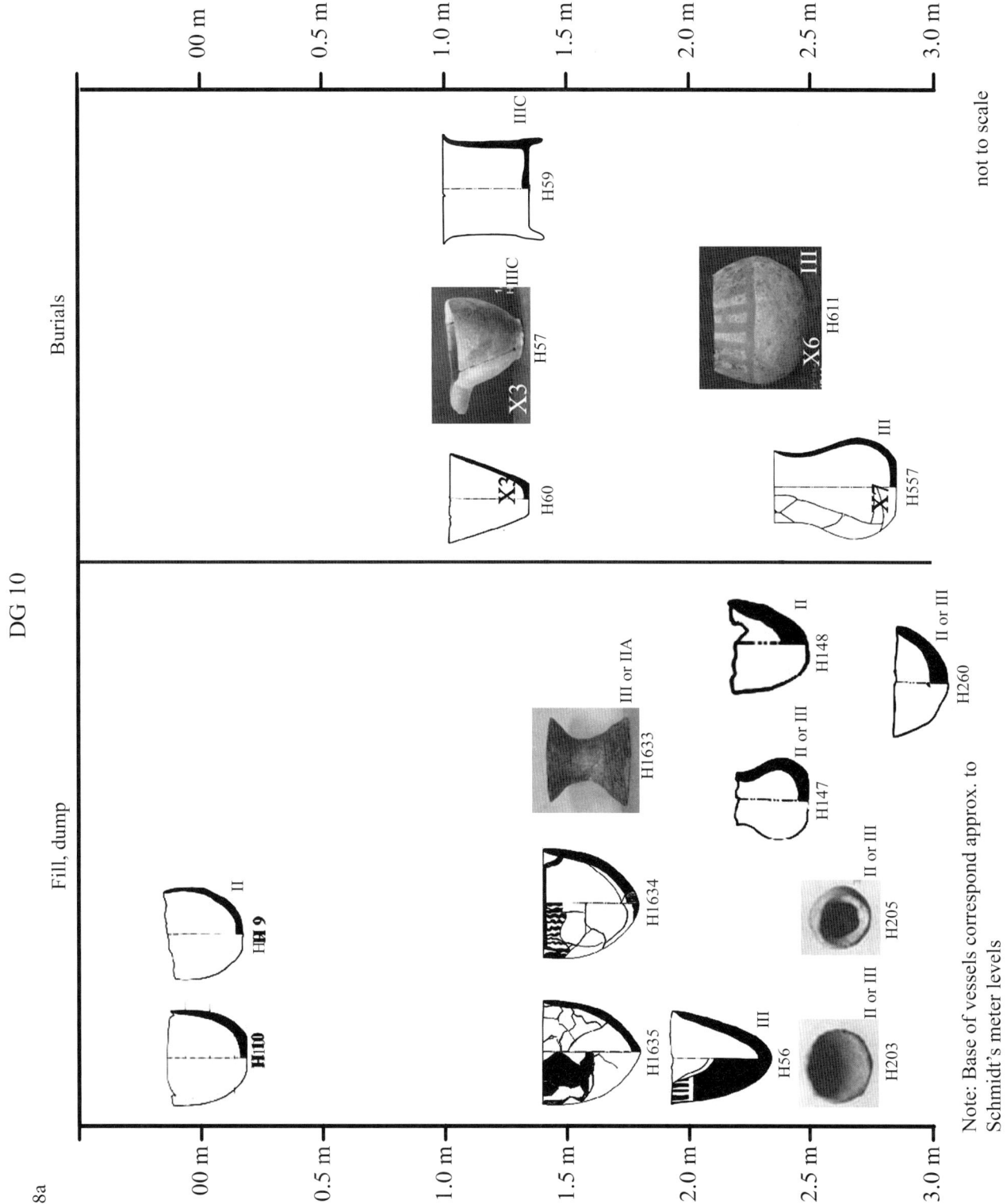

Section 4.9a

DG 11

Fill, dump | Burials

Note: Base of vessels correspond approx. to Schmidt's meter levels

not to scale

APPENDIX 1: POTTERY CHARTS 307

Section 4.11a

DG 20
Burials

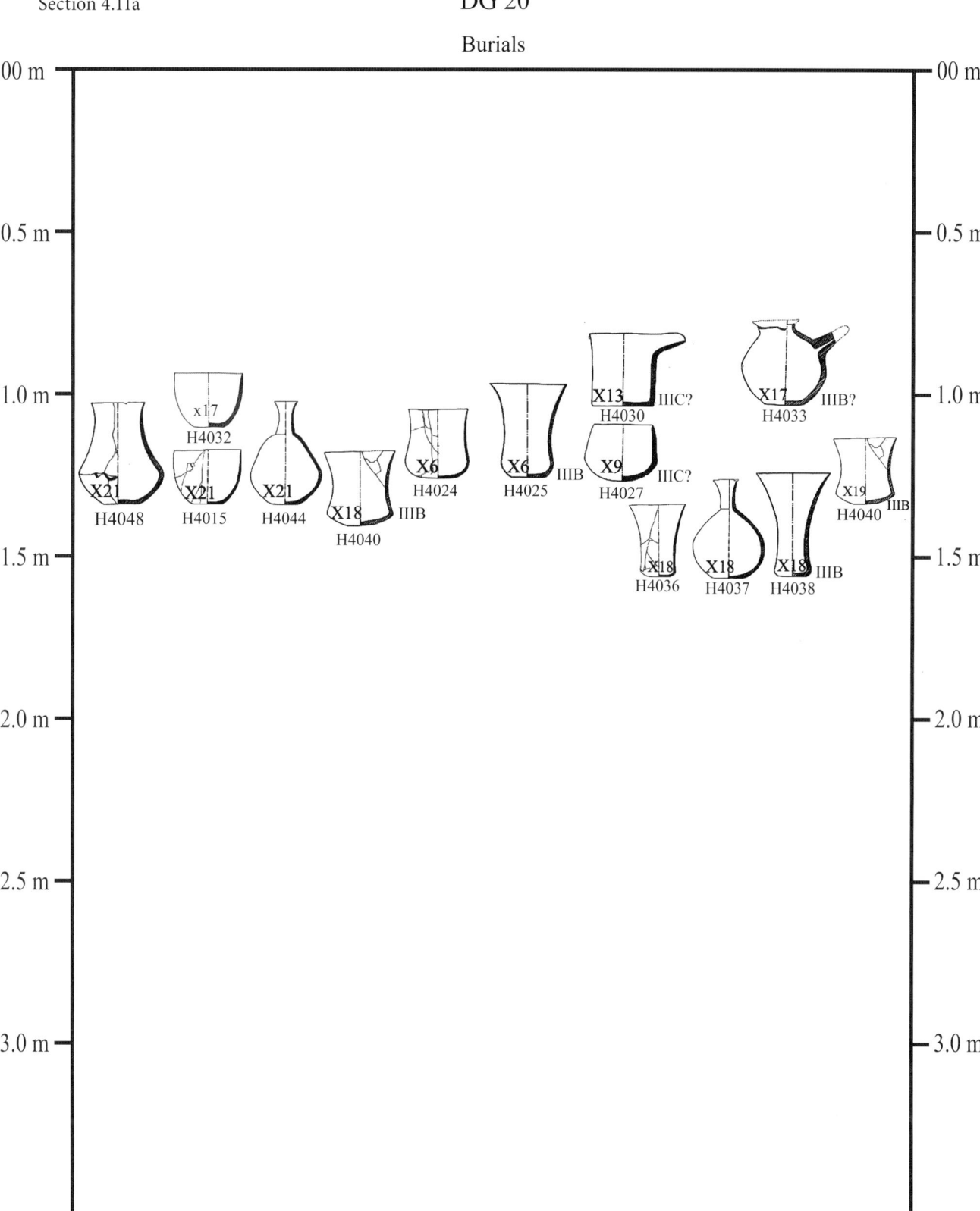

Note: Base of vessels correspond approx. to Schmidt's meter levels

not to scale

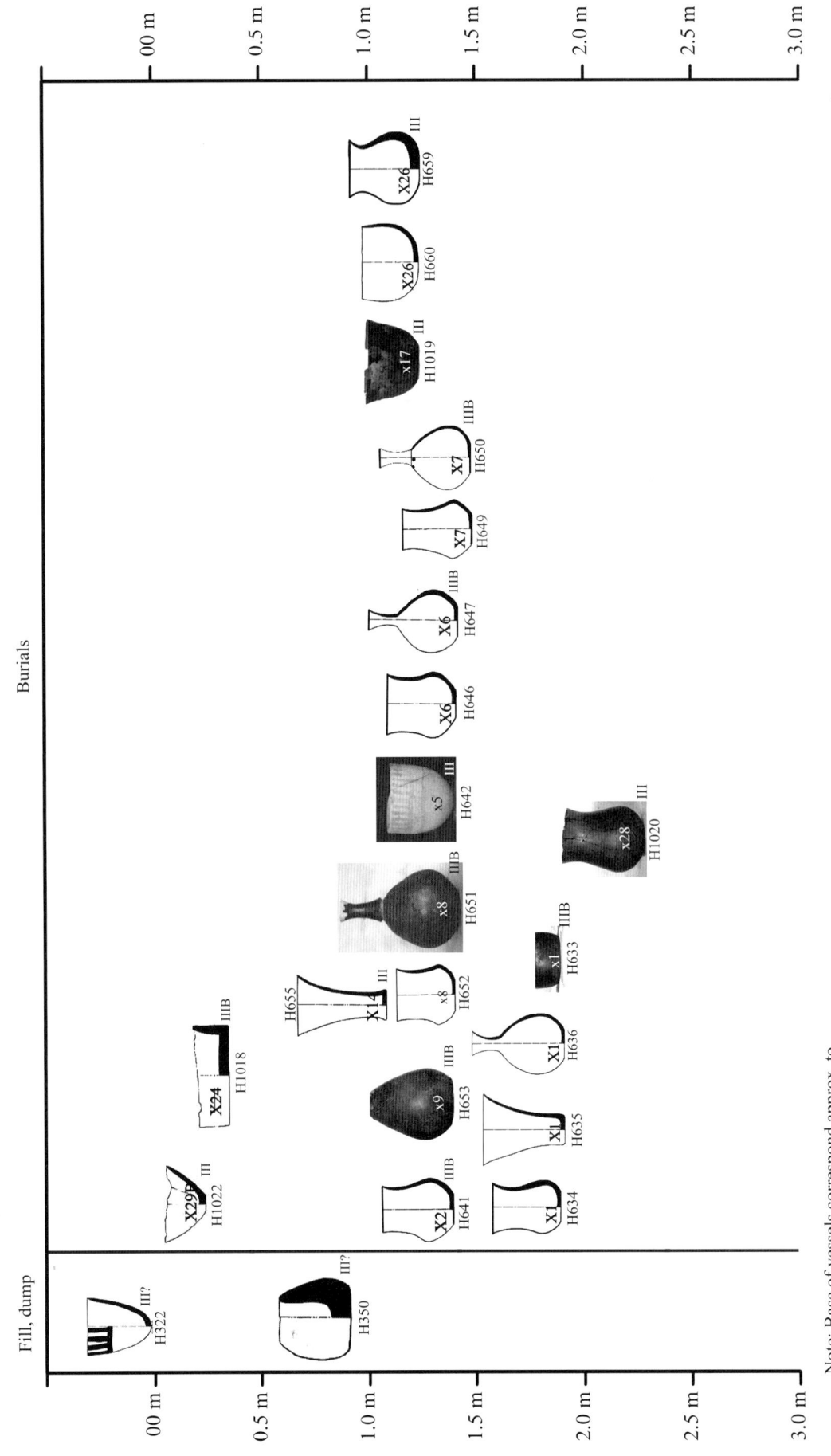

Section 4.12a

DF 29 Burials

Note: Base of vessels correspond approx. to Schmidt's meter levels

not to scale

Section 4.13a

DF 18 Burials

Fill, dump

Note: Base of vessels correspond approx. to Schmidt's meter levels

not to scale

Section 4.14a

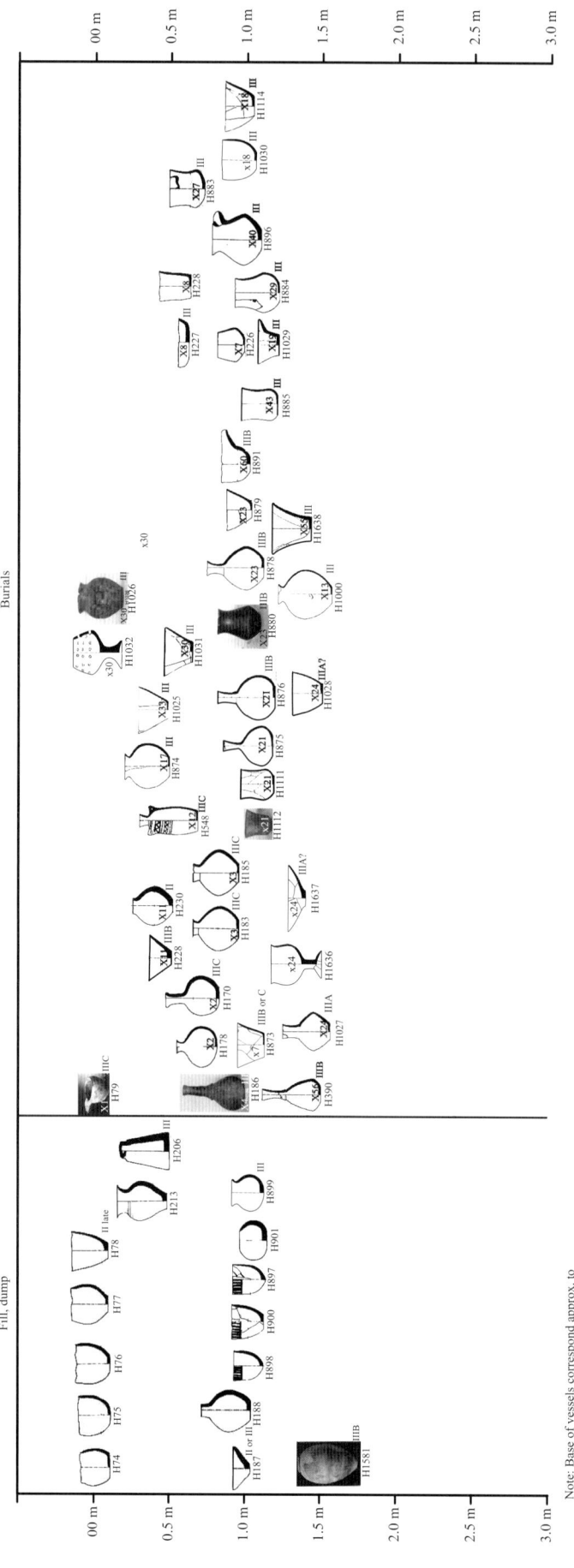

APPENDIX 1: POTTERY CHARTS 311

Section 4.15a CF 88
Burials

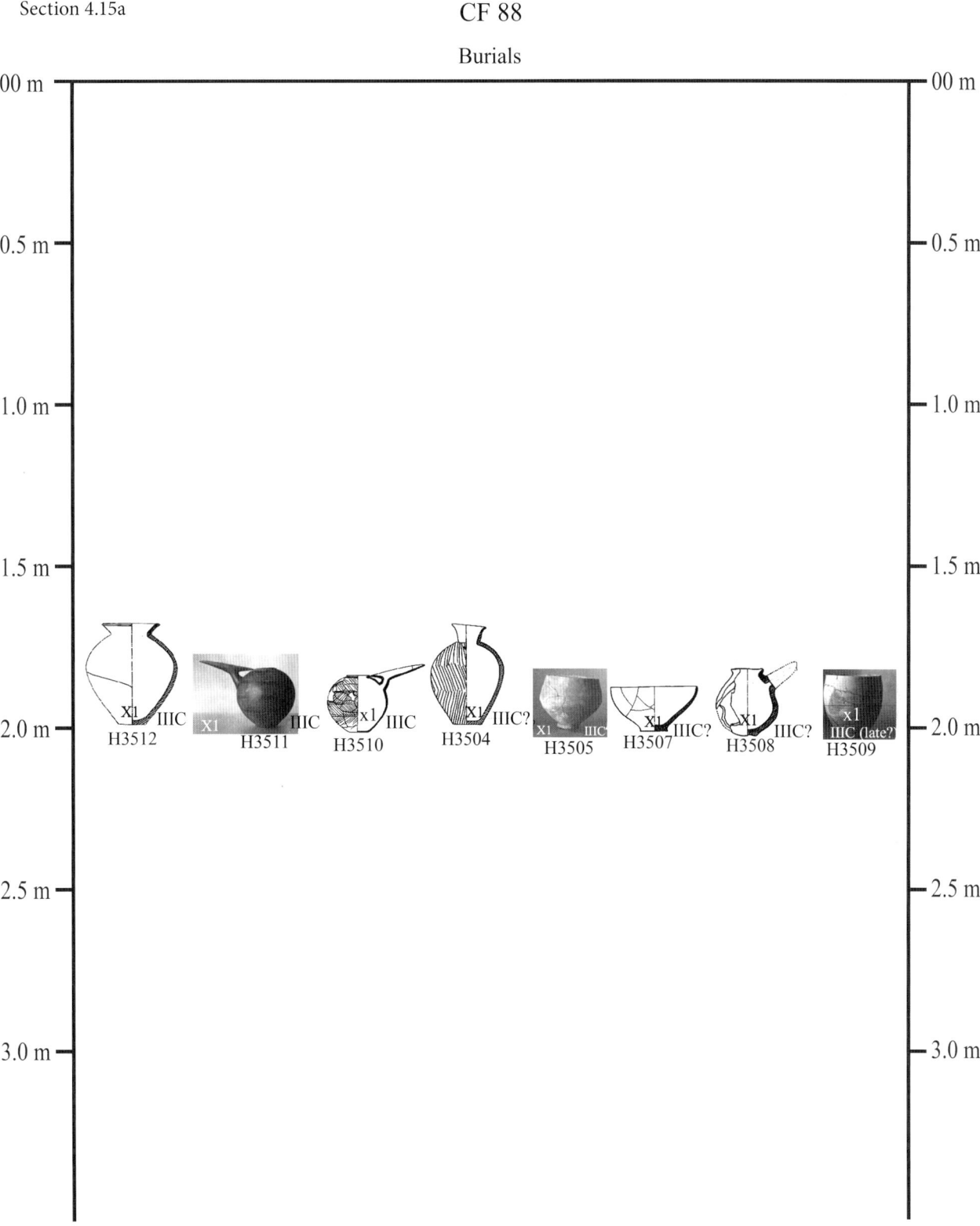

Note: Base of vessels correspond approx. to
Schmidt's meter levels

not to scale

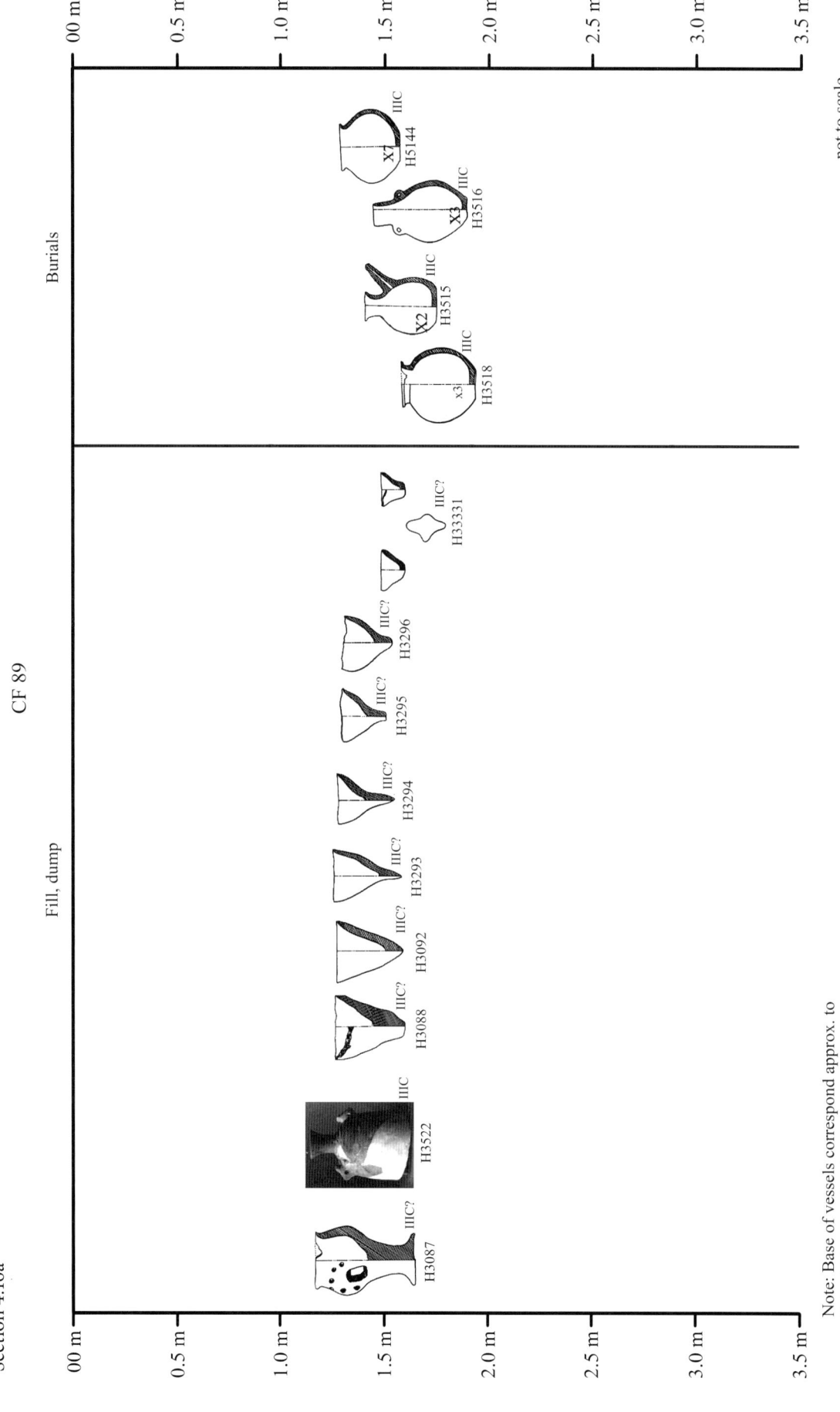

Section 4.18a CF 99

Section 4.20a

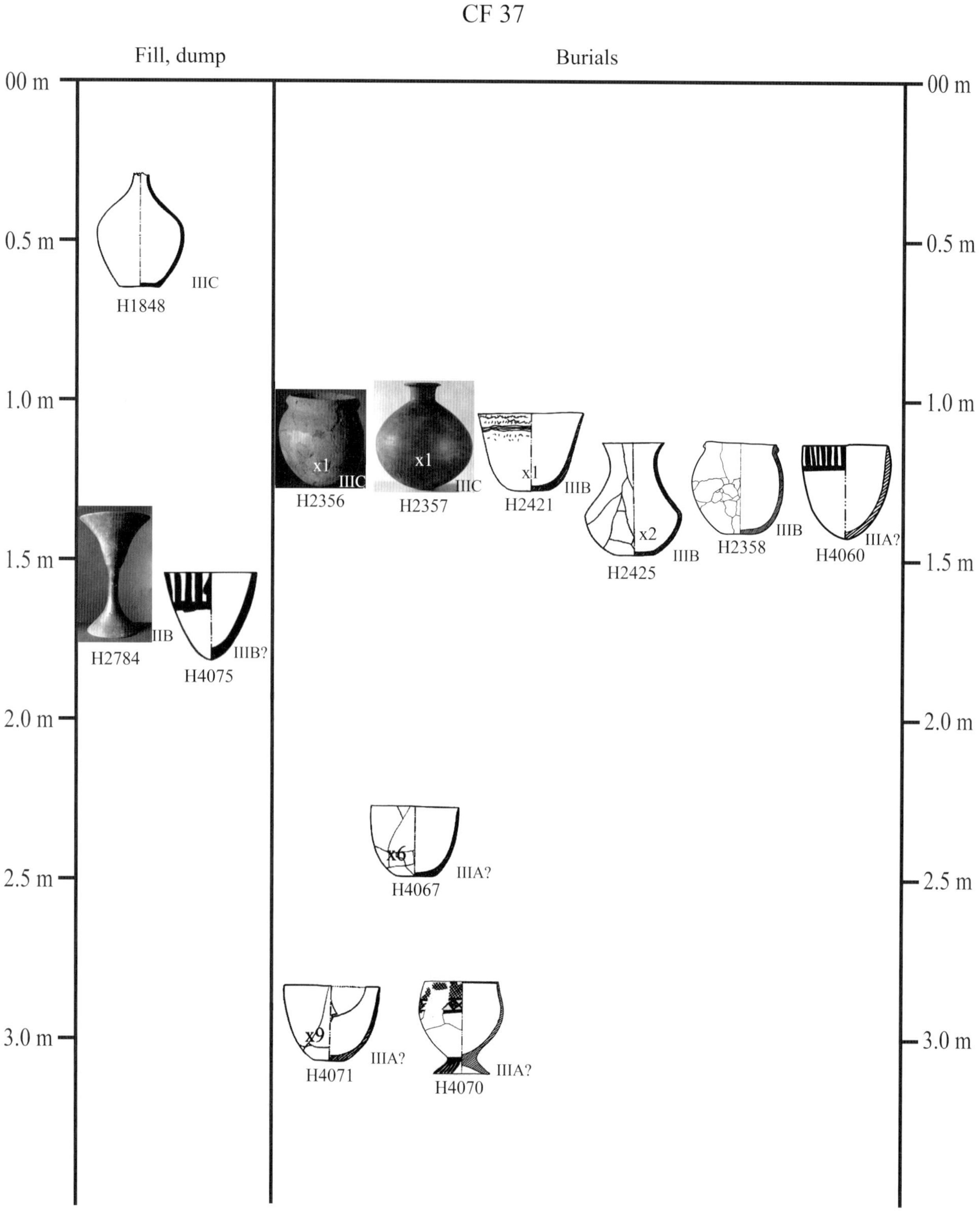

CF 37

Fill, dump | Burials

- H1848 — IIIC (0.5 m)
- H2784 — IIB (1.5 m)
- H4075 — IIIB? (1.5 m)
- H2356 — IIIC, x1 (1.0 m)
- H2357 — IIIC, x1 (1.0 m)
- H2421 — IIIB, x1
- H2425 — IIIB, x2
- H2358 — IIIB
- H4060 — IIIA?
- H4067 — IIIA?, x6 (2.5 m)
- H4071 — IIIA?, x9 (3.0 m)
- H4070 — IIIA? (3.0 m)

Note: Base of vessels correspond approx. to Schmidt's meter levels

not to scale

APPENDIX 1: POTTERY CHARTS 315

Section 4.20b

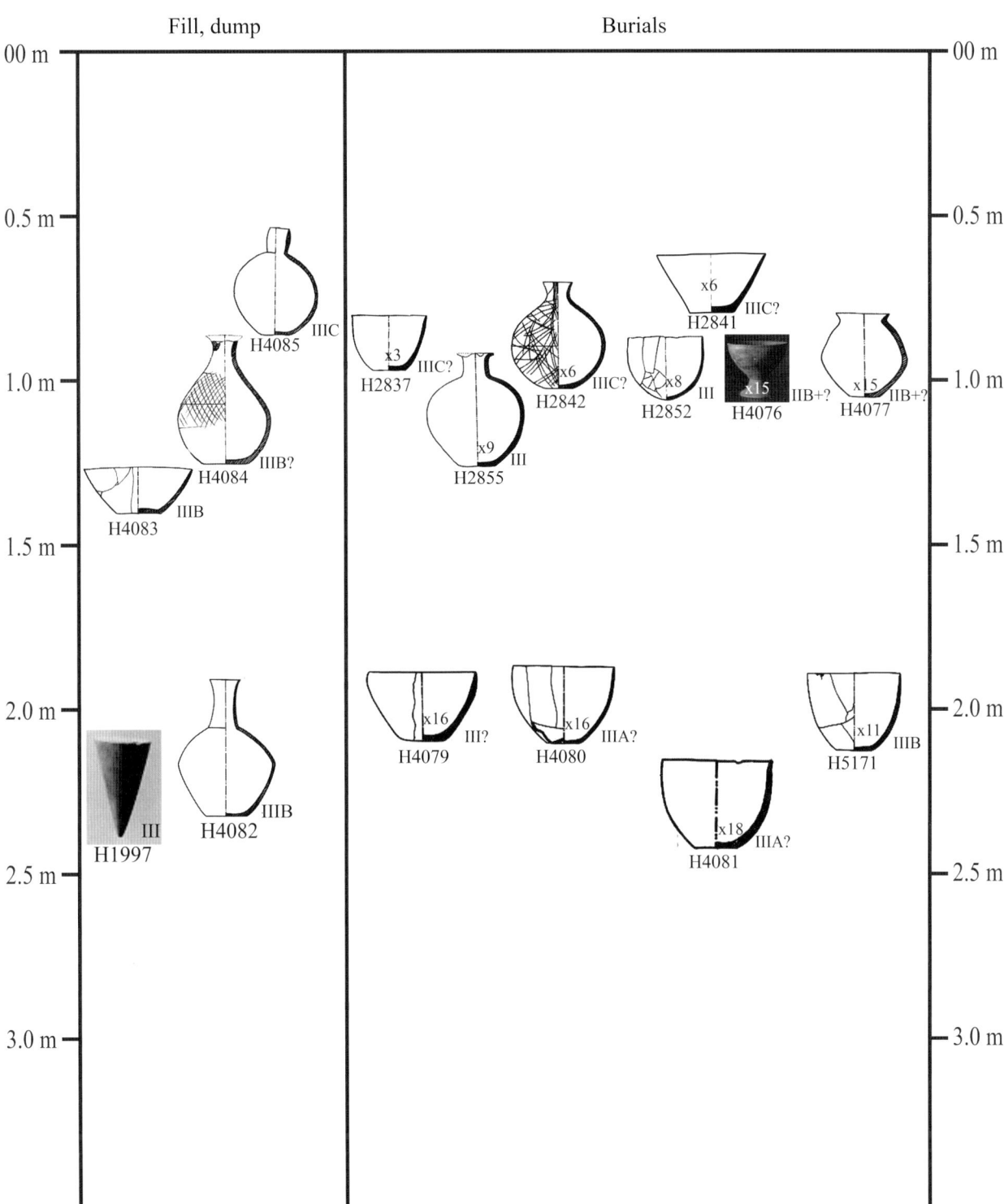

Note: Base of vessels correspond approx. to Schmidt's meter levels

not to scale

Section 4.21a

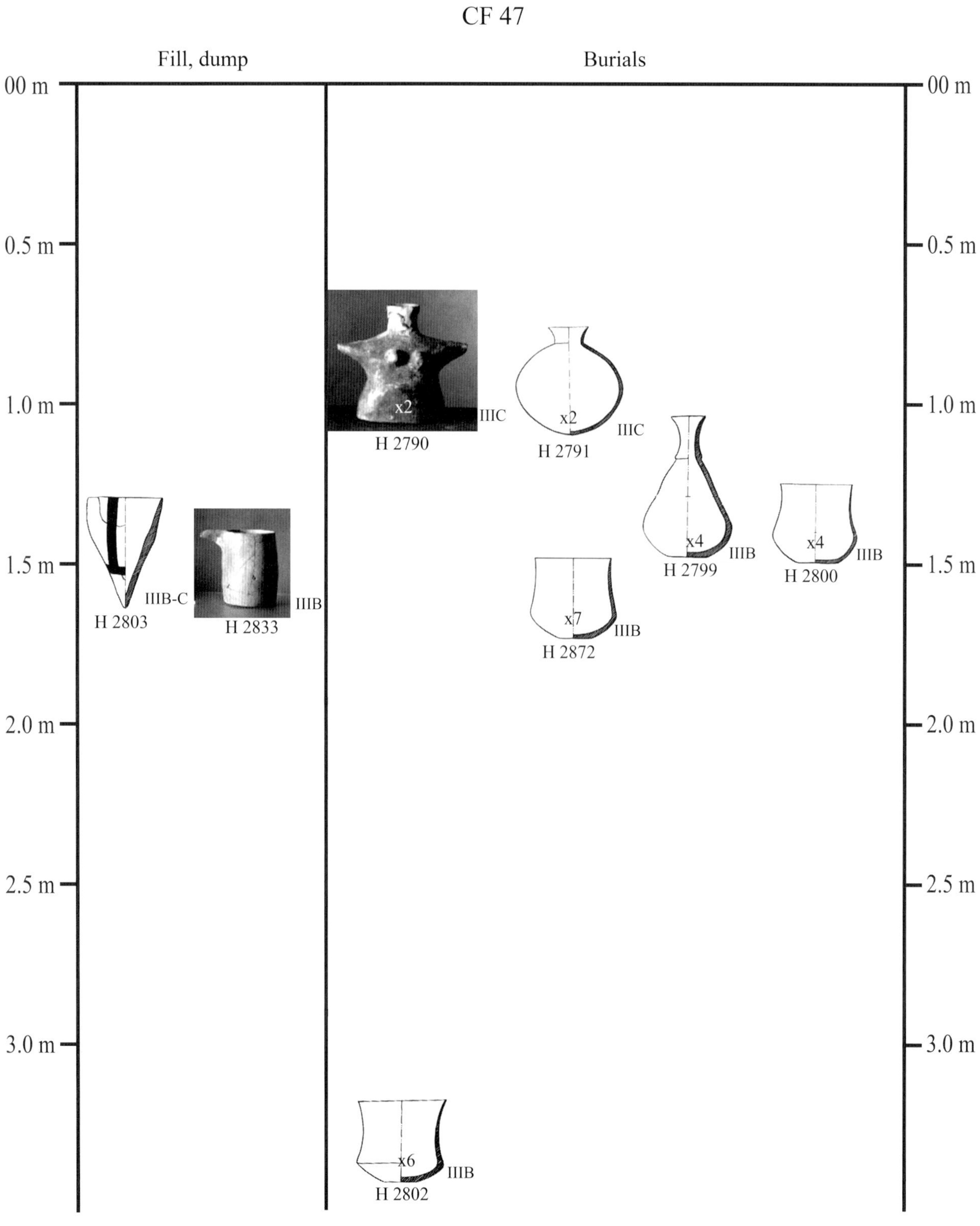

CF 47

Fill, dump | Burials

- H 2790 IIIC (x2)
- H 2791 IIIC (x2)
- H 2803 IIIB-C
- H 2833 IIIB
- H 2799 IIIB (x4)
- H 2800 IIIB (x4)
- H 2872 IIIB (x7)
- H 2802 IIIB (x6)

Note: Base of vessels correspond approx. to Schmidt's meter levels

not to scale

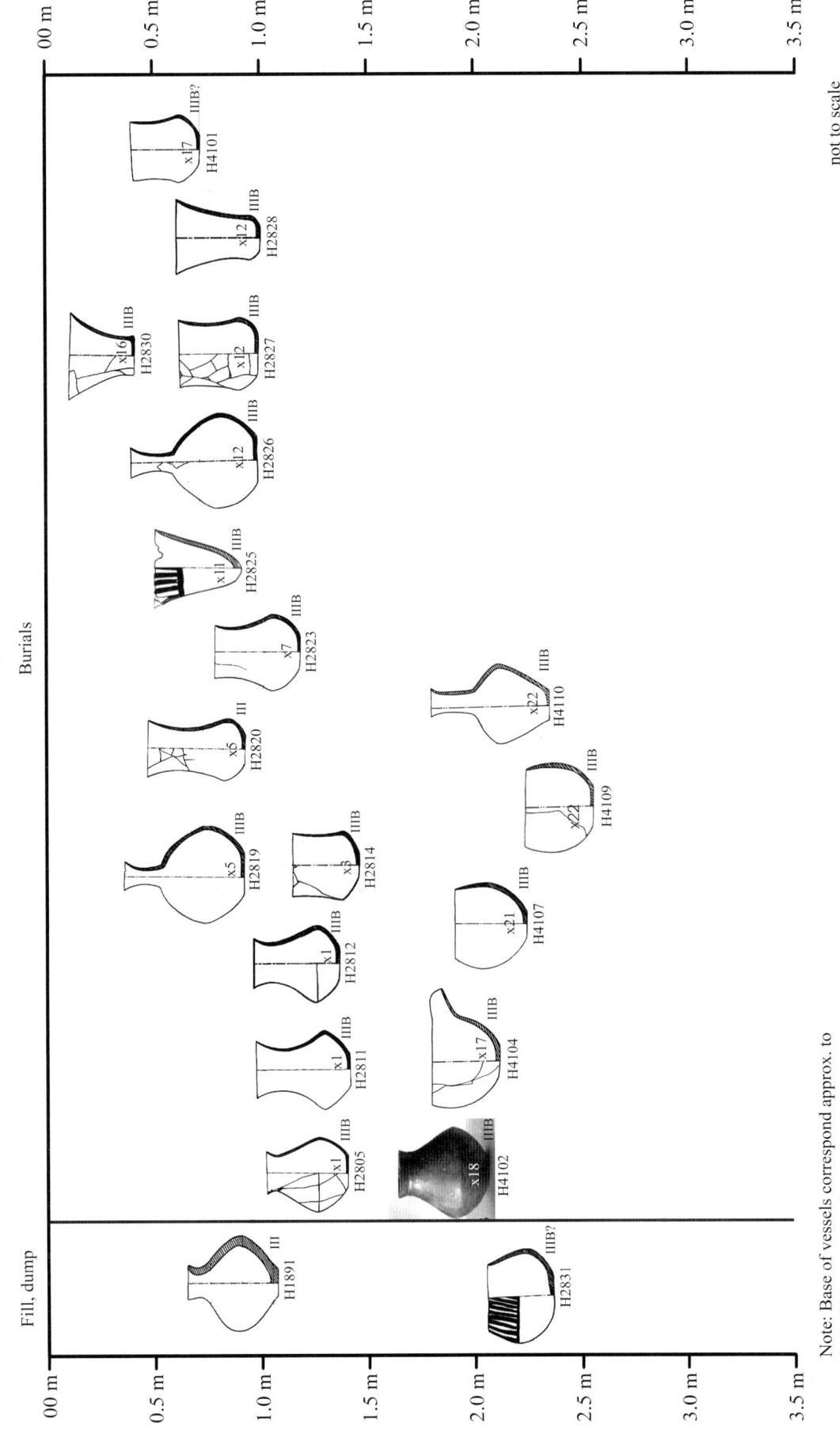

Section 4.22a

CF 57

Fill, dump   Burials

Note: Base of vessels correspond approx. to Schmidt's meter levels

not to scale

Appendix 2

Low and High Outlier Burial Tables

Table A2.1a–e: The "Low Outliers"—Dated Burials

1. Abbreviations for Tables A2.1a–e and A2.2a–b concerning each burial's age, sex, and body position [in that order under the excavated grids in the Square column]:

M	is	male	Inf	is	Infant	Su	is	supine
F	is	female	Juv	is	juvenile	Pro	is	prone
Un	is	unknown	Adu	is	adult	L	is	left lateral
Mat	is	mature	Sen	is	senile	R	is	right lateral

2. Ceramics and notable, non-ceramic objects are listed. Notables always include metals [copper, silver, gold, lead], stone [alabaster, separately, but also flint, lapis, gypsum, etc.] and bone. Notables also sometimes include unusual forms of ceramic vessels such as goblets, chalices, nursing cups, vases, and painted wares. The object descriptions are copied verbatim from Gardner's data, as reorganized by Mueller following the project's 5-group chronological model that was adopted in 2011.

3. Burials that Gardner listed as "Missing" [completely] have been deleted in this table.

Table A2.1a: GROUP 1: Low Outliers

Square and Body Data	Burial No.	Ceramic Vessels	Ornaments	Notables Weapons, Tools and Figurines	Object Location	Inventory No.
			North Flat			
no dated burials						
			Main Mound			
DF09						
Inf Un R	50		Stone Necklace, tan		Neck	H5033
Inf Un R	51		Stone Necklace, tan gypsum		Neck	H5034
Mat F R	52	Bowl, Pedestal, grey			Head	H5035

Table A2.1b: GROUP 2: Low Outliers

Square and Body Data	Burial No.	Ceramic Vessels	Ornaments	Notables Weapons, Tools and Figurines	Object Location	Inventory No.
			North Flat			
CF37						
Mat M L	9	Cup, Pottery, checkerboard pattern			Foot	H4070
		Cup, Pottery, grey			in H4070	H4071
CF38						
Sen M R	15	Footed Bowl			Pelvis	H4076
		Jar			Pelvis	H4077
		Cup			Pelvis	H4078
CF47						
Adu F R	4	Bottle-pitcher			Pelvis	H2799
		Bowl			Pelvis	H2800
			Pendant, stone, carnelian		Neck	H2801
Inf Un Su	6	Beaker			Skull, top	H2802
Inf Un R	7	Bowl, grey			Lumbar	H2872
CF57						
Adu M R	33	Jar, buff			Arm, lower R	H4148
		Cup, large			Arm, lower R	H4149
			Main Mound			
DF09						
Mat M L	13	Jar, shell shaped			Occipital	H3887
Adu M L	29	Cup, buff painted			Chest	H3902
		Goblet, conical			Chest	H3903
		Jar, globular			Face	H3904
		Beaker, cylindrical			Face	H3905
Adu M Un	30	Jar, small			Skull	H3906
Inf Un Un	31	Bowl, stemmed			Missing	H3907
Adu M R	33	Bowl, stemmed found w. oval stone slate #			Back	H3908
Mat F L	35	Jar, grey			Arm, lower	H3909
			Necklace, stone, lapis		Neck	H3910
			Ring, copper		Finger	H3911
			Ring, copper		Finger	H3912
Mat M Un	36	Cup, broken			Skull	H3913

Table A2.1b (cont'd)

Square and Body Data	Burial No.	Ceramic Vessels	Ornaments	Notables Weapons, Tools and Figurines	Object Location	Inventory No.
Mat F Su	41	Goblet, grey			Pelvis	H3915
		Bowl			Pelvis	H3916
		Goblet, grey			Pelvis	H3917
Mat F L	42	Jar, coarse, buff			?	H1388
		Jar, grey, globular, stemmed			near Femur	H3918
		Cup, small, grey burnished			near Femur	H3919
			Pin, double scroll, copper		near Femur	H3920
Adu F Su	43	Cup, lozenge pattern			Foot R	H3921
		Cup, light grey, coarse				H1389
Un Un R	45	Jar			Shoulder, behind	H3922
		Cup			Same	H3923
Juv F L	54	Cup, grey			Skull	H5036
			Beads, alabaster & lapis		Neck	H5037
			Earring, silver, purple grey		Neck	H5038
DG11						
Inf Un R	21	Beaker, buff painted			Knee	H3960
		Bowl, grey			Face	H3961
Inf Un L	47	Cup, buff painted			Skull, top	H3990

Table A2.1c: GROUP 3: Low Outliers

Square and Body Data	Burial No.	Ceramic Vessels	Ornaments	Notables Weapons, Tools and Figurines	Object Location	Inventory No.
		North Flat				
CF38						
		Bowl, grey			Shoulder L	H5171
		Jar, grey			Face, front	H5172
			Bracelet, copper		Arm L	H5173
			Earring, copper		Forehead	H5174
Adu F R	11		Diadem, copper		in H5172	H5175
			Tubes, lapis		in H5172	H5176
			Tubes, copper		in H5172	H5177
				Female fig, copper	in H5172	H5178
			Bracelet, silver		Arm	H5179
Mat F Un	16	Bowl, coarse			Occipital	H4079
		Bowl, grey, burnished			?	H4080
Adu M Su	18	Cup			Feet	H4081
CF48						
		Cup, grey			Forehead	H2805
		Jar, small			Skull, Front	H2811
		Jar, small			Skull, Front	H2812
			Bracelet, copper		Skull, Front	H2806
Adu M R	1		Band, copper		Skull, Front	H2807
			Band, copper		Skull, Front	H2808
			Necklace Silver		Skull, Front	H2809
			Band, copper		Skull, Front	H2810
				Dagger, Copper	Skull, Center	H2804
		Cup, grey			Back	H2814
			Bracelet, copper		near Femur	H2815
Inf Un Un	3		Bracelet, copper		near Femur	H2816
			Necklace, gypsum (stone) & shell		Neck	H2817
Inf Un Un	4		Bracelet, 7 coils, copper		Missing	H2818
		Bottle-pitcher, grey			Lumbar (lower back)	H2819
Adu M L	5	Cup, grey			Lumbar (lower back)	H2820
				Knife, copper	Wrist R	H2821
			Bracelet, copper		Wrist R	H2822

Table A2.1c (cont'd)

Square and Body Data	Burial No.	Ceramic Vessels	Ornaments	Notables Weapons, Tools and Figurines	Object Location	Inventory No.
Adu F L	7	Cup, grey			Wrist L	H2823
			Bracelet, wire, copper		Wrist R	H2824
Inf Un L	11	Cup			Occipital, behind	H2825
Adu M R	12	Bottle-pitcher, grey			Vertex, behind	H2826
		Jar, grey			Occipital, behind	H2827
		Beaker, jar			Occipital, behind	H2828
			Bracelet, copper		Occipital, behind	H2829
Adu M R	16	Bowl, grey			Arm L	H2830
Adu F R	17	Cup, grey			Back	H4101
Inf Un Su	18	Cup, grey			Knee	H4102
			Bracelet, copper		in H4102	H4112
			Bracelet, copper		in H4102	H4113
Juv Un Un	19		3 Earrings, copper		Ear R	H4103
		Spouted cup, grey			near Femur L	H4104
			Earring, copper		Lumbar (lower back)	H4105
Adu F Su	21		Bracelet, copper		Elbow L	H4106
		Bowl, grey			Pelvis R	H4107
Adu M Su	22			Spearpoint, copper	Arm R	H4108
		Bowl, grey			Face, front	H4109
		Bottle-pitcher, grey			Face, front	H4110
CF57						
Juv Un Pro	6	Cup, grey			Shoulder R	H2432
		Jar, grey			Shoulder R	H2433
		Beaker, grey			Shoulder R	H2434
		Spouted cup			Shoulder R	H2435
		Jar, grey			Foot R	H2436
			Bracelet, copper		Wrist L	H2437
		Bottle-pitcher, grey			Shoulder R	H2477
Adu M Un	11	Beaker			Skull	H2443

Table A2.1c (cont'd)

Square and Body Data	Burial No.	Ceramic Vessels	Ornaments	Notables Weapons, Tools and Figurines	Object Location	Inventory No.
Juv Un L	14	Carinated beaker, grey			Lumbar	H2447
		Carinated beaker, grey			Femur	H2448
			Bracelet, copper		Arm R	disc.
Adu F Un	20	Jar, carinated, grey			Leg L	H2457
			Earring and Bracelet, copper		Skull	H2458
		Cup, grey			?	H2496
		Jar, carinated, grey, collar around neck			?	H2497
Inf Un L	21		2 Earrings, silver and copper		near Mouth	H2459
		Bottle, grey			Face, front	H2459b
		Bottle, miniature, grey			Skull R	H2460
		Bottle-pitcher, grey			?	H2502
		Bowl, grey			?	H2503
Adu F L	23	Ladle with cylinder handle			Arm R	H2462
Adu F R	27	Cup, bell-shaped, light grey			Head	H2507
Adu M L	29			Spear point, copper, with wood stem	Femur	H2475
			Beads, lapis, 3, blue		Toes, Foot L	H2476
		Bowl, carinated, grey				H2508
Mat M R	35	Jar, grey, coarse			Face, front	H4150
		Stem goblet, grey, burnished			Skull R	H4151
		Stem goblet, large, grey, burnished			?	H4152
Adu M Su	38	Cup, grey			Vertex	H4155
		Goblet, grey, burnished			?	H4156
			Bracelet, copper, 4 coils		Wrist R	H4157

Table A2.1c (cont'd)

Square and Body Data	Burial No.	Ceramic Vessels	Ornaments	Notables Weapons, Tools and Figurines	Object Location	Inventory No.
Adu M Su (cont'd)	38		Bracelet, copper, 4 coils		Arm L	H4158
Mat M L	40	Bowl, conical, grey			Shoulder	H4160
		Stem goblet, grey, burnished			?	H4161
		Stem goblet, grey, burnished			?	H4162
		Cup, grey			Vertex	H4163
			Necklace, alabaster & lapis		?	H4164
Adu F Un	43	Jar, "metallic", 4 triple rows of stipples			Head	H4169
		Globular jar, reddish brown			Head	H4170
Main Mound						
CG90						
Mat F L	3	Bottle-pitcher			Leg R	H4116
Mat F L	7	Jar, grey			Shoulder, behind	H4117
			Bracelet, copper		?	H4118
			Bracelet, copper		?	H4119
			Earring, copper		?	H4120
			Earring, copper		?	H4121
		Bowl, large, grey			Shoulder, behind	H5091
		Cup, grey			Shoulder, behind	H5092
Inf Un R	8	Jar			Pelvis	H4122
Adu M R	13	Cup			Chest	H5095
Mat F L	14	Cup, grey			Scapula R	H5096
		Jar, grey			above Face	H5097
Adu F Su	15	Bowl, grey			Pelvis R	H5098
		Bottle-pitcher, grey			Pelvis R, in H5098	H5099
Mat M Su	16	Cup, grey			Knee R	H5100
		Bottle-pitcher, grey			Leg R	H5101
			Bracelet, copper		Arm R	H5102
Adu F Un	18	Bowl, grey			Skull behind	H5104
Adu M Pro	19	Bowl, spouted			Skull	H5105

Table A2.1c (cont'd)

Square and Body Data	Burial No.	Ceramic Vessels	Ornaments	Notables Weapons, Tools and Figurines	Object Location	Inventory No.
Inf Un L	20		Bracelet, lapis		Arm	H4124
Juv M L	22	Cup			Shoulder R	H4125
Adu M Su	25	Bottle-pitcher, grey			Skull	H5108
			Bracelet, copper		Arm L	H5109
DF09						
Inf Un R	15	Cup			Forehead	H3888
Inf Un Un	17		Necklace, lapis, frit & crystal		near Body	H3886
		Bowl, carinated, grey, wide			near Body	H3885
Adu M L	23	Beaker, grey			Face, front	H3890
		Bottle-pitcher, grey			Face, front	H3891
		Tulip beaker, grey			Face, front	H3892
Inf Un L	46	Cup, grey			Heels, between pelvis	H3924
Juv F Un	48	Cup, grey			Skull	H5031
DF18						
Mat M R	13	Bottle, grey			Pelvis	H0614
		Cup			Pelvis	H0787
				Knife, copper	Elbow	H0542
Adu M Un	17	Bottle-pitcher, grey			Skull	H0789
Mat F Su	20	Jar, carinated, grey			Chest	H0942
		Bottle-pitcher, cylindrical neck, grey			Arm L	H0943
Juv Un Un	21		Band, copper		Head	H0624
Mat M Un	22		Rings, 3, copper		Head	H0625
Adu F Su	24	Bowl, polished, vertical burnishing marks			Feet	H0788
		Bottle, herringbone pattern burnish, grey brown			Feet	H0626
Inf Un Su	31	Cup			Head	H0944
Adu Un L	43	Cup			Pelvis	H1010

Table A2.1c (cont'd)

Square and Body Data	Burial No.	Ceramic Vessels	Ornaments	Notables Weapons, Tools and Figurines	Object Location	Inventory No.
Adu M R	46	Cup			Head	H1006
		Bottle-pitcher			Head	H1007
			Bracelet, copper		Wrist	H1008
			Beads, alabaster & lapis		Wrist	H1009
DF29						
Adu M Su	1		Bracelet, copper		Arm	H0628
			Bracelet, copper		Arm	H0629
				Knife, copper	Head	H0630
				Mattock, copper	Elbow	H0631
		Bowl, grey			Pelvis	H0633
		Cup, grey			Pelvis	H0634
		Bowl			Pelvis	H0365
		Bottle-pitcher			Femur	H0636
			Tube, copper		Head	H0632
Adu M R	2	Bowl			Foot	H0641
			Bracelet, copper		Arm	H0637
			Earring copper		Head, mandible	H0638
			Tube, copper		Head, mandible	H0639
			Bead, alabaster		Head, mandible	H0640
Mat M L	5	Cup, nursing			Head	H0642
Inf Un L	6	Cup			Head	H0646
		Bottle-pitcher			Head	H0647
			Bracelet, copper		Arm	H0644
			Beads, frit		Head	H0643
			Earring, copper		Head	H0645
Adu M L	7	Beaker, grey			Pelvis	H0649
		Bottle-pitcher, grey, burnished			Feet	H0650
			Tube (fragments), copper		Head	H0648
Mat M L	8	Jar, ceramic			Knee	H0652
		Bottle-pitcher, necked, ceramic			Head	H0651
Inf Un Un	17	Cup			Skull	H1019
Mat F L	20	No items				
Inf Un Su	22	No items				
Adu M R	23	No items				

Table A2.1c (cont'd)

Square and Body Data	Burial No.	Ceramic Vessels	Ornaments	Notables Weapons, Tools and Figurines	Object Location	Inventory No.
Inf Un R	24	Plate/tray, buff coarse			No data	H1018
Adu F L	28	Beaker, grey, burnished			?	H1020
			Earrings, 2, silver		?	H1021
Inf Un Pro	29	Cup			Arm	H1022
DG00						
Inf Un L	6	Bowl, grey			Leg, lower L	H0560
		Jar, grey			Leg, lower L	H0561
		Jar, grey			Leg, lower L	H0562
			v-shaped Pendant, copper		Leg, lower L	H0563
			Bracelet, copper		Leg, lower L	H0564
			Tube, copper		Leg, lower L	H0565
Adu M Un	10	Cup, buff painted			near Body	H0505
Adu M R	14	Bowl, grey			Legs	H0566
Adu M R	16	Bottle-pitcher, grey			Face	H0568
		Bowl, grey			Chest	H0569
		Bowl, grey			Chest	H0570
		Bowl, grey			Pelvis L	H0571
		Jar, grey			in H0569	H0572
			Bracelet, copper		Arm L	H0573
			Bead, alabaster		Chin	H0574
			Tube, copper		Humerus	H0575
				Female fig., copper	Hand	H0576
Adu M Un	19	Beaker, cylindrical neck, grey unburnished			near Body	H0567
Sen Un L	22	Jar			Neck, back of	H0578
		Bowl			Pelvis	H0579
		Jar, little			in H0579	H0580
		Jar			Knee R	H0581
			Beads, alabaster		Arm, lower R	H0582
DG01						
Mat F L	32	Jar, grey			Pelvis	H2519
		Cup, grey			Leg	H2520
			Bracelet, copper		Mouth	H2514

Table A2.1c (cont'd)

Square and Body Data	Burial No.	Ceramic Vessels	Ornaments	Notables Weapons, Tools and Figurines	Object Location	Inventory No.
Mat F L (cont'd)	32		Bracelet, copper		Mouth	H2515
			Ring, copper		Wrist	H2516
			Ring, copper		Wrist	H2517
			Pin, copper		Wrist	H2518
			Pin, copper		Wrist	H2521
			Pin, copper		Wrist	H2522
			Ring, silver		Jaw	H2523
			Ring, copper		Jaw	H2524
			Necklace, lapis & crystal		Jaw	H2525
Adu M L	36	Cup, grey			Arm	H2525
DG10						
Inf Un L	6	Bowl, brown, buff painted			Tibia L	H0611
Adu M L	7	Jar, grey			Ribs	H0557
DG11						
Inf Un L	5	Cup			Head	H3942
		Cup			Head	H3943
Mat M L	9	Cup			Pelvis	H3944
Inf Un R	17	Beaker, grey			Forehead	H3950
			Beads, lapis #		Hand R	H3951
Adu F L	20	Spouted bowl, grey			Thorax	H3956
		Bottle-pitcher, small, grey			Pelvis	H4006
			Bracelet, copper		in H3956	H3957
			Spiral pendant, copper		in H3956	H3958
			Earrings, copper		Ear	H3959
Adu M Un	24	Cup, spouted, grey			Missing	H3963
Adu F L	33	Bottle-pitcher			Vertex, behind	H3969
		Cup, grey			Femur, above	H3979
Adu F L	36	Tulip beaker, grey burnished			Occipital, behind	H3970
Inf Un R	48	Bottle-pitcher, necked			Chin	H3973
		Tulip beaker			Head	H3971
			Necklace, lapis		Neck	H3972
Adu M Su	52	Bowl, grey			Femur L	H3980

Table A2.1c (cont'd)

Square and Body Data	Burial No.	Ceramic Vessels	Ornaments	Notables Weapons, Tools and Figurines	Object Location	Inventory No.
Juv M L	54	Beaker, grey			Torso	H3983
		Tulip beaker, grey burnished			Torso	H3984
Mat F R	66	Bowl, grey			Pelvis, behind	H3988
		Jar, grey			Pelvis, behind	H3989
Adu M Su	68	Tulip beaker, bell-shaped, grey, burnished			Skull	H3991
Adu M R	74	Bottle-pitcher, grey			Femur L	H3994
			Earrings 2, copper #		Ear R	H3995
DG20						
Un	6	Cup, grey			Skull	H4024
		Tulip beaker, bell-shaped, grey burnished			in H4024	H4025
		Cup, grey			Skull	H4026
Adu M Un	9	Cup, buff color			Occipital	H4027
			Beads, lapis		Occipital	H4028
			Beads, alabaster		Occipital	H4029
Juv F R	17	Cup, grey			Vertex	H4032
		Jar, spouted, grey			Face, front	H4033
Adu M L	18	Tulip beaker, bell-shaped, grey burnished			Forehead	H4036
		Bottle-pitcher, grey			Forehead	H4037
		Tulip beaker, grey burnished			Forehead	H4038
			Necklace, lapis		Neck	H4039
Inf Un L	19	Cup, grey			Scapula R	H4040
				Needle, copper	Wrist R	H4041
Adu M Su	21	Bottle-pitcher, grey			Feet	H4044
		Bowl, grey			Feet	H4045
		Cup, grey			in H4045	H4046
			Tube, copper		Neck	H4042
			Beads, lapis		Wrist R	H4043

Table A2.1d: GROUP 4: Low Outliers

Square and Body Data	Burial No.	Ceramic Vessels	Ornaments	Notables Weapons, Tools and Figurines	Object Location	Inventory No.
			North Flat			
CF38						
Adu F R	6	Bowl, grey			Vertex	H2841
		Bottle-pitcher, short neck, grey			Vertex	H2842
			Bracelet, copper		Vertex	H2843
			Bracelet, copper		Vertex	H2844
			Necklace, chalcedony		Vertex	H2845
			Band, silver		Vertex	H2846
			Earrings, copper, 1 large, 2 small		Vertex	H2847
			Earring, copper		Vertex	H2848
			Earring, copper		Vertex	H2849
			Band, silver		Vertex	H2850
Adult M R	9	Bottle-pitcher, short neck, grey burnished			Scapula L	H2855
			Necklace, alabaster, frit, lapis, chalcedony		Neck	H2856
CF55						
Adu F L	1	Dancer, 14 items, see Table A2.2a				
Adu M Su	5	Bowl, grey			Shoulder L	H2390
		Jar, hour-glass shape, grey			Shoulder L	H2391
Adu Un Un	5a	Bottle-pitcher, grey			Femur L	H2392
		Jar, grey			Foot L	H2393
Un Un Su	8	Jar, grey			Pelvis R	H2394
Adu M Su	10	Bowl, grey			Lumbar R	H2395
		Jar, grey			Feet	H2396
			Beads, lapis		Femur R	H2397
			Main Mound			
CG90						
Adu F R	9	Bowl, grey-brown, Unburnished			Chest	H5093
		Bottle-pitcher, tube spout, grey burnished			in H5093	H5094

Table A2.1d (cont'd)

Square and Body Data	Burial No.	Ceramic Vessels	Ornaments	Notables Weapons, Tools and Figurines	Object Location	Inventory No.
Mat F L	10			Wand, Copper	Forehead	H4123
Adu M L	23	Bottle-pitcher, "metal ridge", grey			Back lower	H5106
		Cup, conical, grey, with lip			Back lower	H5107
DF09						
Sen F Su	6	Cup, spouted			Pelvis	H2347
Adu M Su	9		Tube, copper		Scapula L	H2349
		Bottle-pitcher, grey			Scapula L	H2350
		Cup, grey			Scapula L	H2351
Inf Un Un	24	Cup, coarse			Head	H3893
			Necklace, beads, lapis		Neck	H3894
Inf Un Su	25	Jar			Back	H3895
DF18						
Inf Un L	4	Jar			Face, front	H0993
		Jar, small			Face, front	H0994
Adu M R	5			Muller/grinder, stone	Knee L	H0800
Adu M Su	15	Jar			Pelvis, behind	H0622
		Bottle			Pelvis, behind	H0623
Inf Un R	25	Tulip beaker, grey, burnished			Head, behind	H0790
		Jar, carinated, grey, burnished			Shoulders, behind	H0627
Juv M L	36	Tulip beaker, grey burnished			Feet	H0794
			Tube, copper		Neck	H0795
Adu M Su	38	Cup			Foot R	H0799
		Bottle			Leg R	H0796
		Bottle			Arm L	H0998
		Cup			Head	H0798
				Wire, copper, heavy (tool)	Arm R	H0797
Adu M Su	39	Jar			Foot R	H1386
Adu Un L	39a	Bowl			Leg R	H1644
			Bracelet, copper		Arm R	H1353
Juv Un L	41	Cup fragment			Shoulder	H1001

Table A2.1d (cont'd)

Square and Body Data	Burial No.	Ceramic Vessels	Ornaments	Notables Weapons, Tools and Figurines	Object Location	Inventory No.
Juv UN L (cont'd)	41	Cup			Shoulder	H0947
		Cup			Elbow R	H1387
				Tack, copper	Shoulder, under	H1002
Adu M	52	Bowl, grey, unburnished				H0801
DF19						
Adu M Un	13	Jar, large, grey			Skull	H1000
Inf Un Su	18	Cup, grey			Face, front	H1030
Adu Un L	19	Bowl, grey			Pelvis R	H1029
Adu M Su	21	Bottle-pitcher, grey burnished			Shoulder L	H0875
		Bottle-pitcher, grey burnished			Elbow L	H0876
			Bracelet, copper		Skull	H0877
		Cup, grey un-burnished			Pelvis	H1111
		Beaker, bell-shaped, grey burnished			Pelvis	H1112
Adu F Su	24	Bottle-pitcher			Elbow R	H1027
		Bowl, Large, grey, burnished			Elbow R	H1028
		Bowl			Shoulder R	H1113
		Goblet, grey, unburnished			Skull	H1636
		Plate, grey, stem bowl reground			Pelvis	H1637
Inf Un L	40	Jar, short beak spout			Knee	H0896
Inf Un L	43	Cup, grey			Knee	H0885
Adu F R	55	Cup, grey			Elbow L	H1638
DG00						
Adu M Un	7	Jar, grey			Forehead	H0504
DG11						
Adu M L	16	Beaker, grey burnished			Foot R	H3945
		Bottle-pitcher, grey burnished, mended at neck, 4 pairs of repair holes			Foot R	H3946

Table A2.1d (cont'd)

Square and Body Data	Burial No.	Ceramic Vessels	Ornaments	Notables Weapons, Tools and Figurines	Object Location	Inventory No.
Adu M L (cont'd)	16		Earring, copper		Ear R	H3947
			Tube, copper		Neck	H3948
			Beads, 2, alabaster		Neck	H3949
Inf Un R	18		Tube, copper		near Chin	3952
			Bracelet, copper		Wrist	3953
				Wand, Copper	Leg	3954
			Earring, copper		Ear	3955
Adu M L	32	Cup, grey			Forehead	H3967
		Bottle-pitcher, grey			Forehead	H3968
Adu M L	62	Bottle-pitcher			Femur R	H3987

Table A2.1e: GROUP 5: Low Outliers

Square and Body Data	Burial No.	Ceramic Vessels	Ornaments	Notables Weapons, Tools and Figurines	Object Location	Inventory No.
		North Flat				
CF37						
Adu F Pro	1	Cup, grey			Skull	H2356
		Bottle-pitcher, small			Scapula R	H2357
CF47						
Inf Un R	1			Cow figurine, grey, ceramic	Face, front	H2785
			Necklace, stone		Neck	H2786
Adu M R	2	Cup, alabaster			Skull	H2787
			Bead, alabaster		Scapula L	H2788
				Globe (counter), ceramic	Knee	H2789
				Female figurine, ceramic	Pubic bone R	H2790
		Jar, necked			Femur L	H2791
		Cup, alabaster			Ankle	H2792
				Hammer, copper	Ankle	H2793
				Pin, bone	Ankle	H2794
				Pin, bone	Ankle	H2795
			Bead, frit		Ankle	H2796
			Ring, bone		Ankle	H2797

Table A2.1e (cont'd)

Square and Body Data	Burial No.	Ceramic Vessels	Ornaments	Notables Weapons, Tools and Figurines	Object Location	Inventory No.
			Main Mound			
CF79						
Adu M L	1	Cup, grey burnished				H3931
		Canteen, small, grey burnished			Occipital	H3932
		Globular Jar, narrow neck, flaring rim, burnishing in lattice pattern			Shoulder	H3933
			Earrings, copper		Head	H3934
		Cup, alabaster			Head	H3935
			Bead, alabaster			H3936
			Gypsum rings and beads of a pendant		Head	H3637
			Bone, frit, stone		Face, front	H3938
		Cup, alabaster			Chest	H3939
		Cup, alabaster, biconical			Occipital	H3940
		Jar, grey storage, zigzag ornamental burnishing				H5231
CF88						
Juv M Su	1	Jar, grey			Arm	H3504
		Cup, red			Arm	H3505
		Stemmed plate, alabaster			Pelvis	H3506
		Bowl, red			Pelvis	H3507
		Bowl, red			Knee	H3509
		Jar, beak spout, grey, herringbone burnish			Leg	H3510
		Jar, bridge-beak spout, grey burnish			Feet	H3511
		Jar, pattern burnish, concentric bands			Feet	H3512

Table A2.1e (cont'd)

Square and Body Data	Burial No.	Ceramic Vessels	Ornaments	Notables Weapons, Tools and Figurines	Object Location	Inventory No.
CF89						
Mat M R	2		Necklace, frit		Head	H3513
		Bottle-pitcher			Back	H3514
				Stamp seal, copper	Arm	H3515
Mat M Pro	3	Canteen, grey, 2 cord handles			Head	H3516
		Stemmed plate, alabaster			Head	H3517
		Jar			Back	H3518
		Stemmed plate, alabaster			Os coxae	H5199
			Bead, frit		Feet	H3520
Inf Un Su	7	Jar, buff, coarse			Chest	H5144
Mat F Su	10	Cup, alabaster			Chest	H3521
		Jar, spouted, alabaster			Legs	H5145
CF99						
Juv F L	1	Jar, grey			Head	H5138
CG90						
Adu M L	1	Canteen, grey-brown, 2 cord handles			Elbow L	H5090
DF08						
Adu M Pro	1	Priest, 47 items, see Table A2.2b				
DF09						
Adu M Pro	1	Warrior 2, 68 items, see Table A2.2b				
Mat M R	2	Jar, alabaster			Occipital	H0536
		Canteen, grey burnished			Chest	H0537
		Cup, alabaster			Face, front	H0538
				Knife, copper	Scapula R	H0539
				Spearpoint, copper	Scapula R	H0540
		Cup, lead			Chest	H0541
Mat M R	5	Plate, alabaster			Feet	H1390
		Bottle-pitcher, peak spout			Feet, inverted beside H1390	H1646
				Polishing stone	Feet, near H1390	H1575

Table A2.1e (cont'd)

Square and Body Data	Burial No.	Ceramic Vessels	Ornaments	Notables Weapons, Tools and Figurines	Object Location	Inventory No.
DF18						
Inf F R	1	Little Girl, 33 items, see Table A2.2b				
DF19						
Adu M Su	2	Warrior 1, 15 items, see Table A2.2b				
Adu Un R	3	Plate, alabaster			Head	H0182
		Jar, alabaster			Head	H0181
		Cup			Head	H0184
		Jar, grey			Head	H0185
			Bead, alabaster		Head	H0164
Adu F R	4	Bottle-pitcher, necked, grey burnished			Head	H0186
Adu M R	7	Bowl			Torso	H0873
		Jar			Torso	H0226
				Spatula, copper	Torso	H0224
			Earring, copper		Head	H0225
Inf Un Un	8	Cup			Torso	H0227
		Plate			Torso	H0228
Inf Un Un	11	Bowl, grey			Torso	H0229
		Jar			Torso	H0230
Adu M R	12	Canteen			Forehead	H0548
		Cup, cylindrical, disk base & rim, alabaster			Forehead	H0549
				Double headed ram, rod, copper	Forehead	H0550
			Ear pendant, copper		Oral region, L	H0551
				Weapon point, copper	Elbow	H0552
			Pendant, copper		Knee, R	H0553
				Quadruped figurine, copper	Knee, Right	H0554
Adu M Su	17	Jar, globular, grey			Shoulder L	H0874
Adu M R	23	Bottle-pitcher, necked			Scapula R	H0878
		Bowl			Pelvis R	H0879
		Jar			in H0879	H0880
				Tube, copper	Head	H0881

Table A2.1e (cont'd)

Square and Body Data	Burial No.	Ceramic Vessels	Ornaments	Notables Weapons, Tools and Figurines	Object Location	Inventory No.
Inf Un R	27	Cup, small, grey			Vertex	H0883
Mat M Su	29	Jar, grey			Elbow R	H0884
Adu M Pro	30	Jar, coarse, grey			Face front	H1026
		Bowl, coarse, grey			Face front	H1031
		Brazier, buff, coarse			Skull R	H1032
Adu M Su	60	Cup, lateral beak spout, grey burnished			Shoulder	H0891
				Cylinder seal, alabaster, on it: a man, one arm suspended, the other arm raised, in front of a horse	Pelvis	H0892
			Beads, 2, alabaster		Pelvis	H0893
			Pendant, beaded, alabaster & gypsum		Chest	H0894
DG00						
Sen M Su	1	Canteen, grey burnished, 2 string handles			Knee R	H0610
		Cup, alabaster			Knee R	H0612
Adu M L	4	Bottle-pitcher, beak spouted, grey, pattern burnishing			Head	H0501
		Bottle-pitcher, beak spouted, grey, pattern burnishing			Head	H0502
Adu F R	5	Bottle-pitcher, necked, grey burnished			Torso spine	H0558
		Cup, grey			Torso, behind	H0559
DG01						
Juv F R	1	Jar			Hand L	H2481
		Cup			Hand L	H2482
Inf Un Un	6	Bottle-Pitcher			Pelvis	H2483

Table A2.1e (cont'd)

Square and Body Data	Burial No.	Ceramic Vessels	Ornaments	Notables Weapons, Tools and Figurines	Object Location	Inventory No.
Adu M R	9	Jar			Knee	H2484
Adu M Pro	15	Cup, grey			Scapula R	H2486
Adu M L	16	Bottle-pitcher, grey			Foot R	H2487
		Cup, grey			Knee R	H2488
Adu M Un	17	Bowl, grey			Head	H2489
		Jar, grey burnished			Head, in H2489	H2490
		Bottle-pitcher, grey, unburnished			Head, behind	H2491
			Bracelet, copper		?	H2541
Adu M Su	18	Jar			Face	H2492
Sen M R	21	Bottle-pitcher, necked, grey			Elbow L	H2502
		Bowl, grey			Pelvis	H2503
Mat M Un	22	Bowl, grey			Skull	H2504
		Beaker			?	H0578
		Bowl			?	H0579
		Jar, carinated			?	H0580
		Jar, carinated			?	H0581
			Bead, alabaster		?	H0582
Adu M R	38	Beaker, grey			Hand L	H2527
			Coiled earring, copper		Ear R	H2528
Adu M L	39	Beaker, grey			Scapula R, behind	H2529
			Earring, copper		Ear R	H2530
Inf Un Su	41	Beaker, grey			Forehead	H2532
DG10						
Sen F R	3	Bowl, beak spout, alabaster			Shoulder, L	H0057
		Vase, alabaster			Chest, front	H0058
		Cylindrical container, tripod, coarse			Lumbar, vertebrae	H0059
		Bowl, grey			Pelvis	H0060
			Beads, frit		Forehead	H0061
			Earrings, copper		Head	H0062

Table A2.1e (cont'd)

Square and Body Data	Burial No.	Ceramic Vessels	Ornaments	Notables Weapons, Tools and Figurines	Object Location	Inventory No.
DG20						
Adu M R	13	Cup, buff			Knee R	H4030
			Necklace, white stone		Neck	H4031
Inf Un Un	17	Cup			Skull, behind	H1019

Table A2.2a–b The "High Outliers" —Schmidt's Five Named Burials

Table A2.2a: Group 4 North Flat: High Outliers

	Vessel	Ornament	Weapon	Tool	Seal	Figurine	Object Location	Inventory No.
CF55 x1 Dancer								
Adu F L		Earrings, copper					Ear, Mastoid R	H2375
		Earrings, copper					Ear, Mastoid L	H2376
		Ring, silver with gold					near Finger	H2377
		Bracelet, eight coils, copper					Wrist L	H2378
		Bracelet, eight coils, copper					Wrist R	H2379
	Jar, silver, small						Elbow R	H2380
	Cup, copper, cylindrical						Elbow R	H2381
		Band, copper (fragments) repoussé decoration					Elbow, R	H2382
	2 Cups, copper						Elbow, R	H2383
	Box, copper						Elbow, R	H2384
	Bowl, grey polished, large, ceramic						Foot	H2385
		Necklace, lapis & copper (stone)					Elbow R, below copper items	H2386
		Necklace, lapis & copper (stone)					Elbow R, below copper items	H2387
Total = 14		Necklace, lapis & copper (stone)					Elbow R, below copper items	H2388

Table A2.2b: Group 5 Main Mound: High Outliers

	Vessel	Ornament	Weapon	Tool	Seal	Figurine	Object Location	Inventory No.
DF08 x1 Priest								
Adu M Pro		Diadem, silver					Forehead	H0449
	Cup, alabaster						Scapula R	H0450
		"Fan," coiled disk w. handle, copper					Skull, rear	H0451
			Trident, copper				Knees	H0452
	Bowl, large, copper						Knees	H0453
	Bowl, copper						Knees	H0454
	Bowl, copper						Knees	H0455
	Bowl, copper						Knees	H0456
			Dagger, copper				Knees	H0457
					Square, copper		Skull	H0458
		Pendant, copper					Skull	H0459
	Pedestal, copper						Arm R	H0460
		Cross, copper					Skull	H0461
	Cup, small, copper						Arm R	H0462
		Ornament, wand, copper					Knees	H0463
		Ear pendant, copper					Auditory R	H0464
		Pendant, copper					Knees	H0465
		Bracelet, two coils, copper					Arm R	H0466
		Bracelet, copper					Arm R	H0467
		Pins, copper					Skull	H0468
		Pins, copper					Skull	H0469
		Pins, copper					Skull	H0470
		Pins, copper					Skull	H0471

Table A2.2b (cont'd)

	Vessel	Ornament	Weapon	Tool	Seal	Figurine	Object Location	Inventory No.
	Cup, lead						Mouth	H0472
	Cup, spouted, lead						Knees	H0473
	Cup, lead						Knees	H0474
	Cup, lead						Knees	H0475
	Vessel, alabaster						Knees	H0476
	Cup, alabaster						?	H0477
	Plate, alabaster						Back	H0478
	Jar, alabaster						Knees	H0479
	Cup, alabaster						Knees	H0480
	Cup, alabaster						Knees	H0481
						Female, translucent, alabaster	Pelvis R	H0482
DF08 x1 Priest (cont'd)	Jar, alabaster						Skull	H0483
	Bottle-pitcher, grey, ceramic						Knees	H0484
				Pestle, diorite			Knees	H0485
						Animal, serpentine	Scapula R	H0486
						Animal, serpentine	Scapula R	H0487
						Animal, serpentine	Scapula R	H0488
						Animal, serpentine	Scapula R	H0489
		Beads, frit, alabaster					Back	H0490
		Pendant, silver					Skull	H0491
		Beads, frit, alabaster					Skull	H0492
		Beads, amber, white stone					Arm R	H0493
		Bead, large, serpentine					Knees	H0494
Total = 47		Bead, small, serpentine					Knees	H0495

Table A2.2b (cont'd)

	Vessel	Ornament	Weapon	Tool	Seal	Figurine	Object Location	Inventory No.
DF09 x1 Warrior 2								
Adu M Pro						Horse, two-headed, copper	Arm L	H0718
		Fragments, copper					Arm L	H0719
					Circular, copper		Arm L	H0720
			Arrowhead, chalcedony				Scapula R	H0721
			Arrowhead, chalcedony				Scapula R	H0722
			Arrowhead, chalcedony				Scapula R	H0723
			Arrowhead, chalcedony				Scapula R	H0724
			Arrowhead, chalcedony				Scapula R	H0725
			Arrowhead, chalcedony				Scapula R	H0726
			Arrowhead, chalcedony				Scapula R	H0727
			Arrowhead, chalcedony				Scapula R	H0728
			Arrowhead, chalcedony				Scapula R	H0729
			Arrowhead, chalcedony				Scapula R	H0730
			Arrowhead, chalcedony				Scapula R	H0731
			Arrowhead, chalcedony				Scapula R	H0732
			Arrowhead, chalcedony				Scapula R	H0733
			Arrowhead, chalcedony				Scapula R	H0734
			Arrowhead, chalcedony				Scapula R	H0735
			Arrowhead, chalcedony				Scapula R	H0736
			Arrowhead, chalcedony				Scapula R	H0737
						Quadruped, clay	Scapula R	H0738

Table A2.2b (cont'd)

	Vessel	Ornament	Weapon	Tool	Seal	Figurine	Object Location	Inventory No.
						Quadruped, clay	Scapula R	H0739
						Quadruped, clay	Scapula R	H0740
						Quadruped, clay	Scapula R	H0741
						Quadruped, clay	Scapula R	H0742
						Quadruped, clay	Scapula R	H0743
						Quadruped, clay	Scapula R	H0744
						Bird, clay	Scapula R	H0745
						Quadruped, alabaster	Scapula R	H0746
						Quadruped, alabaster	Scapula R	H0747
						Quadruped, alabaster	Scapula R	H0748
DF09 x1 Warrior 2 (cont'd)						Quadruped, alabaster	Scapula R	H0749
						Quadruped, alabaster	Scapula R	H0750
						Quadruped, alabaster	Scapula R	H0751
						Quadruped, alabaster	Scapula R	H0752
						Quadruped, alabaster	Scapula R	H0753
						Quadruped, alabaster	Scapula R	H0754
						Quadruped, alabaster	Scapula R	H0755
						Quadruped, alabaster	Scapula R	H0756
						Quadruped, alabaster	Scapula R	H0757
						Quadruped, alabaster	Scapula R	H0758
						Quadruped, alabaster	Scapula R	H0759
						Quadruped, alabaster	Scapula R	H0760

Table A2.2b (cont'd)

	Vessel	Ornament	Weapon	Tool	Seal	Figurine	Object Location	Inventory No.
						Quadruped, alabaster	Scapula R	H0761
						Quadruped, alabaster	Scapula R	H0762
						Ram, double-headed, copper	Scapula R	H0763
		Beads, Amber & Frit					?	H0764
		Pendant, gold					Mastoid L	H0765
				Chisel, copper			Chest	H0766
			Spearhead, copper				Chest	H0767
			Dagger, copper				Chest	H0768
			Dagger, copper				Chest	H0769
		Fragments, copper					Chest	H0770
DF09 x1 Warrior 2 (cont'd)			Macehead, copper				Elbow L	H0771
	Bowl, copper						Chest	H0772
			Blade, large, copper				Feet	H0773
	Vessel, copper						Arm L	H0774
			Bident, bent, copper				Chest	H0775
	Bowl, copper						Pelvis R	H0776
	Bowl, copper						Chest	H0777
	Bowl, alabaster						Chest	H0778
	Vessel, alabaster						Arm L	H0779
	Jar, alabaster						Scapula L	H0780
	Lid, ceramic						Scapula L	H0781
	Cup, alabaster						Pelvis R	H0782
	Cup, alabaster						Skull	H0783

Table A2.2b (cont'd)

	Vessel	Ornament	Weapon	Tool	Seal	Figurine	Object Location	Inventory No.
DF09 x1 Warrior 2 (cont'd)		Earring, copper, gold coating					?	H0784
Total = 68	Cup, alabaster						Skull	H0785
DF18 x1 Little Girl								
Inf F R						Dog, Silver	?	H0370
						Dog (or Sheep), Silver w/ quartz between legs	?	H0371
		Silver pin					?	H0372
		Silver pin					?	H0373
	Bottle-Pitcher, silver						near Chest	H0374
	Bottle-Pitcher, silver						Head	H0375
	Bottle-Pitcher, silver						Head	H0376
	Jar, silver						Head	H0377
	Bottle-Pitcher, silver						Scapula L	H0378
	Cup, silver						Forehead	H0379
	Fragments of silver vessel						?	H0380
	Jar, alabaster						Pelvis L	H0381
	Cup, alabaster						Pelvis L	H0382
	Cup, alabaster						Head	H0383
		Bead collector, frit					Forearm	H0384
	Jar, glazed, frit (stone)						Pelvis L	H0385
	Box, alabaster						Forearm	H0386
	Box, alabaster						Pelvis L	H0387
	Cup, cylindrical, alabaster						Scapula L	H0388

Table A2.2b (cont'd)

	Vessel	Ornament	Weapon	Tool	Seal	Figurine	Object Location	Inventory No.
DF18 x1 Little Girl (cont'd)	Cup, cylindrical, alabaster						Pelvis L	H0389
	Jar, alabaster						Pelvis L	H0390
	Cup, green stone						Pelvis L	H0391
				Awl, bone			Pelvis L	H0392
				Awl, bone			Pelvis L	H0393
				Awl, bone (fragment)			Pelvis L	H0394
	Jar, grey, ceramic						Pelvis L	H0395
	Jar, grey, ceramic						Pelvis L	H0396
	Jar, grey, ceramic						Pelvis L	H0397
	Pitcher, grey, ceramic						Pelvis L	H0398
	Pitcher, grey, ceramic						Pelvis L	H0399
		Necklace, lapis lazuli, carnelian, gold leaf					Neck	H0400
		Earring, coppper					Clavicle	H0401
		Beads, stone					Neck	H0402
		Ramhead, copper, rod					Pelvis L	H0403
				Pin, copper			Pelvis L	H0404
	Bowl, copper						Pelvis L	H0405
	Bowl, copper						Pelvis L	H0406
Total = 38	Jar, ceramic, grey, vertical burnishing						?	H0498
DF19 x2 Warrior 1								
Adu M Su			Bident, copper				Leg lower R	H0166
			Lancehead, Copper				Humerus R	H0167
			Battle axe, copper				Scapula R	H0168

Table A2.2b (cont'd)

	Vessel	Ornament	Weapon	Tool	Seal	Figurine	Object Location	Inventory No.
DF19 x2 Warrior 1 (cont'd)				Chisel, copper			Elbow R	H0169
						Wand, copper [bird on bulbous base]	Leg R	H0170
			Helmet, copper				Leg lower R	H0171
						Metal fragments, lead	in H0171	H0172
	Teapot, oval, spouted, silver						Leg R	H0173
		Disc, alabaster					Leg R	H0174
	Pedestal, alabaster						Leg R	H0175
	Plate, alabaster						Elbow R	H0176
	Bowl, alabaster						Leg R	H0177
	Jar, large, grey, ceramic						Leg R	H0178
	Jar, small, grey, ceramic						Leg R	H0179
Total = 15		Beads, lapis, onyx, 2 (ear) rings of gold					Hand L	H0180

High Outlier (Groups 4 and 5) Object Total = 182

Appendix 3

Maps

Map 1	CF37
Map 2	CF38
Map 3	CF47
Map 4	CF48
Map 5	CF55
Map 6	CF57
Map 7	CF88
Map 8	CF89
Map 9	CF99
Map 10	CG90
Map 11	DF08
Map 12	DF09
Map 13	DF18
Map 14	DF19
Map 15	DF29
Map 16	DG00
Map 17	DG01
Map 18	DG10
Map 19	DG11
Map 20	DG20

APPENDIX 3: MAPS

Map 1

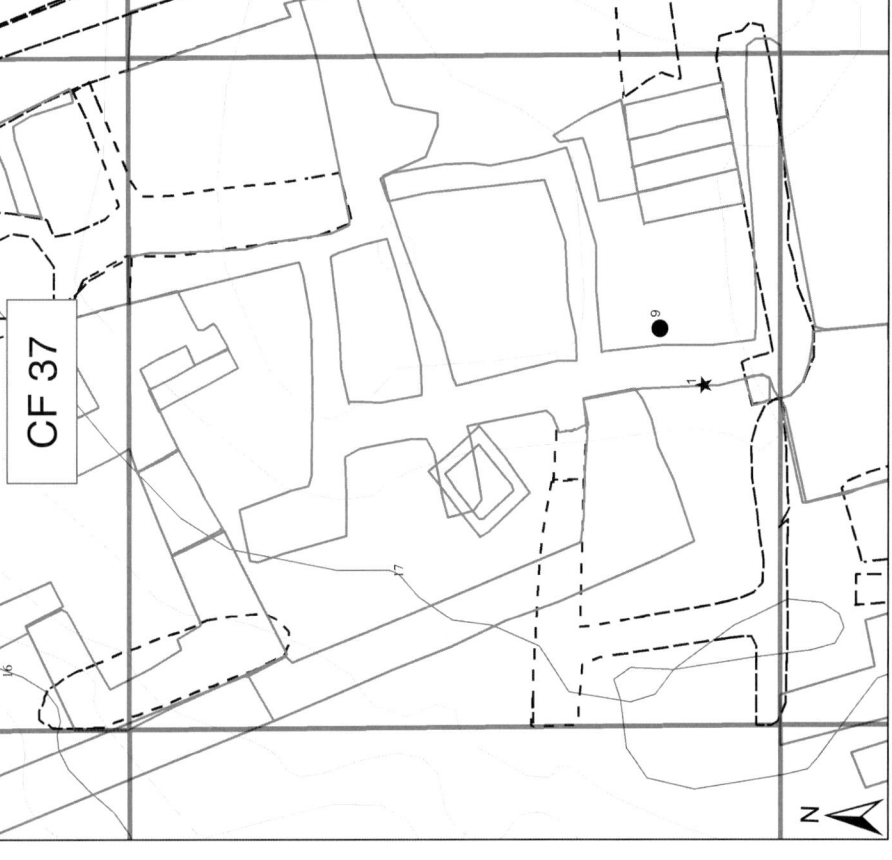

TEPE HISSAR
1931 - 1932 BURIALS
The Main Mound and The North Flat

Distribution of Dated Burial Groups
according to the New Ceramic
Sequence

* ✱ Late Hissar I-Early Hissar II
* ● Early-Mid Hissar II
* ⬟ Late Hissar II-Early Hissar III
* ◆ Mid Hissar III
* ★ Late Hissar III
* ◯ High Outliers

1931-32 Periods
Architecture
- ----- IC / IIA
- ——— IIB / IIIA
- ——— IIIB
- - - - IIIB / IIIC

Aysem Kilinc Unlu - Joseph C. Torres - James T. Rowland

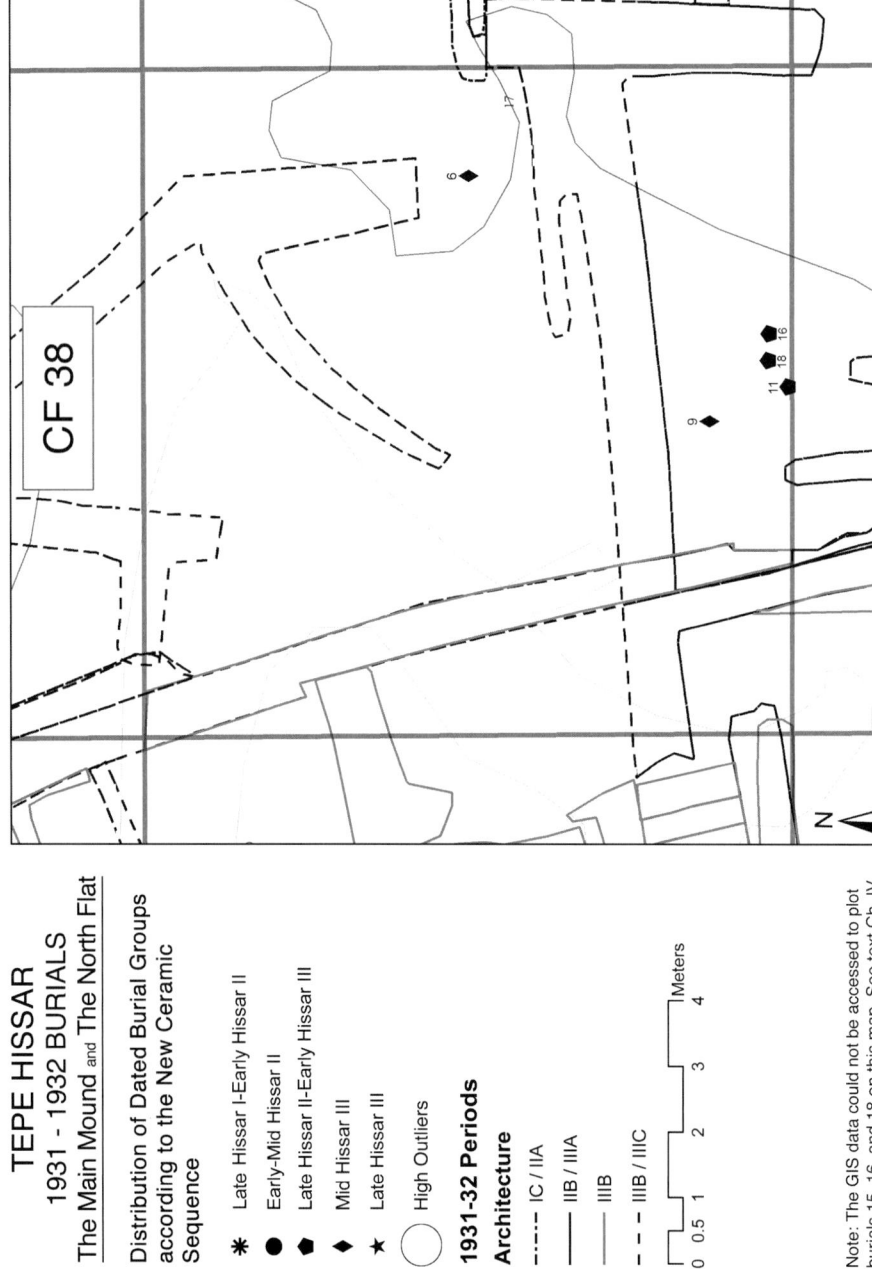

APPENDIX 3: MAPS

Map 3

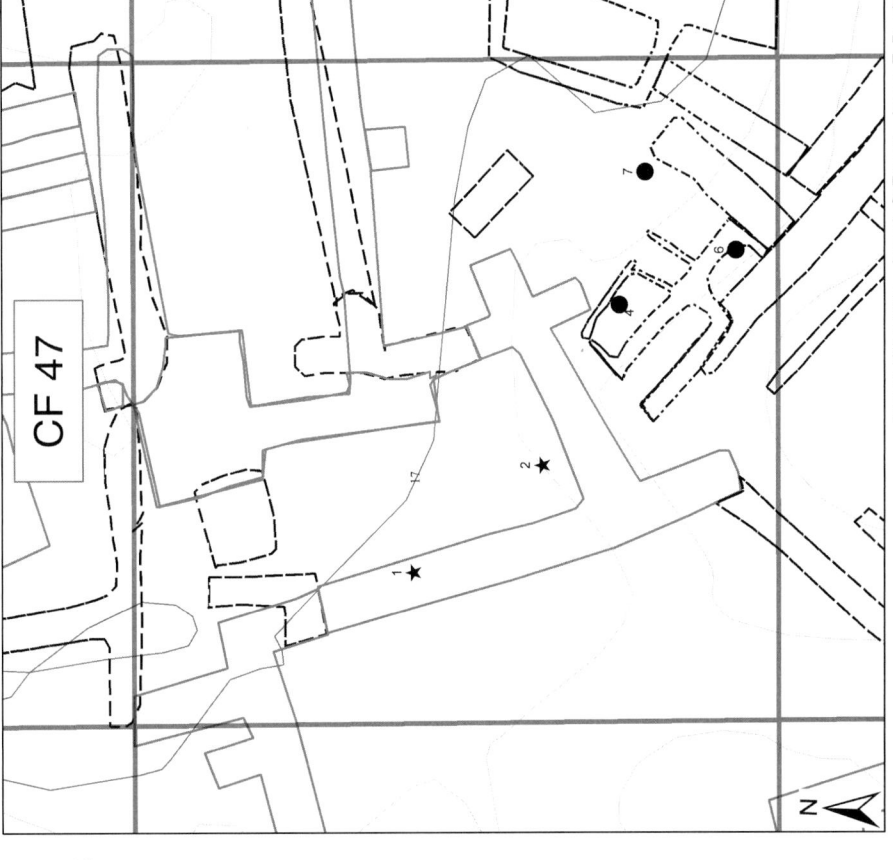

TEPE HISSAR
1931 - 1932 BURIALS
The Main Mound and The North Flat

Distribution of Dated Burial Groups according to the New Ceramic Sequence

✸ Late Hissar I-Early Hissar II
● Early-Mid Hissar II
⬟ Late Hissar II-Early Hissar III
◆ Mid Hissar III
★ Late Hissar III
○ High Outliers

1931-32 Periods
Architecture

----- IC / IIA
——— IIB / IIIA
——— IIIB
- - - IIIB / IIIC

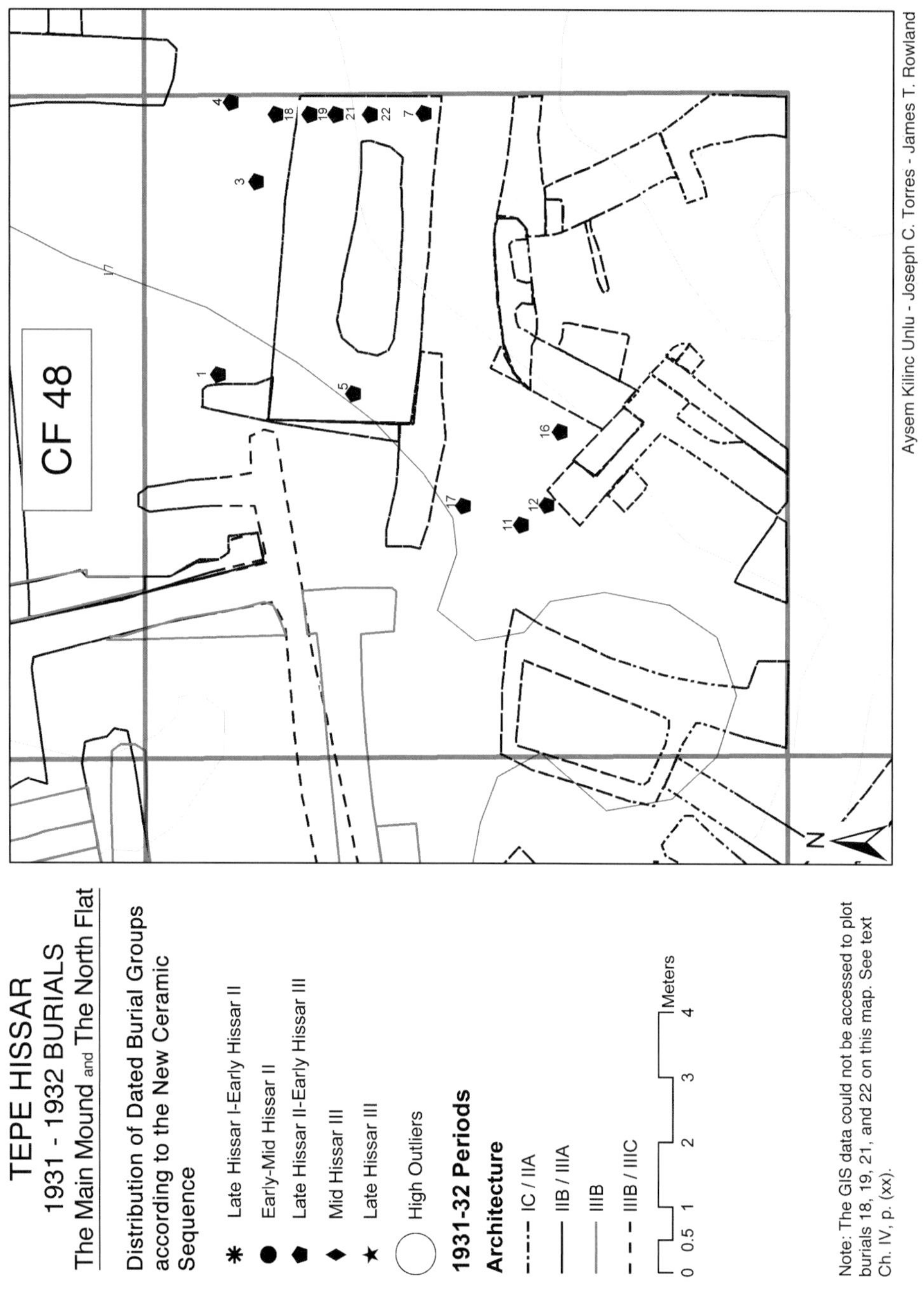

APPENDIX 3: MAPS 355

Map 5

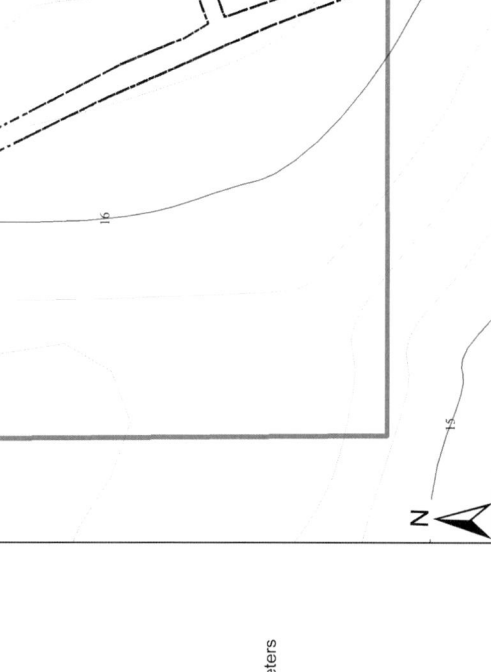

TEPE HISSAR
1931 - 1932 BURIALS
The Main Mound and The North Flat

Distribution of Dated Burial Groups
according to the New Ceramic
Sequence

✱ Late Hissar I-Early Hissar II
● Early-Mid Hissar II
⬟ Late Hissar II-Early Hissar III
◆ Mid Hissar III
★ Late Hissar III
○ High Outliers

1931-32 Periods
Architecture
---·--- IC / IIA
——— IIB / IIIA
——— IIIB
— — — IIIB / IIIC

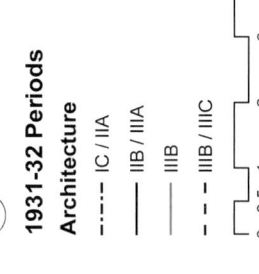

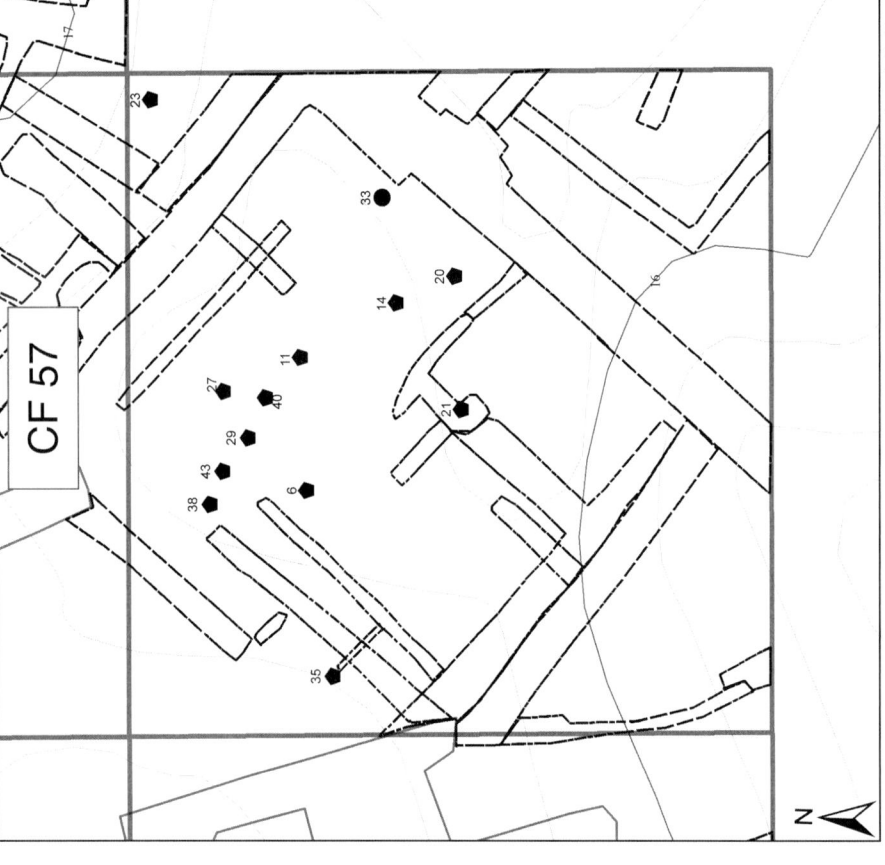

Map 6

TEPE HISSAR
1931 - 1932 BURIALS
The Main Mound and The North Flat

Distribution of Dated Burial Groups according to the New Ceramic Sequence

✱ Late Hissar I-Early Hissar II
● Early-Mid Hissar II
⬢ Late Hissar II-Early Hissar III
◆ Mid Hissar III
★ Late Hissar III
○ High Outliers

1931-32 Periods
Architecture
----- IC / IIA
------ IIB / IIIA
―――― IIIB
- - - IIIB / IIIC

APPENDIX 3: MAPS

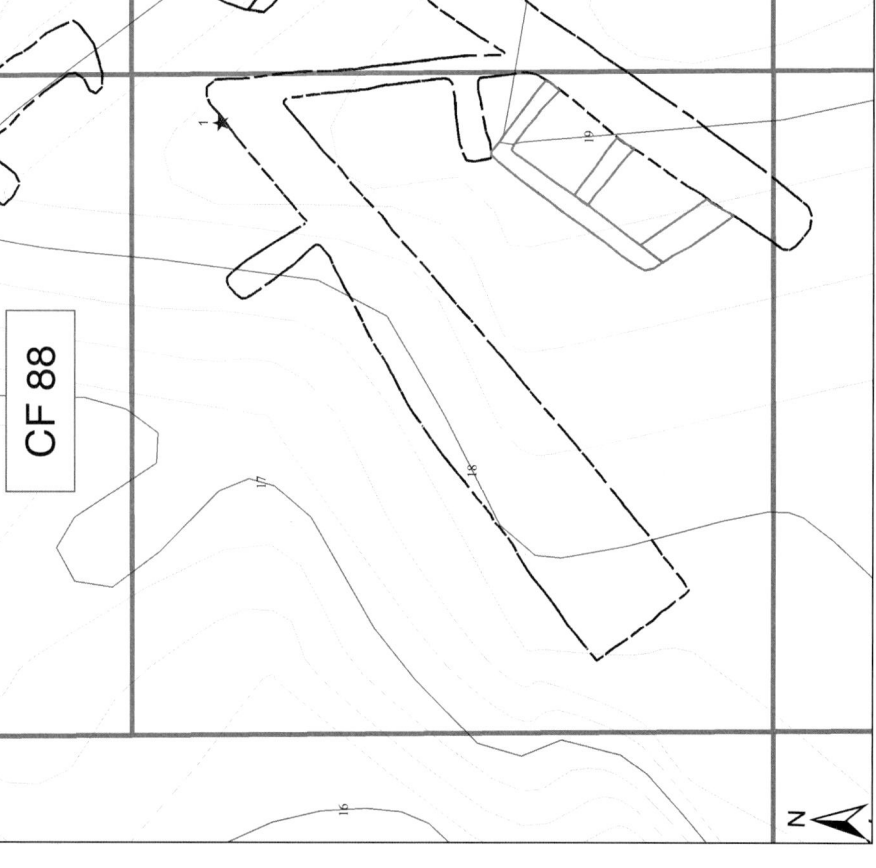

Map 7

TEPE HISSAR
1931 - 1932 BURIALS
The Main Mound and The North Flat

Distribution of Dated Burial Groups
according to the New Ceramic
Sequence

* Late Hissar I-Early Hissar II
● Early-Mid Hissar II
⬟ Late Hissar II-Early Hissar III
◆ Mid Hissar III
★ Late Hissar III
○ High Outliers

1931-32 Periods
Architecture
---- IC / IIA
——— IIB / IIIA
——— IIIB
--- IIIB / IIIC

0 0.5 1   2   3   4 Meters

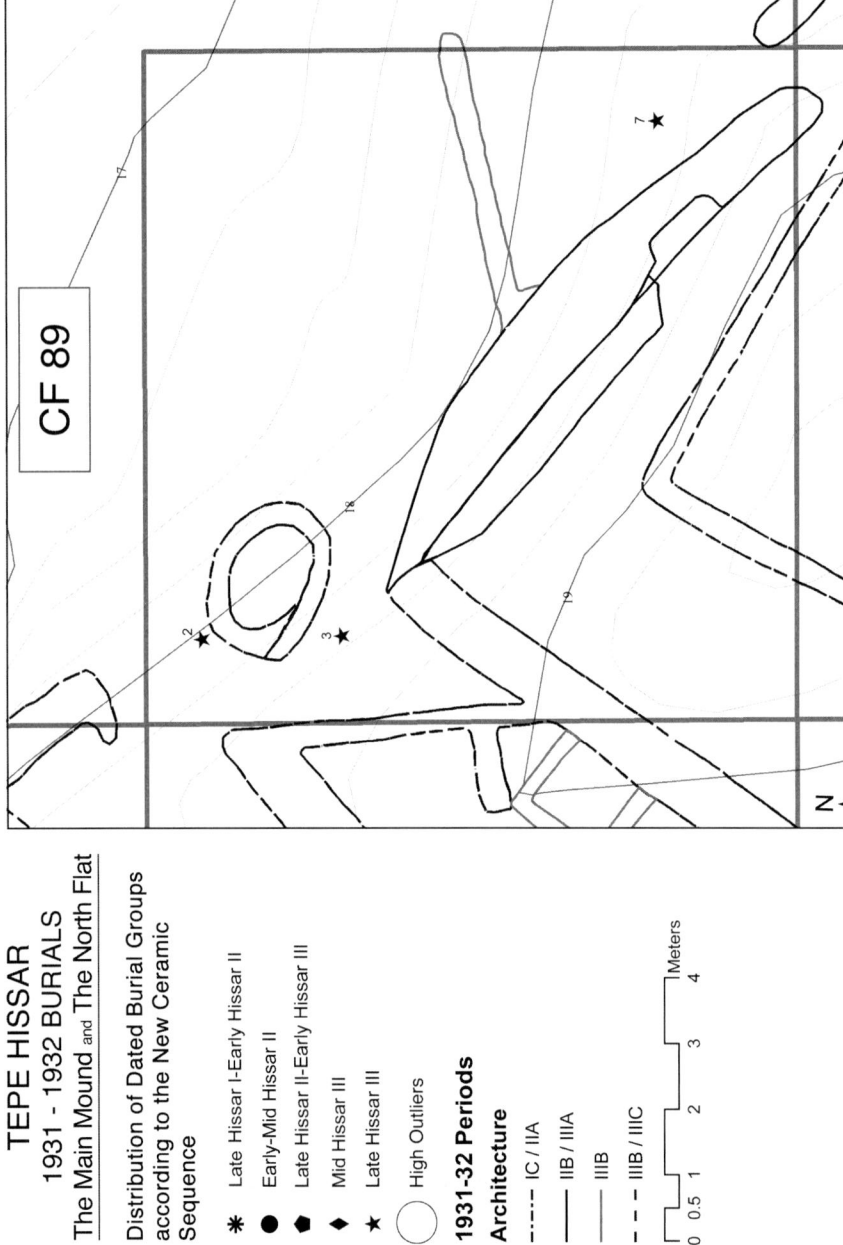

Map 8

APPENDIX 3: MAPS

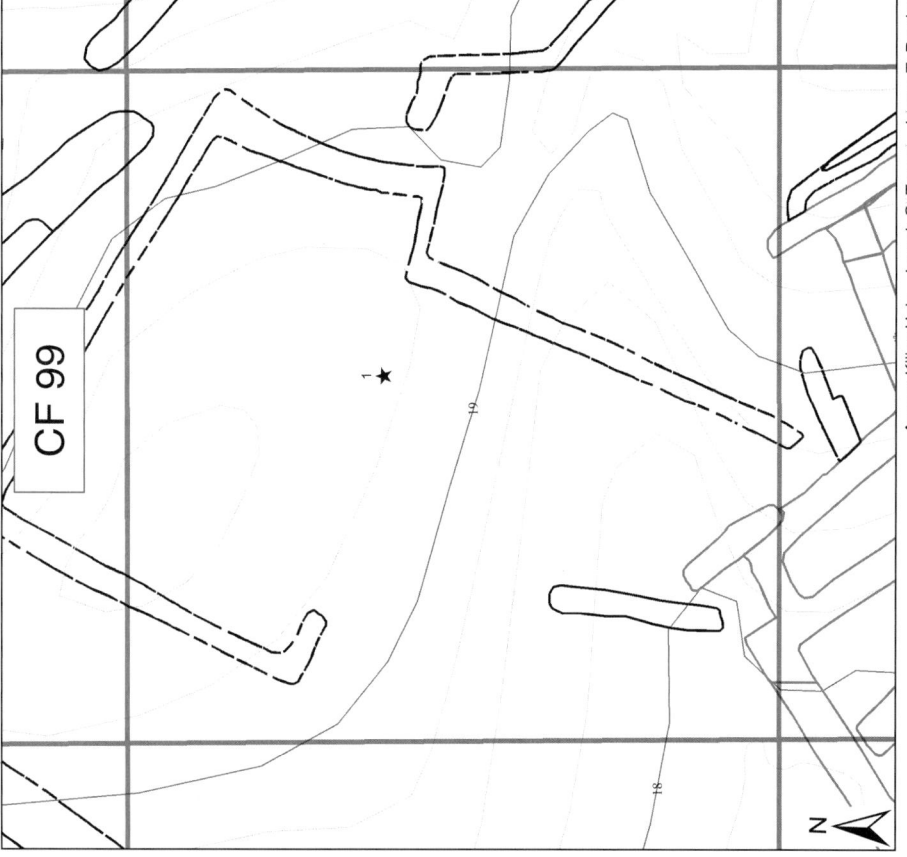

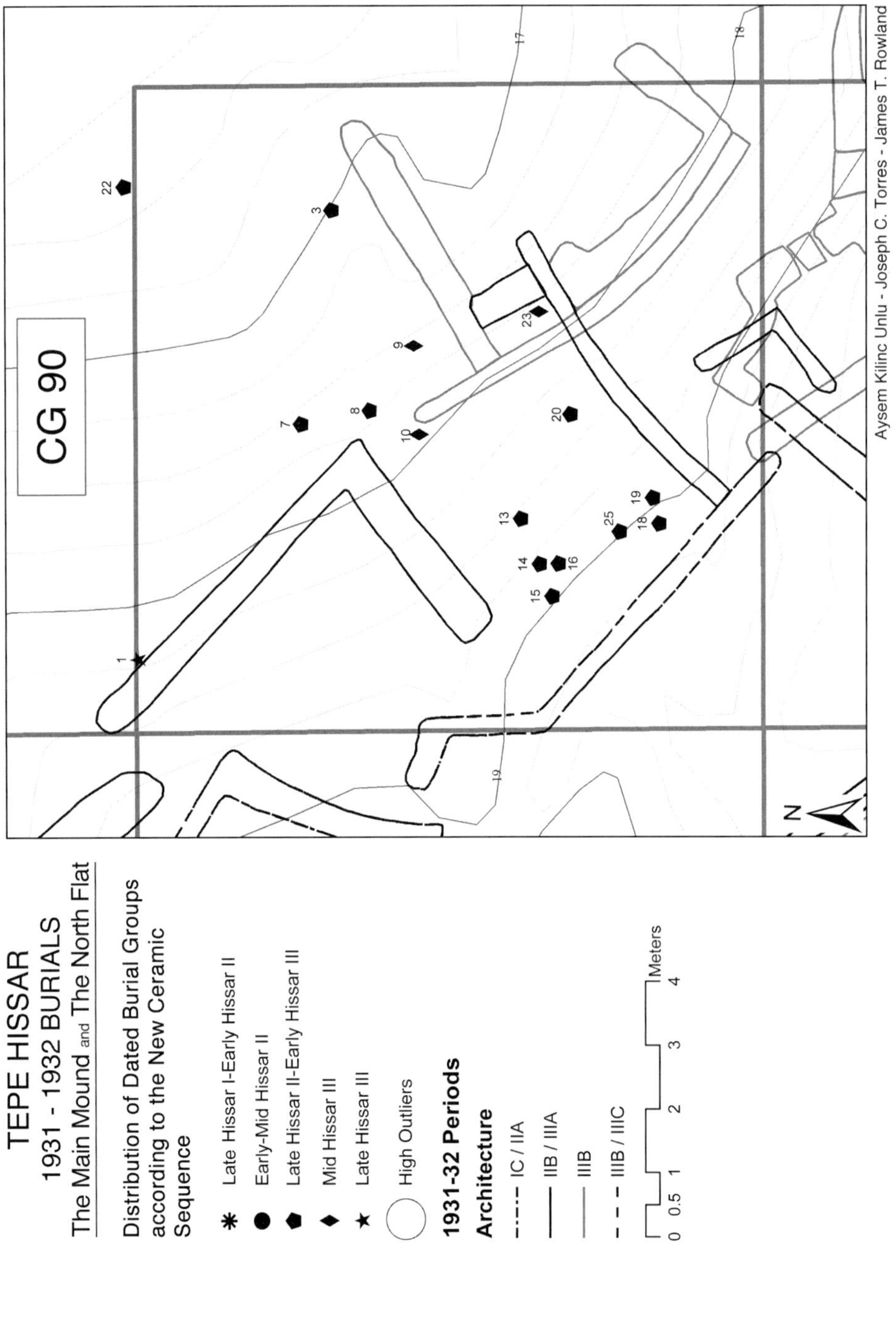

APPENDIX 3: MAPS 361

Map 11

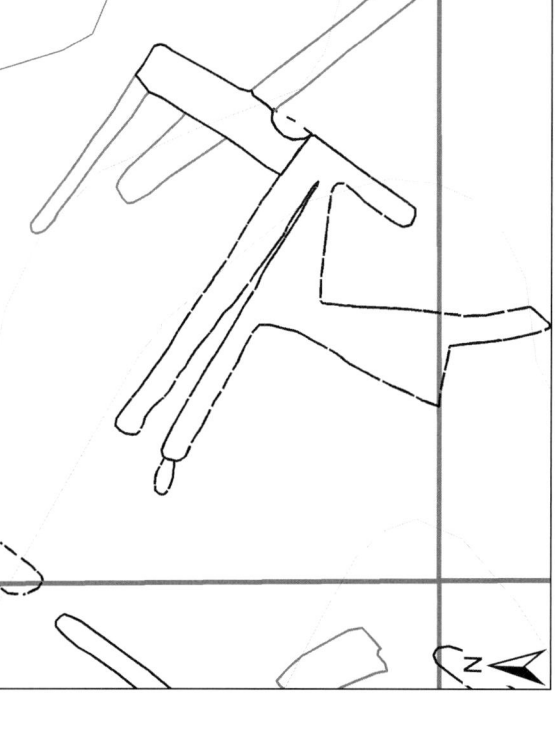

TEPE HISSAR
1931 - 1932 BURIALS
The Main Mound and The North Flat

Distribution of Dated Burial Groups according to the New Ceramic Sequence

✱ Late Hissar I-Early Hissar II
● Early-Mid Hissar II
⬟ Late Hissar II-Early Hissar III
◆ Mid Hissar III
★ Late Hissar III
○ High Outliers

1931-32 Periods
Architecture
---- IC / IIA
—— IIB / IIIA
—— IIIB
---- IIIB / IIIC

Aysem Kilinc Unlu - Joseph C. Torres - James T. Rowland

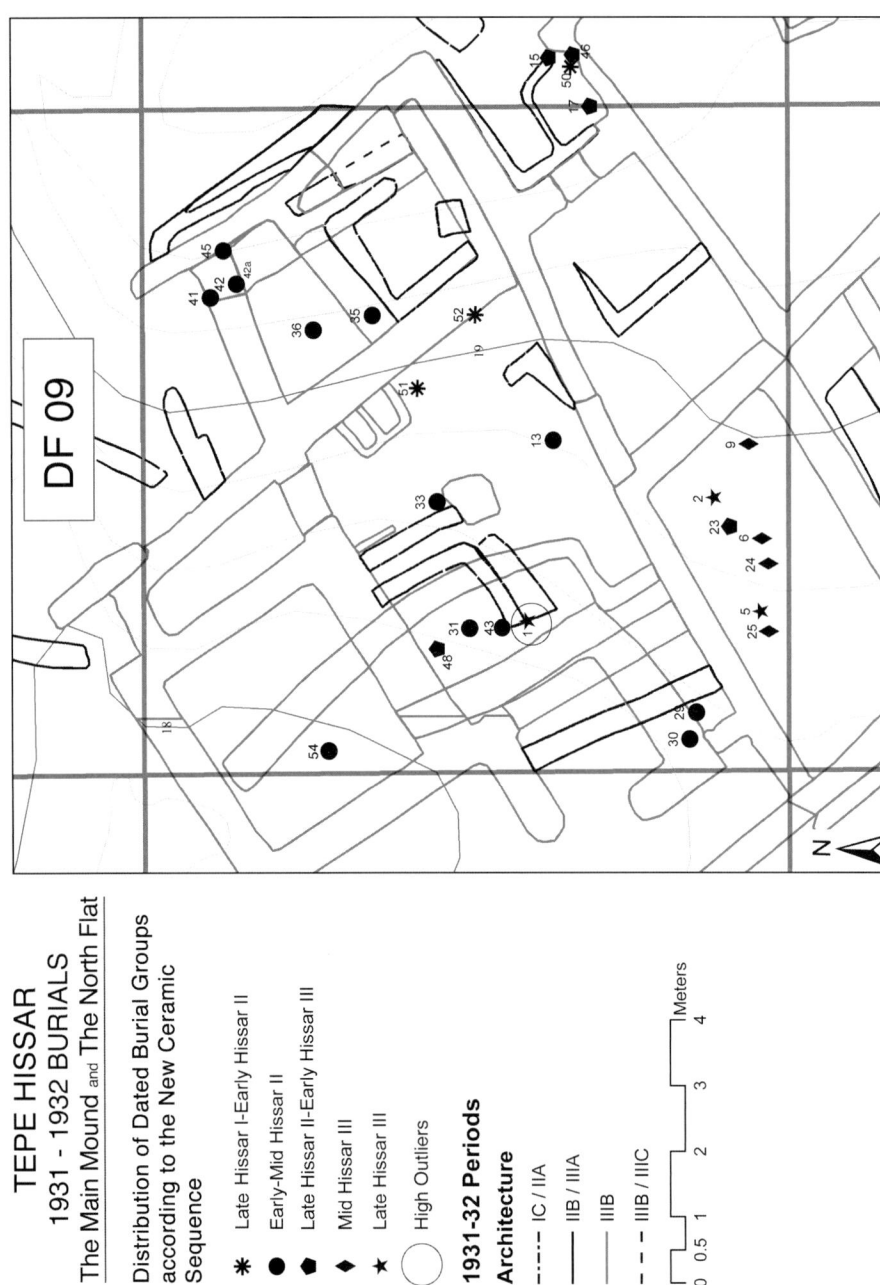

Map 12

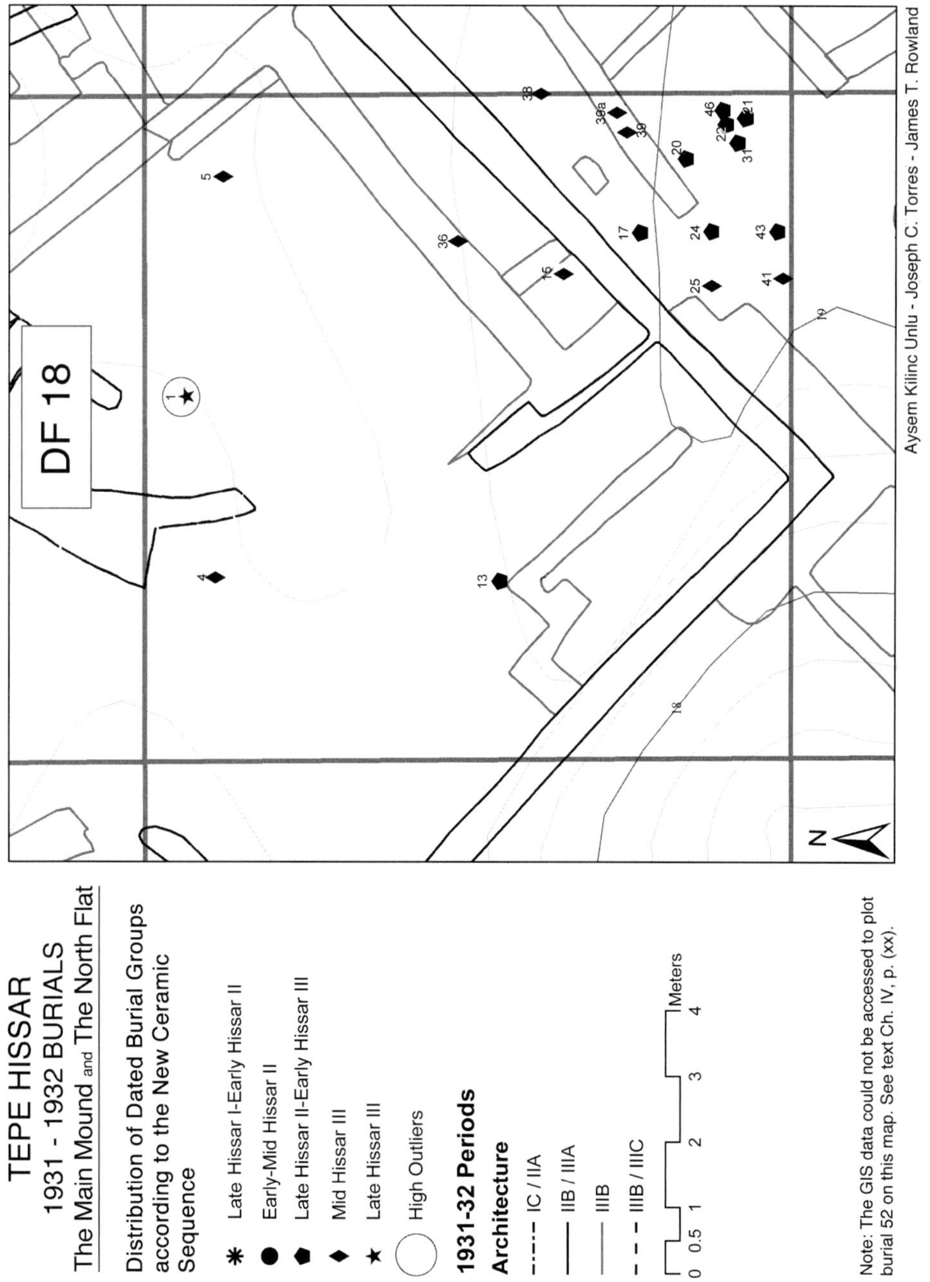

364 THE NEW CHRONOLOGY OF THE BRONZE AGE SETTLEMENT OF TEPE HISSAR, IRAN

Map 14

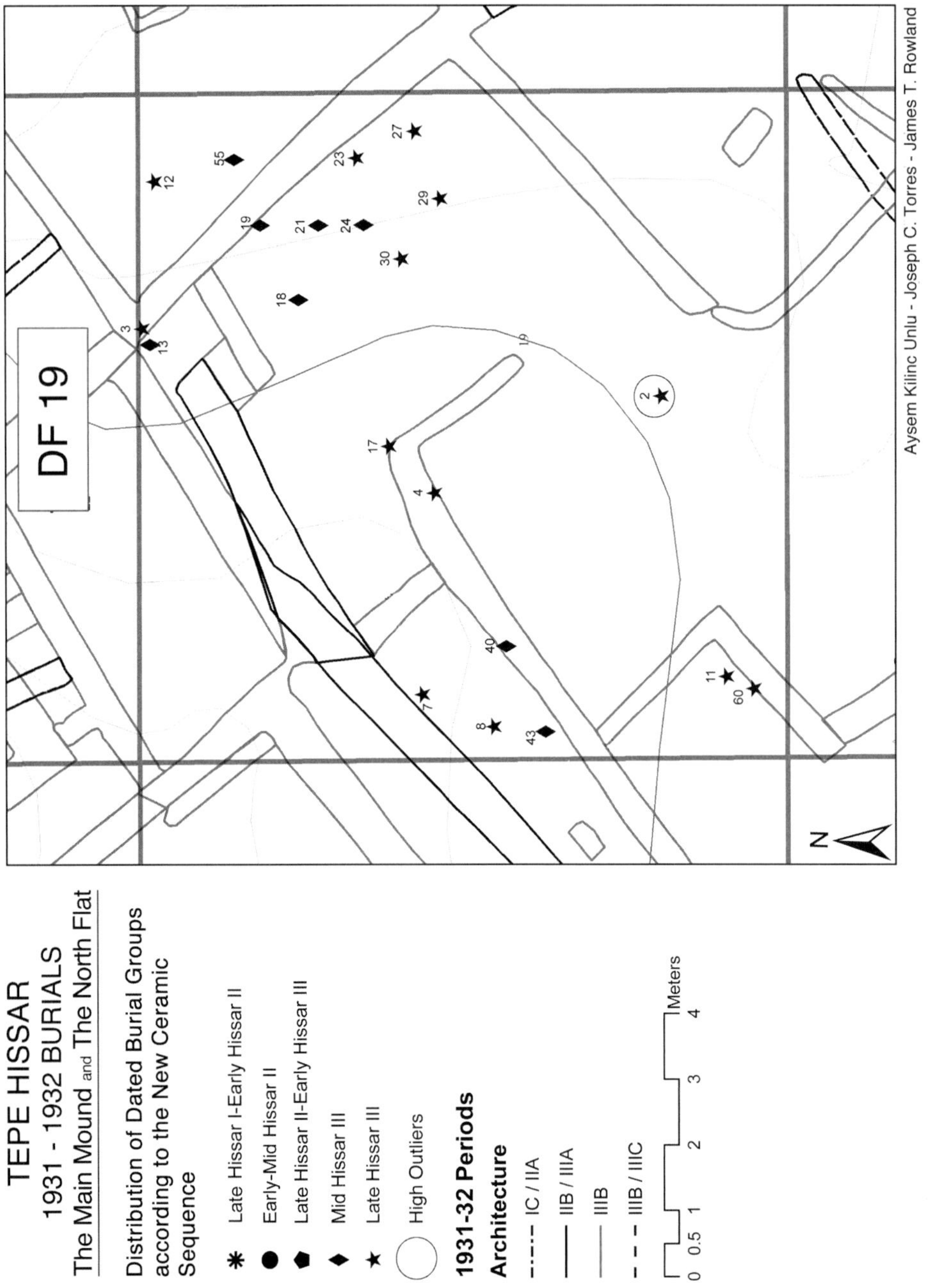

TEPE HISSAR
1931 - 1932 BURIALS
The Main Mound and The North Flat

Distribution of Dated Burial Groups according to the New Ceramic Sequence

✱ Late Hissar I-Early Hissar II
● Early-Mid Hissar II
◆ Late Hissar II-Early Hissar III
★ Mid Hissar III
◯ Late Hissar III
  High Outliers

1931-32 Periods
Architecture
----- IC / IIA
——— IIB / IIIA
——— IIIB
- - - IIIB / IIIC

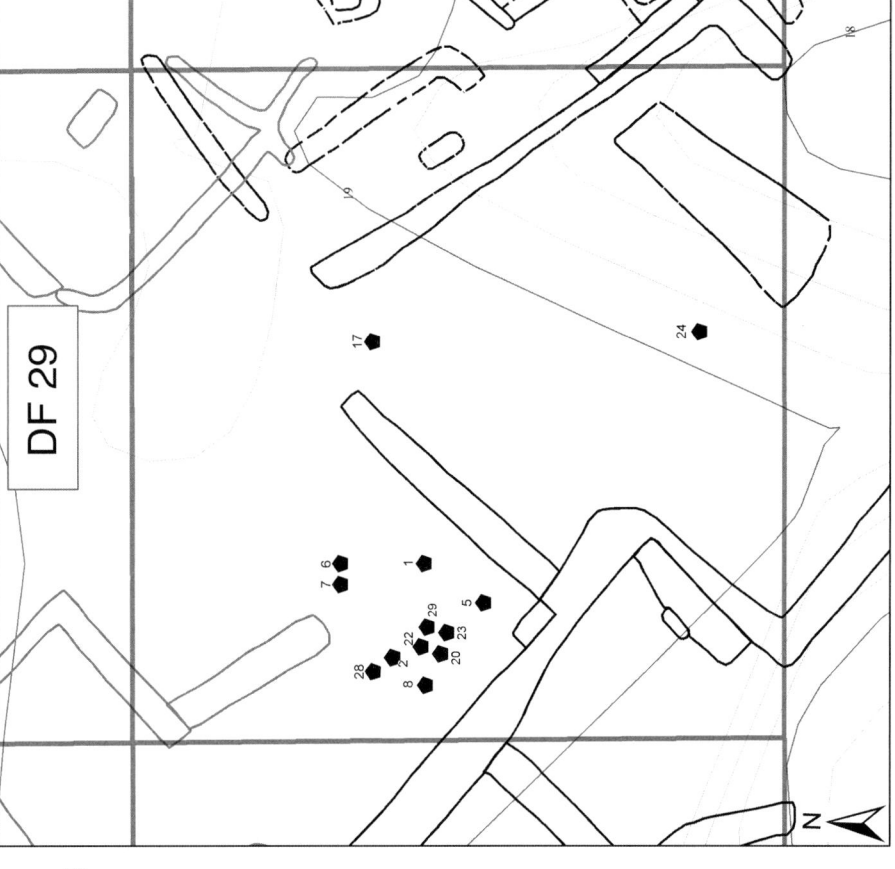

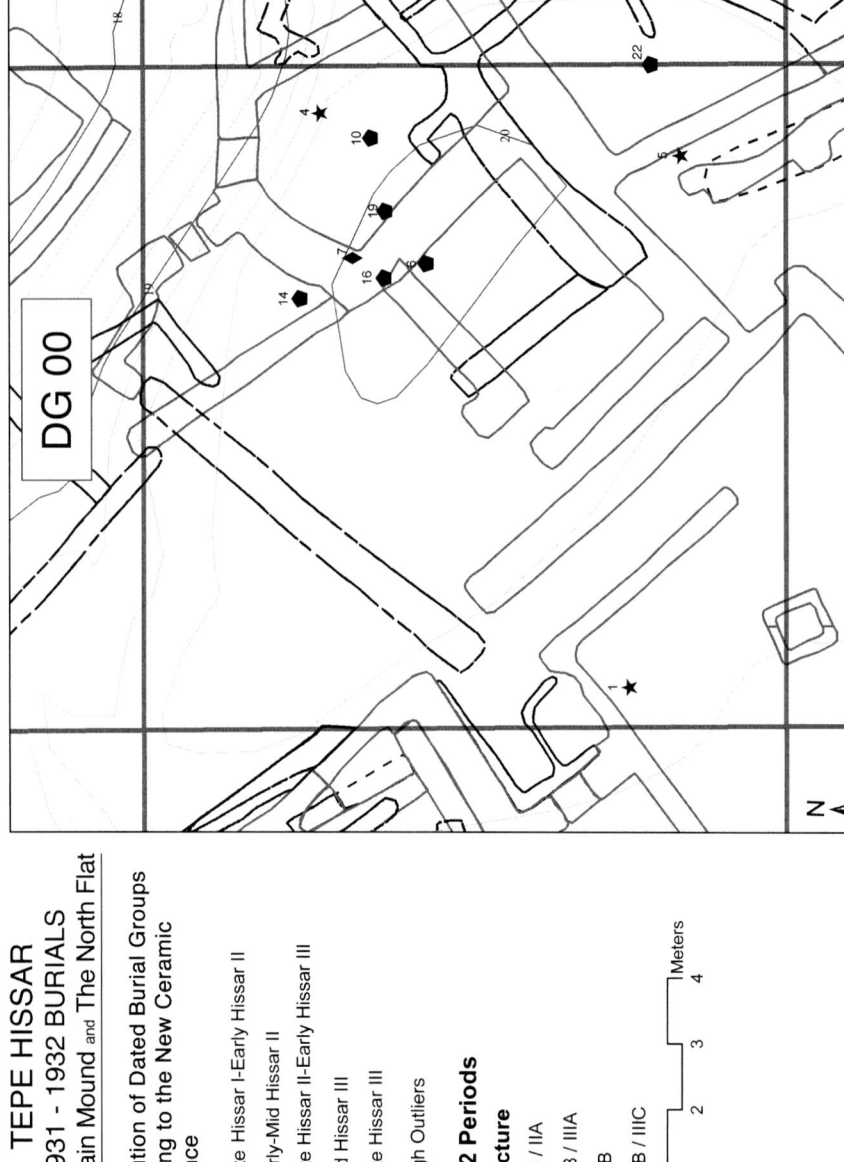

APPENDIX 3: MAPS

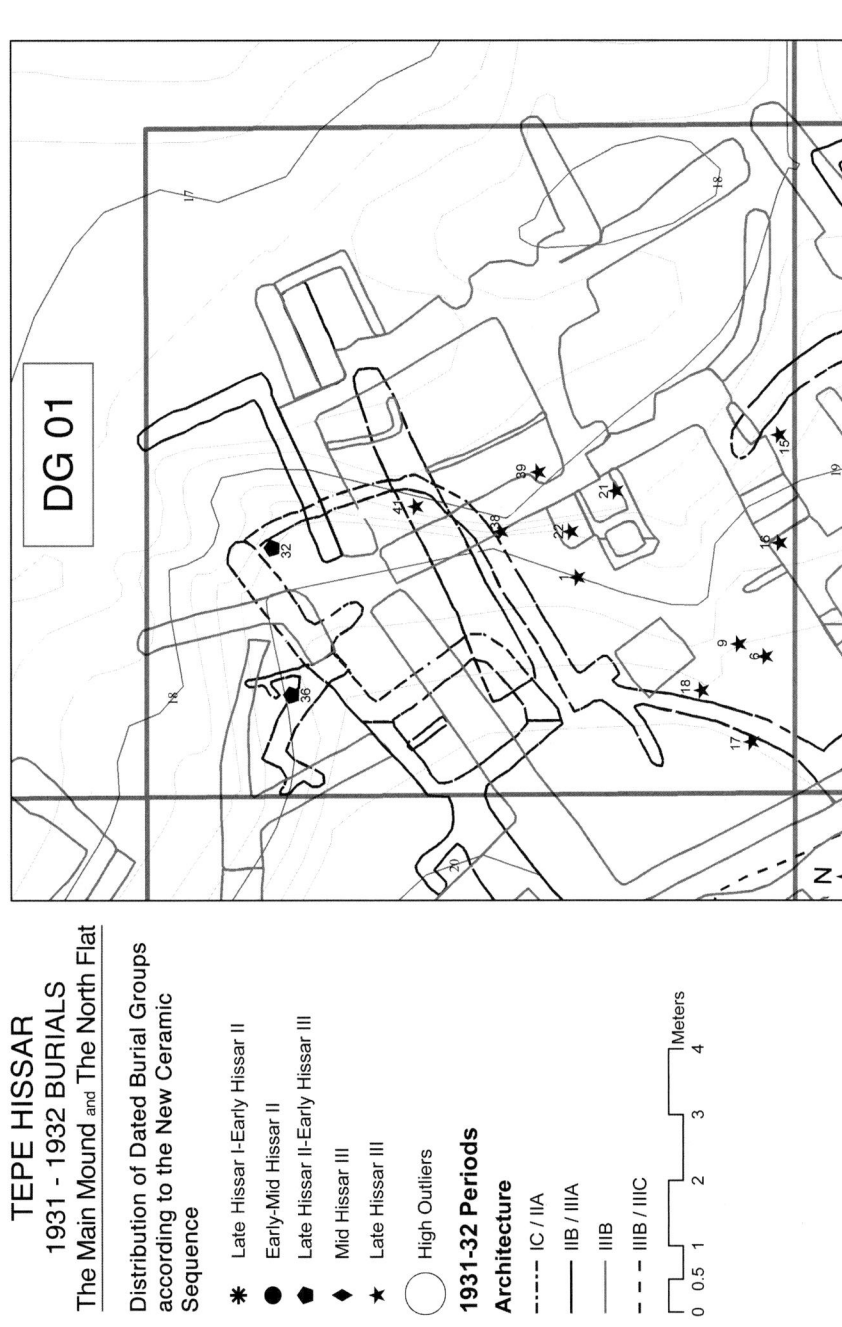

Map 17

TEPE HISSAR
1931 - 1932 BURIALS
The Main Mound and The North Flat

Distribution of Dated Burial Groups
according to the New Ceramic
Sequence

✱ Late Hissar I-Early Hissar II
● Early-Mid Hissar II
⬣ Late Hissar II-Early Hissar III
★ Mid Hissar III
☆ Late Hissar III
◯ High Outliers

1931-32 Periods

Architecture
---·--- IC / IIA
——— IIB / IIIA
——— IIIB
– – – IIIB / IIIC

0 0.5 1 2 3 4 Meters

Aysem Kilinc Unlu - Joseph C. Torres - James T. Rowland

Map 18

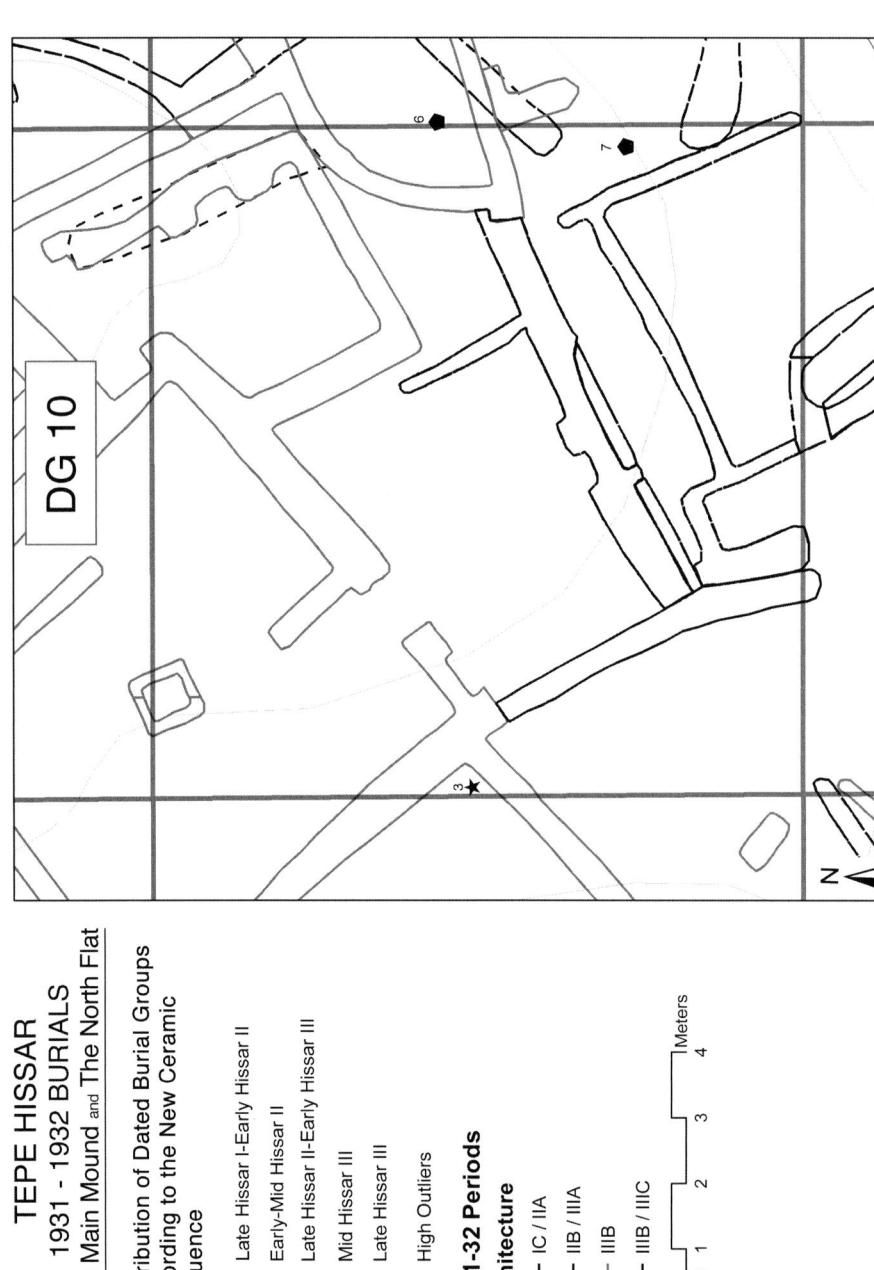

APPENDIX 3: MAPS 369

Map 19

TEPE HISSAR
1931 - 1932 BURIALS
The Main Mound and The North Flat

Distribution of Dated Burial Groups according to the New Ceramic Sequence

✳ Late Hissar I-Early Hissar II
● Early-Mid Hissar II
⬢ Late Hissar II-Early Hissar III
◆ Mid Hissar III
★ Late Hissar III
○ High Outliers

1931-32 Periods
Architecture
- - - - IC / IIA
─── IIB / IIIA
─── IIIB
- - - IIIB / IIIC

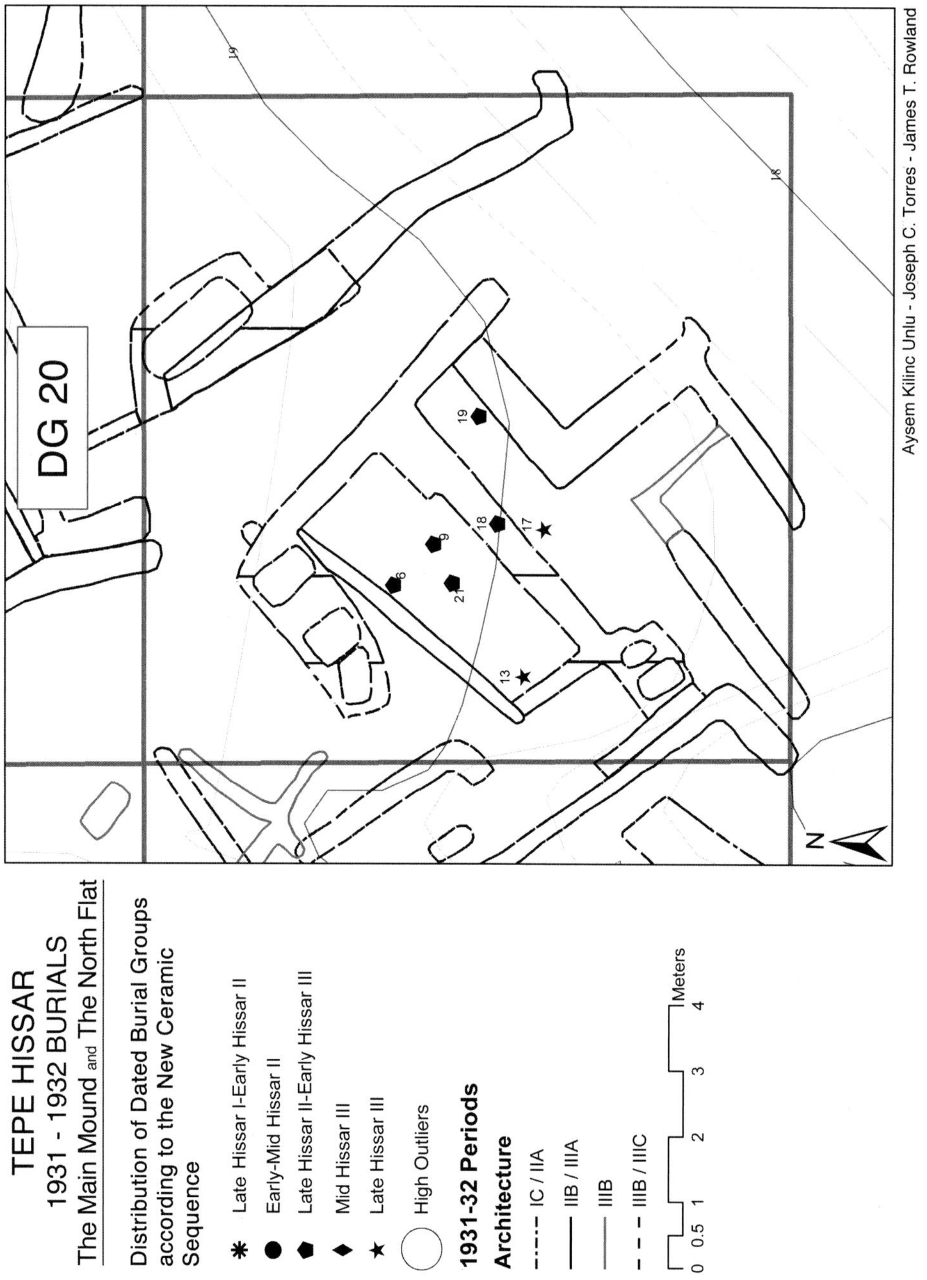

Appendix 4

Radiocarbon Dates from the 1976 Restudy Project

This appendix presents two sets of radiocarbon dates from the 1976 Restudy Project at Tepe Hissar.*

*All samples were wood charcoal.

Dates calibrated using Calib 5.01 (Reimer et al. [2004] calibration)

"P-…" numbers come from PENN XXII in Hurst and Lawn (1984)

"TUNC-20" comes from Bovington et al. (1974)

"SI-6015" comes from Voigt and Dyson (1992)

372 THE NEW CHRONOLOGY OF THE BRONZE AGE SETTLEMENT OF TEPE HISSAR, IRAN

Table A4.1: Radiocarbon Dates from the 1976 Restudy Project

Sample #	C14 date	Context	Schmidt Period	Phase	Date Range (2-sigma)
P-2615	4350±50 BP	NF CF58 Burned Rooms	Hissar II	D-C Transitional Phase	3099–2888 cal BC
P-2617	4420±50 BP	NF CF37 below BB	Hissar II	Phase D?	3328–2916 cal BC
P-2618	3950±60 BP	MM DG20 ovens	Hissar III	Phase B	2606–2271 cal BC
P-2619	4830±60 BP	NF CF57 test trench lot 3	Hissar IC/IIA	Phase E	3737–3506 cal BC
P-2620	3610±70 BP	MM CG90 P-4	Hissar III	Phase A	2153–1761 cal BC
P-2621	4550±70 BP	MM Bldg 3 Area 2, lot 23	Hissar II	Phase D	3393–3025 cal BC
P-2622	5060±320 BP	MM DF09 DS-12	Hissar IC/IIA	F-E Transitional Phase	4534–3029 cal BC
P-2623	5200±70 BP	NF CF57 SW corner lowest	Hissar IC/IIA	Phase F?	4237–3918 cal BC
P-2698	4280±70 BP	NF CF58 Burned Rooms	Hissar II	D-C Transitional Phase	3089–2659 cal BC
P-2699	4410±60 BP	NF CF57 SW corner niche	Hissar II	Phase D	3329–2908 cal BC
P-2700	4370±70 BP	NF CF58 Burned Rooms	Hissar II	D-C Transitional Phase	3135–2884 cal BC
P-2701	3860±60 BP	NF CF47 grey ash (BB)	Hissar III	Phase B	2476–2153 cal BC
P-2703	4270±60 BP	NF CF37-38 below BB	Hissar II	Phase D?	3031–2664 cal BC
P-2704	4340±60 BP	NF CF57 NW corner	Hissar II	D-C Transitional Phase	3113–2872 cal BC
P-2706	4240±70 BP	NF CF58 Burned Rooms	Hissar II	D-C Transitional Phase	3010–2616 cal BC
P-2707	4530±60 BP	MM Bldg 3 kiln 3, lot 35	Hissar II	Phase D	3375–3023 cal BC
P-2708	4440±50 BP	MM Bldg 3 Rm 11, lot 31	Hissar II	Phase D	3331–2937 cal BC
P-2709	4540±60 BP	MM Bldg 3 Rm 1, lot 11	Hissar II	Phase D	3379–3033 cal BC
P-2710	4380±70 BP	MM Bldg 3 Rm 7, lot 37	Hissar II	Phase D	3328–2890 cal BC
P-2711	4570±60 BP	MM Bldg 3 Rm 3, lot 35	Hissar II	Phase D	3397–3092 cal BC
P-2715	4450±60 BP	SH DG61 Bldg 4	Hissar II	Phase D?	3339–2941 cal BC
P-2759	4790±60 BP	SH DF89 lapis/Cu workshop	Hissar II	Phase E? (Tosi phase 5-6)	3684–3379 cal BC
P-2760	4530±50 BP	MM CG90 P-15	Hissar II	Phase D	3369–3076 cal BC
P-2763	4870±70 BP	SH DF79 "below Cu working"	Hissar IC/IIA	Phase E? (Tosi phase 7)	3802–3510 cal BC

APPENDIX 4: RADIOCARBON DATES FROM THE 1976 RESTUDY PROJECT

Table A4.1 (cont'd)

Sample #	C14 date	Context	Schmidt Period	Phase	Date Range (2-sigma)
P-2764	4910±70 BP	TTw Pted Pottery	Hissar IC/IIA	Phase F?	3819–3615 cal BC
P-2765	5020±70 BP	SH DF88 "below Cu working"	Hissar IC/IIA	Phase F? (Tosi phase 7)	3958–3675 cal BC
P-2766	4700±50 BP	SH DF89 lapis/Cu workshop	Hissar II	Phase E? (Tosi phase 5-6)	3626–3367 cal BC
P-2767	4410±60 BP	TTw Grey Ware levels	Hissar II	Phase D?	3329–2908 cal BC
P-2773	4500±50 BP	SH DG80 lapis stratum	Hissar II	Phase D? (Tosi phase 4)	3356–3037 cal BC
P-2774	5750±60 BP	MM DF09 DS-5	Hissar IC/IIA	Phase E	4730–4466 cal BC
SI-6015	4110±60 BP	NF oven in Rm 7, BB	Hissar III	Phase B?	2877–2555 cal BC
TUNC-20	3483±63 BP	TH CH86 below x-9	Hissar IIIC	Phase A	1960–1645 cal BC

Legend for Abbreviations in Context Column of Table A4.1:

MM = Main Mound

NF = North Flat

SH = South Hill

TH = Treasure Hill

TT = The Twins

Bibliography

Abdi, K. 2002. *Strategies of Herding: Pastoralism in the Middle Chalcolithic Period of the West Central Zagros Mountains.* Ann Arbor: University of Michigan.

———. 2003. The Early Development of Pastoralism in the Central Zagros Mountains. *Journal of World Prehistory* 17(4):395–447.

Afshar, Zahra. 2014. Mobility and Economic Transition in the 5th to the 2nd Millennium B.C. in the Population of the Central Iranian Plateau, Tepe Hissar. PhD diss. Durham, England: Durham University.

Ajango, K.M. 2010. New Thoughts on the Trade of Lapis Lazuli in the Ancient Near East c. 3000–2000 B.C. Unpublished manuscript, University of Wisconsin-La Crosse.

Alden, J. 1982. Trade and Politics in Proto-Elamite Iran. *Current Anthropology* 23(6):613–40.

Alizadeh, A. 2003. Some Observations Based on the Nomadic Character of Fars Prehistoric Cultural Development. In *Yeki bud, yeki nabud: Essays on the Archaeology of Iran in Honor of William M. Sumner*, ed. N. Miller and K Abdi, pp. 83–97. Los Angeles: University of California.

———. 2008. Archaeology and the Question of Mobile Pastoralism in Late Prehistory. In *The Archaeology of Mobility: Old World and New World Nomadism*, ed. H. Barnard and W.Z. Wendrich, pp. 78–114. Los Angeles: University of California.

Algaze, G. 2005. *The Uruk World System: The Dynamics of Expansion of Early Mesopotamian Civilization.* Chicago: University of Chicago Press.

———. 1993. *The Uruk World System.* Chicago: Chicago University Press.

Amiet, P. 1986. *L'Age des échanges inter-Iranien.* Paris: Ministère de la Culture et de la Communication, Editions de la Réunion des Musées Nationaux.

Arne, T.J. 1945. *Excavations at Shah Tepé, Iran.* Stockholm: Goteborg, Elanders boktryckeri aktiebolag.

Azarnoush, M., and B. Helwing. 2005. Recent Archaeological Research in Iran—Prehistory to Iron Age. *Archäologische Mitteilungen aus Iran und Turan* 37:189–246.

Beale, T.W. 1973. Early Trade in Highland Iran: A View from a Source Area. *World Archaeology* 5(2):133–48.

Bennett, L. 1989. The Seals of Tappeh Hesar. In *Tappeh Hesar: reports of the Restudy Project, 1976*, ed. R.H. Dyson Jr. and S. Howard, pp. 127–30. Firenze: Casa editrice Le Lettere.

Bilgi, Ö. 1984. Metal Objects from İkiztepe-Turkey. *Beiträge zur Allgemeinen und Vergleichenden Archäologie* 6:31–97.

———. 1990. Metal Objects from İkiztepe-Turkey. *Beiträge zur Allgemeinen und Vergleichenden Archäologie* 9(10):119–219.

———. 1999. İkiztepe'de Ele Geçen Son Buluntular Işığında Orta Karadeniz Bölgesi Protohistorik Çağ Maden Sanatı Hakkında Yeni Gözlemler. *Türk Tarih Kongresi* 7:41–50.

———. 2005. Distinguished Burials of the Early Bronze Age Graveyard at İkiztepe in Turkey. *Anadolu Araştırmaları Dergisi* 18(2):15–113.

Biscione, R. 1976 Unpublished field notes on Tepe Hissar, in Italian. Philadelphia: University of Pennsylvania Museum Archives.

Bloch, M. 1971. *Placing the Dead: Tombs, Ancestral Villages, and Kinship Organization in Madagascar.* London: Seminar Press.

———. 1974. Symbols, Song, Dance, and Features of Articulation. *Archives européenes de sociologie* 15:55–81.

———. 1994. *Placing the Dead: Tombs, Ancestral Villages and Kinship Organization in Madagascar.* Prospect

Heights, IL: Waveland Press.

Bloch, M., and J.P. Parry. 1982. *Death and the Regeneration of Life*. Cambridge: Cambridge University Press.

Bouchez, R.. 1976. Determination des Modes de Cuisson de Ceramiques de l'Iran Proto-historique, d'apres leurs proprietes magnetiques et leurs specters. *IXème Congrès de l'UISPP*, pp. 13–18. Nice: Union Internationale des Sciences Préhistoriques et Protohistoriques.

Bourdieu, P. 1977. *Outline of a Theory of Practice*. Cambridge: Cambridge University Press.

———. 1990. *The Logic of Practice*. Stanford: Stanford University Press.

Bovington, C.H., R.H. Dyson, Jr., A. Mahdavi, and R. Masoumi. 1974. The Radiocarbon Evidence for the Terminal Date of Hissar IIIC Culture. *Iran* 12:195–99.

Brady, I. 1999. Review Essay: Ritual as Cognitive Process, Performance as History. *Current Anthropology* 40:243–48.

Bradley, R. 1990. *The Passage of Arms: An Archaeological Analysis of Prehistoric Hoards and Votive Deposits*. Cambridge: Cambridge University Press.

Brown, J. 1981. Mortuary Practices for the Third Millennium: 1966–2006. In *Performing Death: Social Analyses of Funerary Traditions in the Ancient Near East and Mediterranean*, ed. N. Laneri, pp. 299–308. Chicago: The Oriental Institute of the University of Chicago.

Bulgarelli, G.M. 1972. Il Paleolitico della Grotta di Torre Nave (Praia a Mare-Cosenza). *Quaternaria* 16:149–88.

———. 1973. Survey of Excavations in Iran 1971–72: Tepe Hissar. *IRAN: Journal of the British Institute of Persian Studies* 11:206.

———. 1974. Tepe Hissar. Preliminary Report on a Surface Survey, August 1972. *East and West* 24(1–2):15–27.

———. 1979. The Lithic Industry of Tepe Hissar at the Light of Recent Excavation. In *South Asian Archaeology* 1977, ed. M. Taddei, pp. 39–54. Naples: Istituto Universitario Orientale.

Campbell, S. 1995. Death for the Living in the Late Neolithic in North Mesopotamia. In *The Archaeology of Death in the Ancient Near East: Proceedings of the Manchester Conference, 16th–20th December 1992*, ed. S. Campbell and A. Green, pp. 29–34. Oxford: Oxbow Books.

Carter, E. 1993. Michèle CASANOVA. 1991. – La vaisselle d'albâtre de Mésopotamie, d'Iran et d'Asie centrale aux IIIe et IIe millénaires avant J.-C. *Paléorient* 1213–14.

Casanova, M. 1991. *La vaisselle d'albâtre de Mésopotamie, d'Iran et d'Asie centrale aux IIIe et IIe millénaires avant J.-C.* Paris: Editions recherché sur les civilizations.

———. 1992. The Sources of Lapis-lazuli Found in Iran. In *South Asian Archaeology 1989*, ed. C. Jarrige, pp. 49–56. Madison, WI: Prehistory Press.

Chapman, R. 2003. *Archaeologies of Complexity*. London: Routledge.

Chapman, R., and K. Randsborg. 1981. Approaches to the Archaeology of Death. In *The Archaeology of Death*, ed. R. Chapman, I. Kinnes, and K. Randsborg, pp. 1–24. Cambridge: Cambridge University Press.

Chesson, M.S. 2007. Remembering and Forgetting in Early Btonze Age Mortuary Practices on the Southeastern Dead Sea Plain, Jordan. In *Performing Death: Social Analyses of Funerary Traditions in the Ancient Near East and Mediterranean*, ed. N. Laneri, pp. 109–23. Chicago: The Oriental Institute of the University of Chicago.

Clark, J.E. and W.J. Parry. 1990. Craft Specialization and Cultural Complexity. Research in *Economic Anthropology* 12:289–346.

Cleuziou, S. 1986. Tureng Tepe and Burnished Grey Ware: A Question of "Frontier"? *Oriens Antiquus* 25:221–56.

———. 1991. Ceramics IX: The Bronze Age in Northeastern Persia. *EIr* 5(3):297–300.

Contenau, G., and R. Ghirshman. 1933. Rapport préliminaire sur les fouilles de Tépé-Giyan, près Néhavend (Perse) Première campagne (1931). *Syria* 14:1–11.

Contenau, G., R. Ghirshman, and H. Vallois. 1936. *Fouilles du Tepe-Giyan*. Paris: E. Leroux.

Costantini, L., and R.H. Dyson Jr. 1990. The Ancient Agriculture of the Damghan Plain: The Archaeological Evidence from Tepe Hissar. In *Economy and Settlement in the Near East*, ed. N.F. Miller, pp. 46–64. Philadelphia: MASCA Research Papers in Science and Archaeology.

Crossland, R.A. 1971. Immigrants from the North. In *Cambridge Ancient History Volume 1 Part 2; Early History of the Middle East*, ed. I.E.S. Edwards, C.J. Gad, and N.G.L. Hammond, pp. 824–76. Cambridge: Cambridge University Press.

Cultraro, M. 2007. Combined Efforts till Death: Funerary Ritual and Social Statements in the Aegean Early Bronze Age. In *Performing Death: Social Analyses of Funerary Traditions in the Ancient Near East and Mediterranean*, ed. N. Laneri, pp. 81–108. Chicago: The Oriental Institute of the University of Chicago.

Daher, A.G. 1968. A Study of Grave Groups from Tureng Tepe in Late Third and early Second Millenium B.C. in Northeast Iran as Reconstructed from the Excavations During 1931–32. Master's thesis, University of Pennsylvania.

De Morgan, J., G. Coutteau, V. Gauthier, H. Douvillé, and C. Huart. 1896. *Mission Scientifique en Perse*. Paris: E. Leroux.

Deshayes, J. 1968. Tureng Tepe and the Plain of Gorgan in the Bronze Age. *Archaeologia Viva* 1:35–38

———. 1969. New Evidence for the Indo-Europeans from Tureng Tepe, Iran. *Archaeology* 22(1)10–17.

———. 1975. T*essons de ceramique peinte de Tappeh Hesar*. Tehran: Iranian Centre for Archaeological Research.

———. 1977. A propos des terrasses hautes de la fin du liie millénaire en Iran et en Asie centrale. In *Le Plateau iranien et l'Asie Centrale des origines à la conquete islamique: Leurs relations a la lumiere des documents archeologiques*, ed. J. Deshayes, pp. 95–111. Paris: CNRS.

Dyson Jr., R.H. 1957. Iran, 1956. *University Museum Bulletin* 21(1):27–39.

———. 1965. Problems of Protohistoric Iran as Seen from Hasanlu. *Journal of Near Eastern Studies* 24:193–217.

———. 1972. The Hasanlu Project, 1961–1967. In *The Memorial Volume of the Vth International Congress of Iranian Art and Archaeology, Tehran-Isfahan-Shiraz, 11th–18th April 1968, Vol. 1*, ed. A. Tajvidi and M.Y. Kiyānī, pp. 39–58. Tehran: Ministry of Culture and Arts.

———. 1976. Unpublished Archival Field Notes. Philadelphia: Penn Museum Tepe Hissar Archive.

———. 1987. The Relative and Absolute Chronology of Hissar II and the Proto-Elamite Horizon of Northern Iran. In *Chronologies in the Near East*, ed. O. Aurenche, J. Elvin, and F. Hours, pp. 647–78. Oxford: Archaeopress.

———. 1989. The Burned Building of Tepe Hissar IIIB: A Restatement. *Bastan Chenassi va Honar-e Iran* 9–10:57–83.

———. 1991. Ceramics: i. The Neolithic Period through the Bronze Age in Northeastern and North-Central Persia. *Encyclopedia Iranica* 5(3):266–75.

Dyson Jr., R.H., and S.M. Howard. 1989. *Tappeh Hesar: Reports of the Restudy Project, 1976*. Firenze: Casa editrice Le Lettere.

Dyson Jr., R.H., and B. Lawn. 1989. Key Stratigraphic and Radiocarbon Elements for the 1976 Hesar Sequence. In *Tappeh Hesar: Reports of the Restudy Project, 1976*, ed. R.H. Dyson Jr. and S.M. Howard, pp. 124. Firenze: Casa Editrice Le Lettere.

Dyson Jr., R.H., and W.S.C. Remsen. 1989. Observations on Architecture and Stratigraphy at Tappeh Hesar. In *Tappeh Hesar: Reports of the Restudy Project, 1976*, ed. R.H. Dyson Jr. and S.M. Howard, pp. 69–109. Firenze: Casa editrice Le Lettere.

Dyson Jr., R.H., and C.P. Thornton. 2009. Shir-i Shian and the Fifth Millennium of Northern Iran. *IRAN: Journal of the British Institute of Persian Studies* 47:1–22.

Dyson Jr., R.H., and M. Tosi. 1989. Introduction. In *Tappeh Hesar: Reports of the Restudy Project, 1976*, ed. R.H. Dyson Jr. and S.M. Howard, pp. 1–6. Firenze: Casa editrice Le Lettere.

Dyson Jr., R.H., and M.M. Voigt. 1989. Bronze Age. *Encyclopaedia Iranica* 4(5):472–78.

Earle, T. 2002. *Bronze Age Economics*. New York: Westview Press.

Fahlander, F., and T. Oestigaard. 2008. *The Materiality of Death: Bodies, Burials, Beliefs*. Oxford: Archaeopress.

Finlayson, B. 2010. Agency in the Pre-Pottery Neolithic A. In *The Development of Pre-State Communities in the Ancient Near East: Studies in Honour of Edgar Peltenburg*, ed. D. Bolger and L.C. Maguire, pp. 141–46. Oxford: Oxbow Books.

Gerasimoff, I. 1931. Potsherd Catalogue Tepe Hissar 1931. Philadelphia: University of Pennsylvania Museum Archives (Box 9).

Ghirshman, R. 1938. *Fouilles de Sialk près de Kashan, 1933, 1934, 1937*. Paris: Geuthner.

———. 1977. *L'Iran et la migration des Indo-Aryens et des Iraniens*. Leiden: E.J. Brill.

Giddens, A. 1984. *The Constitution of Society: Outline of the Theory of Structuration*. Oakland: University of California Press.

Gürsan-Salzmann, A. 1992. Alaca Höyük: A Reassessment of the Excavation and Sequence of the Early Bronze Age Settlement. PhD diss., University of Pennsylvania.

———. 2007. *Exploring Iran*. Philadelphia: University of Pennsylvania Museum of Archaeology and Anthropology.

Hakemi, A. 1972. Catalogue de l'exposition LUT Xabis (Shahdad). In *Premier Symposium Annuel de la recherche Archéologique en Iran, Téhéran*.

———. 1978 Découverte d'une civilisation préhistorique à Shahdad au bord ouest du Lut, Kerman. In *Memorial Volume of the VIth International Congress of Iranian Art and Archaeology, Oxford, 1972*, ed. M.Y. Kiani, pp. 131–50. Tehran: Iranian Centre for Archaeological Research.

———. 1997. The Original Place of Production of Chlorite Stone Objects in the 3rd Millennium B.C. *East and West* 47(1–4):11–40.

Harris, M.V. 1989. Hesar Preliminary Report: Objects by Materials (1976). In *Tappeh Hesar: Reports of the Restudy Project, 1976*, ed. R.H. Dyson Jr. and S.M. Howard, pp. 145–48. Firenze: Casa editrice Le Lettere.

Helwing, B. 2011. The small finds from Arisman. In *Early Mining and Metallurgy on the Western Central Iranian Plateau. Report on the first five years of research of the Joint Iranian-German Research Project (Archäologie in Iran und Turan 9)*, ed. A. Vatandoust, H. Parzinger, and B. Helwing, pp. 254–327. Mainz: Philipp von Zabern.

———. 2012a. Late Chalcolithic Craft Traditions at the North-Eastern 'Periphery' of Mesopotamia: Potters vs. Smiths in the Southern Caucausus. *Origini* 34:201–20.

———. 2012b. The Iranian Plateau. In *A Companion to the Archaeology of the Near East*, ed. D.T. Potts, pp. 501–11. Oxford: Blackwell.

———. 2013. Some Thoughts on the Mode of Culture Change in the Fourth Millenium BC Iranian Highlands. In *Ancient Iran and its Neighbours: Local Developments and Long-Range Interactions in the Fourth Millennium BC*, ed. C. Petrie, pp. 93–100. Oxford: Oxbow Books.

Herrmann, G. 1968. Lapis Lazuli: The Early Phases of Its Trade. *Iraq* 30(1):21–57.

Hertz, R. 1960. *Death and the Right Hand*. London: Cohen and West.

Herzfeld, E. 1988. *Iran in the Ancient East: Archaeological Studies Presented in the Lowell Lectures at Boston*. New York: Hacker Art Books.

Hiebert, F. 1998. Central Asians on the Iranian Plateau: A Model for Indo-Iranian Expansionism. In *Bronze and Iron Age Cultures of Eastern Central Asia*, ed. V. Mair, pp. 148–61. Philadelphia: University of Pennsylvania Museum of Archaeology and Anthropology.

Hiebert, F., and R.H. Dyson Jr. 2002. Prehistoric Nishapur and the Frontier Between Central Asia and Iran. *Iranica Antiqua* 37:113–49.

Hole, F. 1974. Tepe Tūlāʾi: An Early Campsite in Khuzestan, Iran. *Paléorient* 2(2):219–37.

Horne, L. 1989. Ground Stone Tools and Artifacts at Tappeh Hesar, 1976. In *Tappeh Hesar: Reports of the Restudy Project, 1976*, ed. R.H. Dyson Jr. and S.M. Howard, pp. 121–23. Firenze: Casa editrice Le Lettere.

———. 1994. *Village Spaces*. Washington, DC: Smithsonian.

Howard, S.M. 1976. Unpublished Field Notes. Philadelphia: University of Pennsylvania Museum Archives.

———. 1989a. The Stratigraphic Sequence of the Main Mound at Tappeh Hesar. In *Tappeh Hesar: Reports of the Restudy Project, 1976*, ed. R.H. Dyson Jr. and S.M. Howard, pp. 55–68. Firenze: Casa editrice Le Lettere.

———. 1989b Unpublished field notes. Philadelphia: University of Pennsylvania Museum Archives.

———. n.d. Unpublished Manuscript. Philadelphia: University of Pennsylvania Museum Archives.

Hurst, B.J., and B. Lawn. 1984. University of Pennsylvania Radiocarbon Dates XXII. *Radiocarbon* 26(2):212–40.

Katz, D. 2007. Sumerian Funerary Rituals in Context. In *Performing Death: Social Analyses of Funerary Traditions in the Ancient Near East and Mediterranean*, ed. N. Laneri, pp. 167–88. Chicago: The Oriental Institute of the University of Chicago.

Khazanov, A.M. 1994. *Nomads and the Outside World*. Madison, WI: University of Wisconsin Press.

———. 2009. Specific Characteristics of Chalcolithic and Bronze Age Pastoralism in the Near East. In *Nomads, Tribes, and the State in the Ancient Near East*, ed. J. Szuchman, pp. 119–27. Chicago: University of Chicago Press.

Kohl, P.L. 1975. *Seeds of Upheaval: The Production of Chlorite at Tepe Yahya and an Analysis of Commodity Production and Trade in Southwest Asia in the Mid-Third Millennium*. Cambridge: Harvard University.

———. 1977. A Note on Chlorite Artefacts from Shahr-I Sokhta. *East and West* 27(1–4):111–27.

———. 1978. The Balance of Trade in Southwest Asia in the Mid-3rd Millennium B.C. *Current Anthropology* 19(3):483–84.

Kopytoff, I. 1986. The Cultural Biography of Things: Commoditization as Process. In *The Social Life of Things: Commodities in Cultural Perspective*, ed. A. Appadurai, pp. 64–91. Cambridge: Cambridge University Press.

Koşay, H.Z. 1951. *Les Fouilles d'Alaca Höyük: Entreprises par la Société d'Histoire Turque: Rapport Preliminaire sur les Traveux en 1937–39*. Ankara: Türk Tarih Kurumu Basımevi.

Krogman, W.M. 1940a. Racial Types from Tepe Hissar, Iran from the Late Fifth to the Early Second Millennium B.C.: A Chapter in the Protohistory of Asia Minor and the Middle East. *Verhandelingen der Koninklijke Akademie van Wetenschappen te Amsterdam, Afdeeling Natuurkunde: Tweede Sectie* 39(2):1–87.

———. 1940b. The Skeletal and Dental Pathology of an Early Iranian Site. *Bulletin of the History of Medicine* 8:28–48.

———. 1940c. The Peoples of Early Iran and Their Ethnic Affiliations. *American Journal of Physical Anthropology* 26:269–308.

Lamberg-Karlovsky, C.C. 1970. *Excavations at Tepe Yahya, Iran: 1967–1969: Progress Report 1*. Cambridge, MA: Harvard University Press.

———. 2009. Structure, Agency and Commerce in the

Ancient Near East. *Iranica Antiqua* 44:47–88.

Lamberg-Karlovsky, C.C., and T. Beale. 1986. *Excavations at Tepe Yahya, Iran, 1967–1975: The Early Periods.* Cambridge: Harvard University Press.

Lamberg-Karlovsky, C.C., and F. Hiebert. 1992. The Relation of the Finds from Shahdad to Those of Sites in Central Asia. *The Journal of the Ancient Near Eastern Studies* 21:135–40

Lamberg-Karlovsky, C.C., and M. Tosi. 1973. Shahr-i Sokhta and Tepe Yahya: Tracks on the Earliest History of the Iranian Plateau. *East and West* 23(1–2):15–53.

Laneri, N. 2007. An Archaeology of Funerary Rituals. In *Performing Death: Social Analyses of Funerary Traditions in the Ancient Near East and Mediterranean*, ed. N. Laneri, pp. 1–13. Chicago: The Oriental Institute of the University of Chicago.

Le Breton, L. 1957. The Early Periods at Susa, Mesopotamian Relations. *Iraq* 19:79–124.

Leitner, K.1990. Unpublished Field Notes. Philadelphia: University of Pennsylvania Museum Archives.

Mahfroozi, A., and C.K. Piller. 2009. First Preliminary Report on the Joint Iranian-German Excavations at Gohar Tappe, Mazandara, Iran. *AMIT Band* 41:177–205.

Malinowski, B. 1929. *The Sexual Life of Savages in North-Western Melanesia.* New York: Eugencis Pub. Co.

Majidzadeh, Y. 1982. Lapis Lazuli and Great Khorassan Road. *Paléorient* 8(1):59–69.

Mashkour, M. 1997. The Subsistence Economy of Hissar IIIB: The Study of Faunal Remains. In *Archaeological Reports of Iran, Vol 1*, ed. M. Malikzādah, pp. 125–32. Tehran: ICAR.

———. 2003. Mamasani in the Fourth Millennium BC. In *Ancient Iran and Its Neighbours: Local Developments and Long-Range Interactions in the Fourth Millennium BC*, ed. C. Petrie, pp. 171–94. Oxford: Oxbow Books.

———. 2009. Faunal Remains from Tol-e Nurabad and Tol-e Spid. In *The Mamasani Archaeological Project Stage One: A Report on the First Two Seasons of the ICAR – University of Sydney Expedition to the Mamasani District, Fars Province, Iran*, ed. D.T. Potts, K. Roustaci, C.A. Petrie, and L.R. Weeks, pp. 135–46. Oxford: Archaeopress.

Mashkour, M., and E. Yaghmai. 1995. Unpublished Field Notes for Tepe Hissar Salvage Excavations.

———. 1996. Faunal Remains from Tappeh Hessar (Iran), Results of the 1995 Excavation. In *Proceedings of XIII UISPP Congress*, ed. C. Arias, A. Bietti, L. Castelletti, and C. Peretto, pp. 543–51. Forli: Abaco Edizioni.

Masson, V.M. 1988. *Altyn-Depe.* Philadelphia: University of Pennsylvania Museum of Archaeology and Anthropology.

Matthews, R. 2003. *The Archaeology of Mesopotamia: Theories and Approaches (Approaching the Ancient World).* London: Routledge.

Matthews, R., and H. Fazeli 2004. Copper and Complexity: Iran and Mesopotamia in the Fourth Millenium B.C. *Iran-London-British Institute of Persian Studies.* 42:61–76.

Meder, O.G. 1989. The Geomorphological and Ecological Setting of Tappeh Hesar in the Damghan Plain, 1976. In *Tappeh Hesar: Reports of the Restudy Project, 1976*, ed. R.H. Dyson Jr. and S.M. Howard, pp. 7–12. Firenze: Casa editrice Le Lettere.

Metcalf, P., and R. Huntington. 1991. *Celebrations of Death: The Anthropology of Mortuary Ritual.* Cambridge: Cambridge University Press.

Momenzadeh, M. and N. Nezafati. 2000. Sources of Ores and Minerals Used in Arisman: A Preliminary Study. In *Preliminary Report on Archaeometallurgical Investigations Around the Prehistoric Site of Arisman near Kashan, Western Central Iran (Archaeologische mitteilungen aus Iran and Turan, Band 32, sonder druck)*, ed. N.N. Chegini, M. Momenzadeh, H. Parzinger, E. Pernicka, T. Stöllner, R. Vatandoust, G. Weisgerber, in collaboration with N. Boroffka, A. Chaichi, D. Hasanalian, Z. Hezarkhani, M.M. Eskandari, and N. Nezafati. Berlin: Dietrich Reimer Verlag GmbH.

Momenzadeh, N. 2004. Metallic Mineral Resources of Iran, Mined in Ancient Times; A Brief Review (contributed by: Ali Hajisoltan & Mahsa Momenzadeh). In *Persia's Ancient Splendour (Persiens Antike Pracht): Mining, Handicraft and Archaeology*, ed. T. Stöllner, R. Slotta, and A. Vatandoust, pp. 8–21. Bochum: Deutsches Bergbau-Museum.

Mousavi, A. 2008. Late Bronze Age in North-Eastern Iran: An Alternative Approach to Persisting Problems. *IRAN: Journal of the British Institute of Persian Studies* 46:105–17.

Nezafati, N., and E. Pernicka. 2012. Early Silver Production in Iran. *Iranian Archaeology* 3:37–44.

Niedzwiecki, S., and B. Dubensky. 1937. Negatives:83546, 83727, 85066. Philadelphia: University of Pennsylvania Museum Archives.

Nokandeh, J., and N. Nezafati. 2003. The Silversmiths of Sialk: Evidence of the Precious Metals Metallurgy at the Southern Mound of Sialk. In *The Silversmiths of Sialk, Sialk Reconsideration Project Monograph, No.2*, ed. S.M. Shahmirzadi, pp. 21–30. Tehran: Iranian Centre for Archaeological Research.

Nowell, G.W. 1978. An Evaluation of the Miles Method of Ageing Using the Tepe Hissar Dental Sample. *American Journal of Physical Anthropology* 49:271–76.

———. 1989. An Evaluation of Tappeh Hesar, 1931–1932 Skeletal Sample. In *Tappeh Hesar: Reports of the Restudy Project, 1976*, ed. R.H. Dyson Jr. and S.M. Howard, pp. 131–32. Firenze: Casa editrice Le Lettere.

Özgüç, T., and R. Temizer. 1993. The Eskiyapar Treasure. In *Aspects of Art and Iconography: Anatolia and Its Neighbors: Studies in Honour of Nimet Özgüç*, ed. M.J. Mellink, E. Porada, and T. Özgüç, pp. 613–68. Ankara: Türk Tarih Kurumu Basımevi.

Pader, E.J. 1982. *Symbolism, Social Relations and the Interpretation of Mortuary Remains*. Oxford: B.A.R.

Parker Pearson, M. 1982. Mortuary Practices, Society and Ideology: An Ethnoarchaeological Study. In *Symbolic and Structural Archaeology*, ed. I. Hodder, pp. 99–114. Cambridge: Cambridge University Press.

———. 1999. *The Archaeology of Death and Burial*. College Station, TX: Texas A&M University Press.

Pernicka, E. 2004. Copper and Silver in Arisman and Tappeh Sialk and the Early Metallurgy in Iran. In *Persia's Ancient Splendour (Persiens Antike Pracht): Mining, Handicraft and Archaeology*, ed. T. Stöllner, R. Slotta. and A. Vatandoust, pp. 232–39. Bochum: Deutsches Bergbau-Museum.

Petrie, C. 2013. *Ancient Iran and its Neighbours: Local Developments and Long-Range Interactions in the Fourth Millennium BC*. Oxford: Oxbow Books.

Pigott, V.C., 1989. Archaeo-metallurgical Investigations at Bronze Age Tappeh Hesar, 1976. In *Tappeh Hesar: Reports of the Restudy Project, 1976*, ed. R.H. Dyson Jr. and S.M. Howard, pp. 25–34. Firenze: Casa editrice Le Lettere.

Pigott, V., L. Horne, S. Cleuziou, T. Berthoud, P.G. Warden, R. Maddin, T. Stech, J.D. Muhly, and H. Schenck. 1982. Special Issue: Archaeometallurgy. *Expedition* 25(1). Philadelphia: University of Pennsylvania Museum.

Pigott, V.C., S.M. Howard, and S.M. Epstein. 1982. Pyrotechnology and Culture Change at Bronze Age Tepe Hissar (Iran). In *Early Pyrotechnology: The Evolution of the First Fire-Using Industries*, ed. T.A. Wertime and S.F. Wertime, pp. 215–36. Washington, DC: Smithsonian.

Possehl, G.L. 2007 The Middle Asian Interaction Sphere: Trade and Contact in the 3rd Millennium BC. *Expedition* 49:40–42.

Potts, T.F. 1993. Patterns of Trade in 3rd Millennium BC: Mesopotamia and Iran. *World Archaeology* 24(3):379–402.

Potts, D.T. 2014. *Nomadism in Iran: From Antiquity to the Modern Era*. New York: OUP.

Rathbun, T.A. 1989. Recent Research in Physical Anthropology on Tappeh Hesar, Iran. In *Tappeh Hesar: Reports of the Restudy Project, 1976*, ed. R.H. Dyson Jr. and S.M. Howard, pp. 133–34. Firenze: Casa editrice Le Lettere.

Ratnagar, S. 2001. The Bronze Age: Unique Instance of a Pre-Industrial World System? *Current Anthropology* 42(3):351–79.

———. 2004. *Trading Encounters: from the Euphrates to the Indus in the Bronze Age*. New Delhi: Oxford University Press.

Ravin-Haque, K.A. 1992. Dental Paleopathology: An Example from Teppe Hissar, Iran. Master's Thesis. Philadelphia: University of Pennsylvania.

Reimer, P.J., M.G.L. Baillie, E. Bard, A. Bayliss, J.W. Beck, C.J.H. Bertrand, P.G. Blackwell, C.E. Buck, G.S. Burr, K.B. Cutler, P.E. Damon, R.L. Edwards, R.G. Fairbanks, M. Friedrich, T.P. Guilderson, A.G. Hogg, K.A. Hughen, B. Kromer, F.G. McCormac, S.W. Manning, C.B. Ramsey, R.W. Reimer, S. Remmele, J.R. Southon, M. Stuiver, S. Talamo, F.W. Taylor, J. van der Plicht, and C.E. Weyhenmeyer. 2004. IntCal04 Terrestrial Radiocarbon Age Calibration, 0–26 cal kyr BP. *Radiocarbon* 46(3):1029–58.

Rice, P.M. 1987. *Pottery Analysis: A Sourcebook*. Chicago: University of Chicago Press.

Robb, J. 2007. Burial Treatment As Transformations of Bodily Ideology. In *Performing Death: Social Analyses of Funerary Traditions in the Ancient Near East and Mediterranean*, ed. N. Laneri, pp. 288–90. Chicago: The Oriental Institute of the University of Chicago.

Rose, C.B. 2014. *The Archaeology of Greek and Roman Troy*. Cambridge: Cambridge University Press.

Rosenberg, M. 1989. The Evidence for Craft Specialization in the Production of Chipped Stone Blades at Tappeh Hesar. In *Tappeh Hesar: Reports of the Restudy Project, 1976*, ed. R.H. Dyson Jr. and S.M. Howard, pp. 111–18. Firenze: Casa editrice Le Lettere.

Roustaei, K. 2004. Tappeh Hesar: A Major Manufacturing Centre at the Central Plateau. In *Persia's Ancient Splendour (Persiens Antike Pracht): Mining, Handicraft and Archaeology*, ed. T. Stöllner, R. Slotta. and A. Vatandoust, pp. 222–31. Bochum: Deutsches Bergbau-Museum.

———. 2010. Tepe Hesar, Once Again. In *Proceedings of the 6th International Congress on the Archaeology of the Ancient Near East, Vol 2*, ed. P. Matthiae, F. Pinnok, L. Nigro, and N. Marchetti, pp. 613–34. Rome: Sapienza University of Rome.

Roux, V. 2003. A Dynamic Systems Framework for Studying Technological Change: Application to the Emergence of the Potter's Wheel in the Southern Levant. *Journal of Archaeological Method and Theory* 10:1–30.

Sajjadi, S.M.S. 2003. Excavation at Shahr-I Sokhta: First Preliminary Report on the Excavations of the Graveyards, 1997–2000. *IRAN: Journal of the British Institute of Persian Studies* 41:21–97.

Salvatori, S. and M. Vidale 1982. A Brief Survey of the Protohistoric Site of Shadad (Kerman Iran): Preliminary Report. *Rivista di Archeologia* 6:5–10.

Schindler, A.H., and J.D. Schmeltz. 1887. *Brief van A. Houtum Schindler aan Johannes Diedrich Eduard Schmeltz (1839–1909) BPL 2404*. Teheran.

Schmandt-Besserat, D. 1992. *How Writing Came About*. Austin, TX: University of Texas Press.

Schmidt, E.F. 1932. Unpublished communication to Jayne Horace, Director of the University of Pennsylvania Museum. Philadelphia: University of Pennsylvania Museum Archives.

———. 1933. *Tepe Hissar Excavations, 1931*. Philadelphia: University of Pennsylvania Museum of Archaeology and Anthropology.

———. 1937. *Excavations at Tepe Hissar Damghan*. Philadelphia: University of Pennsylvania Museum of Archaeology and Anthropology.

———. 1940. *Flights Over Ancient Cities of Iran*. Chicago: University of Chicago Press.

Schwartz, G.M. 2007. Status, Ideology, and Memory in Third-Millennium Syria: "Royal" Tombs at Umm El-Marra. In *Performing Death: Social Analyses of Funerary Traditions in the Ancient Near East and Mediterranean*, ed. N. Laneri, pp. 39–68. Chicago: The Oriental Institute of the University of Chicago.

Shanks, M., and C. Tilley. 1993. *Re-Constructing Archaeology: Theory and Practice*. London: Routledge.

Shepard, A.O. 1965. *Ceramics for the Archaeologist*. Washington, DC: Carnegie Institute of Washington.

Shepherd, D.J. 1999. *Funerary Ritual and Symbolism: An Interdisciplinary Interpretation of Burial Practices in Late Iron Age Finland*. Oxford: B.A.R.

Sinopoli, C.M. 1991. *Approaches to Archaeological Ceramics*. New York: Plenum Press.

Stein, A. 1936. *An Archaeological Tour in the Ancient Persis*. London: British School of Archaeology in Iraq.

Stöllner, T., G. Weisgerber, M. Momenzadeh, and E. Pernicka. 2004. The Significance of the Lead/Silver Mines at Nakhlak in Antiquity. In *Persia's Ancient Splendour (Persiens Antike Pracht): Mining, Handicraft and Archaeology*, ed. T. Stöllner, R. Slotta. and A. Vatandoust, pp. 478–93. Bochum: Deutsches Bergbau-Museum.

Sumner, W. 1986. Proto-Elamite Civilizations in Fars. In *Jemdet Nasr, Period or Regional Style?*, ed. U. Finkbeiner and W. Röllig, pp. 199–211. Wiesbaden: Ludwig Reichert.

———. 1988. Prelude to Proto-Elamite Anshan: The Lapuli Phase. *Iranica Antiqua*, 23:23–44.

Thornton, C.P. 2009a. Archaeometallurgy: Evidence of a Paradigm Shift? In *Metals and Societies. Studies in Honour of Barbara S. Ottaway*, ed. T.K. Kienlin and B.W. Roberts, pp. 25–33. Bonn: Universitätsforschungen zur prähistorischen Archäologie.

———. 2009b. The Chalcolithic and Early Bronze Age Metallurgy of Tepe Hissar, Northeast Iran: A Challenge to the Levantine Paradigm. PhD diss. Philadelphia: University of Pennsylvania.

———. 2012. Iran. In *A Companion to the Archaeology of the Near East*, ed. D.T. Potts, pp. 596–606. Oxford: Blackwell.

———. 2014. The Emergence of Complex Metallurgy on the Iranian Plateau. In *Archaeometallurgy in Global Perspective: Methods and Syntheses*, ed. B.W. Roberts and C.P. Thorton, pp. 665–89. New York: Springer.

Thornton, C.P., A. Gürsan-Salzmann, and R.H. Dyson Jr. 2013. Tepe Hissar and the Fourth Millennium of North-Eastern Iran. In *Ancient Iran and its Neighbours: Local Developments and Long-Range Interactions in the Fourth Millennium BC*, ed. C. Petrie, pp. 131–44. Oxford: Oxbow Books.

Thornton, C.P., and T. Rehren 2009. A Truly Refractory Crucible from Fourth Millennium Tepe Hissar, Northeast Iran. *Journal of Archaeological Science* 36:2700–12.

Thornton, C.P., T. Rehren, and V.C. Pigott. 2009. The Production of Speiss (Iron Arsenide) during the Early Bronze Age in Iran. *Journal of Archaeological Science* 36:308–16.

Tosi, M. 1974. The Northeastern Frontier of the Ancient Near East. *Mesopotamia* 8(9):21–76.

———. 1983. The Development of Urban Societies in Turan and the Mesopotamian Trade with the East: The Evidence from Shahr-i- Sokhta. In *Mesopotamian und Seine 1*, ed. H.J. Nissen and J. Renger, pp. 57–77. Berlin: Berliner Beitrage zum Vorderen Orient.

———. 1984. The Notion of Craft Specialization and its Representation in the Archaeological Record of Early States in the Turanian Basin. In *Marxist Perspectives in Archaeology*, ed. M. Spriggs, pp. 22–52. Cambridge: Cambridge University Press.

———. 1989 The Distribution of Industrial Debris on the Surface of Tappeh Hesar in the Damghan Plain, 1976. In *Tappeh Hesar: Reports of the Restudy Project, 1976*, ed. R.H. Dyson Jr. and S.M. Howard, pp. 13–24. Firenze: Casa editrice Le Lettere.

Tosi, M., and G. Bulgarelli. 1989. The Stratigraphic Sequence of Squares DF88/89 on South Hill, Tappeh Hesar. In *Tappeh Hesar: reports of the Restudy Project, 1976*, ed. R.H. Dyson Jr. and S.M. Howard, pp. 35–54. Firenze: Casa editrice Le Lettere.

Trinkhaus, K.M. 1989. Archaeological Survey of the Damghan Plains, Northeast Iran, 1976–1977. In *Tappeh Hesar: Reports of the Restudy Project, 1976*, ed. R.H. Dyson Jr. and S.M. Howard, pp. 135–42. Firenze: Casa editrice Le Lettere.

Van Gennep, A. 1960. *The Rites of Passage*. Chcago: University of Chicago Press.

Verhoeven, M. 2010. Social Complexity and Archaeology: A Contextual Approach. In *The Development of Pre-State Communities in the Ancient Near East: Studies in Honour of Edgar Peltenburg*, ed. D. Bolger and L.C. Maguire, pp. 11–21. Oxford: Oxbow Books.

Vidale, M. 2005. Resource Exploitation and Craft Technologies in Eastern Iran in the Third Millennium BC. In *The Halil Rud Civilization Discussions on Recent Discoveries*, ed. M.R. Sarfi, pp. 1–3. Jiroft: Free Islamic University.

von der Osten, H.H. 1937. *Researches in Anatolia Vol 7: The Alishar Hüyük Seasons of 1930–32, Part 1*. Chicago: University of Chicago Press.

von der Osten, H.H. and E.F. Schmidt. 1930. *Researches in Anatolia Vol 2: The Alishar Hüyük Season of 1927, Part 1*. Chicago: University of Chicago Press

Voigt, M.M. 1987. Relative and Absolute Chronologies for Iran Between 6500 and 3500 cal. B.C. In *Chronologies in the Near East. Relative Chronologies and Absolute Chronology 16,000–4,000 B.P. British Archaeological Reports International Series 379*, ed. O. Aurenche, J. Evin, and F. Hours, pp. 615–46. Oxford. B.A.R.

Voigt, M.M., and R.H. Dyson Jr. 1992. The Chronology of Iran, ca. 8000–2000 B.C. In *Chronologies in Old World Archaeology, 3rd ed., vol. 1*, ed. R.W. Ehrich, pp. 122–78. Chicago: University of Chicago Press.

Wheeler, M. 1956. *Archaeology from the Earth*. Baltimore: Penguin Books.

Wheeler Pires-Ferreira, J. 1975–77. Tepe Tūlā'i: Faunal Remains from an Early Campsite in Khuzestan, Iran. *Paléorient* 3:275–80.

Williams, H. 2003. Introduction: The Archaeology of Death, Memory and Material Culture. In *Archaeologies of Remembrance: Death and Memory in Past Societies*, ed. H. Williams, pp. 1–24. New York: Kluwer Academic/Plenum Publishers.

Wulsin, F.R., and M.B. Smith. 1932. *Excavations at Tureng Tepe, near Asterabad*. New York: American Institute for Persian Art and Archaeology.

Yule, P. 1982. *Tepe Hissar. Neolithische und kupferzeitliche Siedlung in Nordostiran*. München: Verlag C.H. Beck.

Zagarell, A. 1989. Pastoralism and the Early State in Greater Mesopatamia. In *Archaeological Thought in America*, ed. C.C. Lamberg-Karlovsky, pp. 280–301. Cambridge: Cambridge University Press.

Index

abandonment of site 1, 53, 169, 176, 267, 279, 295
administrative devices. S*ee also* regional/interegional interaction, trade
    seals 24, 25, 38, 39, 184, 227, 244, 246, 248, 255, 259, 261, 277, 280, 281, 291, 294
        cylinder 25, 39, 176, 216, 242, 266, 291, 294, 295, 338
        seal-shaped ornaments 24, 246, 259, 280
        stamp 24, 38, 184, 221, 232, 241, 244, 259, 273, 277, 280, 281, 294
            medallion 25
            terraced square pattern 294
    sealing/label 25, 39, 291, 293, 295
    tablet blanks 279, 291
    tokens/counters
        cones 37, 157
Alaca Höyük 6, 295
Arabian Peninsula 294
architecture 6, 11, 13, 16, 22, 25, 37, 39, 41, 60, 67, 73, 81, 159, 171, 174, 176, 178, 184, 186, 192, 195, 203, 207, 209, 256, 279
    building technology
        chineh 34, 35, 271, 272
        mold-made bricks 35, 159, 279, 280
    buttress 32, 34, 36, 37, 38, 52, 53, 59, 68, 81, 87, 99, 111, 144, 158, 174, 207, 279, 280, 294
    "crescent-shaped" niches 30, 32, 53, 236, 266, 279
archival data 6, 7, 13, 169, 170, 217
    Dyson excavations 1, 2, 5, 6, 7, 11, 14, 18, 32, 36, 37, 42, 48, 54, 58, 59, 68, 69, 72, 110, 111, 144, 158, 180, 203, 214, 271
        C14 Dates 38, 39, 46, 47, 58, 59, 68, 69, 170, 171, 209, 214, 266, 267, 295, 372, 373
        Howard, Susan H. 7, 42, 45, 46, 61, 68, 72, 73

Main Mound
    Building 1 5, 15, 26, 28, 31, 32, 37, 38, 42, 47, 48, 53, 68, 69, 74, 79, 81, 98, 111, 170, 171, 180, 184, 192, 195
    Building 2 5, 15, 22, 23, 25, 26, 28, 30, 31, 32, 36, 37, 38, 42, 47, 48, 52, 53, 57, 68, 69, 74, 81, 98, 111, 170, 174, 176, 178, 180, 186, 192, 242, 279
    Building 3 6, 15, 18, 32, 37, 42, 48, 52, 53, 56, 57, 68, 69, 74, 81, 87, 98, 125, 126, 127, 170, 176, 186, 221, 222, 279
North Flat 6, 7, 11, 20, 21, 23, 24, 26, 28, 31, 32, 33, 34, 36, 37, 38, 39, 41, 42, 48, 52, 57, 59, 62, 63, 68, 69, 71, 72, 74, 81, 87, 98, 99, 111, 126, 127, 144, 158, 159, 162, 167, 170, 176, 180, 186, 192, 195, 197, 202, 203, 209, 213, 214, 217, 221, 226, 227–36, 239–41, 243, 251, 256, 261–65, 271, 275, 279–82, 285–86, 290, 292, 295
Burned Building 6, 26, 31, 32, 33, 34, 38, 42, 48, 57, 58, 59, 63, 68, 69, 74, 81, 111, 127, 144, 158, 159, 167, 186, 192, 195, 197, 203, 207, 209, 213, 214, 231, 246, 261–65, 279–81, 294
    entrepôt 281
    platform hearth 65, 280
    storeroom 38
Pigott, Vincent. *See also* metallurgy 42, 46, 273
Remsen, William C. 41, 217
site survey 2, 4, 6, 14, 18, 21, 23, 41, 42, 46, 273, 295
    Trinkhaus, Kathryn 6, 14, 42, 46, 273, 291
South Hill 1, 6, 7, 11, 15, 18, 21, 23, 24,

26, 28, 31,37, 38, 41, 42, 58, 16, 209, 256, 273,274, 276, 279, 291, 293
    Bulgarelli, Grazia M. 41, 42, 46, 273, 279
    Building 4 26, 28, 31, 37, 42, 59, 279
        industrial workshop 6, 273, 279, 290, 291, 294, 295
        lapis blanks 273, 279, 291, 293, 294
    Reindell, Ingrid 42
    Tosi, Maurizio 1, 41, 42
    storerooms 32, 34, 48, 56, 57, 58, 68, 186, 221, 222, 279
    stratigraphy
        horizontal 6, 11, 36, 38, 39, 42, 46, 47, 48, 52, 59, 71, 78, 82, 87, 98, 111, 126, 127, 164, 169, 170, 171, 178, 217, 267
        vertical 11, 42,46,48, 50, 57, 82, 83, 169
            pinnacle 41, 42, 44, 45, 46, 47, 48, 50, 57, 69, 74, 81, 98, 111, 126, 144, 158, 176, 178, 285
    Twins Hillock, Quadrant FF 6, 18, 21, 23, 36, 38, 42, 47, 59, 68, 271
        Biscione, Raffaelo 42, 47, 271
    reconstruction 7, 22, 32, 58, 73, 170, 174, 176, 280
        burial stratigraphy 7, 11, 36, 39, 69, 71, 111, 159, 164, 166, Ch. 4
            sections 172, 173, 177, 179, 181, 182, 185, 187, 188, 189, 190, 192, 193, 194, 196, 200, 201, 204, 205, 206, 210, 212, 214
                correlated with 1976 sequence 170, 171–83, 206, 207, 208, 209, 210, 211
                uncorrelated with 1976 sequence 170, 184–205, 212, 213
        databases 6, 73
Bactria-Margiana Archaeological Complex (BMAC) 195, 285
burials
    burial groups 6, 158, 180, 195, 209, 217, 226, 227, 230, 231, 232, 233, 234, 235, 238, 239, 242, 243, 246, 247, 267, 297, App.2
        group 1 226–28
        group 2 228–30
        group 3 230–34, 260
        group 4 235–36, 246
        group 5 239–51
        High Outliers 243–51
            Dancer 25, 38, 232, 235, 236, 243, 244, 331, 341
            Little Girl 25, 38, 192, 240, 241, 242, 243, 246, 247
            Priest 25, 38, 184, 234, 235, 240, 241, 242, 243, 244, 245–51, 256, 264, 266, 284, 336, 337, 342, 343
            Warrior 1 25, 38, 171, 195, 240, 241
            Warrior 2 171, 174, 195, 222, 240, 241, 264
        Low Outliers 226, 227, 228, 232, 233, 234, 235, 239, 242, 295, App. 2
    burial rituals 195, 197, 217, 252, 253, 256
        burial with animal bones 252, 253, 256
        gift placement on body parts. *See also* Low Outliers, High Outliers, and secondary burial 253, 255, 256
        performance 217, 252, 255, 256, 257, 260
        Trobriand Island 252
    burial types
        communal 219, 222, 224, 259, 231, 255
        double 35, 37, 38, 222, 231
        secondary 218, 230, 252, 253, 254, 261, 264
CT (Computerized Axial Tomography) Scan 226, 295
GIS Burial Maps 11, 217, 244, 246, 248, App. 3
grave types 221
    cist 23, 37, 221, 222, 239, 244, 259, 261, 273
    vault 221, 222, 239, 261
hoard
    Main Mound
        CF89-99 195, 197, 256, 258, 259
    Treasure Hill
        hoards 1 and 2. *See also* BMAC 246, 282, 283, 284, 285 286
human skeletal and dental studies 217, 223, 224
    isotope analysis 226, 297 (note 6.24)
    Nowell, G.W. 224, 226
    Krogman, Wilton M. 222, 224, 226
    Rathbun, T.A. 223
    Ravin-Haque, K.A. 224, 226
pathologies 224
    cranial 226, 232
    dental 224
    skeletal 226, 232, 297 (note 6.24)
Caspian red ware 291
Central Asia 7, 14, 246, 294
ceramics
    ceramic typology 15, 18, 25
        Howard's 72, 73
        Schmidt's 25, 72
    new ceramic classification/typology 73–75
        ceramic samples 74, 81
        context of the selected sample 74
            Main Mound
                DF09S. *See also* stratigraphy, vertical 69, 72, 73, 74

CG90P. *See also* stratigraphy, pinnacle
  6, 69, 73, 74, 81
 decoration 26, 36, 37, 73, 75, 76, 78, 79, 83,
  99, 127, 154, 158, 264, 277, 341, Ch. 3
 ceramic illustrations and legends
 form attributes 71, 72, 73, 74, 79
 forms 81–163 Ch. 3 pottery illustrations of
  forms through all phases, App. 1 pottery
  charts
   bridge-beak-spouted jar 144, 158, 160,
    164, 195, 286, 335
   tulip-shaped beaker 127, 143, 144, 145,
    186, 192, 207, 209, 256, 280, 289, 329,
    330, 332
 ware attributes 71–75
 ware types
  buff 76–78
  buff painted 78
  coarse 78
  grey 79
  grey burnished, metallic 79
  grey stone 79
  red, red painted 76
 new ceramic chronology
  phases Tables 2.2, 3.4, Fig. 2.6
   F, Early Hissar I 82
   F-E, Late Hissar I/Early Hissar II 84–86
   E, Early Hissar II 87–98
   E-D, Early-Mid Hissar II 98–111
   D, Mid-Hissar II 111–26
   D-C, Late Hissar II/Early Hissar III
    126–43
   C, earlier than B in North Flat 144
   B, Mid Hissar III 144–59
   B-A/A, Late Hissar III 159–64
 technical innovations. *See also* metallurgy 79,
  277, 279, 286, 291
  industrial/technical ceramics 279, 291
  firing reduction 14, 74, 164, 273, 277, 293
  slag as temper 78, 87, 98, 99, 116, 117, 120,
   121, 125, 127, 130, 131, 158, 160, 161,
   162, 273, 277
  ceramic kiln 78, 87, 125, 273, 279
chipped stone 279
Cleuziou, Serge 291
debitage
 alabaster 273, 278, 279, 294
 metal 46, 59, 279
decorative motifs 75–76
Deshayes, Jean 41, 73
donkey, for transport 294
Eskiyapar 295

figurines
 animal 24, 25, 37–39, 171, 174, 180, 207, 226,
  243, 244, 245, 247, 248, 255, 259, 264, 270,
  271, 280, 293, 294
 effigy vessel 25
  female (ceramic, alabaster) 207, 243, 246,
   249, 280, 281
 human 1, 3, 5
  female hourglass shape (copper, silver) 25,
   197, 247, 255
  male and female (copper) 38, 197, 256
flint blades 171, 180, 270
geography
 Cheshmeh Ali River 1, 35, 36, 267
 Damghan Plain 6, 13, 14, 20, 24, 25, 46, 291
  Damghan River 2, 291
  Elburz Mountains 1, 13, 246, 267, 291
  Shir-e Shian (Pre Phase F, Early Hissar I) 15,
   271, 272
 Dasht-i Kavir 1, 267
 Gorgan 35, 41, 291, 293
  Shah Tepe 36, 268, 291
  Tureng Tepe 6, 24, 35, 36, 41, 158, 246, 268,
   291, 293
 southern Iran
  Dasht-i Lut 294
  Shahdad 246, 268, 294
  Shahr-i Sokhta 41, 253, 268
geomorphology 46
 erosion 25
Gohar Tepe 158, 293
 Mahfroozi, Ali 158
ground stone 180, 294
Harris, Mary V. 42
Hindu Kush 293
ICAR 2, 41
ideological order 291
İkiztepe 295
metallurgy xix, 6, 38, 273, 277
 Arisman 293, 294, 296
  Helwing, Barbara xx, 293, 294, 296, 297
 arsenic 273, 277, 294, 296
 furnace 273, 279, 293
 furnace linings 38, 59
 hematite ore 180
 ingot 197, 179, 280
 metals 38, 226, 227, 243, 247, 248, 277, 280,
  285, 291, 293–96
  copper 1, 25, 37, 38, 39, 46, 78, 87, 164,
   171, 180, 184, 195, 197, 213–15, 221–23,
   227, 228, 230–32, 235–38, 242, 244–48,
   250, 251, 256, 257, 259–61, 264, 265,

273, 277, 279, 280, 282, 285, 286, 291, 293–97
   gold 1, 25, 37–39, 215, 227, 244–48, 261, 262, 277, 280, 285, 286, 295
   lead 1, 227, 232, 244, 246–48, 266, 270, 277, 279, 280, 296, 297
   silver 5, 37, 58, 59, 180, 184, 192, 213, 215, 221, 222, 227, 229–32, 235, 236, 244, 246–49, 259, 261, 264, 273, 277, 278, 280, 286, 294–97
mining districts 296
   Anarak 296
   Anaru 296
   Badakshan 295, 296
Momenzadeh, Mozteza 296
Nezafati, Nima 293, 296, 297
Pernicka, Ernst 293, 296, 297
Pigott, Vincent. *See also* archival data, Dyson excavations xix, 6, 38, 42, 46, 69, 87, 273, 277, 279, 297
prill 39, 78, 277
slag 38, 42, 46, 59, 69, 74, 78, 87, 98, 99, 116, 120, 125, 127, 130, 158, 160, 162, 164, 209, 273, 277, 279, 297
smelting 39, 46, 87, 273, 279, 291, 293, 294, 297
technical innovations 291
   cupellation, silver 273, 297
   firing 74, 75, 78, 79, 83, 86, 99, 111, 164, 277
   molds 38, 78, 279, 290, 291
      bi-valve 290
      open face casting 279
      refractory technical ceramics 279
   repoussé 38, 144, 213, 231, 236, 246, 248–50, 264, 265, 280
Tepe Sialk III1-3 270
Tepe Sialk III3-4 271
Tepe Sialk III6-7 273, 293
workshop 6, 39, 209, 264, 270, 273, 279, 290, 291, 294, 295, 297
   industrial workshop 6, 279, 294
Monge, Janet 226, 280
natural resources 1
Nishapur Plain 293
nomad 295, 296
Painted Pottery Flat 18, 21, 23, 24, 26, 34–36, 83, 164, 467, 209, 226, 253, 271, 279
prestige objects 7, 215, 264, 280, 281, 285, 286, 291, 297
   alabaster 24, 25, 32, 38, 39, 167, 171, 180, 184, 186, 192, 197, 202, 207, 222, 226, 227, 231, 232, 235, 239, 242, 244–49, 255, 256, 259, 261, 263, 264, 273, 277, 278, 280, 283, 285, 286, 294–97
      disc, column 25, 32, 38, 195, 207, 215, 246, 263, 285, 290, 294, 297
      vase 72, 127, 130, 192, 286
   beads 25, 37–39, 180, 202, 213, 221, 222, 226, 229–31, 235, 236, 242, 244–48, 253, 259, 261, 264, 273, 277, 280, 291, 293–95, 297
      copper 25, 37–39, 180, 213, 221–23, 235–38, 242, 244-248, 259–61, 264, 273, 277, 280, 291, 293–97
      gold 25, 37–39, 244-248, 261, 277, 280, 295
   semiprecious stones
      amber 39, 226, 244, 246, 291
      carnelian 25, 39, 221, 226, 229, 230, 248, 259, 264, 273, 277, 293, 294, 297
      lapis lazuli 25, 39, 46, 59, 221, 226, 229, 230, 235, 236, 245–48, 259, 561, 264, 273, 277, 279, 291, 293, 294, 297
      rock crystal 25, 37, 235
      turquoise 1, 37, 39, 213, 221, 226, 235, 248, 291, 293
   silver 25, 37, 180, 221, 222, 229–32, 235, 236, 244, 246–49, 259, 261, 264, 273, 277, 280, 286, 294–97
ivory 39
seals. *See also* administrative devices 24, 25, 38, 39, 184, 227, 242, 244, 246, 248, 255, 259, 261, 273, 277, 280, 281, 291, 294–97
cylinder 25, 39, 176, 216, 242, 266, 291, 294, 295
seal-shaped ornaments 25, 259
stamp 24, 25, 38, 39, 189, 221, 32, 242, 244, 245, 239, 273, 278, 280, 281, 294, 296, 297
   medallion 25
social identity symbols
   diadem 25, 38, 184, 213, 231, 235, 246, 249, 255, 264, 280
   double spiral pins 37
   fan/mirror 150
   figurine. *See* figurines
   macehead 25, 37, 171, 174, 231, 244, 291, 293
   wands 25, 38, 180, 184, 195, 222, 227, 231, 232, 237–39, 244-248, 250, 255, 256, 260, 261, 264–66, 280, 284, 291
Proto-Elamite 12, 36, 52, 68, 216, 293, 294, 297
   Elamite 294
   horizon 297
   tablet 12, 294

regional/interregional interaction
   exchange network 286
   long distance 1, 15, 246, 264, 267, 291, 294–96
      Great Khorasan Road 270, 291
   southern Mesopotamia 6, 291, 295
      Uruk 68, 293, 297
   trade 1, 11, 12, 264, 267, 270, 280, 281, 290, 291, 293–97
      Central Plateau 271, 291, 293, 295, 296
         Tepe Sialk 14, 36, 271, 291, 293, 294
      Gorgan 13, 35, 41, 291, 293
         Shah Tepe 36, 291
         Tureng Tepe 6, 12, 24, 35, 36, 41, 158, 286, 291, 293
      southern Iran 15, 215, 246
         Jiroft 294, 297
         Shahdad 246, 294, 297
         Shahr-i Sokhta, cemetery 41, 253, 294, 297
         Tepe Yahya 294
      Turkmenistan xix, 24, 195, 293, 294
         Altyn Tepe 294
         Anau 271, 272
         Namazga Tepe 294
Rosenberg, Michael 270, 279
social complexity 286, 290, 291
   administrator 264, 277, 281, 291, 296
   agent 270, 291, 296
      social networking 270
      Roux, Valentine 296
   social practice 267
      Shanks, Michael 267

shared technical knowledge 279, 293
social and technical interdependence 277
   Tilley, Christopher 267
subsistence 1, 267, 270
   fauna 1, 12, 267, 295, 296
      domestic 1, 24, 296
         cattle 1
         caprine. *See also* figurines, animals 1, 267
         onager 1
      Mashkour, Marjan 1, 12, 269
      wild 1, 12, 72, 246
         fishing 266, 267, 270
            fish 1, 12
            mollusks 12
         hunting 76, 78, 232, 267, 270
            boar 1
            gazelle 1, 78
            red deer 1
   irrigation agriculture 270
      cereals 224, 256, 267
      Costantini, L. 1, 7, 12
      lentil 1
   grapes 1, 12
   olives 1, 12
tools 20, 25, 38, 41, 59, 180, 184, 215, 226, 231, 232, 244–46, 248, 255, 256, 259, 265, 266, 270, 271, 279, 290, 291, 294, 296, 297
transitions to 178, 281, 290, 293, 297
   Iron Age 2, 12, 24, 36, 39, 215, 295, 297
   Late Bronze Age 215, 281, 297
Voigt and Dyson, chronology 297